UNDERSTANDING TEXTILES

SIXTH EDITION

BILLIE J. COLLIER
University of Tennessee

PHYLLIS G. TORTORA
Queens College

Upper Saddle River, New Jersey 07458

Library of Congress Cataloging-in-Publication Data
Tortora, Phyllis G.
  Understanding textiles / Phyllis G. Tortora, Billie J. Collier.—6th ed.
    p. cm.
  Includes bibliographical references and index.
  ISBN 0-13-021951-7
    1. Textiles industry.   2. Textile fibers.   3. Textile fabrics.   I. Title.
TS1445 .T55 2000
677–dc21

                                                  00-032396

Publisher: Dave Garza
Director of Production and Manufacturing: Bruce Johnson
Acquisitions Editor: Neil Marquardt
Marketing Manager: Ryan DeGrote
Editorial Assistant: Susan Kegler
Managing Editor: Mary Carnis
Manufacturing Manager: Ed O'Dougherty
Production Liaison: Denise Brown
Production Editor: Silvia Freeburg
Interior Design and Composition: Clarinda Company
Art Director: Marianne Frasco
Cover Design Coordinator: Miguel Ortiz
Cover Design: Joe Sengotta
Cover Art: PictureQuest
Printing and Binding: Courier Westford, Inc.
Cover Printer: Coral Graphics

Prentice-Hall International (UK) Limited, *London*
Prentice-Hall of Australia Pty. Limited, *Sydney*
Prentice-Hall Canada Inc., *Toronto*
Prentice-Hall Hispanoamericana, S.A., *Mexico*
Prentice-Hall of India Private Limited, *New Delhi*
Prentice-Hall of Japan, Inc., *Tokyo*
Prentice-Hall Singapore Pte. Ltd.
Editora Prentice-Hall do Brasil, Ltda., *Rio de Janeiro*

---

10 9 8 7 6
ISBN 0-13-021951-7

Dedicated to
John and Vincent
for their continuing help and support

PREFACE

The purpose of this book is to provide a common background for students who are making a study of textiles. Some students may be planning to enter one of the many career areas that require some knowledge about textiles. Others may be interested in becoming better-informed consumers. Whatever may motivate students to enter an introductory course in textiles, certain basic concepts are essential to their understanding of the subject. It is our hope that these concepts are presented in a clear, logically developed format.

The text begins with an overview of the textile industry. The majority of students are likely to begin their study of textiles without any prior knowledge of the origin, manufacture, and distribution of the wide variety of textile products they use daily. The first chapter presents an overview of the journey of textile products that begins with fiber production and goes on to manufacture of yarns or other components, to fabric production, to design, and to manufacture of the final product. It is our intention to set a context for the chapters that follow in which basic processes, rooted in science and technology, are explored in depth, beginning with the basic building blocks of fabrics: fibers. In subsequent chapters emphasis is placed on the interrelationships of fibers, yarns, fabric constructions, dyes, and finishes. What is known about each of these components is applied to the understanding of textile behavior and performance. The chapters build on each other, much as the textile structure itself is built, and summaries at various stages in the text review the properties that affect performance. We reinforce this view of analyzing component parts of a textile by case studies of particular end use products.

Diagrams and photographs have been selected with care to illustrate the concepts and processes described in the text. Many students study in parts of the country where they have no access to field trips to textile manufacturing sites; therefore, we have included photographs of various types of machinery.

Each chapter includes review questions that invite students to summarize and apply the concepts presented in the text.

The recommended readings at the end of each chapter have been selected to complement the subject matter of the chapters. We have made a conscious effort to include both relatively elementary and highly technical material so as to introduce students to the variety of resources in the field. We have also tried to include readings from the most widely used periodicals in the field. An extensive bibliography, broken down under special subject headings, appears at the end of the book.

After chapter 1 introduces the reader to the various elements from which textiles are made, their historical development, and the present-day organization of the textile industry, chapter 2, a combination of the second and third chapters of the last edition, establishes the relationship of fiber properties to fiber behavior. It includes the chemical and physical concepts basic to understanding the behavior of textile fibers, and is written for the reader who has had little previous chemistry training. Students should be able to gain some understanding of these elementary concepts and to appreciate not only the integral role that chemistry plays in the manufacture and finishing of textile products but also the role of chemistry in the use and care of textiles by consumers. Often this kind of material is integrated into varying parts of a text. We have not done so here because a separate chapter on the subjects offers a better opportunity to explain elementary chemical and physical terminology and concepts and to relate these concepts to the science of textiles in later discussions. Some instructors may prefer to emphasize this chapter a great deal, whereas others may wish to discuss it only briefly. Either approach may be taken, and the chapter is divided into three parts to enable further flexibility in assigning the material.

The chapters on textile fibers (chapters 3 to 12) begin with the natural fibers (chapters 3 and 4). Cellulosic fibers are discussed first because they are simpler in structure than the protein fibers and because cotton is so widely used. Protein fibers, with emphasis on wool and silk, follow. In chapter 5 we introduce important concepts about manufactured fibers, after which we review manufactured cellulosic fibers in chapter 6. Chapters 7 to 12 cover related groups of manufactured fibers.

Chapters about fibers are all organized in the same way, with many of the topic headings being repeated in each chapter. These topic headings are also used in chapter 2, "Textile Fibers and Their Properties," in order to facilitate comparisons between fibers. Some common brand names of manufactured fibers that are produced under a number of trademarks are mentioned. As companies merge and change products, trademarks become outdated. Readers can keep current through obtaining information on the Internet. Each chapter ends with a table summarizing some of the more important characteristics of the major fiber groups discussed.

From fibers the text moves to yarns and their production (chapter 13), and then discusses fabric structures. Those who have used previous editions of this text will note that chapters dealing with fabric manufacture have been reorganized, with weaving and woven fabrics separated into two chapters (14 and 15), followed by chapter 16 on knitted fabrics. The chapter on nonwovens from previous editions (now chapter 17) has been renamed "Other Fabric Construction Methods" because not all the fabrics discussed are classified as nonwovens. Chapter 19, on multicomponent fabrics, concludes the presentation of fabric construction methods.

For both yarns and fabrics, summaries in the chapters show how fiber, yarn, and fabric construction contribute to the total structure of the fabric and how the structure of the fabric is in turn related to its performance. Performance factors affecting durability, appearance, and comfort are discussed. The intent is to enable readers to begin to put together the parts of a textile product and think in terms of end use properties. Examples of specific end uses are presented as case studies under the heading "Putting It All Together. . . ."

The various methods of finishing fabrics and adding color and design are discussed in chapters 19 to 23. New to this edition is a chapter 19, devoted to the preparation steps that fabrics undergo before being dyed and finished. Chapter 24, "The Care of Textile Products," is entirely devoted to the care of textiles, even though some material on this subject appears in preceding chapters. This chapter is important because of the importance of care in relation to consumer satisfaction with textiles. Chapter 25 explores the important topic of "Textiles and the Environment, Health, and Safety."

Consumer Briefs appear throughout and explore in depth topics of particular interest to consumers. These features include such diverse topics as how to select carpet, developments in manufacture of recycled polyester, washable silk apparel, and ink jet printing.

The final chapter summarizes standard test methods used in the textile industry to evaluate the performance of textile products. Performance is related to specific end uses by additional case studies on sail cloth, outdoor clothing, and automotive textiles.

Special reference tools within the text are provided in appendices. These include the aforementioned bibliography, a glossary of terms (many from the *Annual Book of ASTM Standards*), and a summary of textile legislation.

A Basic Textiles Swatch Kit is available for use in conjunction with this edition of *Understanding Textiles*. The swatch kit consists of 120 fabric swatches, mounting sheets, a master list with fabric name/description/fiber content, and a three-ring binder. It is available through Textile Fabric Consultants, Inc., P.O. Box 111431, Nashville, TN 37222/615-459-7510.

ACKNOWLEDGMENTS

We have received assistance in the preparation of this revision from many individuals and organizations and would like to acknowledge those that provided assistance with previous editions as well as those more directly involved in the current edition. We are grateful for the encouragement and support provided by our families, especially our respective husbands, Dr. John R. Collier and Vincent Tortora, as well as for the assistance of colleagues and students. A special thanks is due to Madalina Romanoschi at Louisiana State University who helped with many aspects of the revision.

A number of reviewers from academic institutions and professional organizations provided invaluable input. These included: Dr. Peggy Ott and students in her class at Louisiana State University, who reviewed the revised chapter 2: Wendy Bourg, Emily Caldwell, Charli DeMent, Amber Lea Dunavant, Eva Hickey, Adele Kelty, Lindsey Leggio, Elizabeth Motta, Kathryn O'Quin, Andrew Pham, Mary B. Renfro, Christy Smith, Samantha A. Stormo, and Andrea N, Wilson; and Dr. Robert Barker, American Fiber Manufacturers Association, for reviews of manufacturing flowcharts.

We extend our thanks to the librarians and staff of the libraries at Fashion Institute of Technology, New York; Louisiana State University; the University of Tennessee; Queens College; the Port Washington, N.Y. Public Library; and the New York Public Library.

It is impossible to acknowledge all the help we received in obtaining illustrative material. We have specified the sources in the figures caption, and thank the many individuals who worked on our behalf to find these illustrations and grant permission for their use. Among those we wish to offer special thanks are Judy Gloston, a handweaver of Huntington, N.Y., for giving us the opportunity to photograph her spinning and weaving supplies; Dr. Dong Zhang, the University of Tennessee; Dr. Jenna Kuttruff, Louisiana State University; and Pati Bel-Berger, Southern Regional Research Center.

Finally, we want to thank the many individuals and trade and professional associations that provided both information and illustrations. Information provided by Seth Walters, Continental General Tire, and Dr. Danny Akin, United States Department of Agriculture, Agricultural Research Service (USDA ARS), is gratefully acknowledged. Among the trade associations that provided useful information were the American Association of Textile Chemists and Colorists (AATCC); the American Fiber Manufacturers Association (AFMA); the American Textile Manufacturers Institute (ATMI); the American Society for Testing and Materials (ASTM); Crafted with Pride in the U.S.A. Council, Inc.; INDA, the Association of the Nonwovens Industry; and the International Fabricare Institute (IFI).

BRIEF CONTENTS

CONTENTS

CHAPTER 3
Natural Cellulosic Fibers

65

CHAPTER 4
Protein Fibers

95

CHAPTER 5

Introduction to Manufactured Fibers   129

CHAPTER 6
Manufactured Celluosic Fibers   143

CHAPTER 7
Nylon and Aramid Fibers   165

CHAPTER 18

Multicomponent Fabrics   379

CHAPTER 23
Finishes that Affect Performance   457

CHAPTER 24
The Care of Textile Products   485

CHAPTER 25
Textiles and the Environment, Health, and Safety   511

CHAPTER 1

INTRODUCTION

Each day each of us makes decisions about textiles. From the simplest choice of what clothes to wear to the commitment of a major portion of the family budget to buy a new carpet, judgments about the performance, durability, attractiveness, and care of textiles are consciously or unconsciously made. The economic implications of decisions about fibers, yarns, and fabrics obviously increase if someone is involved professionally with textiles. But whether or not understanding textiles is required for personal or for professional purposes, the key to informed decision making is knowledge about fibers, yarns, fabrics, and finishes and the ways in which these are interrelated.

Textiles fulfill so many purposes in our lives that their study can be approached in a number of ways. Textiles may be seen as being purely utilitarian, in relationship to the numerous purposes they serve. On awaking in the morning, for example, we climb out from under sheets and blankets and step into slippers and a robe. We wash our faces with washcloths, dry them with towels, and put on clothing for the day. Even the bristles of our toothbrushes are made from textile fibers. If we get into a car or bus, we sit on upholstered seats; the machine moves on tires reinforced with strong textile cords. We stand on carpets, sit on upholstered furniture, and look out of curtained windows. The insulation of our houses may be glass textile fiber. Not only are golf clubs, tennis rackets, and ski poles reinforced with textile fibers, but so are roads, bridges, and buildings. Strong, heat-resistant textile fibers in the nose cones of spaceships travel to distant planets. Physicians implant artificial arteries made of textiles or use fibers for surgery that gradually dissolve as wounds heal. Few of our manufactured products could be made without textile conveyor belts. Even our processed foods have been filtered through textile filter paper. There is truly no aspect of modern life that is untouched by some area of textiles. (See Figure 1.1.)

FIGURE 1.1

Fibers are used in applications that range from apparel to high technology. (a) Mountain climber in activewear made from polypropylene fiber. Courtesy of Helly Hanson; (b) Sofa upholstered in fabric made from olefin fiber. Courtesy of Amoco Fabrics and Fibers/Westpoint Pepperell; (c) Automobile airbags usually made from nylon or polyester fiber. (d) Nonwoven textile fabric used to stabilize the banks of a river; (e) Protective clothing made from high temperature resistant Basofil fiber; (f) Fabrics used as architectural structures at the MGM Conference Center in Las Vegas, NV. (Photographs in a and b provided by the American Polyolefin Council; c, d, and f by Industrial Fabrics Association International; and e by BASF Corporation.)

f

e

Some individual or some group of persons will be the ultimate consumer of each textile product. The ultimate consumer selects the product for a particular end use, whether that use be a fashionable garment or a fabric used to reinforce high-technology building materials. In all cases, consumers want to select products that will perform well in the projected end uses. Most also seek to minimize cost. The ways in which textiles are produced affect their costs. Some steps in manufacturing are more expensive than others. Manufacturers may be able to choose one procedure instead of another. When alternatives are available, manufacturers are likely to select processes that will maximize their profits while making products that will sell at competitive prices and also fulfill the customers' desire for satisfactory performance. Many products must also meet the demands of current fashion.

Even though we all personally experience textiles at home, at work, and at play, we usually encounter only the complete product; rarely do we deal with the individual components. But each finished product makes a long journey from its beginnings in the laboratory or on the farm to the place where it is acquired by the ultimate consumer. An introductory course in textile study can be a sort of road map or itinerary of that journey; therefore, this text is organized to begin with the first steps in the long progression from fiber to completed fabric and goes on to examine subsequent steps in a generally chronological sequence.

If you were to take the shirt or sweater that you are wearing at this moment and break it down into its components, you would have to work backward, taking apart the fabric structure. Most likely your garment is woven or knitted. Weaving and knitting are the two most common means of creating fabrics for apparel, although other methods do exist. Both weaving and knitting are subject to a great many possible variations, and these differences contribute to the enormous variability in appearance, drapability, texture, wrinkle recovery, durability, feel, and many other qualities of fabrics.

To take a woven or knitted structure apart requires that the fabric be unraveled into the yarns from which it was constructed. The yarns (with some few exceptions) are likely to have been made from short or long continuous fibers that are twisted together. By untwisting the yarns, it should be possible to separate the yarn into a number of small, fine, hairlike fibers. These fibers are the basic units that make up the majority of textile products encountered in apparel and home furnishings. (See Figure 1.2.)

FIBERS

Textile fibers exist in nature or are created through technology. Technical definitions of the term *textile fiber* such as that of the American Society for Testing and Materials (ASTM) tend to stress their dimensions: "a generic term for any one of the various

FIGURE 1.2

Fabric unravels into separate yarns. Yarns untwist into individual fibers.

types of matter that form the basic elements of a textile and that is characterized by having a length at least 100 times its diameter" (ASTM 1986).[1]

Although this may explain how a fiber looks, some materials that do fit this definition are not suitable for use in textiles. The fibrous structure of an overcooked pot roast, for example, is obviously not suitable for use in a textile. Fibers appropriate for use in textiles must have not only fineness and flexibility but also sufficient strength and durability to withstand conditions encountered in use.

To understand and evaluate suitability of different fibers for particular products, professionals in the textile field and consumers need to understand the physical and chemical properties of fibers. Particular fibers may be suitable for use in some textile applications but not in others. Carbon fiber, excellent for use in high-technology products and sports equipment, is not useful for wearing apparel. Even among those fibers used in many apparel and home furnishing items, some are preferred for particular applications. Nylon has become synonymous with sheer women's hosiery—women may refer to their stockings as "nylons" although in fact, in the past, fibers such as silk or rayon were used to make women's dress hosiery.

On reflection, then, it is obvious that we tend to prefer some kinds of fibers for certain uses because those particular fibers offer some special advantages. For example, a particular fabric may seem to be more comfortable in warm or cool weather, may soil less easily, may dry more quickly, or may have an appearance that is best suited to a particular kind of occasion. The reasons for these differences among fibers reside in the specific properties of each fiber. If we are to have a clear understanding of the finished products and what qualities are to be expected of them, we need to know the fibers from which the product is made—and the characteristics of those fibers.

---

1. A glossary of technical terms is provided in Appendix B.

YARNS

Fibers alone cannot make a textile. Although it is possible to entangle groups of fibers or to bond them together in some way to create a textile (as is done with felt, for example), most of the cloth that is made into wearing apparel is formed from yarns. *Yarns are assemblies of fibers twisted or otherwise held together in a continuous strand.* An almost endless variety of yarns can be created by using different fibers, by twisting fibers more or less tightly, by combining two or more individual yarns to form a more complex yarn, or by giving yarns a wide range of other special treatments.

Just as different fibers will vary in their individual properties, different kinds of yarns have varying characteristics. (See Figure 1.3.) And to complicate matters still further, two yarns of the same structure will have different properties if they are made from markedly different kinds of fibers.

FIGURE 1.3

Fabrics made from the same fiber and in the same (plain) weave look different because different kinds of yarns are used.

a

b

c

FABRIC STRUCTURES

Yarns must be united in some way if they are to form a cohesive structure. The transformation of individual yarns into textile fabrics can be accomplished by an individual with a pair of knitting needles, a crochet hook, or a hand loom or through the use of powerful machines that combine yarns by weaving, knitting, or stitch bonding to produce thousands of yards of completed fabrics. As with fibers and yarns, the potential for variations in the structure is enormous, and a walk through any department store will reveal to even the most casual observer the almost endless variety of textile structures produced and consumed by the public in the form of apparel or household textiles.

And, once again, if the construction being used is varied, the resulting properties will differ. Furthermore, even when the same weave or knit construction is used, the end product will be distinctive if the fiber or yarn type is varied. (See Figure 1.4.)

COLORING AND FINISHING

Appearance—color, pattern, or texture—is one of the major factors that leads consumers to purchase one product over another. Most textile fabrics intended for personal, household, or architectural use have been decorated in some way, by dyeing the fabric, printing designs on it, or weaving with varicolored yarns. Large segments of the textile industry are devoted to dyeing and/or printing fabrics, yarns, or fibers.

As the reader will learn, certain properties are inherent to each fiber, yarn, or fabric structure. Consumers find some of these properties desirable, while others are not valued. For example, fabrics of synthetic fibers dry quickly after laundering. Most consumers value this quality. But the same fabrics may tend to build up static electric

FIGURE 1.4

Fabrics made from the same fiber and from similar types of yarns look different because different types of weaves were used in their construction.

charges, producing small electrical shocks or "static cling." Consumers do not like this quality. When a fiber, yarn, or fabric has unacceptable properties, special treatments called *finishes* may be applied to the fiber, yarn, or fabric to overcome undesirable properties. Finishes may be used to give to the fibers, yarns, or fabrics some properties that they do not normally possess but that will enhance performance. Static cling can thus be decreased or overcome. Most people are familiar with durable press finishes, for example, or may have purchased upholstered furniture with soil-resistant finishes. Other examples are discussed in chapters 22 and 23 dealing with finishes.

TEXTILE HISTORY

No one knows exactly when the spinning and weaving of textiles began. Recent archeological discoveries of the imprint of woven material on clay pots dating from some 27,000 years ago indicate that people knew how to weave even before they domesticated plants and animals (Fowler 1995). The oldest actual fragment of cloth found thus far is from archeological excavations at a site in southern Turkey called Cayonu. This piece of white fabric, probably linen, has been dated at about 7000 B.C. (Wilford 1993b). Sandals made from fibers that date from as early as 6000 B.C. have been found in caves in Missouri (Kuttruff et al. 1998). (See Figure 1.5.)

People used fibers found in nature and hand processes to make fibers into cloth. Even with limited technology, skilled weavers created a wide variety of fabrics. Some fabrics, such as the simple, plain homespun cloth used daily, were strictly utilitarian. Others were elaborately patterned, printed, or dyed in order to satisfy the universal human need for beauty.

More complex social and political organizations of people evolved. With the growth of cities, nations, and empires came improvements in technology and the development of international trade, both of which involved textiles.

Chinese silk was among the most prized items of commerce. Historians have long thought that silk from China first reached ancient Greece and Rome along a trade route called "the silk road" in the latter part of the second century B.C., but recent archeological evidence indicates that silk may have reached ancient Egypt as early as 1000 B.C. (Wilford 1993a).

The Romans also imported cotton from nearby Egypt and from India. Archeologists have found facilities for dyeing and finishing cotton fabrics in settlements throughout the Roman world.

During the Middle Ages the production and trading of the plant called *woad*, an important source of dye, was a highly developed industry. Crusaders returned from the Middle East to their homes in Europe with luxurious silk and cotton fabrics. These "foreign novelties" became important items in international trade. During the fifteenth century, trade fairs in southern France provided a place for the active exchange of wools from England and silks from the Middle East. The economic activities surrounding these events gave rise to the first international banking arrangements.

Even the discovery of America was a result of the desire of Europeans to find a faster route not only to the spices but also to the textiles of the Orient. Textile trade quickly took root in America, as colonists sold native dyes such as indigo and cochineal to Europe and bought cottons from India. Although advances were being made in the technology of textile production, the manufacture of cloth in Western Europe in 1700 was still essentially a hand process. Yarns were spun on a spinning wheel and fabrics were woven by hand-operated looms.

FIGURE 1.5

This prehistoric fibrous sandal was recovered from Arnold Research Cave, Missouri. It is approximately 8,000 years old and was made and worn by Early Archaic hunters and gatherers. It is the earliest dated footwear specimen recovered in North America east of the Rocky Mountains. The fibrous leaves of the rattlesnake master plant (*Eryngium yuccifolium*) were used in its construction. Photograph courtesy of Jenna Tedrick Kuffruff, Louisiana State University; specimen from the collection of the Museum of Anthropology, University of Missouri–Columbia.

A major reorganization of manufacturing of a variety of goods occurred during the latter half of the 1700s in Western Europe. These changes, known as the Industrial Revolution, altered not only technology, but also social, economic, and cultural life. The production of textiles was the first area to undergo industrialization during the seventeenth and eighteenth centuries as the result of an economic crisis. Good-quality textile products, produced inexpensively in India and the Far East, were gradually replacing European goods in the international market. In Britain it became imperative that some means be found to increase domestic production, to lower costs, and to improve the quality of textiles. The solution was found in the substitution of machine or nonhuman power for hand processes and human power.

Many important inventions, most importantly spinning machines, automatic looms, and the cotton gin, improved the output and quality of fabrics. These inventions provided the technological base for the industrialization of the textile industry. Each invention improved one step of the process. For example, an improvement that increased the speed of spinning meant that looms were needed that consumed yarn more rapidly. More rapid yarn production required greater quantities of fiber. The growth of the textile industry was further hastened by the use of machines that were driven first by water power, then by steam, and finally by electricity.

The textile industry was fully mechanized by the early part of the nineteenth century. The next major developments in the field were to take place in the chemist's laboratory. Experimentation with the synthesis of dyestuffs in the laboratory rather than from natural plant materials led to the development and use of synthetic dyes in the latter half of the nineteenth century. Other experiments proved that certain natural materials could be dissolved in chemical solvents and re-formed into fibrous form. This principle was used to produce "artificial silk" (now called rayon) from cellulosic materials such as wood chips or cotton linters. By 1910 the first plant for manufacturing rayon had been established in the United States.

The manufacture of rayon marked the beginning of the manufactured textile fibers industry. Since that time, enormous advances have been made in the technology for making fibers, spinning them into yarns, constructing fabrics, and coloring and finishing them. Today, the textile industry utilizes a complex technology based on scientific processes and vast economic organizations. With the application of advanced technology to the textile field, textile use has expanded from the traditional areas of clothing and home furnishings into the fields of construction, medicine, aerospace, sporting goods, and industry. These applications have been made possible by the ability of textile scientists to "engineer" textile fibers, yarns, and fabrics for specific uses. At the same time that textile technology is making strides in new directions, the fabrics that consumers buy for clothing and household use also benefit from the development of new fibers, new methods of yarn and fabric construction, and new finishes for existing fibers and fabrics.

THE MODERN TEXTILE INDUSTRY

Today, a huge international industrial complex encompasses the production of fiber, spinning of yarns, fabrication of cloth, dyeing, finishing, printing, and manufacture of goods for purchase. Consumers purchase many different products made of textiles. The story of the journey that these products make as they progress from fiber to yarn to fabric to finished product is not just the story of spinning yarns, weaving or knitting fabric, or constructing the end product. It is also the story of a complex network of interrelated industries, as demonstrated by the diagram, by no means inclusive, in Figure 1.6.

The Fiber Producer

Natural Fibers

The producer of natural fibers and the producer of manufactured fibers are engaged in two very different businesses. The farmer who raises cotton, the rancher who herds sheep, or the grower of silkworms is trying to produce a maximum quantity of fiber from animal or vegetable sources. The grower may attempt to improve the quality of the seeds or breeding stock but is limited in production by natural factors. If the demand for the product increases or decreases, the grower cannot, like the manufactured fiber producer, simply increase or decrease the short-term supply of fiber.

The natural fiber producer sells fibers to mills or to wholesalers for resale. Except for cotton, which is produced in large quantities domestically, much of the supply of natural fibers such as wool, flax, and other vegetable fibers is produced abroad and imported into the United States. There are, however, a number of small wool growers, over 75,000, with production in almost every state in the country. Cotton farms are typically larger enterprises; in 1997 there were 35,000 cotton growers, mainly in the southern states.

FIGURE 1.6

Overview of the textile business flow in the apparel industries.

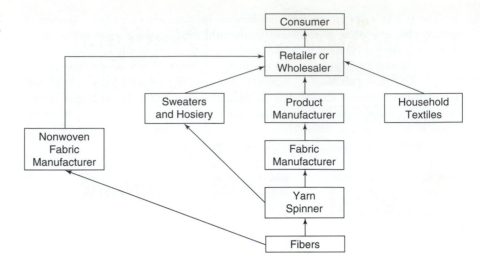

Natural fiber producers have little direct involvement in what happens to their products after they have been sold. The fabrication and finishing of the textiles are undertaken by other segments of the industry. There is, of course, economic self-interest on the part of the fiber producer in the promotion of the fiber. To stimulate interest in or demand for products made of wool, cotton, linen, or silk fibers, fiber producers and others involved in their manufacture, processing, and sale have formed trade associations. The purpose of such trade associations is to stimulate interest in fabrics made from natural fibers through advertising, educational materials, and other promotional campaigns.

Some trade organizations maintained by natural fibers groups include the American Wool Council, the National Cotton Council of America, Cotton Inc., the Mohair Council, and MASTERS OF LINEN, International Linen Promotion. These organizations produce educational materials for use in schools and by consumer groups, provide publicity photographs and information to the press, and sponsor a variety of advertising and public relations campaigns designed to keep the name of the fiber constantly before the public. Such publicity emphasizes the name of the fiber, not the fiber producer. (See Figure 1.7.)

Manufactured Fibers

The term *manufactured fiber* describes a fiber produced commercially through regeneration from natural materials or synthesized from chemicals.[2]

Trade associations in the manufactured fibers industry may be industrywide or specific to particular fibers. The American Fiber Manufacturers Association, Inc. (AFMA) is the trade organization for the manufactured fibers industry, conducting many of the same kinds of promotional activities as described for the natural fibers associations. AFMA always uses generic fiber names—such as polyester, nylon, rayon, and so on—in printed materials, while its individual fiber producing members concentrate on their trademarked fiber names, such as DuPont's Dacron® (polyester) or Wellman's Fortrel® (polyester). Producers of particular fibers may also join together to form fiber-specific trade associations. The Acrylic Council, the Polyester Council, and the American Polyolefin Association are examples of fiber-focused trade associations.

---

2. The term *manufactured fiber* has superceded the older term *man-made fiber* in most segments of the textile industry.

FIGURE 1.7

Examples of some trade association logos for both natural and manufactured fibers.

Production in the manufactured fibers industry differs from the production of natural fibers in a number of ways. While the manufactured fibers industry must depend on available supplies of the raw materials from which fibers are made, this industry is not dependent on natural forces that regulate the supply of fiber. A great many manufactured fibers are made from materials derived from petroleum, and therefore supplies and costs of raw materials may be affected by changes in the price of oil. Manufacturers can regulate production according to supply and demand. Manufacturers can also help to create demand for increased quantities of fiber products through advertising and other publicity.

Many manufactured fiber producers and firms are, or were originally, chemical companies. The fiber manufacturer generally sells the fibers produced to a firm that will make yarns and/or fabrics. These fibers may be sold as unbranded products or commodities. When fibers are sold in this way, the purchaser has no obligation to the fiber manufacturer to produce a product of any specific quality. Products must meet no minimum standards. In short, the buyers can do whatever they wish with the fibers they have purchased.

Other fibers may be sold as *trademarked fibers*. The manufacturer owns the trademark, which is denoted by placing either the symbol ® or ™ after the trademarked name. Trademarked names are always capitalized—for example, Micrell® polyester. The owner of a trademark can bring court action to prevent unauthorized use of the trademark. When the fiber manufacturer's trademarked name is carried by the finished product, the fiber manufacturer has some control over the quality of the fabric, although it is still possible that a poorly made garment could be constructed from the fabric. One advantage to the fabric and garment manufacturers of buying a trademarked fiber is that they can capitalize on the publicity and promotional materials distributed by the fiber manufacturer.

Licensed trademarked fibers are sold only to those manufacturers whose fabrics meet the standards established by the fiber manufacturer. Standards may be set in regard to the construction of fabrics, the manufacture of apparel or other products, and, in blends or combinations of two or more fibers, the appropriate proportion of fibers to be combined.

As an alternative to trademarking, some fiber companies assign *certification mark* names to yarns or fabrics made from their fibers. Such designations require that the items identified with the certification mark meet criteria established by the fiber manufacturer.

Not only do the fabric and garment manufacturers benefit from customer familiarity with the brand name of the fiber, but the fiber manufacturer often shares the costs of advertising or mounts intensive publicity campaigns to promote the fabric, the final product, and even retail outlets where the products are sold.

The interest of manufactured fiber producers in their products does not end when the fiber is sold. Because techniques for spinning and fabricating manufactured fibers may not be uniform for all fibers, the fiber producer provides technical assistance to the fabric manufacturer. Technical bulletins are published that recommend the most effective ways of processing fibers. Consultants from the fiber companies provide information about new developments in textile machinery and finishing. Research and development in fiber-producing companies is often focused on more effective ways of handling manufactured fibers during fabrication.

Fiber producers assist manufacturers of fabrics, garments, or other products to locate sources of yarns and fabrics. The marketing department of a fiber-producing company also maintains a library of fabrics that can be used by manufacturers and their designers.

A wide variety of other services is offered to the direct customers of the fiber companies and to the general public. Exhibits of current products are presented, often at trade and professional meetings. Educational materials for schools, retailers, and consumers are prepared and distributed. Retail stores may be assisted in promoting trademarked products through fashion shows, publicity materials, or cooperative advertising in which the fiber producer pays some part of the advertising costs. Fashion consultants may be available to assist the designers of fabrics, clothes, and furnishings.

Many of these activities are part of an organized advertising and public relations program. In addition to the services offered that result indirectly in publicity and goodwill for the company, direct advertising is also utilized. Besides advertising cooperatively with manufacturers of retail products and retail stores, fiber companies also advertise in publications ranging from those for the trade to general magazines.

Research and development (often abbreviated as R & D) is an important function in most large textile fiber companies. Researchers are constantly looking for new fibers, fiber modifications, and improvements in processing at all steps of manufacture. The whole synthetic fibers industry might be said to have grown out of the research and development program at the chemical company DuPont, for it was in this program that W. H. Carothers first synthesized nylon.

From the Fiber Manufacturer to the Fabric Producer

Fiber must be converted into yarn, except in some specialized "nonwoven" products where the fibers themselves are bonded into a cohesive structure. The production of yarns from short, staple fibers is done by *spinners*. When continuous filament yarns are given special treatments such as texturing, this is done by *throwsters*. *Yarn converters*, who may also be throwsters, dye yarns or add special protective finishes that facilitate knitting or weaving. Textile mills produce knitted, woven, or nonwoven goods. Completed cloth that has not been given any special finishes or coloration is known as *greige goods*. All of these enterprises make up the textile mill product segment of the industry, that also includes dyeing and finishing.

For many years the United States Department of Commerce (DOC) has used a standard industrial classification (SIC) system for all manufacturing establishments for the purpose of collecting and reporting statistics. Textile mill products were coded with the number "22" as a primary classification. Different sub-categories were then coded with three or four digit numbers beginning with 22. Knitting mills, for example, had the

SIC code "225," and companies making women's hosiery were further classified under "2251." Reference to the product chain in Figure 1.6 shows this structure in the industry, where knitted and nonwoven end products are classed under textile mill products.

Data are collected every five years by the DOC in their *Census of Manufactures.* In 1997 the United States adopted a new classification system, the North American Industrial Classification System (NAICS), that is also used by North American Free Trade Agreement (NAFTA) partners Mexico and Canada. Instead of two primary categories for textiles and apparel, there are now three:

1. NAICS 313: includes fabric and yarn producers
2. NAICS 314: includes home furnishings and industrial products (formerly classified under the 23 apparel code) and carpets (which had been coded 22 as textile mill products)
3. NAICS 315: includes knits and sewn apparel products

Professionals in textiles and apparel will encounter and may have to make use of SIC and NAICS codes in their employment. It is possible to track industrial production, employment, inventories, and other activities. Figure 1.8 shows the employment in textile mills (all firms classed under SIC code 22) from 1991 to 1998. It can be seen that this segment represents 3 to 4 percent of all manufacturing employment in the United States.

The industrial classification codes help keep track of product categories since organization of the textile manufacturing industry differs from company to company and also exhibits some differences from one type of textile to another. Cotton fabrics, for example, may be made in a series of steps. One mill may take the raw fiber and turn it into yarn. Then the yarn may be sold to another mill that, in turn, weaves it into cloth. The cloth may be sold to yet another plant where it is dyed or finished. There are separate SIC codes for cotton spinning mills, cotton weaving plants, and dyeing and finishing. The wool industry, by contrast, has traditionally processed the fiber from beginning to end. The same mill buys the fiber, spins the yarn, weaves or knits the goods, and finishes the cloth.

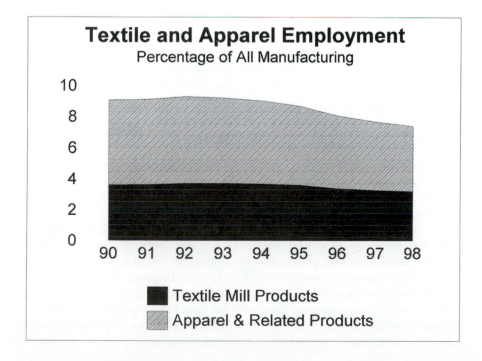

FIGURE 1.8

Employment in the textile and apparel industries. Courtesy of *Textile HiLights,* American Textile Manufacturers Institute.

Since World War II there has been an increased tendency for all segments of the fabric manufacturing industry to follow the pattern of the wool mills. Although all the operations may not necessarily be carried out in the same location, one company performs all these operations as part of the overall production of the fabric. This form of business organization is known as *vertical integration*. Vertically integrated companies produce their own yarn, make that yarn into fabric, and finish the fabrics. Some textile firms, especially those making knits, may also manufacture the final product. Statistics on each of these segments would be reported separately in a vertically integrated mill.

The mills sell their products to apparel or home furnishings manufacturers. This buying or *sourcing* of fabrics and other materials by manufacturers is increasingly international, as further discussion in the section on International Textile Concerns details (see page 19). The mill may also sell yard goods to retail stores for resale to the home sewer and unfinished fabric to jobbers and converters.

Since the number of vertically integrated companies has expanded, converters no longer play as important a role in the textile business as they once did. In these large integrated companies, the conversion of unfinished fabrics (called greige goods) is done within the framework of the company. The traditional role of the converter has been to buy greige goods from mills, to arrange for dyeing and finishing companies to dye or finish the fabric, and then to resell the finished goods.

Mills and converters may have excess fabrics to dispose of. These are often sold to a *jobber*, who buys lots of fabrics for resale to manufacturers or retail stores. The jobber sells in smaller quantities, as a rule, than does the mill or the converter. Manufacturers of garments who want to buy small yardages or specialty fabrics may be able to obtain these more easily from a jobber than from a mill or a converter.

Recently, some companies have begun a reverse trend of *deverticalization*, where they shed some of their operations, for instance yarn spinning, and *outsource* these components, purchasing them from other mills. Some fabric producers have moved into *horizontal integration* of functions. Here, a parent company joins with other companies that produce related kinds of goods. For example, one company may manufacture apparel fabrics, upholstery fabrics, and carpet fabrics.

The advertising and publicity functions of fabric manufacturers are similar to those of the fiber producers. As noted above, the fiber producers and fabric manufacturers may cooperate in publicity campaigns. Fabric producers provide fashion consultants to work with designers and manufacturers, participate in trade and professional shows, produce educational materials, and assist retailers in promoting retail items made from their fabrics.

From the Fabric Manufacturer to the Retailer

After the fabric manufacturer has sold its cloth to the garment manufacturer or to the manufacturer of household goods, the fabrics are converted into the products found on the racks and shelves of the retail store. The apparel and household textile industries are grouped under the SIC code "23." The relative size of this industry segment is shown in the graph in Figure 1.8; companies manufacturing apparel and other textile products employ around 5 percent of all industrial workers in this country.

Producers of apparel, and increasingly of household textiles, must be involved in the identification of current fashion trends. The usual practice in the apparel industry has been to work four to five months in advance of the time at which a garment will be sold. This requires that the textiles for these garments be prepared 12 to 18 months before the garments are sold. With the introduction of computer-based, automated procedures for textile manufacture and management of apparel production, some firms have instituted more rapid production and delivery systems to respond quickly to fashion trends. These procedures can cut delivery time from months to weeks, and in combination with a more flexible approach than the traditional piece-work assembly of garments, have resulted in *agile manufacturing* in the U.S. industry. Industry leaders see agile manufacturing as one advantage of American manufacturers in the competition with foreign producers. (Computerization, agile manufacturing, and quick response techniques are discussed more fully later in this chapter.)

Textile manufacturers must keep up with current trends in design in general and with fashion trends in particular. They must anticipate the direction in which fashion will move, not only for apparel but also for household textiles, to supply the manufacturer with fabric in a timely manner.

Designs for garments come from fashion designers. Some fashion designers have attained sufficient prominence that they own their own manufacturing companies. Others work for specific manufacturing houses; still others may work on a freelance basis, selling individual designs to smaller fashion houses. The fashion designer often works closely with the textile company. The fabric company provides the fashion designer with swatches of fabrics from its new lines, or in some instances, the company may make an "exclusive" fabric that will be sold only to a particular fashion house. It is rare for fabric manufacturers to grant exclusive rights to a fabric to one apparel producer. When this is done, the fashion house is generally a very good customer, and the exclusive rights to the fabric usually last for only a limited time before the fabric becomes available more widely.

After the designs for a particular season have been prepared, the garment manufacturer shows the line to retail buyers and to the press. Retail store buyers place orders for the items shown in the line. If sufficient orders are placed, the garment is manufactured, and the orders are delivered to the store for sale.

Because the garment manufacturer does not sell directly, but through retail outlets, advertising and promotional campaigns of manufacturers are most often tied directly or indirectly to retail store promotions. Some garments are selected by manufacturers for national or regional advertisements. Knowing that a particular garment is slated for advertisement in *Vogue, Bazaar*, or *Seventeen* magazine may encourage a buyer to place orders for the item. The additional press exposure may enhance the salability of the garment. Retail stores that are especially good customers may be singled out for cooperative advertising in which the names of several stores at which the item is available are specifically mentioned in the advertisement. Other cooperative promotional efforts between retail store and manufacturer include fashion shows, provision of counter cards and other display materials for the retailer, and training programs for sales personnel.

In addition to apparel, which accounts for about 39 percent of the textile market, consumers purchase a wide variety of household textiles. Household textiles account for 39 percent of the textile market.[3] Many household textile products, such as sheets, towels, tablecloths, curtains, bed coverings, and area carpets are constructed in the appropriate dimensions and require only some simple finishing such as hemming before they are sold to wholesalers or to retailers.

Wall-to-wall carpet and wall covering materials are usually installed by skilled technicians who work for the retailer. Vertically integrated manufacturers will sell materials directly to the retailer. Other firms may sell to wholesalers who, in turn, supply retailers. Fabric used for coverings of mattresses and upholstery for furniture is sold to the manufacturer where it is cut and applied to the mattress or furniture body.

---

3. Statistics provided by American Textile Manufacturers Institute, 1998. Washington, DC: Fiber Economics Bureau.

Fashion is an important consideration in household textiles as well as in apparel. Designers' names are used in merchandising products such as curtains, bedcovers, sheets, and towels.

INDUSTRIAL TEXTILES

Most consumers are not aware of the segment of the textile industry known as *industrial textiles*, even though they encounter these products every day. Industrial textiles is the most commonly used name for textile applications in agriculture, air and water filtration, architecture, automobiles, banners and flags, casual furniture, environmental protection, earth stabilization, medical products, recreational products, and transportation vehicles. Apparel items in this category are those in which performance is paramount: cleanroom garments, protective gloves and clothing for industry and farming, industry garments that don't develop electrostatic charges (World of Industrial Fabrics n.d.)

Other descriptive terms applied to this segment of the industry are *industrial fabrics*, *technical textiles*, *engineered fabrics*, and *technical fabrics*. Industrial textiles may be woven, knitted, or nonwoven, often of manufactured fibers. Fashion is not a factor in industrial textiles, but instead such functional characteristics as strength, stability, chemical resistance, and weight are likely to be important. Examples of industrial textiles range from small products such as filters and auto safety belts to enormous structures such as roofs, tents, and storage tanks. Roofs and other building structures encompass the field of *textile architecture*, a growing area of interest that combines engineering and art design. Consumers of industrial products include the construction, mining, sanitation, and transportation industries; medicine; and the military.

The industrial fabric segment of the textile field has grown rapidly in recent years. Some of the more dramatic examples of progress in textile technology have come in this area, particularly fiber-reinforced composites for the aerospace industry and *geotextiles*. Geotextiles are textiles used in soil and soil-based structures such as roads, dams, and erosion-control products. (See Figure 1.9.)

FIGURE 1.9

Flexible geotextile channel with 100% coconut fiber matrix sewn between two heavy-weight, ultraviolet-light-stabilized nets. Channel is placed on roadsides and in ditches to prevent erosion of soil after construction. Product of North American Green. Photograph by Julia Thames.

AUTOMATION AND COMPUTER USE

As with practically every other endeavor of our lives, computers and electronic technologies have had a tremendous impact on textile-related industries and businesses. Computerization has made a difference in design, decision making, communication, and process control in manufacturing. Feedback on consumer preferences and product sales is readily available to fiber and fabric producers, apparel manufacturers, dyers, and finishers. The computer has become a routine tool for apparel and interior designers and for product developers; and control of manufacturing processes is increasingly a job for computer programmers.

The textile and apparel industries have formed an organization called the Textile/Clothing Technology Corporation or (TC)^2. The purpose of TC^2 is to conduct research about applications of electronic technology in the textile and apparel industries and to educate executives, engineers, technologists, and educators about automated systems, their potential, and their use. (TC)^2 is funded jointly, largely by matching grants, by the industry and the federal government.

Computer-Aided Design (CAD)

Computer-aided design (CAD) in textiles is applied to the design of yarns and fabrics and to coloration. In those firms that are vertically integrated, CAD may also be applied to apparel design and manufacture. Programs allow the textile designer to develop and modify designs interactively, speeding up the process and providing electronic links to production.

Recent techniques in three-dimensional (3-D) imaging enable simulation of the actual fabric structure and texture on screen and advances in color printing allow better reproduction of the design on paper or other media. Designs can be scanned into the system and then modified or redesigned. CAD applications for knitted fabrics and garments have advanced rapidly. A variety of CAD systems that interface design and construction in the production of woven fabrics and knitted goods are currently available and in use.

New technologies have also been developed to predict the drape of fabric on 3-D moving figures, integrating the fabric and apparel design stages. This involves mathematical modeling using fabric behavioral properties. The fabric's physical characteristics are separated from the surface design so that different types of motion can be applied to any design (Gray 1994; Gray 1998). (See Figure 1.10.) This, along with the textile design capabilities described above, allows merchandisers to create "virtual samples" for customers (Ross 1998).

Computer figures are also used in *3-D scanning*, a development in CAD, that is moving the apparel manufacturing toward *mass customization*, which is the mass production of custom garments. Women's jeans produced through such a process were first marketed in November 1994 (Rifkin 1994). Custom Clothing Technology, Inc., developed the specific process used by Levi Strauss & Company.

Today *made-to-measure* (MTM) allows consumers to input body measurements and select style, fabric, and color. This information is transmitted electronically to a factory where a robot cuts a pattern to the correct individualized measurements. The garment is assembled and shipped to the retailer or to the customer in about three weeks. Using this technology, an increasing number of companies are offering standard items such as pants, jeans, swimwear, and even household textiles through the Internet, joining other industries in *electronic commerce*.

FIGURE 1.10.

Images from a computer screen of predictions of the three-dimensional draping qualities of textiles. Photographs courtesy of Stephen Gray and Anthony Rosella, researchers, Nottingham Trent University, Nottingham, U. K.

Computer-Aided Manufacturing (CAM)

Computer-aided manufacturing (CAM) helps with textile production processes. Computer systems can be used to plan factory layouts and production schedules of maximum efficiency, guide robots, to monitor and control specific operations, and to diagnose and correct problems. Looms, knitting machines, and dyeing processes can now be controlled by computer. All of these provide opportunities to shorten the design to store time for manufacturing textile products.

In assembly plants electronic robots perform tasks that range from transport of materials within the plant to storing and retrieving products. Robotic control of construction techniques for apparel and household textiles is somewhat more challenging than in automobile and other industries. Fabrics are soft materials with fuzzy edges, and robotic manipulation of these materials is not easy.

Electronic on-line inspection of fabrics is however fairly standard. In addition the more accurate control of processes, that is now available in fiber manufacturing for example, can eliminate some of the testing of finished products and provide better quality control. Digital printing, a new technique that is similar to ink jet printing on paper, allows fast implementation of designs and contributes to mass customization.

Especially important to the success of quick response technologies and mass customization is the ability of computers to monitor inventories and store and retrieve data about raw materials, the progress of orders during manufacturing, and linkages with customers. Systems that permit intersystem communication are called computer-integrated manufacturing (CIM). As electronic technologies were adopted by the textile industry, incompatible systems inhibited communication between the different segments of the industry. Significant progress has been made, however, in standardizing the various computer systems installed within the textile manufacturing sector.

INTERNATIONAL TEXTILE CONCERNS

Driven by relative costs, and enabled by the electronic information flow around the world, the textile product chain depicted in Figure 1.6 has spread across national borders. All the operations mentioned thus far—namely, fiber production, yarn manufacture, spinning, weaving or knitting, coloration and finishing of textiles, and fabrication of products can be and are carried out in many different countries.

Many factors ranging from the wages paid to laborers to the exchange rate paid for American dollars tend to make textiles and textile products manufactured abroad cheaper than those produced in the United States. As a result, retailers have tended to increase the quantity of imported apparel and household textiles. The domestic textile production industry has suffered severe economic losses as penetration of imports into the U.S. market has continued to increase each year. (See Figure 1.11.)

The General Agreement on Tariffs and Trade (GATT) was originally established in 1947 to govern trade negotiations between countries. Renegotiation of the GATT, which covers international trade not only in textiles but in a wide variety of goods, began with a series of talks in 1986 known as the Uruguay Round. The U.S. Senate approved the new agreement in December 1994.

Before renegotiation the GATT had included a special Multifiber Arrangement (MFA) that established quotas and other procedures intended to protect both the importer and exporter of textile goods. Under the new GATT, MFA agreements are being phased out so that by 2004, all quotas will be terminated, not only in the developed countries of the world but also in the developing countries. A Textiles Monitoring Body (TMB) was established to oversee the phase-out of restrictions and tariffs. (For a detailed description of the provisions of the new GATT agreement, see Khanna 1994.)

Another agreement that has removed trade barriers is the North American Free Trade Agreement (NAFTA). This agreement involves trade among the United States, Canada, and Mexico.

FIGURE 1.11

Graph shows the growth of imports of textile and apparel into the United States between 1986 and 1997 as compared with exports. Courtesy of *Textile HiLights*, American Textile Manufacturers Institute.

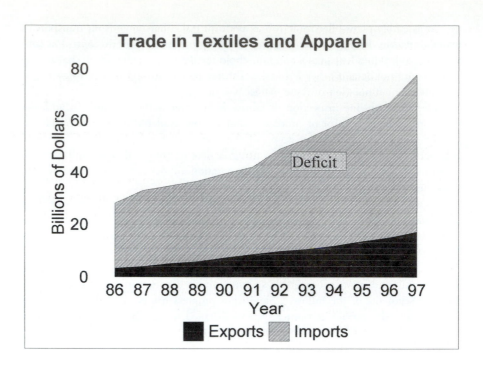

The effects of these agreements on trade in textiles and apparel can be seen by referring again to Figures 1.8 and 1.11. The trade deficit has widened and employment has decreased more sharply in recent years. The number of employees in apparel manufacturing particularly is down, while yarn and fabric producers have had a slower decline, undoubtedly due to higher productivity and adoption of newer technologies.

As imports have made increasing inroads into the U.S. textile and apparel markets, these industries have tried to increase the awareness of consumers about imports and their effect on the American industry. Congress has acted in support of American textiles by passing legislation requiring that all textile products carry labels indicating the country of origin, including a designation to show products produced in the United States. Campaigns supporting domestic textile products have been sponsored by a number of trade organizations and textile- and apparel-producing companies. Print and other media publicity continues to tell the consuming public about American products and the importance of purchasing textiles that are "Made in America."

An important advantage the American textile industry has over foreign competition in the long run is its technological sophistication and, particularly, its potential for automation. Increased automation can cut costs and make American products more competitive and responsive to the need of the retail industry for a "fast turn-around." For example, if a particular item of fashionable apparel sells exceptionally well and fast, the retailer cannot reorder the item from Hong Kong and expect to have it for the same season. If American manufacturers can supply products quickly and dependably, some retailers have indicated that they are willing to pay slightly more for products.

In response to the freer trade environment under GATT and NAFTA, U.S. textile firms have concentrated on automating their operations and on products with the greatest export potential, such as industrial fabrics, finished apparel fabrics, warp knits, specialty yarns, and home furnishings textiles. Manufacturers and trade associations are likely to accelerate their efforts to educate the public about domestically made products. They will intensify research to improve manufacturing technology, emphasizing increased automation and mass customization to improve their ability to meet customers' needs for merchandise quickly.

The Responsibility for Quality

All segments of the textile products industry—the fiber producer, the fabric manufacturer, the product manufacturer, and the retailer—are responsible to some extent for maintaining quality and for complying with legal requirements for labeling. Unless product labeling or promotion makes specific claims about performance, no standard of performance is required by law for most products purchased by consumers. Nevertheless, many companies in the textile and apparel industries accept the maintenance of quality as an ethical responsibility.

Most purchased textile products are from retail or mail-order merchants. If these merchants value their reputations, they respond to justified customer complaints by promptly exchanging goods or refunding purchase price. Retailers can usually obtain refunds for defective products from manufacturers.

Labeling

Some labeling information, however, is required by law. Provisions of the Textile Fiber Products Identification Act mandate labeling of fabrics for fiber content and country of origin. Care labeling regulations require that permanent labels giving care instructions be affixed to apparel. (See Appendix C for a summary of regulatory legislation applied to textiles.) The textile manufacturer must supply information for the labels to the product manufacturer. The product manufacturer must attach any required labels to the product. In two instances the retailer is responsible for label contents: when the retailer is also the importer and when the retailer affixes a private label.

Textile Standards

Manufacturers of textile products are sometimes required to conform to *standard specifications*, defined levels of performance that products must achieve to be considered acceptable for use. The shortened term *standards* refers to established standard specifications. Products must conform to textile product standards when mandated by legislation such as the Flammable Fabrics Act. Some retailers direct the manufacturers from whom they buy to meet certain standards for products. The Department of Defense establishes minimum specifications for textiles used by the military and some federal agencies. Funding regulations for federally financed construction products require that carpets, draperies, and the like conform to stated specifications. Standard specifications also provide a basis for comparing the results of textile studies by different researchers.

Organizations that Establish Standards

The organization most actively involved in establishing textile standards is the American Society for Testing and Materials (ASTM). ASTM is an organization of industrial and academic professionals that establishes standard test methods and specifications through a system of technical committees. One of these committees, D-13, deals with textile materials and products. The American National Standards Institute (ANSI) is a nonprofit federation whose membership is composed of trade, labor, technical, and consumer organizations and governmental agencies. ANSI does not originate standards but serves as a clearinghouse and coordinator for standards in many fields. Textile fabric performance standards developed by ASTM Committee D-13 are accepted by ANSI.

Activities related to the setting of standards are not limited to the United States. International standardized systems of measurement and standard specifications have been developed by the International Organization for Standardization (ISO). Development of international standards facilitates the exchange of goods as global trade increases. A new system of measurement, *Systéme international d'unités* (SI), or the International System of Units, has been adopted by most countries. Its details are published and controlled by an international treaty organization called the International Bureau of Weights and Measures.

Textile Testing

Products must be tested to determine whether they meet established standards. Two groups in the United States have been closely involved in developing testing methods. The American Association of Textile Chemists and Colorists (AATCC) is composed of persons from the textile wet processing industry, textile chemists, others working in varying segments of the textile industry, and educators. The association establishes testing methods, largely in the area of chemical testing, and maintains an active educational program implemented through national and regional meetings and a monthly journal, the *Textile Chemist* and *Colorist*, The *Technical Manual* describes specific test methodologies.

Tests established by ASTM are focused more specifically on physical testing and the testing of fabric construction. ASTM publishes *ASTM Standards*, a compilation of test methods, and *ASTM Standard Performance Specifications for Textile Fabrics*, a group of voluntary fabric performance standards that serves as a guide to manufacturers and consumers. Chapter 26 discusses textile testing in greater detail.

ISO 9000

A series of quality management standards for industry (called ISO 9000) has been established by the ISO and adopted by ANSI. ISO 9000 does not mandate specific standards for a manufacturer or product but seeks to ensure that a product is what the customer expects. Under the program a company can receive ISO 9000 registration by developing, and having approved, quality control programs for the design, production, inspection, and installation of its products. Most fiber manufacturers in the United States are registered under ISO 9000.

CAREER OPPORTUNITIES IN THE TEXTILE FIELD

From the preceding discussion of the organization of the textile industry, it is evident that a wide variety of employment opportunities exists in this field and its related areas. (See Figure 1.12.) The following brief, and very general, list provides not only a view of the breadth of the field but also an appropriate summary for this chapter.

FIGURE **1.12**

Professionals working with textile products. (a) Retailer orders apparel products. (b) Interior designers select home furnishing fabrics. (c) Engineers and textiles scientists install geotextiles for testing. Photograph for (a) by Shea Firnberg, for (b) by Teresa A. Summers, and for (c) by John R. Collier.

a

b

c

Textile careers include the areas of:

1. Marketing and merchandising
   - Wholesale and retail merchandising of fiber, fabric, apparel, interior, and industrial products
   - Advertising and public relations
   - Market research
   - Manufacturer sales of textile products and equipment
   - Buying of products for production and retailing establishments

2. Management
   - Store or department management
   - Business management of production facilities

3. Production
   - Fiber, yarn, and fabric processing
   - Textile dyeing and finishing
   - Production of apparel and household and industrial textiles
   - Technical assistance to producers

4. Product design and development
   - Design of textiles, apparel, and interior furnishings
   - Developing and/or evaluating new products

5. Care, preservation, and restoration
   - Laundering and dry-cleaning of textile products
   - Conservation and exhibition of historic textiles

6. Education
   - Educating professionals in industry, trade organizations, technical schools, colleges and universities, continuing education, and cooperative extension.

In the accompanying Career Brief, professionals in several fields explain how knowledge of textiles helps them in their jobs.

CAREER BOX 1.1   Professionals Speak. . . .

Apparel Designers

As an assistant designer, it is vital that I have a good understanding of the materials that I am working with. I must know the physical characteristics of each fabric that is selected for a collection. I must be able to determine immediately if I am working with a terry fleece or a brushed terry; the wrong decision could be disastrous. Without a strong background in textiles, I would not be able to successfully complete my daily tasks.

As a pattern maker, it is very important to have a good working knowledge of textile components, such as fiber, yarn, and weave. Such knowledge allows me to predict how a fabric will respond in a particular design and better determine the necessity of internal, structural components of the garment.

Interior Designers

It has been very beneficial having a working knowledge of fibers and their properties. I can help advise clients about the end use of a particular fabric, as well as about durability and care. You would be amazed at the people in the trade who haven't a clue and therefore give bad advice. I wish I had taken more textiles courses.

Paint is often cited as an inexpensive and quick way to change the look of a room. I prefer textiles. I contend that textiles, even the most humble and economical varieties, can add color, depth and great interest to an interior space. I recently utilized generous quantities of a wonderful good fabric draped over a makeshift table constructed from ordinary wood doors. These fabric-draped tables provided a sensual and theatrical backdrop for antiques and fine art in a high-end residential living room.

Merchandisers/Retailers

Knowledge of textiles helps me do my job as a retail merchandiser by strengthening my credibility with clients making purchase decisions. Use of proper terminology of fabric types and constructions helps me communicate product features. I am enabled to provide advice regarding comfort, care, and performance of garments and can help justify prices of specialty fibers and fabrics. Knowledge of textiles is a powerful selling tool in the retail environment.

Working in the outerwear department of a large department store, I am frequently called on to suggest items for specific needs. My knowledge of textiles allows me to explain features of these items to make them more appealing to customers. For example, I recently was called on to provide information on the sandwich type construction in jackets and ski wear that makes them lightweight and fashionable, yet functional because of the manufacturing technique and fibers used.

Testers/Quality Control Specialists

As lab manager of the textile testing service, I deal with textiles that have varying constructions, fiber contents, and end uses. On occasion, the scientist is unaware of which test methods would provide them with the information they need, or the specifications for the textile's end use. A background knowledge of textile manufacturing and fiber processing helps us handle samples and interpret the results of testing. Recently we assisted an outside agency with determining finish on samples. That required understanding everything from differences in fibers, in fiber processing, in yarn manufacturing, fabric manufacturing, and finishing.

The quality control of apparel products involves not only the control of workmanship, but also determination of the properties of fabrics. Therefore, a good understanding of the mechanical, physical and chemical properties of fibers and fabrics, and their manufacturing process, is essential for quality control. This knowledge allows the quality control engineer to determine if the fabric properties correspond to the values indicated by the manufacturer, and to set the limits for accepting apparel products for their intended end use and consumers' expectations.

References

ASTM. 1986. *Compilation of ASTM standard definitions.* Philadelphia: American Society for Testing and Materials.

Fowler, B. 1995. Find suggests weaving preceded settled life. *New York Times*, May 9, C1.

Gray, S. 1994. Formula for a fashion show. *Bobbin* 34 (January): 54.

Gray, S. 1998. In virtual fashion. *IEEE Spectrum* 35(2): 18.

Khanna, S. R. 1994. The new GATT agreement: Implications for the world's textile and clothing industries. *Textile Outlook International* 52(March): 10–37.

Kuttruff, J. T., S. G. DeHart, and M. J. O'Brien 1998. 7500 years of prehistoric footwear from Arnold Research Cave, Missouri. *Science* 281: 72.

Rifkin, G. 1994. Digital blue jeans pour data and legs into customized fit. *New York Times*, November 8, A1.

Ross, T. 1998. Made-to-measure: Finding a fit with the industry. *Apparel Industry* (April): 56–60.

Wilford, J. N. 1993a. New finds suggest even earlier trade on fabled silk road. *New York Times*, March 16, C1, C8.

Wilford, J. N. 1993b. Site in Turkey yields oldest cloth ever found. *New York Times*, July 13, C1, C8.

World of industrial fabrics (n. d.). St. Paul, Minn.: Industrial Textiles International.

Review Questions

1. Explain the difference between fibers, yarns, and fabrics.
2. Identify at least three specific instances of trade in textiles before the Industrial Revolution.
3. Describe the role of trade associations in the natural fibers industry. Describe their role in the manufactured fibers industry.
4. What is the difference between a trademark and a certification mark?
5. Describe the flow of textile products in the apparel industry from the procuring of the fiber until the product reaches the ultimate consumer.
6. Describe the steps in mass customization of: an apparel product; a household textile product.
7. What changes have taken place in the American textile and apparel industries as a result of GATT and NAFTA?
8. Give the full name of the organization represented by each of the following acronyms and explain the functions of each organization: AATCC, ASTM, ANSI, ISO.

Recommended Readings

Barber, E. J. W. 1991. *Prehistoric textiles.* Princeton, N.J.: Princeton University Press.

Berkstresser, G. A., and D. R. Buchanan. 1986. *Automation and robotics in the textile and apparel industries.* Park Ridge, N.J.: Noyes.

Dickerson, K. G. 1995. *Textiles and apparel in the global economy.* 2d ed. Englewood Cliffs, N.J.: Prentice Hall.

Ellis, K. 1993. Think Quick. *New York Apparel News*, March, 34*ff.*

Hall, A. J. 1994. Developing international and European standards. *Textile Chemist and Colorist* 26 (May):17.

Kalogerdis, C. 1994. Whatever happened to Quick Response? *America's Textiles International* 23 (October): 43.

Moore, L. 1994. Protection and competition in the U.S. market for textiles and clothing. *Journal of the Textile Institute* 85 (2): 244.

Novina, T. 1993. Home textiles market evolves. *America's Textiles International* 22 (November): K/A 11.

Roberts, M. 1993. Computerization in textiles. *Textile Horizons* (December): 59.

Scheller, H., and L. C. Rabon. 1997, Mass customization affords product variety. *Bobbin* 39 (3): 43.

Tait, N. 1999. Internet users exploit global channels. *Textile Horizons* (May): 8.

——— Textile architecture spreads its wings over the world. 1998. *Technical Textiles International* 7(6): 17.

——— Towards total IT integration. 1998. *Textile Month* (December): 20.

Textile World 140, October 1990. Special issue devoted to U.S. textile industry bicentennial.

TEXTILE FIBERS AND THEIR PROPERTIES

The smallest unit used in making the garment you wear, the upholstery fabric you sit on, or any other product that is part of your daily life is usually a textile fiber. Textile fibers, which are small threadlike structures, may be obtained from natural materials or created through technology. Natural fibers are taken from animal, vegetable, or mineral sources. The most important animal fibers are wool and silk. Cotton and flax (from which linen is made) are the most important vegetable fibers. Asbestos, a mineral fiber, had been used for special products where nonflammable materials were important, but it proved to be carcinogenic and has been replaced in most applications by manufactured fibers.

Manufactured fibers are created through technology. They are generally divided into two classifications: *regenerated fibers* and *synthetic fibers*. Regenerated fibers can be made from natural materials that cannot be used for textiles in their original form but that can be regenerated (re-formed) into usable fibers by chemical treatment and processing. The first commercially successful manufactured fiber was a forerunner of modern rayon, a regenerated cellulose fiber, production of which began around the beginning of the twentieth century. Synthetic fibers, the second type of manufactured fiber, are synthesized from chemical substances. Nylon, a generic name given to the first synthetic fiber by its manufacturer DuPont, was developed by W. H. Carothers. Although nylon was first marketed in 1938, wartime demands for chemicals and nylon fabrics meant that it was not until after World War II that commercial nylon production for the civilian market was initiated on a large scale.

The invention of nylon, and its successful marketing after the war, stimulated the synthesis of additional fibers. Gradually, a wide variety of manufactured fibers

FIGURE 2.1

Major classifications of textile fibers.

were introduced. See Figure 2.1 for a list of all fibers that fall into the aforementioned classifications.

These natural and manufactured textile fibers differ in a number of specific ways. If you could magically enlarge a single atom so that you could enter its interior as if you were entering rooms decorated by different interior designers, you would see that each is unique. With so many individual types of fibers which, to the naked eye, do not really look all that different, those who work with textile materials have evolved ways of describing these differences. They speak of different properties of textiles. By *properties* they mean the various characteristics of textile fibers, yarns, and fabrics.

PART I. FUNDAMENTAL CHEMICAL AND PHYSICAL CONCEPTS

Understanding Polymers

What gives each fiber type its unique qualities is its chemical composition. In the chapters that follow it will be difficult to understand fully the properties of textile fibers and the fabrics into which they are made without some elementary understanding of polymers. The discussion that follows gives a simple explanation of the basic concepts related to polymers. It also introduces a number of terms that appear frequently in technical writing and research about textiles.

Textile fibers are classified according to their chemical composition. Definitions of textile fibers (which are provided in the chapters dealing with each fiber) identify the major chemical repeating units that make up the fiber. In most of these definitions, the unit is named and its formula shown. For example, acrylic is defined as a "manufactured fiber in which the fiber-forming substance is any *long-chain synthetic polymer* composed of at least 85 percent by weight of *acrylonitrile units*." To understand these definitions and some of the properties of textile fibers, it is useful to understand terms such as "long-chain synthetic polymer" and to have some elementary understanding of the chemical structure of textile fibers.

Almost all fibers, whether natural or manufactured, are *organic;* that is, they contain the element carbon. Organic compounds such as textile fibers are made up of carbon together with a few other elements such as hydrogen, oxygen, nitrogen, the halogens (fluorine, chlorine, bromine, and iodine), and sulfur. Carbon atoms frequently combine with each other in a linear, chainlike arrangement as in the following diagram:

Carbon to carbon to carbon to carbon:

$$C \rightarrow C \rightarrow C \rightarrow C$$

The connections, which are strong chemical bonds between atoms, may be shown by drawing lines to indicate the bonds:

$$C-C-C-C-, \text{ and so on.}$$

If a double bond is formed between two atoms, a double line may be drawn: $C=C$. Double bonded carbon atoms are not as free to rotate as those with single bonds and so molecules with double bonds are less flexible.

Carbon atoms can combine not only in a linear fashion but also to form a ring:

This ring structure is usually drawn without showing all the carbon atoms:

Rings in a molecular compound can confer rigidity and stiffness to the material.

A common structure in organic chemistry is the benzene ring, which occurs in the molecules of a number of different textile fibers and dyes. Benzene consists of six carbon atoms in a ring structure with six hydrogen atoms, one on each carbon, and bonded in alternating, or *conjugated,* single and double bonds:

The electrons in the double bonds do not remain at specific bonds but are spread over the ring, or delocalized. Consequently, benzene is more commonly represented as:

Compounds containing one or more benzene rings or more complex fused rings are called *aromatic* compounds. The name derives from the fact that these rings are often part of the structure of substances with strong, and usually pleasant, odors.

Formulas of organic compounds are extremely complex. The formula for the repeating unit of cellulose, the basic material of which cotton, rayon, linen, and other vegetable fibers are composed, is shown here as the chemist would write it.

Polymers and Polymerization

The definition of acrylic given earlier used the term *polymer*. The word *polymer* means "many parts," and these molecules, also known as *macromolecules*, contain hundreds or thousands of atoms bonded together. Analysis of these large molecules shows that they are composed of molecular subunits containing perhaps 3 to 20 or more atoms and that the polymers were built up from many of these smaller units, or *monomers*, joined together. In cellulose, for instance, the subunit is glucose. Interestingly, glucose is also the subunit of another well-known polymer, starch. Starch and cellulose have completely different properties, however, because the monomers are bonded to each other differently; starch is not fibrous and can be digested by humans, whereas the opposite is true for cellulose.

Types of Polymers. The formation of polymers, or *polymerization*, is accomplished through the joining of monomers, one to the other. In the formation of polymers, several intermediate steps take place. Two monomers may join to form a *dimer* (two-monomer molecule), a dimer and a monomer join to form a *trimer* (three-monomer molecule), two dimers join to form a *tetramer* (four-monomer structure), and so on. These compounds, that have a small number of repeating units, are usually classified as *oligomers*. As oligomers grow into large polymer molecules, the number of repeating units in the molecule becomes important. This number is the *degree of polymerization* (DP). Longer polymers, with high DPs, contribute strength to fibers.

Monomers may be combined and can be arranged in a variety of ways to make polymers. *Homopolymers* are polymers composed of identical units of the same monomer substance. Polypropylene, which is made only of propylene monomers, is a homopolymer. *Copolymers* contain two or more different units. Copolymerization is likely to be used to create textile fibers with desirable properties not present in the homopolymer.

To illustrate the differences in polymer arrangements, imagine that M below represents identical units of the same monomer in a homopolymer.

$$-M-M-M-M-M-M-M-M-M-$$

Copolymer structures may have any of several different arrangements. Using M to represent one monomer type and m to represent a second monomer type, copolymer structures may have several different arrangements:

1. Random arrangement with no clear pattern in the alternating of monomers:

$$-M-M-m-m-M-m-M-M-m-m-M-m-$$

2. Alternating copolymer arrangement:

$$-M-m-M-m-M-m-M-m-M-m-M-m-$$

3. Block copolymer arrangement, with individual monomers grouped together and these groups alternating:

$$-M-M-M-M-m-m-m-m-M-M-M-M-m-m-m-m$$

Sometimes a small amount of a third monomer may be added to impart some desired quality otherwise lacking in the polymer. For example, the polymer may benefit from having some sites that would react with certain types of dyes or to form *crosslinks*, that are strong chemical bonds between polymers. Imagine that x represents the third monomer added to a random polymer arrangement:

$$-M-M-m-x-m-M-m-m-x-M-M-m-$$

These representations show polymer arrangements that are "linear," that is, the monomers are predominantly in a long straight chain. Yet another structure can also be formed, that of graft polymers that are made by attaching monomers, or short-chain oligomers, onto long-chain polymers. The long chain forms the base structure, rather like the trunk of a tree, with the side chains branching off. Grafting makes possible the addition of qualities not present in the "mother" fiber. Grafting of monomers can reduce static electricity buildup, improve dyeability, improve soil resistance, or decrease shrinkage.

In contrast to a linear copolymer, a graft copolymer might be represented as follows:

```
        m                                                m
        |                                                |
        m                                                m
        |                                                |
        m                                                m
        |                                                |
M—M—M—M—M—M—M—M—M—M—M—M—M—M—M—M—M—M—M—M—M—M—M—
```

Formation of Polymers. Linear polymers are formed either by *condensation polymerization* or by *addition polymerization*. In condensation polymerization, monomers join other molecules as a small molecule (usually water, ammonia, or methanol) is eliminated:

monomer + monomer → dimer + water (eliminated)
dimer + dimer → tetramer + water (eliminated)

Monomers may link up with monomers, monomers with polymers, polymers with polymers, and so on to form a growing chain, with the elimination of water or another compound during the process. Examples of this process are, among the natural fibers, cellulose from glucose and, among the manufactured fibers, nylon from its components. (See Figure 2.2.)

Addition polymerization differs from condensation polymerization in that no compound is split off. Monomers with the capacity to react (unsaturated monomers) can add to each other in a chemically effected chain reaction to join into a long-chain molecule. This is generally accomplished under conditions of high pressure and high temperature and in the presence of a *catalyst* (a substance that does not take part in the reaction but facilitates the reaction):

```
                    reactive     reactive
monomer =  monomer  =  dimer  →  polymer
    +          +          +
activator   monomer    monomer
```

(See Figure 2.3.) An example of this process is the polymerization of acrylonitrile to create acrylic fibers. Acrylonitrile is a nitrogen-containing three-carbon molecule.

This, in highly simplified terms, is part of the chemical process that takes place in the manufacture of synthetic fibers. Most of the specific processes used by companies to make their trademarked textile fibers are carefully guarded secrets. Such confidential processes are known as *proprietary processes*. Textile chemists, however, can make reasonably accurate estimates of the processes used by each company by reading research reports and by analyzing the properties and physical structure of the fibers.

Arrangement of Polymers in Fibers

The arrangement of the polymer chains in a fiber affects many properties such as strength, elongation, absorbency, and dyeability. This arrangement can vary from random to parallel. A random, unorganized arrangement of long-chain molecules creates an *amorphous* area within the fiber. (See Figure 2.4.) Orderly, parallel arrangement of polymer segments in a three-dimensional pattern is known as *crystallinity*, but crystalline regions may lie in a variety of positions relative to fiber length. If the crystalline structures are parallel to the length, or axis, of the fiber, they are said to be *oriented*. (See Figure 2.5.)

Most fibers possess largely crystalline structures, but they also have some amorphous areas. The amorphous areas are weaker than the crystalline areas, and fibers with the highest levels of crystallinity are the strongest fibers. If the crystalline areas are oriented, the fiber strength is enhanced.

FIGURE 2.2

Schematic representation of condensation reaction. (a) Unreacted monomer units with chemically reactive groups shown as shaded area at each end of the molecule. (b) Collisions between moving monomer units; collisions 1, 2, and 3 occur at reactive sites on each unit, leading to bond formation and release of by-product molecules. The molecules bounce off each other in collision 4. (c) New dimer units have formed, each with reactive site at both ends. (d) Larger fragments have formed by further reaction with monomer units. (e) End of reaction; fragments have joined together to form part of molecular chains. The by-product is removed at the end of the reaction or preferably as it is liberated on bond formation. Reproduced from *Textiles*, and permission granted from *Textiles Magazine,* a publication of The Textile Institute, Manchester, U.K.

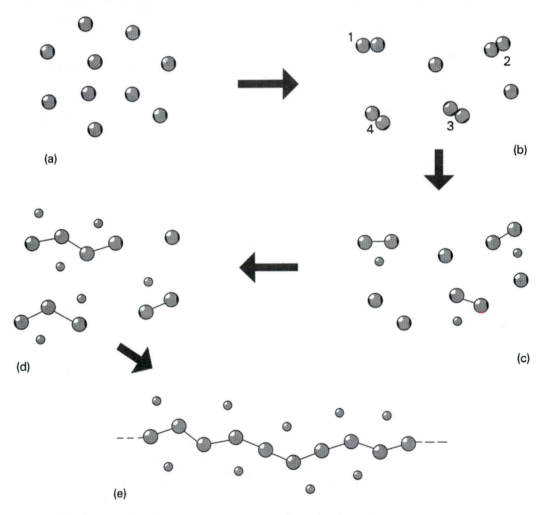

While the crystalline areas affect fiber strength, the amorphous regions contribute other important properties. Dyes and finishes, as well as moisture, are absorbed primarily in the disordered regions because there is more space there. In addition, amorphous fibers are more flexible and stretchable. The random or coiled polymers in these areas can be pulled into a linear arrangement, allowing the material to stretch. Table 2.1 summarizes some differences between crystalline and amorphous fibers and Consumer Brief 2.1 discusses the effect that polymer arrangement can have on fiber properties.

FIGURE 2.3

Schematic representation of addition reaction. (a) Unreacted monomer units approached by highly reactive initiator molecule (shaded black). (b) Chemical bond formed between initiator molecule and monomer unit. The reactive site, marked by an asterisk, transfers to the opposite end of the new molecule. (c) Chain propagation, another monomer unit added. (d) Chain propagation continues with successive addition of monomer units and transfer of reactive sites. (e) End of reaction; the initiating molecule is at one end of the chain. Reproduced from *Textiles* and permission granted from *Textiles Magazine*, a publication of The Textile Institute, Manchester, U.K.

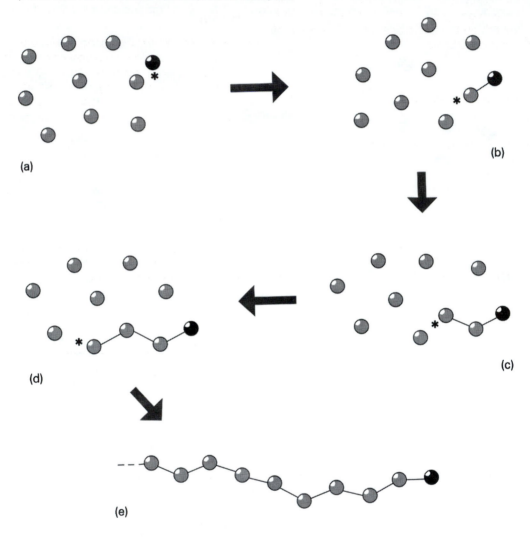

(a) (b) (d) (c) (e)

FIGURE 2.4

Schematic representation of amorphous arrangement of polymers within a fiber. A real fiber would have tens of thousands of polymers instead of the few shown here.

CONSUMER BRIEF 2.1   Cotton, Flax, and Rayon: The Same, But Not the Same

Cotton, flax, and rayon are all composed of the same polymer: cellulose. One would think therefore that, although their physical appearance differs, their chemical and other properties would be the same. The arrangement of the cellulose polymers in each of the three fibers however confers distinctive characteristics on the fibers, primarily in the areas of strength and absorbency.

Strength

Comparing three fibers with the same chemical structure can illustrate the effect of crystallinity and orientation on fiber strength. Cotton is about 70 percent crystalline and 30 percent amorphous. Rayon is only about 30 percent crystalline. As a result, cotton is stronger than rayon.

Flax is stronger than cotton not only because it is slightly more crystalline, but also because its polymers are oriented. In cotton, while some molecules are parallel to the fiber length, many are not oriented but rather lie at an angle. In this position they are not able to bear as much load as are the more oriented molecules in flax, and so it takes less force to break them.

Strength is also affected by the degree of polymerization of the cellulose molecules. Both cotton and flax have higher numbers of repeating units in their molecules than rayon and are stronger.

Stretch

Fibers that are less crystalline, with more amorphous material, can stretch more easily as the chains in the amorphous area are pulled into a straighter configuration. This behavior is seen in rayon fibers that can be easily stretched to a longer length. Cotton and flax, with their more crystalline and oriented structures, resist stretching.

Absorbency

Cellulosic fibers are more absorbent than synthetics, but within the cellulose family, differences exist here as well. Rayon, with its more amorphous polymer arrangement is very absorbent. This is why it is often the fiber used in "cotton balls" and other absorbent products. Cotton and flax are more crystalline and therefore absorb less moisture.

FIGURE 2.5

Schematic representation of crystalline arrangements of polymers in a fiber, with molecules oriented to fiber length.

The structures of some manufactured fibers have a low degree of crystallinity when they are formed. By stretching, or *drawing*, the fiber, the polymer chains become aligned and ordered, resulting in a higher degree of crystallinity. This principle can be seen by taking a strip of polyethylene plastic cut from a storage bag and slowly stretching it. As the strip narrows, the plastic becomes clearer, finer, and much stronger. (See Figure 2.6.)

Textile scientists have studied the arrangement of polymers in fibers, or *fiber morphology*, for many years. With continued research and investigation into the chemical structure of fibers, new theories and knowledge concerning the arrangement of molecules evolved. It was necessary to explain the presence of both crystalline and amorphous regions, as well as the fact that the crystalline areas, in cotton for example, were smaller than the length of the polymers. A model consistent with these observations proposed that the long polymer molecules can pass in and out of crys-

TABLE 2.1
Effect of Crystallinity and Orientation on General Fiber Properties

Crystalline Fibers with High Orientation	Amorphous Fibers with Low Orientation
Stronger	Weaker
Stiffer	More flexible
Less stretchable	Stretchable
Increased luster	Low luster
Less absorbent	More absorbent
Harder to dye	Easier to dye

FIGURE 2.6

Effect of drawing of fibers on polymer orientation.

talline regions and into amorphous regions. The *fringed fibril theory* put forth by Hearle and Peters (1963) illustrates this model. (See Figure 2.7.) The polymers are close together in the crystalline areas and then pass into more disordered regions. Morton and Hearle (1975) used the analogy of a pile of beads to describe this fiber morphology:

> If the beads have hooks on them and several people start fastening them together, each person will build up a compact region of strings of beads fastened together in regular order. But, after a time, the actions of one person will begin to interfere with those of another: it will not be possible for some chains to be fastened up any further because they are already fixed elsewhere. The hooking-together of the strings continues until finally there are several regions of beads fastened together, whereas between them the strings go off in various directions and can only be fastened together where two beads happen to pass close to one another. (p. 26)

Further research into the internal structure of fibers showed that crystalline areas could be formed not only from molecules close to each other, but also by polymers folding back on themselves. Current theory about the structure of manufactured fibers holds that in many fibers these crystalline areas (called crystallites) are stacked in rows of fiberlike formations (microfibrils) that are tied together by polymer molecules that pass through amorphous regions. (Follow the lines representing the polymers in Figure 2.8 for a visual representation of this.)

Internal Bonds or Forces

Polymers are held together by strong chemical bonds or atomic forces along the polymer chains. However, there are also bonds formed between the polymers that lie close together in the crystalline areas of the fiber. In many fibers these, bonds, represented in Figure 2.9 as lines between adjacent polymers, are *hydrogen bonds*. In this type of bonding the oxygen, nitrogen, or fluorine in one molecule is slightly negative and attracts the slightly positive hydrogen in another molecule.

FIGURE 2.7

Fringed fibril structure.

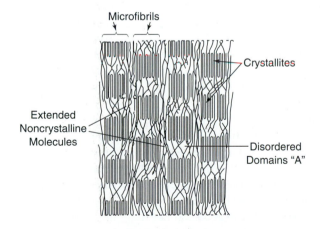

Microfibrils

Crystallites

Extended
Noncrystalline
Molecules

Disordered
Domains "A"

FIGURE 2.8

A model of the structure of polyester proposed by Prevorsek and his colleagues. Reprinted by permission from J. W. S. Hearle, Understanding and control of fibre structure," *Textile Horizons,* February 1994, 11–14.

FIGURE 2.9

Hydrogen bonding (electrostatic attraction) between polar groups on adjacent chains. Reproduced courtesy of *Textiles* and permission granted by *Textiles Magazine,* a publication of The Textile Institute, U.K.

Hydrogen bonds, while weaker than the atomic forces that hold molecules together, are still important in the form and behavior of substances. Take a common substance like water for example. It is a chemical material we experience as a gas (steam), as a liquid, and as a solid (snow and ice). The very fact that water exists as a liquid or solid means that there is something holding the individual water molecules together. That something is the *polarity* that results from positive and negative parts in the molelcule. The negative oxygen of one molecule is attracted to the positive hydrogen of another one. Hydrogen bonding also occurs in the cellulose, as shown in the following illustration, where the oxygen in one molecule is attracted to the hydrogen on another molecule. This attraction holds the chains together in the crystalline areas of the fiber.

Bodies with opposite magnetic charges (polarity) are attracted to each other. All molecules have some polarity and, thus, they tend to stick together. When the molecules are polymers, small positive and negative electrical charges exist all along their length and provide a substantial total intermolecular bonding force. The overall effectiveness of this force depends on how strong the polarities are, how parallel the molecules are to one another, how smooth or bumpy they are, and how long the molecules are.

When long polymers are attracted to parallel long polymers by hydrogen bonds or polar forces, fibers are stronger than if short polymers are attracted to short polymers. In long molecules the area over which these forces bond is greater, increasing the cumulative effect and requiring more force to pull the chains apart. Consequently, the fiber with longer molecules bonded together is stronger. This generalization is true only up to a certain point, however. Chain length will eventually reach the point where any further increase will not result in an increase in strength. At the same time, no decrease in strength takes place either.

Although most polymers are fairly linear, some polymeric substances react to form side chains as well. These side chains cause the molecules to function differently than long, straight molecules. Such polymers do not crystallize as readily as do regular, unbranched polymers because the side chains prevent the polymer chains from coming in close enough contact for hydrogen bonds to operate. (See Figure 2.10.) Starch, the other cellulose polymer, is very highly branched, and is therefore not a fiber-forming substance.

Another means by which molecules are held together is crosslinking. *Crosslinking* is the attachment of one polymer molecule to another by *covalent* chemical bonds

FIGURE 2.10

Polymers with side chains within fiber.

that are equivalent in strength to those along the polymer chain. Since crosslinks are covalent, they are stronger than the hydrogen bond. They may be thought of as ties that hold adjacent chains together. The chains can move but only to a limited extent.

Some fibers, such as spandex, are formed with crosslinks. (See Chapter 11 for a discussion of spandex.) Wool and animal hair fibers have naturally crosslinked structures. The crosslinks in wool are one of the factors responsible for the excellent resiliency of this fiber. The polymers in fibers can also be crosslinked as part of an applied finish to give such properties as improved wrinkle resistance and chemical stability. The crosslinks in finished cotton serve to return the molecules to their original position within the fiber after it has been bent or folded, thus providing wrinkle recovery. (See Chapter 23.)

Some Physical Concepts

Understanding textiles requires not only some knowledge of chemistry but also an understanding of the physical world. In processing and in use, textiles are exposed to physical forces and conditions. The behavior of textiles when subjected to these forces determines how and where they can be used.

Measurements of fiber properties are expressed in units, for example, inch or pound in the British system and centimeter or gram in the metric system. There are seven basic units in the SI system (described on pages 42-47); these are listed, along with their symbols, in Table 2.2. These units cover the three main dimensions of the physical world: length, time, and mass. All physical quantities can be expressed in units of length, time, and mass. The speed of a car is expressed in terms of length and time, in miles per hour or in kilometers per hour. The density of fibers is expressed in units of length and mass: grams per cubic centimeter.

TABLE 2.2
Basic Units of Measure in the SI System

Quantity	Name	Symbol
Length	meter	m
Mass	kilogram	kg
Time	second	s
Temperature	kelvin	K
Electric current	ampere	A
Number of particles	mole	mol
Luminous intensity	candela	cd

Mass and Weight

Length and time are familiar concepts, but there is often confusion over the units of mass and weight. These two terms are especially confusing because when used as scientific measurements, the words are defined differently than when they are used in ordinary conversation. In order to be certain that scientific measurements are accurate they are made in comparison to an established standard. This is known as *standardization*. For standardization purposes mass is defined in comparison to a 1-kilogram standard cylinder maintained in Paris, France. Mass is really a measure of the inertia of matter, that is, the tendency of matter to remain at rest or its tendency to resist increasing its speed. This is not the same as weight, although the two are related. On Earth, *weight* is the force with which gravity pulls on an object. Therefore in the science of physics weight is defined as mass times the acceleration due to gravity. Objects dropped from a height pick up speed, or accelerate, as they move toward the ground. At the same gravity, mass and weight will be the same.

Force

When someone pulls on an object, such as a piece of fabric, he or she is exerting a *force* on the object. The resistance of a fabric to an applied force is a measure of its strength. Force is measured in terms of length, time, and mass. The standard unit of force is the *newton*. One newton is the force required to accelerate a 1-kilogram mass 1 meter per second squared. The force of gravity accelerates objects 32 feet per second squared. The strength of a fiber is often measured in *grams force*, which is about 100 times smaller than a newton.

Heat and Energy

Aside from forces, another condition to which textiles are exposed is heat. Heat is thermal energy transferred from a warm object to a cooler one. Heat, or thermal energy, may be transferred to a textile fabric from a hot iron or from an abrasive action. The molecules in fibers absorb thermal energy and may change their chemical structure or their physical arrangement. *Thermoplastic* polymers under high enough heat will rearrange within the fiber, often assuming a more random or amorphous form as the weakest intermolecular bonds begin to give way. The temperature at which these fibers begin to show such changes in form and structure, and appear to soften, is the *glass transition temperature*, abbreviated T_g. The temperature at which the fibers melt is the melting temperature, T_m.

This behavior under imposition of heat is used in heat setting fabric made from thermoplastic fibers. Not only can fibers be heat-set to make their dimensions permanent, but also many fabrics can be heat-set into pleats, creases, or other permanent shaping. For heat setting to take place, the fabric is deformed into the desired shape. When heat is then applied above the T_g but below the T_m, the molecules assume the deformed shape to accommodate the strain. Upon cooling, new intermolecular bonds form that tend to hold the molecules in their new shape. The fiber after cooling will remain in this position until the heat-setting temperature is again reached or exceeded. If the T_g of a fiber is low, the fiber cannot be successfully heat-set for ordinary uses because hot water in washing or heat from a dryer will negate the effect of heat setting.

If, in use and care, a heat-set fabric is subjected to a temperature above its respective heat-setting temperature, heat setting will be lost. Likewise, a wrinkled thermoplastic fabric lying in a very hot dryer may have wrinkles set in if the dryer temperature goes above the heat-setting temperature.

PART II. CLASSIFYING AND LABELING FIBERS

Generic Fiber Classification

As a result of legislation known as the Textile Fiber Products Identification Act, the Federal Trade Commission (FTC) has established names and definitions for fibers which are placed into *generic* classifications. These generic names or generic classifications are based on the chemical repeat units in the polymers that compose the fibers.

Fibers that are members of the same generic group have similar chemical and physical properties. (See Figure 2.1.) Groups of fibers that are related in their chemical structure may be compared with large, extended families. Each fiber family group is made up of smaller family units. These smaller family units are, in turn, composed of a number of individual units. For example, some fibers have a structure made of protein (the large extended family). Subunits of the "protein" family include silk, which has no other close relatives; and animal hair fibers, including wool, mohair, cashmere, camel's hair, and the like. Regenerated protein fibers have been made from corn, soybean, peanut, and milk protein, but were not commercially successful.

Within the family are certain "family resemblances," or ways in which the members of each group are alike. Most protein fibers, for example, show these similarities: they are harmed by the same chemicals, are fairly resilient, are harmed by dry heat, and are weaker wet than dry. Like human family members, however, each fiber has its own talents or eccentricities: silk has high luster, wool does not; vicuña and cashmere are exceptionally soft and luxurious to the touch; and the color of camel's hair cannot be removed easily.

Producers of manufactured fibers also give each of their fibers a name that is known as the *trademark*. Mary Smith, John Smith, and George Smith may be members of the same human family, each with the same family name, but each has a different given name. In the same way, Dacron® polyester, Fortrel® polyester, and Trevira® polyester are all members of the generic group of polyesters, but each has a different trademark. These trademarked variations in structure, usually less than 15 percent by weight, are not sufficient to produce significant changes in the chemical or physical properties of the different members of the generic family.

By law, all manufactured items must (at the point of purchase) carry the generic name of the fiber on the label. Most producers of manufactured fibers use the generic term along with their own trademark, so that the consumer will find such terms as Dacron® (trademark of E. I. du Pont de Nemours & Company) polyester (generic name) or Fortrel® (trademark of Wellman, Inc.) polyester on labels of textile products. Trademarks protect the exclusive rights of one manufacturer to a particular product, in this case a generic fiber.

Textile Fiber Products Identification Act

Fiber manufacturers introduced ever-increasing varieties of new fibers to the public after World War II. No regulation was made of the use of manufactured fiber names, so that each manufacturer that made its own version of a fiber gave it its own trademark. The consumer was confronted with a variety of fiber names and had no ability to distinguish one from the other. Furthermore, two or more fibers might be blended together without the consumer's knowledge. The purchaser of a man's shirt had no way of knowing whether it was made of cotton, rayon, or a cotton and polyester blend.

The consumer confusion resulting from this situation led to enactment of the Textile Fiber Products Identification Act (often abbreviated TFPIA), which requires fiber content labeling of all textile products. An earlier law, the Wool Products Labeling Act of 1939, had set a precedent in textile labeling and served as a model for the TFPIA. The TFPIA became effective March 3, 1960, and has been amended several times since that date. The legislation assigned responsibility for the enforcement and drafting of rules and regulations under the act to the FTC.

Provisions of the TFPIA. Under the provisions of the TFPIA, all fibers, either natural or manufactured, all yarns, fabrics, household textile articles, and wearing apparel are subject to this law. One of the first tasks assigned to the FTC was the establishment of generic names or classifications for manufactured fibers. (See Figure 2.1.)

A *natural fiber* is defined in the act as "any fiber that exists as such in the natural state." The common English names of natural fibers, *cotton, linen, silk,* and *wool,* appear on labels as generic names.

A *manufactured fiber* is defined as "any fiber derived by a process of manufacture from any substance which, at any point in the manufacturing process, is not a fiber." These categories or generic classifications established by the FTC were based on similarities in chemical composition. Along with similarities in chemical composition, fibers in these groupings had many common physical properties, care requirements, and performance characteristics. New generic classes may be added when manufacturers are able to demonstrate that fibers are sufficiently unique to warrant a separate classification from those already in existence, so that it is possible that further generic classes may be established in the future as new fibers are synthesized.

The criteria that warrant approval of a new generic fiber name are "that the fiber must have a chemical composition 'radically different' from other fibers and that chemical composition must give it significantly different physical properties; the fiber must currently be, or soon be, in active commercial use; and the granting of the generic name must be of importance to the consuming public 'at large,' rather than to a small group of knowledgeable professionals."[1] Recently approved generic names are melamine and fluoropolymer.

Labeling Requirements. The TFPIA requires that all textile products have a label attached that lists the names of the fibers from which they are made.[2] Fiber listing must be done in order of the percentage of fiber by weight that is present in the product. The largest amount must be listed first, the next largest second, and so on. Thus, for example, a fabric might be labeled

60% polyester

30% cotton

10% spandex

The manufacturer must list the generic name of the fiber but may also list the trademark. So, for example, the same label could also read as follows:

---

1 Federal Trade Commission information sheet requesting public comment, May 28, 1985.

2 With these exceptions: upholstery stuffing; outer coverings of furniture, mattresses, and box springs; linings, interlinings, stiffenings, or paddings incorporated for structural purposes and not for warmth; sewing and handicraft threads; and bandages and surgical dressings.

60% Dacron® polyester

30% cotton

10% Lycra® spandex

Note that the trademark is capitalized but that the generic term is not.

Fiber quantities of less than 5 percent must be labeled as "other fiber," unless the fibers serve a specific purpose in the product. If the fibers are listed, the function of these minor components must be stated. For example, a manufacturer could say, "96 percent nylon, 4 percent spandex for stretch," because spandex is an elastic fiber and does perform a specific function. The intent of this provision is to prevent manufacturers from implying that 5 percent or less of a fiber will produce some positive benefit. Quantities of less than 5 percent of most fibers normally have little or no effect on fabric performance. Exceptions are the use of elastic fibers such as spandex or metallic fibers that control static.

Where products are made from fibers that have not been identified, for instance, from mixed reused fiber, the label may indicate that such a product is "composed of miscellaneous scraps, rags, odd lots, textile by-products, secondhand materials, or waste materials." Such a label might read, for example,

45% rayon

35% acetate

20% miscellaneous scraps of undetermined fiber content

No trademarks or other terms may be used that imply the presence of a fiber that is not actually a part of the product. For example, it would be illegal to use the following labels:

SILK-SHEEN Blouses	or	Wooly Warm Blankets
100% nylon		100% acrylic

(Also see Figure 2.11.)

The law also requires that either the name of the manufacturer of the product, a registered trademark, or a registered identification number appear on the label. All the mandated information must appear on the same side of the label, and all fiber content information must appear in type or lettering of equal size or conspicuousness, except for the manufacturer's name or identification number. This information

FIGURE 2.11

Label that violates the TFPIA. Not only is the fabric labeled both as "washable silk" and 100% polyester, but the print identifying the fabric as polyester is also partially obscured by the overprinting of an American flag.

may be placed on the reverse side of the label or on a separate label close to the fiber content label. The main provisions of the TFPIA are summarized in Table 2.3.

Country of Origin Labeling. Amendment to the TFPIA in 1984 sought to clarify and improve country-of-origin labeling requirements and to increase consumer awareness of origin. (A parallel amendment was added to the aforementioned Wool Products Labeling Act at the same time.) (See chapter 4.)

The specific requirements under the amendment are as follows. The country of origin, whether foreign or domestic, must be disclosed in a label placed in the neck of any garment having a neck; for those without necks, it must be placed on a conspicuous spot on the inside or outside of the product. All products are to be separately labeled except when several pairs of hosiery are enclosed in one retail package that will not be opened before its sale. Not only the product itself but also packages must be labeled unless the individual product label can be seen clearly through the package. Mail-order catalogs and mail promotional materials such as department store advertising flyers must disclose whether a product advertised was made in the United States or imported or both, if the products are intended for customer purchase by mail or by phone without prior examination.

Products made entirely in the United States must carry a label that says "Made in the U.S.A." or some other "clear and equivalent" term. (Acceptable examples include "Crafted with Pride in the U.S.A." or "Made in New York, U.S.A.") Those made in the United States using foreign materials must carry a label such as "Made in the U.S.A. of imported fabric" or equivalent terms. The FTC requires only that the manufacturer go back one manufacturing step to determine origin. For example, the manufacturer of knitting yarn sold at retail needs to identify the origin of the fiber; the manufacturer of retail piece goods needs to identify the origin of the yarn but need not identify the origin of the fiber; and the apparel manufacturer must identify the origin of the cloth. The specific country of origin need not be identified, although it may be given. Therefore, for example, a knitting yarn spun in the United States of Australian wool would need to be labeled as "Made in U.S.A. of imported wool fibers." However, if the manufacturer wished, it could say "Made in U.S.A. of Australian wool fiber."

Country of Origin Labeling was important under the trade rules of the Multifiber Arrangement and has remained an issue as trade barriers in textiles are phased out. (See chapter 1, page 19.) The United States Customs Service examines articles carefully to determine if importers misrepresent the country of origin by *transshipment* of textile or apparel products. Under this practice, companies in countries that have exceeded their import limits ship their goods to the United States through a third

TABLE 2.3
Provisions of Textile Fiber Products Identification Act

Label Must	Label Must Not	Label May
List general fiber names in order of percent by weight	Imply presence of fibers not included	List trademark with generic name
List manufacturer name, registered trademark, or registered identification number	List fibers less than 5% unless they serve specific purpose	Designate fibers as "unidentified"
List country of origin		

country. If a country refuses to allow the Customs Service to verify production by on-site inspections, the United States can limit imports from that country or modify the phase-out of quotas under the new General Agreement on Tariffs and Trade (GATT) rules.

PART III. PROPERTIES OF TEXTILE FIBERS

Fibers are the primary materials from which most textile products are made. Many substances found in nature can be classified as fibers according to this definition; however, only a limited number of these materials are useful in the production of yarns or fabrics.

Whether a fiber can be used in the creation of a yarn or fabric depends upon the physical, mechanical, and chemical properties of the fiber. Many fibrous substances lack one or more essential qualities required of textile fibers. They may not, for example, be sufficiently long to be spun into a yarn. Or they may be too weak to use, too inflexible, too thick in diameter, or too easily damaged in spinning and weaving.

Comparison of fiber qualities and characteristics requires the use of certain basic terms and a technical vocabulary. Definition of these terms and of their meanings as they relate to textile performance and/or behavior is important for communication and understanding. Some qualities of textile fibers are closely related to their physical characteristics, while others may be more dependent upon their chemical structure. For the most part, both physical and chemical properties play an important role in how textiles can be expected to behave.

Determination of Textile Properties and Performance

A number of specific textile properties are defined and discussed in the following pages. The determination of the properties of specific fibers is made through one or more of a variety of different fiber-, yarn-, or fabric-testing methods. Test methods are standardized by organizations such as the American Society for Testing and Materials (ASTM), the American Association of Textile Chemists and Colorists (AATCC), or by the government through federal test method standards.

A precise technical vocabulary is used in describing textile properties and reporting the results of textile testing. These terms are explained in the sections of this text that discuss various textile properties. Textile measurement terminology that was unique to different countries or regions developed over a number of centuries. As a result, methods of measurement have, in the past, been difficult to compare from country to country. As textile trade has become more global, the industry has attempted to develop worldwide, standard terminology.

Part of this effort involves adopting the metric measurements of the International System of Units (SI). Its details are controlled by the International Bureau of Weights and Measures. The textile industry tends to be traditional, and not all segments of the textile industry use the SI system consistently. However, researchers and those writing technical literature do prefer the SI system.

Physical Properties

Since most single fibers are so small that they cannot be examined adequately with the naked eye, the physical appearance of these fibers is best observed under a microscope. With a microscope, it is possible to observe such properties as length, diameter, shape, and color. The physical characteristics of each individual fiber affect the appearance and behavior of the yarns and fabrics into which the fibers are manufactured.

Color

The color of natural fibers varies. Some, like linen, have just enough pigment to make them yellow or off-white; others, like wool, may range from white to black. If their color interferes with dyeing or printing, the color may be removed by bleaching. Manufactured fibers are usually white or "bright."

Shape and Contour

The shape of a fiber can be examined both in *cross section* and in its *longitudinal* form. Since a cross-sectional view is a practical way in which to view the three-dimensional form of a fiber, cross sections are often used as a means of comparisons. Cross sections vary from fiber to fiber, ranging from circular to oval, triangular, dog-bone-shaped, U-shaped, trilobal to multilobal, and hollow. (See Figure 2.12.) Cotton fibers have a peanut-shaped cross section while silk fibers have a somewhat irregular triangular shape. Fibers with three- and five-lobed shapes have been manufactured. Three-lobed fibers are known as *trilobal* fibers; those with five lobes are known as *pentalobal*. The term *multilobal* is used to refer to all fibers with a number of lobes in the cross section.

Some fibers have smooth, even contours when examined longitudinally; others are rough and uneven. Wool, for example, is covered with many small scales that cause wool fibers to cling closely together. Cotton is twisted, making it reflect light unevenly and giving it a dull appearance. Horizontal lines or other markings may appear in the length of some manufactured fibers as a result of irregularities in the cross-sectional shape of the fiber. The valleys between the lobes of multilobal fibers cause shadows that (under the microscope) appear as dark lines and are known as *striations*. (See Figure 2.13.) Differences in shape and contour contribute to differences in fiber characteristics such as luster, covering power, appearance, hand or feel, and surface texture.

FIGURE 2.12

Typical variations in manufactured fiber cross-sectional shape together with the resulting longitudinal appearance: (a) dog bone, (b) trilobal, (c) serrated, (d) round. Notice how the shape of the cross section forms visual lines and/or shadows in the appearance of the longitudinal view.

a

b

c

d

FIGURE 2.13

A longitudinal view of rayon showing striations. Courtesy of E. I. DuPont de Nemours & Company.

Luster. *Luster* is the amount of light reflected by the fiber. Luster may be desirable in some products and undesirable in others. Current fashion trends may increase or decrease consumer acceptance of bright or dull fabrics. Some irregularities appear in natural fibers, and although the range of differences is slight enough that fabric appearance is not much affected, these slight irregularities produce a more subtle luster than that of most manufactured fibers.

Manufactured fibers, on the other hand, may have bright luster. If it is desirable to decrease the luster, the chemical titanium oxide is added to the material from which the fiber is made. The small particles of the chemical break up the reflected light, giving the fiber a lower luster. They are said to *deluster* the fiber. Untreated fibers may be known as *bright* fibers; delustered fibers may be called *dull* or *semidull* fibers.

Other cross-sectional shapes can affect the luster of fibers as well. Completely flat cross sections have a high luster, and some manufacturers have produced flat fibers with a glittering luster. But those with less regular surface, such as cotton, which has a somewhat flat but irregular cross section, do not have high luster. Trilobal fibers, whether silk or manufactured, have an increased luster. The luster results from the reflection of light not only from the surface of the fiber but also from the light being reflected from one lobe to another. (See Figure 2.14.) Pentalobal fibers also have this tendency to reflect light from one lobe to another, but because there are more lobes among which the light can be reflected, the fibers have a soft, subdued sheen. When the lobes of the fiber are increased still further, light rays are broken up and the luster decreases. Eight-lobed or *octolobal* fibers have been made to decrease luster or glitter.

Covering Power. Fabrics are often used to conceal what is placed beneath them. The ability of a fabric to obscure an object is known as its *covering power*. The covering power of fibers and fabrics has two aspects: the visual and the geometric. Visual covering power is related to the ability of the fiber to hide what is placed beneath it. The more transparent the fiber, the less covering power it has. The second aspect, that of geometric covering power, might be described as the quantity of fiber required to make a fabric that will cover a specific area. The better the geometric covering power,

FIGURE 2.14

Diagrams showing differences in reflection of light in round, trilobal, and pentalobal fibers.

the less expensive it will be to manufacture a yarn or fabric, because a smaller quantity of fiber will be required.

The covering power of round fibers is poor, because the surface area of fibers is less than that of any other shape. Also being both round and smooth, the fiber will pack closely together into a yarn. Dog-bone-shaped and flat cross-section-fibers have excellent covering power.

Smooth, round filaments with little variation in surface contour show soiling more readily than do striated or multilobal fibers. W. J. Morris (1989) has compared smooth, round fibers to smooth surfaces such as a polished mirror or silver plate on which finger marks and smears are very visible. When the smoothness of these surfaces has been altered by frosting or a matte finish, these smudges are less obvious. In the same way, altering the surface of the fiber helps to decrease obvious soiling. The ability to hide soil is especially important in some products, such as carpets, for which a variety of special multilobal fibers have been developed.

Crimp

Some fibers possess a wavy, undulating physical structure. This characteristic is called *crimp*, and can affect both the warmth and resiliency of fabrics. Wool has a natural three-dimensional crimp. A number of texturing processes can be used to add crimp to manufactured fibers or yarns. Fabrics made from crimped fibers and/or yarns tend to be more resilient and have increased bulk, cohesiveness, and warmth. *Cohesiveness* is the ability of fibers to cling together and is important in making yarns.

Length

By microscopic examination of textile fibers, one can readily observe the ratio (or comparison) of the length of the fiber in relation to its width. Although fibers are, by definition, always long and narrow, the length of the fiber is one basis for division or classification. Fibers of relatively short length, measured in centimeters or inches, are called *staple* fibers. Indefinitely long fibers, those measured in yards or meters, are known as *filaments*.

All natural fibers except silk are staple fibers. Manufactured fibers are usually extruded in filament form, but the filaments can be cut into shorter, staple lengths. Therefore, manufactured fibers may be found in either staple or filament form.

The length of the fiber will have an effect on the appearance of the yarn into which it is made. Filaments can be made into yarns with little or no twisting. These will look smooth and lustrous. Staple fibers, being short, must be twisted together or otherwise assembled to make them into a long, continuous yarn. Shorter fibers will produce more fiber ends on the surface of a yarn, thus creating a duller appearance. Staple fibers that are crimped, twisted, or rough have better cohesiveness for forming into yarns.

The *hand*, or feel, of the fabric is affected by the use of either filament or staple fibers. If a smooth filament form is selected, there are fewer fiber ends on the surface of a fabric, creating a smooth, even surface. If staple fibers are used, the short fiber ends on the surface of a fabric can create a fabric that feels soft and fluffy to the touch. Filament fibers can be crimped or coiled in a *texturing* process to make them less smooth. (See chapter 13.) Judicious selection of short staple, longer staple, or textured or untextured filament yarns enables the manufacturer to vary the appearance, the texture, and other properties of fabrics.

Diameter or Fineness

The *diameter* of a fiber is the distance across its cross section. In natural fibers the diameter usually varies from one part of the fiber to another because of irregularities in fiber size. Unless specifically made to have an uneven diameter, manufactured fibers usually have a uniform diameter throughout.

Fiber diameter is measured in millimeters or in microns. One micron (called a micrometer in the SI system) is 1/1000th of a millimeter or 0.000039th of an inch. As an example, cotton fibers are usually from 12 to 20 microns in diameter. One of the properties that distinguishes textile fibers from other fibrous materials is their high *aspect ratio*, which is the ratio of length to diameter. Wood fibers, which have a low aspect ratio, are used to make paper, but are not appropriate for textiles.

Fiber diameter is an aspect of *fineness*, usually expressed as *linear density*, or weight per unit length. Instead of measuring the distance across the fiber, a calculation is made of the weight of a specified length of fiber. Measurements used in the textile industry can be reported either in *denier*, which is the weight in grams of 9,000 meters of fiber or yarn, or in *tex*. Tex, the SI measurement, is the weight in grams of 1,000 meters of fiber or yarn. (To convert from denier to tex measurements, divide denier by 9 or multiply it by 0.11.) Fibers with lower denier or tex numbers are finer; those with higher denier or tex numbers are coarser.

Manufactured fibers can have any diameter that the manufacturer chooses, and the selection of diameter is generally related to the projected end use of the fiber. Clothing fibers are made in relatively small diameters, whereas heavy-duty fibers for household items or industrial uses are made with larger diameters. Fineness of fibers is related to softness, pliability, and hand, characteristics that consumers often take into account when choosing products. Fine manufactured fibers are more costly to produce than are coarser sizes, and finer natural fibers generally command higher prices as well.

Microfibers. Among the recent technological advances in the production of manufactured fibers has been the development of extremely fine fibers called *microfibers*. This term is generally applied to fibers that are less than 1 denier. The term *ultrafine fibers* is used for fibers that are 0.01 denier per filament or less. (For purposes of comparison, consider that hosiery fibers are generally about 15 denier.) (See Figure 2.15.)

FIGURE 2.15

Relative fiber diameters. Reprinted with permission from the American Association of Textile Chemists and Colorists. *Textile Chemist and Colorist,* **26**(8), p. 13

Microfibers are being promoted for use in lightweight, soft fabrics. They can be fabricated into cloth with extremely fine pores and a dense surface. In addition to their use in apparel fabrics with attractive hand and draping qualities, microfibers are being used in specialized applications such as surgical masks, filtration materials, ski jacket insulation, and surgical wrapping materials.

Density and Specific Gravity

Density and *specific gravity* are terms that are used in relation to the weight of fibers. Both terms show a relationship, but each has a somewhat different technical definition.

Density is the ratio of a mass of a substance to a unit of volume. In the case of a fiber, density is expressed as grams of fiber per cubic centimeter of fiber.

The concept of specific gravity is an alternative and more common and convenient means of expressing density. Specific gravity is defined as the density of the fiber in relation to the density of an equal volume of water at a temperature of 4° C. The specific gravity of water is 1. If a fiber has a specific gravity of more than 1, it is heavier than water; if it has a specific gravity that is less than 1, it is lighter than water. Only a few textile fibers have a specific gravity that is less than that of water, so that the specific gravity of most fibers will range from 1.0 to 2.0 or slightly above. Since specific gravity is a relative value, it cannot be reported in units such as grams or centimeters.

Density has significance for the consumer in a number of ways. Olefins, with a specific gravity less than water, will float on top of water during laundering. The low density of olefin fibers makes possible the manufacture of fibers from smaller weights of raw materials. This results in lower costs for the fiber. Cotton has a moderate specific gravity, and glass fiber has a high specific gravity. Therefore, if a cotton fabric and a glass fabric are made of yarns of comparable size and of similar weave, the glass fabric will be much heavier than the cotton.

Mechanical Properties

The *mechanical properties* of textiles are those that describe the textile material's behavior under applied forces and deformation. *Deformation* is a change of shape or size, usually as a result of application of some type of force. The applied force may cause the textile to stretch, compress, bend, or twist.

Strength

The most important of these behaviors for fibers is their resistance to stretching, that is, to forces applied parallel to the fiber axis. The stretching, or tensile, force required to break a fiber is called *tensile strength.* *Tenacity* of fibers is strength relative to linear density and is measured in *grams per tex* (g/tex) or *grams per denier* (g/d).

To understand the importance of relative strength, consider spider webs, nature's microfibers. It is said that spider silk is among the strongest of fibers (Warner, 1996). Yet we all know how easily these fine filaments can be broken, much more easily than breaking a human hair, which is bigger but relatively weaker. If breaking strength is related to size, however, the different fibers can be more appropriately compared.

Since linear density is used in the calculation of tenacity, fiber density affects these tenacity values. When a nylon and a polyester fiber of the same diameter break under identical tensile forces, the nylon fiber will actually have a higher tenacity. This is because it has a lower density, and therefore a smaller tex, which is the denominator in the calculated tenacity.

Modulus

An important property related to tensile strength is fiber *modulus*. This refers to the fiber's initial resistance to the tensile force, before it breaks, and is a measure of fiber stiffness. If this initial resistance is low, the material will stretch considerably with very little force applied. Examples of materials with low modulus are rubber bands and spandex fibers. High-modulus materials exhibit much lower stretch under tensile force. A steel wire has a high modulus, as do glass and flax fibers.

Elongation and Elastic Recovery

Elongation is the amount of stretching or lengthening of a fiber under a tensile force. Elongation does not imply that the fiber will return to its original form but merely that the fiber length can be elongated or extended. Measurement of elongation is commonly made as "elongation to break," the amount of stretch the fiber can withstand before it will break. A fiber that will stretch or elongate more before breaking will show greater "toughness," or durability, than a stiffer fiber that breaks at the same load but at lower elongation.

If recovery after a stress is removed occurs instantaneously, like a rubber band, it is *elastic recovery*. A slow return to original length is called *creep recovery*. Elastic recovery can be quantified or measured and is calculated in numerical terms as the percentage of elastic recovery. A measured fiber (or fabric) is elongated or stretched to a specific degree, for a specified period of time. The stress is then removed, and the fiber is allowed to recover for a short period of time. After recovery the fiber is remeasured, and the percentage of recovery is calculated. A fiber with 100 percent recovery has returned to its original length. A fiber with 80 percent recovery is 20 percent longer after stretching.

Elongation and elastic recovery are separate qualities. One fiber (fiber A) may stretch (elongate) but not return to its original length, while another (fiber B) may stretch to the same extent and return to (recover) its original size. Both fibers show similar qualities of elongation, but they differ in their elastic recovery. For the manufacturer who wishes to produce a serviceable product that has some "give" but will not stretch out of shape, use of fiber B will produce the better product. For example, good elastic recovery is highly desirable in a product such as pantyhose. Without it, wearers would notice bags of stretched fabric at the knees.

Resiliency

Resiliency refers to the ability of a fiber to spring back to its natural position after folding, creasing, or compression. Fibers differ in their natural resiliency, and those that are resilient are likely to recover from creasing or wrinkling more quickly. Although resiliency and elasticity are not the same, high elastic recovery is associated with good resilience. Wool is an exception because much of its resiliency is due to the natural crimp in the fibers.

The term *loft* is related to resiliency. Sometimes known as *compressional resiliency*, loft is the ability of fiber assemblies to return to their original thickness after being flattened or compressed. A fabric with loft is one that is springy and resists flattening, an especially important property for carpet fibers.

Flexibility

Flexibility of fibers is their ability to be easily bent or folded and is an essential quality of textile fibers. The consumer perceives fiber flexibility in terms of stiffness. Not only is it difficult to spin inflexible, high-modulus fibers into yarns, but fabrics made from such fibers also feel stiff, do not drape well, and are not comfortable to wear. Except for special uses for household or industry, fabrics that lack flexibility have poor consumer acceptance.

Flexibility is of course related to fiber fineness. Heavy, coarse fibers will be relatively inflexible and fabrics made from them will be feel stiff. Microfibers have low bending stiffness, producing drapeable fabrics with a soft hand.

Fibers must bend or flex often without breaking or splitting since the textiles in many end products are subject to manipulation that causes fibers to bend or fold. Glass fiber, for example, can be made into woven textiles, but its uses are limited because the fibers are relatively inflexible. Fabrics made from glass fiber are stiff and tend to break where they are folded.

Chemical Properties

Absorbency

The ability of a fiber to absorb or take water into itself affects many aspects of its use. The ability of a bone-dry fiber to absorb moisture is called *moisture regain*. In calculating the properties of textiles, textile technologists will take a sample of fibers or fabric, dry it thoroughly, and return the sample to a controlled atmosphere in which temperature and humidity are accurately maintained at a temperature of 70° F and 65 percent relative humidity. The amount of moisture that is taken up by the sample is then measured to determine the *standard regain*. This figure is reported in percentage and is calculated using the formula:

$$regain = (moist\ weight - dry\ weight) \times 100/dry\ weight$$

Saturation regain, measured at 95 to 100 percent relative humidity, is numerically higher.

A fiber that has a high regain is *hydrophilic*, meaning "water-loving." Conversely, fibers that do not absorb moisture readily are *hydrophobic* or "water-hating." Cotton, a hydrophilic fiber, is comfortable to wear, especially in hot weather. The fiber removes moisture vapor or liquid water from the skin of the wearer who feels dryer and less clammy. Polyester, with low regain, is less comfortable in hot humid conditions.

Another factor to consider is that when water is absorbed, heat is given off. For fibers with low regain this heat, called the *heat of sorption*, is negligible. Wool fibers, though, which are extremely absorbent, can liberate much more heat when going from a dry to a wet atmosphere, providing additional warmth.

Absorbent fibers accept waterborne dyes and special finishes readily and are easy to launder. On the other hand, fibers that absorb moisture readily dry slowly and may be stained by waterborne soil.

Some fibers *adsorb* moisture rather than absorb it. (See Figure 2.16.) When water is adsorbed, it is held on the surface of the fiber rather than being taken into the fiber itself. If such fibers have a low moisture regain, they dry more quickly than do absorbent fibers and stain less readily. *Wicking* takes place when liquid moisture travels along the surface of the fiber but is not absorbed into the fiber. Some fibers both absorb moisture and also have wicking ability. Most synthetics have low absorbency, but some also have excellent wicking properties that make them more comfortable to wear, since perspiration can travel to the surface of the fabric where it can evaporate.

FIGURE 2.16

(a) Adsorption of water molecules on fiber surface (b) Absorption of water molecules into fiber.

The strength of some fibers is affected by the moisture that they contain. Cotton, for example, is stronger when wet than when dry, whereas rayon and wool are weaker wet than dry. For the consumer this means that handling some fabrics during laundering may require greater care. For the manufacturer, it means that processing of fibers during dyeing or finishing must be modified.

Electrical Conductivity

Electrical conductivity is the ability of a fiber to carry or transfer electrical charges. Fabrics with low or poor conductivity build up electrical charges with the result that these fabrics cling or produce electrical shocks. The mechanical action of automatic dryers also serves to build up static electricity on fabrics of low conductivity, thereby producing static cling. Many synthetic fibers have low conductivity, and when several layers of clothing of low electrical conductivity are worn, the problem of charge buildup is aggravated.

Poor conductivity is related to low moisture regain. Water is an excellent conductor of electricity, and fibers with good absorbency are not as likely to build up static electricity as are those that are nonabsorbent. Furthermore, some fibers with fairly good moisture absorbency but poor conductivity display static buildup, and fabrics cling only when weather conditions are dry. Treatments given to fabrics to decrease static accumulation involve finishes that enable fibers to hold moisture on the surface or to absorb more moisture. Some manufactured fibers are modified in chemical structure during manufacture so as to increase electrical conductivity.

Effect of Heat

Textile products may be subjected to heat not only during manufacture and processing but also in use. In home care, for example, fabrics may be pressed or dried in a hot dryer. The way in which various fibers respond to the application of heat depends on their chemical composition. Many synthetic fibers soften or melt at various temperatures. Cellulosic and protein fibers scorch or turn brown. The specific behavior exhibited by each fiber will, of course, determine the way in which the fiber must be handled during manufacture and use.

How thermoplastic fibers soften and melt on exposure to heat is discussed on page 42. In fabrics made from thermoplastic fibers, heat may be used to permanently set pleats or shape into the fabric, fuse seams, and make buttonholes.

Flammability. Some fibers ignite and burn, some smoulder, and others are noncombustible. Fibers that ignite but then do not continue to burn, whether or not the ignition source is removed, are designated as *flame resistant.* Fibers that do not shrink or burn readily when heat is applied are said to have high *thermal stability.*

Burning of small quantities of textile fibers may be used as a means of differentiating one fiber group from another. Although precise identification of individual fibers cannot be made by burning, burning behavior can help to establish the general fiber group to which the fiber belongs. Cellulosic fibers, for example, exhibit flammability characteristics much like that of paper, protein fibers burn in a manner similar to hair, and some synthetics melt when they burn. The odor produced when a fiber burns and the kind of ash that remains after burning aid in the identification of the fiber.

The flammability of textile fibers may be related to their selection for use in particular products. Certain fibers are inherently noncombustible, whereas others exhibit flame retardant or flame resistant properties. Special finishes are applied to fabrics to retard flammability. Children's sleepwear and certain household products, such as carpets and mattresses, must, by law, be tested to determine whether they pass established test standards relating to flammability. (See Chapter 23.)

Chemical Reactivity and Resistance

Many of the substances used in the manufacture of fibers, in their finishing, and in the care of fabrics in the home are common household chemicals. Therefore, the behavior of textiles when they are exposed to these chemical substances is important to the consumer as well as to the textile technologist.

Effect of Acids. The action of *acids* when they come into contact with various textile fibers varies not only with the type of textile fiber but also with the strength and type of acid. It is important for the textile manufacturer to be acquainted with the effect of acids on textile fibers to avoid damaging fibers or fabrics during finishing. Also, some specialized textile processes rely on the action of acids on various textile fibers.

Acids can break polymer molecules of some fibers into shorter chains, a reaction called *hydrolysis*. In these cases, the bonds connecting the subunits are unstable to acid, and the result is a loss of tensile strength. If the reaction goes on for a sufficiently long time, susceptible fibers will actually be dissolved. Cellulosic fibers are damaged by strong mineral acids and are harmed even by diluted concentrations of these substances. Acid hydrolysis, in a highly controlled process, is used to make permanently stiffened sheer cotton fabrics. The acid is applied so that it breaks down the outermost layer of fabric. The outer layer softens, the reaction is stopped, and the fabric is given a hard press that forms the outer fabric layer into a smooth, clear, permanently stiffened finish.

Because dilute acids do not readily harm protein fibers (the bonds connecting the subunits are relatively stable to acid), especially wool, acid treatments can be used to clean vegetable matter from wool before spinning or after fabrication into cloth. The controlled acid solution destroys the sticks and burrs caught in the wool, the acid is neutralized, and the wool is left unharmed. (See the discussion of carbonization of wool in Chapter 19.) Such processes are carried out under rigidly controlled conditions to avoid any harm to the fibers. Strong mineral acids will damage wool fiber.

Effect of Bases. Sodium hydroxide is a chemical *base* or *alkali* that is used in several textile finishing processes. Bases, even strong bases at high temperatures, do not appreciably harm natural cellulosic fibers. They do, however, cause radical physical changes that improve the strength and appearance of cellulosic fibers. For this reason, a special treatment with sodium hydroxide is sometimes given to these fibers.

Sensitivity to bases is important in the care of protein fibers (silk, wool, and animal hair fibers) in which the bonds between the subunits are broken by the alkali.

Some synthetic fibers are also negatively affected by bases. Many strong soaps and detergents have alkaline material added to increase their cleaning power. These soaps and detergents should be avoided for use with fibers that are sensitive to the action of bases.

Oxidation. Many fibers are not white enough in their natural state or after manufacture to permit dyes to be fully effective. Colors and/or stains accumulated during spinning and weaving are removed by the action of bleaches that *oxidize* the stains or colors. The oxidation interferes with the conjugated double bonds in the colored material, converting it into a colorless substance. However, the oxidizing agent may also react with the fiber itself. If the fiber is sensitive to the action of the oxidizing agent, the fiber may be damaged.

Chlorine bleach is an oxidizing agent that may damage protein fibers and spandex. Chlorine bleach must be carefully controlled in bleaching cellulosic fabrics, but it does no appreciable harm to other fibers such as polyester or nylon. Other bleaching agents made from substances such as sodium perborate will oxidize stains without damage to fibers, although they must be used at higher temperatures to be effective. Both the consumer and the manufacturer benefit from understanding the action of oxidizing agents on different fibers.

Effect of Chemical Solvents. Dyeing and finishing of textiles, as well as laundering and dry cleaning, involve chemical *solutions* and *solvents*. We are all familiar with water solutions of sugar or salt in which the sugar or salt, the *solute*, is uniformly distributed in water, the solvent. Solutions where water is the solvent are *aqueous* solutions.

A substance is dissolved if it is distributed as individual atoms or molecules within the solvent. If instead the molecules of a substance aggregate or gather together in a solvent, they are said to be *dispersed*. Most dyes are applied to textiles from aqueous solutions. Exceptions are disperse dyes, used on polyester, nylon, and acetate, which are dispersed rather than dissolved in water.

It is evident, therefore, that not all solvents will dissolve all solutes. An important consideration is the polarities of the solute and solvent. The rule to remember here is that "like dissolves like." As discussed earlier, water, the most common solvent, is a polar molecule. It will therefore dissolve charged or polar molecules. Many dyes have negatively charged sulfonic acid (SO_3) groups in their structure and dissolve readily in water. Nonpolar solvents such as carbon tetrachloride or perchloroethylene are used to dissolve nonpolar substances such as oily stains on textiles.

Textiles and other materials can be classified based on their attraction for polar or nonpolar solvents. A hydrophilic material attracts polar water molecules, while one that is hydrophobic attracts and absorbs nonpolar organic solvents. Laundering with water removes water-based stains that are often polar in nature. Organic solvents used in dry cleaning help to dissolve oily dirt and stains. (See Chapter 24.)

Environmental Properities

A number of general environmental conditions may have an adverse effect on textile fibers. These include exposure to sunlight and air pollution. For example, many fabrics lose strength after long exposure to sunlight, whereas others may be discolored. Certain dyes used on acetate fibers may be discolored by air pollution, and some fibers lose strength or degrade as they age.

Some fibers support the growth of microorganisms (such as molds or mildew) that will deteriorate the fibers. Others may permit such bacterial growth without damage to the fabric. Still other fibers do not support bacterial growth at all. Fiber characteristics in this respect will affect the choice of fibers for certain uses. Boat sails are subject to the conditions favorable to the development of mildew when they become wet. Synthetics, which resist mildew, thus compete favorably with cotton in making sails for boats. Mildew will develop on most fabrics if they are stored in warm, dark, damp areas.

Carpet beetles, clothes moths, and silverfish are the most common insect pests that attack certain textile fibers. Special finishes may be given to vulnerable fabrics to make them resistant to insects. Proper care and storage of susceptible fabrics, notably wool, can prevent insect damage.

Other Properties

Dimensional Stability

Fibers that neither stretch nor shrink when exposed to moisture or heat are dimensionally stable. *Shrinkage* is a decrease in the length of fibers and may be accompanied by an increase in the width of the fiber. Fibers that absorb moisture readily will exhibit this behavior.

Many fibers are described as being inherently dimensionally stable, yet the fabrics into which they are made may shrink. This fabric shrinkage results from the stretching of fabrics during their construction and/or finishing. Fabrics that are distorted during processing tend to relax to their natural dimensions after the first few launderings. This type of fabric shrinkage is called *relaxation shrinkage*. If fabrics continue to shrink each time they are washed, even after many launderings, then they are displaying *progressive shrinkage*.

Manufactured fibers that are thermoplastic or heat sensitive may shrink when subjected to heat. Special treatment with heat called *heat setting* (discussed on page 42) can, however, be used to set the fiber and make it dimensionally stable. The manufactured fibers or fabrics that have been heat-set do not shrink unless the heat-setting temperature is exceeded.

Abrasion Resistance

One of the most important properties of a fiber in relation to durability of textile products is its ability to withstand abrasion. *Abrasion* is the rubbing or friction of fiber against fiber or fiber against other materials. Fibers with poor abrasion resistance break and splinter, which produces worn or broken areas in fabrics.

Abrasion of fabrics may take place when they are flat, folded, or curved, so that fibers can be subjected to three types of abrasion: flat, flex, and edge abrasion. For example, flat abrasion may be seen on carpets as the feet of passersby constantly rub against the surface; flex abrasion takes place at the back of the knee in trousers or with the folding and unfolding of linens as they are stored; and edge abrasion occurs at the permanently folded edges of collars, cuffs, and hems. Color change in dyed textiles as a result of abrasive wear is known as *frosting*.

Prediction of durability in relation to abrasion is considered to be difficult as many factors influence abrasion. Morton and Hearle (1975), who note that abrasion depends largely on construction of yarn and fabric, state that no way has been found to eliminate the influences of these factors and calculate a basic fiber property.

An intrinsic fiber property that is related to abrasion resistance is *toughness*. Toughness takes into account both the tenacity and elongation to break of a material. Flax, for example, has high strength, but low elongation. Consequently the abrasion resistance of a linen fabric would be lower than one made from polyester that has similar fiber tenacity and much higher elongation.

Pilling takes place when a fabric has been subject to abrasion that causes fiber ends to break, migrate to the surface, and form into a small ball that clings to the surface of the fabric. Pilling is a more serious problem in strong fibers, as weaker fibers tend to break and fall off the surface of the fabric when pills are formed, whereas the stronger fibers do not break away and the pills stay on the surface of the cloth.

Table 2.4 summarizes properties of the most commonly used fibers.

TABLE 2.4
Selected Properties of Some Manufactured and Natural Fibers

Fibers	BREAKING TENACITY[a] (G/D)		Specific Gravity[b]	Standard Moisture Regain (%)[c]	Effects of Heat
	Standard	Wet			
Acetate (filament and staple)	1.2–1.5	0.8–1.2	1.32	6.0	Sticks at 350°F (177° C)–375° F (191° C) Softens at 400° F (205° C)–445° F (230° C) Melts at 500° F (258° C) Burns relatively slowly
Acrylic (filament and staple)	2.0–3.5	1.8–3.3	1.14–1.19	1.3–2.5	Sticks at 450° F (232° C)–497° F (258° C), depending on type
Aramid					
Meta	5.3	4.1	1.38	4.5	Does not melt Decomposes above 700° F (370° C)
Para	26–28		1.44	4.5	Does not melt Decomposes above 660° F (350° C)
Flax	5.5–6.5	6.0–7.2	1.54	8.0–12.0	Burns, does not melt
Cotton	3.0–5.0	3.3–6.4	1.54	7.0–11.0	Burns, does not melt
Modacrylic	2.0–3.5	2.0–3.5	1.30–1.37	0.4–4.0	Will not support combustion Shrinks at 250° F (121° C) Stiffens at 300° F (149° C)
Nylon					
Nylon 66 (regular tenacity filament)	3.0–6.0	2.6–5.4	1.14	4.0–4.5	Sticks at 445° F (229° C) Melts at 500° F (260° C)
Nylon 66 (high tenacity filament)	6.0–9.5	5.0–8.0	1.14	4.0–4.5	Same as above
Nylon 66 (staple)	3.5–7.2	3.2–6.5	1.14	4.0–4.5	Same as above
Nylon 6 (filament)	6.0–9.5	5.0–8.0	1.14	4.5	Melts at 414° F (212° C)–428° F (220° C);
Nylon 6 (staple)	2.5	2.0	1.14	4.5	Same as above
Olefin (polypropylene filament and staple)	4.8–7.0	4.8–7.0	0.91	0.01	Melts at 325° F (163° C)–335° F (168° C)

TABLE **2.4** CONTINUED
Selected Properties of Some Manufactured and Natural Fibers

| Fiber | BREAKING TENACITY[a] (G/D) | | Specific Gravity[b] | Standard Moisture Regain (%)[c] | Effects of Heat |
	Standard	Wet			
Polyester					
Regular-tenacity filament	4.0–5.0	4.0–5.0	1.38	0.4	Melts at 480° F (249° C)–550° F (288° C)
High-tenacity filament	6.3–9.5	6.2–9.4	1.38	0.4	Same as above
Regular-tenacity staple	2.5–5.0	2.5–5.0	1.38	0.4	Same as above
High-tenacity staple	5.0–6.5	5.0–6.4	1.38	0.4	Same as above
Rayon (filament and staple)					
Regular tenacity	0.73–2.6	0.7–1.8	1.50–1.53	13.0	Does not melt Decomposes at 350° F (177° C)–464° F (240° C) Burns readily
Medium tenacity	2.4–3.2	1.2–1.9	1.50–1.53	13.0	Same as above
High tenacity	3.0–6.0	1.9–4.6	1.50–1.53	13.0	Same as above
High wet modulus	2.5–5.5	1.8–4.0	1.50–1.53	13.0	Same as above
Silk	2.4–5.1	1.8–4.2	1.25 (degummed)	10.0–11.0	Burns slowly, sometimes self-extinguishing when flame is removed
Spandex (filament)	0.6–0.9	0.6–0.9	1.20–1.21	0.75–1.3	Degrades slowly at 300° F (149° C) Melts at 446° F (230° C)–518° F (270° C)
Wool	1.0–1.7	0.8–1.6	1.32	15.0–18.0	Burns slowly, sometimes self-extinguishing when flame is removed

Source: Manufactured fiber data from American Fiber Manufacturers' Association.

Note: Standard laboratory conditions for fiber tests were 70° F and 65% relative humidity. Data given in ranges may fluctuate according to fiber modifications or additions and deletions of fiber types.

[a]*Breaking tenacity*: the stress at which a fiber breaks, expressed in grams per denier.

[b]*Specific gravity*: the ratio of the weight of a given volume of fiber to an equal volume of water at 4° C.

[c]*Standard moisture regain*: the moisture regain of a fiber (expressed as a percentage of the dry weight) at 70° F and 65% relative humidity.

Relation of Care Procedures to Properties

Care procedures that are appropriate for fabrics are determined by an evaluation of the behavior of the fiber in relation to many of the factors discussed earlier in this chapter. Laundering or dry cleaning and ironing procedures must be determined by taking into account the reaction of the fiber to the chemical substances used in home and professional cleaning and the fiber's sensitivity to heat. Resistance to microorganisms, insects, and environmental conditions affects the type of care that is necessary in the storage of textiles.

Care procedures are not determined by fiber content alone. In ready-to-wear garments, the care requirements for all components from trimmings to interfacings must be taken into account. Chapter 24 gives a more complete discussion of the care of textile products.

Summary

Interrelatedness of Fiber Characteristics

The particular qualities that distinguish one textile fiber from another result from the combination of the characteristics that have been discussed in this chapter. No one single fiber characteristic stands alone, but each property contributes to, and modifies, fiber behavior. For example, a fiber might have good tenacity but poor abrasion resistance. This fiber would, therefore, be less serviceable than a fiber of moderate strength with better abrasion resistance. Another fiber might possess excellent abrasion resistance but have poor resiliency or poor elastic recovery. *In short, it is the sum of its qualities or characteristics that determines the usefulness of a fiber.*

Selection of fibers for particular end use products is made not only on the basis of fiber properties but also with an eye to cost. The less common fibers (wool, silk, flax, spandex, and high-performance fibers such as aramids) are more expensive. The price of cotton is subject to the vagaries of the weather, which greatly influence the supply of cotton, while the synthetics are affected by the price of the petroleum products from which they are made. The trade journal *Women's Wear Daily* publishes the prices of the most commonly used fibers each month. More detailed information is available in the *Textile Organon*, an industrial publication.

Contributions of Fibers, Yarns, Fabric Structures, and Finishes to Textile Performance

The way a textile product will behave during its useful life is affected not only by fiber characteristics, but also by the types of yarns, fabric constructions, and special finishes that have been used. The general aspects of fabric performance that are affected by these factors might be classified as *durability*, *appearance*, and *comfort*.

Durability. Among the properties of textile fibers that are most important in assessing durability of a fabric are strength, elongation and recovery, and abrasion resistance. However, the choice of yarn type; the specific weave, knit, or nonwoven structure; and addition of special finishes may either enhance or detract from the overall strength, elongation and recovery, or abrasion resistance of a fabric even if it is made from a durable fiber.

Appearance. Major factors in maintaining the appearance of fabrics include wrinkle resistance and dimensional stability. When a manufacturer begins with a fiber that is resilient, the wrinkle recovery of the yarn into which it is made and the fabric into which that yarn is woven or knitted will be enhanced. When the fiber has poor wrinkle recovery, the opposite is true. Nevertheless yarns and fabric constructions play an important role in wrinkle resistance. Fiber content is also a critical element in dimensional stability of yarns and fabrics. Fibers with high moisture regain will swell when wet. Thermoplastic fibers that have not been heat stabilized may be plasticized by heat and shrink when agitated in hot water. Both poor resiliency and lack of dimensional stability of some fibers can be overcome by special finishes.

Pilling and frosting from abrasion will adversely affect the appearance of fabrics. Not only the fiber characteristics, but also the type of yarn can influence pilling. Frosting, as well as fading of dyes, are results of complex interactions of fibers, dyes, and processing.

Comfort. Comfort, especially in wearing apparel, is related to the characteristics of heat transfer, moisture vapor transport and water repellency, air permeability, and softness. An important consideration in providing resistance to heat transfer is the amount of trapped air contained within a textile structure. This so-called *dead air* is a poor thermal conductor, so that if more dead air is held within the structure, more heat will be kept near the body. Some fibers have physical characteristics that enhance this effect. For example, wool is a good fiber for insulation because its natural crimp maintains a high volume of dead air. Manufactured fibers may be given a degree of crimp to increase their insulative value. However, if fibers that trap air are spun into smooth yarns and woven into fabrics with wide spaces between the yarns, the good insulating qualities of the fibers will be negated by the yarn or fabric structure.

Another physical phenomenon that affects comfort is transport of moisture vapor or of liquid water. Moisture is produced by the body in the form of perspiration: either *insensible perspiration*, moisture that evaporates within the skin layers and is emitted as vapor; or *sensible perspiration*, liquid perspiration produced under hot or strenuous conditions. The contribution of textile fabrics to comfort depends on their ability to carry away moisture vapor or water. Fabrics that enhance the transport of vapor are said to breathe. This quality differs from permeability to air, which is discussed later.

Water vapor may be absorbed by fibers, transported through the fibers, and desorbed to the outside. This process depends on the inherent absorbency of the fibers or their affinity for water. Moisture vapor can also pass through air spaces between fibers, and yarns and looser structures will augment this movement.

Some finishes for fabrics made from thermoplastic fibers decrease air permeability by causing fibers to fuse slightly. Here both the fiber characteristics, the fabric structure, and the finish work together to produce the desired result.

Softness is a quality consumers generally associate with comfort. Some fibers feel smooth and cool. Others, such as wool, have scaly rather than smooth surfaces and might be irritating to some people. The "prickle" often associated with wool fabrics is due to the presence of a few short coarse fibers in the yarn. Fabrics made from microfibers have an exceptionally soft feel because the flexibility of the yarn is enhanced by finer fibers.

Approach of This Text to Understanding Textiles

Throughout this text readers will see how characteristics of fibers, yarns, fabrics, dyes, and finishes contribute to performance. At the close of chapters dealing with these topics, the text will provide specific examples of how these each of these elements combines with other factors to produce positive or negative qualities. By the end of the text the authors hope that the reader will be able to view textiles as the sum of their various parts and to have a more complete understanding of the meaning of that equation.

References

Hearle, J. W. S. and R. H. Peters. 1963. *Fibre Structure.* London: Newnes-Butterworth.
Morris, W. J. 1989. Fiber shape and fabric properties. *Textiles* 18(1): 6.
Morton, W. E., and J. W. S. Hearle. 1975. *Physical properties of textile fibers.* New York: Wiley.

Warner, S. B. 1996. Structure and properties of natural and synthetic spider silk. In *AATCC Book of Papers*. Research Triangle Park, N.C.: American Association of Textile Chemists and Colorists, pp. 454–460.

Review Questions

1. What is a polymer? What is the difference between addition polymerization and condensation polymerization?
2. If a fiber producer wanted a strong fiber, why would the producer be likely to look for a fiber that is more crystalline and less amorphous?
3. What is the difference between a generic fiber and a fiber trademark? Which must be included on labels under the TFPIA and why?
4. To what kind of products is the TFPIA applicable? Summarize its requirements.
5. List and define those properties that describe how a textile fiber looks either to the naked eye or under the microscope.
6. Differentiate between:
   a. fiber strength and fiber modulus
   b. elongation, elastic recovery, and resiliency
   c. electrical conductivity, the effect of heat, and flammability
7. Describe some ways in which chemical reactions between textile fibers and chemical substances such as acids, bases, and oxidizing agents can be used in textile processing.
8. What fiber properties affect the dimensional stability of fabrics?
9. Using Table 2.4 compare the properties of cotton, rayon, and polyester, and recommend the most appropriate fiber for a knitted top. Include current cost estimates for each fiber.
10. Explain what is meant by the statement, "It is the sum of its qualities or characteristics that determines the usefulness of a fiber."

Recommended Readings

Cook, J. G. 1984. *Handbook of textile fibers*. 2 vols. Watford, England: Merrow Textile Books.

Ford, J. E. 1985. Textile units for fibers and yarns. *Textiles* 14 (Spring): 17.

Gohl, E. P. H., and D. Vilensky. 1981. *Textile science: An explanation of fiber properties*. London: Longman.

Morton, W. E., and J. W. S. Hearle. 1975. *Physical properties of textile fibers*. New York: Wiley.

Quantifying yarn abrasion. 1994. *High Performance Textiles* (September): 3.

Wada, O. 1992. Control of fiber form and yarn and fabric structure. *Journal of the Textile Institute* 83(3): 322.

Warner, S. B. 1995. *Fiber Science*. Englewood Cliffs, N.J.: Prentice Hall.

NATURAL CELLULOSIC FIBERS

Cellulosic fibers are composed of natural cellulose, regenerated cellulose, or re-generated chemical variants of cellulose. Natural cellulosic fibers are derived from a wide variety of plant sources, which are classified as follows:

1. Seed hair fibers, or those fibers that grow in a seed pod on plants
2. Bast fibers, or those fibers that are removed from the stems of plants
3. Leaf fibers, or those fibers that are found on the leaves of plants
4. Miscellaneous fibers from mosses, roots, and the like

Manufactured cellulosic fibers (discussed in chapter 6) include rayon and lyocell, which are regenerated cellulosic fibers; and acetate and triacetate, which are modified cellulosic fibers.

THE CELLULOSE FAMILY

Table 3.1 lists fibers of the cellulose family. Included in this list are not only those fibers that have extensive commercial production and distribution but also fibers that have little or no importance to the consumer.

Each of these cellulosic fibers possesses distinctive qualities or properties that distinguish it from others and make it especially suitable for certain end uses. Most cellulosic fibers also share a "family resemblance" in their physical and chemical properties.

As pointed out in chapter 2, statements about fiber characteristics are made in relation to the characteristics of other fibers. For example, when flax is said to be a relatively strong fiber, what is meant is that, in comparison with other fibers, flax is fairly strong. If the strength of flax were measured against that of a strand of steel or aluminum wire, for example, it would seem relatively weak.

General Characteristics of Cellulosic Fibers

The following discussion summarizes the general characteristics of natural cellulosic fibers and rayon as a class or group. Cellulose acetate and cellulose triacetate are chemical variants of cellulose and, as such, do not share in many of the family characteristics. Their specific fiber characteristics are discussed at length later, in chapter 6.

The density of cellulosic fibers tends to be relatively high, making fabrics woven from yarns of these fibers feel comparatively heavy. Cellulosic fibers have relatively

TABLE 3.1
Fibers of the Cellulose Family

Natural Fibers	Manufactured Fibers
Seed hair fibers	**Rayon**
Cotton	Viscose rayon
Kapok	High-wet-modulus rayon
Milkweed	Cuprammonium rayon
Bast fibers	Lyocell
Flax	**Modified cellulose fibers**
Jute	Acetate
Ramie	Triacetate[b]
Hemp	
Kenaf	
Leaf fibers[a]	
Abaca	
Sisal	
Henequen	
Piña	
Miscellaneous[a]	
Coir	
Spanish moss	
Sacaton (root fiber)	

[a]Of limited use.
[b]No longer produced in the United States.

low elasticity and resilience. As a result, they wrinkle easily and do not recover from wrinkling readily. Absorbency and moisture regain are generally high. Most cellulosic fibers are, therefore, slow to dry after wetting, comfortable to wear, and easy to dye.

Cellulosic fibers are good conductors of heat and electricity. As good conductors of heat, they carry warmth away from the body and are favored for use in hot weather and warm climates. Since they conduct electricity, cellulosic fibers do not build up static electricity, which produces shocks when garments are worn.

Cellulosic fibers tend to burn easily, with a quick, yellow flame, much as paper (which is also cellulose). Most cellulosic fibers can, however, withstand fairly high dry heat or ironing temperatures before they scorch. On an electric iron, cotton and linen settings are the highest settings on the dial.

Chemical properties of cellulosic fibers include good resistance to bases. Excessive bleaching will harm cellulosic fibers, although carefully controlled bleaching is not detrimental. Strong mineral acids are extremely damaging. Most natural cellulosic fibers will withstand high water temperatures. Such properties permit laundering of cellulosic fibers with strong detergents, controlled bleaching, and hot water temperatures. Regenerated cellulosic fibers are more sensitive to chemicals and require more careful handling and gentle agitation with lower water temperatures.

Most insects do not attack cellulosic fibers. However, silverfish are likely to attack heavily starched cellulosic fabrics. Most cellulosic fabrics are susceptible to attack by fungi, especially mildew. Extended exposure to sunlight tends to damage the fibers.

SEED HAIR FIBERS

Seed hair fibers belong to a class in which the fibers grow from the seeds that are formed in pods on certain plants. The most widely used seed hair fiber is cotton. Other seed hair fibers include kapok, milkweed, and cattail.

COTTON

History

The cotton plant appears to have been native to the area known today as India and Pakistan. The earliest evidence of actual woven cotton fabrics was found in India during the excavation of Mohenjo-Daro, a city dating from the third millenium B.C. Fabrics of comparable age have been unearthed in excavations of Peruvian grave sites, which lead some archeologists and anthropologists to believe that cotton was imported into South America from Asia during prehistoric times. Others, who point out that cotton plants of South America differ genetically from the Asian varieties, believe that cotton cultivation and spinning developed independently in the Western Hemisphere (Barber 1991).

From the Indian subcontinent cotton cultivation spread west to Egypt and east into China and the South Pacific. Roman writers speak of importing cotton fabrics from Egypt and the East. Unable to cultivate this plant in their cooler climates, Europeans of the Middle Ages imported cotton fiber and fabrics. Because Europeans had never seen cotton plants, some believed that cotton came from the fleece of a beast that was half-plant and half-animal (Anderson 1973).

One of the purposes of Columbus's voyage was to find a shorter trade route to India to import the fine Indian cotton fabrics. When Columbus found the Indians of Santo Domingo wearing cotton garments, he was convinced that he had, indeed, discovered a new route to India.

Large-scale cotton cultivation in the American colonies is thought to have begun as early as 1556 when cotton seeds were planted in Florida. By 1616 colonists in Virginia were growing cotton along the James River.

Cotton provides an interesting illustration of the ways in which the value of a textile fiber can vary. In the eighteenth century and before the invention of the cotton gin, cotton fabric was a costly luxury used chiefly by the wealthy. After its processing became less labor intensive through mechanization, the price decreased, and for many decades cotton was a utilitarian fabric available at relatively low cost. Since the development of manufactured fibers, cotton production and manufacture has had its ups and downs with its price affected not only by fluctuations in supply, but also by fashion trends toward or away from natural fibers.

The southern states of the United States, where the production of cotton became a major factor in the economy, proved especially hospitable to the cultivation of cotton. As Americans migrated westward, cotton production also moved west in those areas where the climate was suitable. Texas is the single largest producer of cotton in the United States, with over 5.3 million acres harvested in 1997. Georgia was second with over 1.4 million acres, followed by California with 1.1 million acres, Arkansas and Mississippi with about 1 million acres each. While California is only third in the number of acres planted and harvested, the yield of cotton in this and other western states is much higher (over 1,000 pounds per acre) than the yield of many of the south central and southeastern states where the yield may be only 500 to 800 pounds per acre.

Economic Importance of Cotton Production

Worldwide more cotton is used than any other single fiber. The dominance of natural fibers however is being reduced as production of manufactured fibers is growing. In 1997 cotton accounted for 43 percent of total world fiber consumption, down from 49 percent in 1991. In the United States about 32 percent of the total fiber used by textile mills was cotton, while at the retail level cotton represented about 38 percent of total consumption.

In 1998 total world cotton production was over 84 million bales.[1] China was the largest producer, growing 24 percent of the world total, followed by the United States (16 percent), India (15 percent), Pakistan (9 percent), and Uzbekistan (a republic of the former Soviet Union with 5 percent). These five countries produce 70 percent of the world cotton crop.[2] Production in the United States as a proportion of the world cotton crop has decreased over the last five years.

Botanical Information

Cotton fiber is removed from the boll, or seed pod, that grows on a plant of the botanical genus *Gossypium*. (See Figure 3.1.) Cotton is a member of the mallow family, related to the common garden hollyhock, hibiscus, and okra. Each fiber is a single plant cell that develops as an elongation of a cell in the outer layer, or epidermis, of the cotton seed. (See Figure 3.2.) These seed hairs are called *lint*. A secondary

---

1. One bale weighs 480 pounds.

2. Statistics provided by the National Cotton Council of America, 1998.

FIGURE 3.1

(a) Cross section of a cotton flower showing seeds in boll at the bottom of the flower, (b) closed boll, (c) mature, open boll. (a): Micrograph by J. McD. Stewart, (b) and (d): Courtesy of United States Department of Agriculture.

a   b   c

FIGURE 3.2

Cotton seed showing fibers growing, two days after flowering. Micrograph by J. McD. Stewart.

growth of much shorter fibers accompanies the growth of cotton lint. These fibers, which are too short to be spun into yarn, are called *linters*.

Types of Cotton

Many different species are included within the genus *Gossypium*, and each species of cotton includes many varieties that will produce different results under various field and weather conditions. Robert Merkel has likened these differences to those that can be seen among wine grapes grown in different climates and soils.[3]

---

3. Comment to author by Dr. Robert Merkel, Florida International University, in review of manuscript, spring 1985.

Cotton fibers are sometimes classified according to the length to which they grow. Longer fibers command higher prices since they are usually also finer. Major classifications are:

1. *Short-staple fiber:* $\frac{3}{8}$ to $\frac{3}{4}$ inches in length. Short fibers come from Asiatic species of cotton that are both short and coarse. (Botanically, these species are classified as either *G. arboreum* or *G. herbaceum*.)
2. *Intermediate-staple fiber:* $\frac{13}{16}$ to $1\frac{1}{4}$ inches in length. The variety known as American Upland is of intermediate length and coarseness. This variety of cotton makes up by far the largest quantity of cotton fiber grown in the United States. (Botanically, this variety is classified as *G. hirsutum*.)
3. *Long-staple fiber:* $1\frac{1}{2}$ to $2\frac{1}{2}$ inches. This includes varieties known as Sea Island, Egyptian, and pima (or American-Egyptian), all of which are used for good-quality cotton fabric. Peruvian and Brazilian fibers also fall into this classification. However, the Peruvian variety, known as *tanguis*, has a slight crimp and rougher feel, somewhat like that of wool, with which it is sometimes blended. (Botanically, this variety is classified as *G. barbadense*.)

Cultivation

For optimum growth the cotton plant requires a warm climate, with adequate rain or other water supply. A favorable distribution of rain is more important than is the quantity of rain because the plant needs plenty of moisture during the growing season and warm, dry weather during harvesting. For this reason, cotton is also grown successfully in warm, dry climates with adequate water for irrigation.

Blooms appear on the plant from 80 to 110 days after planting. The blooms are creamy white or yellow when they first appear. From 12 hours to 3 days after the blooms have appeared, they have changed in color to pink, lavender, or red and have fallen off the plant, leaving the developing boll on the stem. Fifty to 80 days later the pod matures and bursts open, and the cotton is ready to be picked. The mechanism that causes the opening of the cotton boll is not fully understood. It is believed to be related to hormonal changes in the maturing plant. Whatever the specific cause, the result is that the boll walls crack, the boll dries, and the cotton fiber is exposed, mature, and ready for picking. (See Figure 3.1c.) Failure to pick the ripened cotton promptly detracts from the quality of the fiber.

A particular problem in growing cotton is the susceptibility of the plant to insect pests like the boll weevil, necessitating the extensive use of pesticides. The most efficient method is spraying of pesticides from airplanes, a frequent sight during the growing season in southern states.[4] Concern for the impact of pesticides on the environment has spawned interest in "organically grown cotton" which is cultivated without the use of fertilizers or pesticides. (See chapter 25.)

The federal government and cotton producing states have established a boll weevil eradication program that includes targeted pesticide application and use of pheromone traps in an initial year. The impact is sufficient to allow significantly reduced use of pesticides in subsequent years, providing both environmental and economic benefits.

To facilitate harvesting, plants may be treated with defoliants that cause a shedding of the leaves and prevent further development of the plant or with desiccants

---

4. The large commercial airline, Delta, began many years ago as a crop dusting enterprise in the Mississippi Delta.

that kill the plant by causing a loss of water from the tissue. When desiccants are used, the leaves remain on the plant and contribute to the trash content of harvested cotton, whereas defoliants remove and thereby decrease this material.

Picking of the cotton is done either by hand or machine. In the United States a great deal of cotton production and harvesting has been mechanized (See Figure 3.3), but in underdeveloped parts of the world, much of the cotton planting, cultivation, and harvesting is done by hand. Technological and agronomic advances here have vastly improved cotton cultivation to the point that the same amount of cotton can be grown on only one third of the land area that was required 60 years ago. However, as noted on page 68, the yield in pounds per acre varies widely among the cotton producing states.

Production of the Fiber

Once the cotton fiber has been picked, it must be separated from the cottonseeds. This is accomplished by ginning. The cotton gin removes the fibers from the seeds. (See Figure 3.4.) Cotton linters, too short for spinning, are used in making manufactured cellulosic fibers; as stuffing materials for mattresses, upholstery, and pillows; and in nontextile materials such as paper. Seeds are used for cottonseed oil and fertilizer.

FIGURE 3.3

Cotton harvesting machine. Photograph courtesy of USDA Agricultural Research Service.

FIGURE 3.4

Schematic of operation of a cotton gin in which cotton fibers are separated from cotton seeds. Courtesy of Queensland Cotton Corporation Limited, Australia.

The quality of cotton fiber varies not only as to the length and variety of fiber but also as to physical condition from ginning; the amount of vegetable matter, dirt, and sand present; and color. The U.S. Department of Agriculture has established a classification system that provides information to the sellers and buyers of unprocessed cotton so that they can determine its value and the requirements for further processing. Raw cotton is "graded" according to the trash content, color, ginning preparation, and brightness. Standards for length of staple fiber have also been established. Evaluation of cotton quality has been made easier with the introduction of high-volume instruments (HVI) for the automated measurement of length, strength, fineness, and color.

Measures for fineness and maturity are made by an indirect method, known as *micronaire* fineness. This is based on the air flow past a standard weight of cotton compressed to a standard volume. Under these conditions fine and immature fibers will impede the air flow more than coarser fibers because they present a more tortuous path for the air through the sample. Lower readings indicate immaturity, and higher readings may be produced by fibers that lack the fineness required for some high-quality products.

In the past many individuals working in jobs where they came into contact with large quantities of cotton contracted a serious lung disease called "brown lung." Known medically as *byssinosis*, the disease is caused by toxins from bacteria or fungi associated with small fibers that are inhaled. Recent developments of machinery for processing cotton have focused on closed systems that protect workers from cotton dust exposure. Air quality is monitored, and legislative requirements for safe levels of exposure have been established under the Occupational Safety and Health Act (OSHA), so that what was once seen as a pervasive problem in the cotton industry has been largely brought under control.

Molecular Structure

Cotton is composed of polymer chains of cellulose. The repeating unit of cellulose is:

The cellulosic polymers in cotton have a high degree of polymerization. The hydroxyl (—OH) groups on the chains are responsible for many of the properties of cellulosic fibers. They attract water and dyes, making cotton absorptive and easy to dye. They also enable hydrogen bonding between adjacent cellulosic chains in the crystalline areas of the fiber.

Cotton is about 70 percent crystalline and 30 percent amorphous (see Figures 2.3 and 2.4). Although the degree of crystallinity is high, the crystalline portions are often not oriented but are at an angle to the fiber axis.

Properties of Cotton

Physical Properties

Color. Cotton fiber is generally white to tan in color. During the past decade naturally colored cotton fibers were developed by Sally Fox of Natural Cotton Colours, Inc., through selective breeding. Brown, tan, and green fibers were marketed under the name FoxFibre®. (See Figure 3.5.) Naturally colored cottons do not require either dyeing or bleaching, processes that produce significant levels of waste water. Prices for products made from these fibers are higher than those of other cottons because of the more limited supply.

Shape. The length of an individual cotton fiber is usually from 1,000 to 3,000 times its diameter. The diameter may range from 16 to 20 microns. In cross section, the fiber has a U or kidney bean shape with a central canal known as the *lumen*. During growth this channel carries nutrients to the developing fiber.

After the fiber has reached its full length, layers of cellulose are deposited on the inside of the thin, waxy, exterior wall. The fiber grows much as a tree does, with concentric rings of growth. (See Figure 3.6.) Each layer is made up of small fibrils, or minute fibrous segments. As these fibril layers are deposited, they form a complex series of spirals that reverse direction at some points. When the boll opens and the fiber is exposed to air, it dries and collapses into the flat shape seen in the microscopic view

FIGURE 3.5

Woven fabric with stripes created by using two different colors of Fox Fibre®, a naturally colored cotton fiber.

of cotton in Figure 3.7. The spiraling of the cellulose fibrils causes the characteristic twists, or *convolutions*, in the lengthwise direction of the fiber. These twists give the magnified cotton fiber the appearance of a twisted ribbon, and they make cotton easier to spin into yarns. Long staple cotton has about 300 twists per inch; short cotton has less than 200. In spite of the twisted shape of the cotton fiber, it is relatively uniform in its size.

FIGURE 3.6

The structure of cotton fiber. As the cotton fiber matures, the cell formed by the primary wall (a) is filled by successive daily deposits of cellulose in layers; (d) is the first layer deposited within the original cell; (b) shows the central layers; (c) is the innermost layer; (e) is the lumen. Courtesy of the National Cotton Council of America.

FIGURE 3.7

Photos of cotton fibers taken through an electron scanning microscope; (a) cross-section and (b) longitudinal view. *Source:* Reproduced courtesy of the British Textile Technology Group (BTTG).

a   b

Luster. The luster of cotton is low, unless it has been given special treatments or finishes. This is, in part, a consequence of the natural twist of cotton and its resultant uneven surface that breaks up and scatters light rays reflected from the fiber surface.

Specific Gravity. Cotton has a specific gravity of 1.54. (Compare with that of polyester at 1.38 or nylon at 1.14.) This means that cotton fabrics feel heavier in weight than comparable fabrics made from polyester or nylon.

Mechanical Properties

Strength. Strength of cotton on a scale of high, medium, and low would rank as medium. (Tenacity is 3.0 to 4.9 g/d.) It has a fairly high degree of crystallinity but somewhat lower orientation. The strength is increased by the length of the polymer chains. In comparison with other cellulosic fibers, cotton is weaker than flax and stronger than rayon.

Cotton is 10 to 20 percent stronger when wet than when dry. Its strength can be increased by a process called *mercerization* in which yarns or fabrics held under tension are treated with controlled solutions of sodium hydroxide. The alkali causes the fiber to swell and straighten out and to become stronger and more lustrous.

Modulus. Cotton fibers have a moderately high modulus, similar to that of polyester. This helps the two fibers to blend well.

Elongation and Recovery. Like most other cellulosic fibers, cotton has low elongation and elastic recovery. Knitted cotton cuffs and bands may stretch during wear and care and may not recover fully.

Resilience. Cotton fabrics also wrinkle easily and do not recover well from wrinkling. In stretching or wrinkling, hydrogen bonds between chains are broken and then reformed in the new position, holding in the wrinkle or other deformation. Through the application of durable press finishes, however, resilience can be improved. Unfinished cotton fabrics generally must be ironed after laundering.

Flexibility. Compared to many other fibers cotton is fairly flexible. However, when fineness is taken into account, its bending resistance on a relative scale is high, affecting the drapeability of cotton fabrics.

Chemical Properties

Absorbency and Moisture Regain. Because of its many hydroxyl groups, which attract water, cotton is an absorbent fiber. Its good absorbency makes cotton comfortable in hot weather and suitable for materials where absorbency is important (such as diapers and towels). It is relatively slow to dry because the absorbed moisture must be evaporated from the fiber. For the same reason, cotton fibers take waterborne dyes readily. The percentage moisture regain of cotton is 7 to 8 percent at standard temperature and humidity.

Heat and Electrical Conductivity. Cotton conducts electricity and thus does not build up static electrical charges. It has moderately high heat conductivity, which makes the fabric comfortable in hot weather.

Effect of Heat; Combustibility. Cotton is not thermoplastic and not melt. Exposure to dry heat at temperatures about 300° F, however, does cause gradual decomposition and deterioration of the fiber. Excessively high ironing temperatures cause cotton to scorch or turn yellow.

Cotton is combustible. It burns upon exposure to a flame and continues to burn when the flame has been removed. Burning cotton fabric smells like burning paper, and a fluffy, gray ash residue remains. It is not possible to distinguish cotton from other cellulosic fibers by burning.

Chemical Reactivity. Cotton that has been cleaned and bleached is about 99 percent cellulose. Its chemical reactions are typical of cellulosic materials. Table 3.2 shows the reaction of cotton to treatment with certain chemical substances in the laboratory.

Some of the chemicals listed in Table 3.2 are used in the finishing of cotton. For example, acids may be employed to stiffen permanently the cotton fabric called organdy. The reaction of cotton to strong bases, in which the fiber swells and becomes stronger with (when the process is carried out under tension) an increase in luster as well, is used for mercerization (See chapter 19). The same process done without tension and under slightly different conditions has been used to make stretch fabrics. Dyestuffs that are too acidic in reaction cannot be applied to cotton fabrics.

Environmental Properties

Resistance to Microorganisms and Insects. Mildew grows on cotton fibers, especially if they are stored under conditions of dampness, warmth, and darkness. This fungus stains the fiber and eventually rots and degrades it. Other bacteria and fungi that grow in soiled, moist areas will also deteriorate or rot cotton fabrics.

Moths and carpet beetles do not attack cotton, but silverfish may eat the fiber. Heavily starched fabrics are liable to be damaged by silverfish.

TABLE 3.2
Reaction of Cotton to Selected Chemicals

Substance	Effect on Cotton Fiber
Acids	
Mineral acids: sulfuric, hydrochloric, nitric, etc.	Concentrated acids destroy. Cold concentrated acids, if not neutralized and washed out, degrade and destroy.
Volatile organic acids: formic, acetic	No harmful effect.
Nonvolatile organic acids: oxalic, citric, etc.	Degrade fiber slightly if not removed.
Bases	
Strong bases: sodium hydroxide, etc.	No harmful effect. High concentrations used in *mercerization* cause fiber to swell and become stronger.
Weak bases: borax, soap, etc.	No harmful effect.
Oxidizing agents	
Chlorine bleaches	Destroy if uncontrolled.
Organic solvents (used in spot and stain removal)	
Perchloroethylene	No harmful effect.
Naptha	No harmful effect.

Resistance to Environmental Conditions. Although cotton shows better resistance to sunlight than do many fibers, extended exposure to sun will cause weakening and deterioration of cotton fabrics. Cotton draperies will last longer if lined with another layer of fabric.

Age does not seriously affect cotton fabrics; however, it is important that the fabrics be stored in clean condition and in dry areas to prevent mildew. Special acid-free tissue paper can be used to store antique cotton garments, cotton quilts, and spreads. Ordinary tissue paper should not be used for wrapping fabrics for long-term storage because the paper contains an acid residue that may damage the cloth.

Other Properties

Dimensional Stability. Cotton fibers swell considerably in the transverse direction when wet. Unfinished woven or knitted cotton fabrics will shrink in the first few launderings because the laundering releases tensions created during weaving or finishing. The relaxation of these tensions may cause changes in the fabric dimensions. Cotton fabrics can be given special finishes to prevent this *relaxation shrinkage.*

Abrasion Resistance. Fabrics made from cotton generally have low abrasion resistance. Garments will show wear at hems, cuffs, and collars; all cotton sheets will not be as durable as those that are blends with more abrasion resistant fibers such as polyester. Cotton fabrics will not, however, pill badly.

Uses

The range of items for which cotton fabrics are used is enormous. In wearing apparel, the qualities of comfort, dyeability, and launderability have led to its wide use in articles ranging from underwear to evening gowns. In the home, bed linens, table linens, draperies, upholstery and slipcover fabrics, and towels are frequently made from cotton. Over the last several years, there has been a slight shift toward interior furnishings. This category accounted for 33 percent of cotton usage in 1997, up from 29 percent in 1995.[5] Cotton's versatility and reasonable cost make it a popular fiber for many products.

Cotton has been increasingly blended with other fibers, especially with manufactured fibers. This blending may be done to create cottonlike fabrics with better wrinkle resistance and dimensional stability. It also appears in blends with flax and ramie, often in apparel items. Various finishes developed for cotton can also compensate for less desirable qualities. Special finishes are discussed in chapters 22 and 23.

Care Procedures

Cotton can be cleaned successfully using either synthetic-built detergents, which are generally quite alkaline, or natural soaps. The alkalinity of the detergents has no effect on the fiber. Dry cleaning solvents do not harm cotton, so, where construction details or trim would make wet laundering undesirable, or when shrinkage is likely to occur, dry cleaning could be used.

Cotton's lack of resiliency causes significant wrinkling in laundering. Care labels may recommend that consumers dry cotton items flat because when hung on clotheslines they may stretch and not recover.

Stains can be removed from white cotton using strong bleaches as long as water temperature, concentration of bleaching agent, and time of exposure are controlled. Strong chlorine bleaches should not be poured directly on cotton since pinholes can be formed in the fabric from direct contact with the bleach.

MINOR SEED HAIR FIBERS

Kapok

Kapok, like cotton, grows in a seed pod. The kapok tree, sometimes called the silk cotton tree, is native to the tropics. Seed pods are gathered when they fall or are cut from the tree. The dried fiber is easily separated from the seeds.

The fiber has exceptional resiliency and buoyancy, but it is too brittle to be spun readily into yarns. As a result, the uses of kapok have been limited chiefly to stuffings and insulation materials. Because of its buoyancy and resistance to wetting, kapok has been used as a filling for life preservers. Having a hollow, air-filled structure, kapok can remain in the water for hours without an appreciable absorption of water, while holding up considerable weight.

Some kapok stuffings are used in household furnishings. The fibers have a tendency to deteriorate and to break down after a time. In general, kapok is little used, having been replaced by synthetic foam.

---

5. Statistics from National Cotton Council of America.

Milkweed

The light airy fibers on the common milkweed plant have been used for some time in textile structures. Composed of 100% cellulose, these are classified as seed fibers because they grow as single cells on the large "seed" of the plant. The limited uses of milkweed fibers are strongly related to their unique structural features. The fibers are hollow, with a thin wall relative to their diameter, and are therefore lightweight. This physical structure has led to their use in items where good insulation or buoyancy properties are needed: as filling fibers for comforters, life vests, and winter jackets. A disadvantage is the high moisture regain of milkweed, which can cause the fiber masses in these items to become damp and clump together.

The smooth, straight fiber contour of milkweed makes the fibers difficult to spin into yarns. They may be blended with other fibers to increase cohesion in the blended yarns, but since they also have low strength because of the thin fiber wall, there is little incentive to produce such yarns.

Bast Fibers

Bast fibers are those that grow in the stems of plants. Located in the inner bark of the stalk, these fibers are often several feet in length. The best known of the bast fibers is linen, which comes from the flax plant. Other important bast fibers include jute, ramie, kenaf, and hemp. Minor fibers of historical interest but of little or no commercial importance are urena and nettle.

Flax

History

Flax had the widest distribution of any of the fiber-bearing plants during prehistoric times. Archeological evidence shows that flax plant stems were used in basket making long before flax fiber came into use for cloth. Techniques for removing the long fibers from flax stems were developed later. At first, wild flax was gathered, but subsequent cultivation of the plant spread it rapidly throughout the Middle East, Northern Africa, and Europe.

The hot, dry climate of Egypt has preserved samples of both coarse and fine linen materials dating from 4000 B.C. Linen fabrics thought to be as much as 7,000 years old have been excavated from the dried-out lake mud of prehistoric villages in Switzerland (Schaefer 1945).

Cooler northern climates were not suited to the cultivation of cotton, but they did permit the growth of flax, and consequently linen fabrics were used widely for most of the items in which cotton is used today. The widespread use of linen for many purposes is reflected in terminology still employed, such as *bed linens* or *table linens*. Modern bed linens and table linens are, however, often made from fibers other than flax.

Interest in linen was stimulated in the early 1990s by ecological concerns of consumers, since flax is grown virtually free of herbicides and pesticides. The United States imports linen fibers, yarns, fabrics, and completed garments, although flax for fibers is not cultivated here. It is, however, being grown here experimentally and new processing methods are being investigated. Precise statistics on the quantity of finished fabrics and manufactured goods are hard to obtain, as economic data on all hard or leaf fibers (such as sisal) and bast fibers (such as linen and ramie) are grouped together; however, the linen share of world fiber consumption remains at about 2 percent. Countries exporting the largest quantities of linen are Poland, Ireland, Belgium, China, France, Spain, Italy, Egypt, and the countries of the former Soviet Union.[6]

Botanical Information

The botanical name of the flax plant is *Linum usitatissimum. Usitatissimum* is Latin for "most useful." Before cotton was available in Western Europe, linen was used extensively in household textiles, for practical and washable garments, and for tents and sails for boats. Its many uses are clearly reflected in the Latin name given to the plant. Some varieties of the plant are grown for fiber, whereas others are grown for seeds. The plant grows to a height of 2 to 4 feet. The varieties grown for fiber have long stems, with few branches and seeds.

Cultivation

In most countries the flax crop is sown in the early spring. The plant thrives best in temperate climates with adequate rainfall. Harvesting is done about 80 to 100 days after sowing when about one-half of the seeds are ripe and leaves have fallen from the lower two-thirds of the stem. In those countries where inexpensive labor is readily available, flax is still harvested by hand, but in developed countries, much of the labor of flax pulling is now done by machine. (See Figure 3.8.) Whether done by hand or machine, the flax plant is pulled completely from the ground. Removing plants from the ground retains as long a stem as possible and prevents discoloration of fibers through wicking.

Stalks are dried sufficiently so that they can be threshed, combed, or beaten to remove the flax seeds, which are used for sowing future crops or for making linseed oil or livestock feed.

Preparation of the Fiber

Bast fibers require extensive processing to remove the fibers from the woody stem in which they are held, a factor that adds considerably to the cost. The procedure is similar for all bast fibers. The deseeded flax straw has to be partially rotted to dissolve the substances that hold the fiber in the stem. This first step in preparing the fiber is called *retting*.

Retting is accomplished through the breakdown of the materials that bind the fibers into the plant stems. Highly specific enzymes that attack only the binding materials and not the fibers are secreted by fungi and bacteria. Retting processes are of three types:

1. *Dew retting* takes place in the field. The flax is laid out in swaths in the fields where the action of rain and dew together with soil-borne microorganisms causes the bark of the stems to become loosened. This may take

---

6. Information from the MASTERS OF LINEN and the *Euroflax Newsletter*, No. 2(10), December 1998, p. 21.

FIGURE 3.8

Flax harvesting and processing. (a) Pulling machine used during the harvesting of flax plants. (b) Worker scutches flax during fiber processing. Photographs courtesy of MASTERS OF LINEN.

a   b

from 3 to 6 weeks, depending on weather conditions. After retting, the bark is removed, and retted straw bundles are set up in the fields to dry.

2. *Water retting* takes place when flax is submerged in water for 6 to 20 days. When water temperature is cooler, the process takes the longer amount of time. Water retting may be done in ponds, in vats, or in sluggish streams. As in dew retting, the bacterial action causes the bark to be loosened.

   Water retting produces finer fiber but is more costly; therefore, the less expensive and more easily mechanized dew retting process is generally preferred except for certain qualities of fiber needed for fine, wet-spun yarns.

3. *Chemical retting* processes of several types have been developed. In one, flax is sprayed with a systemic herbicide that kills the flax as it grows. If weather conditions are right, retting takes place in the standing plant, and the dry, retted flax can be pulled. This approach, however, has been found to be too dependent on weather. Acceptable fibers have also been obtained from harvested flax by chemical or enzyme treatments to act on binding materials. (Akin et al. 1998).

Retting only loosens the bark from the stem. (See Figure 3.9.) Following retting, *breaking* and *scutching* finish the job of separating the fiber from the stem. In breaking, the flax straw is passed over fluted rollers or crushed between slatted frames. This breaks up the brittle, woody parts of the stem but does not harm the fiber. In scutching, the broken straw is passed through beaters that knock off the broken pieces of stem. (See Figure 3.8.) The fibers are baled and shipped to spinning mills.

At the mill the fibers go through yet another process before they are ready for spinning. The fibers are *hackled*, or combed, to separate shorter fibers (called *tow*) from longer fibers (called *line fibers*) and to align fibers parallel preparatory to spinning.

FIGURE 3.9

Diagram of a portion of a cross section of a flax stem. As a result of retting, clumps of fibers along the outer edge are starting to separate from the woody core.

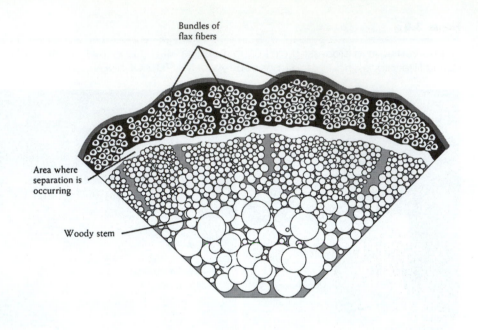

Bundles of flax fibers

Area where separation is occurring

Woody stem

Even with all this processing, individual fibers do not separate out, and bundles of fibers continue to cling together.

Flax fibers are long; therefore, they must be processed on specialized machinery. (See chapter 13 for discussion of spinning flax fibers.)

Properties of Flax

Physical Properties

Color. Unbleached flax varies in color from a light cream to a dark tan. Different types of retting may produce differences in fiber color.

Shape. Fiber bundle length may be anywhere from 5 to 30 inches, but most line (longer) fiber averages from 20 to 30 inches, whereas tow (shorter fiber) is less than 15 inches. Single fiber diameter averages 15 to 18 microns.

In microscopic cross section, flax has a somewhat irregular, many-sided shape. Like cotton, it has a central canal, but its lumen is smaller and less distinguishable than that of cotton. Looking at the lengthwise direction of fiber under the microscope is rather like looking at a stalk of bamboo. Flax has crosswise markings spaced along its length that are called *nodes* or *joints*. (See Figure 3.10.)

Luster. Because it is a straight, smooth fiber, flax is more lustrous than cotton, but it does not have the smooth surface that most manufactured fibers display. A special finishing technique called *beetling* can be employed to increase the luster of linen fabrics. (See chapter 19.)

Specific Gravity. The specific gravity of flax is the same as that of cotton (1.54). Linen fabrics are, therefore, comparable in weight to cotton fabrics but feel heavier than silk, polyester, or nylon, even in cloth of similar weave.

FIGURE 3.10

Photographs of flax fibers taken through an electron scanning microscope: (a) cross-section and (b) longitudinal view. Photographs reproduced by courtesy of the British Textile Technology Group (BTTG).

a   b

Mechanical Properties

Strength. Flax is stronger than cotton, being one of the strongest of the natural fibers. It is more crystalline and more oriented than cotton. It is as much as 20 percent stronger wet than dry.

Modulus. Flax fibers have a high modulus. In former days sails were made of linen because it resisted the wind forces without deforming greatly.

Elasticity and Resilience. The elongation, elasticity, and resilience of flax are lower than those of cotton because linen lacks the fibril structure that gives some resilience to cotton. Linens crease and wrinkle badly unless given special finishes.

Flexibility. Just as flax fibers resemble bamboo stalks, they also display the brittleness one associates with bamboo. Although fairly soft fabrics can be made from very fine yarns, generally linen fabrics feel stiff because the fibers have high resistance to bending.

Chemical Properties

Absorbency and Moisture Regain. Moisture regain of linens is higher than that of cotton (11 to 12 percent). Unlike cotton, linen has very good wicking ability; that is, moisture travels readily along the fiber as well as being absorbed into the fiber. Both absorbency and good wicking ability make linen useful for towels and for warm-weather garments.

Heat and Electrical Conductivity. Linen conducts heat more readily than does cotton and is even more comfortable for summer wear. Conductivity of electricity prevents static electricity buildup.

Effect of Heat; Combustibility. Higher temperatures are required to scorch linen than to scorch cotton. Linen is slightly more resistant to damage from heat than is cotton. The burning characteristics of linen are similar to those of cotton; it is combustible, continues to burn when the flame is removed, and burns with an odor like that of burning paper.

Chemical Reactivity. The chemical reactions of linen closely parallel those of cotton because both are composed of cellulose. Like cotton, linen is destroyed by concentrated mineral acids, not harmed by bases or decomposed by oxidizing agents, and not harmed by organic solvents used in dry cleaning. Linen could be mercerized, but because the flax is naturally stronger and more lustrous, mercerization offers few advantages.

Environmental Properties

Resistance to Microorganisms and Insects. If linen is stored damp and in a warm place, mildew will attack and harm the fabric. Dry linen is not susceptible to attack. It generally resists rot and bacterial deterioration unless it is stored in wet, dirty areas. Moths, carpet beetles, and silverfish do not usually harm unstarched linen fabrics.

Resistance to Environmental Conditions. Linen has better resistance to sunlight than does cotton. There is a loss of strength over a period of time, but it is gradual and not severe. Linen drapery and curtain fabrics are quite serviceable.

The resistance of linen to deterioration from age is good, especially if fabrics are stored properly. Linen, however, has poor flex abrasion resistance. To avoid abrasion and cracking at folded edges, a linen fabric should not be repeatedly folded at the same place.

Other Properties

Dimensional Stability. Like cotton, linen has poor dimensional stability because the fibers swell when exposed to water. Tension from manufacturing therefore results in relaxation shrinkage of fabrics. Preshrinkage treatments can be applied to linen fabrics to prevent relaxation shrinkage.

Abrasion Resistance. Linen fabrics have fairly low abrasion resistance. Because of their high bending stiffnes, their flex abrasion is also low.

Table 3.3 compares characteristics of cotton and linen.

Uses

Linen fabrics are found in wearing apparel and in household textiles. Yarns spun from flax range from extremely fine for weaving into sheer, soft "handkerchief" linens to coarse, large-diameter yarns for "crash," a fabric that is frequently used for making dish towels.

In wearing apparel, linen fabrics are popular for summer clothing. The major disadvantage of linen clothing, its wrinkling, may be somewhat overcome by giving the fabrics special wrinkle-resistant finishes. Producers are also using high-twist yarns and crepe weaving to improve crease resistance. Blending of fabrics with synthetics may help to improve wrinkle recovery as well. Many casual linen garments today are prewashed for a soft, slightly wrinkled look.

Linen fabrics are often used in for household textiles. (See Figure 3.11). The launderability of linen combined with its good luster and attractive appearance make it

TABLE 3.3
Selected Properties of Cotton and Flax Fibers

Property	Cotton	Flax
Specific gravity	1.54	1–54
Tenacity (g/d)		
Dry	3.0–5.0	5.5–6.5
Wet	3.3–6.4	6.0–7.2
Breaking elongation	5–7%	3%
Modulus	Moderate	High
Resiliency	Poor	Poor
Moisture regain	7–11%	11–12%
Burning	Burns, does not melt	Burns, does not melt
Conductivity of		
Heat	High	High
Electricity	High	High
Resistance to		
Fungi	Damaged	Damaged
Insects	Silverfish damage	Silverfish may eat sizing
Prolonged exposure to sunlight	Loss of strength	Loss of strength
Chemical resistance to		
Strong acids	Poor resistance	Poor resistance
Strong bases	Excellent resistance	Excellent resistance
Oxidizing agents	Good	Good
Solvents	Good	Good

Source: Data on this and subsequent fiber characteristics tables (Tables 4.2, 6.3, 7.2, 8.1, 9.2, 10.1, 11.1) from *Man-made fiber fact book* (Washington, D.C.: American Fiber Manufacturers Association, 1978); "Man-made Fiber desk book," *Modern Textiles*, 62 (March), 1981; "Identification of fibers in textile materials," *Bulletin X-156*, (Wilmington, De.: DuPont, 1961); *Textile Handbook* (Washington, D.C.: American Home Economics Association, 1974); R. W. Moncrieff, *Man-made fibers* (New York: Wiley, 1975); W. E. Morton and J. W. S. Hearle, *Physical properties of textile fibres*, (Manchester, U.K.: The Textile Institute, 1975); and "Textile World man-made fiber chart," *Textile World*, 130 (August 1990).

popular for use in tablecloths and place mats. Other important uses for linen fabrics in the home include tea towels; because flax fibers are longer, linen produces less lint (small bits of fiber that break off from the yarn) than does cotton and is, therefore, preferred for drying glassware. Linen is used alone or in blends for household products such as curtains and in slipcover and upholstery fabric. Linen is also used in vintage aircraft for making the wings and bodies of biplanes.

Since the fabric is in relatively short supply and the fibers require extensive processing, linen tends to be rather expensive. Both the cost factor and desirability of increasing wrinkle resistance have led to blending flax with other fibers.

Care Procedures

Linen can be dry cleaned or laundered at home with heavy-duty detergents. Being stronger wet than dry, the fabric requires no special handling during laundering.

FIGURE 3.11

FIGURE 3.11

High-quality household linens are often made from flax fiber and take advantage of its high luster. Photograph courtesy MASTERS OF LINEN.

Excessive chlorine bleaching damages linen, but linen fabrics can be whitened by the periodic, controlled use of chlorine or other bleaches.

Even though linen can be laundered, many care labels on linen garments carry the instructions "Dry Clean Only." This is because garments are less likely to shrink and appearance is usually better. Fabrics do not wrinkle or suffer as much color loss after dry cleaning as they do after laundering.

Ironing temperatures for linen are at the highest end of the dial on electric irons. Linen fabrics can be ironed safely at a temperature of 450° F. Dryer drying at the highest setting is satisfactory.

OTHER BAST FIBERS

Ramie

Ramie, or China grass, comes from a plant in the nettle family. The fibers are taken from the stalk. A perennial shrub, the ramie plant grows in semitropical regions. At the present time, ramie growth and processing are concentrated in the Philippines, Brazil, and the People's Republic of China. Hong Kong, Taiwan, Korea, and Japan process but do not grow ramie.

Ramie stalks are planted and the fiber is harvested the third year after planting. Three crops may be cut each year. After cutting the stems, the leaves of the plant are beaten off, the stems are split lengthwise, and the bark is stripped from them. This yields "ribbons" of bast that are soaked in water until the green outer layer can be scraped off. After drying, this substance, sometimes called China grass, is bundled and shipped.

Before spinning, the fiber must be retted out of the ribbons. Both dew and wet retting, similar to that used with flax, can be done. A chemical retting process that uses sodium hydroxide and an acid rinse has been patented and is used in the industrially developed countries.

Ramie has properties similar to flax, but is more lustrous. It is the strongest of the natural fibers and the most crystalline. Like flax it has fairly low resiliency and flexibility and a high modulus. It is white in color, its absorbency is excellent, it dyes rapidly, and it has good resistance to attack by microorganisms.

The commercial use of ramie had been limited by processing difficulties that made it expensive to produce. Until the chemical retting process was developed, only hand methods could be employed to remove the fiber from the stem. Controlling fiber quality was also difficult. Researchers have developed controls for growth and processing that have made possible the production of uniform quality fibers. Advances in the processing of ramie fibers are proprietary; that is, they are not made available to the public by the manufacturers.

Ramie is used alone or in blends. Blends are most frequently made with cotton, linen, and polyester. One hundred percent ramie fabrics do not require any special care. They are machine washable but require ironing and may shrink. If blended with adequate quantities of polyester or other synthetics, these fabrics will have easy-care characteristics and little shrinkage. The major use of ramie fabrics, especially ramie blends, in wearing apparel is in sweaters, suits, and pants. (See Figure 3.12.) It is also used in table linens and fabrics for home furnishings.

The case of ramie is an example of the effect that international trade agreements described in Chapter 1 can have on production and distribution of textile products. It became a popular fiber in the 1970s and 1980s after the Multifiber Arrangement (MFA) was enacted. Since it was excluded from import controls, blended fiber textile items that were over 50% ramie could be shipped to large markets such as the United States; and indeed many ramie/cotton and ramie/linen blended apparel items were imported and sold. In 1986, however, ramie was included in the group of fibers covered under MFA agreements between trading countries and this economic incentive for ramie production was reduced.

Jute

Jute fiber is taken from the stem of the jute plant. Successful cultivation of the plant requires fertile soil and a hot, moist climate. Jute is grown in India and Bangladesh and, to a lesser extent, in China, Thailand, and other southeast Asian countries.

Jute plants grow from 6 to 16 feet high. The stalks are cut just after the flowers begin to fade. Like other bast fibers, separation of the fiber requires retting. Many jute producers use chemical retting processes with chlorine compounds. After retting, the stems are broken and the fiber is removed.

Jute and other bast fibers such as kenaf and hemp are shorter than flax. The actual fibers in the plant stalk, called "ultimate fibers" have aspect ratios (length divided by width) of only about 150, which makes them difficult to spin. Compare this to the aspect ratio of cotton fibers which is considerably over 1,000. Since the ultimate fibers are so short, jute is not processed to separate out individual fibers but only to separate fiber bundles, which can be quite long. The fibers in the bundles are held together by lignin and other substances that act as glues.

Jute ranges in color from light to dark brown. Its strength is somewhat lower than that of other bast fibers, but it has similar bending properties. On exposure to air, jute becomes somewhat brittle. It absorbs moisture readily, resists deterioration by microorganisms more than some cellulosic fibers, and is weakened by exposure to sunlight.

Jute has long been in demand as a cheap, useful packaging material. Burlap is one of the major jute bagging fabrics. Jute has also traditionally been used for carpet backings and cordage. In recent years polypropylene, a manufactured fiber, has be-

FIGURE 3.12

"Ancestral Heritage," three-piece ensemble in ramie designed by Kue Nam Shim, Mokpoo National University, Korea, and Nancy Bryant, Oregon State University. Winner, Best in Show Award, at Runway Show of ITAA, Dallas, Texas, November 1998.

come a major competitor for jute in many of these uses. As a result, the jute-producing countries have been looking for additional and innovative applications. Some of these have been as geotextiles in erosion control, as a cheap replacement for cotton filling yarns in handwoven fabrics in India, and as reinforcement fiber in resin composites used to make chests and boxes for shipping tea and fruit. Some high-quality jute fabrics also have been used to make golf bags, soft luggage, and sports handbags (Atkinson 1993).

Continued competitive success for jute will depend on economical production to keep costs down and on marketing strategies. Recently efforts have been made to promote jute for apparel and decorative household fabrics.[7] One advantage jute enjoys is that spinning processes for the fiber are more developed than those for other bast fibers such as kenaf and hemp.

Kenaf

Kenaf is also a bast fiber, similar to jute in that it is composed of short ultimate fibers that are separated from the stalk as fiber bundles. Botanically, it is related to both cotton and okra. Grown predominantly in Africa and India, kenaf has sparked renewed interest as an alternative crop in the South and West of the United States. When harvested, the plant stems are decorticated to remove the inner part of the stalk and then retted to obtain the fiber bundles. (See Figure 3.13).

Mechanical fiber properties are similar to those of jute, but kenaf is stronger. It is also whiter, more lustrous, and can be bleached and dyed more easily. While kenaf has a high moisture regain, it is not wet as quickly as cotton.

Traditionally, kenaf was used in making rope and twine for which its high strength was important. Recent developments have focused on the use of these fibers in paper making since paper of kenaf fibers is smoother and whiter than that made from wood pulp. New methods for processing the kenaf stalks to obtain longer fibers have led to the production of nonwoven and woven textiles. For example, a nonwoven mat of kenaf fibers containing grass seeds is now marketed as a lawn starter. Apparel, wall coverings, and awning and tent fabrics have been constructed of kenaf and kenaf blends. (See Figure 3.14.) The woody core of the kenaf plant can be used for animal bedding, packing, and as an absorptive material for oil spill cleanup.

---

7. *Fantasy in Jute—The Golden Fibre, Indian Jute Industries,* Calcutta, India: Research Association, n.d.

FIGURE 3.13

Photomicrograph of kenaf fiber bundle. Reproduced from W. Tao, J. P. Moreau, & T. A. Calamari: Properties of nonwoven mats from kenaf fiber, *TAPPI Journal,* vol. 78, no. 8, 165–169.

FIGURE 3.14

"Sunset," original design in a kenaf blend, created by Kyeong-Sook Cho, Janice Huck, and Gita N. Ramaswamy, Kansas State University. Awarded first prize in Best of Fashions—Graduate Students at Runway Show of International Textile and Apparel Association (ITAA), Dallas, Texas, November 1998.

Hemp

The hemp plant, *Cannabis sativa*, is a member of the mulberry family and a type of marijuana plant. The fiber bundles come from the bast layer of the stem. Mature plants are cut off and spread on the ground where they are left to dry for 5 or 6 days. Leaves and seeds are beaten off, and bundles or sheaves of hemp are formed after additional drying. Retting, breaking, and scutching complete the fiber extraction process.

Hemp has tensile strength comparable to that of linen; it is one of the strongest of the natural fibers. It has good absorbency and poor elasticity. In its chemical properties, hemp is similar to cotton and flax.

The major uses of hemp are in the production of industrial fabrics, twine, and ropes because of its great tensile strength and high modulus that provides initial resistance to force. Interest in apparel and household fabrics made from hemp, as well as craft items, has increased recently. Imports of hemp to the United States showed marked increases from 1995 to 1996: in hemp tow and waste fiber, 416 percent; of yarns, 58 percent; and of woven fabrics, 31 percent. A number of well-known fashion designers have added designs containing hemp fibers and fabrics to their lines.

Although it is legal to import hemp fibers and fabrics into the United States, cultivation of hemp plants is illegal because the Federal Drug Enforcement Agency does not differentiate between the various subspecies of cannabis plants. Those who are trying to have this plant (which they call "industrial hemp") legalized say that it contains too little of the hallucinogenic substance found in marijuana to have any effect, and that furthermore trying to smoke the plant would make a person ill. Canada has legalized cultivation of hemp and its first hemp crop came onto the market in 1998 (Gross 1997).

LEAF FIBERS

Leaf fibers are of limited usefulness and, for the most part, are made into cordage. They are taken from a variety of plants, most of which are perennials that produce fiber for 5 to 20 years. The leaves are harvested, and through mechanical methods, the extraneous matter is scraped and broken away from the fiber.

The most widely used leaf fibers are those from cactuslike plants, such as those that have long, fleshy leaves with spiny edges (agave, henequen, sisal), yuccas, the banana family (abaca or Manila hemp), and the bromeliad family (piña or pineapple). Piña cloth is used in the Phillippine Islands to make a sheer, lustrous fabric that is often used in Phillippine national costumes. Spun yarns from leaf fibers can also be fashioned into baskets, placemats, and other craft items. (See Figure 3.15.)

FIGURE 3.15

Handmade basket from Zimbabwe constructed of spun sisal yarns. Photograph by Madalina Romanoschi.

MISCELLANEOUS FIBERS

The most well-known fiber in this group is coir, a fiber obtained from the outer hull of the coconut. The production of the fiber is carried out by hand using primitive methods. The coconut is picked, the nut is removed, and the husks are collected. Fiber is separated from the husks by a process that includes soaking to loosen the fiber, drying, and pulling the fiber from the husks.

The brown coir fibers, which are from 5 to 10 inches long, are used for brushes, ropes, and mats. Among the useful qualities of coir are resistance to rot, lightness coupled with elasticity, and resistance to abrasion. Coconut fibers are also used in geotextiles, primarily for erosion control. (See Figure 1.9.)

A few fibers are obtained from roots and mosses. Sacaton, a coarse, stiff, root fiber from Mexico, has been used as bristle for brushes. Spanish moss, an air plant, has been used for inexpensive upholstered furniture and mattress filler. In recent years, synthetic fibers have, to a large extent, replaced these materials.

SUMMARY

Natural cellulosic fibers can be produced by the seeds, stalks, or leaves of plants. The most important of these economically is cotton. While most cellulosic fibers have similar chemical properties, their physical appearance and mechanical properties can vary widely. This variation can be seen in the different fabrics produced from cellulosic fibers, from soft cottons to crisp linens. Among the common properties of cellulosic fabrics are high absorbency, low wrinkle resistance, and poor dimensional stability.

References

Anderson, F. 1973. Medieval beasties. *Natural History* 82 (January): 61.

Akin, D. E., W. H. Morrison, III, G. R. Gamble, L. L. Rigsby, G. Henriksson, and K.-E. L. Eriksson. 1998. Effect of retting enzymes on the structure and composition of flax cell walls. *Textile Research Journal* 67: 279.

Atkinson, R. 1993. Jute economy faces drastic industrial restructuring. *Textiles* 22 (3): 17–20.

Barber, E. 1991. *Prehistoric textiles*. Princeton: Princeton University Press.

Gross, E. 1997. Hemp: Historic fiber remains controversial. *Textile World* 147 (11) (November): 42.

Schaefer, G. 1945. On the history of flax cultivation. *CIBA Review* 9 (April): 1763 *ff.*

Review Questions

1. What are some of the physical and chemical properties common to most natural cellulosic fibers?
2. Define the following terms used in conjunction with cotton growing and processing.

   boll   byssinosis
   ginning   convolutions
   linters   naturally colored cotton

3. What are the major economic and environmental concerns in cotton production?

4. What care procedures are recommended for cotton garments? How are these related to the chemical properties of cotton?

5. Compare the structural differences of cotton and flax. How do these differences affect fiber properties?

6. List the steps in processing flax. What is the purpose of each step?

7. What are some of the specific properties of ramie, jute, and kenaf that determine their use in particular end products?

8. Identify some of the uses of each of the following minor cellulosic fibers: hemp, coir, and piña.

Recommended Readings

Batra, S. 1985. Other long vegetable fibers. In *Handbook of fiber science and technology*. Vol. IV, *Fiber chemistry*, ed. M. Lewin and E. M. Pearce, 728. New York: Marcel Dekker.

Buxton, A. 1988. A profile of the linen industry. *Textile Outlook International* 18 (July): 91.

Cheek, L. 1990. Dyeing and colorfastness characteristics of direct-dyed ramie in comparison to flax and cotton. *Clothing and Textiles Research Journal* 8 (Winter): 38.

Crews, P. C., S. A. Sievert, L. T. Woeppel, and E. A McCullough. 1991. Evaluation of milkweed floss as an insulative fill material. *Textile Research Journal* 61: 203.

Dickerson, D. K., E. F. Lane, and D. F. Rodriguez (1996). *Evaluation of selected performance characteristics of naturally colored cotton knit fabrics*. CATI # 961003. Fresno, Calif.: California Agricultural Technology Institute.

Doraiswamy, I., and P. Chellamani. 1993. Pineapple leaf fibres. *Textile Progress* 24 (1).

Hickman, W. S. 1994. Linen—the way ahead. *Journal of the Society of Dyers and Colorists* 110 (5/6): 170.

Kohel, R. J., and C.F. Lewis. 1984. *Cotton*. Madison, Wisc.: American Society of Agronomy, Crop Science Society of America, Soil Science Society of America.

Linen—versatility from the catwalk to the skies. 1992. *Textiles* 21 (4): 6–7.

Ramaswamy, G. N., C. G. Ruff, and C. Boyd. 1994. Effect of bacterial and chemical retting on kenaf fiber quality. *Textile Research Journal* 64: 305.

Stout, H. P. 1985. Jute and kenaf. In *Handbook of fiber science and technology*. Vol. IV, *Fiber chemistry*, ed. M. Lewin and E. M. Pearce, 702–726. New York: Marcel Dekker.

Thompson, J. 1994. King of fibers [cotton]. *National Geographic* 185 (June): 60–87.

Wustrow, K. 1994. Quality management: Working with environmentally grown cottons. *Knitting Times* 63 (August): 14.

PROTEIN FIBERS

P*rotein fibers* are those fibers in which the basic chemical structure is composed of amino acids joined in polypeptide chains. They may be separated into two basic groups:

1. *Animal hair fibers.* The major fiber in this group is sheep's wool. Other fibers of commercial importance come from animals such as the alpaca, camel, cashmere goat, llama, vicuña, guanaco, and the angora goat, whose fleece provides mohair. Also used are qiviut, or hair from the musk ox; angora rabbit hair; fur fiber from animals such as beaver, mink, and rabbit; and cow and horsehair.
2. *Fibers formed from extruded filaments.* Silk, produced by the silkworm caterpillars, is the only important fiber in this group. Spider silk, whether naturally or artificially produced, is now being studied for textile uses.

In the past manufactured fibers were produced from a variety of protein sources such as corn, soybeans, and milk, but none were commercially successful. See Table 4.1 for a list of protein fibers.

TABLE 4.1
Fibers of the Protein Family

Natural Fibers	Manufactured Fibers
Animal hair fibers	Azlon[a]
Major fibers	
Wool (from sheep)	
Specialty hair fibers	
Camel family	
Alpaca	
Huarizo	
Guanaco	
Misti	
Vicuña	
Llama	
Goat family	
Cashmere	
Mohair (from the angora goat)	
Qiviut (from the musk ox)	
Cashgora	
Fur fiber	
Beaver	
Fox	
Mink	
Chinchilla	
Rabbit (especially angora rabbit)	
Other	
Horsehair	
Cow hair	
Extruded fibers	
Silk (from the silkworm)	
Spider silk	

[a]No longer produced.

THE PROTEIN FAMILY

All protein fibers contain the elements carbon, hydrogen, oxygen, and nitrogen. Wool contains sulfur as well. In each protein fiber these elements are combined in different arrangements. As a result, properties of the various protein fibers may show some striking differences.

Even so, these fibers share a number of common properties. Protein fibers, except silk, tend to be weaker than cellulosic fibers, and they are weaker wet than dry. Fabrics made from protein fibers must be handled with care during laundering or wet processing. They do, however, as a general rule have greater resilience than cellulosic fibers. They are more resistant to wrinkling and hold their shape better.

Specific gravity of protein fibers tends to be lower than that of cellulose. Fabrics made from these fibers feel lighter in weight than do comparable fabrics made from cellulosic fibers.

Fibers from the protein family do not burn readily. When set aflame, they may extinguish themselves. Burned fibers smell like burning hair, flesh, or feathers. Protein fibers tend to be damaged by dry heat and should be ironed with a press cloth or steam. Wool and silk require lower ironing temperatures than do cotton and linen, with recommended temperatures around 300° F.

Chemical properties common to most protein fibers include susceptibility to damage by bases and by oxidizing agents, especially chlorine bleach. Like human hair they should be cleaned with solutions that are "pH balanced," that is, that are neutral or slightly acidic. Strongly alkaline soaps and detergents can damage fabrics made of protein fibers, but acids have less effect than on cellulosic fibers. Fabrics can be bleached safely with hydrogen peroxide, as can human hair, but chlorine bleaches are harmful to these fibers.

Sunlight discolors white fabrics made from protein fibers, turning them yellow after extended exposure. Although wool has better resistance to sunlight than does cotton, it will degrade on prolonged exposure. Silk degrades readily on exposure to sunlight.

ANIMAL HAIR FIBERS

The hair of a number of different kinds of animals has been used for textile fibers for many centuries. It is not clear when sheep or goats were domesticated. The ancestors of modern sheep living during prehistoric periods probably did not have the "wooly" type of fleece that modern sheep have but were covered with a straight, hairlike pelt. Straighter fibers do not spin into yarns easily, so that sheep may have originally been domesticated only for food. As woolier breeds evolved, people probably noticed these fibers could be spun into yarn and used to construct cloth. The earliest actual remains of wool fibers and fleece come from Egypt in the fourth millennium, considerably later than the first remains of flax (Barber 1991).

After people recognized that these fibers were useful in constructing cloth, sheep, goats, and other animals such as camels, llamas, alpacas, and the like were domesticated in different parts of the world, and their hair was removed for spinning and weaving. Of the many varieties of animal hair from which textile fibers are derived today, the fleece of the sheep is most widely used. In Central Asia the camel is an important source of textile fiber, and South America is the home of a number of camel-like animals that produce fibers used for spinning and weaving. The alpaca and llama are native to the Andes Mountains regions and have been domesticated. Vicuña and guanaco are wild or semiwild animals from the same geographic region. Other animal hair fiber comes from domesticated goats such as the angora goat and the cashmere goat.

Hair from other wild or domesticated animals such as rabbits, musk oxen, horses, and cows have some minimal use in textile products.

SHEEP'S WOOL

Under the Wool Products Labeling Act of 1939, wool is defined as "the fiber from the fleece of the sheep or lamb or hair of the angora or cashmere goat (and may include the so-called specialty fibers from the hair of the camel, alpaca, llama, and vicuña)" (Federal Trade Commission 1986). Fiber taken from the domesticated sheep makes up by far the largest quantity of fiber sold under the name of wool.

Types of Wool

Approximately two hundred different breeds and crossbreeds of sheep produce wool fiber. The fiber produced by these animals varies widely in quality not only because of the conditions under which the sheep may graze and the quality of the pasture land but also because some breeds of sheep produce finer quality wool than do others.

The sheep that produces the most valuable and finest wool is the Merino variety. (See Figure 4.1.) This type of wool accounts for about 30 percent of wool production. Merino sheep originated in Spain but are now prevalent all over the world, the largest proportion of Merino fleeces today coming from Australia. Merino wool is fine and elastic, though relatively short—from 1 to 5 inches. French Rambouillet sheep, descendants of the Merino bloodline, were imported to the United States in 1840 and make up 27 percent of all the sheep in the United States. These, too, produce fine, high-quality wool.

A second group of sheep that originated in the British Isles produces fibers that are not as fine as Merino and Rambouillet but are also of good quality. Fibers range

FIGURE 4.1

Merino rams with full coats of wool prior to shearing. Photograph courtesy of the Wool Bureau, Inc.

from 2 to 8 inches in length. Some of the breeds of sheep from this group are Devonshire, Dorset, Hampshire, Oxford, Southdown, and Wiltshire. Like Merino sheep, these breeds are raised worldwide.

Coarser, longer fiber is produced by a group of sheep known as Long British or Long Crossbreeds. The fiber length is 4 to 16 inches, and the better known breeds include Leicester, Lincoln, Cotswold, Romney Marsh, and Cheviot. Much of this fiber is made into outerwear in tweed, cheviot, homespun, and shetland fabrics.

A fourth group of sheep is made up of a variety of crossbred sheep that produce fibers, from 1 to 16 inches in length, that are coarse and have lower elasticity and strength. These wools are used largely for carpets and inexpensive, low-grade cloth.

Climatic conditions can adversely affect the quality of the wool, as can the condition of the grazing area. Australian flocks are enclosed in large fenced areas where underbrush and burrs are kept to a minimum, whereas American sheep are permitted to graze on open ranges. This free grazing results in fleece in which sticks, leaves, burrs, and other vegetable matter may be caught.

Wool Consumption

In 1997 less than one percent of the fibers processed by mills in the United States were wool and only 1.5 percent of imported textile and apparel items were wool.[1] Of the wool apparel items purchased in the United States during the 1998–1999 winter season, over 50 percent were imported.[2] Worldwide the market demand for wool fibers dropped from 6 percent in 1977 to 3 percent in 1997.[3] Australia, New Zealand, and South Africa are major producers of wool. In the United States, Texas, California, and Wyoming produce the largest quantities of wool.

Wool Harvesting and Processing

Shearing

Sheep are sheared to remove the fleece in the spring season. (See Figure 4.2.) Expert shearers move from place to place removing fleece or clip wool. In Australia fleece is removed in sections with the underbelly section kept separate from the sides. This is done because the fleece from the undersection and legs tends to be inferior in quality to that of the sides—it contains more vegetable matter and is more tangled, matted, and torn. In the United States shearers remove the fleece in one piece.

Fleece that is sheared from sheep at 8 months of age or younger is called *lamb's wool*. Because this is the first growth of hair with tapered ends, it tends to be softer and finer. Products made from this soft, fine wool are generally labeled "lamb's wool."

Wool removed from animals that have been slaughtered for meat is referred to as *pulled wool*. Wool is taken from hides by one of several methods. A chemical depilatory, a substance that loosens the wool from the hides, may be used. This material does not seriously damage the hide and is the preferred method because it allows full use of both hides and fleece. Another method is to allow bacterial action to loosen the fiber so that it can be pulled from the hide.

1. Statistics from American Textile Manufacturers Institute.

2. American Sheep Association, Inc.

3. Fiber Facts, www.fibersource.com. 1999.

FIGURE 4.2

Worker shearing wool from a sheep.

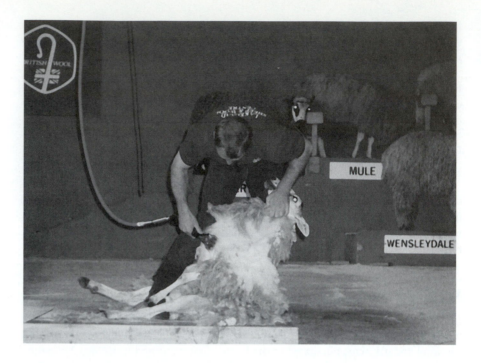

Pulled wool is inferior in quality to fleece or clip wool because it is less lustrous and elastic. Pulled wool is generally blended with other types of wool. The chemical treatment given to the pulled wool in its removal from the skin degrades the fiber and allows the fiber to swell more readily in the dyebath. For this reason, pulled wool dyes more unevenly than does sheared wool.

Experimentation with other methods of fleece removal is ongoing. In a new process, called "Bioclip," epidermal growth factor (EGF) is injected into sheep (Bioclip Harvesting, 1998). Hair growth stops for one day, then resumes. The point where growth stopped creates a weak place in each hair of the fleece. When this weak point reaches the surface, the fleece can be removed by hand. This method requires less than half the time that shearing requires, and the fibers are more uniform with less damage and fewer skin pieces. The sheep, however, lack adequate covering to protect them from the sun if the fleece is removed too soon.

Grading

Grading of wool is done at the time the fleece is sheared. In grading, the fleece is judged for its overall fiber fineness and length. An alternative to grading is found in *sorting*, in which the fleece is divided into sections of differing quality. The best fiber comes from the sides and shoulders; the poorest comes from the lower legs.

Preparation for Spinning

The first step taken to prepare the fleece for use is *scouring*, which removes oil, grease, perspiration, and some of the dirt and impurities from the fleece. The fleece is washed a number of times in a warm, soapy, alkaline solution. A fleece of about 8 pounds will be reduced by scouring to about 3 to 4 pounds. Much of the weight loss results from the removal of lanolin, a natural oil secreted by the sheep, which keeps the fleece soft and waterproof. This lanolin is recovered for use in cosmetics and other oil-based preparations. Even though lanolin can be recovered, the refuse produced by scouring of wool may be a cause of water pollution in areas where wool is processed.

If wool retains significant quantities of vegetable matter after scouring, it must be carbonized to remove this substance. *Carbonization* is the treatment of the fleece or fabric with sulfuric acid to destroy burrs, sticks, or other cellulosic material. Careful control is maintained to ensure that fibers are not damaged by the process. An alternative method is to lower the temperature of the fleece below freezing so that dirt, burrs, or vegetable matter become brittle and can be knocked or brushed from the fleece.

As a result of these processes, the wool may become overly dry and brittle. To avoid this, a small amount of oil is added to the fiber to keep it flexible, and the wool is kept somewhat moist during handling.

All wool fibers are *carded*. Fine wire teeth, mounted on a cylinder, separate the fibers and make them somewhat, although not completely, parallel. This procedure also helps to remove remaining vegetable matter from the fiber.

Wool Products Labeling Act

Wool fabrics can be made from new or from used wool, but one cannot tell by looking at the fabric whether the wool it contains is new or reused. To ensure that products made from used fibers are clearly labeled as such, the Wool Products Labeling Act of 1939 was enacted. This legislation regulated the labeling of sheep's wool and other animal hair fibers. The provisions of this act may be summarized as follows:

1. All wool products must be labeled.
2. The fibers contained in the product, except for ornamentation, must be identified.
3. The following terms, defined by the statute, should be used in identifying wool products (Federal Trade Commission 1986, 28).
   a. The term *wool* means fiber "which has never been reclaimed from any woven or felted wool product."
   b. The term *recycled wool* means (1) "the resulting fiber when wool has been woven or felted into a wool product which, without ever having been utilized in any way by the ultimate consumer, subsequently has been made into a fibrous state," or (2) "the resulting fiber when wool or reprocessed wool has been spun, woven, knitted, or felted into a wool product which, after having been used in any way by the ultimate consumer, subsequently is made into a fibrous state."
   c. The terms *new wool* or *virgin wool* shall not be used when "the product or part (of a product) so described is not composed wholly of new or virgin fiber which has never been reclaimed from any spun, woven, knitted, felted, bonded or otherwise manufactured or used product."

Recycled wools are often made from the cutting scraps left from the manufacture of wool items. The fibers are pulled apart and returned to the fibrous state through a process known as *garnetting*. In the garnetting procedure, fibers may be damaged and can, therefore, be lower in quality than some new wool. Less frequently, wool is recycled from fabrics used by the ultimate consumer. These fabrics are also returned to the fibrous state by garnetting. Because these fibers have been subject to wear not only from the garnetting process but also by the normal wear and tear of a garment or product in use, these are the lowest-quality wool fibers. Recycled wools are often made into interlining materials for coats and jackets, or other inexpensive wool products. They are sometimes referred to as *shoddy*.

Although the terms *virgin wool* or *new wool* guarantee that fabrics are made from wool that has not been previously fabricated, the terms carry no guarantee of quality. It is possible that a fabric made from poor-quality virgin wool may be inferior to one made from excellent-quality recycled wool.

In pile fabrics the face and the backing may be made of different fibers. The contents of the face and the backing may be listed separately, such as "100% wool face, 100% cotton back." If listed separately, the proportion of these fibers must also be indicated in percentage, so that in addition to the designation of "100% wool face, 100% cotton back," the label must also say "Back constitutes 60% of the fabric and pile 40%." The contents of paddings, linings, or stuffings are designated separately from the face fabric and must be listed.

The 1984 amendments to the Wool Products Labeling Act requiring country of origin labeling are the same as those required by the Textile Fibers Products Identification Act (TFPIA) and are described in chapter 2.

Molecular Structure

Wool is made of a protein substance called *keratin*, a polymer composed of 18 different amino acids connected by peptide bonds. Molecules composed of more than two different amino acids joined by peptide bonds are called polypeptides; therefore the wool molecule is a *polypeptide*. The peptide bonds are *amide* linkages made up of carbon, nitrogen, oxygen, and hydrogen:

$$
\begin{array}{c}
\text{O} \\
\parallel \\
-\text{C}-\text{N} \\
| \\
\text{H}
\end{array}
$$

The relative amounts of amino acids vary from one type of wool to another. Within the fiber the polypeptide molecules are arranged in a helical (spiral) form, which under a tensile force can be stretched to an extended, pleated structure. The wool molecule contains three types of intermolecular and intramolecular bonds. (See Figure 4.3.) Listed in order of bond strength, these are:

1. Cystine or sulfur linkages where the sulfur atoms of two amino acids are covalently bonded
2. Ionic bonds or salt bridges between two oppositely charged amino acids
3. Hydrogen bonds

The sulfur bonds can be broken by chemical treatment and then reformed with the molecules in an altered position. This is the principle behind the permanent waving of hair, where hair is formed into curls, a solution is applied to break the sulfur bonds, and then a neutralizer reforms the sulfur linkages in the curled position.

The hydrogen bonds are important in shaping wool fabrics during apparel construction and also in imparting pleats and creases. The bonds can be broken by moisture and then reformed in the new position when the fabric is dried. Also, because these bonds contribute to the strength of the wool, the fiber is weaker when it is wet and the hydrogen bonds are broken. The ionic bonds are broken under either acid or basic conditions.

FIGURE 4.3

Structural formula for the wool molecule.

$$-CH \begin{cases} CO \\ NH \end{cases} \qquad \begin{cases} CO \\ CH- \end{cases}$$

$$\begin{cases} CO \\ NH \end{cases} CH-CH_2-S-S-CH_2-CH \begin{cases} CO \\ NH \end{cases}$$

cystine linkage

$$NH \begin{cases} CO \\ -CH \end{cases} \qquad \begin{cases} CO \\ CH- \end{cases}$$

$$-CH \begin{cases} CO \\ NH \end{cases} \qquad \begin{cases} CO \\ CH- \end{cases}$$

$$CO \begin{cases} CH-CH_2-CH_2-COO^- \ {}^+NH_3-CH_2-CH_2-CH_2-CH_2-CH \end{cases} NH$$

glutamic acid   lysine

$$NH \begin{cases} CO \\ -CH \end{cases} \qquad \begin{cases} CO \\ CH- \end{cases}$$

$$CO \begin{cases} CH-CH_2-COO^- \ {}^+NH_3-\underset{\underset{NH}{\parallel}}{C}-NH-CH_2-CH_2-CH_2-CH \end{cases} NH$$

aspartic acid   arginine

salt linkage

Because of the helical structure and bulky side chains on the polymers, wool is only about 30 percent crystalline. The high amount of amorphous material decreases the strength but increases the absorption of water and dyes.

Properties of Wool

Physical Properties

Color. Wool fibers vary in natural color from white to creamy white to light beige, yellow, brown, and black. Wool may be dyed easily; however, it is difficult to keep white wool snow-white. The fiber tends to yellow from exposure to sunlight and with age. Bleaching is not a fully satisfactory means of keeping wool white, as chlorine bleaches are harmful to the fiber and bleaching itself tends to cause some yellowing. Among the bleaches used in textile manufacture are oxygen bleaches such as hydrogen peroxide, sodium peroxide, and sodium perborate. An alternative bleaching process is called reduction bleaching; one such process, *stoving*, uses sulfur dioxide. Peroxide is the most common treatment.

Shape. The length of the fiber depends on the breed of sheep from which it comes and on the fiber's growing time. In general, fiber length ranges from 1 to 14 or more inches, with finer fibers usually being shorter and coarser fibers usually being longer.

Wool fibers range from 8 to 70 microns in diameter. Merino fleece fibers are usually about 15 to 17 microns in width. In cross section the fiber is oval or elliptical. The cross section may show three parts: the innermost part is called the *medulla*.

FIGURE 4.4

(a) Wool fiber closeup, cross section. (b) Wool fiber closeup of scale structure along the fiber length. Photographs Courtesy of the U.S. Department of Agriculture.

a

b

Not all wool fibers possess a medulla, which is the section in which the pigment or color is carried and which provides air space. Most finer wools do not have a medulla. The next segment is the *cortex*, which makes up most of the fiber. Research has shown that the cortex is made up of microscopic cells that pack this area. The outer layer consists of a fine network of small overlapping scales. The scale structure is responsible for the behavior of wool in felting and in shrinkage. (See Figure 4.4.)

The scales on the surface of the fiber overlap "like the tiles on a roof, with the protruding end of the scales pointing toward the fiber tip" (Boston 1984, 523). Because of the way the scales are arranged, the fiber can move in only one direction. As fibers are placed close together in a mass of fiber, or in yarns, or in fabrics, they entangle with one another. During washing, the cloth is compressed and manipulated, and the individual fibers are bent. The fiber, being highly elastic, slides through the entanglement but can move only in one direction. As all the fibers exhibit this unidirectional movement, the fibers are drawn closer together, causing the whole structure to become smaller, or *shrink*.

Wool fiber possesses one further quality that is important in its physical appearance and behavior: most types have a natural crimp, or curly, wavy shape. The crimp is due to chemical differences in the two halves of the cortex that cause them to react differently to environmental conditions. One side swells and stretches more, resulting in slight curvature. The bilateral structure of the cortex spirals around the fiber, producing a three-dimensional crimp. (See Figure 4.5.) The crimp increases the bulk and springiness of wool and makes it resilient. It also makes wool fiber relatively easy to spin into yarns.

FIGURE 4.5

Three-dimensional crimp in wool showing spiraling of fiber.

Mixed into wool fleece are a number of *kemp* hairs. Kemp hairs are coarse, straight hairs that are often white and shiny and do not absorb dye easily. A large proportion of kemp hairs lowers the quality of the fleece.

Luster. The luster of wool is low because of the scaly, rough surface. Luster varies among different breeds of sheep, different sections of the fleece, and the conditions under which an animal has been raised. In general, the luster of poor-quality wool is greater than the luster of better grades of wool.

Specific Gravity. The specific gravity of wool is 1.32. This relatively low density makes wool fabrics feel light in relation to their bulk. The ability of wool fibers to trap air also gives them an ability to provide warmth without excessive weight. This is fortunate since wool is so weak that a large amount of fiber is usually necessary to make fabrics of adequate strength.

Mechanical Properties

Strength. Wool is a relatively weak fiber (tenacity is 1.0 to 1.7 g/d). The low strength is mainly due to the low degrees of crystallinity and orientation in the fiber. The strength decreases in wet wool because the hydrogen bonds are broken by water. Although the strength of wool is low, the fiber has high elongation owing to the helical structure.

Modulus. Wool fabrics stretch easily because of the low modulus of the fibers.

Elongation and Elastic Recovery. Wool is easily extended, but has fairly low recovery. As a result garments that are stretched at the elbows or knees will often bag.

Resilience. The resilience of wool is excellent, a result of its natural crimp. Elasticity and resilience contribute to the appearance of wool products by giving them good resistance to, and recovery from, wrinkling. Wrinkles will hang out of wool garments, especially if they are hung in a damp atmosphere, as will creases, pleats, or other shape provided by pressing.

Chemical Properties

Absorbency and Moisture Regain. Wool is an extremely absorbent fiber because it has a number of chemical groups that attract water and also because it has such an amorphous molecular structure. Wool also gives up its moisture slowly. Paradoxically, wool is also water-repellent. Spilled liquids run off wool because the scale structure of wool inhibits wicking of moisture along the fiber surface. Surface moisture is absorbed slowly.

The behavior of wool in relation to moisture can be summarized by saying that wool is naturally water-repellent, but upon prolonged exposure to moisture, the fiber does absorb substantial quantities of water. The moisture is held inside the fiber, not on the surface, so that wool can absorb a significant amount of moisture without feeling wet to the touch. Wool has a high heat of sorption providing additional warmth in a moist atmosphere as heat is evolved when the fibers absorb water. A further advantage is that wool retains its resilience even when wet, so that wool can become wet yet still insulate the wearer from cold.

Heat and Electrical Conductivity. The conductivity of wool of both heat and electricity are low. Both the poor heat conductivity of wool fiber and its ability to trap air between the fibers contribute to its excellent qualities for cold-weather clothing. Even though the electrical conductivity of wool is rated as poor, wool fibers do not build up static electrical charges unless the atmosphere is very dry. The ability of the fiber to absorb moisture improves its conductivity when humidity is present in the atmosphere. For this reason, wool garments sometimes generate static electrical charges indoors in winter when central heating of homes makes them warm and dry.

Effect of Heat; Combustibility. Wool will burn if a flame is held to the fabric, but it burns slowly, and when the flame is removed, the fabric may self-extinguish. The danger of flammability exists, but this factor is not so great as with many other fabrics. Wool can be treated for fire retardancy. Dry heat damages the fiber, producing a negative effect on both appearance and strength.

Chemical Reactivity. Wool fibers are damaged quickly by strong basic solutions; even relatively weak bases have a deleterious effect on wool. Strong laundry detergents and soaps have "free" alkali added to increase their cleaning power, and extended exposure to this additional alkali may be harmful to wool. Wool fabrics should be washed with special mild detergents.

Acids do not harm wool except in very strong concentrations. This makes it possible to carbonize wool fleece to remove vegetable matter without harming the wool fiber.

Chlorine compounds used for bleaching damage wool. Hydrogen peroxide or sodium perborate bleaches can be used safely. Organic dry-cleaning solvents will not harm the fiber.

Environmental Properties

Resistance to Microorganisms and Insects. Mildew will not form on wool unless the fabric has been stored in a damp condition for an extended period of time. Fabrics should be put away only after they are completely dry.

One of the major problems in the care of wool is its susceptibility to damage from insect pests. Moths and carpet beetles are particularly destructive because the chemical structure of the crosslinks in wool is especially attractive to these insects. Care in the storage of wool is required to minimize attack by insects. Soiled clothing is damaged more readily than are clean fabrics, as the insects may attack the spilled food as well as the wool. Wool fabrics with special finishes that prevent moth attack are referred to as being "mothproofed." Some of these finishes can be applied at the time of dry cleaning.

Consumers must exercise caution when using moth-repellents such as paradichlorobenzene crystals or napthalene flakes. These substances are poisonous if ingested by children or animals. Because prolonged inhalation of the fumes is also dangerous, treated textiles must be placed in airtight storage containers or in areas separated from living or working space. These chemicals should be placed above the garments since their vapors are heavier than air.

Resistance to Environmental Conditions. Exposure to sunlight will cause deterioration of wool, although it is less severely affected than cotton. Sunlight also yellows white wool fabrics. Age will not affect wool adversely. However, because of their susceptibility to attack by moths, wool fabrics require careful storage.

Other Properties

Dimensional Stability. Wool has poor dimensional stability. As mentioned earlier, the tendency of wool to shrink and felt can cause fabrics and garments to decrease in size. The shrinkage of wool is progressive. In the first laundering, fabrics stretched in the weaving process tend to relax. But wool will continue to shrink with subsequent launderings if it is not washed in cool water with a minimum of handling.

Consumers should preshrink wool fabrics before sewing unless the fabric is labeled as having been treated to prevent shrinkage. Purchasers of wool ready-to-wear garments should look for labels indicating shrinkage control. Finishes can be given to wool to render the fabric washable. Such finishes are discussed at length in chapter 23.

Abrasion Resistance. Wool is not an inherently abrasion resistant fiber. However, its resilience and flexibility in fabric structures help to absorb energy and provide durability. This property, as well as resistance to pilling, are dependent on yarn and fabric construction. Loose yarn and fabric constructions will allow individual fibers to pull out and form pills that can be held onto the fabric surface by the rough fiber scales (Hopkins 1953).

Uses

The excellent insulating qualities of wool lead to its use for cold-weather clothing. Winter coats, warm sweaters, and men's and women's suits are frequently made of wool fabrics or blends of wool and other fibers.

Wool's capacity for temporary setting makes the fiber ideal for tailored garments that are shaped through pressing techniques. By using different kinds of wool yarns and variations in weave, a wide variety of attractive garments and accessories can be manufactured from wool.

In the home, wool fabrics are made into carpets, blankets, upholstery fabrics, and sometimes draperies. Special coarse, resilient, durable wool fibers are produced for manufacture into carpets. Blankets of wool are warm without excessive weight and have the advantage of inherent flame resistance. The durability of upholstery fabrics will depend on the construction of the yarn and fabric, and those fabrics made from tightly twisted yarns with close, even weaves are most serviceable.

The disadvantages of wool used for apparel and in the home center on the tendency of fabrics to shrink and the susceptibility of wool to moth damage. Fabrics that have been finished to overcome both these problems are available, and appropriate handling during use and care will minimize these disadvantages. A disadvantage of wool for some individuals is that they may have allergic reactions from contact with the fiber. Some wool fabrics may have a rough or "scratchy" feel because of short coarse fibers that stick out of the yarn.

Consumer Brief 4.1 details some new wool products and interests.

Care Procedures

Wool fabrics can be either laundered or dry-cleaned, although dry cleaning is preferable for wool fabrics that have not been specially finished to make them "washable." Dry cleaning minimizes shrinkage problems. Also, commercial dry-cleaning solvents may include mothproof finishes that will protect wool garments from moth attack during storage.

Fabrics that have been given special finishes to render them washable should be laundered according to care directions attached to the fabric. Fabrics without special finishes must be handled gently because the fabric is weaker wet than dry and also to prevent felting of fibers because of friction. Wool products should be washed in lukewarm water, and special synthetic detergents without added alkali used. Washing can be done by hand or machine, provided that the wool fabrics are submitted to

CONSUMER BRIEF 4.1   What's New with Wool?

With the price of wool fiber down worldwide, producers are concentrating on better marketing and on expanding the variety of products in which wool and wool blend fabrics are used (Warner, 1998). The effort is led by The Woolmark Company, an international textile organization based in Australia, that licenses to manufacturers throughout the world.

Apparel, especially tailored suits and jackets, are still the primary products for wools. Other garments and different types of interior textiles are now being made from wool and modifications of wool fabrics make them more versatile. Lightweight wools in many designs are being promoted for seasonless garments that look and feel good and are wrinkle resistant (Online Textile News Network).

Wool blends fit this model and are being seen in traditional and new products. Tropical suitings with wool blend yarns provide the tailoring and draping qualities consumers appreciate. These fabrics are made with premium fine wool fibers. Another blend that is being produced is with cotton for jeans. The wool in the denim fabric adds warmth and bulk (Warner 1998). A new technology to stretch wool fibers, making them smaller, will enable development of other products where fine fibers are desirable.

A new product for the home is quilts filled with lamb's wool and Merino wool. The wool filling is covered with a cotton face and back and stitched to keep the filling in place. Wool fibers have also been used in blankets of knitted fleece.

Wool has long been used in hand woven oriental carpets and rugs. New carpets are being produced in the United States from yarns of 75 percent mohair and 25 percent wool. The luster of the mohair provides subtle shades and colorations in the carpets.

Even the staid and traditional Harris tweed is showing a new personality. No longer relegated to classic tailored jackets, this rugged fabric handwoven in the Outer Hebrides of Scotland has recently inspired designers of recent fashions. Apparel that appeals to women and younger consumers is being produced to maintain the market for Harris tweed. Brighter colors and modern silhouettes appeared in recent shows, accented with fur collars and bright accessories. The narrow width of the handwoven tweeds (30 inches) has been a problem in expanding its use, but several weavers are now using looms that are twice as wide.

One of the widely publicized scientific breakthroughs of the past decade was the cloning of the sheep, Dolly, in the United Kingdom. When Dolly was sheared, the precious 90 ounces of fiber from her fleece were carefully dyed and spun at Leeds University and a national competition conducted to design a sweater memorializing this discovery.

minimal agitation. Agitation and friction produced in handling wool are more detrimental to the fabric than are high washing temperatures, so that care must be taken to avoid placing undue stress on wool fabrics during laundering. Knitted garments, such as sweaters, should be measured before laundering, and while the garments are drying they can be gently reshaped into their original size.

Chlorine bleach will damage wool fabrics. Hydrogen peroxide may be used for bleaching. Solvents used for spot and stain removal do not harm wool fabrics. However, care should be taken in the application of spot remover. Excessive friction or rubbing on the fabric surface may cause matting and felting of fibers in the treated spot. Pat the fabric gently rather than rubbing hard.

Wool fabrics should not be dried in an automatic dryer. The pounding action caused by tumbling damp fabrics may cause excessive felting shrinkage of the fabrics. The dryer provides all the conditions conducive to felting: heat, moisture, and friction. Drying fabrics flat will prevent strain on any one part of the garment.

Because of the detrimental effect of heat on wool fibers, ironing temperatures should not exceed 200° F, and fabrics should always be pressed with a press cloth or steam.

SPECIALTY HAIR FIBERS

Many hair fibers possess qualities similar to those of wool. These fibers are produced in comparatively small quantities, but they do have an important place in the textile industry, particularly in high-status, prestige clothing items.

Cashmere

Cashmere fiber comes from the fleece of the cashmere (or kashmir) goat, an animal that is native to the Himalaya Mountains region of India, China, and Tibet. (See Figure 4.6.) Iran and Iraq also produce cashmere fiber.

The goats are "double-coated" with fine underhairs and longer coarser guard hairs. Shearing of the entire coat would result in a fleece of mixed fibers, so the fiber is gathered by combing hairs from the animals during the shedding season. Only the fine underhair is useful for cashmere fabrics, and one goat can produce 4 to 16 ounces of usable fiber. Chinese cashmere goats have denser underwool than other types and hence give a higher yield of fibers (Ryder 1993).

The softest fibers are $1\frac{1}{2}$ to $3\frac{1}{2}$ inches in length. Coarser and stiffer fibers range from 2 to 5 inches. Fibers are finer than are those in wool, about 15 microns in diameter. The natural color of cashmere is gray, brown, or, less often, white.

Microscopically, cashmere displays a scale structure like that of wool, but the scales are spaced more widely apart. The cross section of cashmere fibers is round.

The chemical and physical behavior of cashmere is much like that of wool, although cashmere is more quickly damaged by bases.

FIGURE 4.6

(a) Cashmere goat. (b) Female worker in Inner Mongolia commune removes fleece from a cashmere goat, using a special hand-made comb with a wood handle and an adjustable bar that allows the iron comb to open wider as the supply of fleece increases. Photographs courtesy of Kairalla Agency. Photograph by Boris Shlomm, president of Amicale Industries.

a   b

The softness and luster of cashmere combined with its scarcity put this fiber in the category of luxury fibers that are expensive. The fiber abrades easily, because of its softness, and since many of these fabrics are constructed with napped or fleecy surfaces, they require careful handling. Sweaters, coats, and soft luxurious fabrics and yarns account for the largest proportion of the items made from cashmere.

Camel's Hair

The two-humped Bactrian camel of Central Asia is the source of camel's hair fiber. (See Figure 4.7.) Early accounts of the harvesting of camel's hair stated that hair was gathered during the molting season in the spring by "trailers" who followed the camel caravans. The process currently used in obtaining camel's hair is hand shearing similar to the method used for sheep shearing before the invention of high-speed electric clippers (Shlomm 1985). The aforementioned trailers may have existed at a time when local inhabitants were more nomadic, but now with more settled populations in China and other Asian countries, the harvesting of camel's hair has become more like sheepherding. Camels are, however, also used as a means of transportation.

About 30 minutes to an hour is required for one to two people to shear one animal. Shearing takes place in May in the north and about a month earlier in the southern part of the region. Adults produce up to 10 kilograms of fiber, which is sorted by herdsmen as either coarse or fine. A re-sorting into various grades is done in a central warehouse. Within the collected hair are found both fine, soft down called *noils*, and coarse bristly hairs. The soft noils, which make up about 30 percent of the fiber, are used for making apparel.

Under the microscope camel's hair shows a scale structure similar to that of wool, but the scales are less visible and less distinctly seen. The cortex is distinct; the

FIGURE 4.7

Two-humped Bactrian camel being sheared by Chinese worker. Courtesy of Kairalla Agency. Photograph by Boris Shlomm, president of Amicale Industries.

medulla is discontinuous. Both the cortex and medulla are pigmented. This pigment produces the light brown or tan color associated with camel cloth, and because it is not discolored by oxidation, it cannot be removed by bleaching. Therefore, camel fabrics are usually left in their natural color or are dyed to darker shades.

Camel's hair provides excellent warmth without weight. It is said to have better insulating qualities than any of the other hair fibers. It is a relatively weak fiber and is subject to damage from abrasion because of its softness. Other physical and chemical properties of camel's hair are like those of wool.

Most fine camel's hair fiber is used for clothing, especially coating fabrics. Like other hair fibers, there is great variety in quality of camel's hair fibers, and the consumer must evaluate these products carefully. Because it is easy to dye wool camel color to blend it with camel's hair, a final product may be misrepresented as "camel's hair" when, in fact, the quantity of camel's hair is relatively low. Camel's hair fabric is expensive and should not be selected for its durability, as it tends to wear readily. Coarse camel's hair is used for industrial fiber, ropes, and paintbrushes.

Mohair

Mohair fiber is taken from the angora goat. (See Figure 4.8). Although South Africa produces the largest quantity of mohair (about 13.5 million pounds per year), the United States is responsible for 45 percent of world production.

Angora goats, unlike their cashmere counterparts, have a single coat of hairs and so are sheared in the same way as sheep. Fleece is removed twice a year. Each animal

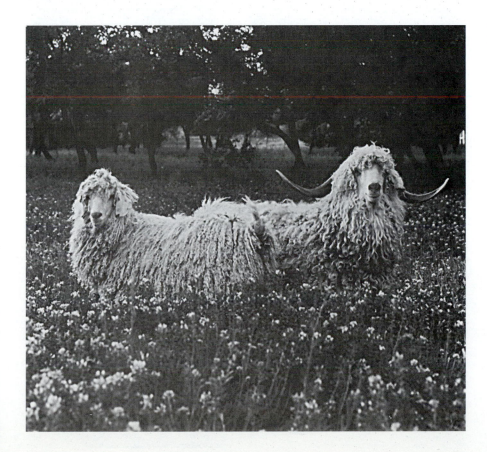

FIGURE 4.8

Angora goats, source of mohair fleece. Photograph courtesy of the Mohair Council.

yields from 3 to 5 pounds a year of 4- to 6-inch fiber. To obtain a supply of slightly longer fiber, some goats are sheared only once a year, in which case the fibers are 9 to 12 inches in length.

The natural color of unscoured fleece is yellow to grayish white. Cleaning removes 15 to 25 percent of the weight. The clean fibers are white in color, silky, and fine in feel and appearance. Fibers are graded, with kids' or young goats' fleeces especially valued for their fineness. The cross section of the fiber is round, with the medulla being only rarely visible. Small air ducts are present between the cells of the fiber, which give it a light, fluffy feeling. The microscopic appearance of mohair is similar to that of wool.

FIGURE 4.9

Photograph of mohair suiting fabrics by William Halstead shows the luster and draping qualities of these fabrics. Photograph courtesy of William Halstead & Co., Bradford, U.K. and the International Mohair Association.

Most of the physical and chemical properties of mohair are very similar to those of wool. The major differences between wool and mohair are the very high luster of mohair and its slippery, smooth surface. Mohair is especially resistant to abrasion. When viewed under the microscope, mohair shows fewer scales than does wool. As a result, the fiber sheds dust and soil and neither shrinks nor felts as readily as wool. Mohair is easier to launder, as well.

The current uses of mohair stress products where its luster can be used to good advantage, and these include men's and women's suitings, upholstery fabrics, carpets, and draperies. Novelty yarns, such as looped or bouclé yarns, are often made of mohair, and mohair is blended with other fibers. (See Figure 4.9.)

The cost of mohair fabrics tends to be higher than that of wool. The quality of mohair can vary a good deal, so the consumer must evaluate mohair products carefully.

Cashgora

New Zealand cashgora is a relatively new specialty fiber from the cashgora goat. This animal was bred in New Zealand by crossing wild female cashmere goats and angora goats. The underhairs, which become dominant in the crossbred goats, are similar to mohair but finer in size.

Cashgora fiber diameter ranges up to 22 microns. Luster is low to medium. Cashgora has a soft hand, dyes well, and is strong. Spun into either 100 percent cashgora yarn or blended, cashgora is used for knitting yarns, knitwear, blankets, and yard goods. Attempts to market this fiber have not been very successful and it is rarely found outside of New Zealand.

Qiviut

Qiviut is the underwool of the domesticated musk ox. (See Figure 4.10.) Herds of musk oxen are cultivated in Alaska. These animals shed in the spring, at which time

FIGURE 4.10

Domesticated musk oxen (with horns removed) being raised in Alaska.

they are combed and the fine underwool is machine spun. Yarns are sent to Eskimo women in about 50 to 60 villages in the region, and they hand-knit a variety of products. Each village has a distinctive pattern unique to that settlement. The fiber is similar to cashmere in texture and softness. One-half pound of qiviut will make a large, warm sweater. An equivalent garment in sheep's wool would require 6 pounds of fiber. Quiviut, like many specialty hair fibers that are in short supply, is very expensive.

Alpaca

Native to Peru, Bolivia, Ecuador, and Argentina, the domesticated alpaca produces a fleece of fine, strong fibers that have a glossy luster. (See Figure 4.11.) Recently, raising of alpacas has begun in Australia. The alpaca is sheared once every 2 years in the spring (November and December in the Southern Hemisphere). Hairs average 8 to 12 inches in length and range in color from white to brown to black.

Alpaca fiber is used in suits, dresses, and upholstery fabrics. It may be made into blends with other fibers.

Llama

Another domesticated Andean animal, the llama produces a fine, lustrous fleece, similar to alpaca. (See Figure 4.12.) Its colors are predominantly black and brown, but some lighter colors are found. Slightly weaker than alpaca or camel's hair, llama fleece is used by many Indian artisans to produce decorative shawls, ponchos, and other

FIGURE 4.11

Alpaca.

FIGURE 4.12

Llama.

products. The fibers, which are often blended, are used for coatings, suitings, and dress fabrics.

Llamas and alpacas have been crossbred, and the resulting animals have fleece with many of the same qualities and characteristics as those of the parents. An animal with a llama sire and an alpaca dam is called an *huarizo*. One with a llama dam and an alpaca sire is a *misti*.

Vicuña

A wild animal, the vicuña lives at very high altitudes in the Andes Mountains. (See Figure 4.13.) Although attempts are being made to domesticate this animal, most of the fiber must be obtained by hunting and killing the vicuña. One vicuña yields 4 ounces of extremely fine fiber and 10 to 12 ounces of less fine fiber. The Peruvian government sets a limit on the number of vicuña that can be taken in any year, so that the fiber is in very short supply.

One of the softest fibers known, vicuña is also the costliest. A vicuña coat is comparable in cost to a good fur coat. Its use is limited to luxury items. The natural color—a light tan or chestnut brown—is usually retained, as the fiber is hard to dye.

FIGURE 4.13

Vicuña herd. Photograph by William L. Franklin.

Guanaco

Another wild animal, the guanaco, has been domesticated successfully. Although supplies of the fiber are more readily available than vicuña, it remains a relatively expensive fiber.

Guanaco is a soft, fine fleece of reddish-brown color. Often blended, guanaco is similar to alpaca in its qualities.

Fur Fiber

Fiber from the pelts of fur-bearing animals are usually left on the skin, which must be treated in a process similar to tanning. (See chapter 17.) The fibers can, however, be removed and blended with other wool fibers to provide interest and soft texture. Fur fibers from animals such as the beaver, fox, mink, chinchilla, rabbit, and the like are used.

Angora rabbits have long, fine, silky, white hair. (See Figure 4.14.) These rabbits are raised in France, Italy, Japan, and the United States. The fiber is obtained by combing or clipping the rabbits. Angora rabbit fiber is exceptionally fine (13 microns) and is slippery and hard to spin. Angora is used chiefly in novelty items and is often knitted. Sweaters are often made of angora blended with nylon and wool. The fibers tend to slip out of the yarns and increase in length on the surface of the fabrics so that some persons have the mistaken notion that angora hair "grows."

Fur Products Labeling Act

Relatively small quantities of fur fibers are used in the production of textiles. If fur fiber has been removed from the skin and incorporated in a textile product, it is des-

FIGURE 4.14

Angora rabbit. Photograph courtesy of Amicale Industries.

ignated as "fur fiber" and is subject to regulation under the TFPIA and the Wool Products Labeling Act of 1939. Fur that is attached to the animal skin is regulated by the Fur Products Labeling Act of 1951. This legislation requires that all fur products carry the true English name of the fur-bearing animal from which the fur comes. It also requires that furs be labeled with the country of their origin.

No fur may be given a trademark name of a fictitious or nonexistent animal. If furs have been worn or used by the ultimate consumer, they must be designated as "used fur." When fur is damaged from natural causes or from processing, it must be labeled as containing damaged fur. Any dyeing or bleaching or other treatments given to artificially color the fur must be disclosed.

Cow Hair and Horsehair

Cow hair is sometimes blended with wool in low-grade fabrics used for carpeting and blankets and in felts. Horsehair serves as a filling or stuffing material for mattresses and upholstered pieces. In the past it was woven into a stiff braid for use in millinery or dressmaking, but this use has been replaced, for the most part, by synthetic fibers. Rubberized horsehair has been used to make carpet underlays.

SILK

History of Silk Culture

Silk originated in China, the first habitat of the silkworm which grew wild and lived on the leaves of a species of mulberry tree. Although some animal hair and flax fibers can grow to considerable length, silk is the only natural fiber that is hundreds of meters long.

Silk is made by the silkworm as it builds its cocoon. The substance is *extruded* from its body in one continuous strand from beginning to end. It is possible to unwind the cocoons and obtain long silk filaments. The Chinese discovered this process and, recognizing the potential value of the fiber it produced, guarded the method closely for hundreds of years. Silk has a natural beauty, and its history has been surrounded by legends. Chinese folklore credits the discovery of silk to Princess Si Ling Chi, who reigned about 2650 B.C. According to legend, after watching a silkworm spin its cocoon in her garden, she attempted to unwind the long filaments. After much experimentation she succeeded. She instructed her serving women in the art of weaving rich and beautiful fabrics from the long silk threads. So grateful for her discovery were the Chinese that they transformed Princess Si Ling Chi into a goddess and made her the patron deity of weaving (Lewis 1937).

History agrees with legend at least insofar as the approximate dates for the first use of silk by the Chinese. In spite of the close guarding of the secret of *sericulture,* or the controlled production of silk, other countries managed, often by somewhat devious means, to obtain silkworms. The Japanese supposedly abducted four Chinese maidens who were experts in sericulture and forced them to disclose the process. Another princess carried silkworm eggs and the seeds of the mulberry tree in her headdress when she left China to marry a prince of another kingdom. Even as late as the sixth century A.D., the secrets of silk manufacture were sought by the Byzantine emperor Justinian, who sent two monks to the East to discover how to produce and weave these handsome fabrics. The monks returned from a lengthy trip with silkworm eggs and mulberry seeds in their hollow bamboo walking sticks. From these seeds a flourishing silk industry developed in Byzantium. The cultivation of the silkworm spread to Italy and later to France (Lewis 1937).

Silk Production

Cultivation of the Silkworm

Silk is the only natural filament fiber that has significant commercial value. Produced by a caterpillar known as a "silkworm," silk can be obtained either from cultivated silkworms (*Bombyx mori*) or wild species.

Silk from wild species is limited in quantity and produces a coarser, stronger, short fiber known as *tussah silk*. Tussah silk has short fibers because the cocoons from which it is taken have been broken or pierced. When wild silk is spun by caterpillars that feed on oak leaves, the silk is light brown or tan in color and cannot be bleached.

By far the largest quantity of silk comes from sericulture, the controlled growth of domesticated silkworms to produce the silk fiber. Whether the silkworms be domesticated or wild, they go through four basic stages of development:

1. Laying of the eggs by the silk moth.
2. Hatching of the eggs into caterpillars, which feed on mulberry leaves.
3. Spinning of a cocoon by the caterpillar.
4. Emerging of the silk moth from the cocoon.

The science of sericulture has been perfected over many thousands of years. Today, all stages of development are carefully controlled, and only the healthiest eggs, worms, and moths are used for the production of silk. (See Figure 4.15.)

Selected moths of superior size lay from 400 to 600 eggs or seeds on prepared cards or strips of cloth. Each seed is about the size of a pinhead. These eggs can be stored in cool, dry places until the manufacturer wishes to begin their incubation.

Incubation is done in a mildly warm atmosphere and requires about 30 days. At the end of this time, the silkworms hatch. They are about $\frac{1}{8}$ inch in length. The young silkworms require constant care and carefully controlled diets. Shredded or chopped young mulberry leaves are fed to the worms five times each day. Some recent research has been conducted on an artificial diet, primarily of tofu, for silkworms (Ito et al. 1995). Worms that appear to be weak or deformed are discarded. The areas in which worms are grown are kept scrupulously clean. For about a month the worm grows, shedding its skin four times. When fully grown, worms are about $3\frac{1}{2}$ inches in length.

When its size and activity show that the worm is about ready to begin to spin a cocoon, the silkworm is transferred to a surface of twigs or straw. From two sacs located in the lower jaw, the worm extrudes a substance made up of two strands of silk (fibroin) and a gummy material (sericin) that holds them together. Moving its head in the shape of a figure eight, the worm surrounds itself with a cocoon of perhaps 1,000 meters of fiber. The completed cocoon is about the size of a peanut shell and takes 2 to 3 days to spin. If the worm is permitted to live, it will change into a pupa or chrysalis and then to a moth. After 2 weeks the moth breaks through the cocoon and emerges, mates, lays eggs, and begins the cycle again.

Only those moths selected as breeding stock are permitted to complete the cycle. These are selected from the largest and heaviest cocoons. The remainder of the cocoons are subjected to dry heat that kills the pupa.

FIGURE 4.15

(a) Silk moth laying eggs, (b) silkworms on a bed of mulberry leaves, (c) silkworm beginning to spin cocoon, and (d) completed cocoon. Photographs courtesy of the Japan Silk Association.

Occasionally, two silkworms will spin a cocoon together. This produces a cocoon made of a double strand of silk and is known as *doupion* silk (*doupioni*, in Italian).

Reeling of Silk

The whole, unbroken cocoons are sorted according to color, texture, size, shape, and other factors that will affect the quality of the fiber. Reeling of silk is, to a large extent, a hand operation done in a factory called a *filature*. Several cocoons are placed in a container of water of about 140° F. This warm water serves to soften the *sericin*, the gum that holds the filaments of silk together. Little of this gum is actually removed in reeling. The outer fibers are coarse and short and not useful in filament silk. They are separated and are used for spun silk, which is made from short fiber lengths.

The filaments from four or more cocoons are held together to form a strand of yarn. As the reeling continues, a skilled operator adds or lets off filaments as needed to make a smoother strand of uniform size. Several skeins of silk weighing 50 to 100 grams each are combined into a bundle. Each bundle is called a *book* and weighs from 5 to 10 pounds. These are packaged into bales for shipping.

Silk Yarns

The making of silk filament yarns is called *throwing*. Reeled silk filaments can be combined into yarns immediately. Short, staple-length silk fibers must be spun. Short outside fibers of the silkworm's cocoon, the inner fibers from the cocoon, and the fiber from pierced cocoons are known as *frisons* and are made into spun silk yarns. Fibers are cut into fairly uniform lengths, combed, and twisted into yarns in the same way that other staple fibers are spun.

Gum Removal

As mentioned earlier, the sericin that holds the silk filaments in place in the cocoon is softened but not removed in reeling. This gummy material makes up about 25 percent of the weight of raw silk. It is removed before throwing, after throwing, or after the fabric has been woven. A soap solution is used to wash the gum from the silk. In some silk fabrics, called *raw silk*, the sericin has not been removed.

Regulation of Silk Weighting

During the latter part of the nineteenth century, the technique of *weighting* was employed extensively to add body and weight to silk fabrics after removal of the gum. In passing silk through a solution of metallic salts, the salts are absorbed by the fiber, with a corresponding increase in the weight of the fabric. Silk can absorb more than its own weight in metallic salts, so that this excess weight on the fiber will, eventually, cause the fabric to break.

This practice had become so widespread that a good deal of poor-quality fabric was being sold. Because the buyer could not tell from its appearance or hand that the silk had been weighted, the Federal Trade Commission (FTC), in 1938, began overseeing silk weighting by passing its pure silk regulations.

These FTC regulations are still in effect. Other than some weighting of silk for neckties and for products requiring especially heavy fabrics, few silk fabrics are now weighted. The regulations require that fabrics labeled "silk" or "pure dye silk" contain from 0 to 10 percent of weighting. All silk fabrics that have more than 10 percent weighting must be labeled as weighted silk, unless they are black in color. Black silks are able to hold a greater quantity of weighting than are other colors without degradation, and so black silks can be weighted up to 15 percent.

Locale of Production

Because the culture of silkworms requires so much hand labor, sericulture has been most successful in countries where labor is less expensive. No silk is produced in the United States. China is the largest silk producer in the world. India and Thailand both produce substantial quantities of silk, but most of it is consumed within those countries and is not exported. Although Japan is the world's largest consumer of silk per capita, it produces almost no silk for export. Italy is the largest exporter of finished silk goods but imports the silk fiber from which those goods are made. This is also true of England and France, which also produce finished silk fabrics.

Molecular Structure of Silk

Like wool, silk is composed of polypeptide chains, but it has fewer amino acids and no sulfur linkages. The polymer molecules are not coiled but are extended. This structure allows the chains to be more tightly packed, increasing the crystallinity of the fiber. Hydrogen bonds and salt bridges crosslink adjacent molecules, contributing to the strength.

Properties of Silk

Physical Properties

Color. The natural color of cultivated silk is off-white to cream. Wild silk is brown.

Shape. The cross section of silk is triangular in shape. (See Figure 4.16.) The double silk filaments lie with the flat sides of the triangles together, surrounded by the sericin coating. (See Figure 4.17.)

The fiber has a smooth, transparent, rodlike shape with occasional swelling or irregularities along its length. It is fine, having a diameter of 9 to 11 microns, and filaments may be as short as 300 meters or as long as 1,000 meters. Individual filaments as long as 3,000 meters have been measured.

Luster. The luster of degummed silk is high but not so bright as manufactured fibers with round cross sections. Although the surface of the fiber is smooth, the roughly triangular shape changes the pattern of light reflection.

Specific Gravity. The specific gravity of silk is less than that of cellulose fibers and is similar to that of wool. Lightweight fabrics can be made of silk because of the fine diameter of the fiber and its high tenacity.

a   b

FIGURE 4.16

Photos of (a) cross-section and (b) longitudinal view of silk fibers taken through an electron scanning microscope. Reproduced courtesy of the British Textile Technology Group (BTTG).

Silk Fibers

"Gum"

FIGURE 4.17

Position of silk fibers within "gum" before processing.

Mechanical Properties

Strength. Silk is one of the strongest of the natural fibers. (Its tenacity is 2.8 to 5.2 g/d.) It is stronger than wool because of its higher crystallinity. Its wet strength is slightly less than its dry strength because the hydrogen bonds between protein polymers are broken by moisture.

Modulus. Silk has a moderately high modulus. This means that it will resist an initial tensile force more than will wool and will not stretch as easily.

Elongation and Recovery. The elongation of silk fibers before breaking is about half that of wool but considerably higher than cotton. It has fairly good recovery if stretched only slightly, but will not recover completely from high extensions.

Resilience. Silk has a moderate degree of resilience. Creases will hang out of silk, particularly under moist conditions, but its wrinkle recovery is slower and not as good as that of wool.

Chemical Properties

Absorbency and Moisture Regain. The absorbency of silk is good (the moisture regain is 11 percent), making it a comfortable fiber to wear. Although silk is more difficult to dye than wool, it can be printed and dyed easily to bright, clear colors if appropriate dyes are used.

Heat and Electrical Conductivity. The heat conductivity of silk is low, so densely woven fabrics can be relatively warm. However, because sheer, lightweight fabrics also can be woven from silk, it can be used for lightweight, summer clothing.

Because the electrical conductivity of silk is not high, silk tends to build up static electricity charges, especially in dry atmospheres.

Effect of Heat; Combustibility. When placed in a direct flame, silk will burn, but when the flame is removed, the silk may self-extinguish. Therefore, silk is not considered an especially combustible fabric. Like wool, silk is damaged by dry heat and should be ironed damp, at low temperatures and using a press cloth.

Chemical Reactivity. Like other protein fibers, silk is sensitive to the action of bases. Acids will harm silk more quickly than they harm wool. Chlorine bleach deteriorates the fiber, but hydrogen peroxide or other oxygen bleaches can be used. Organic chemical solvents used in dry cleaning will not affect silk. Perspiration will cause deterioration of the fabric. Perspiration can have a negative effect on dyestuffs, causing discoloration after repeated exposure; therefore, silk fabrics should always be cleaned before they are stored.

Environmental Properties

Resistance to Microorganisms and Insects. Mildew is not a problem with silk. Moths do not harm clean silk, but carpet beetles will attack the fabric.

Resistance to Environmental Conditions. Sunlight deteriorates silk even more rapidly than wool, causing white fabrics to yellow. Age will lead to eventual deterioration of fabric strength. Silk fabrics should be stored away from light. Antique fabrics should be sealed off from the air.

Weighting of silk causes it to crack, split, and deteriorate much more quickly than it would otherwise. (See Figure 4.18.) Historic costumes made of silk before silk

FIGURE 4.18

Silk fabric from the skirt of an historic costume of the 1890s that has deteriorated as a result of silk weighting.

weighting was introduced are still in good condition. Weighted silk garments dating from the 1870s to the 1930s often shred and break apart.

Other Properties

Dimensional Stability. The dimensional stability of silk is good. It does not stretch to any significant extent but may exhibit relaxation shrinkage because of its higher moisture absorbency.

Abrasion Resistance. Silk is not resistant to abrasion. While the fibers themselves have some ability to absorb energy their fineness makes them vulnerable to wear. Filament silk fabrics will not pill under abrasive action.

Special Finishes Applied to Silk

Silk has long been considered a luxury fabric, delicate and requiring special care. Beginning in 1977 one company, Go Textiles, introduced popular casual garments, such as shirts and jeans, made of silk. Given a special finish called *sandwashing* (see the discussion of sueding in chapter 22), these garments had an attractive faded appearance; they were soft, supple, and washable. Washed silks, even though expensive, became popular, and by the 1980s major American designers had put them into their collections.

As washable silks gained in popularity, other finishes were used to alter their hand. *Sueded silk* was finished with a slight nap. Treatment with alkali broke down the sericin coating, caused small pits in the fibers, and raised short fibers during tumble drying. To make apparel easier to care for, soil- and stain-resistant finishes were applied.

Uses

The beauty of silk fabrics is legendary. For many centuries silk was synonymous with luxury and was used for garments worn on feast days, festivals, and other occasions of great importance. Wall hangings of silk were used to decorate the homes of the wealthy, and carpets woven of silk were used in the homes of the rich in Persia and China.

The increased use of washable silk in casual clothing and larger supplies worldwide as a result of silk's exclusion from textile import limitations have made silk items increasingly available to most consumers. Although the quality may vary, the range of apparel for which silk is used has expanded in recent years, and silk or silk blends can be found in women's dresses, blouses, slacks, and lingerie; men's trousers, shirts, and neckties; knitted cold weather underwear; and various accessories. Raw silk is popular for summer-weight suits and jackets.

Silk may also be found in some high-priced drapery and upholstery fabrics. The performance of silk fabrics in these uses is rather poor. Upholstery fabrics of silk are often made in weaves that show up the luster of the fabric but abrade easily. Sunlight will deteriorate drapery fabrics of silk. Draperies made of silk should be lined with some other fabric to protect the silk from constant exposure to the sun.

Table 4.2 offers a comparison of the two major protein fibers: silk and wool.

Care Procedures

Silk fabrics should be stored away from direct sunlight, both to avoid yellowing of white fabrics and to prevent loss of strength. Long-term storage of silk wedding gowns or other items is best done in containers that are sealed against air and carpet beetles. Care labels should be followed to determine the best care procedures for individual silk garments. The following recommendations for care of silk fabrics were made by the Silk Institute.

1. Some dyes used on silk are susceptible to bleeding or loss of the dye. Check by wetting a small and inconspicuous spot (perhaps a seam or facing area) and blot the damp area between paper towels, pressing hard. If color appears on the paper towel, the fabric is not colorfast and should be dry-cleaned.
2. Fabrics that should generally be dry-cleaned include chiffon, georgette, taffeta, silk satin, and charmeuse; dark colors or bright patterns; those with embroidery, lace, pleats, or ruffles; items with linings, interfacings, or covered buttons.
3. Among the fabrics made from silk that can often be hand-washed are China silk, India silk, crêpe de chine, pongee, shantung, tussah, doupioni, jacquard, and spun silk.
4. Raw silk garments will gradually loose the residual silk gum if laundered.

Consumer Brief 4.2 discusses the care of washable silks.

Spider Silk

Protein filaments are spun not only by wild and cultured silkworms, but also by many species of spiders. The chemical make-up of spider silk is determined not only by the spider species, but also by diet, weather, and other factors. It is similar to silk from silkworms in that it contains no sulfur.

Spider silk has some unique features, which have spurred researchers to attempt to produce an artificial spider silk. Spider silk fibers are round in cross section and,

CONSUMER BRIEF 4.2   Care of Washable Silks

Even for silk items labeled as washable, care labels should be followed closely to avoid problems. When washing items by hand, launder in a mild detergent that contains no added alkali. Use lukewarm water and handle carefully. Do not wring or scrub, especially on fabrics made from smooth, sold color filaments where wear is more likely to show. Chlorine bleach should never be used on silk. If fabrics must be bleached, use hydrogen peroxide. Rinse garments thoroughly and then roll in a clean bath towel to absorb excess moisture.

If machine washing is recommended, use a gentle, two-minute wash cycle; lukewarm water; and mild detergent. Do not tumble dry, unless care labels direct, as the surface may be abraded or the fabric may be more likely to shrink. To dry, place garment on plastic hangers (wire hangers can cause rust stains).

Iron while the garment is still damp, on the wrong side of the garment, keeping ironing temperatures low, at 300° F or lower. Test silk fabrics to be sure they will not watermark before using steam or a damp press cloth. Although badly wrinkled silk fabrics will require pressing, many creases will hang out of silk fabrics without ironing. When ironing silk, protect the fabric with a dry press cloth.

The International Fabricare Institute (IFI) has noted a number of problems with some washable silks. Dyes have actually dissolved in water, causing dye transfer to other items being washed at the same time. Pastel colors tend to be more colorfast than dark colors. Some sizings or finishes used on washable silks discolor on contact with moisture from rain, water-soluble food and beverages, or perspiration. Spilled alcohol or perfume or cosmetics that contain alcohol may remove or change colors. Dyes, especially blues and greens, may lose or change color if they come into contact with alkaline substances such as soaps, shampoos, detergents, or toothpaste. Both sunlight and artificial light will sometimes cause fading.

Washable silks should not be dry cleaned because their dyes can be removed or lightened by dry cleaning solvents. Care labels should provide thorough information about how to wash these fabrics. Products that do not perform in a satisfactory manner when directions have been followed should be returned to the retailer for a refund.

with a diameter of about 5 microns, are much finer than filaments spun by silkworms. The fibers that anchor the web and support the spider are known as *dragline silk.*

The fibers in spider webs have much higher strength than silk with similar elongation values, giving them the ability to absorb impact energy needed to catch and hold the spider's prey. The ability to manufacture such fine strong fibers in filament lengths sufficient for textile purposes would be a significant achievement.

REGENERATED PROTEIN FIBERS

With the commercially successful regeneration of cellulosic fibers, research was undertaken to find suitable protein materials for regeneration in the hope of creating fibers with the highly desirable qualities of wool. The generic name of regenerated protein fibers is *azlon.* Materials that have been used to make azlon fibers include corn, peanuts, soybeans, and the protein from beetles. However, although experimentation continues, azlon fibers have never succeeded in gaining a significant place among textile fibers.

TABLE 4.2
Selected Properties of Wool and Silk Fibers

Property	Wool	Silk
Specific gravity	1.32	1.25 (degummed)
Tenacity (g/d)		
Dry	1.0–1.7	2.4–5.1
Wet	0.8–1.6	1.8–4.2
Breaking elongation (%)	30–40	24
Modulus	Low	Moderate
Resiliency	Good	Moderate
Moisture regain	~15%	11–12%
Burning	Burns, does not melt	Burns, does not melt
Conductivity of		
Heat	Low	Low
Electricity	Low	Low
Resistance to		
Fungi	Good	Good
Insects	Damaged by moths	Damaged by moths
Prolonged exposure to sunlight	Loss of strength	Significant loss of strength
Chemical resistance to		
Strong acids	Good	Poor
Strong bases	Poor	Poor
Oxidizing agents	Poor	Poor
Solvents	Good	Good

SUMMARY

Protein fibers can be produced by a number of different animals, the most widely used being wool from sheep and silk from silkworms. The common properties of protein fibers were summarized in the beginning of the chapter, and the distinctive features of each fiber detailed in other sections. In learning the properties of protein fibers, it is appropriate to distinguish between those grown as hair on animals and those extruded as filaments by silkworms or spiders. The latter are the only natural continuous filament fibers and differ both physically and chemically from wool and other animal hair fibers. Table 4.2 compares some selected properties of wool and silk fibers.

References

Barber, E. 1991. *Prehistoric textiles*. Princeton, N.J.: Princeton University. Press, 20–25.

Bioclip harvesting 1998. *Textile Horizons* 18(June): 18.

Boston, W. S. 1984. Wool. In *Encyclopedia of textiles, fibers, and nonwoven fabrics*, ed. M. Grayson, 523. New York: Wiley.

Federal Trade Commission. 1986. *Rules and regulations under the Wool Products Labeling Act of 1939*. Washington, D.C. Federal Trade Commission.

Hopkins, G. E. 1953. *Wool as an apparel fiber*. New York: Rinehart and Co.

Ito, H., Y. Muraoka, T. Yamazaki, T. Imamura, H. Mori, M. Ichida, M. Sumida, and F. Matsubara. 1995. Structure and chemical composition of silk proteins in relation to silkworm diet. *Textile Research Journal* 65 (12): 755.

Lewis, E. 1937. *The romance of textiles*. New York: Macmillan.

Ryder, M. 1993. The distinction between cashmere and mohair. *Premier Fibre News* (December): 22.

Shlomm, B. 1985. Gaining an insight into camel hair production. *Wool Record*, November.

Warner, J. J. 1998. Wool research: In search of lost magic. *Textile Horizons* (November): 5.

Review Questions

1. What are some of the physical and chemical properties common to most protein fibers?
2. Define the following terms that are applied to wool: lamb's wool, pulled wool, virgin wool, recycled wool, shoddy.
3. Explain how the chemical structure of wool accounts for (1) its ability to be set into pleats and creases and (2) its resiliency.
4. How does the physical structure of wool affect its properties?
5. What are the distinguishing characteristics of each of the following specialty hair fibers

   cashmere   alpaca
   camel's hair   vicuña
   mohair   angora rabbit
6. Define the following terms that are applied to silk: degumming, raw silk, tussah silk, doupion, throwing, weighting, sandwashing, spun silk.
7. Under what conditions should silk products be dry-cleaned? Under what conditions should they be washed?
8. What are the differences in mechanical properties between spider silk and silk from silkworms?

Recommended Readings

Arnold, L. N., and A. De Boos. 1998. Tropical-weight wool-rich blend fabrics with unique draping characteristics. *Textile Research Journal* 68 (8): 564.

Burroughs, J. 1993. Making a case for mohair fashions. *America's Textiles International* 22 (November): K/A 11.

Deshpande, P. 1999. Silk centre runs like clockwork. *Textile Month* (June): 49.

Higgs, W. 1987. The musk ox and its wool. *Journal for Weavers, Spinners, and Dyers* 142 (April): 14.

Hunter, L. 1993. *Mohair: A review of its properties, processing, and applications*. Manchester, England: Textile Institute.

Hyde, N. 1984. The queen of textiles [silk]. *National Geographic* 165 (January): 2.

Hyde, N. 1988. Wool—fabric of history. *National Geographic* 173 (May): 554.

Kaplan, D., W. W. Adams, B. Farmer, and C. Viney, eds. 1993. *Silk polymers: Materials science and biotechnology.* Washington, D.C.: American Chemical Society.

Madeley, T., R. Postle, and T. Mahar. 1998. Physical properties and processing of fine merino lamb's wool. Part I: Wool growth and softness of handle. *Textile Research Journal* 68(8): 545.

Madeley, T., R. Postle, and T. Mahar. 1998. Physical properties and processing of fine merino lamb's wool. Part II: Softness and objective characteristics of lamb's wool. *Textile Research Journal* 68(9): 663.

McCurry, J. W. 1994. Is mohair in for more woes? *Textile World* 143 (December): 67–73.

Rheinberg, L. 1991. The romance of silk. *Textile Progress* 20 (4).

Russell, K. P. 1977. The specialty animal fibres. *Textiles* 6 (February): 8.

Ryder, M. L. 1997. Silk—the epitome of luxury. *Textiles Magazine* (1): 17.

Sueded/sandwashed silk. 1992. *IFI bulletin: Fabrics, fashions* 2.

———. 1994. Wool works. *Textiles* 23(2): 14.

Warner, S. B., M. Paindavoine, and M. Jain. 1996. Structure and properties of natural and synthetic spider silk. *AATCC Book of Papers.* Research Triangle Park, N.C.: American Association of Textile Chemists and Colorists (AATCC).

INTRODUCTION TO MANUFACTURED FIBERS

The chemical principles outlined in chapter 2 apply to both natural and manufactured fibers. In manufactured fibers chemists have succeeded in creating through chemical means substances that have the qualities necessary to make them useful in textiles. Manufactured fibers may be either regenerated or modified natural substances, or synthetic.

In the manufactured fibers industry, all the early procedures started with materials similar in structure to natural fibers. These materials were dissolved chemically and were then re-formed into long, filament fibers. It was not until chemists came to understand the chemical structure of fiber molecules that they realized that it might be possible to create fibers entirely from simple chemical substances.

An analytical technique called X-ray diffraction revealed that fibrous qualities depended on the presence of long-chain polymers. This understanding led to attempts to put together long-chain polymers in the laboratory from chemical materials. Chemists had synthesized the large polypeptide molecules similar to the proteins in wool and silk, containing an abundance of amide linkages. Scientists believed that synthesis of polypeptides might lead to the invention of a totally synthetic fiber that was not derived from any natural substance.

In the early part of this century, E. I. du Pont de Nemours & Company, a chemical manufacturing firm, established an extensive basic research program, and those doing research in this program were given wide latitude as to the areas in which they might work. In particular, W. H. Carothers, a chemist at DuPont, chose to work in the synthesis of long-chain molecules; he was not searching for textile fibers, but the work he initiated in the formation of long-chain polymers was applied widely to the creation of a number of fibers and to their subsequent manufacture. The direction in which Carothers was working might be described as follows: "Take molecules that can react at both ends, react them, and long molecules will result. If these molecules are very long in relation to their dimensions, they will exhibit fiber-forming properties" (Moncrieff 1975, 319).

The basic research done by Carothers resulted in the invention of nylon, the first truly synthetic fiber to be marketed. Nylon is, according to chemical classification, a polyamide.

FIBER FORMATION

The basic steps in producing manufactured fibers are shown in Figure 5.1. First, polymers, whether natural or synthetic, must be converted into liquid form to be spun. This is done either by dissolving the polymer in a suitable solvent or by melting it. This polymer solution or polymer melt is sometimes referred to as the spinning *dope*. Cellulose, the raw material for most naturally derived manufactured fibers, is not easily dissolved. Accordingly, the cellulose polymer is usually modified before it is dissolved. Synthetic polymers are put together in the plant before the dissolution or melting step.

Before actually forming the fiber, certain characteristics can be added to the polymer material. Many manufactured fibers are naturally bright, with a high luster. If dull or semidull fibers are wanted, delustering agents can be added to the molten polymer to break up light rays and decrease shine. Colored pigments, flame retardants, and compounds to absorb ultraviolet light can also be added. Occasionally substances are added during polymer synthesis so that they are incorporated into the polymer molecules themselves.

The liquid polymer is then *extruded* through a *spinneret*. Each spinneret has a number of holes, and each hole produces one filament. As they exit the spinneret the filament fibers are solidified by cooling of melted polymers, by evaporating the solvent, or by precipitating the polymer from solution. These methods of solidification are the bases of the three primary fiber manufacturing processes. Other spinning methods that have been developed are described later in this chapter.

Filament yarns are described by denier (that is, size) and number of filaments; for example, filaments described as 70/34 represent 70 denier/34 filaments. When fibers being extruded are intended for conversion into staple lengths, spinnerets with larger numbers of holes are used to produce more filaments that are later cut into staple lengths. Spinneret holes are spaced to allow the filaments to be extruded without touching each other. The holes must be exactly the same size to produce uniform fibers. The metal used in the plate must be capable of withstanding high pressures or corrosive spinning solutions.

Most fiber spinning processes include a final step of *drawing* in which the filaments are stretched around rollers.

Melt Spinning

Melt spinning takes advantage of the thermoplastic characteristics of polymers. Chips of solid polymer about the size of rice grains are dropped from a hopper into a melter

FIGURE 5.1

Flowchart for producing manufactured fibers.

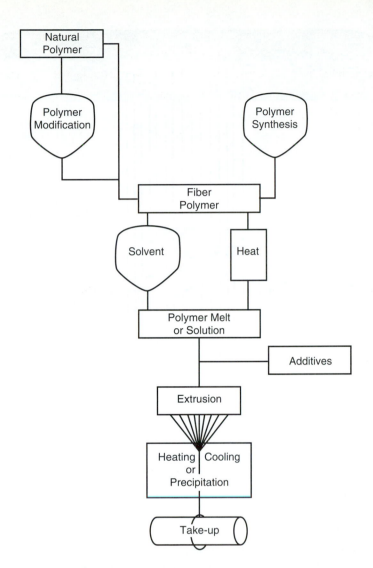

where heat converts the solid polymer into a viscous liquid. The liquid forms a "melt pool" that is pumped through filters to remove any impurities that would clog the spinneret and is delivered to the spinneret at a carefully controlled rate of flow. Melt spinning is simpler and cheaper than other spinning methods; therefore, it is used except when polymers cannot be melt spun.

The spinneret holes are usually round, but noncircular holes are also used to make filaments of various cross-sectional shapes. Melt-spun fibers may be made through Y-shaped holes that yield a three-lobed fiber or C-shaped holes to produce a hollow filament, for example.

The diameter of the fiber is determined by the rate at which the polymer is supplied to the hole in the spinneret and the windup speed, not by the diameter of the hole. When the molten polymer emerges from the spinneret hole, a cool air current is passed over the fiber, causing it to harden. (See Figure 5.2.) Failure to maintain constant feeding speed of molten polymer or changes in the temperature of cooling will cause irregularities in the diameter of the fiber. Nylon and polyester are the most common melt-spun fibers.

FIGURE 5.2

Melt spinning. Illustration courtesy of the American Fiber Manufacturers Association, Inc.

COOL AIR FLOW

Melt Spinning

One of the latest developments in melt spinning has been the significant increase in spinning speeds. Processing speed has increased from less than 1,000 meters per minute in the 1960s to over 7,000 meters per minute today. This is the equivalent of a car traveling over 250 miles per hour. Higher-speed spinning is cost-effective and up to a certain point increases the orientation of the polymers in the fibers. Beyond a speed of about 6,500 meters per minute, however, this advantage disappears as there is not enough time for the polymers to crystallize and the fibers may break (Demir and Behery, 1997).

Dry Spinning

Many polymers are adversely affected by heat at or close to their melting temperatures. Polymers that cannot be melt spun undergo other methods of spinning, such as dry spinning, to produce filaments. Dry spinning requires the dissolving of the polymer in a solvent to convert it into liquid form. Substances used as solvents are chosen not only because they will dissolve the polymer but also because they are safe and can be reclaimed and reused.

The polymer and solvent are extruded through a spinneret into a circulating current of hot gas that evaporates the solvent from the polymer and causes the filament to harden. (See Figure 5.3.) The solvent is removed and recycled to be used again.

Dry-spun filaments generally have an irregular cross section. Because the solvent evaporates first from the outside of the fiber, a hard surface skin of solid polymer forms. As the solvent evaporates from the inner part of the fiber, this skin "collapses" or folds to produce an irregular shape. If the rate of evaporation is slowed, the cross section of the filament will be more nearly round. Acetate fibers and some acrylic fibers are dry spun.

Wet Spinning

Wet-spun polymers are, like dry-spun polymers, converted into liquid form by dissolving them in a suitable solvent. The polymer solution is extruded through a jet

WARM AIR FLOW

Dry Spinning

FIGURE 5.3

Dry spinning. Illustration courtesy of the American Fiber Manufacturers Association, Inc.

Wet Spinning

FIGURE 5.4

Wet spinning. Illustration courtesy of the American Fiber Manufacturers Association, Inc.

into a liquid bath. The bath causes coagulation and precipitation of the fiber. (See Figure 5.4.) Solvents are usually recovered from the liquid bath and are recycled. Viscose rayon and some acrylics are wet spun.

It is possible to add special chemical reagents to the liquid bath that produce selected changes in the fiber. This is done in the manufacture of some high-strength rayons, for example.

A variant of wet spinning, called dry-jet wet spinning, has been developed to produce some of the newer fibers such as the aramids described in chapter 7. Instead of the spinneret being immersed in the spinning bath, it is placed slightly above the bath so that there is a small air gap, usually less than an inch. The fibers exiting the spinneret can be stretched to orient the molecules before they enter the bath to be solidified. This process develops high orientation and crystallinity in one step, rather than drawing in a separate step as described below (Jaffe and Jones 1985).

Other Spinning Methods

Although melt-, dry-, and wet-spinning techniques are used to form the vast majority of manufactured fibers, several other spinning techniques also exist and may be applied in a limited number of specialized situations. High-molecular-weight polymers, such as those in Spectra® polyethylene, are formed by *solution spinning* or *gel spinning*. As in wet and dry spinning, the polymer is dissolved in a solvent. The polymer and solvent together form a viscous gel that can be processed on conventional melt-spinning equipment to form a gel-like fiber strand. Later in the processing, the solvent is extracted and the fibers stretched.

Fibers made from polymers that have extremely high melting points and are insoluble present obvious difficulties in spinning. Such materials may be spun by a complex process called *emulsion spinning* in which small, fibrous polymers are formed into an emulsion, aligned by passing the emulsion through a capillary, then fused or sintered (combined by treating with heat without melting), passed through the spinneret into a coagulating bath, and subsequently stretched.

Drawing or Stretching

Both crystalline and amorphous arrangements of molecules exist within newly formed filaments. It is possible to orient these molecules to make them more parallel to the walls of the filament, and therefore more crystalline and stronger, by stretching the filament before it is completely hardened. (See Figure 2.4, page 36.)

Newly formed filaments are, therefore, subjected to drawing or stretching. Depending on the fiber type, this may be done under cold or hot temperature conditions and has the additional effect of making the filament both narrower and longer. Fibers made from polymers that have a low glass transition temperature, such as nylon, can be drawn at room temperature. The polymers are mobile and can be pulled into positions parallel to the fiber length. Polyester, on the other hand, has a higher glass transition temperature and so must be heated to be drawn. Drawing is accomplished by stretching the fibers between two rollers, called *Godet rolls,* with the second roller rotating faster.

Not all yarns are drawn to the maximum amount possible, because when a fiber reaches its maximum length, the extensibility of the yarn and fiber are lowered. Yarns that have not been fully drawn are called *partially oriented yarns* (POY). Those that have been fully drawn are called *fully oriented yarns* (FOY). Lower speeds in melt spinning produce fibers with lower orientation. As is true of many other textile processes, precise control of the process must be maintained so that the manufacturer can achieve the qualities needed in the final product.

Other steps may be added, such as texturing (in which crimp is added to the filaments) or heat-setting treatments to ensure very low shrinkage as is required in fibers for automobile tires. Sometimes two or more steps may be combined into consecutive operations to reduce manufacturing costs, so that the fibers may go from spinning directly to drawing, or from spinning to drawing to texturing. Texturing of filament yarns is discussed more fully in chapter 13.

Heat Setting

Thermoplastic manufactured fibers may shrink when exposed to heat. To prevent shrinkage, such fibers are treated with heat during manufacturing to "set" them into permanent shape. Exposure during use and care to temperatures greater than the heat-setting temperature will counteract the heat setting, resulting in fiber shrinkage or loss of heat-set pleats or creases.

FIBER SPINNING MODIFICATIONS

As the technology for producing manufactured fibers has become more highly developed, manufacturers have turned to increasingly sophisticated techniques for creating new fibers. Different fiber shapes and sizes, as well as unique combinations of polymer types in the same fiber, are but several examples of these techniques.

Hollow Fibers

Hollow fibers are made of a sheath of fiber material and one or more hollow spaces at the center. (See Figure 5.5.) These hollows may be formed in a number of different ways. The fiber may be made with a core of one material and a sheath of another, and then the central material is dissolved out. Or an inert gas may be added to the solution from which the fiber is formed, with the gas bubbles creating a hollow area in the fiber. Other experimental or proprietary techniques have been used to make hollow fibers. One involves spinneret holes with solid cores around which the polymer flows.

Hollow fibers provide greater bulk with less weight. They are, therefore, often used to make insulated clothing. For absorbent fibers such as rayon, hollow fibers provide increased absorbency. Some have been put to such specialized uses as filters or as carriers for carbon particles in safety clothing for persons who come into contact with toxic fumes. The carbon serves to absorb the fumes.

FIGURE 5.5

Photograph of the cross section of a hollow rayon fiber mounted in wax and photographed through a scanning electron microscope. Photograph courtesy of Courtaulds North America, Inc.

Bicomponent Fibers

As the technology for producing manufactured fibers has become more highly developed, manufacturers have turned to increasingly sophisticated techniques for creating new fibers. Not only are new generic fibers being created but also different polymers or variants of the same polymer can be combined into a single fiber to take advantage of the special characteristics of each polymer. Such fibers are known as *bicomponent fibers*. The American Society for Testing and Materials (ASTM) defines a *bicomponent fiber* as "a fiber consisting of two polymers which are chemically different, physically different, or both."[1] Bicomponent fibers can be made from two variants of the same generic fiber (for example, two types of nylon, two types of acrylic) or from two generically different fibers (for example, nylon and polyester or nylon and spandex). The latter are called *bicomponent bigeneric fibers*.

Components in bicomponent fibers may be arranged either side by side or as a sheath core. In making a *side-by-side bicomponent fiber*, the process requires that the different polymers be fed to the spinneret together so that they exit from the spinneret opening, side by side. (See Figure 5.6.)

Sheath-core bicomponent fibers require that one component be completely surrounded by the other, so that the polymer is generally fed into the spinneret as shown in Figure 5.6. Variation in the shape of the orifice that contains the inner core can produce fibers with different behavioral characteristics.

---

1. Reprinted, with permission, from the *Annual Book of ASTM Standards* (1994), copyright 1994 American Society for Testing and Materials, West Conshohocken, PA 19428.

FIGURE 5.6

Formation of bicomponent fibers.

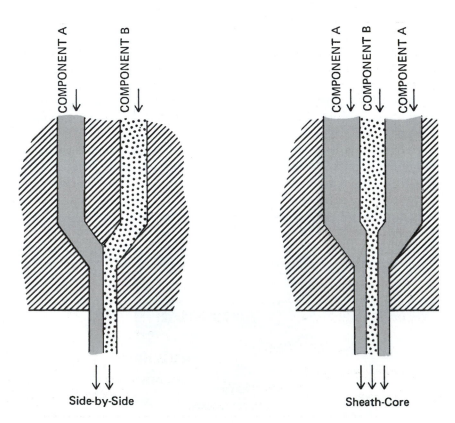

COMPONENT A   COMPONENT B

COMPONENT A   COMPONENT B   COMPONENT A

Side-by-Side

Sheath-Core

Most side-by-side bicomponent fibers are made to provide stretch or crimp to the fiber. Each of the polymers used in the bicomponent fiber has slightly different characteristics. Often one polymer is made to shrink in heat or chemical treatment more than the other, which pulls the fiber into a permanent crimp. If sufficient crimp is provided or if the fiber is elastic, the bicomponent fiber may also have increased stretchability. Other uses for bicomponent fibers have been suggested. For example, components with different melting points could be used to bond fibers together in the construction of nonwoven fabrics. When heat is applied, one fiber softens, serving as a glue to hold the other fiber in place. A less absorbent core fiber could be sheathed in a more absorbent fiber to increase comfort or increase dyeability.

Another type of bicomponent fiber is the *matrix fiber* in which one polymer is dispersed within the other before they are extruded. Figure 5.7 illustrates the structure of a matrix fiber. Few commercial matrix fibers have been manufactured. One, Cordelan®, a Japanese fire-retardant fiber recommended for children's sleepwear, was distributed in the United States for a time but is no longer available.

Under the Textile Fiber Products Identification Act (TFPIA) those products made from bicomponent bigeneric fibers must have listed on their labels the generic fibers present. Constituents are to be listed in the order of "predominance by weight" and must state the "respective percentages of such components by weight." The ruling goes on to state, "If the components of such fibers are of a matrix-fibril configuration, the term 'matrix-fibril' or 'matrix fiber' may be used." [TFPIA, section 303.10]

The label of a Cordelan® fiber product might, therefore, read as follows:

100% matrix fiber
(50% vinal, 50% vinyon)

Bicomponent fibers made from the same generic fiber are not covered by this regulation. They are composed of the same generic fiber type throughout, even though the different types of the same polymer may each exhibit somewhat different characteristics.

Microfibers

Several different methods have been developed for the spinning of microfibers. It is possible to produce microfibers through conventional melt spinning; however, to create such fine filaments requires very strict process controls and a uniformly high quality of polymer. There is a limit to the fineness of fibers extruded directly. Filaments smaller than 0.6 denier are too fine to withstand the tensile forces in the melt spinning process (Warner 1995).

A more common method is a bicomponent process using two different polymers that do not mix. After spinning, the filament yarns are woven into a fabric.

FIGURE 5.7

Longitude and cross section of matrix fiber structure. The black areas represent fibrils of one generic fiber; the second fiber is represented by the white.

The fabric is then treated with a solvent to dissolve or shrink away one component of the fibers, leaving the fine microfibers. The fabric is soft and drapeable, and this sequence of steps minimizes the stress on the fibers until after the fabric is constructed.

Two different types of bicomponents are currently used to produce microfibers. In the *citrus* configuration, wedge-shaped polyester segments are held within a star-shaped core of nylon or a different type of polyester. The core can be dissolved or separated by a chemical treatment of the fabric. The family of Belima® fibers produced by the Japanese company Kanebo are manufactured by this method. The other procedure currently used for making microfibers begins with extrusion of bicomponent *islands-in-the-sea* fibers, akin to the matrix-fibril fibers described above. Dissolution of the "sea" leaves the tiny microfibers. (See Figure 5.8.)

The search for better methods to make ever finer fibers continues. One (still experimental) method, called *electro-spinning*, uses a high voltage to overcome the forces holding the molecules in a liquid together. The polymer solution or melt is split into extremely fine filaments, some as small as 500 nanometers in diameter (1 nanometer is 1/1000th of a micron).

FIGURE 5.8

Formation of microfibers: (a) citrus type; (b) islands-in-the-sea type.

a

Part A   Part B

b

HIGH-PERFORMANCE FIBERS

The natural fibers and fibers regenerated from natural materials are often referred to as the first generation of fibers. Second-generation fibers are those manufactured fibers synthesized after Carothers's discovery of nylon. These were new generic fibers based on chemical differences. For the third generation fibers of the last two decades, technology has focused primarily on developing manufacturing processes and fiber modifications to produce *high-performance* or *high-technology* fibers (Hongu and Phillips 1998).

The terminology and classification of these fibers is still evolving. They are generally considered to be fibers produced by the advanced technological methods of today. They include the super strong and heat resistant fibers as well as those with special functions such as biodegradability and microbial resistance. A polyester fiber with the cross section of silk and microslits to simulate silk's luster and rustle is one such high-technology fiber. Microfibers are another example of high-technology fibers.

Super fibers are manufactured to have exceptionally high strength (tenacities higher than 20 g/d). The gel-spinning technique described in this chapter was developed to produce crystalline fibers with strengths in this range. Methods have also been developed to convert acrylic fibers into carbon super-fibers. (See chapter 12.)

MANUFACTURED FIBERS INDUSTRY PRACTICES

Trademarks

Most companies that manufacture fibers assign trademarks to their fibers. Those trademarks are promoted to the public and within the industry. Although the TFPIA requires that both generic and trademark names be listed on labels attached to products at the point of purchase, companies are not required to list both generic and trademark names in promotional materials. As a result, companies that want to build demand for their specialized fibers often run advertisements in trade publications using only trademark names.

Frequently, fiber manufacturers assign a trademark to a fiber that is used for particular products. For example, BASF Company manufactures nylon fibers for use in carpets and produces a series of variants of this carpet fiber, each with some properties that are unique. The company uses the name Zeftron® as a general trademark for its nylon carpet fibers and then adds numbers and letters to designate the specific variants: Zeftron 200®, Zeftron 500ZX®. This makes it possible for the carpet manufacturers who are BASF's customers to more easily order the most appropriate fiber.

Terminology, Acronyms, and Abbreviations

Producers and purchasers of manufactured fibers use a number of terms and their acronyms or abbreviations to refer to fibers. These terms often are not familiar to the general public. Table 5.1 provides a brief introduction to some of the more commonly used terms and their acronyms and abbreviations. The table also provides a cross-reference to the place in the text where each concept is explored in more detail.

TABLE 5.1
Acronyms and Abbreviations Commonly Used in the Manufactured Fibers Industry

Acronym or Abbreviation	Term	In-text Discussion
F	Filament	Chapter 2, page 50
M	Monofilament	Chapter 13, page 283
S	Staple	Chapter 2, page 50
T	Tow	Chapter 13, page 249
BCF	Bulk continuous filament	Chapter 13, page 248
FF	Fibrillated film	Chapter 13, page 266
FOY	Fully oriented yarn	Chapter 5, page 134
POY	Partially oriented yarn	Chapter 5, page 134
PT	Producer textured	Chapter 13, page 247

SUMMARY

This chapter has provided a general introduction to the techniques used to produce manufactured fibers and to some of the specialized terminology used by those working in this field. Manufactured fibers are made by melting or dissolving a polymeric material and then extruding it through a spinneret to be hardened by cooling, drying, or precipitation. The fibers are stretched or drawn either during the spinning operation, or afterward, to induce orientation of the polymers and provide strength.

Many spinning processes for particular fibers are patented and/or proprietary, and new techniques for producing superstrong fibers, microfibers, and other specialty fibers have been developed. Chapters 6 to 12 will acquaint readers with the characteristic properties and special processing methods of different types of manufactured fibers.

References

Demir, A. and H. M. Behery (1997). *Synthetic Filament Yarn Texturing Technology.* Upper Saddle River, NJ: Prentice Hall.

Hongu, T., and G. O. Phillips. 1990. *New Fibres.* New York: Ellis Horwood.

Jaffe, M., and R. S. Jones. 1985. High-performance aramid fibers. In M. Lewin and J. Prestion, eds. *High technology fibers,* 349. New York: Marcel Dekker.

Moncrieff, R. W. 1975. *Man-made fibres.* New York: Wiley.

Single molecule fibres. 1998. *Textile Horizons* 18(6): 18.

Warner, S. B. 1995. *Fiber science.* Englewood Cliffs, N.J.: Prentice Hall.

Review Questions

1. What are the steps that are common to all fiber manufacturing processes? What is the purpose of each step?
2. What are the differences between melt spinning, dry spinning, wet spinning, gel spinning, and emulsion spinning?

3. Define the following terms and explain how and why these fibers might be used.

    bicomponent fibers   side-by-side bicomponent

    bicomponent bigeneric fibers   fibers

    sheath-core bicomponent fibers   matrix fibers

4. Describe two ways of forming microfibers.

5. If fibers are described as *delustered, partially oriented, heat-set, microfibers*, at which stage of manufacture is each of the four italicized characteristics given to the fibers?

6. How does spinning speed affect the properties of melt-spun fibers?

Recommended Readings

Achwal, W. B. 1994. Microfibers—characteristics, properties, and processing. *Colourage* 41 (August): 35.

American fiber manufacturers special report [special issue]. 1994. *Southern Textile News* (December 12).

Holme, I. 1994. Microfibers: Present and future prospects. *Synthetic Fibers* 23 (April/June): 13.

Hongu, T., and G. O. Phillips. 1998. *New fibres.* Manchester, U.K.: Woodhead/The Textile Institute.

Issacs, M., and J. W. McCurry. 1994. Race is on to find new uses for microfibers. *Textile World* 144 (August): 45.

Kanebo ultrafine fibers. 1998. *JTN Monthly* 528 (November): 32.

Miroslawska, M. 1990. Spinning ultrafine filaments. *America's Textiles International* 19 (January): FW-2.

Mukhopadhyay, S. K. 1993. High performance fibres. *Textile Progress* 25 (3/4).

Seymour, R. B., and R.S. Porter, eds. 1993. *Manmade fibers: Their origin and development.* London: Elsevier.

Talele, A. B., R. K. Datta, and R. S. Gandhi. 1994. New profiled fibers: An overview. *Textile Industry of India* 33 (March): 11.

Ultrafine microfibers. 1994. *JTN Monthly* 480 (November): 49.

CHAPTER

6

MANUFACTURED CELLULOSIC FIBERS

For thousands of years the only fibers used for textiles were those found in nature, even though, as early as 1664, English scientist Robert Hooke suggested that people ought to be able to create fibrous materials that had the same qualities as natural fibers. However, neither Hooke nor any of his contemporaries were equal to the task. In the nineteenth century a number of scientists had begun to look seriously for techniques for creating fibers. Their search was successful. Nitrocellulose, the first rayon fiber, was obtained as early as 1832. Further experimentation and development followed, and by the end of the century, Count Hilaire de Chardonnet, a Frenchman, had set up a factory for the production of "artificial silk" (rayon), the first "manmade" fiber (Moncrieff 1975).

RAYON

The earliest processes for making rayon used natural materials that were fibrous, such as short cotton linters that could not be spun into yarns or fibrous wood pulp. Chardonnet used the pulp of mulberry trees because silkworms ate the leaves. The pulp was dissolved in chemicals that broke down the molecular structure of the fiber somewhat, while still retaining a substantial quantity of polymer molecules. The solution was forced through a metal plate that had small holes in it, exposed either to heated air or to a chemical solution, and then formed into a long, hairlike filament. This substance was called "artificial silk."

This fiber was given the name *rayon* in 1924. It is a regenerated cellulose. The specific process that was used is now obsolete in the United States and has been replaced by other methods of manufacture, but the basic principle of taking a natural material that is not usable in its original form and regenerating it into usable textile form remains the same. The manufacture of artificial silk by Chardonnet in 1891 marked the beginning of the manufactured fibers industry.

FTC definitions of generic fiber names always are written to specify the chemical makeup of the fiber. The FTC definition of rayon identifies rayon as "a manufactured fiber composed of regenerated cellulose, as well as manufactured fibers composed of regenerated cellulose in which substituents have replaced not more than 15 percent of the hydrogen of the hydroxyl groups." FOOTNOTE: the source for this and all subsequent fiber definitions is The Textile Fiber Products Identification Act, section 303.7. The major fiber groups that fall within this definition are viscose rayon, cuprammonium rayon, high-tenacity rayon, and high-wet-modulus (HWM) rayon. Viscose rayon accounts for by far the largest amount of rayon manufactured.

VISCOSE RAYON

Raw Materials

Wood pulp is the major source of cellulose used to produce viscose rayon. Cotton fibers, especially the short cotton linters, can also be used. Most of the timber used comes from 8- to 12-year-old eucalyptus, spruce, or southern pine trees that are raised in nurseries. Harvested trees are stripped of their bark, sun-dried, then cut into strips, and finally reduced to chips. Chips are treated to remove lignin (binding agents) and to remove as much of the resin as possible.

The resulting pulp consists of about 94 percent cellulose. It is pressed and cut into blotterlike sheets for further processing.

Manufacture

The following steps are employed in the process for manufacturing viscose rayon from these sheets of cellulose. Since cellulose is not easily dissolved, it is treated to produce a soluble form that can be spun into fibers. Figure 6.1 shows the process in a flowchart.

1. *Steeping* or *slurrying*. The quantity of cellulose is measured carefully by weight and then placed in a soaking press, or slurry press, where it remains immersed in a solution of caustic soda (sodium hydroxide) for about an

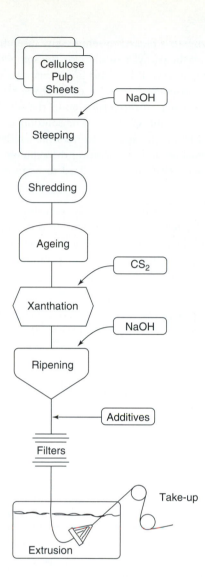

FIGURE 6.1

Flowchart showing the manufacture of viscose rayon fiber.

hour. The action of the sodium hydroxide is similar to that in mercerization, swelling of the structure and separation of the polymer chains. The excess solution is pressed out of the pulp material, leaving a slurry consisting
of a substance called alkali cellulose.

2. *Ageing.* Alkali cellulose is shredded into small fluffy particles called *white
   crumbs.* These are aged under carefully controlled conditions for several
   days. During this time the cellulose chains are broken into shorter polymers
   that can be dissolved more easily.

3. *Xanthation.* Carbon disulfide is then added to the white crumbs, which produces sodium cellulose xanthate and changes the color to bright orange-yellow. The large xanthate groups push the polymers farther apart and the cellulose xanthate is then soluble in sodium hydroxide.

4. *Dissolving and Ripening.* The orange-yellow crumbs are placed in dissolving
   tanks of dilute sodium hydroxide. The resulting solution is thick and viscous and is known as *viscose.* In color, it is gold with a consistency similar to
   that of honey.

5. *Filtration.* The viscose is filtered to remove any insoluble particles. This is important because the particles would clog the spinneret holes and interfere with the spinning process. It is at this point that delustering agents (such as titanium dioxide) or pigment dyes for coloring the fiber may be added.

6. *Extrusion.* The final step in the formation of the fiber is the forcing of the viscous liquid through the spinneret. The solution is wet spun into a dilute sulfuric acid bath. The acid hydrolyzes the xanthate, thereby reversing the xanthate formation and regenerating the cellulose in the form of long, continuous filaments that are then washed to remove chemicals or other impurities.

Environmental problems associated with the viscose process have reduced the number of producers in the United States. The evolution of hydrogen sulfide gas during the regeneration step and the run-off from the sulfuric acid bath are difficult to control. The viscose process is still, however, the most commonly used and economical production method worldwide.

Process Modifications

High-Tenacity Rayon

Rayon fibers produced by the process described are weak fibers. The final spinning step can be modified to increase the strength resulting in *high-tenacity* (HT) viscose rayon. To accomplish this a zinc compound is added to the spinning bath to slow down the regeneration while the fibers are being stretched. The polymer molecules are more oriented and crystalline.

High-Wet-Modulus Rayon

Attempts have been made to produce rayon fibers that possess some of the advantages of cotton. These experiments have centered on the development of rayon fibers with fibril structures similar to that of the natural cellulose fibers.

A Japanese researcher, S. Tachikawa, discovered a process for manufacturing rayon that develops a physical structure more like that of cotton. In this process the severity of the chemical processing was decreased, the manufacturing time was decreased, and careful control was maintained over the chemical materials used. More specifically, Tachikawa's process eliminated the aging of alkali cellulose, dissolved the cellulose xanthate in water rather than in caustic soda, and eliminated the ripening of cellulose xanthate. A lower concentration of acid was used in the spinning bath with little or no salts.

These rayons are known as *high-wet-modulus* (HWM), which means rayons that have greater resistance to deformation when wet. They are also called *polynosic rayon*. Although HWM rayons are no longer manufactured in the United States, they are manufactured abroad. The Lenzing Fibers Corporation of Austria manufactures *modal* fibers, a European generic name for HWM fibers and distributes these fibers in the United States.

Vertical Spinning

A recent process improvement in the spinning of viscose rayon is placement of a row of spinnerets in a vertical position facing upward. This reduces the space and the volume of acid formerly required for long sulfuric acid regeneration baths. The fibers are collected not in a rope, but as a ribbon that is pulled around pins to stretch the fibers. The ribbon form allows better penetration of water to wash out the acid and sulfur that is evolved during the spinning process. Not only is space reduced, but environmental conditions in the plant are greatly enhanced.

Molecular Structure

Rayon is composed of cellulose, like cotton. In viscose rayon, however, the cellulosic chains are much shorter. The degree of polymerization is only about 400 to 700, compared to 6,000 to 10,000 for cotton. The molecules are also less ordered, the crystalline areas are smaller in size, and the fiber has a higher amount of amorphous material. HWM fibers have longer polymer chains and a more crystalline structure, but the degree of polymerization is still less than 1,000.

Properties of Viscose Rayon

In the production of manufactured fibers, many qualities can be built into the fiber. For this reason, it is difficult to generalize about all rayon fibers, since each manufacturer may produce viscose rayons that differ somewhat.

Rayons have generally been used in many of the same kind of products for which cotton is used. When compared with cotton, rayons have displayed certain disadvantages. They are not equal in firmness and crispness; they have poorer dimensional stability, stretching and shrinking more than cotton; and they lose strength when wet so that rayons must be handled carefully both in industrial processing and in home laundering. Table 6.1 gives the properties of the major manufactured cellulosic fibers.

Physical Properties

Color and Luster. Rayon fibers are normally white in color. Their luster can be modified by adding titanium dioxide, a delustering agent, to the solution before the fibers are extruded.

Shape. Manufactured fibers can be manufactured in any length and diameter. In cross section the viscose rayon fibers appear as irregular circles with serrated edges. When lengthwise fibers are examined microscopically, longitudinal lines called *striations* are seen. (See Figure 6.2.) The striations on the surface of viscose rayon are a visual effect caused by the appearance of the serrations created when the skin of the fiber formed at a faster rate than the core. When the core is formed, the skin, which is larger, collapses slightly to form an irregular "wrinkled" surface. High-tenacity (HT) and HWM rayons have a rounder cross section because the regeneration of the cellulose is retarded in the spinning bath, resulting in less of a skin and core structure.

If carbon dioxide or some other gas-generating material such as sodium carbonate is injected into the viscose solution, that gas will be trapped inside the fiber when it is extruded. Depending on how this process is controlled, the resulting fibers may be hollow or may have hollow spaces (cells) within the fibers. (See Figure 5.5.)

Specific Gravity. The specific gravity of rayon is 1.51. Rayon fibers have densities comparable to those of cotton and linen (1.54), which are also composed of cellulose. Viscose, cotton, and linen fabrics of similar weave and construction will be of comparable weight.

TABLE 6.1.

Comparison of Characteristics of Regenerated Cellulosic Fibers and Cellulose Derivative Fibers

Property	Regular Viscose Rayon	High-Wet-Modulus Rayon	Lyocell	Acetate	Triacetate
Specific gravity	1.51	1.51	1.56	1.32	1.3
Tenacity (g/d)					
Dry	1.0–2.5	2.5–5.5	5.0	1.2–1.4	1.1–1.3
Wet	0.5–1.5	1.8–4.0	4.3	0.8–1.0	0.8–1.0
Moisture regain (%)	11–15	11–14	11	6	4
Resilience	Poor	Fair	Good	Poor	Fair
Burning	Burns, does not melt	Burns, does not melt	Burns, does not melt	Burns, melts at 500° F	Burns, melts at 575° F
Conductivity of					
Heat	High	High	High	Moderate	Moderate
Electricity	High	High	High	Moderate	Moderate to high
Resistance to damage from					
Fungi	Damaged	Damaged	Damaged	Fair resistance	Resistant
Insects	Attacked by silverfish	Attacked by silverfish	Attacked by silverfish	Silverfish may eat sizing	Silverfish may eat sizing
Sunlight	Loss of strength	Some loss of strength	Some loss of strength	Some loss of strength	Moderate resistance
Chemical resistance to					
Strong acids	Poor	Poor	Poor	Poor	Poor
Strong bases	Poor resistance	Excellent resistance	Excellent resistance	Causes saponification	Causes saponification
Oxidizing agents	Good	Good	Good	Good	Good
Solvents	Good	Good	Good	Dissolved by acetone	Damaged by acetone

FIGURE 6.2

Electron scanning photograph of regular viscose rayon in cross section (left) and longitudinal view (right). Photographs courtesy of British Textile Technology Group (BTTG).

Mechanical Properties

Strength. The strength of viscose rayon is low because of its lower polymer chain length (when compared with cotton and flax). (See Consumer Brief 2.1.) Furthermore, rayon is weaker than cotton because its physical structure is different. During the growing process, cotton develops a fibril structure, the layers or rings of which protect the fiber and provide greater strength. Ordinary rayon has no fibril layers in which the crystallinity of the physical structure is increased. Instead, rayon has a more amorphous inner structure. There is a considerable decrease in strength when the fiber is wet. Rayon fabrics must be handled carefully during laundering. Figures cited by manufacturers of regular-tenacity rayons available in the United States range from 1.0 to 2.5 g/d for dry fibers, and for wet tenacity, 0.5 to 1.5 g/d.[1]

High-tenacity and HWM rayons have higher strengths: from 3.0 to 5.7 g/d, dry, and 1.9 to 4.3 g/d, wet. It should be noted that, while these fibers are stronger than regular rayons, their tenacities are similar to, or lower than, those of most nylon and polyester fibers. (See Table 2.2, page 35.)

Modulus. Viscose rayon fibers have a fairly low resistance to stretching. HWM fibers, on the other hand, were specifically designed to have a high modulus, more comparable to that of cotton and polyester.

Elongation and Recovery. Viscose rayons stretch and, having low elastic recovery, tend to remain stretched. For some time after stretching, the distorted fabric tends to "creep" toward, but not completely to, its original length.

Resilience. The elastic recovery of rayon is low, as is its resiliency. Untreated rayons tend to stretch and wrinkle badly. Durable press finishes are generally not applied to viscose rayon because they weaken the fiber.

---

1 Data from *Textile World Man-made Fiber Chart* 130 (August 1990).

Chemical Properties

Absorbency and Moisture Regain. The molecular structure of viscose is more amorphous than is that of cotton or linen, making the viscose fibers more absorbent than the natural cellulosic fibers. Moisture regain is 11 percent. Viscose accepts dyes readily, because of its increased accessibility. Also, fibers with larger surface areas dye more readily, and the serrated edge of the rayon fiber provides greater surface area. The absorbency of the fiber makes clothing of viscose comfortable to wear.

Heat and Electrical Conductivity. The conductivity of both heat and electricity of viscose rayon is satisfactory, so that the fiber is reasonably comfortable in hot weather and does not build up static electricity.

Effect of Heat; Combustibility. Viscose fabrics must be ironed at lower temperatures than cotton. Too-high ironing temperatures will produce scorching. The recommended ironing temperature of viscose rayon is 250° F. Long exposure to high temperatures deteriorates the fiber.

The fibers burn with characteristics similar to those of cotton. Viscose rayon fabrics continue to burn after the source of the flame has been removed, and burning fabrics have the odor of burning paper. A soft, gray ash remains after burning.

Chemical Reactivity. The amorphous molecular structure of viscose makes it more susceptible to the action of acids and bases. Acids attack viscose more readily than cotton or other cellulosic fibers. Viscose is more susceptible to damage from bases as well.

Environmental Properties

Resistance to Microorganisms and Insects. Viscose is subject to damage from mildew and rot-producing bacteria. Silverfish will attack the fiber. Care in storage is necessary to prevent exposure of the fabric to conditions that encourage mildew and silverfish.

Resistance to Environmental Conditions. Exposure to sunlight will deteriorate viscose rayons more rapidly than cotton. Although it is often used in curtains and draperies, viscose rayon is not especially satisfactory for these products unless they are lined to protect against sunlight. Age does not have a deleterious effect on viscose rayons if care is taken to be sure fabrics are stored in a clean, dry condition.

Other Properties

Dimensional Stability. Rayon fabrics may be stretched during processing and exhibit relaxation shrinkage upon a first laundering. Since the regain of rayon is high, the amount of shrinkage is usually fairly high as well. Fibers may continue to shrink in subsequent launderings. Special finishes can be given to viscose to overcome some of the problems of shrinkage. Rayon fabrics can be prewashed or treated with special finishes to stabilize them.

Abrasion Resistance. The resistance of rayon fibers to abrasion is extremely low, and the resistance decreases when the fibers are wet. Durability is not a quality generally associated with rayon.

Uses

Viscose rayon is used in fashionable wearing apparel, ranging from millinery to lingerie, suits, dresses, and sportswear. Its use is dictated by its aesthetic rather than its durability properties. Viscose rayon is often blended with other fibers that may be more durable. The HWM modal fibers produced in Europe are found in knit tops, lingerie, and other apparel. In the home rayon fabrics or blends of rayon with other fibers can be found in tablecloths, slipcovers, upholstery, bedspreads, blankets, curtains, and draperies.

Because of their absorbency, rayon fibers are used in the manufacture of a wide variety of nonwoven fabrics, both disposable and durable. Often they make up the "cotton balls" sold for cosmetic uses and are the absorbents in disposable diapers. High-tenacity rayons were developed for tire cords and are still found in some brands and in other industrial products. They have been used as a starting material for carbon fibers.

Care Procedures

Fabrics made from rayon have had a broad range of quality and price. Dry cleaning is usually recommended for regular viscose fabrics because of their low strength, abrasion resistance, and dimensional stability. Consumers should be sure to follow care-labeling instructions closely.

Some rayon fabrics, particularly HWM rayons, may be washed, but laundering requires care because the fiber is weaker when wet and can be damaged more easily by rough handling. Drying in an automatic dryer may accentuate rayon's tendency to shrink. When pressing rayon fabrics, use lower ironing temperatures. Chlorine bleaches must be controlled carefully to avoid fabric deterioration. Oxygen (or perborate) bleaches are safer for rayon fabrics, if bleaching must be done.

CUPRAMMONIUM RAYON

Cuprammonium rayon is different from viscose rayon in that it is made by dissolving cellulose in a copper ammonium solution and extruding the fiber into a water bath. The manufacture of cuprammonium rayon was discontinued in the United States in 1975. It is still being manufactured in Italy, Japan, and eastern Germany. Water waste from the cuprammonium process is contaminated with chemicals, mainly copper, that must be removed to meet clean-water standards in the United States. The cost of removing chemical pollutants from the water is significant, and this factor has resulted in discontinuance of its manufacture in the United States.

Properties of Cuprammonium Rayon

Properties of this type of rayon are similar to those of viscose rayon. The fiber has a somewhat more silklike appearance and feel and is often manufactured in finer diameters. It is also slightly stronger.

Under the microscope cuprammonium rayon appears to have a round cross section and a smooth, longitudinal appearance. No striations, or extremely fine striations, appear on the surface.

The fiber can be made into lightweight fabrics. A brand name fabric, Bemberg Rayon, often used in linings, is made of cuprammonium fibers. Good conductors of heat and fairly absorbent, these fibers are especially suitable for use in warm-weather clothing. Consumers may find cuprammonium rayon fibers labeled as *cupro.*

Films and hollow fibers of cuprammonium rayon are used in making artificial kidneys as they exhibit superior performance in removing impurities and cause less blood clotting than do other manufactured fibers.

LYOCELL

Courtaulds, a European fiber manufacturer, developed and introduced the trademarked fiber Tencel®, which is produced by a process known as solvent spinning. This fiber has been designated by the FTC as *lyocell*, a separate generic name, but classified as a subcategory of rayon. Tencel® is now produced by Acordis, a new fiber company formed when the Dutch firm of Akzo Nobel bought Courtaulds. The Lenzing Company in Austria also markets a lyocell fiber called Lyocell by Lenzing®.

Manufacture

The raw material for lyocell, like that for viscose rayon, is wood pulp. The solvent, *N*-methylmorpholine-*N*-oxide (NMMO) is mixed with the pulp and when the mixture is heated, the cellulose dissolves. There is no degradation of the polymer as is necessary in the viscose process, because the cellulose dissolves directly at the high temperature. The resulting clear, viscous solution is filtered, then extruded through an air gap into a bath of dilute NMMO in which the cellulose is precipitated as a fiber. (See Figure 6.3.)

A major advantage of this process is that it is self-contained. The solvent, which is not toxic, is reclaimed from the spinning bath and is recycled. Since this solvent-spinning technology can more readily meet environmental regulations, lyocell is often billed as the "green" fiber.

FIGURE 6.3

Flowchart showing the spinning process Tencel® lyocell fibers. Illustration courtesy of Courtaulds Fibers, Inc.

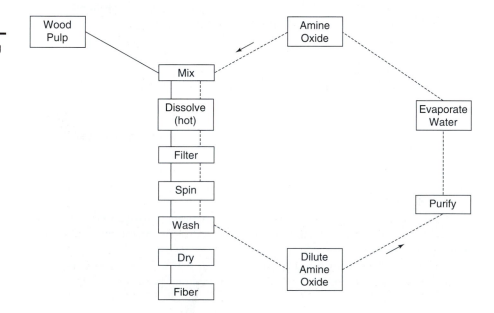

Properties of Lyocell

Chemical and environmental properties of lyocell are similar to those of rayon. It has high moisture regain, is comfortable to wear, and dyes readily. Physical structure, however, is somewhat different and lyocell has better mechanical properties.

Physical Properties

Tencel® lyocell has a smooth cross section, without the serrations characteristic of viscose rayon. Because of the manner in which the fibers form during spinning they are highly crystalline and as a result small fibrils tend to splinter off from the surface. This *fibrillation* gives lyocell a fuzzy appearance and reduces the luster of the fibers. (See Figure 6.4.) The amount of fibrillation can be controlled by finishing treatments to give a soft or "peach skin" effect (Wilmot 1998).

Mechanical Properties

Lyocell has high strength for a regenerated cellulosic fiber. The tenacity of Tencel® lyocell is 5.0 g/d dry, and up to 4.3 g/d when wet. It has a higher modulus as well, making it a good fiber for blending with cotton. Elongation is between that of regular and HWM rayon, and wrinkle recovery is better. In addition, lyocell can be treated with durable press finishes without diminishing its strength severely.

Other Properties

Lyocell fabrics do not exhibit the high shrinkage of rayon fibers. Their durability is also higher, but abrasion, especially wet abrasion, will increase the fibrillation of the fibers.

FIGURE 6.4

Fabric with lyocell yarns (vertical) and viscose rayon yarns (horizontal). Fibrillation of the lyocell fibers and the striations in the rayon fibers are visible.

Uses

Lyocell is used in men's and women's apparel such as shirts, blouses, pants, and dresses. (See Figure 6.5.) It also is used in some household textiles. Its combination of mechanical properties have enabled textile producers to successfully blend it, not only with cotton, but with wool, linen, silk, nylon, and polyester.

Lyocell fibers were originally used only in fairly tightly woven structures to inhibit fibrillation. New versions of the fibers have been produced by crosslinking the fibers as they are spun to control fibrillation. They can therefore be used in a wide variety of knits, which are looser fabric structures.

Care Procedures

Easy-care properties are a significant advantage for lyocell fabrics. They have good dimensional stability and moderately good wrinkle resistance and so can be washed, although drycleaning may be recommended for some items. Finishes can be applied to increase wrinkle recovery and lyocell fabrics require less finish than cotton or rayon.

A problem in laundering that must be considered is the fibrillation that can occur. Fabrics rub against each other in laundering and in the wet state this can increase the fibrillation, altering the appearance, and ultimately the strength of the fabrics.

FIGURE 6.5

Garments made from Tencel® lyocell fibers. Left: blazer and pants of 100% Tencel® manufactured by Thane Barnes. Right: Linda Allard suit for Ellen Tracy made from 50% Tencel® and 50% wool. Photograph courtesy of Acordis Cellulosic Fibers Inc.

CONSUMER BOX 6.1 **Lyocell: The "Green" Fiber**

Lyocell is the first new manufactured fiber to be developed in many years. The name was derived from "lyo", meaning solution, and "cell", for cellulose. The process for making lyocell is environmentally friendly in that the solvent used to dissolve the cellulose is non-toxic and has actually been used in a number of cosmetic and hair products. In addition, the solvent is almost completely recycled during the manufacturing of the fiber.

Acordis, which makes Tencel®, and Lenzing AG, which calls their version Lyocell by Lenzing®, manufacture fibers for high-end apparel uses where the aesthetics of rayon, with added durability qualities, have appeal. Lyocell fabrics have good drape and are comfortable to wear because of their high moisture absorbency. They can also be dyed in a wide range of colors.

The tendency of lyocell to fibrillate, that is to have very small microfibrils break off from the fiber surface, is utilized to produce various surface textures. The fibrils create a fine, soft finish which is variously referred to as "peach skin," "mill wash," or "soft touch." The amount of fibrillation can be controlled by fiber spinning processes and by finishing treatments that deliberately cause fibrillation by subjecting wet fabric to agitation and abrasion and then shearing it to produce a fine, even surface. The intensity of the treatment and the manner of shearing can be controlled to produce a range of fabric surface textures. Acordis is currently manufacturing a new lyocell version, Tencel® A100, that is crosslinked during spinning to reduce fibrillation. It is intended for products in which a smoother surface is desired.

Lyocell fibers are considerably stronger than rayon, both wet and dry and therefore can be laundered. Fabrics are usually given a finishing treatment to stabilize them so that they will have low shrinkage. The propensity of lyocell to fibrillate is considered an aesthetic advantage, but can be a drawback when items are laundered. After numerous washings the fibrillation becomes worse, and can cause changes in surface appearance as well as decreases in strength.

When first marketed, lyocell was used primarily in woven fabrics, because the woven structure was tighter and helped to control the fibrillation. The desire to make knitted fabrics from lyocell fibers led to the development of lower fibrillating fibers such as Tencel® A100. These fibers will retain their original appearance better in the looser knitted fabric structure.

The severe conditions in commercial laundering may accelerate this effect. Consumer Brief 6.1 provides more information on lyocell's use and care.

CELLULOSE ACETATE AND CELLULOSE TRIACETATE

In the 1920s experimentation with regeneration of cellulosic materials led to the discovery of a by-product called cellulose acetate. This substance, a chemical derivative of cellulose, was used as a coating for the fabric wings of World War I airplanes. It caused the fabric to tighten up and become impervious to air. After the war the demand for this material decreased, and the manufacturers of cellulose acetate sought another market for their product. Intensive research yielded a process for converting cellulose acetate into a fiber with high luster and excellent draping qualities. Like rayon, acetate was known as "artificial silk."

The resulting confusion between real silk and artificial silk led the FTC to establish a separate name for the manufactured fibers. In 1924 the term *rayon* was established to include both regenerated cellulose and cellulose acetate. In 1953 an FTC ruling established separate categories for rayon and acetate and for triacetate, another derivative cellulose fiber.

Cellulose acetate and cellulose triacetate are classified as *derivative cellulose fibers*. These fibers should be distinguished from the rayons and lyocell, which are *regenerated cellulose fibers*. The production of both fibers begins with cellulose but, unlike rayon and lyocell, the chemical composition of acetate and triacetate fibers is not cellulose but a chemical variation of cellulose known as an ester. For this reason, the behavior of cellulose acetate and cellulose triacetate differs somewhat from the other cellulosic fibers.

Manufacture

In the chemical reactions that take place during the manufacture of cellulose acetate (and cellulose triacetate), acetyl groups ($-OCOCH_3$) are substituted for $-OH$ groups on the cellulose molecule. This process is known as *acetylation*.

All three available hydroxyl groups in the cellulose molecule are acetylated. When a substance is formed from cellulose in which all three hydroxyl groups have been acetylated, the material is called cellulose triacetate. If one-third of the acetyls are removed by hydrolysis, the substance is called cellulose acetate or cellulose diacetate. Both are used in forming textile fibers, but triacetate is no longer produced in the United States.

The initial stages of formation of both cellulose acetate and cellulose triacetate are the same. (See Figure 6.6.) Purified cellulose pulp is steeped in acetic acid for a time to make the material more reactive. After further treatment with still more acetic acid, acetic anhydride is added. This mixture is stirred until it is thoroughly blended, but no reaction takes place until sulfuric acid is added to the mixture. The sulfuric acid begins the acetylation reaction. The temperature is kept low because the reaction gives off a great amount of heat, and the mixture stands for 7 or 8 hours until it takes on a thick, gelatinlike consistency. The material formed is triacetate, also known as *primary acetate* since it is made first. From this point, the procedure differs, depending on whether cellulose acetate or triacetate is being made.

Triacetate. To produce triacetate fibers, water is added to the viscous solution. The triacetate can no longer be held in this weak solution and precipitates out in the form of small, white flakes. These flakes are collected, dried, and then dissolved in a solution of methylene chloride and a small quantity of alcohol. The fibers are dry spun through a spinneret into warm air, solidified, and are formed into yarns. The hazards associated with methylene chloride and the engineering challenges of recovering the

FIGURE 6.6

Flowchart showing the manufacture of cellulose acetate.

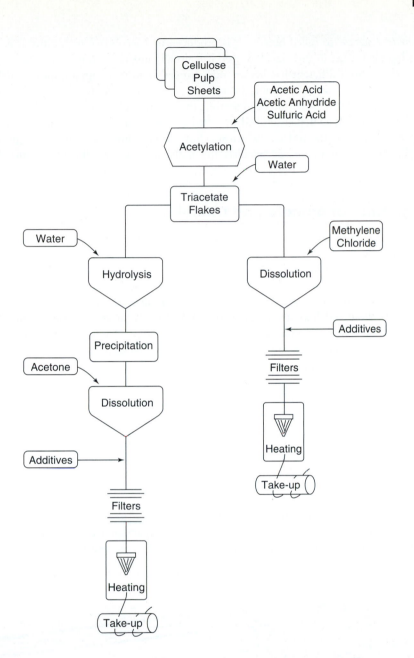

solvent were the primary reasons for discontinuing production of this fiber in the United States.

Acetate. To follow the steps in the spinning of regular acetate, we must return to the formation of triacetate, or the primary acetate. The next step is the conversion of the base acetate into a diacetate. The primary acetate, excess acetic acid, and acetic anhydride from the first reaction are combined with sufficient water to produce a 95 percent solution of acetic acid. This mixture stands for 20 hours, during which time acid hydrolysis takes place and some of the acetylated hydroxyl groups are reconverted to their original form. This mixture is tested constantly so that the reaction is stopped at the appropriate point. The mixture is poured into water, and the cellulose acetate precipitates into chalky white flakes that are collected, washed, and dried. This is the *secondary acetate*, so called because it is produced in a secondary step. Since it is the predominant fiber in this class however, it is usually just referred to as acetate.

Flakes from different batches are mixed together to maintain a uniform quality of acetate. The flakes are soluble in acetone, a common, nontoxic solvent. Before spinning, the flakes are dissolved in acetone to form the solution, or dope. This takes about 24 hours. The dope is filtered and then extruded through spinnerets into warm air that evaporates the acetone. When winding the fiber into yarns, fibers are given a slight stretch that orients or parallels the molecules, making the fiber somewhat stronger.

Properties of Acetate and Triacetate

The properties of acetate and triacetate are summarized in Table 6.1.

Physical Properties

Shape. In microscopic appearance acetate and triacetate are similar. Normally, both fibers are clear and have an irregular, multilobed shape in cross section rather like popcorn. Acetate may be manufactured in other cross sections as well; however, most commercially available acetate fibers with unusual cross-sectional shapes have been withdrawn from manufacture.

The longitudinal appearance of regular acetate and triacetate fibers shows broad striations. It is not possible to distinguish regular acetate fibers from triacetate fibers by microscopic examination. (See Figures 6.7 and 6.8.)

Luster and Color. If acetate and triacetate have not been treated to decrease luster, both fibers will have a bright appearance and good luster. Fibers that have been delustered show small, black spots of pigment in the microscopic longitudinal view and cross section. Fibers are white unless they have been solution dyed.

Specific Gravity. Acetate and triacetate are both lower in specific gravity, at 1.32 and 1.3, respectively, than rayon or cotton. Comparable fabrics, therefore, feel lighter when made of acetates or triacetates than if they are woven of cotton, linen, or rayon.

FIGURE 6.7

Photomicrograph of cellulose acetate fiber in: (a) cross section; (b) a longitudinal view. Photomicrograph courtesy of the DuPont Company.

a   b

a

b

FIGURE 6.8

Photomicrograph of delustered cellulose triacetate fiber in:
(a) a cross section;
(b) longitudinal view.
Photomicrographs courtesy of the DuPont Company.

Mechanical Properties

Strength. Both acetate and triacetate have very low strength. These fibers were, however, developed for end uses where strength is not a primary consideration. Both are weaker wet than dry, but the effect is not as great for triacetate since it is less absorbent.

Modulus. Both fibers have a low modulus, similar to that of rayon and lower than cotton. They stretch easily and feel soft to the touch.

Elongation and Recovery. Acetate and triacetate differ in their ability to recover from stretching. That of acetate is much lower if it is extended over 5 percent.

Resilience. Triacetate has better wrinkle resistance than acetate and better recovery, especially after wetting.

Chemical Properties

Absorbency and Moisture Regain. Acetate is more absorbent than is triacetate. Acetate has a moisture regain of 6.3 to 6.5 percent, whereas triacetate regains only 3.5 percent of moisture. Acetate has more of the cellulose hydroxyl groups remaining for attracting water.

Heat and Electrical Conductivity. Neither heat nor electrical conductivity of acetate and triacetate is as good as the conductivity of other cellulosic fibers. Both fibers tend to build up static electricity charges, and neither acetate nor triacetate is as cool to wear as cotton, linen, or rayon.

Effect of Heat; Combustibility. Both acetate and triacetate are thermoplastic fibers; they soften and melt with the application of heat. Acetate is particularly sensitive to heat and melts at a lower temperature. Triacetate is normally given a special heat-setting treatment that makes it much less sensitive to heat than acetate. Surface designs such as moiré (see chapter 22) can be heat-set in acetate. If triacetate is stretched during heat treatment, the crystallinity of the molecule can be increased. Heat-treated triacetate can be permanently set into pleats or other shapes.

If ignited, acetate and triacetate burn with melting. When the flame has been put out, a small, hard, beadlike residue remains at the edge of the burned area.

Chemical Reactivity. Acetate and triacetate are fairly resistant to acids and bases, although acetate can be converted back to cellulose with strong bases. Both fibers can be bleached with oxygen bleaches. Acetate dissolves in acetone and triacetate is also affected by this solvent.

Environmental Resistance

Resistance to Microorganisms and Insects. Mildew will grow on acetate or triacetate if the fabrics are stored in a soiled condition. The growth causes discoloration of the fabric but no serious loss of strength. Triacetate is more resistant to mildew than is acetate. Moths or carpet beetles do not attack either fiber. However, heavily starched or sized acetates are prone to attack from silverfish.

Resistance to Environmental Conditions. Extended exposure to sunlight will cause a loss of strength and deterioration of acetate fabrics. Draperies should be lined to protect them from the sun. Triacetate has moderate resistance to sunlight. The resistance of acetate to ultraviolet light is decreased if the fiber has been delustered.

Acid fumes in the atmosphere may adversely affect some dyes used for acetates. The chemical nature of acetates requires that they be dyed with a type of dye known as *disperse dye.* Certain of these dyes are subject to atmospheric fading, or *fume fading.* Blue and gray shades, after exposure to atmospheric gases produced by heating homes with gas, turn pink or reddish. Greens may turn brown.

To overcome this problem, acetate fibers may be colored in the solution before the fiber is extruded from the spinneret. Pigment that is added to the acetate solution is locked into the fiber permanently and cannot change in color. In addition to solution dyeing, special finishing agents called diethanolamine or melamine can be applied to acetate and triacetate fabrics to stabilize colors and prevent fume fading. Also some blue dyes that are not reddened by gas fumes have been developed.

Acetate does lose some strength through aging. Triacetates resist deterioration with age.

Other Properties

Dimensional Stability. Triacetate fibers have good resistance to stretch or shrinkage. Acetate fabrics may exhibit relaxation shrinkage on laundering unless they are pretreated. Knit fabrics are especially prone to relaxation shrinkage, showing as much as 10 percent shrinkage during laundering. Exposure to high temperatures may also cause acetates to shrink.

Abrasion Resistance. Neither acetate or triacetate is abrasion resistant. They are not generally used in items for which durability is an important property, but abrasion can be a problem in acetate linings. Nylon hosiery wearing against acetate satin linings in coats provides sufficient abrasion to cut these fibers.

Uses

Acetate is used for many household and apparel textiles because it has an attractive appearance and pleasant hand, and is inexpensive. Decorative fabrics are woven to take advantage of the high luster and wide color range available in acetate fabrics. Poor abrasion resistance limits their use in products where abrasion resistance is important, such as upholstery.

Acetates are used for items of clothing such as blouses, dresses, lingerie, and garment linings. (See Figure 6.9.) Handsome drapery and upholstery fabrics are often made of acetate brocade, taffeta, or satin. Acetate yarns are used in some fabrics together with yarns of other fibers to provide a contrast between the luster of acetate and dull appearance of, for example, cotton or rayon. One of the highest volume uses of acetate is cigarette filters. The tiny fibers of acetate tow in the filter provide a large surface area for absorbing compounds from the burning tobacco.

Filament acetate is produced by Eastman Chemical Company under the trademarks of Chromspun®, a producer-colored fiber, and Estron®. Celanese Acetate makes acetate fibers in filament, staple, and tow and produces Microsafe AM®, an antimicrobial fiber in filament or staple.

Triacetate fabrics have the advantage of being able to be heat-set. Apparel in which pleat or shape retention is important is often made from triacetate. The major use of this fabric is in wearing apparel; however, the manufacturer recommends its use for comforters, bedspreads, draperies, and throw pillows, as well. Triacetate is manufactured in Belgium, Japan, and the United Kingdom.

FIGURE 6.9

Fashionable red pants suit made from Celanese® acetate fiber. Photograph courtesy of Celanese Acetate. Outfit by Lois Snyder for Dani Max in Symphony Fabrics, modeled by Kristi Yamaguchi.

Care Procedures

Acetate

If handled with care, acetates can be laundered successfully. However, dry cleaning is usually recommended. Woven acetate goods may shrink as much as 5 percent and knits as much as 10 percent in laundering. During laundering, acetate fabrics should not be subjected to undue stress through wringing or twisting. Fibers are weaker wet than dry, and acetates will wrinkle badly if creased or folded when wet.

Hydrogen peroxide or sodium perborate bleaches can be used if necessary for whitening of fabrics. Bleaching should be carefully controlled. Ironing temperatures for acetates must be kept low. The fabric will stick if ironed at temperatures about 350 to 375° F and will melt at 500° F.

Acetone, a component of some fingernail polishes and polish removers, will dissolve acetate. Care should be taken to avoid spilling acetone-containing substances on the fabric.

Triacetate

Triacetate fabrics can be hand or machine washed. Hydrogen peroxide and sodium perborate bleaches can be used. Triacetates have better wrinkle recovery and crease resistance than acetates. If the fabrics require touch-up ironing after laundering, triacetates can be ironed at the rayon setting on the iron dial.

Dry cleaning solvents will not harm triacetates. These fabrics can be successfully drycleaned. Acetone will also damage triacetate fabrics. Spills from nail polish or remover that contains acetone will swell and may dissolve the fabric.

SUMMARY

Manufactured cellulosic fibers can be classified as those that are all cellulose and those that are cellulose derivatives. The cellulose fibers are the various types of rayon: viscose, cuprammonium, and lyocell. Fibers that are made from modified cellulose are acetate and triacetate. All these fibers have desirable aesthetic qualities and can be used in filament form or cut into staple lengths. Generally, low strength, abrasion resistance, and dimensional stability are disadvantages of manufactured cellulosic fibers. Lyocell fibers are superior in these properties, however.

References

Moncrieff, R. W. 1975. *Man-made fibers*. New York: Wiley.

Wilmot, N. J. 1998. Tencel®: The manipulation of fabric aesthetics and performance via the application of chemical finishes. In *AATCC Book of Papers,* 459. Research Triangle Park, N.C.: AATCC.

Review Questions

1. In what ways are cotton and viscose rayon different? How does the molecular structure of these fibers account for these differences?
2. What was the reason for the development of HWM rayon? What advantages does it offer?

3.	How do the mechanical properties of lyocell differ from those of viscose rayon? Why do lyocell fibers fibrillate and how can this be controlled?
4.	Why is cuprammonium rayon no longer manufactured in the United States?
5.	What is the difference in chemical composition of regenerated cellulosic fibers and cellulose derivative fibers? What generalizations can you make about the differences in properties of those fibers that are regenerated and those that are derivative?
6.	What differences in fiber properties of acetate and triacetate can be explained by differences in chemical structure?

Recommended Readings

Artificial silk. 1967. *CIBA Review* 2.

Cellulosic fibers and textiles. 1998. *JTN Monthly* (November): 18.

Kumar, A., and C. Purtell. 1994. Enzymatic treatment of man-made cellulosic fabrics. *Textile Chemist and Colorist* 26 (October): 25.

McCurry, J. W. 1998. Lyocell disciples see lofty future. *Textile World* 148 (March): 47.

Richmond, M. L. 1987. Diverse rayon comes of age. *California Apparel News* (January 16-22): 6.

Summers, T. A., B. J. Collier, J. R. Collier, and J. L. Haynes. 1993. History of viscose rayon. In R. B. Seymour and R. S. Porter, eds. *Manmade fibers: Their origin and development.* London: Elsevier, p. 72.

Nylon and Aramid Fibers

Under the most recent Federal Trade Commission (FTC) definition, *nylon* is "a manufactured fiber in which the fiber-forming substance is a long-chain synthetic polyamide in which less than 85 percent of the amide

$$(-C-NH-)$$
$$\underset{O}{\overset{\|}{}}$$

linkages are attached directly to two aromatic rings." This definition covers a variety of structures, two main classifications of which are used in the United States: nylon 6 and nylon 66. In a 1974 revision of generic fiber categories, the FTC established a separate category of fibers that is designated *aramids*. Like nylons, aramid fibers are polyamides; but in aramids 85 percent or *more* of the amide linkages are attached to two aromatic rings. The benzene rings described in chapter 2 are part of the structure of aramid fibers.

NYLON

Nylon 66 and nylon 6 are isomers; that is, each polymer contains the same elements by weight, but the polymers' molecules are arranged differently. Such differences in structural arrangements cause some differences in fiber properties. However, in an article comparing the two types of nylon, R. A. F. Moore (1989) concluded that "the properties of these two types of nylon are more similar than dissimilar" (p. 22).

Although the processes for making both nylon 66 and nylon 6 have been known since the earliest experimentation on nylon, DuPont, which pioneered the development of nylon in the United States, chose to utilize the nylon 66 process. Nylon 66 predominates in the United States, whereas nylon 6 predominates in Europe, although several U.S. textile companies produce nylon 6.

The generic name *nylon* was proposed by DuPont in 1938 for the first commercially produced fibers. The company had considered such names as *Delawear* (for the state in which the DuPont laboratories were located) and *Duparooh* (for "DuPont pulls *a* rabbit out of hat") before settling on *nylon*. Although nylon production has grown in volume over the last 20 years, its share of the synthetic fiber market has declined. About 14 percent of all manufactured fibers in 1997 were nylon.

Manufacture

Figure 7.1 shows the primary steps in producing nylon. The chemicals from which nylon 66 is synthesized are adipic acid and hexamethylene diamine:

Adipic acid	*Hexamethylene diamine*
$COOH(CH_2)_4COOH$	$NH_2(CH_2)_6NH_2$
$1 + 4 + 1 = 6$	6

Note that there are six carbon atoms in each molecule of adipic acid and six carbon atoms in each molecule of hexamethylene diamine. For this reason, this nylon was designated as nylon 6.6 (six carbons in each molecule of reacting chemical). In time it came to be known as nylon 66. These materials are synthesized from benzene. (See page 31.)

Nylon 6 is made from *caprolactam*, which has the following chemical structure:

Since there are six carbons in caprolactam, the fiber is known as nylon 6.

Because DuPont pursued development of nylon 66, the development of nylon 6 was left to researchers in Europe, where it became the most common type of nylon manufactured. In recent years the high costs associated with the disposal of a large

FIGURE 7.1

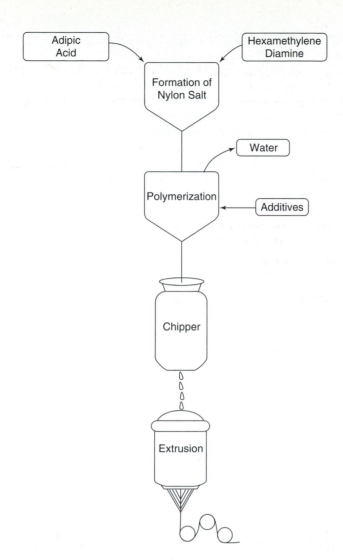

amount of ammonium sulfate (a by-product of the manufacture of caprolactam) have made nylon 6 somewhat more costly to produce than nylon 66. Variants of the nylon 6 structure, nylon 7 and nylon 9, are produced in Russia, but are not commercially competitive.

Polymerization of Nylon 66

The first step in the manufacturing process is preparation of a nylon "salt," which is a compound, but not a polymer, of adipic acid and hexamethylene diamine. The salt is prepared first to ensure the proper ratio of the acid and the amine in the subsequent polymerization step. This condensation polymerization takes place in an air-free atmosphere. Water, which is split off during polymerization, is allowed to escape from the reacting tank. If the manufacturer wishes to produce a delustered nylon, titanium dioxide can be added to the material during this step.

The molten polymer that forms is extruded from the tank as a ribbon, several inches in width. The material is quenched in cold water, which reduces the size of the crystals formed. The ribbon is broken into smaller nylon "chips."

Polymerization of Nylon 6

Caprolactam is polymerized by one of two methods. In one, caprolactam is melted, heated, and filtered under high pressure, during which process condensation polymerization takes place. In the second method, water in the amount of 10 percent of the weight of the caprolactam is added, after which the water and caprolactam are heated to a high temperature, steam escapes, and polymerization takes place.

In both these methods, a certain amount of monomer material remains. The polymerized material is given a water bath in an extractor to remove the monomer, which, if it remained, would weaken the final fiber. The polymer is dried and made into nylon chips.

Spinning

Both nylon 66 and nylon 6 are melt spun, although nylon 66 has a higher melting point (482° F) than nylon 6 (415° F). The chips fall onto an electrically heated grid that is too small to allow the chips to pass through until they have been melted. The melted polymer is delivered from an extruder, from a metal grid melter, or directly from a polymerizer and then passes through a filter that removes any impurities on to a metering pump. The pump delivers measured polymer to the *pack*, which consists of a small filter and spinneret.

As they exit from the spinneret, the molten filaments enter a chimney where they are air-cooled and simultaneously stretched to orient the molecules. Spin finish (a complex mixture of oil lubricants emulsified in water together with additional materials such as wetting agents, antistatic agents, and adhesives) is coated onto the fiber. The finish lubricates fibers for subsequent processing and disperses static electrical charges that would interfere with yarn formation. The finish is eventually washed from the fabric.

Drawing

After addition of the finish, the fiber is wound onto a bobbin. In this state, nylon is not especially strong or lustrous, so fibers are stretched to 400 to 600 percent of their original length. The stretching orients the molecules, making the fiber more crystalline, increasing luster, and improving tensile strength. Since nylon has a low glass transition temperature, little heat is required to orient the molecules during this step.

Molecular Structure

The polyamide chains in drawn nylon are fairly highly oriented in a crystalline structure. When the molecules are straightened during the drawing process, they have no bulky side groups to prevent them from packing closely together. So the crystalline areas form easily, and hydrogen bonds form between the amide links of adjacent polymers. The fibers are 50 to 80 percent crystalline, depending on the amount of drawing. In the amorphous areas the polymers are coiled, allowing for fiber stretch and recovery. Nylon 66 and 6 differ in the chain packing because of differences in the order of groups in the amide linkages.

Properties of Nylon

Physical Properties

Appearance. Normal nylon in microscopic appearance looks like a long, smooth cylinder. Its cross section is circular, and it is naturally lustrous, unless it is delustered. (See Figure 7.2.) The cross-sectional shape of nylon 66 or nylon 6 can be varied to produce fibers with a particularly desirable appearance or performance quality. For example, nylon 66 is sometimes made in trilobal or multilobal forms. The trilobal shape, similar to that of silk, reflects more light, thereby increasing luster.

Specific Gravity. A relatively low-density fiber, nylon has a specific gravity of 1.14, which is lower than most other fibers. (Rayon, for example, has a specific gravity of about 1.5, polyester one of 1.38.) Nylon can be made into very light, sheer fabrics of good strength.

Mechanical Properties

Strength. The strength of nylon is excellent. It is produced in a variety of tenacities. The regular tenacity of nylon 66 is 3 to 6 g/d; that of regular nylon 6, 4 to 7 g/d. High-tenacity nylon 66 that has been drawn more during spinning can range from 6.0 to 9.5 g/d. The exceptional strength of nylon has led to its use not only for tire cords but also for a variety of industrial items. Nylon's high strength has led to its predominance in the field of women's hosiery. Since the fibers are so strong, they can be made in the very fine deniers required for sheer hosiery and lingerie.

Modulus. Even though it is a strong fiber, nylon has a low modulus so that it stretches easily with little force. Although nylons are generally strong compared to many other fibers, their use in some industrial products such as geotextiles and sailcloth is limited by their low modulus. On the other hand this is a plus for sweaters, swimwear, and activewear where low resistance to stretch provides comfort and fit.

F 4B   NYLON   10μm

FIGURE 7.2

Electron scanning photograph of regular nylon (a) in cross section and (b) longitudinal view. Photographs courtesy of British Textile Technology Group (BTTG).

Elongation and Recovery. Nylon exhibits fairly high elongation before breaking, but when extended short of the breaking point, it will recover well. This helps garments made of nylon, or nylon blended with elastic fibers like spandex, to retain their shape and dimensions.

Resilience. Not only does nylon recover well from stretching, but it also has excellent recovery from compression. This feature makes it ideal for carpets and rugs. Nylon is also wrinkle resistant and was used in some of the first "drip dry" garments. Elastic recovery of nylon 6 is claimed to be slightly better than that of nylon 66.

Flexibility. Nylon has low resistance to bending and can be flexed easily. Nylon fabrics are usually fairly drapeable depending on their weight and construction.

Chemical Properties

Absorbency and Moisture Regain. Nylon is moderately hydrophilic, having better moisture regain than many manufactured fibers. Nevertheless, nylon fabrics dry quickly after laundering.

Heat and Electrical Conductivity. Nylon is a poor conductor of electricity, and builds up static electricity, especially when humidity is low. Nylon serves as a good insulator in electrical materials because of its nonconducting qualities. Special nylons have been manufactured to improve conductivity and decrease static electricity. Nylon's heat conductivity is also low.

Effect of Heat; Combustibility. The melting point of nylon 66 is about 500° F. It will soften and may start to stick at 445° F. Nylon 6 is even more heat sensitive. If a hot iron is used on nylons, the fibers may glaze, soften, or stick. The fiber burns in a flame but usually self-extinguishes when the flame is removed. However, nylon fibers do melt, and as with any fiber that melts, if the molten fiber drips onto the skin, it may cause serious burns.

Nylon's reactions to heat can be taken advantage of in manufacturing products. Its thermoplasticity allows it to be heat-set (see chapter 2). Since its softening, or glass transition, temperature is lower than polyester, it can be dyed more easily, because the dyes can penetrate into the regions of the fiber that have become less crystalline and more open. These effects are more significant in nylon 6, which melts at a lower temperature than nylon 66, and place some limitations on its uses. It is not used in industrial applications in which thermal resistance is essential, and it is more difficult to process into textured yarns for hosiery and to finish in yarns blended with other fibers, such as spandex.

Chemical Reactivity. Like most synthetics, nylon is chemically stable. Dry-cleaning solvents will not harm nylon. It is not seriously affected by dilute acids but is soluble in strong acids. Treatment with concentrated hydrochloric acid at high temperatures will break down nylon 66 into adipic acid and hexamethylene diamine, the substances from which it is made. This reaction could be used to reclaim these basic materials and permit this fiber to be recycled after use. Prolonged exposure to acidic fumes from pollution will damage the fiber.

Environmental Properties

Resistance to Microorganisms and Insects. Moths, mildew, and bacteria will not attack nylon.

Resistance to Environmental Conditions. Nylon is less affected by light than natural fibers. It may degrade after long exposure to sunlight, but age has no appreciable effect if fabrics are stored away from sunlight. Sheer nylon fabrics are unsuitable for use in curtains.

Other Properties

Dimensional Stability. Nylon has good dimensional stability at low to moderate temperatures, neither shrinking nor stretching out of shape. At high temperatures nylon fabrics may shrink. Washing and drying temperatures should be kept low. Nylon's moderate regain prevents a high degree of relaxation shrinkage when fabrics are wet.

Abrasion Resistance. This is one of nylon's advantages in many end uses, such as luggage, upholstery, and sportswear. It is a tough fiber, with extremely good abrasion resistance. In addition, nylon fabrics can be folded or flexed repeatedly without showing wear.

A disadvantage is that nylon fabrics have a tendency to pill under abrasive conditions. Because of the high strength of the fibers, the pills remain on the fabric, making wearing apparel unsightly.

Uses

The availability of a wide variety of types of nylon (from fine to coarse, from soft to crisp, from sheer to opaque) has resulted in the use of nylon in a large range of products for apparel, the home, and industry. (See Figure 7.3.) It is important to remember,

FIGURE 7.3

Photographs of a few of the diverse uses of nylon fibers: (a) tires made with nylon tire cord, (b) nylon carpet fibers, (c) luggage made of sturdy nylon fabric. Photographs courtesy of AlliedSignal Fibers.

a

b

c

however, that nylon is more expensive than other synthetic fibers and therefore is targeted for products where its unique combination of properties are critical.

Nylon has long been of major importance in the manufacture of women's hosiery because it is strong and stretches and recovers easily. Sheer fabrics made of nylon have been popular because of their inherent strength and abrasion resistance. Its light weight and durability make it ideal for jackets and running suits, and especially for soft-sided luggage. Because it is resilient and abrasion resistant, it dominates the carpet and rug market. Nylon is often used in blends to contribute abrasion resistance and elasticity.

Nylon's chemical reactivity, particularly its susceptibility to strong acids, has made it useful in the manufacture of microfibers. When formed into composite bigeneric fibers with polyester, the nylon can be easily dissolved after fabrics are constructed by acid treatment of the fabrics. (See chapter 5.)

Nylon Trademarks

Currently nylon fibers are produced in the United States by a number of different companies. Each company establishes one or more trademark names for its different fiber variants, however, these trademarks change often, with new trademarks being instituted and older trademarks being discontinued. The following are a few examples of trademarks that have been in use for extended periods of time. Antron® and Tactel® are nylon 66 fibers made by DuPont. Allied Signal Fibers manufactures Anso®, and Caprolan®, both of which are nylon 6. Nylon 6 fibers with the trademark Zeftron® are made by BASF Corporation, some of which are designed specifically for carpets. Ultron® is one of the nylon fibers from Solutia Inc. (formerly Monsanto Corporation), and Trilene® is a monofilament nylon from Berkley.

Care Procedures

Nylon is an easy-care fiber. Most nylon items are machine washable and can be tumble dried at normal drying temperatures.

However, nylon requires special care in certain circumstances. Like many synthetics, nylon has an affinity for oil-borne stains. These should be removed with a grease solvent before laundering.

Just as nylon is easily dyed, it also has a tendency to "scavenge" colors, picking up surface color easily from other fabrics. This is why many white nylons gradually become gray or yellowed; therefore, it is advisable to wash white nylons alone, never with other colored items, especially if high laundering and drying temperatures are used.

Nylon's resilience usually precludes ironing, but if pressing seems necessary, the heat sensitivity of nylon requires that it be pressed with a warm, not hot, iron. Also, nylon items should be removed from the dryer as soon as the cycle is ended. Nylons that remain in a hot dryer in a wrinkled condition may retain these wrinkles until the item is pressed.

ARAMID

Aramid fibers are composed of polyamides in which at least 85 percent of the amide linkages are attached to two aromatic rings. Recalling the structure of benzene from chapter 2 (page 31), aromatic rings can be seen to be linked through the carbons at different positions on the ring. If the linkages are two carbons apart, the polymer is a *meta*-aramid, whereas in *para*-aramids, the linkages are three carbons apart.

meta   para

Nomex® is a trademarked meta-aramid produced by DuPont. Kevlar® is made from a para-substituted polymer.

Manufacture

Since aramid polymers have such high melting points, they are made by a different process than other synthetics that are heated to effect polymerization. Instead of acids, the more reactive acid chlorides are used so the polymers can be formed in solution at much lower temperatures. The polymer for Nomex® is dissolved in dimethyl formamide, dry spun, and then drawn to produce an extremely crystalline fiber.

The *para*-aramid for Kevlar® fibers is dissolved in sulfuric acid and spun using the dry-jet wet spinning method. During the spinning process, the rigid polymers form *liquid crystals*. This transitional structure, in between the liquid and crystalline forms, is what gives Kevlar® its exceptional strength and modulus (Magat 1997). The polymers are almost completely aligned and the high orientation is locked in when the fiber is solidified, so that drawing is not necessary.

Properties of Aramids

Aramid fibers were engineered for high strength and thermal stability. The aromatic rings make the polymer chains stiffer and more energy is required to break or decompose them. The two types of aramids are nevertheless different, especially in their mechanical properties. (See Table 7.1.)

Para-aramid fibers have extremely high modulus and tenacity, because of the liquid crystalline stage that occurs during spinning. Tenacity of the newest generation Kevlar® fibers is almost 30 g/d, compared to less than 10 g/d for even the highest-strength nylon fibers. The strength of meta-aramid fibers is much less, around 5 g/d. The combination of high strength and modulus makes Kevlar® an extremely tough fiber that affects its end use in selected products (see later discussion).

Figure 7.4 shows a cross-sectional view of Nomex® aramid fibers, which are peanut-shaped. Para-aramid fibers have a rounder cross section. The color range of aramid fibers was originally fairly limited. Nomex® garments, however, are now available in a number of colors, including bright fluorescents for added safety protection. The Kevlar® color range is generally restricted to gold, sage green, royal blue, or black.

Moisture regain of aramids is 5 percent, a moderate degree of absorbency. The more crystalline para-aramids have lower regain.

Aramid fibers have no melting point (they do not melt), and they have extremely low combustibility. The fibers decompose at a temperature above 700° F, and meta-aramid fibers decompose at a slightly higher temperature. This property of Nomex® determines its use in fire-resistant garments.

TABLE 7.1
Selected Properties of Nylon and Aramid Fibers

Property	Nylon 66	Nylon 6	Meta-aramid	Para-aramid
Specific gravity	1.14	1.14	1.38	1.44
Tenacity (g/d)				
Dry	3.0–9.5	2.5–9.5	4.8-5.8	35.0
Wet	2.6–8.0	2.0–8.0	4.8-5.8	35.0
Moisture regain (%)	4.0–4.5	4.5	4.5	4.5
Resiliency	Excellent	Excellent	Excellent	Excelent
Burning characteristics	Burns and melts, usually self-extinguishing when flame is removed	Burns and melts, usually self-extinguishing when flame is removed	Low flammability	Low flammability
Melting point (°F)	500°	428°	Does not melt, decomposes above 700°	Does not melt, decomposes above 660°
Conductivity of				
Heat	Low	Low	Low	Low
Electricity	Low	Low	Low	Low
Resistance to damage from				
Fungi	Excellent	Excellent	Excellent	Excellent
Insects	Excellent	Excellent	Excellent	Excellent
Prolonged exposure to sunlight	Degrades	Degrades	Degrades	Degrades
Acids	Degraded by concentrated acids	Degraded by concentrated acids	Degraded by hot, concentrated acids	Degraded by hot, concentrated acids
Bases	Degraded by hot, concentrated bases	Degraded by hot, concentrated bases	Degraded by hot, concentrated bases	Degraded by hot, concentrated bases

Aramids degrade and lose strength on exposure to ultraviolet rays. Their resistance to radiation from gamma, beta, and X-rays is, however, excellent, and this resistance is utilized for some industrial applications. Their resistance to most chemicals and organic solvents is generally good, but like nylons, they are degraded by strong acids.

Uses

Aramid fibers are used in industrial products and protective clothing, where their high cost is justified by the necessity for specific performance properties. Nomex®, with its excellent thermal stability, is fabricated into clothing for firefighters, race car drivers, petrochemical and refinery workers, utility workers, U.S. Forest Service per-

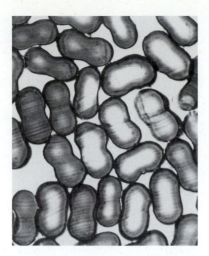

FIGURE 7.4

Photomicrograph of a cross section of Nomex® aramid fiber. Photomicrograph courtesy of the DuPont Company.

sonnel, military flight personnel, and National Aeronautics and Space Administration (NASA) astronauts. It is made into a wide variety of garments, including hoods, shirts, lab coats, jackets, parkas, aprons, gloves, pants, coveralls, jumpsuits, and socks. Its light weight and moderate absorbency make it more comfortable than other materials that might be used. Highly temperature-resistant papers are also made from meta-aramid fibers.

Kevlar®, with high strength and modulus, is used in safety gloves, boots, clothing, chain saw chaps, firefighter clothing, military helmets, and bullet-resistant vests (IFI 1991). Its toughness is an advantage in these products where impact resistance and ability to absorb energy are important. In industry it is an ideal reinforcing fiber material for plastics, given its combination of strength and light weight. It has replaced glass fiber in some aircraft because it is lighter in weight than glass. Sports equipment, such as boats, hockey sticks, tennis racquets, fishing rods, and golf clubs, make use of Kevlar® fibers as well. Whereas aluminum canoes weigh 70 to 80 pounds and those made of fiberglass weigh 50 to 70 pounds, a Kevlar® canoe of the same size weighs only 40 to 50 pounds. However, it costs almost twice as much as the heavier canoes (see Figure 7.5). Para-aramids are also used in automobile tires, ropes, cables, and sailcloth. Strength and light weight are again important here, while the fiber has the added advantage of good resistance to creep, so line, ties, and sails stay taut.

Care Procedures

With increased usage of aramid fibers in protective clothing, consumers and professional launderers and dry cleaners are encountering garments made from these fibers. The International Fabricare Institute makes the following recommendations about caring for garments made from aramid fibers (IFI 1991). Nomex® and Kevlar® garments can be machine washed and dried when laundered at home, but they must be washed separately so that they do not pick up lint from other garments. The lint will impair their flame resistance. Garments soiled with grease or oil can be dry-cleaned. Chlorine bleach should not be used, but oxygen bleaches are safe.

FIGURE 7.5

Canoeist easily portages lightweight Kevlar® aramid canoe between lakes or around impassible stretches of water. Photograph courtesy of We-no-nah Canoe, Inc.

SUMMARY

Nylon fibers are composed of polyamides, and may be referred to as polyamides in other countries. The fibers have a low modulus and therefore stretch easily, making them highly suitable for use in hosiery, swimwear, and athletic apparel. They are the preferred fiber for carpeting because of their compressional resilience and are also strong fibers for industrial uses. They are, however, more expensive than the more widely used polyester fibers to be discussed in chapter 8.

Aramids are specialty polyamide fibers that differ in molecular structure from nylon. Aramid fibers have high thermal stability, making them good candidates for use in protective clothing, and can also be produced to exhibit superior strength and modulus. They are commonly referred to by the trade names of fibers produced in the United States: Nomex®, a fiber with high heat resistance; and Kevlar®, which has high strength and modulus.

References

IFI. 1991. Nomex® and Kevlar®. *International Fabricare Institute Bulletin*, September.
Magat, E. 1997. In the pursuit of strength. *Chemical Heritage* 18 (2): 18.
Moore, R. A. F. 1989. Nylon 6 and nylon 66: How different are they? *Textile Chemist and Colorist* 21 (February): 19.

Review Questions

1. Compare the characteristics of nylon 66 and nylon 6. In what ways are they different? In what ways similar?
2. What properties of nylon make it especially useful in (a) women's hosiery and (b) carpets.
3. Identify some of the products in which meta-aramid fibers are used and some in which para-aramid fibers are used. What differences in the properties of these two fibers account for the different kinds of products in which they are used?

Recommended Readings

Bardsley, T. 1994. Nylon: The name. *Textile Horizons* (December): 34.
Gabara, V. 1994. High performance fibres 1: aramid fibres. In H. Brody, ed. *Synthetic fibre materials*. Essex, U.K.: Longman Scientific and Technical, p. 239.
Meikle, J. L., and S. M. Spivak. 1988. Nylon: What's in a name? *Textile Chemist and Colorist* 20 (June): 13.
Morris, W. J. 1988. Nylon at 50: An industrial success and a personal tragedy. *Chemtech* 18 (December): 725.
Nylon: silky to super strong. 1997. *Textile World* 147 (9): 62.
Scott, B. 1997. Stopping bullets. *Scientific American* (March): 132.
The Nylon Revolution. 1988. *America's Textiles International* 17 (April): 28.
Yang, H. H. 1989. *Aromatic high strength fibers*. New York: Wiley Interscience.
1995. *Kevlar aramid fiber*. New York: Marcel Dekker.

POLYESTER FIBERS

In his first experiments with the synthesis of polymers, W. H. Carothers concentrated his attention on compounds called polyesters. Encountering some difficulties in this research, he turned his attention to polyamides, from which he synthesized nylon.

After the discovery of nylon, a group of English researchers at Imperial Chemical Industries (ICI) concentrated on the polyester group. Their experimentation led to the development and subsequent manufacture of polyester fibers. DuPont bought the English patent, and the first DuPont plant for the production of Dacron® polyester in the United States opened in March 1953.

The FTC defines *polyester fibers* as "a manufactured fiber in which the fiber-forming substance is any long-chain synthetic polymer composed of at least 85 percent by weight of an ester of a substituted aromatic carboxylic acid, including but not restricted to substituted terephthalate units

$$p(-R-O-\underset{\substack{\|\\O}}{C}-C_6H_4-\underset{\substack{\|\\O}}{C}-O-)$$

or parasubstituted hydroxybenzoate units

$$p(-R-O-C_6H_4-\underset{\substack{\|\\O}}{C}-O-)"$$

(as amended September 12, 1973).[1] British publications may refer to polyester as Terylene, an ICI trademark.

---

1. The polyester made from the hydroxybenzoate compound, trademarked as Kodel® in the United States, is no longer produced.

MANUFACTURE

The raw material from which most polyesters are made is petroleum, from which the constituent acids and alcohols are derived. The most commonly used acid is terephthalic acid or its dimethyl ester. The processes that are used for manufacturing different types of polyesters vary. Many of the details of these processes are not known because the companies that hold the patents on the manufacturing processes have not released full information on precisely how these processes are carried out. A generalized description of the process for synthesizing polyesters follows.

Polymerization

The major polyester in manufacture and use is polyethylene terephthalate, abbreviated PET. It is formed by the reaction of terephthalic acid and ethylene glycol. Condensation polymerization takes place during the reaction of terephthalic acid and alcohol, in a vacuum, at high temperatures. Many producers use dimethyl terephthalate, the ester of terephthalic acid, because it polymerizes more easily. Polymerized material is extruded in the form of a ribbon onto a casting wheel or cooling trough. The ribbon hardens, and small polyester chips are cut from the ribbon.

Spinning and Drawing

The chips are dried to remove any residual moisture and are then put into hopper reservoirs ready for melting. The melted polymer (polyester is melt spun, like nylon) is extruded through the spinnerets, solidifies on hitting the air, and is wound loosely onto cylinders. How the solidified filaments are processed next depends on the projected end use of the fiber.

If filaments are to be made into staple fiber, several sets of filaments, each containing 250 to 3,000 filaments, are brought together and coiled in a large can in preparation for drawing. The yarns are then heated and drawn to several times their original length to orient the molecular structure, and then allowed to relax to release stresses and strains and reduce shrinkage of drawn fibers. Drawn tow is crimped, dried, and heat-set for stability. At this point, tow may be cut into required staple lengths, usually 38 to 152 millimeters (1.5 to 6 inches) in length, and baled, ready for sale.

Fiber intended for continuous filament yarn is either drawn directly and packaged for sale or wound on bobbins preparatory for draw twisting or draw texturing. Yarn for weaving or knitting or yarn intended for texturing is often processed on a draw twister that heats, draws the fibers, and imparts a small amount of base twist. Additional heating and drawing is given to high-strength industrial yarns in a second stage of processing.

Although draw-twisted yarns can also be textured, recent developments in spinning polyester have led to the use of an alternative process. High-speed spinning processes yield partially oriented yarn (POY), which is preferred for draw texturing because it eliminates the expensive draw-twisting operation and allows the POY to be both drawn and textured in the same operation, one in which the drawing, texturing, and heat-setting operations are carried out in an integrated manner. Chapter 13 gives a fuller discussion of texturing. The diagram in Figure 8.1 summarizes the manufacture of polyester.

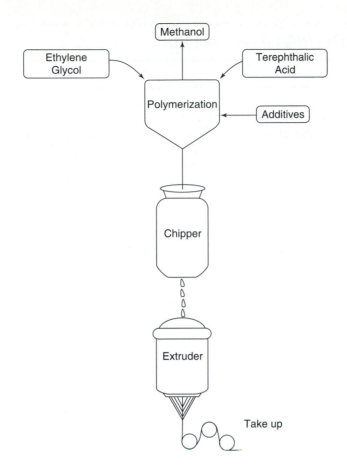

FIGURE 8.1

Flowchart for polyester production.

MOLECULAR STRUCTURE

In polyester fibers the long polymers of PET are arranged in amorphous and crystalline regions, the extent of which is dependent on the amount of drawing during manufacture. Polyester does not crystallize as easily as nylon because of its aromatic rings, which are bulky and inhibit alignment of the molecules. In addition, there are no polar groups in the polyester polymers to form hydrogen bonds between the polymers. The aromatic rings do, however, provide stiffness to the polymer chains, which contributes to modulus, strength, and thermal stability.

PROPERTIES OF POLYESTER

Table 8.1 summarizes selected characteristics of polyester.

Physical Properties

Appearance. Polyester fibers are manufactured in a variety of cross sections, including round, trilobal, pentalobal, and hollow shapes. Under the microscope round fibers appear as long, smooth rods, with spots of pigment if the fiber has been delustered. This pigmented appearance decreases the luster or brightness of polyesters. Longitudinally, multilobal fibers appear striated. (See Figure 8.2.)

TABLE 8.1
Selected Properties of Polyester Fibers

Property	Polyester
Specific gravity	1.38
Tenacity (g/d)	
Dry	4.0–7.0 (regular tenacity); 6.3–9.5 (high tenacity)
Wet	4.0–7.0 (regular tenacity); 6.3–9.5 (high tenacity)
Moisture regain (%)	0.4
Resiliency	Excellent
Burning characteristics	In flame, burns slowly with melting
Melting point (° F)	480–550°
Conductivity of	
Heat	Low
Electricity	Low
Resistance to damage from	
Fungi	Excellent
Insects	Excellent
Prolonged exposure to sunlight	Moderate to good
Acids	Good
Bases	Harmed by strong bases

FIGURE 8.2

(a) and (b). Electron scanning photograph of polyester (a) in cross section and (b) longitudinal view. Photographs courtesy of British Textile Technology Group (BTTG).

a   b

Specific Gravity. Specific gravity of PET is moderate at 1.38. Polyesters have a specific gravity greater than nylon (1.14) and lower than rayon (1.50). Fabrics made from polyesters are medium in weight.

Mechanical Properties

Strength. The strength, or tenacity, of polyester varies with the type of fiber; however, as a general category, polyester would be considered a relatively strong fiber. Its strength is not affected by moisture. Regular filaments have a breaking tenacity of 4 to 7 g/d; high-tenacity filaments are rated at 6.3 to 9.5 g/d.

Modulus. A high modulus distinguishes polyester from other commonly used synthetics. The aromatic rings, that provide stiffness in aramid fibers, also increase the modulus of polyester.

Elongation and Recovery. Polyester fibers will stretch a moderate amount before breaking, with their elongation being primarily dependent on the amount they are drawn during processing. Staple fibers usually undergo less drawing and therefore will have higher elongation. Polyester recovers well from stretching but is inferior to nylon in its elasticity. It has good recovery from low stretch, but recovery decreases when the fiber is highly extended.

Resilience. Resilience of polyester fibers is excellent. For this reason, they are often blended with less wrinkle-resistant fibers to make easy-care fabrics. Polyester's recovery from compression, however, is not as good as that of nylon.

Chemical Properties

Absorbency and Moisture Regain. The moisture regain of polyester is low, only 0.2 to 0.8 percent. Although polyesters are nonabsorbent, they do have wicking ability. This quality increases polyester's comfort in warm weather, as perspiration is carried to the surface of the fiber and evaporated. Multilobal fiber cross sections improve the wicking qualities of polyesters, as liquid moisture is carried down the channels between the lobes. Special finishes can be applied to polyester to make it more hydrophilic.

Effect of Heat; Combustibility. The melting point of polyester is close to that of nylon, ranging from 480° to 550° F. Polyesters usually need no pressing because of their excellent wrinkle recovery. If they must be pressed, it should be with a warm, not hot, iron. Polyesters can be heat-set into pleats with especially good results. Not only will heat setting stabilize size and shape, but wrinkle resistance of polyesters is enhanced by heat setting.

Polyester shrinks from flame and will melt, leaving a hard black residue. The fabric will burn with a strong, pungent odor. Some polyesters are self-extinguishing. Melted polyester fiber can produce severe burns.

Chemical Reactivity. Polyesters are not harmed by solvents used in professional dry cleaning nor are they susceptible to damage from bleaching. Although polyesters are not harmed by acids, they may be adversely affected by strong bases. Alkalinity encountered in detergents is not harmful.

Environmental Properties

Resistance to Microorganisms and Insects. Mildew and moth larvae will not attack polyesters. Bacteria, however, will grow in soiled items, particularly those that have absorbed perspiration.

Resistance to Environmental Conditions. Although the fibers will degrade after long exposure to sunlight, they have better sun resistance than do most fibers. This resistance is enhanced when the fibers are placed behind glass that screens out some of the harmful ultraviolet rays. Polyesters are, therefore, highly suitable for use in curtains and draperies. Age has no appreciable effect on polyesters.

Other Properties

Dimensional Stability. Polyesters that have been given heat-setting treatments have excellent dimensional stability, so long as the heat-setting temperature is not exceeded. If polyester fabrics have not been heat-set, they may shrink at high temperatures. Because of its low moisture regain, polyester does not shrink when wet and can stabilize fabrics when it is blended with other fibers.

Abrasion Resistance. Polyester fibers have good abrasion resistance and are often selected for products where durability is a consideration.

MODIFICATIONS OF POLYESTER

Among manufactured fibers polyester dominates the market. In 1997 52 percent of manufactured fibers produced in the world were polyester. The quantity of polyester in use is a reflection of its versatility. It is produced as staple, filament, tow, and fiberfill, which may be made in either filament or crimped staple form. Filament yarns are textured to create stretch yarns or filament yarns with the aesthetic qualities of yarn spun from staple fibers. Such yarns decrease pilling, which can be a problem in staple polyester yarns.

Cross-sectional shape can be modified to create fabrics for special purposes. Japanese manufacturers have varied cross-sectional shape to produce fabrics with especially attractive hand and drape. These fabrics, called *Shingosen fabrics,* are sold in Japan and abroad. Teijin, a Japanese company, manufactures and sells Wellkey®, a hollow polyester with minute holes in the cross section that are intended to absorb perspiration. (see Figure 8.3.) Hollow polyester fibers are made into fiberfill with good insulating qualities.

Polyester microfibers are produced by a number of manufacturers and used in high-density fabrics for sportswear and rainwear and other apparel such as blouses, shirts, and dresses. In other items, the fine fibers have lower bending resistance and increase the aesthetics and drapeability of the fabrics.

Polyester Trademarks

The following are among the better-known trademarks for polyester fibers produced by manufacturers in the United States. AlliedSignal Fibers manufactures Stay Gard®; American Micrell uses the trademark Micrell® for its microfiber polyester; DuPont's better-known trademarks include Dacron® and Hollofil®, its premium microfiber

FIGURE 8.3

Polyester fiber with unique cross section intended for special purposes. Diagram of Wellkey® which has a hollow center and modified surface that is designed to absorb perspiration. Illustration courtesy of Teijin American, Inc.

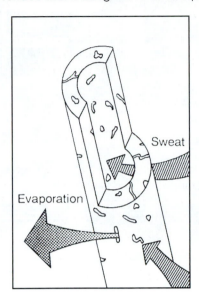

Micromattique®, and CoolMax® fabric made with fibers that wick moisture; Trevira uses the Trevira® trademark; Nan Ya Plastics makes Tairilin®, a microfiber; and Wellman, Inc. makes Fortrel® polyester and also Fortrel Ecospun® which is made from recycled plastic bottles. (See Figure 8.4)

USES

Polyester is used in a wide range of wearing apparel, home furnishings, and industrial products, either alone or in blends. The exceptional resilience of polyester makes it especially suitable for use in easy-care fabrics. Since polyester is a manufactured fiber, its physical and chemical properties can be tailored for specific end uses, such as the microfiber rainwear or industrial tire cords.

Blends of polyester with other fibers are made to take advantage of durability and easy maintenance. Durable press fabrics are frequently made from blends of cotton and polyester. Wool and polyester blends have a wool-like feel and appearance and some of the easy-care aspects of polyester. Furthermore, creases and pleats can be heat-set through the thermoplastic properties of polyester. Other blends with rayon and with acetate as well as blends with other synthetics such as acrylics and with natural fibers such as silk, flax, and ramie are produced.

A large volume of polyester and polyester blend fabrics is used in curtains, draperies, sheets, and pillowcases for the home furnishings market. Increasingly polyester is also seen in carpets. Although cheaper, its lower electricial conductivity and resilience make it less desirable than nylon. Sleeping bags, insulated outdoor clothing, and pillow and comforter fillings of polyester are being promoted by manufacturers

FIGURE 8.4

Ecospun garment designed by Diane Von Furstenberg from Wellman's 1998 Master Apprentice Programme and Collection. Photograph by Eric Weiss.

as easy-care, nonallergenic substitutes for goosedown. Hollow polyester fibers are said to offer advantages in this use over traditional polyester fiber forms.

Industrial uses of polyesters include fire hoses, power belting, ropes, base fabrics for coating, and nets. Tire cord for automotive uses and sails for sports are also made from polyester fibers, where their high modulus is an advantage. Nonwoven polyester fiber webs may be used in construction projects for reinforcement.

CARE PROCEDURES

Polyester is blended with so many other fibers that consumers should consult labels for specific instructions on care. Those procedures that are appropriate for 100 percent polyester fabrics may not be suitable for the fibers with which polyester is blended.

Polyester fabrics are generally machine washable. Water temperatures should be warm, not excessively hot. Ordinary laundry detergents can be used. Household bleaches will not harm white fabrics. Oily stains should be removed before laundering by treatment with a grease solvent.

Polyesters should be dried at moderate temperatures, and items should be removed from the dryer as soon as the cycle is complete to avoid creases that must be removed by ironing. As a general rule, polyesters should not require pressing after drying, although polyester fabrics may be ironed on the wrong side with a moderately

CONSUMER BOX 8.1 — Polyester's Image Today

"Polyester gets no respect!" This was the lead sentence in an article discussing manufacturers' efforts to enhance the image of polyester. After more than two decades of constant growth in demand for and use of polyester by consumers, apparel manufacturers in the 1970s flooded the market with polyester double knits. The public came to associate polyester with these garments, many of which had questionable design quality, aesthetics, and comfort. With the advent of new products and fiber modifications, however, the advantages of polyester are successfully being marketed today to improve its image.

The fiber has long been a natural for blending with cotton because it has a similar modulus, which aids in processing the blended yarns. Its resilience and dimensional stability compensate for cotton's disadvantages in these areas. Cotton/polyester blends still remain one of the most popular fabrics on the market. They are seen, not only in many types of fashion apparel, but also in sheets, comforters, curtains, and other home furnishings. While cotton/polyester blends tend to pill, low-pilling polyester staple fibers are produced for use in blended spun yarns.

Most of the microfibers produced today are polyester and are used in a number of products. Rainwear of polyester microfibers is soft and comfortable and provides water resistance both because of the low absorbency of the fibers and also because the tight packing of the fine microfibers inhibits penetration of water. Microfiber suits, jackets, and pants for both men and women are advertised as ideal for traveling. They are durable, look smart, and will retain their wrinkle-free appearance. Some jackets are being made with a mesh lining to allow the fabric to wick away perspiration in the tiny channels between the fibers. Microfiber fleeces are also being made to provide warmth for outdoor clothing.

The wicking properties of polyester have also promoted its use in high-tech clothing for sportswear. In addition, the absorbency of the fiber can be increased by treatment with sodium hydroxide, which slightly degrades the fiber surface, making it more wettable. Polyesters have also been exposed to plasma, a gas with reactive ions, to create absorbent sites on the fiber surface. Finally, absorbent compounds can be added to the polymer during polymerization.

Other shape and finish modifications of polyester have enabled it to mimic many other fibers. Fabrics made of trilobal polyester fibers have the look, drape, and feel of silk, and the added advantage of being machine washable. Polyester and polyester blends can be spun into yarns with small irregularities to make "linen look" fabrics. The fibers can be given crimp for blending with wool for tailored suits and jackets.

Polyester has almost replaced nylon as the fiber of choice for tire cords. In its high tenacity version, and with its high modulus, it provides the strength, as well as the stretch and impact resistance, that contribute to tire durability. Its strong modulus makes it a good partner with Kevlar® for sailcloth, and, with its high strength, it is a primary candidate for use in architectural structures such as lightweight roofs, stadium covers, and the like.

For many years polyester was a symbol of the throw away society, but now several polyester manufacturers have introduced fibers made from recycled plastic soda bottles. These fibers are used in fabrics for outdoor clothing and other apparel, as well as in blankets. They are advertised as environmentally friendly and are popular with consumers.

Polyester has not only increased its role as the workhorse of the textile industry, but as a result of innovative processes, it has regained its stature as an apparel and interior furnishings fiber. The wide range of tenacities, sizes, and shapes in which it can be produced, as well as its competitive price, ensure its continued versatility and consumer acceptance.

warm iron. Some blends of polyesters and cottons can be difficult to iron because the suitable ironing temperature for polyester fibers may not be high enough to press wrinkles from cotton, whereas the cotton temperature is too high for the polyester.

Most fabrics made from polyesters can be dry-cleaned safely. Some polyester double knits printed with pigment colors cannot be dry-cleaned, because the cleaning solvent will dissolve the adhesive holding the pigment on the surface. Care labels should be checked to determine whether dry cleaning should be avoided.

SUMMARY

Polyester is the most widely used manufactured fiber today. It is made by melt spinning and can be produced in a range of sizes, strengths, and shapes. Its characteristics are good strength, dimensional stability, and wrinkle resistance, but low moisture regain. Polyester and polyester blend fabrics are used in many different consumer and industrial products and polyester dominates the microfibers market. Consumer Brief 8.1 discusses some of the advantages and disadvantages of polyester.

Review Questions

1. What is POY, and why is it preferred over other forms of the fiber for draw texturing?
2. If you had three fabrics that were the same in all other respects but one was made of polyester, one of nylon, and one of rayon, which would feel heaviest? Why?
3. Describe step-by-step care procedures that could be used for a 100 percent polyester garment that can be laundered at home. For each step that you describe, identify one or more properties of polyester that make this type of care appropriate.
4. What are some of the modifications of polyester fibers that can be made to produce fabrics with specific characteristics? To what uses are these modified fibers put?
5. Compare the mechanical properties of polyester and nylon fibers. How are the properties related to their molecular structures?

Recommended Readings

Brunnschweiler, D., and J. W. S. Hearle. 1993. *Polyester: 50 years of achievement.* Manchester, U.K.: The Textile Institute.

Callahan, P. 1994. The fabric of our lives? Polyester makes a comeback. *Forbes* 153 (9 May): 64.

Harris, W. B. 1997. Will polyester production expand outside Asia? *Textile World* 147 (3): 128.

Janeck, C., and H. Lunde. 1983-84. Hydrophilic finishes: Effect on selected properties of polyester fabric. *Clothing and Textiles Research Journal* 2 (Fall/Winter): 31.

Mason, R. W. 1999. Decades later, polyester forges new image. *Textile World* 149 (1): 56

Meyer, D. G., and H. Koopman. 1993. Marketing polyester in the 1990's. Part 7: Business and economics. In D. Brunnschweiler and J. W. S. Hearle, eds. *Polyester: 50 years of achievement*, 323. Manchester, U.K.: The Textile Institute.

Miyoshi, T. 1993. Functional polyester developments. *Textile Asia* 24 (July): 71.

Thomas, M. 1993. At 50 years polyester gains new fashion vitality. *Textile World* 143 (December): 62, 65.

Zeronian, S. H., and M. J. Collins. 1989. Surface modification of polyester by alkaline treatments. *Textile Progress* 20 (2).

ACRYLIC AND MODACRYLIC FIBERS

Acrylic fibers are defined by the FTC as "manufactured fibers in which the fiber-forming substance is any long-chain synthetic polymer composed of at least 85 percent by weight of acrylonitrile units

$$(-CH_2-CH-)$$
$$|$$
$$CN."$$

ACRYLICS

Although acrylonitrile, the polymer of which acrylic fibers are composed, had been synthesized earlier, it could not be melt spun because it tends to decompose if melted. Suitable solvents for the polymer were not found until the 1940s. A number of different fiber producers had been working independently to develop and patent processes for spinning fibers from the acrylonitrile polymer, each proceeding along somewhat different lines. As a result, seven separate production processes were patented: six using wet spinning and one using dry spinning.

The second synthetic fiber to be produced commercially by DuPont, Orlon® acrylic fiber, entered production in 1950. DuPont announced in 1990 that it would phase out its acrylic business by the end of that year. Monsanto entered the acrylic field in 1952 with Acrilan® acrylic, and American Cyanamid introduced Creslan® acrylic in 1958. Global production of acrylic fibers was 2.7 million metric tons in 1997; this represents 10 percent of all fibers produced, down from 13% in 1977.[1]

Manufacture

Acrylic fibers are produced from acrylonitrile usually in combination with one or more comonomers. The reaction that takes place during polymerization is an addition reaction. After the acrylic polymer is made, it is dissolved in dimethyl formamide (DMF). Both dry and wet spinning methods have been used for manufacturing acrylics, but today most are wet spun into baths of lower DMF concentration. (See Figure 9.1.) Acrylic fibers are used in staple form, and the fiber is crimped before cutting.

---

1. American Fiber Manufacturers Association, "Fiber Facts," www.fibersource.com.

FIGURE 9.1

Flowchart for acrylic production.

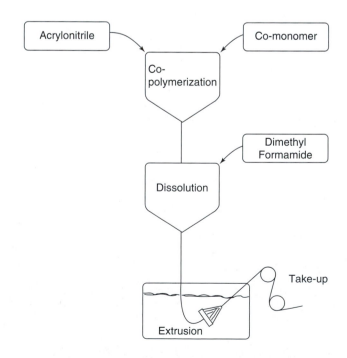

A number of variations in the processes used to manufacture acrylic fibers are possible. Many of these processes are proprietary, and their details are not available. The general characteristics common to most acrylic fibers are as follows.

Molecular Structure

Acrylonitrile polymers in acrylic fibers are highly crystalline because the chains pack together tightly. Most fibers contain up to 15 percent of another monomer to interrupt the regular packing of the polymers and reduce the brittleness of the fiber. Different producers use different comononers, resulting in some variation of fiber properties and processing. Fibers that are 100 percent acrylonitrile are stronger and more thermally stable than copolymer acrylic fibers, but they are also more brittle. They have, however, found an important use as a starting material for producing carbon fibers. (See chapter 12.)

Properties of Acrylics

Physical Properties

Shape. The microscopic cross section of acrylic fibers may be round, bean-shaped, dog-bone shaped, or multilobal, depending on the manufacturing process. Likewise, the longitudinal appearance of acrylics is either smooth or twisted and may have wide striations (lengthwise markings). (See Figure 9.2.) Acrylics are usually crimped to make them more wool-like.

Luster. Acrylics are usually delustered with titanium dioxide and in addition the crimp further decreases the apparent luster.

Specific Gravity. Specific gravity ranges from 1.14 to 1.19, making acrylics lightweight.

Mechanical Properties

Strength. Standard breaking tenacities of acrylic fibers are reported as ranging from 2.0 to 3.6 g/d. The fibers are weak and are therefore not appropriate for end uses requiring high strength.

a   b

FIGURE 9.2

Photographs of acrylic fibers taken through an electron scanning microscope: (a) cross section; (b) longitudinal view. Photographs courtesy of the British Textile Technology Group (BTTG).

Modulus. The range of moduli for acrylic fibers is moderate to low, making them compatible with a number of other fibers and they are often seen in blends.

Elongation and Recovery. Acrylics stretch fairly easily and will extend up to 25 percent before breaking. The elastic recovery of acrylic fibers varies from one trademarked fiber to another. In general, however, it is lower than that for most other synthetic fibers.

Resilience. Resilience ranges from good to excellent. Crimped fibers will have good compressional and bending recovery.

Chemical Properties

Absorbency and Moisture Regain. The moisture absorption of acrylics is low, with a moisture regain of 1.0 to 2.5 percent. This is an important aspect in which acrylics differ significantly from wool.

Electrical Conductivity. The low electrical conductivity of acrylics is related to their low moisture absorption. Antistatic finishes may be added to fibers to eliminate static electricity buildup.

Effect of Heat; Combustibility. Although the literature reports melting points ranging from 450° to 497° F, depending on the specific type of fiber, manufacturers report that acrylics do not exhibit typical melting points but rather tend to decompose over a wide temperature range and eventually char to a brittle residue. Untreated acrylic fibers ignite and burn, leaving a hard, black bead residue at the edge of the fabric. Flame-retardant finishes can be given to acrylics. Fibers shrink in steam but can be safely ironed at 300° F. Exposure to high, dry heat may cause yellowing or further darkening of the fibers. Acrylic fibers and fabrics can be heat-set under appropriate conditions.

Chemical Reactivity. Acrylics are very resistant to acids, except to nitric acid in which they dissolve. Resistance to bases is moderate, and degradation by sodium hydroxide at high concentrations and/or temperatures is cited by Moncrieff (1975) for Acrilan® and Creslan®. Solvents used in commercial dry cleaning do not affect the fiber adversely. Most acrylics are not harmed by household bleaches.

Environmental Properties

Resistance to Microorganisms. Mildew, microorganisms, and moths will not harm acrylic fibers.

Resistance to Environmental Conditions. Resistance to sunlight ranges from very good to excellent. This characteristic has promoted the use of acrylics in awnings and outdoor furniture. Age has no detrimental effect on fabric strength.

Other Properties

Dimensional Stability. Heat setting will produce good dimensional stability in fabrics made of acrylics. Because of the fiber's low moisture absorbency, acrylic fabrics do not shrink when wet. However, there are many varieties of acrylics with somewhat different performance in regard to their dimensional stability. For this reason, instructions on care labels should be followed carefully in laundering acrylics. For example, some fabrics are manufactured from specially crimped fibers that require machine drying after laundering to restore the crimp. If hung wet on a line, some of these fabrics may stretch out of shape.

Abrasion Resistance. The abrasion resistance of acrylics is somewhat lower than that of other synthetics.

Bicomponent Acrylics

Acrylic fibers may be made in bicomponent varieties. (See chapter 5 for full discussion of bicomponent fibers.) Bicomponent acrylic fibers are created by extruding two different types of acrylic material together as one fiber from the spinneret. Each has somewhat different shrinkage properties, and when the fiber is subjected to heat and moisture during processing, one polymer shrinks more than the other and produces a permanent spiral crimp. The crimp provides increased bulk and resilience. Bicomponent acrylics are most often used in knitted goods such as sweaters and socks. Care instructions provided with bicomponent acrylic fibers often indicate that they must be laundered and tumble dried. During laundering the fibers swell, relieving tensions placed on the fibers during use, and the tumble drying is necessary to return fibers to their crimped and bulked shapes. Because line drying will not produce the same results, consumers should be sure to follow care instructions.

Uses

Acrylic fibers are fabricated into woven and knitted fabric constructions in a variety of textures and weights appropriate for different end uses. They are often blended with other fibers, particularly wool. Their wool-like hand and bulk combined with easy-care characteristics make them popular for use in sweaters, fleece fabrics, hand-knitting yarns, and blankets. Their bulk also makes them appropriate for socks, where they can provide both warmth and cushioning for the feet. (See Figure 9.3.)

Resistance to degradation by sunlight leads to use of acrylics in drapery and upholstery fabrics, and increasingly in outdoor products such as awnings and furniture. Not only is their light resistance an advantage, but also their low moisture absorbence helps to protect the fabrics under a variety of weather conditions. (See Figure 9.4.)

Acrylic Trademarks

Two fiber companies in the United States currently produce acrylic fibers. Solutia, Inc. (formerly Monsanto) manufactures a number of types of acrylics. Widely known brand names are Acrilan® and Duraspun®; Sayelle® is produced for knitting yarns. Sterling Fibers, Inc. makes Creslan® and Cresloft®. They also produce Biofresh®, an antibacterial acrylic fiber with the antimicrobial compound incorporated into the fiber during manufacture for enhanced durability.

Care Procedures

Different acrylic fibers may vary in their care requirements. For this reason, it is especially important to follow care labels of these fabrics. In general, acrylic fabrics can be laundered and dry-cleaned. They do not shrink in laundering but may be sensitive to heat, so that when machine drying is recommended for acrylic products, low heat settings should be used, and fabrics should be removed from the dryer immediately after tumbling. Pressing temperatures should not exceed 250° to 300° F.

FIGURE 9.3

Three of the common types of apparel in which acrylic fibers are used (a) hosiery; (b) knitted sportswear; (c) high-pile fabrics for warmth. Photograph courtesy of the Acrylic Council.

a

c

b

MODACRYLIC

Modacrylic fibers were first manufactured commercially by Union Carbide Company in 1949 before the production of acrylics. Because the composition of modacrylics is similar to that of acrylics, both fibers were at first included in the acrylic classification, but in 1960 the FTC ruled that a separate category should be established for them.

Modacrylics are defined by the FTC as "a manufactured fiber in which the fiber-forming substance is any synthetic polymer composed of less than 85 percent but at least 35 percent by weight of acrylonitrile units

$$(-CH-CH_2-)$$
$$|$$
$$CN$$

except fibers under category (2) of paragraph (j) of Rule 7 of the Textile Fiber Products Identification Act."[2]

Manufacture

Modacrylic fibers are made from copolymers of acrylonitrile with other compounds, such as vinyl chloride, vinylidene chloride, or vinyl bromide. The polymer formed in the polymerization reactor is dissolved in an appropriate solvent, dry or wet spun, and then drawn and cut into staple lengths. Varying degrees of crimp may be added to the fiber depending on its projected end uses.

Properties of Modacrylics

Physical Properties

The cross section of acrylic fibers is slightly irregular in shape. The longitudinal appearance usually shows some striations, or it may have a grainy effect. (See Figure 9.5.) The specific gravity of modacrylics is 1.3, which is comparable to wool, so that the fibers feel light but also have good insulating qualities.

Mechanical Properties

Modacrylics are similar to acrylic fibers in their mechanical properties. Modulus and elongation are slightly higher than acrylics. Modacrylics have good recovery from stretching and bending.

Chemical Properties

The absorbency of the fibers is low, and the moisture regain is 2.5 percent. As a result, the stain resistance to waterborne soil is good.

A significant of advantage of modacrylic, that determines many product end uses of the fiber, is its flame resistance. The fibers were generally copolymers of

---

2. This exception refers to certain synthetic rubber products that have a substantial quantity of acrylonitrile in their composition.

FIGURE 9.4

Wicker outdoor furniture upholstered in fabric made from acrylic fiber. Photograph courtesy of Outdoor Wicker from Frontgate.

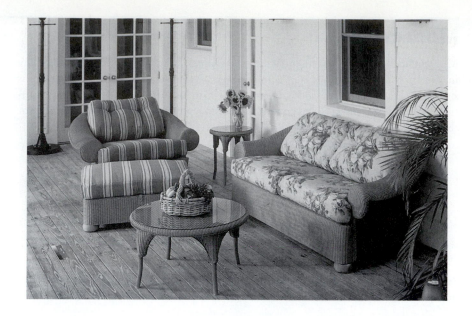

polyacrylonitrile with halogenated monomers to retard burning. They will burn when placed in a direct flame but will self-extinguish as soon as the flame is removed.

The melting point of modacrylics is low (about 370° to 410° F). Only the olefins and saran are more sensitive to heat. If modacrylic fabrics are ironed, very low temperature settings must be used. If a dryer is used, temperatures should be set for low or no heat.

Chemical resistance of modacrylics is good. Dry-cleaning solvents will not affect them adversely. Some modacrylics may be discolored by strong bases, but their resistance to acids is good to excellent.

Environmental Properties

The resistance to deterioration from light is fairly good. Neither moths nor mildew attack modacrylics. Age has no apparent effect.

Other Properties

Modacrylics have good dimensional stability. However, their sensitivity to heat may result in some shrinkage if they are dried in a dryer at high temperatures. The resistance to abrasion of modacrylic fibers is moderate.

Uses

The major areas of use for modacrylic fibers include pile and fleece fabrics for apparel and blankets. Flame-resistant draperies and curtains, paint roller covers, filters, wigs, and hairpieces are also made from modacrylics. Because these fibers have a low softening temperature and a high thermal shrinkage potential, a variety of texturizing treatments can be applied to simulate the textures and characteristics of fur fibers. Many fake fur fabrics are made from modacrylic fibers. The combination of good resilience with abrasion resistance makes modacrylic fibers especially suitable for use in high-pile fabrics, where they can simulate luxurious furs. They are also used in some industrial fabrics that take advantage of their flame resistance and good chemical resistance.

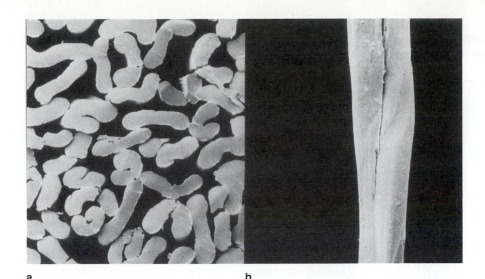

a   b

FIGURE 9.5

Photographs of modacrylic fibers taken through an electron scanning microscope: (a) cross section; (b) longitudinal view. Photographs courtesy of the British Textile Technology Group (BTTG).

Modacrylic Trademarks

Modacrylics were formerly manufactured in the United States by Union Carbide (Dynel®), Eastman Kodak (Verel®), and Monsanto (SEF®), but all have now ceased production. The Kaneka Corporation of Japan makes a modacrylic fiber called Kanecaron, which represents about 65 percent of world production (Pile Fabrics, 1998).

Care Procedures

Deep-pile garments must be cleaned professionally to avoid crushing or altering the appearance of the pile. Other modacrylic fabrics are machine washable, but special care should be taken to avoid exposing them to very high temperatures because of their heat sensitivity. Low dryer temperatures must be used, and ironing should be done only with a warm, not hot, iron. Some modacrylic fibers are discolored by the use of chlorine bleaches. Table 9.1 compares selected properties of acrylic and modacrylic fibers.

SUMMARY

Acrylic and modacrylic fibers both are based on polyacrylonitrile polymers. Acrylics are more than 85 percent polyacrylonitrile, whereas modacrylic fibers are between 35 and 85 percent. Acrylic is produced as crimped staple fibers and has many properties similar to wool. It provides bulk and warmth making it a good fiber for sweaters, suits, coats, and socks. It does not however have the high moisture absorbence of wool and so will not shrink when washed. Acrylics have good sunlight resistance and can be used effectively in outdoor furniture.

TABLE 9.1
Selected Properties of Acrylic and Modacrylic Fibers

Property	Acrylic	Modacrylic
Specific gravity	1.14–1.19	1.3
Tenacity (g/d)		
Dry	3.0–9.5	2.3
Wet	2.6–8.0	2.3
Moisture regain (%)	4.0–4.5	1.0
Resiliency	Good	Good
Burning characteristics	In flame, burns with melting, continues after flame removed	In flame, burns very slowly with melting; self-extinguishing after flame removed
Melting point (° F)	Softens at 450° to 497°; indeterminate melting point.	Approximately 400°
Conductivity of		
Heat	Low	Low
Electricity	Low	Low
Resistance to damage from		
Fungi	Excellent	Excellent
Insects	Excellent	Excellent
Prolonged exposure to sunlight	Excellent	Excellent
Acids	Good, except nitric	Good
Bases	Good to weak bases	Moderate

Modacrylic is produced by a limited number of firms and has found use predominantly in simulated fur items. Its properties are similar to those of acrylic, with the added advantage of flame resistance.

References

Moncrieff, R. W. 1975. *Man-made fibres.* New York: Wiley.
Pile Fabrics. 1998. *World Clothing Manufacturer* 79 (7): 45.

Review Questions

1. What are some of the outstanding properties of acrylic fibers? What are some of the end uses for acrylic fibers, and how do the outstanding properties you have identified contribute to these uses?
2. What cautions must be exercised in caring for acrylics?
3. What are some of the outstanding properties of modacrylic fibers? What are some of the end uses for modacrylic fibers, and how do the outstanding properties you have identified contribute to these uses?
4. What cautions must be exercised in caring for modacrylics?
5. How are bicomponent acrylics different from regular acrylic fibers?

Recommended Readings

Acrylic Council sponsors blind sock test, survey with young football players. 1994. *Southern Textile News* (October 10): 5.

Bajaj, P. 1994. Absorbent acrylic fiber launched. *Textile Month* (August): 38.

Ford, J. E. 1992. Acrylic fibres. *Textiles* 21(2): 12.

Hobson, P. H., and A. L. McPeters. 1994. Acrylic and modacrylic fibers. In M. Grayson, ed. *Encyclopedia of textiles, fibers, and non-woven fabrics*, pg 1. New York: Wiley Interscience.

Improved heat resistance and luster for acrylic. 1990. *High Performance Textiles* 3 (March): pg 8.

Masson, J. C. 1995. *Acrylic fiber technology and applications*. New York: Marcel Dekker.

Scalco, M. 1991. Pil-Trol®. *International Fabricare Institute Bulletin* (September).

OLEFIN FIBERS

Although olefin monofilaments have been manufactured for specialized applications since 1949, the widespread use of olefin fibers for a variety of textile products has been a relatively recent development. These fibers are often called polyolefins, but the FTC specifies the generic name "olefin." According to the FTC, an *olefin fiber* is "a manufactured fiber in which the fiber-forming substance is any long-chain synthetic polymer composed of at least 85 percent weight of ethylene, propylene, or other olefin units, except amorphous polyolefins qualifying under category (1) of paragraph (j) of rule 7."[1]

Two major categories of olefin fibers exist. One is polypropylene; the other is polyethylene. Of the two, polypropylene is used far more extensively for textiles and constitutes the larger quantity of olefin fibers in use today, primarily because of its higher thermal stability. Worldwide the production of olefin fibers has increased significantly. In 1977, they represented 7 percent of manufactured fibers; in 1997 the figure had grown to 16 percent.

---

1. This exception refers to a type of synthetic rubber with a substantial proportion of polyolefin material.

POLYPROPYLENE FIBERS

Manufacture

Polypropylene flakes and chips are manufactured from polypropylene gas, a component of natural gas, or from the cracking of naptha, a product of crude oil refining. The polymerization reaction is an addition reaction in which the polymer is formed from addition of monomers to a growing chain. (See chapter 2.) In the polymerization step, specialized catalysts are used to produce polymer molecules that are capable of crystallizing when formed into fibers. Two chemists, Karl Ziegler and Giulio Natta, won a Nobel Prize in 1963 for developing the catalyst system (Stevens 1999). A new type of catalyst system, using metallocene catalysts, is now being pioneered by several producers. The metallocene system produces purer polymers that are more uniform in size (Ward 1999).

After polymerization the fiber is formed by one of two means: polypropylene may be melt spun as filaments, or it may be mechanically fibrillated. Fibrillated fibers are created by first extruding a film of polypropylene. This film is either stretched and split or slit and drawn into a network of fibers. (See chapter 13 for a discussion of film fibrillation.)

Polyprolylene manufacturing plants tend to be smaller in scale compared to those for other synthetic fibers. Since the fibers are difficult to dye, it is easier to add pigment colors during spinning, and there is an economic incentive for smaller runs of differently colored fibers.

Molecular Structure

The polypropylene molecule has methyl groups ($-CH_3$) on every other carbon in the polymer backbone. For high crystallinity, and optimum fiber properties, the methyl groups are all on one side:

$$-CH_2-CH-CH_2-CH-CH_2-CH-CH_2-$$
$$\begin{array}{ccccccc} & | & & | & & | & \\ & CH_3 & & CH_3 & & CH_3 & \end{array}$$

The Ziegler-Natta catalysts produce this polymer arrangement that allows tight chain packing and crystalline areas.

Properties of Polypropylene Fibers

Physical Properties

Shape. In microscopic appearance melt spun polypropylene fibers may have any of several cross-sectional configurations, depending on the shape of the holes of the spinneret used in extruding the fibers. Under the microscope the surfaces of polypropylene fibers appear to be smooth; however, under the greater magnification of electron microscopy, pigmented fibers may have protuberances along the fiber surface that are thought to be either clumps of pigment particles or part of the fiber structure. (See Figure 10.1.)

The properties of the melt-spun fibers and fibrillated fibers differ somewhat. The denier (size) range of melt-spun fibers is greater than is that of fibrillated fibers. Fibrillated fibers have a branchlike structure that may eliminate the need to add texture to

a   b

FIGURE 10.1

Photographs of polypropylene fibers taken through an electron scanning microscope: (a) cross-section; (b) longitudinal view. Photographs courtesy of the British Textile Technology Group (BTTG).

the fiber. Also, fiber-to-fiber interlocking is better in fibrillated films, but fiber length is not so uniform, and fibrillated fibers are less regular in shape than melt-spun fibers.

Specific Gravity. The density of polypropylene is especially low. Its specific gravity is 0.92, or less than that of water. As a result, olefin fabrics float on water when they are washed. The low density of polypropylene also is related to the relatively low cost of olefin fiber, as a small weight of raw materials can be used to produce a large volume of fiber.

Color. Since polypropylene fibers are hard to dye, pigments are usually added to the melted polymer before the fibers are spun. Unpigmented fibers are clear.

Mechanical Properties

Strength. Polypropylene olefins are strong. The breaking strength of polypropylene filaments is 2.5 to 5.5 g/d, depending on the amount of stretching the fiber undergoes after extrusion (the breaking strength of regular-tenacity nylon 66 is 3.0 to 3.6 g/d).

Modulus. Propylene has good initial resistance to stretch, similar to cotton and polyester.

Elongation and Recovery. The elastic recovery of polypropylene olefin fibers is excellent. They will stretch a moderate amount before breaking. High strength polypropylenes for industrial uses have lower elongation.

Resilience. The resilience of polypropylene is lower than nylon and polyester, and carpet made from the fiber will tend to mat. Newer variants of polypropylene, however, have better resilience.

Chemical Properties

Absorbency. Polypropylene is almost completely nonabsorbent. This low absorbency also makes it difficult to dye, but makes the fiber exceptionally resistant to waterborne soil and stains. Grease and oil do stain polypropylene fabrics, and since they are oleophilic (or oil attracting), stains may be difficult to remove. Depending on their construction, olefin fabrics have good wickability (Crow and Osczavski 1998).

Electrical Conductivity. The electrical conductivity of polypropylene is poor. Its low absorbency contributes to problems of static electricity buildup, although finishes used in the spinning and processing of the fiber can overcome this problem in the finished product.

Effect of Heat; Combustibility. The melting point of polypropylene is low: 338° F. Hot bacon fat dropped on olefin carpets will melt fibers. Hot dryers and heaters can also affect them. Olefins are combustible and melt as they burn. They produce a sooty smoke.

Chemical Reactivity. In general, polypropylene's resistance to bases and to acids is good. Some organic solvents used in dry cleaning may affect the fabrics adversely. Perchloroethylene should not be used. However, Stoddard solvent will not deteriorate the fibers. Home laundering is preferable to dry cleaning in the care of polypropylene fabrics.

Environmental Properties

Mold, mildew, and insects do not attack olefins. Sunlight does deteriorate the fabric, but age has no appreciable effect.

Other Properties

Dimensional Stability. The dimensional stability of heat-set polypropylene is good, as long as it is not subjected to temperatures above 250° F. Elevated temperatures will result in fabric shrinkage. Wet stability is good because the absorbence is so low.

Abrasion Resistance. Polyprolylene fibers have good abrasion resistance, an important factor in their use over many years in upholstery.

The characteristics of polypropylene fibers are summarized in Table 10.1.

TABLE 10.1
Selected Properties of Polypropylene and Polyethylene Fibers

Property	Polypropylene	Polyethylene[a]
Specific gravity	1.14–1.19	1.3
Tenacity (g/d)		
Dry	3.0–9.5	
Wet	2.6–8.0	2.3
Moisture regain (%)	4.0–4.5	1.0
Resiliency	Good	Good
Burning characteristics	In flame, burns with melting, continues after flame removed	In flame, burns very slowly with melting; self-extinguishing after flame removed
Melting point (° F)	Soften at 405°–497°; indeterminate melting point.	Approximately 400°
Conductivity of		
Heat	Low	Low
Electricity	Low	Low
Resistance to damage from		
Fungi	Excellent	Excellent
Insects	Excellent	Excellent
Prolonged exposure to sunlight	Excellent	Excellent
Acids	Good, except nitric	Good
Bases	Good to weak bases	Moderate

[a]Gel-spun polyethylene fibers.

Uses

Polypropylene fibers are used in a variety of products, including carpets and carpet backing, upholstery, and many nonwovens. It has virtually replaced jute in carpet backing in the United States because of its resistance to microorganisms. Being non-absorbent and having good weather resistance, polypropylene can be made into carpets that will withstand exposure to outdoor conditions in areas where sunlight is not intense or prolonged. However, without ultraviolet light stabilizers such carpets will deteriorate in climates like those of the American Southwest. When polypropylene is used for traditional indoor carpets, soil- and water-borne stain resistance are exceptional. Other characteristics such as good abrasion resistance, good lightfastness if solution dyed, and resistance to moths have contributed to the successful use of polypropylene for carpetings. (See Figure 10.2.) A drawback has been its lower resilience which can affect the stability of the carpet pile.

Upholstery fabric manufacturers have made extensive use of polypropylene in a variety of fabrics including velvets. Again, stain resistance and resistance to abrasion

FIGURE 10.2

Carpet and upholstery fabrics made from polyolefin fiber. Photograph courtesy of the American Polyolefin Association.

are important in this application. Automotive interior fabrics also represent a major market for olefin fabrics.

Polypropylene is used in a variety of nonwovens, such as industrial filters and diaper stock, where thermobondability is an essential property. Good wicking qualities also contribute to its use in diaper liners. (See Figure 10.3.)

Industrial applications of olefins are numerous and include ropes, cordage, filter paper, netting, and bagging. Nonwoven olefin geotextile materials are used in road construction and in other engineering projects. Polypropylene geotextiles are placed under the soil or roadbeds where their strength and chemical resistance are advantages, and they will not be degraded by light. They are also used as stitching in geotextiles for control of erosion. These products, placed on top of the soil, should biodegrade after vegetation is established.

Although industrial and home furnishings areas are the major outlets for polypropylene fiber, it is also an apparel fiber. Well established for activewear products such as underwear that are the first layer against the skin, thermal garments, hosiery, and wet suit liners, polypropylene is also beginning to penetrate other markets such as lingerie, bathing suits, and children's clothing. It is also being used as effect and design yarns. Characteristics that encourage activewear applications are excellent wicking qualities (by which moisture is transmitted to the outer surface, thereby reducing the cold, clammy feeling next to the skin), good thermal insulating qualities, and excellent abrasion resistance.

Fine-denier filament polyolefin is difficult to produce as high-quality filament yarn, although research in this area continues. Staple fiber yarns are more easily produced, and most apparel is made from staple yarns. Because the polymer must be colored before it is extruded, polypropylene has the advantage of absolute colorfastness

FIGURE 10.3

Polyolefins are widely used in diaper stock and diaper liners.

but the disadvantage that decisions about color must be made long before the fabrication of final products. Given the impact of fashion on apparel, this may be a limiting factor in use in highly fashion-oriented garments.

Olefin fibers are also being used for insulation materials for gloves, footwear, and apparel. Fine olefin and polyester fibers are made into a nonwoven batting that the manufacturer, 3M, calls Thinsulate®. The batting provides good insulation because the high surface area and low density of the material trap air. The fine size and light weight of the fibers contribute to warmth without excessive bulk or weight.

DuPont manufactures Tyvek®, a spunbonded polyolefin (see chapter 18 for discussion of spunbonding) for use in barrier garments such as clean suits, protective garments for toxic waste cleanup, and the like. One of the major advantages of the fiber is the low cost of production.

Polypropylene Trademarks

Amoco Fibers and Fabrics produces a number of polypropylene fibers including the brand names Alpha®, Impressa®, and Marvess®. Wellman, Inc. makes Polystrand® fibers.

Care Procedures

Polypropylene carpet and upholstery fabrics are relatively care free. Stains can be wiped off with a damp cloth. Routine vacuuming and periodic shampooing will help to maintain and preserve both appearance and durability.

Garments and other items such as blankets can usually be laundered. Polypropylene is injured by some dry-cleaning fluids. Care labels should be checked carefully, as blends of polypropylene with other fibers may require special care.

All polypropylene fabrics can be laundered at moderate temperatures. The fiber, however, is heat sensitive at about 250° F. Most dryers do not exceed temperatures of 180° to 190° F so that drying at low temperatures is permissible; however, line drying may be preferable as it generally eliminates any need for pressing. Hot irons will damage these fabrics, so only cool iron temperatures should be used for pressing.

POLYETHYLENE FIBERS

Polyethylene shares many qualities in common with polypropylene and exhibits some differences, including a lower melting point and some tendency to be deformed if stretched more than 10 percent. Melt-spun polyethylene has not been a textile fiber of major importance; the polymer has been used mostly for plastic films and packing materials. Recently, however, several companies have developed high-strength polyethylene fibers. AlliedSignal Fibers produces Spectra®, a gel-spun polyethylene fiber with an exceptionally high degree of polymer chain orientation.

Spectra® and other high-strength polyethylene superfibers manufactured abroad are characterized not only by high strength and modulus but are also less brittle than many competing high-technology fibers. They resist moisture, chemicals, and ultraviolet light and are lightweight. Disadvantages are a low melting point (300° F or 147° C) and, for some varieties of the fiber, a tendency to "creep," or elongate, under load over a long period of time.

FIGURE 10.4

High-strength products made from Spectra® polyethylene fiber range from (a) protective gloves and sleeves to (b) backpacks considered to be the toughest, lightest internal-frame packs ever produced. (a) courtesy of Golden Needles & Knitting Glove Company, (b) courtesy of AlliedSignal, Inc.

a   b

Products for which these fibers are being used include ropes, cables, sailcloth, cut-resistant clothing, gloves, backpacks, body shields, and a wide range of fiber composite materials for industry. (See Figure 10.4.)

SUMMARY

Polyolefin fibers are composed of polymers similar to those used for plastic films and bags. The predominant fiber in this class is polypropylene, which has a higher melting point and is therefore more appropriate for textiles than the other fiber, polyethylene. Polypropylene fibers are extremely light, can be produced in a range of sizes and strengths, and have almost no moisture absorbence. Industrial-strength polyethylene fibers produced by the gel-spinning process are made for ropes and protective clothing items.

References

Crow, R. M. and R. J. Osczevski. 1998. The interaction of water with fabrics. *Textile Research Journal* 68 (4): 280.

Stevens, M. P. 1999. *Polymer chemistry*. New York: Oxford University Press.

Ward, D. 1999. Synthetic success. *Textile Month* (April): 57.

Review Questions

1. Which properties of polypropylene fibers contribute to their use in the following products:
    carpets
    carpet backing
    diapers
    upholstery
    thermal underwear
    geotextiles
2. What care procedures are recommended for polypropylene garments?
3. What properties of high-strength polyethylene fibers contribute to their use in the following products?
    cut-resistant clothing
    composite materials for industry

Recommended Readings

Barish, L. 1989. Sunlight degradation of polypropylene textile fibers: A microscopial study. *Journal of the Textile Institute* 80 (1): 107.

Cheng, C. Y., and C. R. Davey. 1994. Effects of recycling on polypropylene properties. *International Nonwovens Journal* 6 (Summer): 38.

Dobson, S. 1994. Polypropylene fibers for technical textiles. *Technical Textile Markets* 19 (October): 48.

ELASTOMERIC FIBERS

*E*lastomeric fiber is defined as fiber made of "a natural or synthetic polymer which at room temperature can be stretched repeatedly to at least twice its original length and which after removal of the tensile load will immediately and forcibly return to approximately its original length" (American Society for Testing and Materials 1986, 262). These materials have extremely low glass transition temperatures, and, as is indicated in the definition, will exhibit plastic, or deformable, behavior at room temperature.

Several generic fiber classifications have been established for elastomeric fibers: spandex, rubber, anidex, and elastoester. Of these generic fiber groups, anidex is no longer produced and the newest generic fiber, elastoester, is manufactured in Japan.

RUBBER FIBERS

Rubber is probably the most important and widely used natural polymer for industrial products (Stevens 1999), primarily in tires. Fibers can be made from natural rubber or from several synthetic rubber polymers. Natural rubber comes from rubber plants. The polymer in natural rubber, with the repeating unit of isoprene,

$$-CH_2\overset{\displaystyle CH_3}{\overset{\displaystyle |}{C}}=CHCH_2-$$

does not have sufficient long-term recovery from stretch. It is therefore crosslinked in a process called *vulcanization* that provides a "memory" to the material. Fibers are formed by splitting thin films of crosslinked rubber polymers into fine strands.

For many years natural rubber was used as the core for fiber-covered elastic materials. Its advantages include high stretch, elasticity, flexibility, good strength, and nonabsorbency. Its disadvantages include deterioration by temperatures above 200° F and by sunlight, oils, petroleum, and aging. Many of these problems are caused by other compounds, such as proteins, that are present in natural rubber.

Synthetic rubber products can be produced in purer forms to improve some of the disadvantages of natural rubber. The most common of these, polyisoprene, is classified by the Federal Trade Commission (FTC) in the same subcategory as natural rubber along with polybutadiene and noncrystalline polyolefins. Another subcategory of synthetic rubbers are those made of acrylonitrile and butadiene. These materials, called *lastrile* or *nitrile rubbers*, are particularly resistant to oils. The third type of synthetic rubber fibers designated by the FTC are those that are "polychloroprene or a copolymer of chloroprene in which at least 35 percent by weight of the fiber-forming substance is composed of chloroprene units."

Synthetic rubbers exhibit similar characteristics to natural rubber in their behavior but in general show better resistance to deterioration. They are not commonly produced in the United States as fibers, but are used as film coatings for fabrics. Their low resistance to stretching and elastic recovery provide a coating layer that deforms with the fabric and is therefore not constraining.

Spandex

Manufactured in the United States since 1959, spandex fibers have attained extensive use in stretch fabrics for foundation garments, sports apparel, fashionable clothing, and other products where elasticity is important.

The FTC defines *spandex fiber* as "a manufactured fiber in which the fiber-forming substance is a long-chain synthetic polymer comprised of at least 85 percent of a segmented polyurethane." Spandex is a block copolymer with rigid aromatic segments connected by urethane linkages to polyether or polyester segments. The polyether or polyester segments of the polymer are amorphous and assume a coiled position when fibers are relaxed. When fibers are stretched the coils straighten, thereby providing the high elongation characteristic of spandex. Upon the release of tension, the amorphous, or "soft," segments coil up again, returning the fibers to their prestretched position. The rigid segments form highly hydrogen-bonded crystalline areas that prevent the polymers from sliding past each other and permanently deforming when stretched.

Manufacture

Spandex is manufactured in a process similar to that of aramid fibers. For DuPont's Lycra® spandex the constituents for the block copolymer of polyether and urethane are reacted in solution at a fairly low temperature. The fibers are then dry-spun from a solution of dimethyl formamide. They come into contact with each other while they are still somewhat soft and tacky, resulting in a random fusing or sticking together of individual fibers. (See Figure 11.1.) This fusing of fibers into bundles strengthens them for subsequent processing (Couper 1985).

Another production method is used by the Globe Manufacturing Co. for their Glospan® fibers. In this process, called reaction spinning, a prepolymer of shorter length is extruded into a wet spinning bath. It contacts a compound that completes the polymerization of the long-chain molecules and partially coagulates them into fibers. A subsequent heating step completes the fiber formation. Since the fibers are brought into contact while they are still somewhat soft, they adhere to each other forming fused bundles, as with dry-spun spandex fibers.

Properties of Spandex

Because spandex is used in many products in which rubber might be used, it is helpful to compare the properties of spandex to rubber as well as to other fibers. The characteristics of spandex fibers are summarized in Table 11.1.

Physical Properties

Lycra® spandex fibers are round in cross-section and smooth in the longitudinal view. (See Figure 11.1.) Other spandex fibers may have peanut or dog bone shapes. Rubber monofilaments have a rectangular cross section. Spandex fibers can be made in

FIGURE 11.1

Two cross-sectional views of Lycra® spandex fibers: (a) magnified 500 times; (b) magnified 150 times. Photomicrographs courtesy of the DuPont Company.

a   b

TABLE 11.1
Selected Properties of Spandex[a]

Property	Spandex
Specific gravity	1.21
Tenacity (g/d)	
Dry	0.7
Wet	0.7
Moisture regain (%)	1.3
Resiliency	Excellent
Burning characteristics	In flame, burns with melting, continues after flame removed; sticks at 370° F
Conductivity of	
Heat	Difficult to assess because fiber is used in combination with other fibers
Electricity	Difficult to assess because fiber is used in combination with other fibers
Resistance to damage from	
Fungi	Excellent
Insects	Excellent
Prolonged exposure to sunlight	Resists degradation, but may discolor
Acids	Good; acid fumes may cause yellowing
Bases	Fair

[a]Properties are for Lycra® spandex fibers.

much finer deniers than rubber, giving them a significant advantage for many end uses. Spandex has a moderate density. Specific gravity is 1.0 to 1.2, depending on pigmentation.

Mechanical Properties

Strength. Spandex is relatively weak when compared with nonelastomeric fibers, but much stronger than rubber. Breaking strength is around 0.7 g/d.

Modulus. The modulus of spandex, as that of rubber, is extremely low. It can be easily stretched.

Elongation and Recovery. The most important properties of spandex are its high elongation and excellent recovery. It can stretch 500 to 600 percent without breaking. This amount of stretching is comparable to rubber and the recovery is also similar.

Chemical Properties

Absorbency and Moisture Regain. Although the moisture regain of spandex fibers is low (<1.0 percent), water will penetrate the fiber.

Effect of Heat; Combustibility. Spandex fibers will burn. They melt at temperatures of about 450° F and will become sticky at temperatures around 340° F. Spandex can be heat-set and the fibers can be dried safely in an automatic dryer.

Chemical Reactivity. The resistance to chemicals of spandex fibers is generally good and is another distinct advantage that these fibers have over rubber. Chlorine compounds in strong concentrations will cause the fiber to be degraded and yellowed, but polyether-based fibers especially can withstand chlorine concentrations such as those used in swimming pools. Chlorine bleaches should, however, be avoided.

Seawater has no deleterious effect on spandex fibers. Perspiration and suntan oils do not seriously affect spandex, although some suntan oils may cause yellowing of white fibers. (Suntan oils do deteriorate rubber.)

Environmental Properties

Spandex has satisfactory resistance to microorganisms. Extended exposure to light may cause discoloration of some types of white spandex but does not deteriorate the fiber seriously.

Uses

Spandex fibers are always used in conjunction with other fibers. This combination with other fibers may be made in one of several ways. The spandex fiber may be used as bare yarn, single-covered wrapped yarn, double-covered yarn, or core-spun yarn. Fine-denier spandex is used to give stretch with sheerness in products such as ladies' hosiery.

Bare-core spandex yarns are uncovered filaments. They may be woven or knitted into fabrics in combination with other yarns. This provides additional strength to the spandex and gives stretch to the fabric. To make the monofilament more comfortable and more comparable to other yarns, a spandex filament core is often covered with another fiber. Single-covered yarns have one layer of another filament fiber wrapped around the spandex core. In double-covered yarns one layer is twisted around the core in one direction, and the second layer is twisted around the core in the opposite direction. (See Figure 11.2.) These yarns can be very sheer and are often used for sup-

FIGURE 11.2

Types of elastomeric yarns (length and cross section.)

ELASTOMER
INSIDE COVERING YARN
OUTSIDE COVERING YARN
SPUN STAPLE FIBER COVERING
OUTSIDE YARN
INSIDE YARN
ELASTOMER
SPUN STAPLE FIBER COVERING

Bare Filament   Covered Yarn   Core-spun Yarn

port hose. Where desirable, two different types of fibers can be used, one in each layer. The wrapped yarns will stretch and recover with the spandex core. Core-spun yarns are made by holding spandex filaments under tension while a staple fiber is spun around the core.

Spandex yarns are woven or knitted into a variety of garments in which stretch is desirable. These may include power nets for foundation garments, woven or crocheted fabrics for underwear waistbands, tricot or circular knits for lingerie, and activewear used in sports such as swimming, skiing, golf, and tennis. (See Figure 11.3.) Attractive stretch laces and other decorative fabrics can also be made with spandex.

The cost of spandex fibers is relatively high. As a result, spandex is used chiefly in those applications where alternative forms of providing stretch, such as stretch-texturing nylon or polyester, are inadequate.

Spandex Trademarks

Spandex fibers produced and marketed in the United States are Lycra® by DuPont, Dorlastan® by the Bayer Company, and Cleerspan® and Glospan® that are manufactured by Globe Manufacturing Company.

FIGURE 11.3

Swimwear made from Glospan® spandex type S-17 B by Globe Manufacturing Corporation. Chlorine-resistant Glospan® provides improved protection from damage caused by chlorine, ultraviolet rays, suntan oil, and perspiration. Photograph courtesy of Christina Swimwear.

Care Procedures

Because spandex fibers are used in combination with other fibers, care must take into account not only the characteristics of spandex but also those of the other fibers. Spandex should not be subjected to excessive heat in ironing. It is recommended that ironing temperatures not exceed 300° F or the "synthetic" setting on a hand iron. Dryer temperatures should be moderate. Chlorine bleaches should not be used in laundering spandex, because they can degrade the fiber.

SUMMARY

Elastomeric fibers, those with high elongation and good recovery, can be made from natural or synthetic rubbers, as well as from polyurethane. Spandex fibers, which are polyurethanes, are the most versatile and often used for textile and apparel purposes. They are more resistant to chemicals and environmental conditions and can be laundered. They are, however, expensive and are therefore used in blends with other fibers such as nylon. End uses include underwear, swimwear, activewear, and hosiery.

References

American Society for Testing and Materials. 1986. *Compilation of ASTM standard definitions*, 6th ed. Philadelphia: ASTM.

Couper, M. 1985. Polyurethane elastomeric fibers. In M. Lewin and J. Preston, eds. *High Technology Fibers*, 51. New York: Marcel Dekker.

Stevens, M. P. 1999. *Polymer chemistry*, 3rd ed. New York: Oxford University Press.

Review Questions

1. What is the definition of an elastomeric fiber? How do elastomeric fibers provide high elongation and recovery?
2. What are the advantages of using spandex fibers instead of rubber fibers in bathing suits?
3. Describe the various ways in which spandex is used in combination with other fibers.
4. How are care procedures for fabrics that include spandex determined?

Recommended Readings

Hochswender, W. 1997. Into the stretch. *Esquire* (August): 92.

Morton, M. 1973. *Rubber Technology*. New York: Van Nostrand Reinhold.

Rozelle, W. N. 1997. Spandex: Miracle fiber now coming into its own. *Textile World* 147 (1): 80.

Shivers, J. C. 1998. The search for a superior elastic fiber. *Textile Chemist and Colorist* 30 (12): 17.

Snyder, H. L. 1998. The invention of Lycra® and resulting innovations in textiles. In *AATCC Book of Papers*, 555. Research Triangle Park, N.C.: American Association of Textile Chemists and Colorists.

CHAPTER 12

HIGH-PERFORMANCE AND SPECIALTY FIBERS

In addition to the manufactured fibers discussed in earlier chapters, there are other types of fibers that have somewhat limited use or represent relatively recent developments in the technology of manufactured fiber production. These include the high-performance fibers that have been engineered for or used in industrial and specialty products. (See chapter 5 for a general description of high-performance fibers.) They also include mineral and metallic fibers that have been used for many years for particular functional or aesthetic purposes, as well as several recognized generic types that may appear in only a small number of products.

Most of the applications of the fibers discussed in this chapter are to be found in products used in industry, in building and construction materials, by the law enforcement community and the military, in recreational equipment, or in geotextiles. While most consumers may not ordinarily select or purchase many of the products made from these fibers, we increasingly depend on the machines, equipment, tools, and structures that incorporate these fibers in our homes, our work environments, and our leisure time pursuits. As these segments of the textile industry grow, larger numbers of graduates of textile programs are likely to find employment in the management, manufacture, and distribution of high performance and specialty textiles. For the discussion below, these fibers are grouped according to their distinctive or special characteristics. Characteristics of selected high-performance fibers used today are presented in Table 12.1 on page 223.

HEAT-RESISTANT FIBERS

A number of fibers, natural and manufactured, organic and inorganic, have extremely high (or no) melting points. They thus provide high thermal stability or resistance to heat. Many of these fabrics are strong and stiff, and could also be classified as high-strength, high-modulus fibers. Their primary end uses, however, are determined by their thermal stability.

Asbestos

Asbestos is no longer being made into textile products, but it is of historical interest both because it is the only natural mineral fiber and also because it still remains as an insulating material in many buildings. Since it is naturally fireproof, it was used alone or in blends to make textile products in which fire resistance was important, for example, in insulating materials, protective clothing, fire curtains for theaters, and household products such as ironing board covers or pot holders.

Continued inhalation of asbestos fiber can cause serious lung disease, and asbestos fiber is carcinogenic. For this reason, it is no longer used in textile applications. Asbestos fiber insulation, which was placed in many commercial buildings in the 1950s and 1960s, must be removed if renovation or structural modification of these buildings occurs. This is usually expensive.

Glass Fiber

During World War I, the Germans found that they were running short of asbestos fiber. In an effort to find a substitute fiber that was noncombustible, they attempted to make fibers from glass, with only limited success.

Following World War I, researchers continued to look into ways of using glass to produce fibers. This technology had been sufficiently advanced by the late 1930s, when the Owens-Corning Glass Company initiated the mass production of glass fiber.

Glass fiber is made from glass that has been melted and extruded into long, fine filaments. Glass is made from silica sand and limestone, plus small amounts of other constituents such as soda ash, borax, and aluminum hydroxide. The quantities of these ingredients are varied depending on the qualities desired in the glass fiber.

Manufacture

Glass fiber can be produced in both continuous filament form and in staple lengths. Selected ingredients are mixed together, and the mixture is melted in a high-temperature furnace. Molten glass is then drawn from the furnace in the form of filaments, the diameter of which is controlled by the viscosity of the glass melt, the rate of extrusion, and the size of the spinneret hole.

If staple fiber lengths are required, an air jet "cuts" the filaments and pulls the fibers onto a revolving drum from which they are gathered into a strand. Filament fibers are wound onto a spool by high-speed winders. Bare glass fibers have poor abrasion resistance, so a sizing or lubricating material is applied to fibers to provide some degree of protection. Fibers made of glass are subject to the usual textile processes for making yarns and for weaving. (See Figure 12.1.)

FIGURE 12.1

Strands of glass fiber roving are woven into fabric used in reinforced plastic boats, containers, parts for trucks and recreational vehicles, home furnishings equipment, sporting goods, and corrosion-resistant products such as storage tanks. Photograph courtesy of PPG Industries, Glass Group.

Properties of Glass Fiber

Physical Properties. Under the microscope glass fibers look like small glass rods (which is exactly what glass fibers are). Most glass fibers are manufactured in extremely small diameters (around 5 to 15 micrometers) to provide the flexibility required for textile applications. The longitudinal view of the fiber shows a smooth, round surface that produces a high luster. The fiber is colorless, unless a ceramic pigment is added to the glass melt before it is formed into fibers. Glass fibers have a specific gravity of 2.5 to 2.7, making them extremely heavy.

Mechanical Properties. Glass fibers have high breaking strength and modulus, but low elongation. Resilience is also extremely low.

Chemical Properties. Glass fiber is completely nonabsorbent and therefore has no affinity for dyes. For best colorfastness color can be added to the molten glass before it is spun by incorporating ceramic pigment into the glass melt. Acids do not generally affect glass fiber; however, bases can have a deleterious effect. Organic solvents do not affect the fiber.

Glass conducts neither heat nor electricity. For this reason, it is used in staple form in a variety of insulation materials. The fiber is completely noncombustible. When held in a flame, the finish of the fabric darkens as the pigments and resins used in finishing are destroyed, but the fibers, yarns, and woven structure of the fabric remain intact. Glass fiber softens at 700° C or 1350° F or above.

Other Properties. Glass fiber is attacked by neither mildew nor insect pests. Sunlight does not damage the fabric nor is it harmed by aging. Because of their low absorbency and high melting point, glass fibers have excellent resistance to shrinkage.

One of the major problems encountered in glass fabrics is their low abrasion resistance. They tend to break where creased and to wear at points where the fabric rubs against other objects.

Uses

Except for special items of protective clothing in which glass fiber is one component, glass fiber has never been used for wearing apparel. If the ends of the fibers are broken, they scratch or irritate the skin. Also, glass fiber has poor resistance to abrasion, is not absorbent, and lacks stretch. At one time glass fiber was used fairly extensively in draperies, curtains, lampshades, and window shades; however, at the present time, except for some institutional curtain and drapery products, the only significant application of glass fibers for home use is in vertical blinds. The glass fiber batting material used for insulation in buildings is not classified by the glass fiber industry as a textile fiber.

Today, glass fiber is most widely used for products in aerospace, construction, the electrical industries, transportation, recreation, packaging, and filtration for insulation purposes. Yarns made from glass fiber are used for reinforcement and in the growing field of composites. In fact glass fiber composites dominate the market (No dampening of demand for composites 1998). (Chapter 18 gives a detailed discussion of such fiber-reinforced composites.)

Glass fibers also find applications in the field of fiber optics. Scientists learned that light could be transmitted over long distances through fine strands of transparent materials. These beams of light can be used to carry messages. Glass fiber has proved to be a particularly effective carrier. The strands of glass fiber that form the light-transmitting core of fiber-optic cable are surrounded by a sheath that keeps the light from dispersing or straying. (See Figure 12.2)

Manufactured Aromatic Fibers

The most widely recognized fibers in this category are the aramids, described in chapter 7. There are, however, several other aromatic fibers that exhibit excellent heat resistance. The thermal characteristics of these fibers are compared in Table 12.1.

Polybenzimidazole (PBI) Fibers

Polybenzimidazole (PBI) is defined by the FTC as "a manufactured fiber in which the fiber-forming substance is a long-chain aromatic polymer having reoccurring imidazole groups as an integral part of the polymer chain."

PBI entered commercial production in May 1983. The largest present end use of PBI is in civilian and military protective apparel. (See Figure 12.3.) It is being used as a

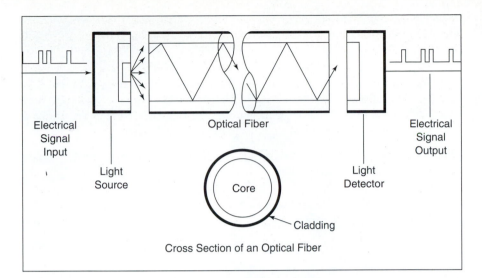

Electrical Signal Input

Light Source

Optical Fiber

Light Detector

Electrical Signal Output

Core

Cladding

Cross Section of an Optical Fiber

FIGURE 12.2

An optical fiber. Electrical signals are converted into light which is transmitted by the optical fiber; the light is then converted back into an electrical signal. Cladding helps keep most of the light inside the fiber by reflecting light waves toward its center as they pass through it. Illustration reprinted courtesy of the National Science Foundation.

successful alternative to asbestos in protective gloves, gaskets, and packing materials in industrial applications and to construct fire-blocking material in places such as aircraft.

The fiber is nonflammable in air, emits little or no toxic gases or smoke up to temperatures of 1040° F, and has excellent resistance to acids, organic solvents, and fuels. The fiber is currently produced by Celanese Corporation in staple form.

TABLE 12.1
Selected Properties of High-Performance Fibers

Fiber	Melting Temperature (° F)	Decomposition Temperature (° F)	Tenacity (g/d)	Modulus (g/d)	Compressive Strength (g/d)
Glass	1300–2900		11–20	330–415	~3.5–5.0
Gel-spun polyethylene	212		30–35	1,400–2,000	2.0
Meta-aramid	Does not melt	700	5.3	1,150	
Para-aramid	Does not melt	660	26–28	980–1,425	2.5–3.8
PBI	Does not melt	625	3.1	360	
PBO	Does not melt	1100	42	1,300–2,000	1.4–2.8
Sulfar	545		3.0–3.5	30–40	
Melamine	Does not melt	700	1.8		
Carbon (PAN)	Does not melt	<1500	13–27	1,500	1.6–2.9
Carbon (pitch)	Does not melt	<1500	16–28	950–4,600	2.5–6.9
Ceramic		1000–1600	5.2	1,100–1,200	21.2

Sources: Data from Kumar, S. 1991. Advances in high performance fibres. *Indian Journal of Fibre and Textile Research* 16 (March): 52; Lewin, M. and J. Preston. 1985-1996. *High technology fibers, parts A-D.* New York: Marcel Dekker; and Warner, S. B. 1995. Fiber science. Englewood Cliffs, N.J.: Prentice Hall.

Note: PAN, Polyacrylonitrile.

Figure 12.3

PBI blends are used extensively in applications such as firefighters' turnout gear (shown here) and industrial protective clothing. Photograph courtesy of Celanese Acetate.

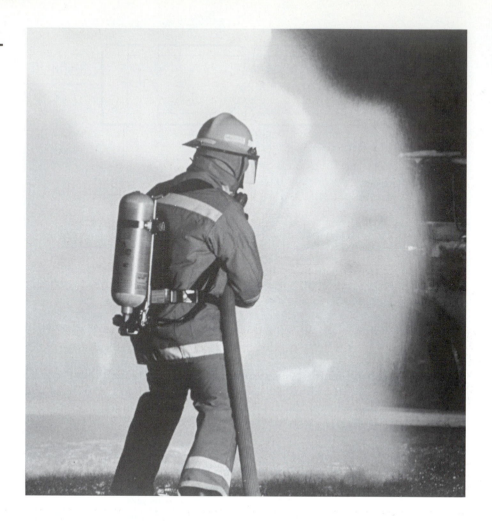

Polyphenylene Benzobisoxazole (PBO) Fibers

PBO fibers are recently developed fibers composed of the polymer polyphenylene benzobisoxazole. They belong to a class of materials known as rigid rod polymers that are extremely stiff and form highly ordered crystalline structures. PBO is synthesized from benzene dihydrochloride and terephthalic acid, the acid also used in the manufacture of polyester. It is spun from a strong acid solution through an air gap into a water bath. Zylon PBO fibers are manufactured by the Toyobo Company in Japan.

Because of its rigid structure, PBO exhibits both excellent thermal stability and high strength and modulus. The fibers do not melt and will not decompose below temperatures of 1200° F. PBO fabrics are light and flexible, but are not easily dyed. They are a gold color as produced.

The fibers are used in protective clothing for firefighters, industrial workers, and racing car drivers. They can also be found in filters for high-temperature devices, sporting goods, ropes, and cables.

Sulfar

Sulfar is defined by the FTC as "a manufactured fiber in which the fiber-forming substance is a long synthetic polysulfide in which at least 85% of the sulfide ($-S-$) linkages are attached directly to two (2) aromatic rings." The aromatic composition of the polymers in sulfar contributes to its high melting point (545° F, 285° C). The fiber is described as having tenacity, elongation, modulus, elastic recovery, boiling water shrinkage, and moisture regain that are satisfactory for textile applications. Chemical resistance is described as excellent.

Suitable applications for sulfar include filter bags for filtration of high temperature materials, woven and nonwoven filter fabrics for gases and liquids, papermaker felts, and protective clothing. Manufacturers suggest that sulfar has advantages over competing high-temperature-resisting, chemically resistant fibers in that it is less expensive and is easy to process. It is, however, not dyeable and is therefore more appropriate for industrial end uses.

Sulfar fibers are manufactured under the trademark name Ryton® by Amoco Fabrics and Fibers Company.

Melamine

A recently approved generic fiber type is melamine, recognized by the FTC as "a manufactured fiber in which the fiber-forming substance is a synthetic polymer composed of at least 50% by weight of a crosslinked melamine polymer." Unlike many synthetic manufactured fibers, melamine is not thermoplastic. Rather it is *thermosetting*. This means that, once formed, the fibers do not deform when heat is imposed. The polymers are in a three-dimensional crosslinked network, similar to the material in melamine dinnerware that was popular a number of years ago.

Because of the rigid structure, melamine fibers have low thermal conductivity and high resistance to heat shrinkage. They are also extremely resistant to chemical degradation. They have applications in protective clothing for firefighters and industrial workers, in airplane seating, upholstered furniture, and high-temperature filters.

A new and limited use fiber, melamine is produced by BASF Corporation under the brand name Basofil®.

HIGH-STRENGTH, HIGH-MODULUS FIBERS

Several of the fibers discussed as heat resistant also have high tenacity and modulus. The para-aramids described in chapter 7 and the gel-spun polyethylene fibers in chapter 10 are considered high-strength fibers as well. The following discussion encompasses several fiber types that are also used where high strength and modulus are the most important characteristics.

Carbon Fibers

Carbon fibers find their major applications in industrial uses. Within the industry the terms *carbon fibers* and *graphite fibers* are sometimes used interchangeably, but graphite fibers are actually a special type of carbon fiber that has a crystal or *graphitic* structure unique to true graphite fibers.

Manufacture

Carbon fibers are made either from rayon or polyacryonitrile (PAN) fibers or from pitch, a material derived from coal tar or petroleum tar. Currently the use of rayon as a starting material for carbon fibers is very small. In the most common production method, PAN fibers are heated to temperatures over 1000° C, driving off most of the hydrogen, nitrogen, and other atoms to leave only carbon. On further heating to

FIGURE 12.4

Photographs of carbon fibers in a composite structure taken through an electron scanning microscope: (a) cross-section; (b) longitudinal view. Photographs courtesy of the British Textile Technology Group (BTTG).

2500° C, a crystalline graphite structure develops which produces extremely high-modulus graphite fibers. Similar processing is given to pitch, which can be formed into fibrous materials. Because the raw material is less expensive, substantial quantities of industrial- and general-grade materials are manufactured from pitch.

Properties of Carbon Fibers

Carbon fibers are black in color, with a fairly smooth appearance. (see Figure 12.4.) They have a stiff hand, high strength, and are light in weight. The high tenacity (13 to 28 g/d) and modulus are due to the crystalline structure of the fiber.

FIGURE 12.5

A variety of sports equipment made using graphite fibers. Photograph courtesy of Hercules Aerospace Products Group.

Uses

Carbon fibers are most often used as a reinforcing material in plastic composites. The high strength of the fiber increases the toughness of the composite material, and the black color is not a detriment because the fibers are embedded in the matrix. Carbon fiber–reinforced composites are used in lightweight structures for aircraft and space-craft and as brake discs for jet airplanes. Carbon fibers also are used in such diverse areas as sporting goods, the construction industry, the automotive industry, and med-icine. (See Figure 12.5.) For example, the spinnaker pole of the yacht *Intrepid* con-tained 23 miles of graphite yarn. Golf club handles have been made with carbon fibers, and tennis racquets and fishing poles are made of carbon. Carbon fibers are used for the reinforcement of bridges and buildings, and graphite materials have been used for implantation to replace bone. Many industrial composites use carbon fibers in their structure.

Inorganic Manufactured Fibers

Several other types of fibers have been developed for use in the aerospace and aircraft industries. These fibers are not used for commercial textile products for the home or in garments.

Ceramic Fibers

Composed of aluminum, or other oxides, these fibers have lower tensile strength than many inorganic fibers, but higher compressive strength. This makes them useful as re-inforcing materials in aircraft, space shuttles, and submarines where high pressures are encountered.

Boron Fibers

Made by depositing boron vapor onto fine tungsten wire, these fibers have uses in re-inforcement, especially of aluminum. Cloth made in part from boron fibers was used in the drill stems for collecting lunar rock samples during NASA's moon mission.

OTHER SPECIALTY FIBERS

Metallic Fibers

Metallic fibers were the first manufactured fibers. Gold and silver "threads" have long been used to decorate costly garments, tapestries, carpets, and the like. These threads were made either by cutting thin sheets of metal into narrow strips and weaving these strips into decorative patterns or by winding a thin filament of metal around a cen-tral core of another material.

Examination of historic costumes and fabrics reveals the disadvantage of using metals in this way. Except for gold, the metals tended to tarnish and become discol-ored. Yarns were relatively weak and broke readily. Durability was limited, and, of course, the cost of precious metals was high.

Fashion fabrics today make use of a variety of metallic fibers that are both inex-pensive and decorative. Metallic fibers are also used in products for purely practical purposes. Many decorative metallic fibers are made in the form of large monofilaments. These are discussed in chapter 13.

Forming fibers from metal is difficult; therefore, metal fibers are largely limited to those made from steel (carbon, stainless, and low-alloy types), aluminum, iron, nickel, and cobalt-based superalloys. These particular metals lend themselves most readily to fiber formation. The manufacture of fibers from metal is usually done by one of three methods. A rod of metal is used as the starting material, and from it fine-dimension metal wire is drawn to form fibers. A more common method begins with the formation of metal foil that is sheared or slit into fibers. Copper scrubs, commonly used in cleaning, demonstrate this method on a macro scale. The metal foil can be coated with a colored adhesive and transparent film for added color and durability of the split fibers. In a more costly process, gold can be plated on aluminum-covered yarns of polyester or other fibers.

Most applications of metal fibers are for aerospace and other industrial applications where such products as filters, seals, abrasives, and insulation are used. The automotive industry uses metal fibers in tires and brake linings. (See chapter 13 for a discussion of tire cords.) There are limited applications of metal fibers in consumer products, particularly in certain household textile products, decorative apparel, military uniform decorations, and others.

Superfine filaments of stainless steel and aluminum are made and added to fabrics in a number of ways. Metal fibers are used as the core of yarns, wrapped around other core yarns, or used alone. Steel and copper and aluminum fibers are blended into some industrial carpets where they cut down on static electricity buildup and have the side effect of decreasing flammability. As the heat of a fire increases, the metallic fibers conduct some of the heat away from the fire, thereby decreasing the heat of the flame. This tends to slow the rate of burning or to lower temperatures below the kindling point. Other projected end uses for metal fibers include upholstery, blankets, and work clothing and in blends with polyester for hospital gowns.

Saran

Saran is a textile fiber of limited use. *Saran* is defined by the FTC as "a manufactured fiber in which the fiber-forming substance is any long-chain synthetic polymer composed of at least 80 percent by weight of vinylidene chloride units ($-CH_2-CCl_2-$)." Introduced by Dow Chemical Company in 1941, saran is no longer made in fiber form the United States. It is much more commonly seen as the plastic film used for the storage of food.

Saran is a stiff, nondrapable fiber with specialized uses in agricultural and industrial fabrics. It has a high density (specific gravity is higher than most other synthetics at 1.70), which along with its inflexibility, eliminates it from use in apparel fabrics. Other properties observed in saran films are also apparent in saran fibers. Its strength is good, and it has excellent elastic recovery and resiliency. Saran is abrasion resistant, has low moisture regain, and is not significantly affected by sunlight, microorganisms, or chemicals. These characteristics led to its use in outdoor furniture and upholstery for public conveyances. Lighter-weight fibers such as acrylic and polypropylene have supplanted saran for some of these applications.

Agricultural fabrics take advantage of the weather and flame-resistant characteristics of saran. Such fabrics are used to provide shade for growing plants. The chemical resistance of the fiber results in a variety of industrial uses. Saran grille fabrics are used in sound systems because they distort sound less than other materials do.

Saran, in combination with other fibers such as modacrylics, is used for making flame-resistant drapery fabrics.

Vinal

The FTC defines *vinal* as "a manufactured fiber in which the fiber-forming substance is any long-chain synthetic polymer composed of at least 50 percent by weight of vinyl alcohol units ($-CH_2-CHOH-$) and in which the total of the vinyl alcohol units and any one or more of the various acetal units is at least 85 percent by weight of the fiber." In some countries vinal fibers are called polyvinyl alcohol fibers.

Most of the development of vinal has taken place in Japan. The fiber has a melting point close to that of nylon 6 (around 425° F) and extremely good chemical resistance and is especially resistant to rot-producing microorganisms.

The use of vinal fibers is largely in industrial applications, although some blends of vinal fiber with cotton, rayon, or silk have been used abroad. Vinal fibers are manufactured in China, Germany, and Japan.

In a preliminary step during manufacture, a soluble form of vinal fiber is created. Nonsoluble vinals or polyvinyl alcohol (PVA) fibers are formed after additional treatments. The water-soluble form of vinal fibers has found specialty end uses. Soluble yarns of PVA may be used as "support" yarns in fabric constructions where open, sheer, or lacelike effects are desired but are not attainable through normal weaving processes. The fabric is woven and then laundered, causing the soluble yarns to dissolve, leaving only the insoluble yarns in a lacy, open pattern.

Soluble yarns may also be used when socks are manufactured in a continuous "string" with a few rows of stitches between the toe of one sock and the top of the next. The socks are cut apart, and when subjected to finishing processes, the remaining soluble threads dissolve out, leaving a smoothly finished edge. Only hot water is required to dissolve the PVA fibers.

Vinyon

Vinyon fibers are used most frequently in industrial applications where their high resistance to chemicals is useful. Vinyon has a low melting point and is, therefore, useful as a bonding agent in nonwoven fabric construction.

The FTC defines *vinyon* as "a manufactured fiber in which the fiber-forming substance is any long-chain synthetic polymer composed of at least 85 percent by weight of vinyl chloride units ($-CH_2-CHCl-$)." They may be called polyvinyl chloride fibers in other countries.

The low melting point of vinyon has prevented its use to any extent in apparel in the United States. Vinyon has high resistance to chemicals. Major uses are as a bonding agent in industrial nonwoven applications and for tea bags and other specialty uses. Vinyon is manufactured in Japan.

Fluoropolymer

Polymers containing fluorine, based on the substance polytetrafluoroethylene (PTFE), have been used for some time in textile and other applications. The FTC has now approved the generic name of fluoropolymer for these fibers.

The polymeric material may be formed into fibers by the emulsion spinning process (see page 134) or may be formed into sheets, extruded in molded form, or applied as a coating to other substances.

Fluoropolymer fibers have excellent chemical resistance, are usable over a wide temperature range, resist abrasion, and are nonabsorbent. Industrial uses include pump and valve packing, gaskets, filtration materials, bearings, and office copy equipment.

Consumers may know Teflon®, a fluorocarbon manufactured by DuPont, as a coating for cooking utensils. Teflon® is also the trade name for DuPont's fluoropolymer fibers. Teflon® fluorocarbon membranes with very tiny openings or pores are used in making Gore-Tex® fabrics, which have wide use in outdoor apparel. Albany International produces monofilament fluoropolymer fibers.

THE FUTURE OF HIGH-PERFORMANCE AND SPECIALTY FIBERS

Using the concept of fiber generations introduced in chapter 5 as a platform from which to look into the future, one can see that "synthetic fibers of the third generation are not simply alternatives to natural fibers as were synthetic fibers of the second generation" (Hongu and Phillips 1998, 3). The future is likely to bring not only modifications of existing generic fibers that will enhance fiber aesthetics and performance for the general consumer but also a wide array of high-technology and superfibers with ever-expanding applications in fields ranging from biotechnology to space exploration. As protecting the environment becomes increasingly important, fibers made from recycled materials and environmentally friendly processes are likely to thrive.

The cutting edge technology that resulted in production of some of the high-strength and heat-resistant fibers described in this chapter will increasingly be the standard, particularly for U.S. fiber manufacturers. Expect to see enhancements and process improvements that will make these fibers even stronger and more thermally stable. Fibers that are modified to store and release heat, provide antimicrobial properties, protect the wearer from the damaging ultraviolet rays of the sun, or absorb perspiration during exercise are considered high-performance fibers as well. The growing area of microfiber production will extend to more and more generic types, resulting in a wider range of microfiber products from apparel to industrial filters.

In this environment, the specialty fibers described in this chapter will probably remain in limited use in targeted products. Saran, vinal, and vinyon are not produced in the United States and have been replaced in many end uses by other more common fibers.

References

Hongu, T., and G. O. Phillips. 1998. *New fibers.* Manchester, U.K.: Woodhead/The Textile Institute.
No dampening of demand for composites. 1998. *Textile Horizons* 18 (October): 21.

Review Questions

1. How do high-performance fibers provide heat resistance or high strength and modulus?

2. Which of the following fibers are consumers likely to find in apparel? Which in household products? Which ones are consumers unlikely to encounter in products they purchase and why?

    PBO   fluoropolymer
    PBI   metallic fiber
    sulfar   vinyon
    vinal

3. What properties of glass fiber prevent it from being used in wearing apparel?

4. Identify at least three uses of carbon fibers and explain which properties make carbon fibers a good choice of these uses.

5. What are some uses for soluble fibers?

Recommended Readings

Brody, H. 1994. *Synthetic fibre materials.* Essex, U.K.: Longman Scientific and Technical.

Donnet, J.-B., T. K. Wang, S. Rebouillat, and J. C. M. Peng, eds. 1998. *Carbon fibers.* New York: Marcel Dekker.

Jackets to make bridges earthquake resistant. 1998. *Southern Textile News* (April 20): 13.

Kumar, S. 1991. Advances in high performance fibers. *Indian Journal of Fibre and Textile Research* 16 (March): 52.

Lewin, M., and J. Preston. 1985-1996. *High technology fibers, parts A-D.* New York: Marcel Dekker.

Mukhopadhyay, S. K. 1993. High performance fibers. *Textile Progress* 25 (3/4): 1.

Smith, W. C. 1998. High-performance fibers protect, improve lives. *Textile World* 148 (10): 53.

MAKING FIBERS INTO YARNS

If fibers are to be woven or knitted into cloth, they must be formed into long continuous strands called *yarns*. Fiber for yarns is supplied either in long filaments or short staple lengths. The type of yarn chosen for a fabric affects its appearance, durability, and hand and draping characteristics. Yarn construction can serve either to enhance or detract from the inherent qualities of the fiber from which the yarn is made. The term *spinning* is generally used to describe the conversion of fibers into yarn.

STEPS IN THE HISTORICAL DEVELOPMENT OF SPINNING

A brief overview of advances in the development of hand spinning will serve to introduce some basic concepts about how staple fibers are made into yarns. Hand spinning is still practiced today as a craft by many people, and the mechanical processes for spinning yarns use the same principles as hand spinning.

Hand Spinning

Before the invention of manufactured fibers, all yarns except those made from silk had to be spun from short, staple fibers. At first these staple fibers were twisted together by hand. A simple experiment will easily demonstrate how this can be done. Take a small bunch of fibers from a roll of absorbent cotton. Pull off a long strand and begin to twist the fibers in one direction. You will soon find that you have a rather short, coarse, but recognizable, cotton yarn. Rolling the fiber between the hand and the leg is another primitive method of spinning. Hand twisting by an experienced spinner can produce an acceptable yarn. Ancient textiles, that were woven from hand-twisted cotton yarns of excellent quality, have been found in Peruvian graves.

Before fibers could be twisted into yarns, some attempt had to be made to bring them into a more parallel alignment. This could be done by hand by running fingers through a bundle of fibers in order to straighten the fibers somewhat. Tools were designed to do the job more efficiently, and hand spinners still use an ancient device called a *carder*, a pair of wooden paddles on which is mounted a leather piece set with bent wire hooks. (See Figure 13.1.) The process of straightening fibers before spinning, done by hand or machine, is called *carding*.

A small quantity of fiber was placed on one carder. The second carder was laid against the first, and they were pulled in opposite directions. This process was repeated several times until the fibers were roughly parallel and any extraneous material had fallen out. The carded fibers were put aside for spinning.

Fibers could be made more completely parallel by a further step called *combing*. Combing was generally reserved for fibers of longer lengths, and the process, using a device shaped like a comb, pulled the fibers into alignment.

After the fiber had been carded or carded and combed, the actual twisting together of the fibers was begun. The spinner who twisted fibers together by hand needed a place to put the completed yarns. The solution was to wind them onto a stick. In time, the stick itself became a tool for spinning. By notching the stick to hold the thread and by adding a weight (called the *whorl*) to the end of the stick, a spindle was made. With the whorl to provide momentum, the spinner could use the stick to help in twisting the yarn. The spinner stood erect and held the mass of fiber under the left arm, leaving both hands free to work. A long, untwisted strand of fiber was fed to the spindle by the left hand. With the right hand, the spinner gave the stick a twist and let it fall, whirling, toward the ground. The momentum and weight of the falling spindle twisted the fibers into a continuous yarn. (See Figure 13.2.) The right hand was used to control the quantity of fiber feeding onto the spindle. When the spindle reached the ground, the spinner bent over, picked up the spindle, and wrapped the newly made yarn around the stick. Pulling out a new bunch of fiber, the spinner twisted the end of the unspun fiber to the end of the completed yarn and began the process again.

For better control of spinning, bundles of fiber were mounted on a long staff. The staff also prevented the fibers from becoming entangled. The Old English word for a bundle of flax was *dis*, and so the staff on which the fiber was placed came to be known as the *distaff*.

So closely were women associated with the tasks of spinning that many of these terms have taken on interesting connotations in modern language usage. The spinning was often done by the unmarried girls and adult women, and so the term *spinster* has become a synonym for an unmarried woman. The distaff was used almost exclusively by women, and in time the term has come to connote women's activities or interests.

For many thousands of years, this hand method of spinning was the only way in which yarn could be made. A major improvement in this technique originated in India when the action of a wheel was added to the spinning of the yarn. The Indian *charka*, or spinning wheel, seems to have been invented sometime between A.D. 500 and A.D. 1000 (Born 1939). Since the production of cotton was paramount in India, this wheel was devised to spin cotton. The spinning wheel did not come into wide

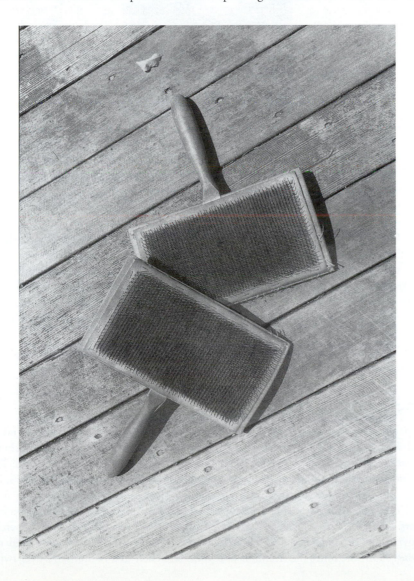

FIGURE 13.1

A set of hand carders used to card wool prior to spinning.

FIGURE 13.2

Hand spinning with a drop spindle. Fibers are drawn from a bundle of fiber and spun by lowering the spindle with a spinning motion. Spun yarn is wrapped around the spindle as it is formed.

use in Europe until the fourteenth century, and it is thought to have been carried to Spain by way of the Arab countries that occupied Spain until the late 1400s. The original Indian spinning wheel that had been used for cotton was small and close to the ground. A modification of this wheel that allowed the spinner to stand was made in Europe, but the same basic wheel, with minor modifications, was used for spinning flax, cotton, or silk. (See Figure 13.3.) Wool, however, required a bigger wheel, and the wool spinning wheel was always made with a much enlarged wheel.

Among the improvements in spinning equipment were a treadle mechanism for turning the wheel, which made it possible for the spinner to sit at the wheel to spin, and a "flyer and detachable bobbin" mechanism. This device allowed the simultaneous spinning and winding of yarn onto the bobbin, thus eliminating the interruptions necessary for winding up the complete yarn.

Throughout the development of all these processes, power was always supplied by the spinner, either through hand or foot and hand motions.

Mechanized Spinning

As part of the search for more efficient means of producing cloth during the Industrial Revolution of the eighteenth and nineteenth centuries, a number of machines for spinning were developed. Each offered some new and more effective process. The invention of the spinning wheel may be thought of as the first mechanization of spinning. In 1741 John Wyatt and Lewis Paul built a machine for spinning cotton which used a roller-drafting principle; that is, they fed a long strand of carded or combed fibers through a series of rollers. Each set of rollers moved at a different speed, thereby drawing out or elongating the strand of fibers. This strand of fibers was called the *roving*. From the roller the strand of fibers was stretched to a bobbin-and-flyer twist-

FIGURE 13.3

WHEEL, CARD, AND REEL.

WOOL WHEEL.

Spinning wheels. The wheel on the left is a flax wheel. On the ground under the shelf stands a device for winding skeins of yarn and one for hackling (carding) flax fibers. The wheel on the right is a wool wheel.

ing mechanism, like that of a spinning wheel. Arkwright used this same principle in 1769 when he constructed a spinning machine called the "water frame," which was given this name because it was operated by water power.

A second spinning machine was invented by James Hargreaves sometime in the 1760s. Utilizing the basic principles of the spinning wheel, Hargreaves's "spinning jenny" made eight yarns at the same time. A later patent shows that the number of yarns that could be made was increased to sixteen, and eventually the jenny was modified to make as many as one hundred yarns.

Both the spinning jenny and the Arkwright machine had certain limitations. Yarns made on these machines were not as strong as hand-spun yarns and were, therefore, not as suitable for use in the *warp* or lengthwise fabric direction, where greater tension was placed on each one.

Samuel Crompton combined the Arkwright machine and the spinning jenny into one basic machine that used both rotating rollers in drawing out the yarn and a moving carriage that provided the twist needed to make strong, fine yarns. This machine, known as the spinning mule, was the basic machine for producing cotton yarn in England until well into the twentieth century.

Although each of these methods made it possible for the quantity of yarn produced by one spinner to be enormously increased, they still required supervisory personnel to keep the machines operating. In about 1830 a device was developed that could be added to the spinning mule to make its operation completely automatic. These first machines were made for spinning cotton yarns, but the spinning jenny and subsequent modifications of this machine allowed the mechanization of wool spinning as well.

At about the same time that the automatic spinning mule was developed, an American inventor named John Thorpe devised a ring spinning machine. This machine has been used in the United States since about 1830 and is a basic machine used for spinning cotton and other staple fibers today.

The most recent development in the spinning of yarns from staple fibers is a process known as *open-end spinning*. In this method, the need to rotate the spindle full of yarn to insert twist is eliminated, allowing much greater spinning speeds.

TYPES OF YARN

The primary classification of yarns is as filament or staple. These terms were introduced earlier to describe the length of fibers, but are also used to distinguish yarns.

Filament Yarns

Filament yarns are made from long, continuous strands of fiber. *Monofilament yarns*, those made from a single filament, find limited use in nylon hosiery (where an exceptionally sheer fabric is wanted), in some open-work decorative fabrics, and in fabric webbing (used in some lightweight beach or casual furniture) as well as in a variety of industrial uses. Monofilament yarns can be made by the extrusion of large single filaments from spinnerets. The slit film technique in which a film of synthetic polymer is cut into strips will also make single filaments, each of which can be used as a monofilament yarn.

More commonly, many filaments are joined to form *multifilament yarns*. Multifilament yarns can be made more cohesive by twisting them together loosely or more tightly. (See Figure 13.4.) The amount of twist together with the characteristics of the fibers (luster, hand, cross-sectional shape, etc.) will determine the appearance and feel of the yarn. For example, a loosely twisted smooth filament yarn made from a bright fiber would be characterized by marked luster, resistance to pilling, and a smooth surface.

Sometimes filament yarns are put through an additional process called *texturing*. Texturing modifies the feel and bulk of filament yarns.

Staple Yarns

Staple, or *spun*, yarns are made from staple length fibers. Being short, staple fibers must be held together by some means in order to be formed into a long, continuous yarn. Although the multiple processes required to make staple yarn add significantly

FIGURE 13.4

Yarns depicted are: (a) monofilament—solid single strand of unlimited length; (b) multifilament—many continuous filaments; (c) staple—many short fibers twisted together: (d) ply yarn— two single yarns twisted together. Drawings reproduced by permission from B. C. Goswami, J. G. Martindale; and F. L. Scardino, *Textile Yarns: Technology, Structure, and Applications* (New York: Wiley, 1977), 2.

(A)

(B)

(C)

(D)

to the cost of the yarn, the aesthetic qualities such as comfort, warmth, softness, and appearance make these yarns highly desirable in many products. Natural fibers, except for silk, are all staple fibers. Silk and manufactured fibers can be cut or broken into staple fibers, so that it is possible to spin any natural or manufactured fiber into a staple yarn.

In addition to identifying yarns as being made from either filament or staple fibers, yarns are also classified based on a number of other characteristics. Authorities often differ when they define yarn types. The following are the most common classifications.

Yarns Classified by Number of Parts

Yarns that have been classified by the number of parts they possess are divided into *single*, *ply*, and *cord yarns*. A *single yarn* is made from a group of filament or staple fibers twisted together. If a single yarn is untwisted, it will separate into fibers. A single yarn might be identified as either a single yarn of staple fibers or a single yarn of filament fibers.

Ply yarns are made by twisting together two or more single yarns. If ply yarns are untwisted, they will divide into two or more single yarns, which, in turn, can be untwisted into fibers. (See Figure 13.5.) Each single yarn twisted into a ply yarn is called a *ply*.

Cord yarns are made by twisting together two or more ply yarns. Cord yarns can be identified by untwisting the yarn to form two or more ply yarns. Cord yarns are used in making ropes, sewing thread, and cordage and are woven as decorative yarns into some heavyweight novelty fabrics.

Yarns Classified by Similarity of Parts

Simple yarns are those yarns with uniform size and regular surface. They have varying degrees of twist, ranging from loose to moderate, tight or hard twist. Single, ply,

FIBERS TWISTED INTO
SINGLE YARNS

TWO SINGLE YARNS TWISTED
INTO PLY YARNS

THREE PLY YARNS TWISTED
INTO A CORD

FIGURE 13.5

Single, ply, and cord yarns.

and cord yarns can all be simple yarns if their components are uniform in size and have a regular surface. When one strand of fibers is twisted together evenly, it is classified as a simple single yarn. Two simple, single yarns twisted together create a simple ply yarn. (See Figure 13.4.)

Yarns made to create interesting decorative effects in the fabrics into which they are woven are known as *novelty yarns*. Some authors also call these yarns *complex yarns*, although complex yarns usually have more than one part. Novelty yarns can be single, ply, or cord, staple or filament.

In the industry novelty yarns tend to be referred to as *fancy yarns*. Terminology identifying these yarns is confusing. A Saurer Corporation (manufacturers of spinning equipment) spokesperson commented on the difficulties in a 1982 presentation, saying "it is most difficult to find the correct terminology, due to the fact that, say, five twisting specialists may have about seven terms for the same yarn alone." The following list of terms and their definitions represents an attempt to define these terms as they appear to be accepted by most authorities. (See Figure 13.6.)

1. *Bouclé yarns* are ply yarns. An effect yarn (so-called because it is used to create decorative effects) forms irregular loops around a base yarn or yarns. Another yarn binds or ties the effect yarn to the base. Some sources use the terms *loop* or *curl yarns* interchangeably with bouclé (Potter and Corbman 1967). *Ratiné yarns* are similar to bouclé in construction. The loops in ratiné yarns are spaced evenly along the base yarn. *Snarl yarns* are another type of loop yarn in which two or more single yarns under different tension are twisted together. The varying tension allows the effect yarn to form alternating unclosed loops on either side of the base yarn.

2. *Flake, flock,* or *seed yarns* are made of loosely twisted yarns that are held in place either by a base yarn as it twists or by a third or binder yarn. These yarns are relatively weak and are used in the filling to achieve decorative surface effects.

3. *Nub yarns* are ply yarns in which an effect yarn is twisted around a base yarn a number of times in a small area to cause an enlarged bump or "nub." Sometimes a binder yarn is used to hold the nubs in place. The spacing of the nubs may be at regular or irregular intervals. Nubs are often different colors than the base yarn. The terms *knot, spot,* or *knop* are also applied to this type of yarn.

4. *Slub yarns* may be either ply or single yarns of staple fibers. The slub effect is created by varying the twist in the yarn, allowing areas of looser twist to

FIGURE 13.6

Some types of novelty yarns. (a) bouclé yarn, (b) flake, flock, or seed yarn, (c) nub, spot, or knop yarn, (d) slub yarn, (e) spiral or corkscrew yarn, (f) chenille yarn. Drawings reprinted by permission from B. C. Goswami, J. G. Martindale, and F. L. Scardino, *Textile Yarns: Technology, Structure, and Applications* (New York: Wiley, 1977), 6.

a. BOUCLÉ YARN[1]

b. FLAKE, FLOCK, OR SEED YARN[1]

c. NUB, SPOT, OR KNOP YARN[1]

d. SLUB YARN[1]

e. SPIRAL OR CORKSCREW YARN[1]

f. CHENILLE YARNS[1]

be created. This produces a long, thick, soft area in the fabric called a *slub*. Slub yarns are irregular in diameter. The surface of fabrics woven with slub yarns shows these irregularities. Yarns made in this way have areas of varying twist, causing weaker areas in the yarn. In many fabrics slub yarns are placed in the filling or crosswise direction where fabrics receive less strain. Slubs are the same color as the rest of the yarn and cannot be pulled out of the fabric without damaging the structure of the fabric. Filament yarns can be spun with varying degrees of twist. These yarns also create a slubbed appearance in fabrics. Such filament yarns are known as *thick-and-thin yarns*.

5. *Spiral*, or *corkscrew*, *yarns* are made of two plies, one soft and heavy, the other fine. The heavy yarn winds around the fine yarn.

6. *Chenille yarns* are made by a totally different process and require several steps in their preparation. First, leno-weave fabric is woven (see page 311). This fabric is cut into strips, and these strips, which have a soft pile on all sides, are used as yarns. These are not yarns in the traditional sense of twisted fiber but have been taken through a series of preliminary stages before being readied for use.

Core-Spun Yarns

Core-spun yarns do not fall into the category of novelty yarns, but are yarns made with a central core of one fiber around which is wrapped or twisted an exterior layer of another fiber. Core-spun yarns may be made with an elastomer core, such as spandex, covered by another fiber to produce a stretch yarn. Other core-spun yarns include sewing thread made with polyester cores and cotton cover. (See Figure 11.2, page 215.)

THREAD

The terms *yarn* and *thread* are sometimes used interchangeably. However, a distinction should be made between yarns, which are fiber assemblies intended for weaving, knitting, or otherwise combining into a textile fabric, and sewing threads, which are used for sewing together sections of garments or other products.

Sewing threads may be made from one or more kinds of fiber. The most important threads have been those made from cotton or from a multifilament core of polyester covered with a cotton, rayon, or spun polyester. Except for yarns made from nylon or polyester, single yarns are not suitable for sewing threads; therefore, two or more plies are used.

To perform well, sewing threads must have high stability to bending, good strength, limited elongation, minimal shrinkage, and good abrasion resistance. Consider the stresses to which sewing thread is exposed. On the sewing machine, it must slide through various thread guides, it is hit back and forth under tension by the sewing machine needle, and it is permanently held in a bent position as it interlocks with the thread from the bobbin. Seams in tarpaulins, shoes, pants, and safety belts are subject to considerable tension and abrasion. If threads used shrink more or less than the fabrics in garments, puckering and wrinkling will appear at seam lines.

Home sewers purchase thread for their personal use, but 95 percent of the sewing thread produced goes to industry. The development of high-speed industrial sewing machines requires that manufacturers of sewing thread constantly improve the quality and performance of these products. A surface lubricating finish must be applied to industrial thread to minimize frictional heating of the sewing needle that could fuse or damage thermoplastic materials.

YARN TWIST

All staple yarns and some filament yarns have twist applied to them to hold the fibers together. The degree of twist given to a yarn affects a number of aspects of its appearance, behavior, and durability. The amount of twist in a given yarn can be measured. The ASTM standard definition of twist is "the number of turns about its axis per unit length observed in a yarn or other textile strand" (ASTM 1998, 49). Twist may be expressed as turns per meter (tpm), turns per centimeter (tpcm), or turns per inch (tpi).

Effects of Twist

The bulkiness of yarns is related to twist. As a general rule, increasing twist decreases apparent yarn size. This can be demonstrated easily by taking a strand of loose fiber, such as absorbent cotton, and twisting it. The more one twists, the smaller in diameter the yarn will become.

Strength increases in staple yarns as twist increases up to a certain point. Beyond this point, the strength of the yarn begins to decrease, and yarns with exceptionally high, tight twist may become brittle and weak.

Elasticity is increased if yarns are twisted tightly. Tightly twisted yarns are known as *crepe yarns*, which are generally very fine. The twist of crepe yarns is so high that they curl up unless they are held under tension, as they would be on a loom during weaving. A simple and easy test to identify crepe yarns is to unravel a yarn from the fabric and run it between the fingernails, thus removing the tension produced by sizing material. If the yarn curls up into corkscrewlike curls, it has been creped. This tendency of crepe yarn to twist makes fabrics constructed from these yarns less dimensionally stable than other fabrics, as they are more elastic, and they have an uneven fabric surface.

More tightly twisted yarns shed soil more easily. Because their surface is smoother, there are fewer loose fiber ends to attract and hold soil. In yarns made from absorbent fibers, absorbency is lower in more tightly twisted yarns.

Abrasion resistance is increased by tighter twist. This is a logical result because in a more tightly twisted yarn many fibers are held in such a way that they appear on the surface, then into the center of the yarn, and then back to the surface again. As a result, more fibers are subject to a relatively even distribution of abrasion. Loose surface fibers in low-twist yarns also snag and pull up, creating points of wear.

The appearance of a fabric can be determined to a large extent by the twist of the yarn. For example, if filament yarns of higher luster are only given low twist, they will reflect greater quantities of light in mirrorlike fashion and, therefore, appear brighter than the same yarns when they are more tightly twisted. Crepe fabrics achieve a nubby, somewhat crinkled, effect by using creped yarns that have a less even surface texture. Unevenly twisted slub yarns can also produce a rough surface. The

FIGURE 13.7

(a) Tightly twisted crepe yarns are used to create a pebbly surface texture; (b) loosely twisted silk slub yarns are used to produce a fabric of the shantung type.

a   b

fabric designer takes advantage of these effects to create a wide variety of surface textures and designs. (See Figure 13.7.)

Direction of Twist

In twisting fibers together to form yarns, the fibers can be twisted either to the right or to the left. In textile industry terminology this twist is called *S* or *Z twist*. (See Figure 13.8). Z twisted yarns are twisted so that the direction of the twist follows the center bar of the letter Z. Z twist is also known as *right twist*. In S twist yarn, the twist direction follows the center bar of the letter S. S twist is also known as *left twist*. This concept will be more easily understood if the reader takes a small bunch of absorbent cotton and makes a vertical line on the fibers with a pen. Then, suspending the fibers from the thumb and forefinger of the left hand to that of the right, rotate the fibers to the right with the upper left-hand fingers. The line you have made will take a diagonal direction similar to that of the bar in a Z. If the upper fingers are twisted to the left, the line will follow the bar of the S.

Most yarns are made with a Z twist. However, in certain fabric constructions special effects can be achieved by combining yarns in which the fibers have been twisted in either the same or opposite directions.

Figure 13.8

S and Z twist yarns.

Yarn Size

Because the textile industry requires some means for distinguishing between yarns of different sizes, standards of measurement have been established. There are different systems of measurement for cotton-type yarn, wool-type yarn, and still other systems for filament yarns.

This variety of measurement systems may seem unnecessarily complicated. The systems had their origins in measurements that were appropriate for particular uses in isolated textile manufacturing localities and may go back for hundreds of years. The present trend is toward use of metric measurements, but traditional terminology is still used.

The basic principles underlying these systems that should be borne in mind are these: the system is different for staple and filament yarns, may vary by type of fiber, and may be either a direct measure of size or an indirect measure.

Direct Numbering Systems

Direct methods of measurement rely on the measurement of fixed lengths of yarn. A specified length of yarn is measured, and this length is weighed. The measures used are tex or denier. As explained earlier, tex is the weight in grams of a 1-kilometer (1,000-meter) length of yarn, and denier is the weight in grams of 9,000 meters of yarn. Yarns may also be specified in *decitex*, which is the weight of 10,000 meters. In all these measures, the higher the number, the coarser the yarn.

The size of filament yarns may be designated by giving the denier or tex of the total yarn or by the denier per filament (dpf). This last measure, in conjunction with the number of filaments, provides additional information about the yarn.

Indirect Numbering Systems

Indirect methods of yarn numbering rely on the measurement of fixed weights of yarn. Each system establishes a number of hanks (skeins) of yarn that make up either a pound or a kilogram of yarn weight. Pounds are used for measurements in the English system and kilograms for measurements in the metric system. The size of the hanks used is different for the different natural fibers, with the measures being as follows: *cotton count* equals the number of hanks of 840 yards in 1 pound; *linen count* (also called *linen lea*) equals the number of hanks of 300 yards in 1 pound; *woolen count* equals the number of hanks of 1,600 yards per pound; *worsted count* equals the number of hanks of 560 yards per pound. All these yarn numbers are reported in technical or research

TABLE 13.1
Comparable Yarn Numbers in Direct and Indirect Systems of Yarn Numbering

	Direct Methods		Indirect Methods				
	Tex (weight in grams of 1,000 m of yarn)	Denier (weight in grams of 9,000 m of yarn)	Cotton (no. of 840-yd hanks per lb)	Linen (no. of 300-yd hanks per lb)	Worsted (no. of 560-yd hanks per lb)	Woolen (no. of 1,600-yd hanks per lb)	Metric (no. of 1,000-m hanks per kg)
Finest	5.6	50	106	298	160	56	180
	8.3	75	71	198	106	37	120
	11.1	100	53	149	80	28	90
	16.6	150	35	99	53	19	60
	22.2	200	27	74	40	14	45
	33.4	300	18	50	27	9.3	30
	44.4	400	13	37	20	7.0	37
	55.5	500	11	30	16	5.6	18
	77.7	700	7.6	21	11	4.0	13
	111	1,000	5.3	15	8.0	2.8	9
	166	1,500	3.5	9.9	5.3	1.9	6
Coarsest	222	2,000	2.7	7.4	4.0	1.4	4.5

Source: Adapted from J. Pizzuto, *Fabric Science* (New York: Fairchild, 1974), 88; data from *Annual Book of ASTM Standards*, Vol. 7.01 (West Conshohocken, Pa.: ASTM, 1998), Standard D2260.

literature followed by the abbreviation *Ne*, which stands for "number in the English system." Metric yarn numbers in the indirect measurement system equal the number of 1,000-meter hanks in each kilogram, and this measurement is followed by the abbreviation *Nm*, which stands for "number in the metric system."

Because different lengths of yarns are used to establish yarn numbers in the varying systems, yarn numbers are not directly comparable unless one uses a table such as Table 13.1. Looking at that table, one can see, reading across the table, that depending on the system being used, comparably sized yarns can have widely divergent numbers assigned. Nevertheless, regardless of the specific yarn numbers, certain basic principles apply. In the direct system the lower numbers indicate fine yarns; higher numbers indicate coarser yarns. Just the opposite is true in the indirect system, where higher numbers indicate finer yarns and lower numbers coarser yarns. For example, if 7 hanks of one linen yarn weigh 1 pound, and 50 hanks of another linen yarn weigh 1 pound, obviously the yarn with the higher number (50) would be finer than the yarn with the lower number (7).

YARN PRODUCTION METHODS: AN OVERVIEW

The following pages provide an overview of the techniques used to transform fibers into yarns. The following outline may help the reader to understand the sequence of that discussion.

1. Making filament fibers into yarns
2. Making bulk filament yarns
3. Transforming filaments into tow
4. Making staple fibers into yarns
   a. Preparation of staple fibers for spinning
      1) Blending staple fibers
      2) Breaking and opening bundles
      3) Cleaning fibers
   b. Systems for processing different types of staple fibers
      1) Fiber preparation by the cotton system
      2) Fiber preparation by the woolen system
      3) Fiber preparation by the worsted system
      4) Processing of flax fibers
   c. Insertion of twist into yarns
      1) Ring spinning
      2) Open-end spinning
5. Ply yarns
6. Other methods of manufacturing yarns

In the chapters devoted to various types of fibers, the term *spinning* was used to describe the formation of manufactured fibers by extruding them through a spinneret. This use of the word should not be confused with the term *spinning* as it is used to describe the formation of a yarn from fibers. Newly formed manufactured fibers were also described as being *drawn*. This term also has two meanings: (1) the drawing of manufactured fibers to orient the molecules within the fiber and (2) a step in certain of the processes for creating yarns from staple fibers.

MAKING FILAMENT FIBERS INTO YARNS

In creating manufactured fibers for use in filament yarns, spinnerets are used that have the exact number of holes (from about 30 to several thousand) needed for a particular type of yarn. Following extrusion, the fibers may be drawn, or alternatively, the drawing may take place during a subsequent step. This is true, for example, of partially oriented yarns (POY) of polyester. The drawn filaments may be twisted together either tightly or loosely, depending on the characteristics desired in the resulting yarn (See chapter 5 for a fuller discussion of manufactured filament fibers).

Much of the silk fiber produced is processed into filament yarns, although short silk fibers can also be made into staple yarns. Creation of filament yarns of silk can be done immediately after reeling fibers from cocoons or later, after the gum has been removed.

TEXTURING FILAMENT YARNS

Yarns made from straight filament fibers are smooth and slippery to the touch. They lack the comfort, bulk, and hand of yarns spun from staple fibers. Bulky yarns are formed from fibers that are inherently bulky and cannot be closely packed because of such characteristics as cross-sectional shape, fiber resilience, natural crimp, or some other quality. Manufactured yarns can be treated with processes that use heat setting or mechanical entangling of fibers to alter their bulk, texture, and stretch.

Yarns can be textured primarily to increase bulk for comfort, resiliency, and hand; or to provide stretch to the yarn. Texturing may be done by the fiber manufacturer (*producer-textured* yarn) or at some later step in the manufacture of the yarn. In the early stages of development, texturing processes were carried out separately from fiber spinning and drawing. The steps of drawing and texturing then became continuous, and now are more commonly carried out in a simultaneous operation using POY yarns (Demir and Behery 1997).

It should be noted that texturing filament yarn is much less expensive than spinning staple yarns. Customers seem to show a preference for spun yarns in many applications; thus, texturing filament yarns, especially those of polyester, has become an important manufacturing step. With the widespread use of POY (see chapter 8 for a fuller discussion), the texturer, who may also be the fiber producer, simultaneously draws and textures the yarn.

Bulk Textured Yarns

Yarns textured for bulk have a relatively large number of randomly spaced and sized loops along the filaments or fibers and very little stretch. They are produced primarily through air-jet texturing in which texture is produced not by heat but by feeding yarns into a system in which slack filaments are formed into loops by jets of air. (See Figure 13.9.) Air-jet texturing can be used for filament yarns of any fiber.

The resultant yarns have little stretch because many of the fibers retain their straight or slightly twisted conformation. These yarns do, however, more closely resemble staple yarns than some of the stretch textured yarns described below.

FIGURE 13.9

Texturing of yarns by the air-jet method. From S. Backer, Yarn, *Scientific American,* (December) 1972. Artist: Dan Todd.

Stretch Textured Yarns

The bulk texturing air-jet process depends on mechanical action only. If fibers in a yarn are mechanically deformed and then heat treated, the resulting yarns have not only increased bulk, but higher stretch as well. There are a number of these *thermomechanical* texturing processes that have been commercially applied to filament yarns. The fibers are twisted, crimped, or curled, passed through a heater to set in the modified conformation, and then relaxed. Only thermoplastic fibers, which deform on imposition of heat, can be durably textured in this way. The bulk continuous filament (BCF) yarns used in carpets are usually crimp textured, not bulk textured as described in the preceding section. The term bulk continuous filament, however, has remained as a carry-over from earlier definitions of textured yarns.

The most common stretch texturing method is the *false-twist* process, so named because the yarn is twisted, heated, and then untwisted. The crimp and waviness of the fibers in the twisted state will remain. The twist can be applied by different mechanisms. The simplest and oldest uses a spindle with the yarn wound around a pin. As the spindle turns, twist is imparted and set in the heating zone. Since the yarn is moving rather than being held stationary at the exit end, the twisted structure is relaxed. (See Figure 13.10.)

FIGURE 13.10

(a) Texturing of yarns through false twist texturing. From S. Backer, "Yarn," *Scientific American* (December) 1972. Artist: Dan Todd. (b) Disk system for insertion of false twist. (c) Yarn is twisted by "twister belts" as it passes between them. (c) Drawing courtesy of Murata of America, Inc.

a

b

c

Further development in the false-twist process has concentrated on better and faster twisting methods. Some machines use a series of revolving disks over which the yarn passes, while others have a friction belt device that rubs the yarn.

Other processes that introduce crimp include the *stuffer box* method, in which fibers are fed into a small chamber where the crimped shape is heat-set. The *gear crimp* process imparts crimp by passing filaments between the teeth of two heated gears. In *knit-deknit*, yarns are knitted into a fabric, the fabric is heat-set, then yarns are unraveled and retain crimp formed in the knitted configuration. These last-mentioned processes account for only about 5 percent of textured yarns (Wilson and Kollu 1987).

Stretch yarns have a moderate to high degree of yarn curl or crimp. When placed under stress, they will stretch, flattening the curls; but when stress is removed, the fibers in the yarn return to the permanent heat-set shape.

Consumers as well as those in the textile industry may use the term *stretch* more broadly, applying it to any yarn or fabric that exhibits stretch and recovery. Most of these alternative routes to provision of stretch are discussed elsewhere, and they include the use of elastomeric fibers (chapter 11), bicomponent fibers with differential shrinkage (chapter 5), and treatment of fabrics to provide moderate amounts of stretch (chapter 19).

TRANSFORMING FILAMENTS INTO TOW

Tow is a bundle of filaments that will be broken or cut into staple lengths. One of the advantages of starting with tow for spinning a staple yarn is that, unlike cotton, wool, and other natural fibers, the tow fibers are aligned and parallel and need not be combed or carded to make them ready for spinning. The fibers can be said to go from tow to *sliver*, a continuous rope of staple fibers, in one operation. The industry terms the process "tow-to-top." Specialized machines make this conversion. For example, the Pacific converter cuts a flat web of tow into the desired staple length. (See Figure 13.11.) A rope of fibers can be chopped by a revolving blade. Fibers may be cut into uniform or variable lengths. The web of cut fibers is then rolled into a sliver of staple fibers.

A second method of converting tow-to-top is to break the fibers into staple lengths. The Perlock system applies tension to the tow and pulls the stretched tow across a tow breaker wheel, a cog wheel with sharp, protruding edges. The filaments

FIGURE 13.11

Filaments are converted to tow. Continuous filaments are fed under a roller (a) with sharp blades that cut the filaments into short lengths. (b) Cut fiber is rolled into a sliver.

(a)　　　(b)

then break on the sharp edges of the tow breaker wheel. Stretch breaking is most effective with synthetic fibers, less useful in cutting regenerated cellulose. A variation of this process, the Turbo-stapler process, is used for producing high-bulk yarns, especially from acrylics.

During stretch breaking, the fibers are extended and must be treated to relax the fiber or yarns will show a good deal of relaxation shrinkage. In the Perlock process, breaking is followed by adding crimp to the fiber, heat-setting the crimp, and relaxing the fiber by a steam heat treatment. If a sliver of stretch-broken, crimped, relaxed staple is blended with a sliver of stretch-broken, crimped, but not relaxed staple, the bulking properties of the resulting yarns are much improved.

The yarns made in this way are woven or knitted into a garment, the garment is treated with hot water, and the unset fibers shrink, causing the preshrunk fibers to stand up in a bulky, fuzzy surface texture.

MAKING STAPLE FIBERS INTO YARNS

From the time staple fibers are supplied to the manufacturer until they have been made into yarns, they go through a series of steps. Some steps are required for all yarns and fibers, and some are optional.

Preparation of Staple Fibers for Spinning

Blending Staple Fibers

It is sometimes desirable to blend two or more different fibers into one yarn. Frequently, manufactured fibers are blended with natural fibers to take advantage of the best qualities of each fiber. In other blends the combination may be made to reduce the cost of the fabric by blending a less expensive fiber with a more expensive one, or blending may be done to achieve decorative effects.

Blending may be done at one of several steps in the preparation of yarns from staple fibers: during opening, during carding, or during drawing out. No matter when blending is done, quantities of each fiber to be used are measured carefully, and the proportions of one fiber to another are consistently maintained.

Breaking and Opening Bundles

Bales of fiber may be opened either by hand or by machine. (See Figure 13.12.) Many modern textile mills have completely mechanized this process. The trend toward mechanization of opening cotton bales has been accelerated by the requirements of the Occupational Safety and Health Act that workers' exposure to cotton dust be limited. As noted earlier, high levels of cotton dust appear to be associated with a lung disease called byssinosis.

Cleaning Fibers

Cotton contains impurities such as sand or grit and particles of leaf, stalk, and seeds. New wool that has not previously been cleaned contains vegetable matter, sand, dirt, and grease. Both may require special cleaning after the bales have been opened.

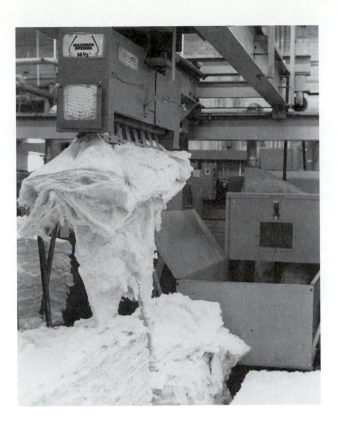

FIGURE 13.12

Bales of fiber are opened. Much of this operation is done automatically to avoid exposing workers to cotton dust. Photograph courtesy of American Textile Manufacturers Institute.

Manufactured fibers do not require cleaning, but if they have been compressed for packing and shipping, they need to be opened and the fibers separated so that bunches of fibers do not cling together and form thick areas, or *slubs*, in the yarn.

Systems for Processing Different Types of Staple Fibers

Processing of fibers in preparation for spinning may be done on one of three major spinning systems: the cotton, the woolen, or the worsted (also called long-staple) system. These systems were developed at the time when only natural fibers were in use; therefore, the different characteristics of the fibers, including their length, helped to shape the processes used. Manufactured staple fibers can be handled on any of these systems. More yarn is produced on the cotton system than on the worsted or woolen systems.

Fiber Preparation by the Cotton System

Increased automation in yarn production has largely eliminated initial steps of loosening and separating lumps of fiber and the subsequent formation of a *lap*, a flattened fairly uniform layer of fibers. Instead, the opening and transport of fiber to the carding machine are done in a more or less closed system.

Carding. The carding machine consists of an inner cylinder and an outer belt, both set with hundreds of fine wires. The intermeshing wires separate the fibers and pull them into somewhat parallel form, much as the old hand carders did. The wire teeth also remove trash and entangled lumps of fibers called *neps*. A thin web of fiber is formed in this machine, and as the web is moved along, it passes through a funnel-shaped device that forms it into the sliver, which is a ropelike strand of roughly parallel fibers. (See Figure 13.13.)

Blending can take place at the point of carding by joining quantities of different fibers. Carding mixes the blend fibers together, distributing them evenly throughout the mass of fiber.

Combing. Whereas carding is a step in the production of all fibers, combing is an optional step in the preparation of some yarns. When a smoother, finer yarn is wanted, fibers are subjected to a further paralleling called *combing.* A comblike device arranges fibers into parallel form. At the same time it removes the short fibers as well as most remaining neps or impurities. (See Figure 13.14.)

Combed yarns have smooth surfaces and finer diameters than do carded yarns. Since the shorter fibers have been removed, fewer short ends show on the surface of the fabric, and the luster is increased. Combed yarns are more expensive to produce, and fabrics made from combed yarns are, therefore, higher in price. Far more of the yarn produced on the cotton system is carded than that which is both carded and combed. When products are made from fabric with combed yarns, this is often advertised to the consumer.

Drawing Out. Carding or combing transforms a fiber mass into a sliver. Several slivers are combined in the drawing-out process. Blending of fibers can be done by combining slivers of different fibers. During the drawing out, a series of rollers rotating at different rates of speed elongates or draws out and attenuates the sliver into a single more uniform strand that is fed into large cans.

FIGURE 13.13

Cleaning and separation of individual fibers takes place in the carding machine. A web of fibers is formed into a thin rope-like strand or sliver. Photograph courtesy of the National Cotton Council of America.

FIGURE 13.14

A lap composed of slivers is passed through a comb that combs out short fibers. The output of the comb is formed again into a sliver. (Not all fibers are combed.) Photograph courtesy of the National Cotton Council of America.

Within the card sliver is a substantial proportion of fibers with hooked ends. These hooks are formed as the fibers are moved along by the carding machinery. Their presence reduces the effective length of the fiber, and if these hooks are not removed, the yarns produced will be weaker. Subsequent drawing steps help to eliminate some hooks.

Carded slivers are drawn twice following carding. Combed slivers are drawn once before combing and twice more after combing.

Roving. The sliver is fed to a machine called the *roving frame*. Here, the strands of fiber are elongated still more by a series of rollers. As they are wound on the bobbins, they are given a slight twist. The product of the roving frame, an elongated, slightly twisted strand of fibers, is called the *roving*. (See Figures 13.15, 13.16, 13.17, and 13.18.)

Fiber Preparation by the Woolen System

A wide range of wool types, but generally the shorter fiber varieties, can be spun on the woolen system. Manufactured staple fibers can be blended with the wool fibers and spun on the woolen system as well.

After cleaning, the fibers are blended, a small amount of oil is added to the fiber to facilitate processing, and the fibers are carded. The carded web is divided into strips by a *condenser*, following which a slight amount of twist is introduced by subjecting the strips to a rubbing motion to form rovings. Final twist and yarn formation are subsequently imparted, usually on a ring spinner. Some authors prefer to call

FIGURE 13.15

Sliver, pulled from large cans, is fed into the roving frame. Photograph courtesy of the National Cotton Council of America.

FIGURE 13.16

On the roving frame, fibers are twisted slightly and drawn into a smaller strand. Photograph courtesy of American Textile Manufacturers Institute.

FIGURE 13.17

Sliver that has been given some twist is wound onto bobbins. Textile plants that use open-end or air-jet spinning do not need the roving process. Open-end and air-jet machines spin yarn directly from the card sliver. Photograph courtesy of the American Textile Manufacturers Institute.

FIGURE 13.18

Roving is fed to ring spinning frame where it is drawn out to final size, twisted into yarn, and wound on bobbins. Photograph courtesy of the American Textile Manufacturers Institute.

the woolen system the "condenser system" because fibers other than wool are often prepared by this system.

Woolen yarns are soft and bulky. They have many fiber ends on the surface of the yarn, giving them a fuzzy appearance and hand. This results from omission of the drawing-out processes that would have straightened the fibers. Woolen yarns are weak and have poor abrasion resistance.

Fiber Preparation by the Worsted System

The worsted system is used for longer varieties of wool and can also be used for manufactured staple fibers in appropriate lengths. If wool fiber is being processed, it is cleaned and then processed either dry or with oil added to lubricate the fibers. Carding is followed by preparation of fibers for combing. Before combing, the fibers are subjected to *gilling* (comparable to drawing out). The fibers pass through gill boxes in which pins control the movement of short fibers and minimize the development of unevenness in slivers while also assisting in straightening of fibers. Slivers are subjected to three gillings, after which they are combed, gilled again, drawn, and, finally, spun.

Worsted yarns are smooth, sleek, and compact in appearance, with few fiber ends on the surface of the yarn. Their strength is better than that of woolen yarns and their hand is crisper. Figure 13.19 provides a comparison of woolen and worsted yarns.

The *semiworsted system* is a variation of worsted spinning that omits combing. Yarns produced are not as smooth, lean, or lustrous as worsted yarns, but processing is cheaper.

Processing of Flax Fibers

The length of flax fibers requires that they be processed somewhat differently from either wool or cotton. The final cleaning of flax is accomplished by a hackling machine, a device that has a revolving belt set with pins that remove short fibers, entangled fibers, and vegetable matter. The pins bring the linen fibers into alignment.

Flax fibers that are comparable to carded fiber after hackling are referred to as *tow* or *hackled fibers*; those comparable to combed fibers are referred to as *line* or *well-hackled fibers*. The same terms are applied to the yarns made from these fibers. Table 13.2 summarizes the terms used in referring to combed and carded yarns from different fibers and some of the properties of the yarns.

FIGURE 13.19

Diagrams of: (a) yarn spun on the woolen system; (b) yarn spun on the worsted system. Illustrations courtesy of the American Wool Council.

A

B

TABLE 13.2
Terms and Characteristics of Combed and Carded Yarns

	Carded Yarn	Combed Yarn
Term for:		
Flax	Tow or hackled yarn	Line or well-hackled yarn
Wool	Woolen yarn	Worsted yarn
Cotton and other staple fibers	Carded yarn	Combed yarn
Properties		
Appearance	Rough	Smooth
Hairiness	High	Low
Strength	Lower	Higher
Twist	Lower	Higher

The processes used in preparing flax fiber for spinning are intended to take advantage of the strength and luster of these long fibers. Precise steps vary, depending on whether tow or line fibers are being handled. Also, either a wet or dry processing can be utilized. Wet processing produces the finest, strongest, and smoothest yarns.

Figure 13.20 compares steps in the major yarn preparation processes.

Insertion of Twist into Yarn

The aforementioned systems for preparation of fibers for spinning are preliminary to the final yarn formation. A variety of different means can be used to join fibers together to form a yarn. Some of these yarn-forming methods are well established, others are beginning to be used commercially, while still others are in various stages of noncommercial research and development.

The predominant commercial systems of yarn formation are ring spinning and open-end spinning. The following text summarizes the methods of spinning that are now used or that are likely to be commercialized in the near future. The major focus of discussion is ring and open-end spinning because of their dominant position in the industry.

Ring Spinning

The ring spinner is made up of the following parts:

1. Spools on which the roving is wound
2. A series of drafting rollers through which the roving passes
3. A guiding ring or eyelet
4. A stationary ring around the spindle
5. A traveler—a small, U-shaped clip on the ring
6. A spindle
7. A bobbin

The roving is fed from the spool through the drafting rollers. The rollers elongate the roving, which passes through the eyelet, moving down and through the traveler. The traveler moves freely around the stationary ring. The spindle turns the bobbin at a constant speed. This turning of the bobbin and the movement of the traveler

FIGURE 13.20

Comparison of the steps in the major yarn preparation systems.

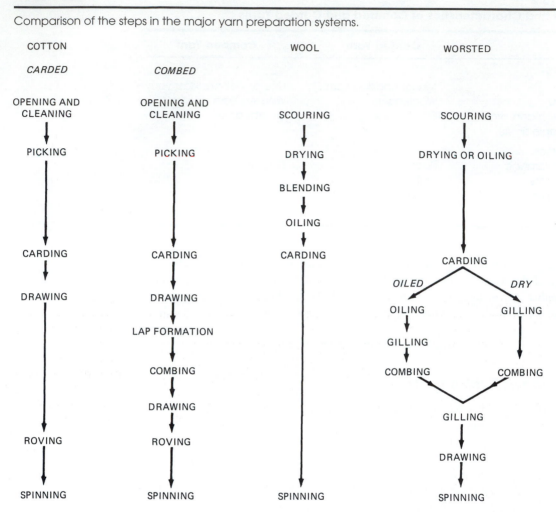

impart the twist to the yarn. The yarn is twisted and wound onto a bobbin in one operation. (See Figures 13.21 and 13.22.)

Bobbins must be removed from the machine when full, a process called *doffing*. From here, bobbins are transported to a *winding* machine where yarn is wound onto packages. Automated systems for doffing and winding have been developed and are widely used. Winding is considered an important step. It provides an opportunity to *condition* yarn, that is, to bring the yarn into equilibrium with the moisture in the atmosphere, and to add wax or other coatings that will facilitate weaving. Winding also allows the identification of flaws in the yarn and formation of larger yarn packages than the spindles on the spinning frame.

The ring spinning technique produces finer and stronger yarns than can be made on other competing processes. However, by the 1960s the rotation speed of the spindle [which began at 4,000 revolutions per minute (rpm)] seemed to have reached an upper limit at about 12,000 rpm. At higher speeds the traveler burns and must be replaced frequently. These maximum speed limitations gave impetus to the development of alternate twisting systems that operated at higher speeds. Although ring spinning continued to hold an important place in the production of yarns, other systems, most notably the open-end spinning systems, seemed likely to replace ring spinning

FIGURE 13.21

Ring spinner.

FIGURE 13.22

Ring spinning machine in operation. Note the cones of roving at the top of the machine. The filled bobbins of spun yarn are being removed automatically at the center of the picture with new bobbins at the bottom ready to be moved into position for spinning. Photograph courtesy of Zinser Textilmaschinen GmbH.

for certain sizes and types of yarns. Recently, ring spinning has made a comeback, however, for the following reasons. Japanese manufacturers of spinning machinery were able to improve ring spinning technology so that maximum speeds have increased to 21,000 rpm. Demand for finer-count yarns has increased in the last several years. Increased automation and improved quality control have helped to lower costs of manufacturing.

Open-End Spinning

Because of the speed limitations in ring spinning, researchers concentrated on developing techniques for inserting twist into yarns that would permit more rapid production. A result of this search was the introduction, in the 1960s, of the *open-end spinning machine*, which operated at higher speeds but produced a yarn with slightly different characteristics than conventional ring-spun yarns.

Open-end spinning omits the step of forming the roving. Instead, a sliver of fibers is fed into the spinner by a stream of air. Figure 13.23 shows an open-end spinner of the rotor type and describes its operation. The sliver is delivered to a rotary beater that separates the fibers into a thin stream. It is carried into the rotor by a current of air through a duct and is deposited in a V-shaped groove along the outer edge of the rotor. Twist is provided by the turning of the rotor.

Fibers fed to the rotor are incorporated into the rapidly rotating "open end" of a previously formed yarn that extends out of the delivery tube; hence, the name open-end spinning. As the fibers join the yarn, which is constantly being pulled out of the delivery tube, twist from the movement of the rotor is conveyed to the fibers. A constant stream of new fibers enters the rotor, is distributed in the groove, and is removed at the end of the formed yarn, becoming part of the yarn itself.

The fineness of the yarn is determined by the rate at which it is drawn out of the rotor relative to the rate at which fibers are being fed into the rotor. In other words, if fewer fibers are being fed in while fibers are being withdrawn rapidly, a thinner yarn will result, and vice versa. The twist is determined by the ratio of the rotor turning speed to the linear or withdrawal speed of the yarn (that is, the higher the speed of the rotor, the greater the twist).

FIGURE 13.23

Open-end spinner. The fibers are separated into a thin stream by a rotary beater. The fibers moved by an air stream enter the rotor and through centrifugal force are carried in a V-shaped groove. The fibers are drawn off from the groove to become attached to the open end of an already formed yarn. The rotor produces the twist. From S. Backer, "Yarn," *Scientific American* (December) 1972. Artist: Dan Todd.

Theoretically, a variety of different means may be used to form the yarn and insert twist. These have been divided into the following categories: mechanical spinning (of which rotor spinning is an example), electrostatic spinning, fluid spinning, air spinning, and friction spinning. Of these, only rotor and friction open-end spinning machines have been commercialized, and most of the open-end spinning machines now in use are of the mechanical rotor spinning type. Friction open-end spinning machines are also available.

Friction spinning systems use friction to insert twist. A mixture of air and fibers is fed to the surface of a moving, perforated drum. Suction holds the fibers against the surface while a second drum rotates in the opposite direction. Twist is inserted and the yarn begins forming as the fibers pass between the two drums. The newly forming yarn is added to the open end of an already formed yarn, and the completed yarn is continuously drawn away. (See Figure 13.24.)

The advantages of open-end spinning are that it increases the speed of production, eliminates the step of drawing out the roving before spinning, and permits finished yarns to be wound on any sized bobbin or spool. (See Figure 13.25.) As a result, it is less expensive. It produces yarns of more even diameter than does ring spinning. Yarns are more uniform in diameter, bulkier, rougher, more absorbent, and less variable in strength than are ring-spun yarns.

Fabrics made from open-end spun yarns compared with ring-spun yarns are more uniform and more opaque in appearance, lower in strength, less likely to pill, and inferior in crease recovery. A number of sources indicated that they are more subject to abrasion.

Neither friction nor rotor spinning will produce yarns as fine and strong as ring-spun yarns, although recent advances have extended the range of yarn sizes possible. Open-end spun yarns have a handle that has been characterized as "harsh." Some of the kinds of products that seem to be especially well suited to the use of open-end spun yarns are in filling yarns for fabrics where yarn strength is not a factor, toweling pile yarns, denim, and heavier weights of bed sheeting. The yarns' even surface makes them desirable as base fabrics for plastic-coated materials. On the other hand, the more acceptable feel of ring-spun yarns has led knitwear manufacturers to prefer them, and they are better for fine blends of polyester and cotton.

FIGURE 13.24

DREF-2 spinning system. The DREF-2 system utilizes friction as the means of inserting twist. Drawing courtesy of Fehrer AG.

FIGURE 13.25

Room equipped with open-end spinning machines. Compare this photograph to Figure 13.22 and note that fibers are fed directly from the cans to the machine and that it is not necessary to mount spools of roving on the machine. Photograph courtesy of the American Textile Manufacturers Institute.

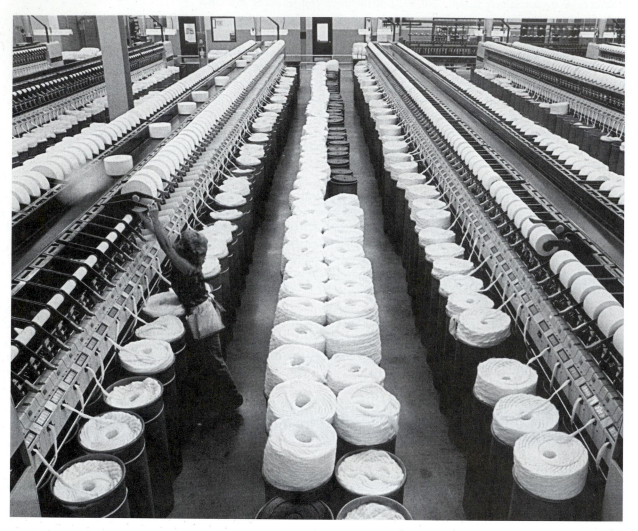

PLY YARNS

Ply yarns are made from two or more single yarns that are twisted together. Ply yarns are much more expensive than single yarns but are nevertheless often produced to achieve certain benefits. Ply yarns made from identical single yarns are more regular in diameter and are stronger. Ply yarns are often made to achieve particular decorative effects.

In general, the steps involved in creating ply yarns include:

1. Winding single yarns and clearing any flaws
2. Placing the required number of component yarns alongside each other, in place, ready for supplying to the machine

3. Insertion of twist to form the ply yarn by any of a number of different machines

4. Winding the finished yarn on a cone or package for delivery to the customer

A number of different machines are used in making ply yarns, which may also be referred to as *folded yarns*. Ring-folding machines, for example, operate on the same principle as ring-spinning machines except that instead of a roving being fed to the traveler, the single yarns to be combined are both fed together for twisting.

A variant on this process is *Sirospun yarn*. To strengthen worsted warp yarns sufficiently to withstand the stresses of weaving, the yarns generally must be *two-folded* or double ply. Instead of feeding two single yarns into the spinning system, two rovings are fed into the ring-spinning machine. Naturally occurring variations in the density of fiber strands and in tension cause randomly inserted levels of twist to be incorporated. The end result, Sirospun yarn, is similar to a single yarn yet has enough of the characteristics of a ply yarn to be satisfactory for weaving.

OTHER METHODS OF MANUFACTURING YARNS

In addition to ring and open-end spinning, techniques that insert true twist into yarn, there are other types of yarn construction. Three of those that have some current commercial application are described in the following sections: false-twist, or self-twist, spinning; yarn wrapping; and splitting or slitting films made from synthetic polymers. The viability of these processes for commercial purposes varies.

False-Twist, or Self-Twist, Spinning

Self-twist spinning, also called false-twist spinning, is used to make ply yarns. In this process two rovings are used. Each one is passed through a pair of rollers that are both rotating and oscillating. Each set of rollers twists its roving in a direction opposite to the other. The uneven motion of the rollers forms a yarn that has both twisted and untwisted areas. Adjacent ends of the two yarns are allowed to untwist around each other. (See Figure 13.26.) Care must be taken to space the untwisted areas of each yarn in such a way that a loosely twisted section of one yarn never coincides with a loosely twisted section of the other yarn, or a weak spot would result.

FIGURE 13.26

Self-twist spinning. Two separate rovings are fed between a pair of rollers that move both forward and side-to-side. The twisted rovings, each with opposite directional twist, when placed side-by-side twist around each other to form a ply yarn. From S. Backer, "Yarn," *Scientific American* (December) 1972. Artist: Dan Todd.

FIGURE 13.27

Diagram of the structure of a fasciated yarn.

Self-twist yarns can, of course, be used only in those fabrics that require two-ply yarns. The process also requires that fiber lengths not be too short. Wool and long-staple manufactured fibers are especially suitable.

Yarn Wrapping

Yarns can be made from a bundle of parallel fibers held in place by surface wrapping of other staple or filament fibers. The first of these wrapped yarns were made by DuPont and were called *fasciated yarns.* (See Figure 13.27.) The term derives from the Latin word *fasces,* meaning "a bundle of rods wrapped with ribbons." Such yarns are no longer made by DuPont; however, wrapped or covered yarns, similar in concept, are being produced.

Air-Jet Spinning

The Murata Company, a Japanese firm, has commercialized an air-jet spinning machine that functions as follows. A largely untwisted sliver is fed into the machine. Two nozzles, each forcing an air jet against the sliver from opposite directions, cause fibers from the outer layer of the sliver to wrap around the interior fibers, thereby forming the yarn. (See Figure 13.28.)

Hollow Spindle Spinning

In hollow spindle spinning, a sliver of core fibers is fed through a hollow spindle where it is wrapped by a filament yarn unwinding from the spindle.

An interesting application of the technique has been in the manufacture of towels and other fabrics, in which the wrapped yarns are used in the pile. In this instance,

FIGURE 13.28

Diagram of Murata jet spinner for wrap spinning.

Sliver Delivery

1st Jet

2nd Jet

the wrapping yarn is made from soluble polyvinyl alcohol (PVA) fibers. After the fabric has been put through the finishing processes, these yarns dissolve, leaving a soft, all-cotton twistless and absorbent yarn in the pile. Figure 13.29 illustrates the differences in appearance of ring-spun and wrap-spun yarns.

Core Spinning

Core-spun yarns are usually made with a continuous filament core surrounded by twisted fibers or other yarns. (See Figure 11.2, page 215.) Recently, core-spun yarns

a

b

c

d

FIGURE 13.29

Comparison of ring-spun and wrap-spun yarns: (a) ring-spun yarns; (b) wrap-spun yarns with soluble filament wrapping; (c) plain weave fabric of ring-spun yarns; (d) plain weave fabric of wrap-spun yarns with filament wrapping dissolved. Microphotographs courtesy of G. F. Ruppenicker, personal communication.

with a staple core of one fiber and an outer sheath of another fiber have been produced by an adaptation of ring spinning. Two rovings, one of polyester and one of cotton, are fed through drafting rollers and then pass through separate channels before being wound on the spindle. The channel for the cotton sheath is longer, ensuring that it will wrap around the polyester core as the twist is inserted. Fabrics from staple core yarns are more durable and have more easy-care features than those of 100 percent cotton yarns.

Making Yarns from Films

Recently, various new techniques have emerged that allow yarns to be formed directly from synthetic polymers without the formation of fibers or the twisting of fibers into yarns. These processes include the formation of yarns by the split-film and slit-film processes. Slit-film yarns could be classified as monofilaments. Yarns made by the split-film process do not fit neatly into the categories of staple or filament yarns.

Split Films

In the creation of yarns by the *split-film* technique, a sheet of polymer is formed. The formed sheet is drawn in the lengthwise direction. Through drawing, the molecules in the polymer are oriented in the direction of the draw, causing the film to be strengthened in the lengthwise direction and weakened in the crosswise direction. This causes a breakdown of the film into a mass of interconnected fibers, most of which are aligned in the direction of the drawing, but some of which also connect in the crosswise direction. The process is known as *fibrillation*. (See Figure 13.30.)

The fibrillated materials can be twisted into strings or twines or other coarse, yarnlike materials. The usefulness of split-film yarns is limited because the yarns created are coarse. Olefins are made into split-film yarns for use in making bags, sacks, ropes, and other industrial products.

Slit Films

Slit films are made by cutting film into narrow, ribbonlike sections. Depending upon the process used for cutting and drawing the film, the tapes may display some degree

FIGURE 13.30

Film fibrillation.

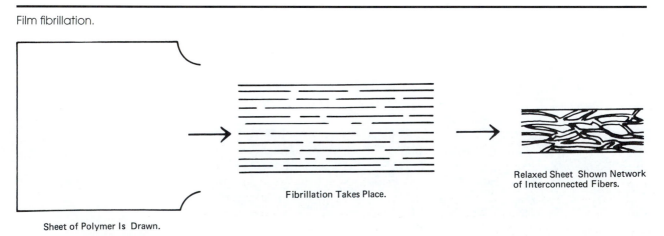

Sheet of Polymer Is Drawn.

Fibrillation Takes Place.

Relaxed Sheet Shown Network of Interconnected Fibers.

of fibrillation, like that described for split films. When tapes are made that do not fibrillate, they are flatter and are more suitable for certain uses. Flat tapes are used as warp yarns in weaving and can be made into carpet backings that will be very stable, remaining flat and even. All types of tape yarns are used in making wall coverings, packaging materials, carpet backing, and as a replacement for jute in bags and sacks.

Lurex®, a flat, ribbonlike yarn with a metallic appearance, is a slit film yarn that is often used to add decorative touches to apparel or household textiles. Lurex® is made from single or multiple layers of polyester film. Multilayered types are made by placing a layer of aluminum foil between two layers of polyester film. Monoply types are cut from metallized polyester film, protected by a clear or colored resin coating. The natural color of Lurex® is silver. Other colors are produced by adding pigments to the lacquer coating or to the bonding adhesive. The width of these yarns ranges from 0.069 to 0.010 inch. The manufacturer claims that the use of polyester film yields a strong, flexible yarn that can be woven or knitted without support, but notes that these yarns are decorative rather than functional.

BLENDS

Blending is the process of mixing fibers together. As noted earlier, it can take place at any of several points during the preparation of a yarn. The purposes of blending are (1) the thorough intermixing of fibers and/or (2) combining fibers with different properties to produce yarns with characteristics that cannot be obtained by using one type of fiber alone. Self-blending of bales of the same fiber is done routinely in processing natural fibers because the fibers may vary from bale to bale. In this type of blending, the mixing of as many bales as possible is done early in the processes preparatory to spinning so that the subsequent steps can help to mix the fiber still more completely.

For the same reasons, even when two or more different fiber types are combined, blending is done as early as possible. Carding helps to break up fiber clusters and intermix fibers more thoroughly. However, if the fibers being blended require different techniques for opening, cleaning, and carding, as with polyester and cotton, then slivers can be blended. For blended yarns of different fibers, the *blend level* is the percentage by weight of each fiber.

Blending is not limited to staple-length fibers. Filament fibers of different generic types can be combined into a single yarn. This can be done either by extruding these fibers side by side, during drawing, or during texturing.

As described earlier, a blended yarn can be core spun with one fiber at the center and a different fiber as the covering or be wrapped with one fiber making up the central section and another the wrapping yarn. As yarn spinning and texturing technologies grow more sophisticated, we expand the possibilities of combining several different fibers into one yarn. Multiple-input texturing machines can produce specialty yarn blends.

It should be noted that fabrics woven from two or more yarns each made of different fibers are not considered blends. These fabrics are, instead, called *combination fabrics*. They do not behave in the same way as those fabrics in which the fibers are more intimately blended and may require special care procedures. Regrettably, the Textile Fibers Products Identification Act (TFPIA) labeling requirements do not distinguish between blended fabrics and combination fabrics when fiber percentage contents of fabrics are given. (See Figure 6.4, page 153.)

Properties of Blended Yarns

Fibers with different characteristics, blended into a yarn, can each contribute desirable properties to the final textile material. The ultimate performance is an average of the properties of the component fibers. For example, a fabric of 50 percent cotton and 50 percent polyester would have an absorbency intermediate between that of cotton or polyester. In some cases, however, the observed fabric property is not determined simply by the relative amounts of each fiber in the blend. In blends of nylon with cotton, the tenacity of the blended yarn initially decreases with increasing amounts of nylon because of differences in the breaking elongation of the two fibers. At the breaking elongation of the cotton fibers, the nylon fibers are not assuming their share of the stress, leaving the cotton to bear the load.

The stage at which blending occurs also affects the properties of the fabrics. In general, the more intimate the mixing of fibers in the blends, the better the resulting properties. Yarns blended at the fiber stage exhibit a more effective averaging of properties than ply-blended yarns.

Even though considerable study and evaluation have been made of optimum fiber proportions required to achieve desired results in blends, no certain conclusions have been reached. It is clear that extremely small proportions of fibers have no appreciable influence on performance, although they may have some effect on appearance.

EFFECTS OF YARN STRUCTURE ON FABRIC PERFORMANCE

As noted in chapter 2, fabric behavior is affected by the interaction of the characteristics of the fibers used, the yarn structure, fabric construction, and special finishes. *Durability*, *appearance*, and *comfort* of textile fabrics are much affected by the types of yarns that are used.

Durability Factors

Yarn strength is of primary importance in determining ultimate fabric strength. Yarn strength is due not only to the inherent strength of the fibers in the yarn but also to the yarn structure. Filament yarns are stronger than spun yarns because all of these continuous fibers are contributing to yarn strength. The yarn breaks when the fibers are ruptured. Spun yarns, which are held together by their twist, are broken by breaking some fibers and by overcoming the twist frictional force holding the fibers together. This takes less force than breaking all the fibers in a comparable filament yarn. As twist is increased in spun yarns, the strength increases (up to a point) because the increased frictional force between fibers prevents slipping. Overtwisting, however, will decrease strength due to increased strain in the yarn. Coarser yarns can withstand tensile forces better than finer yarns and normally contribute more to fabric strength.

The elongation and recovery of fabrics are important in determining their end use and performance. Fabrics that stretch and recover are comfortable and are especially appropriate in products such as hosiery or swimwear. In order to produce yarns with maximum elongation, elastomeric fibers such as spandex or rubber that stretch up to five times their length (500 percent) and then recover can be used. Filament yarns can be textured to provide stretch.

Resistance to abrasion is determined by the ability of a material to absorb the energy applied during abrasion. A number of textile properties affect the resistance of a fabric to abrasion, yarn construction being one. Loosely twisted yarns abrade more easily than do tightly twisted yarns. In the loosely twisted yarns individual fibers are more likely to be plucked out of the fabric surface.

Appearance

Drape and hand, wrinkle resistance, dimensional stability, and covering power all contribute to satisfaction with the appearance of textile products. *Drape* refers to the ability of fabric to form pleasing folds when bent under its own weight. Drape is improved by yarn structures that allow movement or bending within the fabric. Twist also affects the bending of yarns. Highly twisted yarns bend more easily because the fibers are oriented at a sharper angle to the yarn length. This behavior is especially apparent in crepe yarns, which are highly twisted. True crepe fabrics, those made from crepe yarns, have high drapability.

Fabric hand refers to the "tactile sensations or impressions that arise when fabrics are touched, squeezed, rubbed, or otherwise handled" (AATCC 1997, 376). Hand is an important consideration in consumer selection and acceptance of apparel fabrics. Like drape and other properties, it is a complex phenomenon involving a number of different fabric characteristics. One important factor in the assessment of hand is the smoothness of the material. Filament yarns and fine-combed spun yarns feel smoother than textured or crepe yarns. In addition, a fabric that compresses easily and recovers from compression or squeezing will feel soft. This feeling is enhanced by resilient fibers and high-bulk yarns that are not compact.

Yarn properties must be considered in relation to wrinkle recovery. When a crease forms in woven or knitted fabric, the yarns bend. The fibers in the outer side of the yarn are strained, while those on the inner side are compressed. Yarn stiffness, or resistance to bending, is related to twist and size. In looser yarn structures, with lower twist, fibers are freer to move to relieve the stresses of bending. They will, therefore, bend relatively easily. In more tightly twisted yarns the frictional forces within the yarn tend to keep fibers from shifting position, and they tend to return to their original configuration and resist wrinkling. As described earlier, however, overtwisted yarns bend more easily. The most flexible yarn of all should be one in which filaments are combined with little or no twist. The least flexible yarns should be those in which the fibers are bonded together by an adhesive or fused by heat or chemical means.

Yarn size affects stiffness as well. Heavier yarns resist wrinkling more than finer yarns. Yarn size can be increased by putting a larger number of fibers into a yarn, by using fibers of larger diameter, or by plying several yarns. Extremely fine fibers, even in coarse yarns, however, reduce resistance to bending.

The terms *covering power* and *cover factor* refer to both the optical and geometric properties of fabrics. *Optical covering power* is the ability of the fabric to hide what is placed under it. Fiber characteristics affect the optical covering power. So too does yarn structure. Smaller-diameter yarns or smoother yarns cover less well, depending on how tightly packed the yarns are in the fabric structure.

Comfort Factors

Heat transfer is the transfer of heat energy from a generating body to the surrounding atmosphere. Textile fabrics can provide resistance to heat transfer from a body, or in the case of some interior furnishings, from buildings. As noted earlier, trapped air keeps heat near the body. Yarn structure and its related property of fabric thickness are extremely important in determining the thermal comfort of fabrics. A spun yarn or textured filament yarn entraps more air than a flat filament yarn and therefore offers more resistance to heat transfer. The degree of twist also affects thermal comfort, as the higher twist yarns hold less air volume.

Air permeability is the ability of air to pass through a fabric. Where openings between yarns or between fibers within yarns are large, a good deal of air will pass through the fabric. Conversely, when compact yarns are packed tightly into fabrics, with little air space between them, the flow of air through the fabric is diminished. It follows, then, that closely woven fabrics with compact, tightly twisted yarns have lower permeability.

Yarns contribute to fabric softness. Loosely twisted yarns and many novelty yarns have rougher surfaces that decrease the smoothness of fabrics. Filament yarns are generally smoother than spun yarns. Sheets made of filament silk yarns are softer and more luxurious than those of staple linen or cotton fibers.

TABLE 13.3
Properties of Staple, Filament, and Textured Yarns

Property	Staple	Flat Filament	Textured Filament
Appearance and hand	Dull, fuzzy	Lustrous, smooth	Dull, rough
Tenacity	Lowest	Highest	High
Elongation	Low	Lowest	Higher
Bulk	Medium to high, depending on twist	Low	High
Pilling	Can be high	Low	Low
Snagging	Low	High	Highest

Note: Comparison assumes that other factors such as fiber content and yarn size are constant.

Putting it all together for . . .

Tire Cord

As the summary discussion of the effects of yarn structure on fabric performance indicates, the selection of textiles with particular end uses must take into account the properties contributed by the various components of the structure. Tire cords are manufactured to exhibit specific properties, and selection of fiber and yarn features is important in providing optimum performance. This is the first of a series of case studies that looks at the performance characteristics of a particular textile product, and is presented here as an example of how the properties of each component, fiber and yarn, must be carefully selected.

Tensile Properties

Perhaps the most important property one thinks of for tire cords is strength. Cords in tires are embedded in the rubber matrix to reinforce it. As noted in the ASTM test method for tire cords from manufactured fibers, "the force-bearing ability of a reinforced rubber product is related to the strength of the yarn or cord used as a reinforcing material" (ASTM 1998, 243).

In most tires currently produced, both manufactured fiber and steel cords are used. Steel is known for its strength, but it is also heavier than the synthetic fibers and rayon. Therefore, tires are not reinforced with steel cords alone, but also with high-tenacity polyester, nylon, aramid, or rayon fibers. The steel cords are placed parallel to the tread, so they can aid in bearing the load as the tire turns. Polyester and nylon are the most commonly used nonsteel fibers, and a number of fiber manufacturers make versions of these fibers specifically for tire cords. The extremely high-strength fibers such as para-aramid or PBO are not ordinarily used, primarily because of cost. High-tenacity rayon is still used by one tire manufacturer.

Two other tensile properties, modulus and elongation, are also important in tire performance. Higher-modulus fibers, which resist initial tensile forces better, are preferred. This is one reason many tire producers have replaced nylon with polyester in the body of most tires.

Tire cords should also resist elongation so that they are dimensionally stable. One fiber manufacturer currently produces dimensionally stable polyester (DSP) specifically for tire cords. In high-performance tires for high-speed vehicles, however, nylon plies are placed around the bottom and sides of the steel cords. The nylon yarns have heat higher shrinkage than polyester and will compress the tire area that is reinforced with steel. This section of the tire is then better able to withstand the radial forces generated at high speeds.

The yarn structure and type are selected to maximize the strength of tire cords. As the name implies, a cord structure is best, because it is stronger than single-yarn structures. The yarns are ply twisted and then the plies are twisted to form a cord. In some tires, two-ply yarns can be used and smaller tires may even have "monoplies." The yarn structure affects the quality of the tire. All tire cords are made from filament yarns, which are much stronger than staple yarns. The yarns are twisted to increase strength.

Size also affects strength and tire cords are large (often 500 tex and above) compared to most yarns used for apparel or home furnishings. It is not desirable, however, to use large yarns, because the surface area for bonding to the rubber will be decreased.

Linear Density

The weight per length, or linear density, of fibers used in tire cords affects the weight of the tire. This precludes reinforcement of tires entirely with steel cords. Steel fibers have a specific gravity of about 7.8, over five times that of polyester and nylon. Nylon has a slightly lower density than polyester or rayon, giving it some advantage.

Adhesion

Since tire cords are used to make the rubber tires stronger and more resistant to force, it is important for the cords to adhere to the rubber. Good adhesion results in better transmission of the applied forces to the reinforcing material, in this case the steel or

manufactured fiber cords. Textile tire cords have an advantage over steel because they have a larger surface area for bonding. In common manufacturing processes, the textile cords are woven into a sheet and dipped into an adhesive, and then heated to set their length and minimize shrinkage. A good coating of the fibers by the adhesive helps to stabilize them and decrease elongation. The rougher surface of the twisted and/or plied filament fibers increases the penetration and pickup of the adhesive, which is usually a *latex*, or water emulsion.

SUMMARY

Fibers and yarns are the basic building blocks of most fabrics. Predictions about the performance of textile products, however, also require knowledge about the contributions of fabric structure and special finishes to the end products. Although one or more components of textiles may have a powerful influence on the end product, none of the various constituents can function alone.

References

AATCC. 1997. *Technical manual.* Research Triangle Park, N.C.: American Association of Textile Chemists and Colorists.

ASTM. 1998. *Annual book of ASTM standards.* West Conshohocken, Pa.: American Society for Testing and Materials.

Born, W. 1939. The Indian hand-spinning wheel. *CIBA Review* 28 (December): 988.

Demir, A., and H. M. Behery. 1997. *Synthetic filament yarn texturing technology.* Upper Saddle River, N.J.: Prentice Hall.

Potter, M. D., and P. B. Corbman. 1967. *Textiles, fiber to fabric.* New York: McGraw-Hill.

Wilson, D. K., and T. Kollu. 1987. The production of textured yarns by methods other than the false-twist technique. *Textile Progress* 16 (3).

Review Questions

1. Describe the steps in hand spinning that are required to form a yarn. What is the purpose of each step? Which of these steps are also used in mechanized spinning?

2. What are the differences between filament and staple yarns? single, ply, and cord yarns? simple and fancy or novelty yarns? thread and yarn? S and Z twist yarns?

3. What differences would you expect to find between low-twist and high-twist yarns?

4. How do direct and indirect yarn numbering systems differ?

5. What are the differences between bulk and stretch textured yarns? What properties of manufactured fibers are used in texturing yarn?

6. Compare the steps in the cotton spinning system, the woolen spinning system, and the worsted spinning system.

7. For what types of end uses are open-end spun yarns best suited. Why?

8. What is the purpose of blending fibers? What are some of the factors that affect the properties of blended yarns?

9. How does yarn structure contribute to:
    strength
    abrasion resistance
    comfort
    wrinkle recovery
    softness

Recommended Readings

1990. An introduction to textile technology: Yarn manufacturing-spun yarns. *JTN*, 423 (February): 98.

Backer, S. 1993. Staple fibers-the story of blends. Part 2: Development and the future. In D. Brunnschweiler and J. W. S. Hearle, eds. *Polyester—50 years of achievement*, 94. Manchester, England: The Textile Institute.

Barella, A. 1993. The hairiness of yarn. *Textile Progress* 24 (3).

Catling, H. 1983. A history of spinning and weaving. *Textiles* 12 (Spring): 20.

Dyson, E., ed. 1975. *Rotor spinning: Technical and economic aspects.* New Mills, Stockport, U.K.: Textile Trade Press.

Floyd, K. L. 1988. Carding. *Textiles* 17 (2): 34.

Goswami, B. C., J. G. Martindale, and F. L. Scardino. 1977. *Textile yarns: Technology, structure and applications.* New York: Wiley.

Horridge, P., and S. Khan. 1994. Physical properties of cotton-wool blend fabrics. *American Dyestuff Reporter* 83 (July): 38.

Ishida, T. 1990. An introduction to textile technology: Yarn manufacturing—filament yarns. *JTN*, 424 (March): 98.

Krause, H. W. 1985. Staple fiber spinning systems. *Journal of the Textile Institute* 76 (2): 185–195.

Nikolic, M., J. Cerkvenic, and Z. Stejepanovic. 1993. Formation models: Comparing yarn qualities and properties. *Textile Horizons*, December, 47.

Sawhney, A. P. S., et al. 1991. Comparison of fabrics made with cotton covered polyester staple core yarn and 100% cotton yarn. *Textile Research Journal* 61 (2): 71.

Wilson, D. K., and T. Kollu. 1991. The production of textured yarns by the false-twist technique. *Textile Progress* 21 (3).

14

WOVEN FABRICS

F abrics can be constructed in a variety of ways, ranging from the matting together of fibrous materials to the intricate interlacing of complex yarn systems. The following discussion outlines and defines the major classifications of fabric constructions. The specific techniques and processes by which these different fabrics are made are discussed in the chapters that follow.

FABRIC CONSTRUCTION METHODS

Woven Fabrics. Weaving of fabrics consists of interlacing systems of yarn. By varying the interlacings, a wide variety of different fabric constructions can be made.

Looped Fabrics. Fabrics can be constructed from one or more continuous yarns by the formation of a series of interconnected loops. Knitting, though a complex form, is one type of looping construction. Crochet is another.

Knotted Fabrics. Some fabrics are created by knotting yarns together. Lace, nets, macramé, and tatting are created by knotting.

Braided Fabrics. Fabrics may be created by plaiting together yarns or strips of fabrics. The components are interlaced in a diagonal pattern over and under one another to form a flat or tubular fabric of relatively narrow width.

Films. Since films are not made from fibers, they are not considered to be true textiles even though they are often used in products that have traditionally been made from textiles such as shower curtains or upholstery. They are sometimes laminated to textiles and therefore may be part of the structure of some textile products. They are usually synthetic polymers extruded in the form of sheets rather than as fibers. Polymer films can also be deposited on or "cast" on surfaces from solutions in a process analogous to fiber wet spinning. In some cases, these films are eventually made into fibrous form by a process called fibrillation or by cutting the sheet into fibers.

Nonwovens. Webs of fibers can be held together into a fabric by interlocking of fibers by mechanical action or by fusing fibers together with heat, adhesives, or chemicals. Examples of a few fabrics constructed by these means include spunlaced, spunbonded, and needle-punched fabrics, and bonded webs. Felt and bark cloth, older fabric making techniques, are also constructed from webs of fibers, but are not technically defined as nonwovens.

Stitch-Through Fabrics. Stitch through or stitch bonding is a relatively new technique for constructing fabrics in which two sets of yarns or masses of fibers are stitched together into a fabric structure by another set of yarns.

Textile Composites. These materials generally consist of one or more textile components impregnated with or embedded in a resin matrix. Textile composites are generally used for high-technology products for industry, the military, and aerospace.

THE CREATION OF WOVEN FABRICS

Fabrics can be woven from yarns on a simple hand loom or on a highly complex, totally automated power loom. In either case, the fabric that is produced will be made by interlacing one yarn with another. The lengthwise-direction yarns in a woven fabric are called the *warp yarns* or *ends*. Crosswise yarns are called *filling yarns, weft yarns,* or *picks*. Warp and filling yarns normally interlace with each other at right angles.

The Hand Loom

As with spinning, the principles of weaving are easily understood by reviewing the operations performed in hand weaving. Many weavers continue to practice this craft. Weaving requires that the warp yarns be held under tension. Having stretched out one set of yarns, the weaver then takes a second yarn and interlaces it with the warps. The simplest interlacing is made by moving the filling over the first warp, under the second, over the third, and under the fourth, and so on. In the second row, the filling moves under the first warp, over the second, under the third, and so on. The third row repeats the pattern of the first, and the fourth row repeats the pattern of the second row. Known as a *plain weave* or *tabby*, this is the simplest form of weaving.

The filling yarns, those running at right angles to the warps, can be introduced by hand. As the weaving process developed, weavers found it was easier either to use some device such as a needle, or to wrap the yarns around a stick. This latter method had the advantage of allowing the yarn to be unwound as the stick was moved through the warps. Ultimately, yarn was wound onto a bobbin, and the bobbin was placed into a boatlike *shuttle*. The pointed end of the shuttle allowed the carrier to move smoothly, while the bobbin allowed the yarn to unwind as it was needed.

Filling yarns tended to be somewhat loose in placement and had to be pushed into place more firmly. The earliest weavers painstakingly pushed each yarn into place with a small stick. A later, more efficient method used a wooden stick, shaped like a sword, that was slipped behind the filling yarns and pushed them tightly against the fabric that had already been woven. This weaver's sword, or batten, became a permanent part of the loom, although its shape was transformed gradually into a comblike device called a *reed* that was mounted on a frame. The frame retained the name *batten*, and a pull of the hand on the batten frame moved the reed forward, swinging the reed against the filling yarn and pushing it ("beating up") firmly into place.

At first the finished cloth was probably the same dimensions as the loom, but Egyptian fabrics of long dimensions have been found, and it is possible that they may have used a roller beam system. A beam with warp yarns wrapped around it allowed yarns to be fed continuously to the weaver, and as the fabric was woven, it was wrapped around a roller at the other end of the loom. In this way continuous lengths of fabric, longer than the loom, could be constructed.

As long as each warp yarn had to be raised by hand before the filling was interlaced with it, the process of weaving remained slow and tedious. Inventive weavers improvised a means of speeding up the procedure of raising and lowering warp yarns. Alternate rows of warps were placed over a *shed rod*, a stick that lifted them above the level of their neighboring yarns. This formation of raised and lowered warp yarns is called the *shed*. The bobbin could be thrust across the entire width of the cloth through the shed without stopping to raise each individual warp yarn. The alternate set of warp yarns was threaded through a series of string loops that were tied to another rod. This rod could raise the second set of yarns past those on the shed rod. By thrusting the bobbin under this second set of yarns that had been raised by an upward pull on the rod, the filling interlaced with an alternate set of yarns. Alternate raising and lowering of the rod made it possible to interlace warp and filling yarns quickly and efficiently. The rod that held the second set of warps was called a *harness*; the loops were called *heddles*. Variety in weave could be achieved through the use of multiple harnesses, each raising a different set of warps.

The widespread use of silk probably brought about certain improvements in loom structure. Since silk filament yarns were fine and slippery, use of the shed rods made weaving more difficult. In silk weaving, the shed rod was replaced by a second harness with heddles, as the smooth, fine yarns tended to slide against the shed rod, while the heddles held them securely.

The change from hand manipulation of harnesses to operation by foot treadle was another improvement. The loom was constructed so that pressure on a foot treadle raised and lowered the harness frame. This released the hand to operate the shuttle and the batten and increased the speed with which the weaver could work.

Probably the single most important invention that preceded automation of the loom was the flying shuttle. The *flying shuttle*, designed by John Kay and patented in 1733, was a device with a spring mechanism that threw the shuttle across the loom from one side to the other. In hand weaving, Kay's device was activated by a cord on either side of the loom that was pulled by the weaver. When the machine was mechanized, the flying shuttle was incorporated into the loom and operated mechanically.

Figure 14.1 depicts the basic hand loom that had developed by the time of the Industrial Revolution. Hand looms used by weavers today have the same type of structure.

Automation of Weaving

To transform weaving from a hand to a mechanical operation, several conditions had to be satisfied. The various motions made in hand weaving had to be automated. The *Encyclopedia of Textiles* (1980) notes that "the power loom of today is essentially the hand loom adapted to rotary driving" (p. 30). A further requirement of power looms was that a power-operated loom had to stop automatically when a warp or filling yarn had broken. If the loom continued to function, the cloth would be flawed.

The first automatic loom was devised by Edmund Cartwright in 1784. Although it had a number of defects, this loom did work well enough to demonstrate that automatic loom weaving was feasible. Gradually, inventions by different individuals each contributed to the development of an economically viable automatic loom.

FIGURE 14.1

Contemporary weaver's loom with some of the parts labeled. Loom belonging to Judy Glosten, Huntington, N.Y.

Eventually, upper limits on production speed of shuttle looms were reached. Also, shuttle looms are extremely noisy. To overcome these deficiencies, looms were invented that transported filling yarns without a shuttle. These shuttleless weaving machines are faster and less noisy than shuttle looms. Currently, their operations are monitored by computers.

MODERN WEAVING PROCESSES

Present-day looms can be divided into two major classifications: those that produce cloth in flat form and those that produce cloth in tubular form. Looms that produce flat woven cloth predominate. Flat looms can be further subdivided into two categories: (1) those that use a shuttle to transport filling yarns and (2) shuttleless weaving machines, those that use some other means for carrying the filling from side to side.

Preliminary Steps

Preparing the Warp Yarns for Weaving

Before their use on the loom, warp and filling yarns must be prepared for weaving. The essential characteristics of suitable warp and filling yarns differ. Warp yarns undergo greater stress and abrasion during weaving than do filling yarns; therefore, warp yarns must be strong enough to withstand these pressures. Warp yarns must be clean, free from knots, and uniform in size. A single warp yarn is called an *end*.

Warp yarns are wound onto the warp beam from many cylindrical packages of yarn which are called *cheeses*. (See Figure 14.2.) To strengthen and lubricate warp yarns, sizing or *slashing* is added. Size is made up of starches or synthetic polymers such as polyvinyl alcohol (PVA) that act as lubricants. The yarns are passed from one warp beam through a solution of sizing material. The sized yarns are dried immediately after treatment and are wound onto another warp beam. Sizing is not always required on filament yarn warps.

The warp beam containing the sized yarns is placed on the loom. In preparation for weaving, each warp end (yarn) must be threaded through its own drop wire, heddle eye, and reed dent. The *drop wire* is a device that will stop the loom if an end should break, the *heddle eye* is the opening in a heddle that carries the yarn, and the *reed dent* is an opening in the reed, the comblike device that will push each filling yarn close against the completed fabric.

Placing the warp yarns on the loom is done either by *drawing-in* or by *tying-in*. If warp yarns from a previously woven fabric are in place and if that fabric had the same number of warps, the new warps are tied into place by attaching them to the warps already on the loom.

If the new warp is different from that previously woven or if there is no warp on the loom, then the warps must be drawn-in. To draw-in or tie-in each end by hand would be enormously time consuming; therefore, a variety of machines has been developed for drawing-in. A separate machine can be used for each step (that is, drawing through the drop wire, the heddle eye, and the reed dent), or one machine can perform all three steps. When a loom makes the same fabric, warp after warp, the new warp can be tied-in to the old.

Heddle wires are held in frames called *harnesses*. The number of harnesses required for the loom is determined by the weave.

FIGURE 14.2

Warp beam being prepared from several hundred "cheeses" of yarn. Photograph courtesy of the National Cotton Council of America.

Preparing the Filling Yarns for Weaving

Yarn that is to be used for the filling must be packaged in some form that allows it to be unwound easily for transport through the shed. In shuttle looms the device that carries the yarn across the shed is called a shuttle and is made up of a wooden carrier into which a *quill*, or *pirn*, is placed. (See Figure 14.3.) The filling yarn is wound onto the quills from larger packages of yarn. For shuttleless looms this step of winding quills is unnecessary because filling yarn is drawn directly from large packages car-

FIGURE 14.3

The wooden shuttle (into which is fitted a quill or pirn on which yarns are wound) carries yarn across the loom. Photograph courtesy of Steel Heddle.

rying 2 to 3 pounds of yarn that are mounted on the sides of the loom. If yarn that has been prepared for use in the filling is not to be used immediately, it is usually conditioned, kept in a room with hot, humid air. Conditioning allows yarn to relax and helps to prevent the formation of kinks.

BASIC MOTIONS OF WEAVING

Loom Operations

Once the filling yarns have been prepared and the warp yarns have been set into place, the loom goes through a series of motions: shedding, picking, beating up, and letting off. (See Figure 14.4.)

FIGURE 14.4

Steps in the action of a loom when a filling yarn is inserted in a plain-weave fabric. (a) Shed is formed by separating warp yarns to create space through which the shuttle can travel. (b) Shuttle is projected through the shed. (c) Beating up of yarn takes place to push new filling firmly against the others already in place. (d) Positions of warp yarns are reversed to reform shed, and the process is repeated with the shuttle traveling in the opposite direction.

Shedding

The shed is formed by raising the harnesses to form an open area between the sets of warps. The formation of the shed is known as *shedding*.

Picking

While the shed is open, the yarn is transported across the opening, laying a filling yarn across the width of the loom. The insertion of the filling is known as *picking*. A single filling yarn is known as a *pick*. Speed of weaving machines is generally expressed as the number of picks per minute, yards or meters of filling inserted per minute, or yards or meters of fabric per hour. Speed obviously is related to the width of the loom. Wider looms, weaving wider fabrics, would require more time for one filling insertion.

Beating Up

Beating up is done by the reed, the comblike device that pushes the filling yarn close against the woven fabric.

Letting Off

As the woven fabric is formed, it must be moved or *let off* the loom and *taken up* on the cloth beam to make room for the formation of more fabric. All these functions are synchronized so that they occur in the appropriate sequence and do not interfere with one another.

Monitoring Yarn Breakage

There is always the danger that a warp or filling yarn may break during weaving, causing a flaw in the cloth. Warp yarns are threaded through drop wires, small metal plates with holes, which are drawn down when a yarn breaks or they may be monitored by electronic scanners that indicate when a yarn is broken. Through signals resulting from either the drop wires or a break in the electronic contact, the loom is shut off, allowing the broken yarn to be repaired.

YARN TRANSPORT METHODS

The carrier used for transporting the filling yarn may differ from one kind of loom to another. The different devices used form the basis for classifying different types of looms. Within the industry many people refer to newer equipment as *weaving machines* rather than looms. Weaving machines vary from older, shuttle looms to modern shuttleless machines with sophisticated electronic controls. This newer equipment now predominates in the United States textile industry.

Shuttle Looms

In shuttle looms the shuttle traverses the cloth, and the filling yarn unwinds from the quill. Quills in the shuttle must be replaced when the yarn supply is exhausted. The frequency with which a quill has to be replaced depends on the fineness of the filling yarn. Coarse yarns require more frequent replacement; finer yarns need to be replaced less often.

In the mechanical changer, full quills are kept ready in a revolving case. The machine rams them into the shuttle when the shuttle comes to rest briefly after crossing the yarn. The pressure of the full quill crowds the empty quill out of the shuttle. It falls through a slot into a container under the loom. The new quill is pushed mechanically into place in the shuttle, which has a self-threading device that automatically picks up the yarn when the new quill is inserted. This allows the weaving to continue without a stop.

A specialized process has been developed that allows winding of quills to take place at the loom. In the Unifil system, empty quills are carried on a conveyer belt to a point where yarn from a large package is wound onto an empty quill that is then returned to a position where it can be placed in the shuttle. (See Figure 14.5a.) This system requires that fewer wound quills be supplied, but it has several limitations. It is useful only for single-color picks, and because the cost of the system is high, it is most economical for coarse yarns that would require especially frequent quill replacement.

Picking when two or more different colors or types of filling yarn are used requires two or more shuttles and a more complex and costly type of loom arrangement. A conventional shuttle loom has one shuttle box on each side of the machine. (See Figure 14.5b.)

To insert yarns of different colors or types, a number of shuttle boxes must be moved up and down to bring shuttles into position to create the pattern. Such looms are often called *pick and pick looms*. Among the advantages of most shuttleless looms is that they draw yarn for each pick directly from yarn packages, making it easier and less costly to insert a number of different colors or types of yarn.

The rapid crossing of the shed by the shuttle leaves a layer of filling yarn. When the shed is changed, the yarn is locked into place by the change in warp positioning. However, to make the yarn lie flat and in its proper position, it must be beaten into place.

FIGURE 14.5

(a) Box loom. Quills that are being filled on the Unifil system are visible at the point indicated by the arrow. Photograph courtesy of Picanol Corporation. (b) Filled quills are mounted, ready for insertion into the shuttle, which is not visible, Photograph courtesy of the International Linen Promotion Commission.

a　　　　　　　　　　　　　　　　　　b

Shuttleless Weaving Machines

Shuttleless weaving machines were invented to increase the speed of weaving and reduce the literally deafening noise. The modern loom with a shuttle, although much faster in operation than the earliest automatic looms, is not susceptible to further increases in speed because of the variety of operations that the machine must perform. Time is required for stopping the shuttle and accelerating it in the other direction and the weight of yarn on the quill that must be carried across the shed limits the speed. For this reason, future loom developments are likely to be in the area of shuttleless weaving.

Shuttleless machines may be classified as to the method used in inserting the filling yarns. Four basic types have been developed:

1. Machines with grippers or projectiles (throw across)
2. Machines with mechanically operated gripper arms or rapiers (reach across)
3. Machines employing water or air jets to carry the filling (spit or blow across)
4. Machines that form multiple sheds (multiphase)

In hand weaving and automatic shuttle weaving, the filling yarn is continuous and runs back and forth across the fabric, but in most shuttleless weaving, the filling yarn extends only from selvage to selvage, as it is cut off before it passes across the shed. In all shuttleless weaving, the yarn for the filling is unwound from large, stationary packages of yarn that are sometimes set on one side and at other times set on both sides of the loom. Since weaving speed depends on fabric width, there is every incentive to build wider machines for more efficient filling insertion.

Projectile or Gripper Loom

In the gripper or projectile type of weaving machine, a small hooklike device grips the end of the filling yarn. (See Figure 14.6.) As the gripper is projected across the warp shed, it tows the filling behind it. The gripper can move more quickly than a conventional shuttle because of its decreased size; it can travel farther more easily, thereby making possible the weaving of wider fabrics, and it does not require the step of filling the shuttle; it pulls the yarn directly from a prepared yarn package.

Two types of gripper looms are used. In one, the gripper travels only in one direction. It is returned to the starting point by a conveyor belt. To maintain the weaving speed, each machine must have several grippers, although only one is in use at any one time.

In the other type of gripper machine, a single gripper inserts one filling yarn alternately from the right- and left-hand sides of the loom. The gripper serves the same function as a conventional shuttle, but instead of holding a quill, it carries the yarn behind it. Packages of yarn must, therefore, be placed on both sides of the machine.

The gripper machine not only weaves fabric more quickly than does the shuttle loom, but it runs with less noise, making it possible for manufacturers to comply more easily with government regulations that restrict noise levels.

There is also a saving in power costs for wide-width fabrics. Narrow fabrics are not economically woven on this loom since too much time is spent in periods of acceleration of the gripper. Wide fabric widths are quite productive, as the power consumed is less than that for a conventional shuttle loom of the same size. Sheets are woven side by side on some of these machines to take advantage of these savings. Ac-

FIGURE 14.6

Gripper projectile carries the weft yarn into the shed. Photograph courtesy of Sultzer Textile.

cording to data from producers of these machines, the looms can reach speeds slightly over 1,200 meters of filling yarn per minute.

Rapier Loom

As in the gripper loom, a stationary package of yarn is used to supply the filling yarns to the rapier machine. One end of a *rapier*, a rod or steel tape, carries the filling. The other end of the rapier is connected to the control system. The rapier moves across the width of the fabric, carrying the filling across through the shed to the opposite side. The rapier is then retracted, leaving the new filling in place.

In some versions of the machine, two rapiers are used, each half the width of the fabric in size. One rapier carries the yarn to the center of the shed, where the opposing rapier picks up the yarn and carries it the remainder of the way across the shed. (See Figure 14.7.) A disadvantage of both these techniques is the space required for the machine if a rigid rapier is used. The housing for the rapiers must take up as much space as the width of the machine. To overcome this problem, looms with flexible rapiers have been devised. The flexible rapier can be coiled as it is withdrawn and will therefore require less space. However, if the rapier is too stiff, it will not coil; if it is too flexible, it will buckle. The double rapier is used more frequently than the single rapier. Rigid and flexible rapier machines operate at speeds of up to 1,300 meters of filling per minute.

FIGURE 14.7

(a) In the two-rapier type of shuttleless machine, one rapier carries the yarn to the center of the shed where a second rapier grasps the yarn and (b) carries it across the rest of the width of the fabric. Photographs courtesy of American Dornier Machinery Corporation.

a   b

Water-Jet Loom

Water-soluble warp sizings are used on most staple warp yarns. Therefore, the use of water-jet looms is restricted to filament yarns, yarns that are nonabsorbent, and those that do not lose strength when wet. Furthermore, these fabrics come off the loom wet and must be dried. In this technique a water jet is shot under force and, with it, a filling yarn. The force of the water as it is propelled across the shed carries the yarn to the opposite side. This machine is economical in its operation. A water jet of only 0.1 centimeter is sufficient to carry a yarn across a 48-inch shed. The amount of water required for each filling yarn is less than 2.0 cubic centimeters. Water-jet machines can reach speeds of 2,000 meters of filling per minute.

Air-Jet Loom

Air-jet looms operate in a manner similar to water-jet machines. Instead of projecting a stream of water across the shed, a jet of air is projected. The initial propulsive force is provided by a main nozzle. (See Figure 14.8.) Electronically controlled relay nozzles provide additional booster jets to carry the yarn across the shed. Data from manufacturers indicate that air-jet looms operate at speeds up to 2,200 meters of filling inserted per minute. They can weave multicolored yarns to make plaids and are available with both dobby and jacquard patterning mechanisms (discussed later in this chapter).

Multiphase Loom

All the weaving techniques discussed thus far require that the shed be open all the way across the machine for the device carrying the filling yarns to pass through the shed. This imposes a limit on loom speed.

The multiphase machine overcomes this limitation by forming many different sheds at different places across the machine and forming these only as the filling yarn

FIGURE 14.8

Air-jet nozzles spaced across the weaving machine transport filling yarns. Photograph courtesy of Sulzer Textil.

is inserted. In this way, a number of filling yarns can be inserted, one behind the other. As a section of the shed opens, the filling passes, and the shed closes, opening again in the new pattern as the next filling yarn arrives. (See Figure 14.9.) Speed is increased because of the number of yarns that can be inserted almost simultaneously one right after the other, but the actual speed of movement of the filling yarns is lower than in other types of machines. For this reason, filling yarns that are weaker can be used. Sultzer Ruti, the manufacturer of a multiphase machine, states that its loom will insert up to 5,400 meters of filling per minute.

Selvages

Many shuttleless weaving machines insert filling yarns from one side. In the shuttle type of loom, the carrying of the continuous filling back and forth across the fabric creates a closed selvage edge, with no loose yarn ends to fray or ravel. In shuttleless looms, however, one or both of the selvages is fringed. It is necessary to reinforce this edge if the fabric is not to fray at the edges. Methods of reinforcement include providing for tucking the yarns at the open edge or use of a *leno selvage*, a self-selvage in which two warp yarns at the edges of the fabric twist around each filling. The tucked-

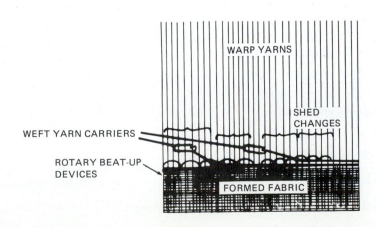

WARP YARNS

SHED CHANGES

WEFT YARN CARRIERS

ROTARY BEAT-UP DEVICES

FORMED FABRIC

FIGURE 14.9

Multiphase loom continually inserts weft yarns from yarn carriers. Rotary beat-up devices press inserted yarn firmly against previously formed cloth. If the pattern changes, small groups of yarns are changed into a new shedding position after each new yarn carrier has passed.

in finish is the more durable. For heavy industrial fabrics made from heat-sensitive or thermoplastic fibers, hot melting devices cause the yarns to fuse together to form a tight selvage. (See Figure 14.10.)

Advantages of Shuttleless Weaving Machines

When patterned fabrics are woven on shuttleless weaving machines, colors can be changed more easily. Unlike shuttle looms in which a different shuttle must be provided for each different color, the shuttleless machines can be provided with a variety of colors directly from yarn packages. Other advantages include lower power requirements, lower sound levels, smaller space requirements, and higher speeds of fabric production. (See Table 14.1.) On the other hand, the higher production rates of shuttleless machines require that yarn quality be high to ensure trouble-free operation.

Trends in loom purchases within the textile industry in the United States show clearly that shuttleless weaving machines are replacing traditional shuttle looms. In 1985 there were 160,000 shuttle looms in place in the United States, and by 1997 that number had dropped to less than 70,000 (Isaacs 1998). Currently the most widely used machines worldwide are rapier and projectile types. Air-jet looms are becoming more popular in North America.

TABLE 14.1
Comparison of Weaving Speeds[1]

Type of Loom	Potential Range of Speeds Reported in Meters of Filling Inserted Per Minute
projectile weaving machines	about 1,200
flexible rapier weaving machines	950 to 1,300
rigid rapier weaving machines	1,000 to 1,300
waterjet weaving machines	1,800 to 2,000
air jet weaving machines	1,100 to 2,200
multiphase weaving machines	5,400
conventional shuttle loom	300[2]

[1]Data reported by weaving machine manufacturers in *Textile World,* May 1998, pages 90 to 109.
[2]Data provided by American Textile Manufacturers Institute.

CONTROL OF LOOM MOTIONS

The essential motions in loom operation are the motion of the harnesses to form the shed and the activation of devices for carrying the filling through the shed.

Cam Loom

In the past the motions in most simple weaves were controlled by mechanical devices called *cams*. The shape or profile of the cam is followed by a device called the cam follower, and the irregularities in the cam shape are translated by the cam follower into the motions of the loom. (See Figure 14.11.) In this way simple repeat patterns can be created. Repeats are limited to six or fewer picks, but this includes a substantial majority of the most commonly used fabrics. More complex designs require dobby or jacquard looms. Such looms are rapidly being replaced by more modern machines with electronic control of motions.

Dobby Loom

The *dobby loom* is a conventional loom with a somewhat enlarged dobby "head." (See Figure 14.12a.) The traditional dobby mechanism uses a pattern chain on which there are pegs. Needles or feelers contact the pegs in the pattern chain and are positioned by the pegs. The feelers cause hooks within the dobby head to be connected or disconnected, and the motion of the hooks is translated to the harnesses that move from up to down or to in-between positions as dictated by the pattern.

From twenty-four to thirty shedding combinations are controlled in this way, so that the repeats are limited to about thirty rows in size. A machine called the double-cylinder dobby loom has been developed that approximately doubles the size of the repeat that can be made. The fabrics woven on this loom are less complex than are jacquard patterns and usually consist of small fancy or geometrical figures or designs. (See Figure 14.12b.) Plain terry towels are also woven on dobby looms. With the development of electronic jacquard looms that can make both jacquard and dobby fabrics, dobby looms are becoming less important.

CAMS

WARP BEAM

HARNESSES

FINISHED CLOTH

CAM FOLLOWERS

FIGURE 14.11

Cam follower translates the motion of the cams to the harnesses, which are raised and lowered according to the "instructions" transmitted by the shape of the cam. In this way variations in the weave can be achieved.

FIGURE 14.12

(a) Electronically controlled dobby head that uses a memory card instead of a pattern card to control loom movements. Photograph of Murata MX-8E machine courtesy of Murata Machinery Ltd. (b) Fabric woven on a machine with a dobby head.

a

b

Jacquard Loom

The *jacquard loom* is the descendant of an oriental loom, the draw loom, which was used to weave complex patterned fabrics. (See Figure 14.13a.) Operation of the draw loom required two workers: the weaver who threw the shuttle and operated the batten and a *drawboy* who raised and lowered a series of cords that controlled the pattern. The drawboy had to work from a platform above the loom while the weaver sat below.

Since the drawboy could make mistakes in the selection of cords, later modifications of the loom structure introduced a mechanical device for raising and lowering the cords. In 1805 Joseph Jacquard, a Frenchman, perfected the principle of the mechanical draw loom. To this day, this same type of loom used in weaving complex patterns is known as the jacquard loom and the weave is known as the *jacquard weave*. (See Figure 14.13b.)

a

b

c

FIGURE 14.13

(a) Photograph of a fabric that illustrates the complexity of designs that can be woven on the jacquard loom and jacquard weaving machines with two different configurations. (b) Dornier rapier weaving machine, Type HTVS 8/J, eight-jacquard type. Photograph courtesy of American Dornier Machinery Corporation. (c) Bonas U.S.A. electronically operated jacquard loom. Photograph courtesy of Bonas U.S.A., Inc.

The ability of the jacquard loom to weave a variety of complex fabrics is a result of the ability of this machine to control each warp yarn separately. Each warp yarn is threaded through a loop in the end of a leash or cord.

Before the loom is set up, a design is worked out on graph paper, and the position of each of the yarns in the design is analyzed. A punched card is prepared that corresponds to each of the filling yarns. The card contains a "code," a set of punched holes that will determine which warp yarns must be lifted for each passage of the filling. The punched cards are laced together in the correct order for the design. As each card advances to the operating position, needles rest against the card. The needles are held under the pressure of a spring. When a needle position coincides with a hole in the card, the needle moves through the hole. The movement of the needle engages a hook, which in turn lifts the cords attached to the hook. The cords raise the yarns they hold to form the shed. When the filling has been inserted, the needles retract, the cards move to the next position, and different sets of needles engage holes in the next card. This, in turn, causes other warp yarns to be lifted to form a different shed.

Some electronically operated jacquard machines require far less space than mechanically operated jacquards. (See Figure 14.13c.) Other advantages of electronic machines are increased speed of operation; the ability to change patterns with greater ease, which makes possible the production of short runs of fabric; and computer interfacing to rapidly translate design to production.

BASIC WEAVING CONCEPTS AND TERMINOLOGY

Woven fabrics, with a few exceptions (such as triaxial fabrics, discussed later in chapter 15) are constructed by interlacing warp (lengthwise) yarns and filling (crosswise) yarns at right angles. In theory, warp and filling yarns should intersect at right angles. When this relationship is perfect, the fabric is said to be on *true grain* or *grain perfect*. As a result of the stresses and strains imposed during weaving or finishing, these yarns may not lie in the proper position, and when this occurs, the fabric is said to be *off-grain*.

The off-grain relationship of warp and filling yarns is described by different terms, depending on how the distortion lies. Warp yarns are usually straight, as they are subject to lengthwise tension throughout the processing of fabrics. Filling yarns are usually responsible for the distortion, but they may be distorted in a straight line (*skewed*) or in a curved line (*bowed*). (See Figure 14.14.)

Woven and other fabrics can be designated as reversible, that is, having the same appearance on both front and back, or not reversible. For fabrics that are not reversible the side to be displayed in the finished textile is termed the *face* of the fabric and the other side is the *back*.

Within the textile and apparel industries, comparative measurement systems are necessary. The concept of yarn size expressed as yarn number was discussed in chapter 13. When dealing with fabrics, comparisons of size are made in terms of the number of yarns per inch or fabric count, the width of the fabric, and the weight of the cloth.

The closeness of the weave is expressed as the *fabric count*. With a small magnifying glass calibrated in inches or centimeters, it is possible to count the number of yarns in 1 inch or centimeter of warp and in 1 inch or centimeter of filling. When the number of yarns in the warp is similar to the number of yarns in the filling, the weave is said to be a *balanced weave*. The fabric count is often expressed in numerical form as 80 × 64, indicating that there are 80 warp yarns per inch by 64 fillings.

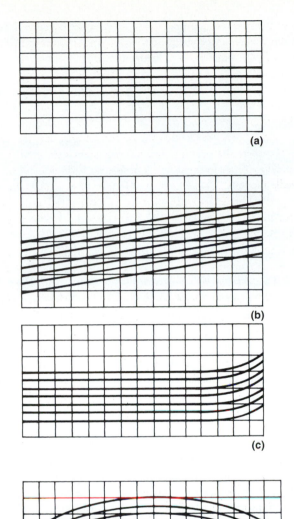

FIGURE 14.14

Grain positions. (a) Warp and filling interlace at 90° angle. Fabric is on "true grain." (b) Filling is off the square, skewed. Though straight, the filling is not at 90° to the warp. (c) Filling is "bowed"—straight for part of the way, then curved toward one selvage. (d) Filling is "bowed" or curved from selvage to selvage.

When warp and filling are perfectly balanced, or equal, the count may be stated as 80 square, meaning there are 80 yarns per inch in the warp and 80 yarns per inch in the filling. Alternatively, the number may be doubled, in which case a count of 180 would indicate a count of 90 yarns per inch in each direction. Balanced-weave fabrics with the same type of yarns in warp and filling are more durable because the fabric wears evenly in both warp and filling directions.

Fabric count is usually measured with a calibrated, square magnifying glass called either a *linen tester* or *pick glass*. (See Figure 14.15.) The glass is marked off in fractions of an inch or in centimeters, and the number of warp and filling yarns beside these calibrations can be viewed in magnified form with the glass and counted.

In those fabrics where fabric counts are not balanced, the larger number of yarns will usually be found in the warp direction. Unbalanced fabrics usually exhibit so-

FIGURE 14.15

Pick counter used to facilitate counting yarns per inch or wales and courses of knitted goods. Photograph courtesy of Alfred Suter Co., Inc.

called rib effects created when numerous finer warp yarns cross over coarser filling yarns. Costs increase more rapidly as the number of picks (filling yarns) per inch increases; therefore, fabrics with balanced weaves or those with more yarns in the filling than in the warp are more costly to manufacture.

Counts are taken in the *greige* (that is, unfinished) goods, and since fabrics may shrink during finishing, the count provided may not be exactly accurate. If only one number appears, it can generally be assumed that the fabric has a balanced weave.

Fabric widths will vary with the size of the loom on which they were woven. Since the introduction of automated looms and with improvements in the technology for transporting the filling yarns, fabric widths have increased dramatically. A survey of the specifications of shuttleless looms, for example, notes width possibilities of as much as 500 centimeters (197 inches), while narrow looms are available for weaving specialty items such as tapes (Issacs 1998.)

Fabric weight is expressed as ounces per linear (running) yard, yards per pound, or ounces per square yard. Woolens, worsteds, and fabrics of similar weight made from blends or manufactured fibers are often measured in ounces per yard. For example, one may see designations such as a 14-ounce tweed or an 8-ounce tropical worsted. In this system of measurement, the higher the number, the heavier the fabric. As measurements tend to move to the metric system, these weights may be expressed in grams per square meter rather than in ounces.

Yards per pound is a measure of the number of yards of cloth in 1 pound. In this measure, higher numbers indicate lighter-weight fabrics. This system of measurement is used mostly for cottons, cotton blends, or lightweight manufactured fabrics.

When measuring ounces per yard or yards per pound, the width of the fabric is not taken into account. These measures are, therefore, less precise than is the measure of ounces per square yard or grams per square meter.

Fabric weights may range widely. Fabrics weighing less than 1 ounce per square yard would be very lightweight, as for example in some sheer curtain fabrics, gauzes, or even mosquito netting. Fabrics weighing from 2 to 4 ounces per square yard are also relatively lightweight. These are often referred to in the industry as *top-weight* fabrics and are typically used for shirts or blouses. Medium-weight fabrics, 5 to 7 ounces per square yard, are referred to as *bottom-weight* fabrics and are used for items such as skirts or slacks. Heavyweight fabrics range from 9 to 11 ounces (for example, some jeans), and weights over 14 ounces are classified as *very heavyweight* (perhaps for upholstery).

SUMMARY

Woven fabrics are made on looms, or weaving machines. The various types of equipment described in this chapter can create an enormous variety of fabrics. Professionals in the textile industries must select not only appropriate equipment but also raw materials—fibers and yarns—from which to produce goods for apparel, home furnishings, and scientific and industrial applications. As businesspersons in a highly competitive global economy, they must make choices that allow them to produce these goods in the most efficient and cost-effective way.

In the next chapter, readers will become acquainted with the wide variety of woven fabrics that are produced on these weaving machines.

References

American Fabrics and Fashions Magazine, 1980. *Encyclopedia of textiles*, 3d ed. Englewood Cliffs, N.J.: Prentice Hall.

Isaacs, M. 1998. Loom makers get ready for ITMA 99. *Textile World* 148 (May): 86.

Review Questions

1. Explain the basic principle of operation of a hand loom inserting weft yarns into the fabric. In what ways does the operation of a modern shuttleless machine differ from the hand loom?
2. Identify the various methods of transporting the filling yarns through the shed in automated weaving.
3. What are the advantages and disadvantages of shuttleless weaving as compared with weaving with a shuttle?
4. When would it be necessary to use a jacquard loom? A dobby loom?
5. What is the difference between a fabric that is on true grain and one that is bowed or skewed?
6. Define fabric count. How is fabric count measured? What is meant by a balanced fabric count?

Recommended Readings

Broudy, E. 1979. *The book of looms*. New York: Van Nostrand Reinhold.

Catling, H. 1984. The development of modern weaving machines. *Textiles* 13 (Spring): 5.

Chadwick, A. 1987. Weaving. *Textiles* 16 (3): 63.

Cherzi, J., and R. R. Gosai. 1999. Weaving to tomorrow. *Textile Horizons* (May): 21.

D'Harcourt, R. 1962. *Textiles of ancient Peru and their techniques*. Seattle: University of Washington Press.

Ishida, T. 1993. Historical developments in weaving machinery: Part 3. Modern weaving machinery, today and tomorrow. *JTN The International Textile Magazine*, 458 (January): 108.

Machinery investment upsurge confirmed. 1998. *Textile Month* (August): 6.

Marks, R., and A.T.C. Robinson. 1986. *Principles of weaving*. Manchester, England: The Textile Institute.

Schwartz, P., T. Rhodes, and M. Mohamed. 1982. *Fabric forming systems*. Park Ridge, N.J.: Noyes.

The weaving evolution. 1998. *Textile Horizons* (June): 10.

15

THE WEAVES

Three types of weave structure form the basis of even the most complex weaves. Known as basic weaves, these are the *plain weave*, the *twill weave*, and the *satin weave*.

Visual representation of weaves is often made on graph paper. Each square of the paper represents the yarn that appears on the upper side or surface of the fabric. Darkened squares represent the warp yarns crossing over filling yarns.

Diagraming of weaves on graph paper is a useful exercise, but readers will probably find that the concepts relating to weaves are made clearer if they use colored yarns or strips of colored paper to create small samples of each of the basic weaves. A small hand loom, or a child's loom, can be used for this purpose.

297

BASIC WEAVES

Plain Weave

The plain weave is the simplest of the weaves and the most common. It consists of interlacing warp and filling yarns in a pattern of over one and under one. Imagine a small hand loom with the warp yarns held firmly in place. The filling yarn moves over the first warp yarn, under the second, over the third, under the fourth, and so on. In the next row, the filling yarn goes under the first warp yarn, over the second, under the third, and so on. In the third row, the filling moves over the first warp, under the second, and so on, just as it did in the first row. (See Figure 15.1.)

The weave can be made with any type of yarn. Made with tightly twisted, single yarns that are placed close together both in the warp and filling, and with the same number of yarns in both directions, the resulting fabric will be a durable, simple, serviceable fabric. If, however, the warp were to be made from a single yarn and the filling from a colorful bouclé yarn, a quite different, much more decorative fabric would result. Both are the product of the same, basic, plain weave.

Plain-weave fabrics are constructed from many fibers and in weights ranging from light to heavy. Weaves may be balanced or unbalanced. Decorative effects can be achieved by using novelty yarns or yarns of different colors. Together with many of these novelty fabrics, a number of standard fabric types are made in the plain weave. In the past these standard fabrics were always constructed from specific fibers. At present suitable manufactured fibers are also woven into many of the standard fabric constructions.

Balanced Plain-Weave Fabrics

The balanced weaves are the most common. Unbalanced weaves, or *rib weaves*, and another variation, *basket weaves*, will be discussed later. It is helpful to classify balanced plain weaves by weight as light, medium, or heavy. (See page 299.)

Lightweight Plain-Weave Fabrics. Lightweight plain-weave fabrics may be light in weight because they have either a low fabric count or are constructed of fine yarns

FIGURE 15.1

(a) Diagram of the plain weave; (b) close-up photograph of plain-weave fabric.

a

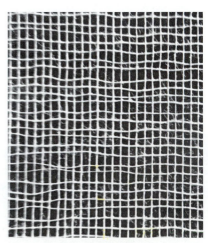

b

and are usually sheer. The following low-fabric-count balanced plain weaves have somewhat specialized uses.

1. *Cheesecloth* is open weave soft fabric originally used in producing cheese, serving as a wrapper or strainer for curds. (See Figure 15.1b.)
2. *Crinoline* and *buckram* are heavily sized to serve as stiffening fabrics.
3. *Gauze,* with a higher count than cheesecloth, is used in theatrical costumes and medical dressings, as well as for blouses and dresses.

The following are high-count balanced plain weaves with fine yarns.

1. *Chiffon* is made from fine, highly twisted filament yarns. Because of the tightly twisted crepe yarns, chiffon has excellent drape, and although it is delicate in appearance, it is relatively durable. Sheer evening dresses, blouses, lingerie, and other dressy apparel are constructed from the fabric.
2. *Ninon,* a sheer plain weave of filament yarns, is often used in sheer curtains and draperies.
3. *Organdy* is a sheer cotton fabric that is given a temporarily or permanently stiffened finish.
4. *Organza* is a stiff sheer fabric made of filament yarns.
5. *Voile,* a soft fabric with somewhat lower fabric count and higher twist yarns, has a distinctive two-ply warp and good drapability.

Medium-Weight Plain-Weave Fabrics. Medium-weight balanced plain weaves usually have fairly high fabric counts, contain medium-weight yarns (12 to 29 tex), and are opaque. Distinguishing characteristics may be design, color, finish, or fabric count.

1. *Calico* is a closely woven fabric with a small printed design.
2. *Chambray* fabrics have colored warp yarns and white filling yarns that produce a heather appearance. Some contemporary chambrays may have warp and filling yarns of different colors.
3. *Chintz* is a fabric printed with large designs that is often given a polished or glazed finish. Solid color glazed fabrics are called *polished cotton.*
4. *Gingham* is a woven check or plaid design made with yarns of different colors.
5. *Muslin,* generally woven from cotton or cotton blends, is made in both heavily sized, bleached qualities and in better grades for sheets and pillow cases. Muslin sheets are not combed and have a lower count (128 to 140 total yarns per inch) than do percale sheets.
6. *Percale,* a closely woven, plain weave of cotton or blended fibers, is made from yarns of moderate twist. Percale yard goods are generally carded, but percale sheets are finer and more luxurious in feel and are made of combed yarns. Percale sheets have a count of 180 to 200 yarns (warp plus filling) per inch.

Heavyweight Plain-Weave Fabrics. The following are common heavyweight plain-weave fabrics.

1. *Butcher linen* is a plain, stiff, white fabric made from heavy yarn.
2. *Crash* is made from thick and thin yarns, giving the fabric a nubby look.
3. *Homespun* is a furnishing fabric made with irregular yarns to resemble hand-spun and hand-woven fabrics.
4. *Osnaburg* is made of low-quality cotton for industrial use and in interior fabrics for curtains and upholstered furniture.

Rib Variations

Ribbed fabrics have an unbalanced weave with many small yarns crossing over a fewer number of large yarns. Most unbalanced weaves have a larger number of warp yarns than filling yarns, forming a crosswise rib. Ribs can be relatively small or quite pronounced. (See Figure 15.2.) *Corded fabrics* can be created by grouping yarns together in one direction before they are crossed by yarns in the other direction or by using large yarns at intervals. (See Figure 15.3.) The following are some standard rib-weave fabrics.

1. *Bengaline* and *ottoman* heavyweight fabrics with large ribs, are used mostly in upholstery and furnishings.
2. *Broadcloth* is a medium-weight unbalanced plain weave with fine ribs. The rib weave makes it crisper than medium-weight balanced weaves. It is often made from cotton or cotton blends.

FIGURE 15.2

Faille fabric with pronounced crosswise rib.

FIGURE 15.3

Dimity fabric with pronounced lengthwise cord.

3. *Faille* has a prominent rib and is made with fine filament yarns in the warp and heavy spun yarns in the filling. It is usually heavyweight, although lighter-weight *tissue failles* are also produced.

4. *Grosgrain* has very prominent ribs and is usually woven in narrow ribbon widths.

5. *Poplin,* a bottom-weight rib weave, is usually made from cotton or cotton blends.

6. *Shantung* has a nubby, irregular rib in the filling. Formerly made almost exclusively of silk, shantung is now made from a variety of manufactured fibers as well.

7. *Taffeta* is a medium-weight weave made from filament yarns that is often used for evening wear.

8. *Bedford cord* is a sturdy fabric constructed with a pronounced lengthwise cord.

9. *Dimity,* a sheer cotton fabric, is often made with a lengthwise cord effect. Some dimity fabrics use larger yarns in both the warp and filling direction to achieve a checked, or *barred,* effect.

Basket Weave

The *basket weave,* a variation of the plain weave, uses two or more warp and/or two or more filling yarns side by side as one yarn. (See Figure 15.4a.) The resultant cloth is fairly loose in weave.

The following are among the more common basket-weave fabrics.

1. *Monk's cloth* is a coarse cloth of large yarns. (See Figure 15.4b.) Monk's cloth uses four or more yarns as one in the weave. Its major uses are in household textiles such as curtains, spreads, and the like.

2. *Hopsacking* is made of many different fibers. This fabric simulates the fabrics used in bags for gathering hops. It has a 2-2 or 3-3 basket weave and is commonly used in upholstery.

3. *Modified basket weaves* may use double yarns in one direction but not in the other. *Oxford cloth*, which is made in this way, is a soft fabric, often made of cotton or cotton blends, that is used for shirts. Frequently, it is made with narrow colored stripes in the warp, or a colored warp.

4. *Duck* and *canvas* are heavy, tightly woven, and very stiff plain-weave fabrics made of even yarn for industrial use. They usually have an uneven weave

a

b

FIGURE 15.4

(a) The basket-weave variation of the plain weave; (b) monk's cloth, a basket-weave fabric with four warp and four filling yarns.

pattern. Because of the tight weave, these fabrics are often used for outdoor purposes.

Twill Weave

Twill fabrics are readily identified by the diagonal lines that the weave creates on the surface of the fabric. Because there are fewer interlacings, the yarns in twill fabrics can be spaced closely together, packed tightly, and held firmly in place. Therefore, twill fabrics are usually strong and durable; they are also supple and drape well. Most twill-weave fabrics are made in bottom weight. The compact structure of twill fabrics enables them to shed soil readily, although when soiled they may be difficult to get clean. Depending on their construction, twill fabrics generally show good resistance to abrasion. Twill fabrics are often used for tailored garments, particularly those made of worsted wool yarns.

The simplest twill weave is created by the warp yarn crossing over two filling yarns, then under one, over two, under one, and so on. In the next row, the sequence begins one yarn down. (See Figure 15.5.) The area in which one yarn crosses over several yarns in the opposite direction is called a *float*.

The lines created by this pattern are called *wales*. When the cloth is held in the position in which it was woven, the wales (diagonal lines) will be seen to run either from the lower left corner to the upper right corner or from the lower right to the upper left. If the diagonal runs from the lower left to the upper right, the twill is known as a *right-hand twill*. About 85 percent of all twill-woven fabrics are right-hand twills (American Fabrics 1980, 325). When the twill runs from the lower right to the upper left, the twill is known as a *left-hand twill*. (See Figure 15.6.)

There are a number of types of twill weaves. All use the same principle of crossing more than one yarn at a regular, even progression. Descriptions of twills may be made in terms of the pattern of warp yarns crossing filling yarns. The description of twill weaves is notated as 2/1, 2/2, 3/2, and so on. The first digit refers to the number of filling yarns crossed over by the warp and the second digit to the number of filling yarns the warp passes under before returning to cross the filling again. When the crossing is over and under the same number of yarns, the fabric is called an *even* or *even-sided twill*. When warps pass over a larger or smaller number of filling yarns than they pass under, the fabric is called an *uneven twill*.

Even-Sided Twill

The even-sided twill has the same number of warp and filling yarns showing on the face of the fabric. Figure 15.7 shows how such a weave is achieved in a 2/2 twill.

FIGURE 15.5

Right-handed, warp-faced twill weave.

FIGURE 15.6

Left-handed twill weave.

Even-sided twills are reversible unless printed or finished or one side.

1. *Serge* is a popular basic twill fabric made from any number of different fibers. When serge is made from wool, it is often woven from worsted yarns. Serge will take a crease well, but wool serge tends to become shiny with wear. It tailors well.
2. *Flannel,* if made of wool, is usually a twill weave with a napped finish.
3. *Plaids* or tartan patterns are yarn-dyed even-sided twills.
4. In a *herringbone twill* the direction of the twill reverses itself to form a broken diagonal that appears like a series of V's: herringbone patterns create a decorative effect. (See Figure 15.8.) Herringbone twills are common in suiting fabrics.

Warp-Faced Twill

Warp-faced twills have a predominance of warp yarns on the surface of the fabric, with patterns of 2/1, 3/1, 3/2, and so on. (See Figure 15.9.)

FIGURE 15.7

Right-handed, even-sided twill (2/2).

FIGURE 15.8

Herringbone twill fabric.

1. *Denim* is a durable heavyweight twill with colored warp yarns and white filling yarns. Since it is a warp-faced twill, the colored warp yarns predominate on the face and the white filling yarns on the back.
2. *Drill* is another heavyweight fabric, usually of a solid color.
3. *Jean* is a lighter-weight twill, usually with colored warp yarns and white filling yarns.
4. *Gabardine* is durable and closely woven. It is made into a variety of weights from many different fibers such as wool, rayon, cotton, and manufactured fibers.

Filling-Faced Twill

Filling-faced twills have a predominance of filling yarns on the surface of the fabric. Filling yarns are generally weaker than are warp yarns, so that relatively few filling-faced twills are made.

FIGURE 15.9

Right-handed, warp-faced, twill weave (2/1).

Twill Angles

When the face of a twill fabric is examined, the diagonal of the wales will be seen to move at a more or less steep angle. The steepness of the angle is dependent on two factors in the construction of the fabric: the number of warp yarns per inch of fabric and the number of steps between movement of yarns when they interlace.

The more warp yarns in the construction, the steeper the angle of the wales, provided that the number of filling yarns per inch remains the same. This is because the points of interlacing of the yarns will be closer together, thereby the diagonal of the wales will make a steep climb upward. When the steepness of the angle is the result of close spacing of warp yarns, these steeper angles are an indication of good strength. If the angle the wale makes with the filling yarn is about 45 degrees, the fabric is a *regular twill.* Fabrics with higher angles are *steep twills,* and those with smaller angles are *reclining twills.*

Generally, the interlacing of yarns in a twill changes with each filling yarn. There are, however, fabrics in which the interlacing of yarns changes only every two filling yarns or every three filling yarns. The less often the interlacing changes, the steeper the angle of the twill will be.

Satin Weave

Satin-weave fabrics are made by allowing yarns to float over a number of yarns from the opposite direction. Interlacings are made at intervals such as over four, under one (using five harnesses); over seven, under one (eight harnesses); or over eleven, under one (twelve harnesses). Floats in satin fabrics may cross from four to twelve yarns before interlacing with another yarn. No pronounced diagonal line is formed on the surface of the fabric because the points of intersection are spaced in such a way that no regular progression is formed from one yarn to that lying next to it.

When warp yarns form the floats on the face of the fabric, the fabric is a *warp-faced satin.* (See Figure 15.10.) When filling yarns float on the face, the fabric is a *filling-faced satin.* (See Figure 15.11.) Satin-weave fabrics made from filament yarns are called *satins;* those from spun yarns are *sateen.* Most warp-faced weaves have filament yarns because filament yarns do not require a tight twist to serve as warp yarns, whereas cotton, being a staple fiber, must be given a fairly high degree of twist if it is to serve as a strong warp yarn. Therefore, sateen fabrics are usually filling faced, although some warp sateens are made.

Satin-weave fabrics are highly decorative. They are usually made from filament yarns with high luster to produce a shiny, lustrous surface and tend to have high fab-

FIGURE 15.10

Warp-faced satin weave. Warp yarns form floats, crossing over seven filling yarns between every interlacing.

FIGURE 15.11

Filling-faced satin weave. Filling yarns form floats, crossing over four warp yarns between every intersection.

ric counts. They are smooth and slippery in texture and tend to shed dirt easily. The long floats on the surface are, of course, subject to abrasion and snagging. The longer the float, the greater the likelihood of snags and pulls. Satins are often used as lining fabrics for coats and suits because they slide easily over other fabrics. The durability of satin-weave fabrics is related to the density of the weave, with closely woven, high-count fabrics having good durability. Satins made from stronger fibers are, of course, more durable than those made from weaker fibers.

The following are some names given to satin fabrics.

1. *Antique satin,* a satin made to imitate silk satin of an earlier period, often uses slubbed filling yarns for decorative effect.
2. *Peau de soie* is a soft, closely woven satin with a flat, mellow luster.
3. *Slipper satin* is a strong, compact satin, heavy in weight. It is often used for evening shoes.
4. In *crepe-backed satin,* loosely twisted, lustrous warp yarns are combined with tightly twisted, creped filling yarns. The floats on the surface are created by the warp, so that the face of the fabric is chiefly made up of warp yarns with a satin appearance, whereas the back of the fabric is made up largely of tightly twisted filling yarns that produce a crepe or rougher surface texture with a flat, less shiny appearance.

Novelty Fabrics from Basic Weaves

Novelty effects in fabrics are in large part a result of selection of novelty yarns for incorporation into fabrics made in one of the basic weaves.

Crepe Fabrics

Crepe fabrics may be defined as fabrics characterized by a crinkled, pebbly surface. (See Figure 15.12.) Originally, crepe fabrics were made from crepe yarns, that is, yarns with an exceptionally high degree of twist, up to sixty-five turns per inch. Most standard crepe fabrics were made in the plain weave, some with rib effects, and some in satin weave, as in crepe-backed satin. With the advent of synthetic fibers, however, many *crepe effects* are achieved through the use of textured yarns, bicomponent yarns in which uneven shrinkage creates a crepelike surface, or embossing or stamping a crepelike texture on the surface of the fabric. Most fabrics made from these more recent processes will be durable only if they are made from heat-treated thermoplastic fibers. Another method uses a special crepe weave that breaks up the surface of the

FIGURE 15.12

Crepe fabric with a pebbly surface created by using tightly twisted crepe yarns and irregular weave.

cloth into a random sequence of interlacings. Careful examination of fabrics having a crepelike appearance will reveal that relatively few of them are actually woven with crepe yarns.

Seersucker

Seersucker, another plain-weave fabric, is created by holding some warp yarns at tight tension, some at slack tension. Those at slack tension puff up to form a sort of "blister effect." Seersucker surface effects are permanent. Often the slack and tight yarns are each made from a different colored yarn, to provide a decorative striped effect. Seersucker should not be confused with fabrics having puffed effects created by chemical finishes, such as *plissé* or *embossing*, which are much less durable.

VARIATIONS OF THE BASIC WEAVES

Dobby Fabrics

The dobby weave is like a jacquard weave in miniature. The Dobby weaves have small, repeated patterns, that are usually geometric. (See Figure 15.13.)

The following are some of the fabrics made on the dobby loom.

1. *Bird's eye,* a cloth made with small diamond-shaped figures, has a weave that is said to resemble the eye of a bird. Bird's eye is also called *diaper cloth.*

FIGURE 15.13

Close-up photograph of fabric woven on the dobby loom.

2. *Piqué* is a medium- to heavyweight fabric, often of cotton, with a pronounced lengthwise cord, often combined with other small figures or patterns such as honeycomb or waffle effects.
3. *White-on-white* has a white dobby figure woven on a white background and is often used for men's shirting.

Jacquard Fabrics

The operation of the jacquard loom was described in chapter 14. Jacquard patterns, when carefully analyzed, may be seen to contain combinations of plain, twill, and satin weaves, even in the same crosswise yarn. Many decorative fabrics are made by the jacquard technique. Jacquard-woven tapestry fabrics should not be confused with true tapestries (see below) even though some fashion promotions may refer to jacquard fabrics as "tapestry fabrics."

The following are some of the best-known jacquard patterns.

1. *Brocade* features an embossed or embroidered appearance. Elaborate patterns, often of flowers and figures, stand out from the background. Pattern and ground are usually different weaves. Brocades are made from a wide range of fibers and with a wide range of price and quality. Fabrics are used for upholstery, draperies, and evening and formal clothing.
2. *Brocatelle* is similar to brocade, but with figures or patterns standing in high relief. Brocatelle is used mostly for upholstery fabrics and draperies.
3. *Damask* is a flatter fabric than brocade and often has a fine weave. Damask figures often use a satin weave to reflect light from the pattern, whereas the background is made in a plain or twill construction. Linen damasks have long been used for luxurious tablecloths. Damasks are reversible. Cotton and linen damasks are made either with four-yarn float or a seven-yarn float in the satin weave. The longer floats are more lustrous, but the shorter floats are more durable, as they are less likely to snag or be subject to abrasion. (See Figure 15.14.)
4. *Tapestry-like fabrics* have an appearance that simulates hand-woven tapestries. Used extensively in fabrics for interiors, these jacquard-woven fabrics have highly patterned designs on the face. Although the back is also figured, the colors within the design differ. For example, a leaf that appears on the face as green will be some other color on the back. (See Figure 15.15.)

FIGURE 15.14

Damask fabric woven on a jacquard loom.

FIGURE 15.15

Tapestry-type fabric woven on a jacquard loom: (a) face; (b) back. Note that design is identical on face and back, but that the colors, as indicated by gradations of black and white, are reversed.

a

b

Hand-Woven Tapestries

Tapestries woven by traditional methods differ from jacquard-woven fabrics having the appearance of a tapestry in that the traditionally woven tapestries are made using hand techniques. Jacquard-woven tapestry fabrics generally use repeated patterns of finite size. Traditional tapestry weaving is used to produce enormous fabrics that can form one large picture. Tapestry weaving may be compared to painting with yarn. (See Figure 15.16.) Since it is basically a hand technique, tapestry is made on an elementary loom.

In the weaving of European tapestries, the loom followed the basic form of the two-bar loom. The loom was set up either vertically or horizontally, and warp yarns were measured and affixed to the loom. Filling yarns were prepared in the appropriate colors. The design of the tapestry was first worked out in a drawing, or *cartoon*, as it

FIGURE 15.16

French or Flemish tapestry of the late fifteenth century woven from wool and silk with metal threads. Photograph courtesy of the Metropolitan Museum of Art, the Cloisters. Gift of John D. Rockefeller, Jr., 1937.

was called. The artist who created the drawing may have been one of great stature, and painters such as Raphael and Rubens served as designers of sixteenth- and seventeenth-century tapestries. The cartoon was sometimes traced onto the warp yarns. In other instances it was mounted behind the loom, and the tapestry weaver looked through the warp yarns to the design, following the plan of the drawing. The tapestry was woven with the wrong side facing the weaver. Sometimes a mirror was set up beneath the tapestry so that the weaver could check the progress on the right side.

The various colors of yarns were wound onto sharp, pointed bobbins that were introduced into the warp, and the weaver proceeded to fill in the area of that particular color. When the weaver reached the end of one color, a new bobbin was used for the next section. This created a problem, because as the weaver worked back and forth in a particular segment of the design, the yarns of one color did not join with the yarns of the adjacent color. This produced slits in the fabric at the place where each new color began. Sections of the tapestry could be sewn shut, but this caused the fabric to be weaker at the spots where the fabric was seamed together. Two other methods were also used to prevent the formation of slits. Where the color of one section ended and another began, both the old and the new color could be twisted around the same warp yarns. This system worked well except that it created a slightly indistinct or shadowy line. Where clear, well-defined lines were required, the yarns of adjacent colors were fastened together by looping one yarn around the other.

In traditional tapestry weaving, all the warp yarns are completely covered by filling yarns, so it is the filling yarns that carry the design. The warp yarns serve only as the base.

Leno-Weave Fabrics

The *leno weave* is the modern descendant of a technique called *twining* that was used thousands of years ago for making fabrics. In leno-weave fabrics, the warp yarns are paired. A special attachment, the *doup* or *leno* attachment, crosses or laps the paired warp yarns over each other, while the filling passes through the opening between the two warp yarns. (See Figure 15.17.)

FIGURE **15.17**

(a) Structure of a leno-weave fabric; (b) closeup of a leno-weave fabric with bouclé yarns in the crosswise direction.

a   b

Leno-weave fabrics are made in open, gauzelike constructions. The twined (not twisted) warp yarns prevent the filling yarns of these open fabrics from slipping. Curtain fabrics are often made with leno weave. Two of the more popular leno-weave fabrics are *marquisette* and *grenadine*. Many fruit sacks are leno-woven of slit films.

Woven Pile Fabrics

Pile fabrics have been defined as "fabrics(s) with cut or uncut loops which stand up densely on the surface" (Klapper 1967, 64). Pile fabrics may be created by weaving or through other construction techniques, such as tufting, knitting, or stitch through. To create the loops that appear on the surface of woven pile fabrics, the weaving process incorporates an extra set of yarns that form the pile. Construction of woven pile fabrics, therefore, represents a complex form of weaving in which there are at least three sets of yarns.

Woven pile fabrics are divided into two categories depending on whether the extra set of yarns is in the warp direction or the filling direction. *Warp pile fabrics* have two sets of warp yarns and one set of filling yarns. *Filling pile fabrics* have two sets of filling yarns.

Pile fabrics are woven by one of several methods, depending on whether they are warp pile or filling pile fabrics.

Warp Pile Fabrics

Warp pile can be made by the wire method, the double-cloth method, or by slack tension weaving.

In the wire method one set of warp yarns and the filling yarn interlace in the usual manner and form the "ground" fabric in either a plain or twill weave. The extra set of warp yarns forms the pile. When the pile yarns are raised by the heddles, the machine inserts a wire across the loom in the filling direction. When the warps are lowered, they loop over the wire to make a raised area. The next several filling yarns are inserted in the usual manner. The wire is then withdrawn, leaving the loop, which is held firmly in place by the other yarns. *Frieze*, a fabric often used for upholstery, is an example of an uncut, looped pile fabric that can be made by the wire method. If the fabric is to have a cut pile, the wire has a knife blade at the end that cuts the yarns as the wire is withdrawn. *Velvets* may be made in this way. (See Figures 15.18 and 15.19.) If the fabric is to have an uncut pile, the wire has no cutting edge.

The double-cloth method is used for cut pile fabrics. Here, two sets of warps and two sets of fillings are woven simultaneously into a layer of fabric. A third set of warp yarns moves back and forth between the two layers of fabric, holding them together

FIGURE 15.18

Construction of pile fabrics by the pile method.

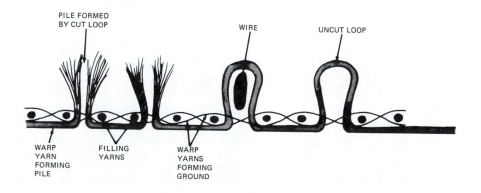

PILE FORMED
BY CUT LOOP

WIRE

UNCUT LOOP

WARP YARN FORMING PILE

FILLING YARNS

WARP YARNS FORMING GROUND

FIGURE 15.19

Velvet fabric in which figure is created by alternating sections of cut pile (the darker areas which reflect more light) with uncut sections (the loops of which are visible in the photograph.)

and being held by each fabric. The resultant fabric is cut apart by a sharp knife, thereby creating two lengths of fabric, each with a cut pile. (See Figure 15.20.)

Velvets and *plushes* can be made with the double-cloth method. Velvets are usually made of filament yarns. Other nonpile fabrics can be made by the double-cloth method, and are discussed later.

Terry cloth is made by the slack tension method. Terry cloth is made with uncut loops. Usually, two sets of warps and one set of filling yarns are used; however, more expensive fabrics may use two sets of yarns in each direction. The ground of the fab-

DOUBLE WOVEN VELVET BEFORE SPLITTING

CUT

PILE TUFTS

FIGURE 15.20

Diagram showing construction of pile fabric by the double-cloth method. Courtesy of the Crompton Company, Inc.

ric is of warp yarns held under tension, the pile of warp yarns that are allowed to relax. Periodically (usually after every three picks), tension is released on the warp pile yarns at the same time as the next three filling yarns are pushed firmly into place. The first two of each three picks are only beaten up part way. The loose warp yarns loop up on the surface to form the terry pile. Loops may remain uncut to form the traditional terry cloth with loops on both sides. (See Figure 15.21.)

Sometimes one side is sheared to make an attractive *velour* face. Such fabrics do not wear as well as uncut loop fabrics. Pile yarns in velour toweling tend to become dislodged more easily, thereby shortening the wear life of the material. Terry pile may appear on one or both sides of the fabric.

Filling Pile Fabrics

Filling pile fabrics are woven by the filling pile method. In this method there are two sets of filling yarns and one set of warp yarns. The extra set of filling yarns forms floats that are from four to six yarns in length. The floating yarns are cut at the center of the float, and these ends are brushed up on the surface of the fabric. (See Figure 15.22.)

In some filling pile constructions, the filling yarn that makes the pile is interlaced with the ground one time before it is cut; in others, the filling pile interlaces twice. Those fabrics in which there are two interlacings are more durable than when only one interlacing has taken place.

Floats for *corduroy* are placed in lengthwise rows, and floats for *velveteen* are spaced to produce an overall pile effect. Velveteens are characterized by a uniform, overall pile.

FIGURE 15.21

Terry cloth fabric. Ground is visible in the spaces between the uncut loops of the pile.

FIGURE 15.22

Construction of corduroy by the filling pile method.

Cut Floats Form Pile

Cross-section of Pile Fabric (Corduroy)

The even spacing of corduroy floats produces a strip or wale characteristic of this fabric Corduroys are given names according to the numbers of wales. *Feathercord* corduroy has about 20 to 25 lengthwise wales per inch; *fine wale* or *pinwale* corduroy, about 16 to 23 wales; *mid, medium,* or *regular wale* corduroy, about 14 wales; *wide wale* corduroy, about 6 to 10 wales; and *broad wale* corduroy, about 3 to 5 ribs per inch. Novelty wale corduroys are also produced in which thick and thin wales are arranged in varying patterns. (See Figure 15.23.) Some corduroy fabrics are now made with 100 percent cotton yarns in the pile filling and polyester and cotton blends in the ground

FIGURE 15.23

Corduroy fabric made with wales of three different widths and types.

yarns. Other decorative effects can be achieved by cutting floats selectively to vary pattern and texture. Most filling pile fabrics are made from spun yarns.

Chenille

Chenille fabrics have a pile that is created by the use of chenille yarns. (See chapter 13.) The loose yarn ends that fluff up on the surface of the chenille yarn to form "caterpillars" create a soft, cut pile when woven into fabrics. The pile in this case is created not by the fabric structure but by the characteristics of the yarn which is itself a narrow strip of lenowoven fabric. Chenille fabrics may be woven or knitted.

DECORATIVE SURFACE EFFECTS

Woven Effects

Hand embroidery has been used for many centuries to add decoration to fabrics. With the invention of the automatic loom came the production of looms that would create ornamental effects similar to that of embroidery.

Clipped or Unclipped Spot Weave

Embroiderylike designs may be achieved through the use of extra warp and extra filling yarns. In the clipped spot weave, either an extra shuttle or an extra set of warp yarns interlace to create a simple woven design. The extra yarns are carried along as a float on the wrong side of the fabric when they do not appear in the design. After the cloth is completed, the long floats may be cut away (clipped) or left uncut (unclipped). If clipped, which is the most common practice, the yarns form a characteristic "eyelash" effect. Sometimes these fabrics are used inside out for design interest. (See Figure 15.24.)

The durability of the design depends on the closeness of the weave of the fabric into which it is woven. Some domestic *dotted swiss* fabric is constructed by the clipped spot weave. This sheer cotton fabric uses small clipped spot yarns in con-

FIGURE 15.24

Clipped spot design.

a

b

FIGURE **15.25**

(a) Close-up of dotted swiss made by the clipped spot method. (b) Close-up of dotted swiss made by the swivel weave. Note that in (a) the fibers only interlace under one warp yarn, whereas in this figure the yarns appear to wrap around the warp yarns.

trasting color to create a dotted surface design (Figure 15.25a). Dotted swiss may also be made with flocking or with plastic dots, much cheaper options.

Swivel Weave

Similar fabrics can be made in the swivel weave, which is sometimes used in decorative fabrics for interiors. The design is made by supplying an extra filling yarn on a small shuttle or swivel. The filling design yarns are carried several times around a group of warps by the motion of the swivel to prevent the yarn from pulling out of the background fabric. The long floats between designs are knotted and clipped off. Occasionally, imported dotted swiss fabrics may use a swivel weave rather than a clipped spot weave. The swivel weave is more durable than the clipped spot weave because the design yarns are woven in and cannot pull out of the fabric as easily as in the latter method. (See Figure 15.25b.)

Lappet Weave

Lappet weaves have an extra warp yarn that may interlace in both the warp and filling direction with the ground fabric. The extra set of warps is threaded through needles set in front of the reed. The yarns are carried in a zigzag direction, back and forth to form an embroiderylike design. The design is created on the right side of the fabric, the excess yarn being carried along on the wrong side. Extra yarn is not clipped away from the back of the fabric but can be seen as it is carried from one design area to another. Imported Swiss braids often use the lappet weave, which is seldom found on merchandise sold in the United States.

Interwoven, or Double-Cloth, Fabrics

Interwoven fabrics are also called double-cloth fabrics. They are made with three, four, or five sets of yarns.

Double-faced fabrics are made with three sets of yarns. Woven either from two sets of warp yarns and one filling yarn or from two sets of filling yarns and one warp yarn, the effect of the weave is to produce the same appearance on both sides of the fabric. Some blankets and double-faced satins are examples of fabrics that are woven in this way.

Fabrics made with four sets of yarns use two sets of warp yarns and two sets of filling yarns. Yarns from both layers move back and forth from one layer to another, as required by the design. In some areas the two fabrics are totally separated; in others, all four sets of yarns are interwoven. *Matelassé* is one fabric made by this process. (See Figure 15.26.) The two layers of these fabrics cannot be separated without destroying the fabric. The cut edge of the fabric will show small "pockets" where fabric layers are separate. The pocket boundaries are the point at which yarn sets interchange from one side of the fabric to the other.

Fabrics with five sets of yarns are produced in the same way as double-woven pile fabrics. Two separate fabric layers are constructed. Extra yarns travel back and forth between the two layers to hold them together. These fabrics are often reversible, with one side being of one color and one side of another color. If the connecting yarn is cut, the two segments of the fabric can be separated into two individual pieces of cloth. (See Figure 15.27.)

Triaxally Woven Fabrics

Research and development of new fabric construction is constantly in progress. Several recent methods of fabric construction that are related to knitting are discussed in chapter 16. There is, however, another method of constructing fabrics that is closely related to traditional weaving, and it is known as *triaxial weaving*. The term is derived from *tri-* meaning "three" and *axial*, meaning "of or pertaining to the axis or center line." In other words, triaxial fabrics have three axes or center lines. (See Figure 15.28.) Traditionally, woven fabrics have a biaxial form or two axes, the lengthwise and crosswise axes.

Triaxial fabrics are usually woven by interlacing two sets of lengthwise yarns with one set of crosswise yarns. Special cams in the loom manipulate the yarns so that the double set of yarns is carried in a diagonal direction. All three sets of yarns interlace.

FIGURE 15.26

Matelasse fabric produced with four sets of yarns. In flat areas all four yarns interlace to form a single layer; in raised areas two separate fabrics are formed.

FIGURE 15.27

Double-woven fabric made with five sets of yarns. Each side of the fabric is a different color, and at the lower right corner the two fabric layers have been pulled apart and the yarns that hold them together can be seen.

FIGURE 15.28

Triaxial fabric structure.

Triaxial weaves are not entirely new. Snowshoes and some forms of basketwork sometimes have been made using a triaxial construction. The major advantage of triaxial weaving is in its stability against stretching not only in the length and crosswise directions but also in the bias. Even those biaxial fabrics with good stability in the warp and filling will stretch in the bias direction. Triaxially woven fabrics have high bursting strength resistance and strong resistance to tearing and raveling. Strength is uniform in all directions.

EFFECTS OF WOVEN STRUCTURE ON FABRIC PERFORMANCE

Durability

The contributions to strength of fibers and yarns have been discussed in chapters 2 and 13. Fabric structure also plays a critical role. Two of the most important fabric variables affecting strength of woven fabrics are weave and fabric count. The more interlacings in a fabric, the higher the fabric count. Fabric weaves with a high number of interlacings, such as plain weaves, can transfer and thereby share the tensile stresses at the intersection points. As a result, if fibers and yarns of comparable strength are used, they tend to have higher breaking strength than fabrics with fewer intersection points, such as satin weaves. On the other hand, tearing strength of fabrics with many interlacings may be reduced. In tightly woven plain weaves the yarns are bound in position and are unable to move to group together to share the stress imposed in tearing. They therefore exhibit a lower tearing strength than twills, oxfords, or satins, all of which have fewer lacing points.

The effect of weave can be altered by changing the fabric count of a woven fabric. A plain-weave fabric with an extremely low fabric count, such as cheesecloth, has a low breaking strength but a high tearing strength. The breaking strength is low because there are few yarns to share the load applied. The yarns in this structure, however, can slide around easily and group together to share the load during tearing. Try to tear a piece of cheesecloth and the strength of this type of structure becomes apparent. (See Figure 15.29.)

Yarns and fabric structure work together in determining elongation and recovery of textile fabrics. Crimp added to yarns, as in textured yarns, and the natural crimp created in all fabrics when yarns interlace are also related to extensibility. When warp and filling yarns cross each other, they cannot continue to move in an absolutely straight line, but each set of yarns must bend over and under yarns in the other set. Each yarn, therefore, develops a wavy configuration. (See Figure 15.30.) As the fabric is stretched, the crimp in the direction of the stretch is removed, permitting the fabric structure to reach its maximum extensibility. The greater the yarn crimp, the more extensible the fabric. Since warp yarns are under more tension during weaving, there is usually more crimp, and greater extensibility, in the filling direction. In unbalanced weaves, however, where there are many warp yarns interlacing with fewer filling yarns, the warp yarns will have more crimp.

In woven fabric construction, the aspect of crimp distribution seems to be particularly important in durability. The crown—the part of the yarn that protrudes above the surface of the fabric—receives the pressure of abrasion. The more crowns of the same height there are in a given area of cloth, the more evenly the wear will be distributed over the surface of the fabric, as shown in Figure 15.30. Prominently ribbed fabrics, such as faille or grosgrain, tend to abrade easily because the crowns of the warp yarns are so exposed. Interrelationships of construction and yarn structure may be observed in a fabric like shantung, in which uneven, loosely twisted slubbed yarns present higher crowns that are unevenly spaced; this is an example of a fabric that has poor abrasion resistance.

Weave also enters into abrasion resistance. In fabrics with floats, yarns and fibers are freer to move to absorb energy and are less consistently exposed to abradants. For this reason, twills and some tightly woven satin fabrics show superior abrasion resistance.

FIGURE 15.29

A cheesecloth under a tearing load showing yarns bunching together at the point of load concentration. Photograph courtesy of Robert Merkel. Reprinted from *Textile Product Serviceability,* Macmillan/Prentice Hall. Robert Merkel, 1991.

FIGURE 15.30

As warp and filling yarns pass over and under each other, they develop crimp. Smaller warp yarns (shown in black) develop greater crimp as they pass over larger filling yarns (shown in white).

Appearance

Drape or the ability of fabric to form pleasing folds is related to bending and shearing behavior, which are in turn affected by yarn and fabric properties. *Shearing* is the deformation of a structure in which a rectangle becomes lozenge shaped. In woven fabrics this results from movement of yarns from what one might call a normal position in which they run horizontally and vertically and interlace at right angles to other positions in which the interlacing is deformed away from the 90 degree angle. (See Figure 15.31.) Yarn and fabric structures that allow movement at the yarn intersections increase shearing. Woven fabrics with smooth yarns, low fabric counts, and higher crimp exhibit lower resistance to shearing.

Fabrics that shear easily are softer and more drapable. To illustrate this principle, think about cutting a half-circle skirt from a fabric. Parts of the garment will lie along the straight grain (true warp or filling directions), but other parts will lie along other directions, some at a diagonal called the *bias*. In the bias direction, fabric is particularly subject to shear deformation.

If the fabric is unable to shear, it remains stiff and will not mold or drape softly. In general, because of the ways in which yarns are combined, woven fabrics have higher shearability than other fabric structures.

To form the graceful folds desirable in draping, fabrics also must have low resistance to bending. Lower fabric counts and fine yarns with flexible fibers give fabrics the ability to bend easily and contribute to draping. Fabrics such as satins that have long floats in the weave are more flexible, bending more easily and improving draping qualities.

Fabric structure affects the ability of yarns and fibers to move. In general, woven fabrics with few interlacings wrinkle less than do other fabrics. This is because loosely constructed fabrics generally allow more fiber redistribution and motion. It follows, then, that plain weaves wrinkle more than twill or satin weaves, and fabrics with higher fabric counts also wrinkle more. Cheesecloth, with an extremely low fabric count, does not wrinkle as much as higher-count plain weaves. (See Figure 15.32.)

Dimensional stability problems are often related to unreleased stresses introduced during fabric manufacturing. Fabrics, and the yarns in them, must be kept under tension during weaving. As a result they may be stretched beyond their natural dimensions. Later when the fabric is subjected to moisture, or heat in the case of thermoplastic fibers, the stresses within the fibers, yarns, and fabrics are relieved, and the whole fabric relaxes. Fabrics containing moisture absorbent fibers will shrink more in laundering because the fibers absorb a significant amount of water and swell. (See chapter 23, page 458 for a discussion of relaxation shrinkage.)

FIGURE 15.31

Shear deformation is the movement of yarns from a normal position (a) where yarns run horizontally and vertically to other position(s) (b) where interlacing is deformed to a less than 90 degree angle. Fabrics with low shearability (c) are not as soft and drapable as fabrics with high shearability (d).

A. NORMAL STATE

B. SHEARED

C. LOW SHEARABILITY

D. HIGH SHEARABILITY

Shrinkage can also be affected by fabric count in woven fabrics. Generally, if there is room in the structure for the yarns to swell without moving closer together, then the fabric will be more dimensionally stable. If there is not much room between the yarns, they move closer together when the fibers swell. Therefore, fabrics with higher fabric counts will shrink more until they reach the point where they are forced together into a "jammed" construction and can no longer move.

FIGURE 15.32

Cotton cheesecloth (left) and cotton print cloth (right) after wrinkling.

Optical covering power is also influenced by weaves. An open-construction fabric will obviously cover less well than a densely constructed fabric. Sheer fabrics are often desired and can be achieved by fine yarns and/or low fabric counts. Differences in covering power can be seen among the three woven fabrics in Figure 15.33. Fab-

FIGURE 15.33

Effects of fabric construction and cover factor on air permeability. Fabric (a) has the highest permeability and lowest cover factor. Fabric (c) has the lowest permeability and highest cover factor. Micrographs by Helen H. Epps, reprinted by permission of International Textiles and Apparel Association.

a

b

c

ric crimp is also related to covering power in woven fabrics. As yarns in one direction cross and exert pressure on the yarns in the opposite direction, these yarns may be flattened somewhat. Flatter yarns provide better cover.

Comfort Factors

Fabric construction plays an important role in insulation. Pile or napped constructions are especially good for cold weather because the yarns or fibers perpendicular to the surface provide numerous spaces for dead air. This effect is maximized if such fabrics are worn with the napped or pile surface next to the body, or if they are covered with another layer.

Moisture vapor transmission and water repellency affect comfort. Most fibers are not naturally water repellent but must be given special treatments to render them water repellent. Dense cotton fabrics, by contrast, may provide water repellency through both fabric structure and fiber properties. The hydrophilic cotton fibers swell on exposure to water, jamming the construction and forming a barrier to keep out water.

Air permeability is decreased in fabrics with high fabric counts. To make garments that are warm enough for sports such as skiing in which moving air may cool the athlete, a fabric with low air permeability (such as closely woven nylon) may be combined with materials of low thermal conductivity (such as a polyester or acrylic fiberfill or a pile fabric) that trap air close to the body.

In these and other products, fiber, yarn, and fabric structure can be seen to work together to create the desired effect.

SUMMARY

When fabrics have been constructed by weaving, the weave used will have a significant influence on durability, appearance, and comfort of a product. Three basic weaves are plain, twill, and satin. Variations and modifications of these weaves allows for a tremendous variety of fabrics constructions, and selection of different fibers and yarns adds to the possibilities.

Assessing the combined effects of fiber, yarn, and weave on performance is essential not only for professionals who produce and utilize fabrics, but also for consumers. The importance of considering these various factors is perhaps best illustrated by looking carefully at a particular use for textiles. Case Study 15.1 is an examination of some of the factors relating to fibers, yarns, and weaves that should be evaluated when selecting upholstery fabrics.

Putting it all together for . . .

Upholstery Fabrics

Appearance is often the single most influential factor in selection of upholstery fabric. Consumers often do not realize that an expensive piece of furniture may be upholstered with a beautiful fabric that will wear out in a relatively short time. The most important considerations in evaluating the durability of upholstery fabrics are its resistance to abrasion, its resistance to soil and stains, and colorfastness to light.

Abrasion Resistance

Upholstered furniture is constantly subjected to abrasion as people sit on it. Some fibers have better abrasion resistance than others. In fabric structures where one set of yarns predominates on the surface, the abrasion resistance of the fibers in that yarn would be a very important factor in durability. In many upholstery fabrics, however, yarn and fabric construction may compensate for lower fiber strength.

Yarns with high twist and even diameter resist abrasion better than those with low twist and/or uneven diameter. Yarns with loops, nubs, or slubs, often used because of their attractive texture, are especially subject to abrasive wear. Heavier yarns result in thicker fabrics that are more abrasion resistant.

In closely woven fabrics with balanced weaves, wear is evenly distributed across the surface of the fabric. If fibers are strong and yarns have high twist and uniform diameter, these fabrics can be very durable. In plain-weave fabrics with large ribs or cords, the raised rib or cord area has the potential for uneven wear.

Twill woven fabric structures are generally strong, durable, and resist abrasion. In satin-weave fabrics, the long floats may catch or snag. Furthermore, to capitalize on the attractive appearance of satin-weave fabrics, manufacturers often use acetate, silk, or nylon fibers in low-twist yarns that are not very durable.

In pile fabrics such as velvet or velveteen, abrasion resistance depends on fiber choice and density of pile. Nylon velvet, for example, can be quite durable thanks to its excellent abrasion resistance and good resilience, whereas silk or rayon pile fabrics are more likely not only to abrade but also to remain flat and worn-looking after the pile has been flattened by sitting on it. Uncut pile fabrics tend to wear better, especially if yarns are tightly twisted and made from abrasion-resistant fibers.

Dobby and jacquard woven fabrics are frequently used in upholstery. Their resistance to abrasion is variable. Factors to assess include fiber content, tightness of twist of the yarns, presence of long floats or raised areas that may catch or wear unevenly, and denseness of the weave.

Soil and Stain Resistance

Most stains on upholstered furniture are water- or liquid-borne. Hydrophobic fibers such as polypropylene, which is almost completely nonabsorbent, resist staining best. It is important to note, however, that even though the upholstery fabric may not absorb moisture, the padding materials underneath may. Consumers should ascertain that there is a moisture-proof barrier between the upholstery fabric and the padding materials. When present, this barrier is often a non-woven layer of nonabsorbent material such as polypropylene. Upholstery fabrics made from fibers that do absorb moisture can have stain-resistant finishes applied to them. (See chapter 23, page 466.)

Colorfastness to Light

Upholstery on furnishings that are placed close to windows may undergo color loss or color change after long exposure to sunlight. Information about the types of dyes used on fabrics is generally not available at the point of purchase, however consumers may be able to ask the retailer about guarantees against color loss.

In selecting the right upholstery fabrics, the purchaser must assess the uses to which the furniture will be put. A sofa for a family room where food and beverages will be served, where children will drag toys across the surface, and where cats and dogs will jump up and down must meet far different demands than a period reproduction chair in a formal living room that is rarely used. Careful evaluation of the expected functions and how fiber, yarn, and fabric construction fulfill those functions can result in selecting upholstery fabrics that will satisfy the buyer's needs and expectations.

References

American Fabrics and Fashions Magazine, ed. 1980. Encyclopedia of textiles. 3rd edition. Englewood Cliffs, NJ: Prentice Hall.

Klapper, M. 1967. *Fabric almanac.* New York: Fairchild.

Review Questions

1. Explain the differences between a plain weave, basket weave, twill weave, satin weave, jacquard weave, and leno weave. Name at least two standard fabrics made with each of these weaves.
2. Describe the different methods by which pile fabrics can be made.
3. Explain what is meant by each of the following: clipped spot weave, swivel weave, lappet weave, double-cloth fabric, triaxial weave. Give one example of some type of product in which fabrics made with these weaves might be used.
4. Analyze the probable contributions of fiber, yarn, and weave to the durability, appearance, and comfort of the following products:
    a. A pair of twill weave, denim blue jeans made of 60 percent cotton and 40 percent polyester. Yarns used have a moderately high twist and the cotton has been combed. The fabric has a high fabric count.
    b. A gauze-type fabric blouse for summer made of fine 100 percent linen yarn.

Recommended Readings

Emery, I. 1966. *The primary structure of fabrics.* Washington, D.C.: The Textile Museum.

Men's dress shirts. 1993. *Consumer Reports*, August, vol. 58(8). 504.

Mueller, C., and O. Bissmann. 1993. Letters, figures, interweaving: An easy task. *Textile World* 143 (November): 61.

KNITTED FABRICS

Few segments of the textile industry have grown so rapidly in recent years as has the knitting industry. Advances in knitting production techniques along with the use of synthetic fabrics, such as acrylics and polyesters, for knit goods have led to the manufacture of knitted items, including such diverse products as men's tailored suits, table linens, blankets, bedspreads, carpeting, wall coverings, upholstery, shipping sacks, paint rollers, and vacuum cleaner bags.

The apparel knitting industry may be divided into four branches: knitted outerwear, knitted yard goods, knitted hosiery, and knitted underwear. Knitted yard goods mills produce a wide variety of fabrics in either flat or circular form that can be cut and sewn into apparel and other items. Those mills that produce outerwear, hosiery, or underwear may knit the item directly or may knit sections of a garment (such as sleeves, body sections, and the like) that are sewn, or cut and sewn, together. These mills complete the garment from knitting right through to assembly in the same mill.

HISTORICAL DEVELOPMENT OF KNITS

Although fragments of knitted cloth have been found at the site of Dura Europos, an ancient Syrian city founded in 280 B.C., and other examples from the Middle East date from the middle of the third century A.D., hand knitting seems to have come to Europe only during the Middle Ages. Apparently, the Arab conquerors of Spain imported the technique of knitting from their homeland sometime after A.D. 1000. Knitting spread gradually to the rest of Europe. Because knits were more elastic than woven goods, they gained popularity, especially for making stockings and gloves.

Today one thinks of hand knitting as a process that uses two or more knitting needles, but the earliest hand knitting was done not on needles but on a frame into which a series of pegs had been set. Yarn was looped around each peg. To make the stitches, the knitter pulled a new loop of yarn through the old loop encircling the peg and placed the new loop around the peg while slipping the old loop off the peg with a hooked needle. The gradually increasing rows of loops formed the fabric. Eventually, a long, pointed knitting needle, such as those used today, replaced the pegs for holding the loops, and a second needle replaced the hook for adding and subtracting loops.

The use of two needles or the knitting frame made a flat fabric. A round tube of fabric could be made by using a circular needle, a round frame, or a set of four needles.

Since the knitting process was relatively simple, it lent itself to mechanization somewhat more easily than did weaving. By the late 1500s a knitting frame machine had been invented by William Lee. This machine made mechanically all of the kinds of knits that had previously been made by hand. Lee's machine continued in use until further refinements of machine knitting were made during the Industrial Revolution. (See Figure 16.1.)

FIGURE 16.1

Knitted cap made in Italy in the seventeenth century.
Photograph courtesy of the Metropolitan Museum of Art, Rogers Fund, 1927.

BASIC CONCEPTS

"Knitting is the process of making cloth with a single yarn or set of yarns moving in only one direction. Instead of two sets of yarns crossing each other as in weaving, the single knitting yarn is looped through itself to make a chain of stitches. These chains or rows are connected side by side to produce the knit cloth" (American Fabrics and Fashions Magazine 1980, 370). The interlocking of these loops in knitting can be done by either vertical or horizontal movement. When the yarns are introduced in a crosswise direction, at right angles to the direction of growth of the fabric, and run or interlock across the fabric, the knit is known as a *weft knit*. (Some sources may refer to these knits as *filling knits*, but the term *weft knit* is used in the knitting industry.) When the yarns run lengthwise or up and down, the knit is known as a *warp knit*.

In knitting terminology, the rows of stitches that run in columns along the lengthwise direction of the fabric are known as *wales*. This corresponds to the warp direction of woven fabrics. Crosswise rows of stitches or loops are called *courses*. The direction of the courses corresponds to the filling of woven goods. (See Figure 16.2.)

Both warp and weft knits are made by machine. Knitting machines may be either flat or circular. The flat-type knitting machine has needles arranged in one or two straight lines and held on a flat needlebed. The cloth is made by forming stitches on these needles. The resulting fabric is flat. Machines with flatbeds are used to make both warp and weft knits.

The circular knitting machine has needles arranged in a circle on a rotating cylinder. (See Figure 16.3.) The resulting fabric is formed into a tube. Circular knitting machines produce weft knits almost exclusively.

For nearly two hundred years after its invention in 1589, Lee's machine was used without further improvement. Using a *spring beard needle*, Lee's machine produced flat knitted fabrics by mechanically passing one loop of yarn through another.

Loop Formation

The spring beard needle is formed from one piece of thin wire. One end of the needle is drawn into thinner dimensions and is curved to form a hook. The flexible outer side of the hook can be pressed against the stem of the needle to close the hook for sliding a formed loop off and beginning a new loop. (See Figure 16.4.)

FIGURE 16.2

Rows of stitches that run in a vertical column along the lengthwise direction of the fabric are called wales; crosswise rows of stitches or loops are called courses.

FIGURE 16.3

(a) Electronically controlled circular weft knitting machine. This model, Monarch F-LPJ/3A, is a 72 feed, 37-step double knit machine. The yarn is held on the spools on a frame at the left of the machine. The completed fabric emerges in tubular form at the bottom of the machine. Photograph courtesy of Monarch Knitting Machinery Company, photographed at Alandale Knitting Co., Inc., Troy, N.C. (b) Electronically controlled flat weft knitting machine. Photograph courtesy of H. Stoll GmbH & Co.

a

b

In 1847 Matthew Townshend invented a different type of hook known as the *latch needle*, which has come to be the most widely used type of needle. Its operation is similar to that of the spring beard needle, except that instead of having to mechanically press the flexible wire of the needle closed so that the forming yarn loop will not slide off, a latch closes to hold the yarn in place. Figure 16.5 illustrates the steps in the cycle of the latch needle:

1. The old loop is held on the stem of the needle. The latch is open (a).
2. The hook grasps the yarn to begin forming a new loop (b).
3. The needle falls, the old loop rises, closing the latch of the needle (c).

FIGURE 16.4

Spring beard needle showing casting off of old loop and beginning of new loop.

FIGURE 16.5

Formation of a loop by a latch needle.

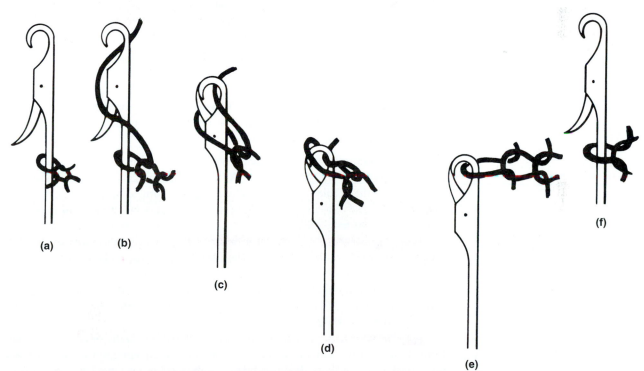

(a)   (b)

(c)

(d)

(e)

(f)

4. The old loop is cast off (d and e).
5. The needle rises, and the new loop slides down to the stem of the needle, pushing the latch open again, and the needle is ready to repeat the cycle (f).

Yet a third type of needle, the compound needle, is used almost exclusively for warp knitting. The compound needle has two components, a tongue and a hook (Figure 16.6). Its motion is as follows:

1. The old loop encircles the hook; the tongue is in such a position as to leave the hook open.

FIGURE 16.6

Tongue (a) of a compound needle moves into position against the hook (b) in order to close the needle.

2. Both tongue and hook rise; a new yarn is fed to the hook.
3. Both tongue and hook descend, but the tongue descends more slowly, thereby closing the hook.
4. As the needle descends, the held loop slides off, forming a new loop.
5. The needle returns to its initial position, the hook ascending more rapidly, thereby opening the hook again.

For weft knitting with either needle type, a cam system provides the action for lifting the needles as the yarn is fed in. A small projection called a butt is located at the bottom of the needle. The butt is held in a groove formed by a system of cams or shaped pieces. The movement of the butt in the grooves between the cams causes the needle to rise and fall. (See Figure 16.7.)

The engaging by the needle of a new piece of yarn is called *feeding*. Devices called feeders are located to introduce the yarn to the needles. The number of feeders can vary, but obviously the more feeders a machine has, the higher will be the speed of fabric forming on the machine, since each needle produces a loop each time it is activated and if many needles are activated more frequently, many courses can be formed at the same time.

Another important element of some knitting machines is the sinker. The already formed fabric may need to be controlled as the subsequent knitting action takes place. A thin steel device called the sinker may be used to hold the fabric as the needle rises, support the fabric as the needle descends, and push the fabric away from the needle after the new loop has been formed. Sinkers are generally mounted between the needles. (See Figure 16.8.) Some machines, however, do not use sinkers but instead use the tensions placed on the completed fabrics for control.

Gauge and Quality

The size of the needle and the spacing of the needles on knitting machines determine the number and size of the knit stitches and their closeness. Each wale is formed on

V

New yarn

SL

Trick
wall

Old
loop

5

4

3

2

1

Stitch
cam

Clearing cam

Upthrow
cam

X

FIGURE 16.7

Cam system for control of
needle action in weft knits.
Reprinted from D. J. Spencer,
Knitting Technology, 2nd ed.
(Oxford: Pergamon Press, 1989),
20. Copyright 1989 by
Butterworth-Heinemann, Ltd.

one needle. The number of needles is equal to the number of wales. The closeness of the stitches determines whether a knit fabric will be lightweight and open or heavier and more dense. The term *gauge* is used to describe the closeness of knit stitches. Gauge is the number of needles in a measured space on the knitting machine. Higher-gauge fabrics (those with more stitches) are made with finer needles; lower-gauge fabrics are made with coarser or larger needles.

The term *cut* is also used to designate the number of needles per inch in the needlebed of a circular weft knitting machine. To describe the stitch density of a

FIGURE 16.8

Sinkers used for weft knits, with latch needles in position ready for formation of new loop.

SINKER

single or double knit fabric, the fabric may be designated as an 18-, 20-, 22-, or 24-cut fabric. The higher the cut, the closer the stitches; the lower the cut, the coarser the fabric.

Varying types of knitting machines measure gauge over different distances on the machine. For example, circular knit hosiery measures the number of needles in 1.0 inch, full-fashioned knitting in 1.5 inches, and Raschel knits in 2.0 inches. Because of these differences, it is best to keep in mind the generalized principle that the higher the gauge, the closer the stitches.

The quality of needles used in manufacturing knit goods is related directly to the quality of the fabric produced. Needles of uneven size and quality will produce knit fabrics with uneven-sized stitches and imperfect surface appearance.

In warp knits, those knits in which the yarns interlace in the long direction, one or more yarns are allotted to each needle on the machine, and those yarns follow the long direction of the fabric. For weft knits, those in which the yarns interlace crosswise or horizontally, one or more yarns are used for each course, and these yarns move across the fabric. In weft knits, one yarn may have from twenty to several hundred needles associated with it. To summarize, weft knits can be made with one yarn, but warp knits must have a whole set of warp yarns, that is, one or more for each needle.

Once the basic distinction between warp and weft knits has been made, further subdivisions of knit classifications are usually based on the types of machines used in their production. The majority of knit fabrics are named after the machines on which they are constructed. For this reason, the discussion of knitted fabrics that follows is organized around the types of machines used in manufacturing knit fabrics and the types of knit fabrics made on these machines.

WEFT KNITS

The most important difference among weft knitting machines is in the number of needlebeds and the number of sets of needles used. On these bases, weft knits are divided among those made on each of these machines:

1. Flat or circular jersey, or single knit, machine: one needlebed and one set of needles.
2. Flat or circular rib machine: two needlebeds and two sets of needles.
3. Flat or circular purl, or links-links, machine: two needlebeds and one set of needles.

Jersey, or Single, Knits

Machines with one needlebed and one set of needles are called jersey machines or single-knit machines. With one set of needles and one needlebed, all needles face the same direction; all stitches are pulled to the same side of the fabric. As a result, jersey fabrics have a smooth face with a vertical grain on the right side of the fabric and a widthwise grain on the back side. The loops formed by the jersey machine are formed in one direction only, which gives a different appearance to each side of the fabric. (See Figure 16.9.) The basic fabric produced by this machine is known alternately as a *plain, single knit*, or *jersey;* the terms are interchangeable.

Jersey stretches slightly more in the crosswise than the lengthwise direction. If one stitch breaks, the fabric may ladder, or *run*. Jersey fabrics tend to curl at the edges and are less stable than are some other types of knits. This is the result of the pressures exerted during knitting. In addition jersey knits may twist or skew after laundering, as the twisting tensions imposed during the knitting process are relaxed. Special finishing techniques are used to overcome these tendencies and maintain fabric stability; the principal ones use starches, gum mixtures, polyvinyl acetate emulsions, and resins.

A great many items of hosiery, sweaters, and other wearing apparel are made from plain jersey knits. Consumer Brief 16.1 highlights one of the common uses of jersey knit fabrics: T-shirts. Plain knit fabrics can also be made into designs of two or more colors by use of a patterning mechanism that controls the selection and feeding of yarns and types of stitches to create jacquard knits. (See Figure 16.10.)

High-Pile Fabrics

High-pile fabrics, such as imitation furs and plushes, are usually knitted by a jersey machine. While the knitting is taking place, a sliver of staple fiber is fed into the machine. These fibers are caught in the tight knit and are held firmly in place. Although any staple fiber can be used for the pile, the greatest quantity of these fabrics are made with acrylic and modacrylic fibers in the pile. (See Figure 16.11.)

By using staple fibers of varying lengths, adding color through fiber dyeing or printing on the surface of the pile, and by shearing or brushing the pile, an enormous variety of effects can be achieved. The use of knitted pile fabric ranges from excellent imitations of furs, such as leopard, tiger, mink, or mouton, to colorful pile outerwear, coat linings, or pile carpet fabrics.

Knitted Terry, Velour, and Fleece

Jersey knits can also be made in the form of knitted terry fabrics and knitted velours. Two yarns are fed into the machine simultaneously, picked up by the same needle,

FIGURE 16.9

Plain or jersey knit stitch. Diagrams courtesy of the National Knitwear Manufacturers Association.

a

TECHNICAL FACE

b

c

TECHNICAL BACK

d

CONSUMER BRIEF 16.1 T-Shirts

T-shirts began life as white knitted cotton undergarments for men during World War II. By the 1990s they were being worn as undergarments and outergarments by men, women, and children; printed with logos and messages; dyed to a wide range of colors; decorated with embroidery, sequins, and beading; and cut to fit loosely or tightly. Between April 1990 and April 1991, more than one billion T-shirts were sold in the United States (Lonsinger 1993.)

The classic T-shirt is constructed of tubular jersey fabric. It has short sleeves set into the body of the garment. Sleeve and bottom hems are usually sewn flat. The neckline consists of a 1 × 1 rib knit strip sewn onto the body of the shirt. Some shirts have pockets sewn onto one or both sides of the front. T-shirts are sometimes made of fine rib knits that, even on close examination, are hard to distinguish from jersey knits. Long-sleeved T-shirts are also made, and these usually have an attached 1 × 1 rib knit cuff.

The characteristics of jersey and rib knits make them the fabric of choice for T-shirts. Jersey knits stretch, moving comfortably with the body. They are resilient, returning to their original shape after stretching. If laundered and tumble dried, they generally require no ironing. The widthwise elasticity of rib knits allows the T-shirt to stretch as it is pulled over the head or wrists but then return to a close fit.

Although many fibers can and have been used to make T-shirt–like garments, the classic T-shirt is usually made from 100 percent cotton or from blends of cotton and polyester. The most common blend is 50/50. Some manufacturers are also making T-shirts of 90 percent cotton and 10 percent spandex for increased stretch and recovery.

The quality of T-shirts depends on the quality of the fibers, yarns, fabric, and construction. Long-staple pima or sea island cottons may be used for high-quality products. Cotton yarns may be mercerized for increased strength, luster, and durability. Yarns may be carded, which will leave more fuzzy fiber ends on the surface of the fabric, or combed for a smoother surface.

Jersey knits can be made in various weights. Those with more stitches per inch and heavier yarns will feel heavier and will be more durable, although in hot weather they will also feel warmer because they allow less air penetration. Less densely constructed knits are likely to snag and pull more readily. If a knit stitch breaks, a run can form, but unlike sheer nylon stockings where the slippery nature of the fiber allows runs to form quickly, the friction of cotton yarns makes runs travel less readily and for less distance.

The major performance problem consumers experience with T-shirts is shrinkage, which occurs during the first several launderings. Jersey knits undergo relaxation shrinkage as a result of the relaxation of tensions placed on fabrics during processing. Shrinkage is usually more pronounced in the lengthwise direction and is often accompanied by growth in the crosswise direction as the knitted loops broaden. Retailers generally anticipate shrinkage of 8 to 10 percent in both width and length, although high-quality knit goods manufacturers try to limit product shrinkage to 5 percent. To ensure satisfactory performance, consumers should look for labels that indicate fabrics have been treated to prevent shrinkage.

In satisfactory construction seams are sewn flat and not puckered, and stitches are close and even. Seams at the back of the neck and also at the shoulder may be covered with a strip of knitted tape, which is more comfortable against the skin than a seam. The tape also prevents the shoulder seam from stretching excessively.

T-shirts can generally be machine washed and tumble dried; however, printing of logos and slogans, and novelty trimmings such as sequins, beads, or embroidery, may require special handling. Consult care labels for recommended procedures.

---

and knitted in such a way that one of the yarns appears on the face of the fabric, the other on the back. The yarn that forms the pile is pulled up to the surface of the fabric. If the pile remains uncut, the resulting cloth is like a one-sided terry cloth. If the pile is cut, the fabric is called *velour*. (See Figure 16.12.)

Terry fabrics made by this process are not as durable as are woven terry cloths, nor do they hold their shape as well. On the other hand, they have softer draping

FIGURE 16.10

Sides of a jacquard patterned plain knit fabric (a) face; (b) reverse.

a

b

qualities. The knitted velours are softer and more flexible than are woven pile fabrics, such as velveteen. Major uses for both fabrics are for sports and loungewear, for infants' and children's clothing, and for household items such as towels and slipcovers.

The soft, fleecy effect produced on the inside of sweatshirts is achieved by much the same techniques as in making velours. The fleece is created by cutting and brushing the loops that are formed on the underside of the fabric.

Plated Fabrics

In creating plated fabrics, the knitting machine feeds two separate yarns at the same time. The two yarns are in the same loop, one behind the other. By varying the color, texture, or type of yarn, interesting decorative effects can be achieved. It is also possible to use one yarn as the face yarn and another as a backing yarn. Using an expensive face yarn with an inexpensive backing yarn can help to keep the cost of the

FIGURE 16.11

A jersey knit, high-pile fabric: (a) back; (b) face.

(a)

(b)

a

b

FIGURE 16.12

A jersey knit, velour fabric; (a) back; (b) face.

fabric lower. Plating varies from relatively simple construction to intricate pattern designs.

Two-Bed Knits

The *Knitting Encyclopedia* (Reichman 1972) states, "From a purely technical point of view, a double knit fabric is any knitted cloth or garment section that has been produced on any type of opposed bed knitting machine with two sets of needles of any range of fineness or coarseness" (p. 96). Those which have the greatest commercial interest can be classified as:

1. narrow and broad rib knits
2. nonjacquard and jacquard double jersey (commonly called double knits)
3. interlock knits

The machines used to produce rib knits, double jerseys, and interlock knits differ from the machines used for plain knits in that they have two needle-holding beds and two sets of needles. For circular machines one set of needles is located on the needle cylinder in the same way as in plain knit machines, and the second set is placed in a dial positioned over the cylinder much as a lid would be placed over a cylindrical jar. The dial is grooved, as is the cylinder, and needles lie within the grooves, called *tricks*, in such a way that the hooks of the horizontal dial needles and those of the vertical cylinder needles are perpendicular to each other. (See Figure 16.13.) The fabric created between the two sets of needles will have the appearance of the face fabric on both sides.

In flat-bed machines the needlebeds are placed so the two rows of needles form an inverted V. These machines are known as *vee bed machines*. (See Figure 16.14.)

FIGURE 16.13

(a) Diagram of a cyclinder and dial arrangement for a circular knitting machine; (b) needles are placed inside the tricks in close-up; (c) diagram of the relative positions of dial and cylinder needles. Diagrams from P. Schwartz, T. Rhodes, and M. Mohamed, *Fabric Forming Systems*. Reproduced courtesy of Noyes Publications.

BACK BED

FRONT BED

TRICKS

(a)

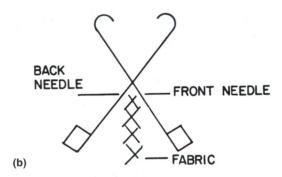

BACK
NEEDLE

FRONT NEEDLE

FABRIC

(b)

FIGURE 16.14

(a) Diagram of a vee bed; (b) diagram showing relative positions of needles from front and back beds. Diagrams from P. Schwartz, T. Rhodes, and M. Mohamed, *Fabric Forming Systems.* Reproduced courtesy of Noyes Publications.

Rib Knits

"A rib knit fabric is characterized by lengthwise ribs formed by wales alternating on the face and back of the cloth. If every other stitch alternates from front to back, it is called a 1 × 1 rib. If every two stitches alternate, it is called a 2 × 2 rib." (Reichman 1972, 354) The larger the number of stitches that alternate, the more pronounced the rib. A 1 × 1 rib made in a fine gauge may hardly be visible to the eye. Fabrics may appear to be a jersey on both sides. (See Figure 16.15.) Rib knits are made on a two-bed machine with one set of needles forming the loops for one wale and the other set of needles forming the alternating wale.

Rib knits have greater elasticity in the width than in the length. They are stable and do not curl or stretch out of shape as do the jersey knits. For this reason, they are often used to make cuffs and necklines on weft knitted garments. Rib knits are reversible unless the number of stitches in the alternating wales is uneven, as in a 2 × 3 rib.

Double Jersey Fabrics

The term *double knit* is generally applied by consumers to fabrics that are, technically, double jersey fabrics. Double jersey fabrics are also made on two-bed knitting machines, but the arrangement of the needles is different from that for knitting rib fabrics. The layers of loops alternate from one side to the other, locking the two layers together. (See Figure 16.16.) Double knit fabrics have the same appearance on both sides of the fabric, that is, exhibiting the appearance of the face or outer side of a single knit on both sides. Twice as much yarn is incorporated into double knit fabrics as into comparable single knits.

FIGURE 16.15

(a) 1 × 1 rib fabric structure. Diagram courtesy of National Knitwear Manufacturers Association. (b) 2 × 2 rib fabric.

a

b

FIGURE 16.16

(a) Diagrammatic representation of a double knit; (b) close-up photograph of front and back sides of a double knit.

a

b

Double knit fabrics are more stable than plain knits. When made from synthetic yarns, double knits should be heat-set for better dimensional stability. They do not run and are easier for the home sewer to handle. During periods when double knits have been fashionable, textured synthetic yarns and wool have been favored for double knit apparel. The home furnishings industry also has utilized double knit fabrics for upholstery.

A wide variety of decorative effects are possible in double jersey fabrics. These include "blister" fabrics with sculptured or raised surface effects and elaborate patterns called "jacquard" patterns because of their similarity to jacquard-woven patterns.

Interlock Knits

Interlock knits are produced on a special machine that has alternating long and short needles on both beds. Long and short needles are placed opposite each other. Long needles knit the first feeder yarn; short needles knit the second feeder yarn. The fabric created is an interlocking of two 1 × 1 rib structures. (See Figure 16.17.)

The resulting fabric, like double knit fabrics, is thicker than single knit fabric, and more stable in the widthwise direction. Interlock fabrics have been traditionally used for underwear. They are produced more slowly than are other rib knits and are generally made in plain colors or simple patterns because the addition of pattern slows down the manufacture even further. (See Figure 16.18.)

Purl Knits

Purl machines have two needlebeds and one set of needles. Because the machine moves only to the left, it is also called a *links-links machine*. *Links* is the German word for "left."

The links-links machine operates somewhat more slowly than do other knitting machines, causing the price of purl fabrics to be higher than that of other knits. The machine has a latch-type knitting needle with a hook on either end that allows the needle to pull stitches to either the back or the face of the fabric. This makes possible the construction of stitches on alternate sides of the fabric. The double needle arrangement makes this the most versatile of the weft knitting machines, as it can make plain, purl, or rib knits.

FIGURE 16.17

Diagram of interlock knitting. Short needles are labeled "S" and long needles, "L". The first feeder yarn is white, the second is dark. Reprinted from D. J. Spence, *Knitting Technology*. Courtesy of Butterworth-Heinemann Ltd.

FIGURE 16.18

(a) Diagrammatic representation of an interlock knit; (b) photograph showing both sides of an interlock knit fabric. (Left is underside of fabric, right is topside.) Diagram reprinted by permission from D. J. Spencer, *Knitting Technology*, 2nd ed. (Oxford: Pergamon, 1989), 20. Copyright © 1989 by Butterworth-Heinemann Ltd.

a

b

The simplest purl fabric is made by alternating courses so that every other course is drawn to the opposite side of the fabric, thereby producing a fabric with the same appearance on both sides. (See Figure 16.19.) The raised courses produce a somewhat uneven texture.

Purl knit fabrics have high crosswise and lengthwise stretch. They are often made into a variety of decorative sweaters. Interesting textures can be achieved by the use of fluffy, soft yarns. The versatility of the machine makes possible the creation of a variety of patterns in these knits; however, relatively small quantities of fabrics are made in the purl stitch.

Weft Knit Stitch Variation

The basic loop formed in the plain knit serves as the starting point for a wide range of weft knit stitches that can be used to vary the surface texture of weft knits. These

FIGURE 16.19

(a) Purl knit structure. Courtesy of National Knitwear Manufacturers Association. (b) Close-up view of stitches in a purl knit fabric.

a

b

include miss or float stitches, tuck stitches, and open stitches variously known as transfer or spread stitches. (See Figure 16.20.)

In miss or float stitches, some needles are immobilized, and instead of catching the stitch, they allow the yarn to be carried across the back of the fabric. The float stitch can be used to hide colored yarns at the back of the fabric when they do not appear in the design on the face. When long, straight floats are used, the elasticity of the fabric is reduced, and long floats are likely to be caught or snagged in use.

The tuck stitch is made by programming certain needles to hold both an old loop and a new yarn without casting off the old stitch. This creates an elongated stitch that appears in the fabric as an opening or variation in the surface pattern.

Loops can be transferred sideways to create decorative effects or open spaces. Transfer of loops can also be used in shaping of knits, as in *full-fashioning*, which is accomplished on specialized machines. Combinations of the tuck, miss, and other stitches with basic rib, plain, or purl knit stitches can create such varied effects as raised cables, open work alternating with plain knit, and a wide range of other deco-

FIGURE 16.20

Basic weft-knitted stitches viewed from the front of the fabric. (Note that only a single purl stitch is shown here. This should not be confused with a purl fabric, shown in Figure 16.20, which is made from many purl stitches.) From J. A. Smirfitt, *An Introduction to Warp Knitting.* Copyright © Watford, Herts, U.K., 1975 Merrow Publishing Company, Ltd. Reproduced by permission.

PLAIN

PURL

TRANSFER

SPREAD

MISS OR FLOAT

TUCK

CROSS

FIGURE 16.21

Close-up photograph of fashion marks in sweater.

rative fabrics. An almost infinite variety of patterns can be created by combining different colored or textured yarns and various stitches.

Weft knits are usually circular unless they are made on full-fashioning machines. In hosiery and sweaters the item itself or sections of the item are made on the specialized knitting machines. When sweaters or stockings are knitted, the desired shape of the fabric piece may be created by increasing or decreasing the number of stitches.

Where stitches have been dropped or added, *fashion marks* appear. Fashion marks—small alterations in the surface caused by the shifting of the needles and the change in position of the yarns—are an indication of better quality in that the consumer can be sure that the shaping of the garment is permanent. Items made in this way are referred to as *full-fashioned*. (See Figure 16.21.) Some manufacturers create mock fashion marks at seamed areas to give the appearance of better quality. A careful examination of the area will show that in a true full-fashioned item, the number and direction of stitches change. In mock fashion marks, this does not occur. Mock fashion marks are usually produced by embroidery and have a long yarn float on the wrong side between marks.

Three-Dimensional Knitting

The techniques employed for full-fashioned garments are also being used to produce three-dimensional knitted structures. Complex shapes can be knitted that serve as reinforcement in molded parts for industrial applications. Covers for chairs and seats can be knitted as one piece, eliminating the cutting and sewing of fabric pieces to fit the forms. (See Figure 16.22.)

WARP KNITS

In warp knitting, each yarn is looped around one needle at a time. The guide bar that carries the yarns moves sideways as well as forward and back so that the yarns are carried both lengthwise and, to a limited extent, diagonally. This diagonal motion is

FIGURE 16.22

Computer-aided three-dimensionally knitted upholstery fabric in which a two-tone effect is achieved by using both lower-luster and bright yarn of the same color and different stitch structures. Photograph courtesy of Teknit, producers of three-dimensional knitted covers for the office furnishing industry in Europe and America.

needed to ensure that the yarns interlace not only with the loop directly below in the same wale but also with loops to the side in adjacent wales. If the yarn interlaced only vertically, there would be no point at which each individual chain of stitches was attached to its neighboring chain.

This construction provides resistance to laddering (running), since each stitch is most directly connected not only with the stitch beneath but also with a stitch placed diagonally and lower. In forming the stitch, diagonal underlay moves the yarn from loop to loop.

Several types of warp knits are made on a number of different warp knitting machines.

Tricot

Tricot machines account for the largest quantity of warp knits. Tricot fabric is knit flat. On the face side the wales create the appearance of a fine, lengthwise line. On the back side crosswise ribs appear in a horizontal position.

In the manufacture of tricot, guide bars move the yarns from side to side. The tricot machines may have from one to four guide bars. The greater the number of bars, the greater the distance the yarn moves between stitches. In moving from one placement to the next, underlay yarns are carried across the back of the fabric. (See Figure 16.23.) This extra yarn creates heavier-weight fabrics.

Tricot fabrics are identified as one-bar, two-bar, three-bar, or four-bar, depending on the number of guide bars used in their manufacture. One-bar, or single-bar, tricot is relatively unstable and is seldom used for garments. It is, however, used as backing for some bonded fabrics. It will run, because the loops interlace close together. Two-bar tricot is stable and fairly light in weight and is used extensively in lingerie, blouses, and the like. Three- and four-bar tricots are used for dresses and men's wear and are heavier than two-bar tricot. (See Figures 16.24 and 16.25.)

FIGURE 16.23

Guide bars on warp knitting machine move from side to side while needles move up and down. Follow the path of each yarn as it changes its position in the fabric structure.

FIGURE 16.24

(a) The simplest single guide bar tricot construction; (b) Diagram of three-bar tricot. Darker areas show how one yarn is carried throughout the fabric. Diagrams courtesy of National Knitwear and Sportswear Association.

a

b

In addition to the basic tricot fabric, a number of variations can be made. A tricot satin is produced by allowing yarns to float further across the back surface of the fabric before they interlace. Other textured tricots known as *brushed tricots* are made with raised, napped surfaces or with small loops. The fabric as knitted is smooth on both sides. The surface effects are achieved during finishing when the fabric is passed through a special machine equipped with wire rollers that either pull loops to the surface of the fabric or break some of the filaments to give a "brushed," soft, napped surface. Brushed and looped tricot fabrics are made with long underlaps that form the pile or loops.

Three- and four-bar tricot constructions permit the carrying of hidden yarns through the fabric. Monofilaments that stabilize the fabric or spandex filaments for stretch may be concealed in the complex structure of the tricot fabric.

Tricot fabrics can be made with a variety of open effects to create interesting lacelike patterns, as well. Figure 16.26 depicts a tricot knitting machine.

FIGURE 16.25

Tricot knitting cycle: (a) the needle is in the up position, old loops are on the needle stems, and guides (bars) are ready to swing through the needles to the back; (b) shows the guides at the back and sideways one space; (c) the yarns are laid across the needles; (d) the needle has risen to get the yarns around the stem; (e) the needle falls, moving the yarn into the hook of the needle while the presser bar presses the needle closes so that the new loops are held inside the hook; (f) a backward motion of the sinker moves the old loops over the closed needle; (g) the old loops have been cast off, and the needle is ready to rise into position as in (a). Diagrams from D. G. B. Thomas, *An Introduction to Warp Knitting*. Copyright © Merrow Publishing Co., Ltd. Reproduced by permission. Watford, Herts, U.K., 1971.

FIGURE 16.26

Tricot warp knitting machine. Example shown is Type HKS-2/3. Photograph courtesy of Karl Mayer Textilmaschinenfabrik GmbH.

Simplex Knits

Simplex knitting machines create warp knits similar to tricot but with a denser, thicker texture—a sort of double knit tricot. Simplex knits are used in products requiring heavier fabrics, such as women's gloves, handbags, and simulated suede-textured apparel fabrics.

Raschel Knits

Raschel knits can range from finely knitted laces to heavy-duty fabrics. Elaborately patterned surface effects can also be achieved with the Raschel machine. The fabrics have lengthwise rows of loops held together by laid-in yarns and may, to the eye, have the appearance of woven goods or lace.

Raschel knitting machines are flat beds with two to forty-eight guide bars. A mechanism called a *fall plate* controls the placement of the laid-in yarns. In the normal knit stitch formation, the needle moves up and down, looping yarns on and off the needle to form a continuous chain. In Raschel machines the fall plate is lowered to prevent the laid-in yarn behind it from forming a normal loop. Instead, the yarn is carried along in the fabric in a horizontal or diagonal direction, according to the pattern desired. In some fabrics this technique is used to simulate the effect of embroidery; in others, it gives a woven appearance. (See Figure 16.27.)

Among the most popular types of Raschel fabrics are power net of elastomeric yarns for foundation garments and swimsuits, thermal cloth for cold-weather underwear, lace, and tailored menswear fabrics. Pile warp knits for fake fur fabrics are made by incorporating an extra yarn in the structure that is then brushed. In power nets for foundation garments, the laid-in yarns are spandex core yarns.

Crochet Knits

An especially versatile variation of the Raschel knitting machine is used to make fabrics that simulate hand-crocheted fabrics. Although the mechanism of the machine varies slightly from that of an ordinary Raschel knitting machine, the principle of forming lengthwise loops held together by laid-in yarns is the same in both machines. The resulting textiles range from narrow trimmings, including those with fancy fringes, to wider fabrics (25 to 75 inches) used for apparel or household textiles.

FIGURE 16.27

Close-up views of two open-structured Raschel knit fabrics.

a   b

CREATING PATTERN AND DESIGN IN KNITTED GOODS

Finished knit goods can be dyed. Patterns can be created by printing on the fabric or through the manipulation of differently colored yarns.

Weft knits are easily knitted into stripes. These stripes always run across the fabric, since the pattern is achieved through varying the colors of the yarns in the different courses. Since the yarns interlace horizontally, it is not possible to knit a vertical stripe in weft single knits.

A jacquard attachment for weft knit machines make it possible to knit a wide variety of patterned fabrics. Like woven jacquard patterns, jacquard knit designs are plotted on paper and then are transferred to the jacquard mechanisms where the machine automatically activates the appropriate needles and colored yarns. Electronically controlled machines are widely used in the knitting industry. (See Figure 16.10.)

The structure of patterns in warp knitting is determined by a system known as the *link-chain system*. Chains with links of variable heights control the movement of the guide bars. The height of the link transfers a motion to the guide bars. The guide bars set the yarn in position over a group of needles to form the pattern, but pattern variations are limited.

WARP AND WEFT INSERTION

Processes have been developed that allow the insertion of warp or weft yarns into knitted structures. Some of these variations of knitting have been purely experimental; others have been commercialized for a time. Their purpose is to provide increased stability to knitted structures. This is accomplished by integrating warp or filling yarns part or all of the way into the lengthwise or crosswise direction of a knitted structure, which holds them in place.

Presently, only weft insertion systems have any substantial commercial distribution. A separate magazine feeds weft yarns to a tricot or Raschel warp knitting machine. The weft yarn crosses the entire width of the fabric. When the fabric is viewed from the back side, it can be seen that the weft always passes under the underlap of the knit stitch and over the loops, as shown in Figure 16.28.

Manufacturers of magazine weft insertion machines recommend the fabrics for a wide variety of apparel, household textile, and industrial applications. The textile literature describes their potential for use in processing high-tenacity yarns that are

FIGURE 16.28

Structure of weft insertion knit fabric. Diagram reprinted by permission of the National Knitwear and Sportwear Association.

difficult to handle in ordinary weaving. High-tenacity yarns will lose some strength as a result of stresses imposed by the interlacing of yarns required in weaving. In weft insertion, the knitting yarns serve to hold the weft yarn in place, and full advantage can be taken of the strength of the inserted yarn.

CARE OF KNITTED FABRICS

Although there is a great variety in the quality of knitted goods sold, and the performance of any individual knit may differ markedly from that of other knits, some general guidelines for the care of knitted goods can be observed. The problems that consumers seem to encounter most often in the performance of knitted fabrics are in the areas of dimensional stability, snagging, and pilling.

Dimensional Stability

One reason for the popularity of knits for wearing apparel is their comfort. The looped construction of knit fabrics permits the fabric to give with the body as it moves. But the stretchiness of knits also results in lessened dimensional stability. Consumers have complained about shrinkage, stretching, and distortion of knits, although interlock and double knit fabrics are usually more stable and display little or no shrinkage. Similarly, fabrics with weft or warp inserted yarns are more stable.

Shrinkage control treatments, heat setting of synthetics, and special resin finishes can provide good dimensional stability for knits. Unfortunately, not all manufacturers provide such treatment for their products. Consumers should check labels for percentage of shrinkage or for other special treatments to judge potential dimensional stability. (About 3 percent shrinkage is one garment size.) If products fail to live up to specified performance standards, items should be returned to the retailer or the manufacturer.

Knits are considered to be easy-care fabrics, and many care labels recommend machine washing. Some labels will also specify that the fabric can be dried in an automatic dryer. In general, however, knits will shrink more in the dryer than if air dried. Knits maintain their shape best if they are dried flat. The weight of a wet knit, hung on a line, may cause the fabric to stretch out of shape. The dimensions of knits usually will be retained best by professional dry cleaning.

Hand knits, sweaters of wool or animal hair fiber, and other knits with an open construction may require special hand laundering and blocking (stretching back into shape). Such items should be laid on a sheet of wrapping paper before washing, and the outlines traced. After washing, the garment should be stretched out on the paper to dry. While still damp, the garment should be gently stretched to fit the outline of the original dimensions.

Aside from stretching or shrinking, an additional problem with knitted items is skewing or twisting as the fabric is relaxed during laundering. Side seams of garments may pull to the front or back and hems may hang unevenly. In general, knits made of synthetics will have better resistance to stretching out of shape than will cotton, acetates, and rayons. Blending of synthetics with cottons, acetates, and rayons will improve the resiliency and dimensional stability of knitted fabrics made from these fibers. Price is a good guide—especially for children's knits.

Knit fabrics have better wrinkle recovery than woven fabrics because the yarns can move more freely. Heavier knits resist wrinkling more than lighter weight single knits.

Mechanical Damage

The loop structure of knitted fabrics makes them especially susceptible to snagging. If a loop catches on another object, it may be pulled up from the fabric surface and a long snag, or pull, of yarn may be formed. If the yarn that has been snagged is not broken, it can be pulled to the back of the fabric. It may be possible to gently stretch the fabric and work the pulled yarn back into place. This is difficult to do with tightly knitted fabric structures.

If the yarn has been broken, the snag may produce a hole in the fabric. A few hand stitches with needle and matching thread should be made to secure the yarns so that the hole does not become enlarged during wearing or laundering.

Synthetic double knits or knits made from loosely twisted yarns may be subject to pilling. Weaker fibers, such as cotton, rayon, acetate, and wool, generally break off the fabric, but the stronger synthetic fibers cling to the fabric, making an unsightly area on the fabric surface. The use of textured yarns for knitting synthetics decreases the likelihood of pilling.

Knits may be damaged by sharp objects puncturing the fabric. If yarns are cut, a hole will result, and further pressure and strain on the fabric may enlarge the open area, as loops are dropped in the interlocking structure.

EFFECTS OF KNIT STRUCTURE ON FABRIC PERFORMANCE

Durability Factors

Strength of knitted fabrics is considered to be less important for durability than it is in woven goods. Knitted fabrics are easily stretched to accommodate changes of shape as a result of stresses imposed in wear and care. When knits are made from resilient fibers and yarns, the ability to stretch and recover from stretching will be enhanced. In comparison to knitted fabrics, woven fabrics are generally firmer and have less elongation. In knits the loops in the structure can be deformed horizontally or vertically, increasing the stretch in both directions. But, as noted earlier, variations in knitting techniques can increase or decrease extensibility of knitted fabrics. Double knit fabrics and warp knit fabrics are usually less extensible than single knit fabrics.

A major problem in the durability of knits is the runs that can develop in weft knits when one of the loops is broken. If stronger fibers and yarns are used in these knits, they will be less likely to run.

Appearance

Shearability, discussed in chapter 15, is an important factor in the appearance of textiles. In general, because of the ways in which yarns are combined, woven fabrics have higher shearability than do knitted fabrics. Knitted fabrics have good flexibility and are easily extended. Warp knits do not shear as easily as weft knits.

These qualities must be taken into account by designers, although they may not be aware of the technical terminology used to describe the fabric properties. For example, a warp knit tricot fabric with low shearability would not be used to make a bias-cut garment in which the intention is to take advantage of high shearability. Instead, the designer would be likely to use a soft, gathered construction where the high flexibility of the fabric would work to good advantage, but where most of the draping would fall in the vertical direction of the fabric.

In general, knits wrinkle less than do other fabrics. This is because loosely constructed fabrics generally allow more fiber redistribution and motion. However, knitted fabrics, because of their greater extensibility, are more likely to lose their shape in laundering. The stresses applied in knitting distort the shapes of the loops rather than just stretching the yarns as in weaving. On relaxation, the loops broaden, shrinking the fabric length and increasing the width. As with woven fabrics, the tighter the structure, the higher the shrinkage until the structure becomes so tight that further shrinkage is not possible. Such fabrics may, however, buckle.

Knitted fabrics tend to have lower cover than do woven fabrics, with weft knits having substantially more porous structures than warp knits, unless the fabric is deliberately made to have an open, lacy construction as in some Raschel knits. Use of thinner or thicker yarns can increase the cover of knitted fabrics.

Comfort Factors

Knits usually entrap more air than woven fabrics, although the tightness of the knit is a factor as well. Pile or napped knit constructions are especially good for cold weather because the yarns or fibers perpendicular to the surface provide numerous spaces for dead air. This effect is maximized if such fabrics are worn with the napped or pile surface next to the body, or if they are covered with another layer.

The flexibility of knits contributes to a feeling of fabric softness. Fibers and yarns used can enhance or detract from the smoothness of knitted fabrics.

Putting It All Together for . . .

Swimwear

Bathing suits are a fairly specialized end use for fabrics; the fabrics chosen must satisfy both fashion and function. For most of the bathing suits worn today, important functional characteristics are stretch and recovery, colorfastness, absorbency, and environmental resistance.

Elongation and Recovery

The majority of bathing suits for women, and many for men, are tight fitting, with stretch required for getting the garments on and off. Since knits have much higher elongation than woven or nonwoven fabrics, they are the preferred fabric construction for bathing suits that fit tightly to the body.

Fibers too play an important role in achieving tightness of fit. Those with lower modulus and high resilience will enhance the stretch and recovery properties of knits. Not only elastomeric fibers but also nylon have low modulus and good recovery. Nylon and spandex are often chosen for swimwear because of these properties. Polyester is not usually used because it has a higher modulus and therefore does not stretch as easily. Knitted fabrics of nylon blended with elastomeric fibers, such as spandex or rubber, will provide the highest amount of stretch. The elastic fibers also have high recovery from stretch.

Colorfastness

Bathing suits are exposed to sunshine, chlorine and other chemicals in swimming pools, and salt water in oceans. Fibers and yarns are both important in maintaining the colorfastness of swimming suits that are often made of bright-colored fabrics. Lightfastness of dyed spandex is fair to good, while that of nylon dyed with acid dyes is good. Spandex normally makes up only a small percentage of the fiber content of swimwear fabrics and is often used in core-spun yarns wrapped with nylon. This helps to protect it from sunlight. Colorfastness of nylon and spandex exposed to pool and salt water is fairly good but these fabrics will show some loss over time.

Absorbency

Since bathing suits are worn while swimming in water, the absorbency of the fabric is a consideration. If a material absorbs and retains a significant amount of water, the weight of the suit will increase, affecting its comfort and function. Synthetic fibers have low water regain and are more appropriate for bathing suits than the natural fibers that were used many years ago.

Environmental Resistance

Light, chlorine, and salt water can also degrade textile fibers. When this occurs, bathing suit fabrics may lose some of their recovery from stretch. Nylon and polyester are more resistant to ultraviolet light and chlorine than spandex. That is another reason why spandex is usually used in small percentages blended with nylon. The use of rubber as an elastomeric fiber in swimwear has decreased because of its susceptibility to degradation by light and other environmental conditions. Because resistance of nylon to degradation by light is higher for fibers that have not been delustered, brighter nylons are usually used in swimwear.

SUMMARY

Knit fabrics are made by interlocking loops of yarn. Two types are knits are produced: weft knits, which are the most common type of knitted fabric; and warp knits. Because the loops in knits can be distorted, they are more stretchable than woven fabrics. Careful examination of a product in which knits are frequently used can show how fiber, yarn, and fabric construction are utilized to achieve maximum durability, appearance, and comfort. The case study on swimwear included in this chapter is an example of selected fiber, yarn, and knitted structures for a specific end use.

References

American Fabrics and Fashions Magazine, 1980 ed. *Encyclopedia of textiles*, 3rd ed. Englewood Cliffs, N.J.: Prentice Hall.

Lonsinger, K. 1993. T-shirts and underwear: The building blocks of fashion. *Knitting Times* 62 (August): 21.

Reichman, C., ed. 1972. *Knitting encyclopedia*. New York: National Knitted Outerwear Association.

Review Questions

1. What is the difference between a weft knit and a warp knit?
2. What determines the number, size, and closeness of knitting stitches? What terms are used to describe the closeness of knit stitches?
3. Describe the various ways that differences in pattern and surface texture can be achieved in weft knits.
4. Which of the following weft knits are made with one needlebed and one set of needles, which are made with two needlebeds and two sets of needles, and which are made with two needlebeds and one set of needles?

jersey knits	velour knits
purl knits	high-pile knits
interlock knits	double knits
rib knits	

5. Explain the differences in weft knit and warp knit structures that make warp knits less subject to developing runs.
6. Identify some common end uses of Raschel knit fabrics, and explain why Raschel knits are often used for these products.
7. Assuming comparable quality and fiber content, compare knitted and woven fabrics in terms of their performance in regard to comfort during physical activity, dimensional stability, snagging, wrinkle recovery, and pilling. Explain what accounts for these differences.

Recommended Readings

Candan, C. 1999. The changing face of knitwear. *Textile Month* (June): 14.

Ghosh, S., and P. K. Banerjee. 1990. Mechanics of single jersey weft knitting process. *Textile Research Journal* 60 (April): 203.

How to buy a sweater. 1994. *Consumer Reports* (December): 791.

King, M. W., R. Guidoin, and B. Soares. 1993. Designing fabrics for hernia repair. *Canadian Textile Journal* 110 (October): 18.

Knitting in the third dimension. 1994. *Textile Horizons* (December): 22.

O'Brien, M. 1997. Flat knitting: Past, present, and future—2. *Textiles Magazine* 3: 5.

Schwartz, P., T. Rhodes, and M. Mohamed. 1982. Knitting and knit fabrics. In *Fabric forming systems*, 76–151. Park Ridge, N.J.: Noyes.

Smith, S. 1994. The history of hosiery in America. *Southern Textile News* (August 8): 2.

Spencer, D. J. 1989. *Knitting technology*, 2d ed. Oxford: Pergamon.

The basic principles of knitting. 1989. *Textiles* 18 (1): 15.

Weft-insertion warp-knits for industrial fabrics. 1983. *Textile Industries* (March): 56.

Willis, D. 1993. More than just T-shirts. *Canadian Textile Journal* 110 (October): 15.

17

OTHER FABRIC CONSTRUCTION METHODS

Although woven and knitted goods make up the largest quantity of fabrics produced, various other construction methods are also used for the fabrication of textiles. Many of these techniques derive from processes used since prehistoric times, others have been developed more recently, and some are the result of new technology within the textile industry. Many of these fabrics are referred to as *nonwovens* even though this term technically applies only to fibers held together in a flexible web.

The fabrication methods discussed in this chapter may be divided into several broad classifications: fabrics made by knotting, by looping, by stitching yarns or fibers together, and by bonding together a web of fibers. Netting, macramé, and lace are created by knotting, either by hand or by machine. Crochet, essentially a hand technique, is made from a series of loops in a process that is similar to knitting. A fabric construction technique, known either as stitch bonding or stitch knitting, combines yarns and/or fibers by sewing them together. Ancient techniques such as felt making or bark cloth construction are similar in principle to the manufacture of modern nonwovens.

FELT

Although evidence is scanty, it is believed that the first means of making fibers into cloth was through felting. Prehistoric remains of felt materials have been found in such diverse parts of the world as Anatolia, Siberia, Europe, Southeast Asia, and South America. To understand the process by which felt is formed, it is necessary to review the structure of the wool fiber from which it is made.

The surface of the wool fiber is covered with a fine network of small scales. (See Figure 4.4.) This scaly structure causes wool fibers to cling closely together, as the scales from one fiber interlock with the scales of another. Furthermore, the natural crimp of wool assists in felting. When masses of wool fiber are placed together, the crimped fibers become entangled. Friction increases this tangling. If the wool is subjected to conditions of heat and moisture, the scales open wider, interlocking with still more scales from neighboring fibers. Wool scales are so oriented that each fiber moves in its root direction, causing the mass to hold together more tightly. When pressure is added, the mass is flattened, producing a web of tightly joined fibers, or felt. The factors essential for producing natural felt from wool are pressure, which increases the tangling, heat, and moisture.

It is not too difficult to imagine a situation in which felt might have been produced accidentally. Suppose a horse rider placed a sheep fleece on the back of a horse as cushioning material. The body of the horse is both warm and moist; the rider provides the pressure and the friction. Over time, the fleece becomes matted, producing a primitive form of felt. Frequent repetition of the procedure could lead to the recognition that this material had potential for some of the same uses as the fleece from which it was made.

Eventually, the natural process was reduced to a series of steps that included applying heat and moisture to a mass of wool fiber, placing the batt (or mass) of fibers on flat stones, and pounding the fibers with hammers or beaters. To vary the texture and quality of the material, fur fibers might have been added, but it was the wool that served to hold the substance together.

In the commercial production of felt, a batt of cleaned wool fiber is fed into a carding machine that lays down a web of fairly even thickness. To improve strength and dimensional stability, two webs of carded fiber are laid across each other with the fibers of one web at right angles to the fibers of the other web. Steam is forced through the mass of fiber, after which a heavy, heated plate or rollers are lowered onto the fibers. The plate or rollers are moved about to produce mechanical motion. The moisture, heat, and friction effectively interlock the fibers.

Following this operation, the fabric is passed through a solution of soap or acid that causes the fabric to compact further. From this stage the fabric goes to a finishing mill in which the fabric is subjected to further agitation, pounding, and shrinkage. This is similar to the fulling finish given to woolen fabrics. (See chapter 19.) After felting is complete, the fabric can be dyed or given any of the traditional finishes used on wool.

To decrease costs, manufacturers may blend other fibers with wool. A woven scrim (a plain, open, woven fabric) may sometimes be added as a framework to support felt to increase its strength.

Felt has the advantage of being easily cut, and because it has no yarns, it will not fray at the edges. Felt can be molded into shape and so has wide use in making hats. Because of its densely packed fibers, felt provides a good deal of warmth, and it is not easily penetrated by water. On the other hand, felt is a relatively weak fabric, may tear under pressure, and is subject to pilling. Being rather stiff, felt does not fall into graceful folds. Its use, therefore, is somewhat limited. Modern manufacturers of wool felt supply material not only for hats and fashion accessories but also for a wide range of industrial uses.

BARK CLOTH

A process similar to that used for felt produces bark cloth or, as it is called in the Polynesian Islands, *tapa*. This nonwoven fabric was also known during prehistoric times in areas as widespread as Asia, Africa, Europe, South and Central America, and the South Pacific.

Made from certain trees, among them the paper mulberry, breadfruit, fig, or related species, bark cloth is produced by first removing strips of the inner layer of bark from the tree. This substance is softened by soaking it in water. The softened bark is placed on an anvil or other flat surface, and special beaters are then used to pound the bark strips to interlace the fibers. When the mass is sufficiently integrated, the material is dried, producing a sheet of fabric. Special texture or surface markings are achieved by pounding the material with incised hammers or embossing the flat surface on which the fibrous materials are spread to be beaten and to dry.

The resulting fabric is somewhat like a soft, supple paper. Pieces of tapa can be joined without sewing. Simply by wetting the edge of two pieces and pounding them together, large pieces of fabric can be made without seams.

Tapa does not drape or sew particularly well and was used chiefly for simple unsewn garments such as ponchos, sarongs, loincloths, or turbans. Small quantities are still made for native religious garb and as an example of native handicrafts.

NONWOVEN FABRICS

Techniques by which fabrics are made directly from fibers, bypassing both spinning and weaving, have been used for centuries in the production of felt and bark cloth. With the development of manufactured fibers, and, in particular, the synthesis of thermoplastic fibers, technologies have evolved that have made possible the large-scale production of nonwoven fabrics. The first nonwoven consumer product, an interlining fabric for the apparel industry, was introduced in 1952 (INDA 1992). Marketed extensively for both durable and disposable items, nonwoven fiber webs range from disposable diapers to blankets, from industrial filters to tea-bag covers.

Nonwoven fabrics are textile structures "produced by bonding or interlocking of fibers, or both, accomplished by mechanical, chemical, thermal or solvent means and combinations thereof" (ASTM 1998). This excludes fabrics that have been woven, knitted, or tufted. The Association of the Nonwovens Fabrics Industry (INDA) in the United States and the European Disposables and Nonwovens Association (EDANA) help to further define what may be called a nonwoven fabric (Jirsák and Wadsworth 1999). Over 50 percent of the weight of a nonwoven must be comprised of fibers with an aspect ratio (length to diameter ratio) of 300. This excludes paper products that are normally made of extremely short fibers. In addition nonwovens must have a density less than 0.4 grams per cubic centimeter, and felted fabrics are usually much heavier.

American Fabrics (1974) magazine recommended that nonwoven fabrics be classified as durable products or disposable products. They defined a durable product as "one which is multi-use. It is not manufactured to be thrown away after a single application" (p. 40). Examples of this type of product are blankets, carpet backings, and furniture padding.

Disposable products were defined as "made to be disposed of after a single or limited number of uses" (p. 40). These are exemplified in disposable diapers, towels, or tea-bag covers. *American Fabrics* pointed out that some items are disposable not because of their durability but because of their purpose. Medical gowns, for example, or airplane and train headrests, might withstand multiple use, but for sanitary reasons they have limited use periods.

Manufacture

There are two steps involved in manufacturing nonwoven fabrics: (1) preparation of the fiber web and (2) bonding of the fibers in the web. A number of possibilities exist for each step, and in addition, the two stages may be distinct or can be carried out as a more or less continuous process. The various combinations are described below and summarized in Table 17.1.

Fiber Web Formation

Staple fiber webs are produced by either *dry forming* or *wet forming*. Dry-forming processes are carding, also called dry laying, and air laying. Carded webs are made in a manner similar to the process for felt webs and slivers for yarn spinning. Thicker webs can be built up by layering the carded webs. In air laying, the fibers are opened, suspended by air, and then collected on a moving screen. The wet laid process is similar to paper making in that a mixture of fibers in water is collected on a screen, drained, and then dried. (See Figure 17.1.)

Webs can also be made by the direct extrusion processes of *spunbonding* and *melt blowing*. Spunbonded fabrics are manufactured from synthetic filament fibers. Continuous filaments are formed by extrusion through spinnerets, and the filaments are blown onto a moving belt where they form a web. As the still hot and partially molten filaments touch, they bond. (See Figure 17.2.) Polymers most often used are polypropylene and polyester.

TABLE 17.1
Nonwoven Fabric Production Methods

Web Formation		
Dry Laid	**Wet Laid**	**Spun Laid**
Carded	Wet laid	Spunbonded
Air laid		Melt blown

Web Bonding		
Chemical	**Mechanical**	**Thermal**
Adhesive bonded	Needlepunched	Calendar bonded
Solution bonded	Spunlaced	Air bonded
	Stitchbonded	Infrared bonded
		Ultrasound bonded

(a)

(b)

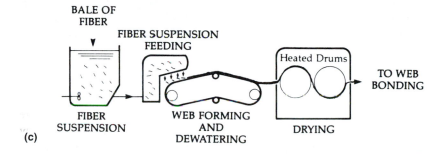

(c)

FIGURE 17.1

Schematic representation of methods of web forming staple fiber webs. (a) Web forming by carding method. (b) Web forming by the air laying method. (c) Web forming by the wet laying method. Diagram reproduced courtesy of INDA, Association of the Nonwovens Fabrics Industry.

Spunbonded fabrics are strong because of the filament fibers and are not easily torn. They are used for a wide variety of products ranging from apparel interlinings, carpet backing, furniture and bedding to bagging and packing material. Spunbonded fabrics may be used in geotextiles to control erosion or in constructing roads. Some spunbonds made from olefins are used as a tough, especially durable substitute for paper in wall coverings, charts, maps, tags, and the like.

Melt blowing also forms fabrics directly from fibers, but it differs from spunbonding in that molten fiber filaments are attenuated and broken into short lengths as they exit from the spinnerets. Cool air distributes the fibers onto a moving screen. As the fibers cool they bond, forming a white, opaque web of fine fibers. (See Figure 17.3.) Because the fibers in meltblown nonwovens are fine, the fabrics make good filter materials.

Specialty products can also be made by layering spunbonded and meltblown fabrics or by entrapping absorbent fibers or other materials within the meltblown structure.

Fiber Bonding

Once a web has been formed, some treatment must be given to bind the fibers together. This can be done by chemical, mechanical, or thermal means.

FIGURE 17.2

(a) Web forming and bonding by the spunbonding process. Photograph reproduced courtesy of INDA, Association of the Nonwovens Fabrics Industry. (b) Close-up photograph of a spunbonded fabric. Photograph courtesy of Dr. Dong Zhang.

a

b

Chemical Bonding. Bonding may be achieved by applying an adhesive material to the web and then setting the adhesive. This, in essence, "glues" the fibers together. Latex adhesives, in which the adhesive substance is suspended in water, are most often used. The fabric web is passed through a bath in which it is impregnated with the latex, and then dried.[1] (See Figure 17.4.)

When adhesive is applied to the surface of the fiber web, it tends to make the fabric stiff and more rigid. Also, fabrics exhibit the characteristics of the adhesive material on the surface rather than those of the original fiber. To overcome this disadvantage, adhesives may be imprinted onto the surface in selected areas. The printing patterns are developed carefully to ensure that adequate bonding takes place among fibers to maintain fabric strength. Such fabrics are less rigid and have better drapability and a more pleasant surface texture than do those that have been completely coated by an adhesive.

Instead of adhesive bonding, fibers may be *solution bonded* by spraying a mixture of chemicals and water onto the surface of the fibers. When subjected to heat, the water evaporates and the chemical vaporizes, dissolving a small amount of fiber, usually where one fiber crosses another. When the dissolved fibers resolidify, bonds are formed that hold the fibers together.

Mechanical Bonding. Fiber webs produced by dry laying methods may be joined by entangling or stitching the fibers in some way. Three such methods used are *needle punching, spunlacing, and stitch bonding.*

---

1. Other, low-wet-pickup, impregnation methods, described in chapter 19 can be used.

FIGURE 17.3

(a) Web forming and bonding by the melt blowing process. Photograph reproduced courtesy of INDA, Association of the Nonwovens Fabrics Industry. (b) Close-up photograph of a meltblown fabric. Photograph courtesy of Dr. Dong Zhang.

a   b

In needlepunching the web is fed into a machine with a bed of barbed needles, like fishhooks. The needles move in and out of the web, entangling the fibers. (See Figure 17.5.) The resulting fabrics are bulky and soft, yet retain their integrity. Products typically made from needlepunched nonwovens are blankets, filters, fabric backings, carpets, apparel, interlinings, road underlays, and automobile trunk liners (INDA 1992).

Spunlaced or *hydroentangled* goods are made by fluid entanglement. High-speed jets of water hitting a fibrous web bind fibers together by causing them to knot or curl around each other. No binder is required. (See Figure 17.5.) Patterns can be created by the use of perforated, patterned screens that support the fiber web. As the fibers become entangled, they assume the pattern of the supports. Depending on the patterns used, spunlaced fabrics may have an appearance similar to fabrics woven from yarns.

Spunlacing is often used in making kitchen wipes. The wipes have a regular pattern of holes surrounded by tightly entangled fibers. Many wipes are also adhesively bonded for increased wet strength.

For the stitchbonding technique fiber webs are stitched through to hold the fibers together. Maliwatt fabrics are fiber webs that have been stitched together. (See Figure 17.6.) The resulting fabrics are used as lining fabrics, furnishing fabrics, insulating materials, base fabrics for tufted goods, and in industrial and geotextiles. Malivlies fabrics, used in felts, packing materials, insulation materials, and utility textiles, are created by

FIGURE 17.4

Application of latex adhesive. Diagrams reproduced courtesy of INDA, Association of the Nonwovens Fabrics Industry.

FIGURE 17.5

(a) Needlepunched process.
(b) Web forming and bonding
by the spunlacing or
hydroentangling process. (c)
Schematic showing how fiber
webs may be held together by
stitchbonding. Diagrams
courtesy of INDA, Association of
Nonwovens Fabrics Industry.

forming stitches from the fibers of the web itself. No additional yarns are required. (See Figure 17.6.)

Other branded processes are kunit and multiknit. Kunit fabrics are formed by feeding a web of fibers into a machine where a type of compound knitting needle (see chapter 16, page 331) forms knitting stitches from the fiber web. These stitches hold the web together and form a fabric that may have either a plushlike, furlike, or flat appearance. (See Figure 17.6.) Uses include linings for clothing and shoes, plush for toys, automotive interior fabrics, acoustical and thermal insulation, packaging material, and base fabrics to which coatings may be applied. In the multiknit process, two fabrics formed by the kunit process are united into a double-sided, multilayered fabric with knitting stitches made by a compound needle with a sharp point that can penetrate both fabrics. Applications include insulation materials, garment interlinings, base materials for molded textile composites, and as a replacement for foam in car and furniture upholstery.

Thermal Bonding. Thermoplastic fibers may be bonded by heat. The application of heat causes the fusing together of heat-sensitive fibers, which effectively fastens them together. As in bonding with adhesives, heat may be applied in a pattern to provide

a Maliwatt

FIGURE **17.6**

Cross-sectional diagrams of pile fabrics made by stitchbonding processes. (a) Maliwatt. (b) Malivlies. (c) Kunit. (d) Multiknit. Drawings reproduced courtesy of Karl Mayer Textilmaschinen-fabrik GmbH.

Cross-lapped carded fleece with mechanical compacting by additional stitchbonding.

b Malivlies

Cross-lapped carded fleece. The mechanical compacting is effected by partial stitching of the fiber structure.

c Kunit

Length-oriented carded fleece. The mechanical compacting is effected by stitching of the fiber structure to pile loops of pre-determined height.

d Multiknit

The ground fabric is Kunit and in a connected process it is subsequently stitched on top of the loops, resulting in two identical plain fabric surfaces.

sufficient bonding for durability and to allow greater flexibility and softness in the end product. Nonwovens can also be formed with a small percentage of binder fibers of lower melting point than the predominant fibers. When the web is heated, the binder fibers melt, providing the necessary adhesion. (See Figure 17.7.)

Spunbond and meltblown nonwovens thermally bond when the molten filaments harden after extrusion. Passing the spunbonded or meltblown fiber webs between

FIGURE 17.7

Two methods of thermal bonding of fiber webs: (a) air bonding; (b) calendar bonding. Diagrams reproduced courtesy of INDA, Association of the Nonwovens Fabrics Industry.

heated cylinders called calendar rolls bonds fabrics more completely. Design effects can be produced if these cylinders have patterns embossed on their surfaces. Heat can also be applied to webs by hot air, infrared radiation, or ultrasound.

Uses of Nonwoven Fabrics

Nonwovens are one of the fastest growing segments of the textile industry. Figure 17.8 shows the rapid increase in consumption of nonwoven fabrics in the United States since 1970 and the prediction of continued growth into the next century.

Table 17.2 provides a summary of the pervasive nature of nonwovens in the United States with new end uses cropping up continually. Many of the applications would be considered industrial fabrics, as they are not used for clothing or home furnishings, but still touch our lives daily. Disposable nonwovens are particularly prominent in the area of medical products. Made cheaply from manufactured fibers, they can be easily sanitized and then disposed of.

An area of strong growth in industrial textiles has been the products known as *geotextiles*. Geotextiles perform functions such as filtration, separation, or reinforcement in ground and soil applications. Although the development of geotextiles is recent, there are historic examples of such textile applications. Hannibal's army in the third century B.C. spread blankets and coats over a marshy battleground before fighting.

Geotextiles can be woven or nonwoven fabrics of polyester, nylon, or polyolefin. The cheaper processing and the wide variety of possible products of nonwovens make them ideal for the large-volume applications in geotextiles. Rugged nonwoven fabrics can be used to stabilize roads by providing a separation layer between the asphalt and the soil roadbed. The geotextile prevents the asphalt aggregate from mixing into the soil and weakening the road surface. (See Figure 17.9.)

FIGURE 17.8

U.S. nonwoven fabric volume output. Chart courtesy of INDA, Association of the Nonwovens Fabrics Industry.

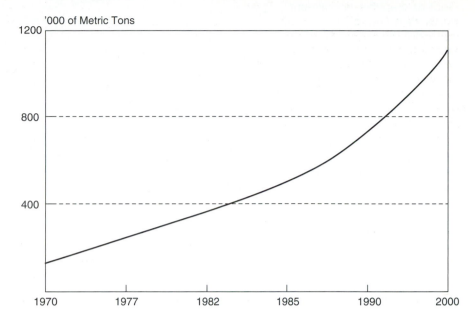

Source: John R. Starr, Inc. estimates

FIGURE 17.9

Typar® nonwoven geotextile provides a tough, durable permeable separation layer, used here in road construction. (a) Road surface without Typar® layer. Soil contaminates and weakens aggregate base placed beneath pavement. (b) Road surface with Typar®. Aggregate will not sink into and intermix with subsoil. Diagram reproduced courtesy of LINQ Industrial Fabrics, Inc.

a   b

Another growing application for nonwoven geotextiles is in soil erosion control. The geotextile fabric, when placed under the sand or gravel cover on an embankment, can prevent soil erosion by holding the soil underneath. (See Figure 17.10.) Nonwoven geotextile mats of biodegradable natural fibers can also be placed on top of newly seeded construction sites to hold the soil until vegetation can grow.

FIGURE 17.10

Geotextile earth embankment application. (1) gravel sand, (2) geotextile fabric, (3) embankment, (4) subsoil. Diagram reprinted from *Industrial Textiles* by Jarmila Svedova. Courtesy of Elsevier Science.

TABLE 17.2
Products That Use Nonwovens

Agriculture
- Seed strips
- Greenhouse covers

Automotive
- Sound and heat insulation
- Interior trim
- Battery separators
- Vinyl roofs
- Upholstery
- Carpet backing

Civil Engineering
- Road and railroad beds
- Soil stabilization
- Drainage
- Dam and stream embankments
- Golf and tennis courts
- Artificial turf
- Sedimentation and erosion control

Clothing
- Interfacings
- Skiwear
- Insulated clothing, gloves
- Swimwear
- Imitation fur
- Underwear
- Bra and shoulder padding
- Robes
- Handbags
- Tailors' patterns
- Shrouds, casket liners
- Shoe liners, insoles
- Rainwear

Construction
- Roofing and tile underlayment
- Acoustical ceilings
- Insulation

Home Furnishings
- Upholstery backings and webs
- Slipcovers
- Wallcovering backings
- Quilts, blankets, bedspreads
- Mattresses, mattress covers, tickings
- Pillows, pillowcases
- Lampshades
- Window shades
- Draperies
- Carpet backings

Household
- Wipes: wet, dry, polishing
- Aprons
- Scouring pads
- Glove liners
- Laundry softeners and antistatics
- Dust cloths, mops
- Tea and coffee bags
- Doormats, bathmats
- Garment bags
- Placemats, napkins
- Ironing board pads
- Laundry bags
- Washcloths
- Tablecloths
- Cheese wrap

Industrial, Military
- Coated fabrics
- Filters
- Clean room apparel
- Air conditioning
- Military clothing
- Abrasives
- Parachutes
- Cable insulation
- Reinforced plastics
- Tapes
- Protective clothing, labcoats

Leisure, Travel
- Sails, kites
- Sleeping bags
- Tarpaulins, tents
- Artificial leather, luggage
- Art canvases
- Airline headrests
- Fiberglass boats

Health Care
- Surgical: caps, gowns, masks, shoe covers
- Sponges, dressings, wipes
- Orthopedic padding
- Bandages, tapes
- Dental bibs
- Drapes, wraps, packs
- Sterile packaging
- Bedpan covers
- Instrument pads
- Privacy curtains
- Bed linen, underpads

- Examination gowns, slippers
- Filters for IV solutions, blood oxygenators and kidney dialyzers
- Transdermal drug delivery

Personal Care and Hygiene
- Buff pads
- Diapers
- Sanitary napkins, tampons
- Incontinence products
- Dry and wet wipes
- Cosmetics applicators, removers
- Bibs
- Vacuum cleaner bags
- Tea, coffee bags

School, Office
- Bookcovers
- Mailing envelopes, labels
- Maps, signs, pennants
- Floppy disk liners
- Towels
- Promotional items

Note: Reproduced courtesy of INDA, Association of the Nonwovens Fabrics Industry.

FIBRILLATED FILMS

Film fibrillation as a means of forming yarns was discussed in chapter 13. Film fibrillation can also be used to create fabrics directly from polymer films. After extrusion the films are embossed, thereby thinning them in selected areas. The embossed film is then stretched in the lengthwise and crosswise directions, and the film breaks apart in the weak areas to form a netting. The fabrics produced by this means may be used alone, as facings for other fabrics, or as supporting scrims between layers of fabric.

STITCH-BONDED FABRICS

Stitch bonding is not only used for mechanically bonding nonwovens, it is also a technique for producing and reinforcing other fabrics. Known variously as *stitch bonding*, *stitch through*, *stitch knitting*, or *mali* (from one machine used in its manufacture), it produces fabrics for industrial, household, and, to a lesser extent, apparel uses. Heinrich Mauersberger, an East German inventor, developed the stitch bonding concept after observing his wife mending a fabric in which the filling yarns had been worn away. Mauersberger assigned the trademark Malimo to his process and the fabric it produced.

Stitch bonding offers manufacturers the advantages of faster speeds than knitting or weaving and can be produced at lower costs, not only because of increased volume of production but also because less fiber or yarn is required. Some stitch-bonded fabrics have greater bursting strength and tear strength than comparable woven fabrics.

One group of stitch-bonding machines constructs fabrics from yarn. Warp and filling yarns are laid loosely, one over the other. A third set of yarns stitches the warp and weft yarns together. (See Figure 17.11.) It is also possible to use filling yarns alone, holding them in place with overstitching. These fabrics are called Malimo fabrics by the Mayer Textile Machine Corporation, which has acquired the Malimo Company. The fabrics are used as industrial textiles, furnishing fabrics, and household textiles. (See Figure 17.12.)

Another yarn-based stitch-bonding technique, Malipol, creates single-sided pile fabrics by stitching pile yarns onto a woven, knitted, nonwoven, or stitch-bonded fabric base. The resulting fabrics have the appearance of plush, terry cloth, or velour and are used in apparel and as lining fabrics, upholstery fabrics, and imitation fur fabrics. The Schusspol stitch-bonding machine also produces pile fabrics by stitching warp, filling, and pile yarns together at the same time, and does not require a preformed base fabric. Applications include carpets and other floor coverings, upholstery, and terry fabrics.

LEATHER

Leather products, made from the skin of animals, are not considered textiles, although they are often used alone or in combination with fabrics in apparel, upholstery, and other products. The skins of large animals are called *hides*, while those from young and small animals are *skins*. Leather is a skin or hide that has been *tanned*, that is treated to avoid decomposition and putrefaction. It is a fibrous material composed of tightly meshed collagen fibers. Collagen is the protein found in the connective tissues of the body.

FIGURE 17.11

Schematic showing how stitch-bonded fabrics are made from warp and filling yarns. (a) Filling yarns, shown in cross section, being fed into the mechanism. (b) Warp yarn. (c) Compound loop-forming hook. (d) Stitch-bonding yarn. (e) Completed fabric with warp and filling yarns held together by stitchbonding yarn.

FIGURE 17.12

Fabrics constructed by the stitch-through technique.

a

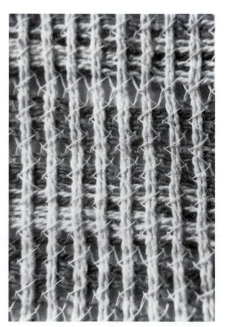

b

Leather processing consists first of soaking the freshly removed skin in a salt solution to inhibit the bacterial decomposition of the proteins and fat. The flesh underlayer and any hair on the top surface are then removed. Traditionally the skins and hides were treated with tannin, extracted from plants, to remove the protein between the collagen fibers. Hence the processing of skins into leather was called *tanning*. In modern tanneries, however, it is much more common to use chrome solutions, which are easier to obtain and control.

The outer layer of the leather is porous, with tiny holes where the hairs were removed. This porous surface is the *grain* which differs from animal to animal. Split leather, that has been cut into layers, does not show the grain and is smoother. The inner, or flesh, side is the softer *suede* face.

Leathers are made into many different products for both apparel and interior and automobile furnishings. Because of the extensive processing, and the limited size of skin pieces, leather products are expensive. Exotic skins, such as alligator, snake, eel, ostrich, and others are extremely costly. The quality of leathers can vary depending on the animal source and the processing.

NETS, MACRÉMÉ, LACE, AND CROCHET

Nets

Nets are created by looping and knotting a continuous strand of yarn into an open mesh. In use since prehistoric times for trapping fish, birds, and other small animals, nets also have a long history as decorative fabrics. Egyptian burial chambers, for example, contained fabric made from open-work net with embroideries of pearls and precious stones.

Most netted fabrics are made with either a square or diamond-shaped mesh. The hand process is a fairly simple one of looping and knotting to form an open-work fabric. The decorativeness of the net can be increased by embroidering designs on the open mesh. The terms *filet* work or *lacis* are applied to decorated nets, which are often classified as a type of lace. (See Figure 17.13.)

Machine-made nets are manufactured on a bobbinet lace machine. Raschel or compound needle tricot knitting machines also produce fabrics similar in appearance but with different structures. Net fabrics range from lightweight tulles to heavy fishing nets.

Macramé

Macramé might be considered as a variation of the principle used in making nets. Like netting, macramé uses the techniques of looping and knotting yarns. Unlike netting, however, the decorative qualities of macramé are determined by the selection and use of a variety of ornamental knots. In netting, it is the open area that is important. In macramé the closed or knotted areas are emphasized.

The word *macramé* seems to be Arabic in origin, and the process itself probably was brought to Europe from the Arab world. Like filet or lacis, macramé may be classified as a lace. Its first use was in finishing off the unwoven yarns at the end of a fabric. In time, macramé was constructed separately and attached to linens or garments in the same way that other trimmings were sewn into place.

The first major surge of interest in macramé came during the seventeenth century during a period of emphasis on lace making in general. Since that time macramé

FIGURE 17.13

Examples of *lacis* or embroidered net fabric from the sixteenth century. Photographs courtesy of the Metropolitan Museum of Art. Gift of Mrs. Magdalena Nuttall.

has experienced periods of great favor and periods of relative obscurity. During the nineteenth century it was an important decoration for clothes and household items. Fashion magazines of the 1800s were filled with instructions for macramé work. Macramé was not used widely during the early 1900s, but has enjoyed a resurgence of interest since the late 1960s.

Since macramé does not require specialized tools, it can be made with a minimum of equipment. During the eighteenth and nineteenth centuries sailors on whaling ships often occupied their spare time by making macramé items that they bartered when they reached port.

FIGURE **17.14**

Macramé fabric, knotted from ivory cotton in the late nineteenth century. Photograph courtesy of the Philadelphia Museum of Art. Given by Mrs. Edward F. Baley, 1955.

The yarns or cords that are used in macramé are fastened to a holding cord, which in turn is clamped or pinned securely so that the cords will not slip. For complex work, the yarns are wound onto bobbins so that they do not become entangled. The work is done by creating a variety of knots that join the cords at different intervals. (See Figure 17.14.) Placement of the knots and judicious selection of the type of knots make possible the creation of a variety of textures and decorative effects. Macramé is essentially a handcraft technique.

Lace

Because of its delicate beauty, lace has been one of the most sought-after fabrics. The precise origins of lace making are unknown, but its development was related not only to knotting and netting but also to embroidery. Among the earliest lacelike fabrics were those that were called *drawn work*. In drawn work, individual yarns were unraveled from a woven fabric, and embroidery stitches were used to fasten groups of these yarns together into a decorative pattern. *Cut work* was also a forerunner of lace. In cut work, areas of fabric are cut out to form a pattern, and the raw edges around the open areas are embroidered both to prevent them from fraying and to add decoration. Ornamentation can be increased by throwing threads across the open area to form geometric patterns, by weaving in and out, or by embroidering over the threads that bridge the gap.

Although fabrics decorated by each of these techniques bear certain similarities to lace, true lace making dispensed with the base fabric and created the design from the threads alone. Laces are generally divided into two categories, according to their construction. One is called *needlepoint lace*, the other *bobbin lace*.

Needlepoint lace, which is slightly older than bobbin lace, probably originated in Venice sometime before the sixteenth century (Goldenberg 1904). In making needlepoint laces, the design for the lace was first drawn on parchment or heavy paper. A piece of heavy linen was sewn to the back of the parchment to hold it straight. Threads were then laid along the lines of the pattern and basted lightly onto the parchment and linen. None of these threads was attached to any other. The lace was created by embroidering over the base threads with decorative stitches. These embroideries connected the base threads. The areas between the threads could also be filled in with fancy needlework, according to the requirements of the pattern. When the embroidery was complete, the basting threads that held the lace to the paper were clipped, and the finished lace was released.

Bobbin lace or, as it is also termed, *pillow lace* uses twisted and plaited threads. It is more closely related to netting and knotting, whereas needlepoint lace stems more from embroidery. Again the design is drawn on stiff paper. Holes are pricked into the paper in the area of the pattern. This pattern is then stretched over a pillow, and small pins are placed at close intervals through the holes in the paper. The pins go through the paper and into the pillow. The thread is wound onto bobbins, and the threads are worked around the pins to form meshes, openings, and closed areas. (See Figure 17.15.) Bobbin lace seems to have originated in Flanders or Belgium.

The techniques for making both bobbin lace and needlepoint lace quickly spread throughout Europe. Each town developed its own style of lace, which had its traditional patterns and construction features. It is this localization of design that has given us the names for most laces. Chantilly lace, for example, was first made in the French city of Chantilly, Venice point lace originated in Venice, Italy, and Val lace was first made in Valenciennes, France.

The production of lace by machine began soon after 1800. Although an earlier machine had had good success in producing manufactured nets, machine-made laces were not perfected until John Leavers invented a machine that could make as much lace in one day as a skilled handworker would produce in six months (Schwab 1951). Only an expert can tell the difference between machine-made and handmade lace. Most modern laces are produced by machine on the Leavers machine. Knitted laces may be made on the Raschel machine, and some lacelike embroidered fabrics are produced by the Schiffli machine. Schiffli fabrics, however, are not true laces; rather, they are embroidered, woven fabrics.

Crochet

The origins of crochet are obscure. The technique of creating fabric by pulling one loop of yarn through another with a hook was brought to the United States by Irish immigrants of the nineteenth century. The craft was evidently practiced in Irish convents as

FIGURE 17.15

Lace making using a lace pillow and bobbins. Yarns from the various bobbins are knotted together following the pattern drawn on a sheet of parchment paper placed over the pillow. The pins hold the knotted yarns in place.

an efficient means of copying lace fabrics. During the potato famine of the 1840s, the nuns taught many poor Irish women to crochet so that they could supplement the family income. When these families came to America, they brought Irish crochet with them, and soon women throughout the United States had learned to crochet.

Crocheting is closely related to knitting. Both join together a series of interlocked yarn loops into a variety of open and/or closed patterns. Crochet is made with a single needle or hook, whereas knitting uses several needles.

EFFECTS OF STRUCTURE ON FABRIC PERFORMANCE

The fabric constructions described in this chapter vary widely, and it is difficult to generalize properties and performance. The following discussion highlights some areas to be considered when assessing the performance of the various fabrics.

Durability Factors

In nonwoven fabrics that do not contain yarns, strength comes from fiber entanglement and adhesion, as well as inherent fiber tenacity. Fiber webs of coarser and higher strength fibers will be stronger than those made from finer, weaker fibers. The bonding of the fibers in the nonwoven structure also provides strength. Fabrics with a large number of bonding points are stronger, and the strength also depends on the strength of the individual bonds. Fiber webs with only fiber entanglement for adhesion, such as needlepunched nonwovens, derive their strength from the frictional forces between the entangled fibers, and can be torn apart. Reinforcing scrims can add strength and more densely entangled webs are stronger.

Some nonwoven fabrics may show lower abrasion resistance if the fibers are not tightly held in the structure. Abrasion will pull fibers out, and the fabric will wear.

In fabrics made from yarns, fiber and yarn characteristics together with the strength or weakness of the methods that hold the yarns together determine durability. Laces and nets are often delicate because of their loose construction and fine yarns, whereas macramé products, with heavier yarns and tight knotting, are stronger and more durable.

Appearance

Nonwoven fabrics made by bonding fibers together rarely resemble woven or knitted fabrics in their appearance. They also lack drapeability. Shearing behavior plays an important role in the drapability of a fabric; therefore a skirt made from felt or a nonwoven fabric appears stiff. Since the fibers are strongly bonded and not able to move at the crossover points, the structure cannot accommodate the shearing force. Instead, when a shearing force is applied, the fabric buckles, much as paper does.

By contrast, the yarns in lace, crocheted, or macramé structures can move, decreasing their shear resistance. Stitchbonded fabrics will vary in their shearing and bending behavior. Varying the fibers and yarns in stitch-bonded, lace, crochet, and macramé fabrics can provide unique and interesting decorative effects.

Comfort Factors

Few nonwoven fabrics are made into wearing apparel except when they are used as interfacing to stiffen some part of a garment, as interlining to provide warmth, or as disposable garments. Comfort is, therefore, not usually a major consideration in evaluating such products. It is, however, a factor for nonwoven protective clothing. These items can sometimes be uncomfortable, both because they may not breathe and also because of their stiffness.

SUMMARY

Although weaving and knitting are the predominant methods by which fabrics are produced, the construction methods described in this chapter are also employed. The most widely widely used of these is the processing of fibers into nonwovens. The rapid growth in nonwoven fabrics made from fiber webs testifies to the versatility of these fabrics in uses ranging from tea bags to high-tech industrial applications. In these products, engineers must pay special attention to the fibers used. In the case of disposable products, cost is likely to be an especially important factor. For high-tech products, fiber strength or the ability to withstand exposure to certain chemicals or temperatures may be the most important considerations. As with all textile products, the interaction of all aspects of fabric structure must be evaluated.

Lace, crochet, and macramé might be considered as somewhat akin to knits, utilizing yarns and keeping those yarns together by knotting or looping. Stitch-bonded fabrics with yarns or fibers held together by a sort of a looped stitch also behave in ways that may be similar to woven or knitted fabrics. And they are used in similar applications in both apparel and home furnishings.

References

American Fabrics, 1974 ed. AAF appraises the non-wovens. *American Fabrics* 101 (Summer): 40.

ASTM. 1998. *Annual book of ASTM standards*. Vol. 7.01. West Conshohocken, Pa.: American Society for Testing and Materials.

Goldenberg, S. L. 1904. *Lace: Its origin and history*. New York: Brentanos.

INDA. 1992. *The nonwoven fabrics handbook*. Cary, N.C.: Association of the Nonwovens Fabric Industry.

Jirsák, O., and L. C. Wadsworth. 1999. *Nonwoven Textiles*. Durham, N.C.: Carolina Academic Press.

Schwab, F. R. 1951. *The story of lace and embroidery*. New York: Fairchild.

Review Questions

1. Explain how the physical properties of wool fibers make the production of felt possible.
2. How can fibers be held together in the manufacture of fiber webs made from manufactured fibers?
3. What are the economic advantages of spunbonding and melt blowing over other nonwoven production methods?
4. Explain the basic principles of forming fabrics by stitch bonding.
5. What are the differences in the techniques for making pillow lace and needlepoint lace by hand?
6. What is the difference between the techniques for making macramé and crochet?
7. How are nonwoven fabrics used in geotextile applications?

Recommended Readings

Bark fabrics. 1940. *CIBA Review* (May).

Felt. 1958. *CIBA Review* no. 129 (November).

Griggs, D. 1989. Machine lace manufacture. *Textiles* 18 (2): 32.

Levey, S. M. 1983. *Lace: A history*. London: Victoria and Albert Museum.

Nonwovens, a growth market. 1992. *Textile Horizons*, December: 83.

Rise of the 'super suppliers.' 1999. *Textile Month* (June): 54.

United Nations Industrial Development Organization. 1976. *Acceptable quality levels in leathers*. New York: United Nations.

MULTICOMPONENT FABRICS

W hen readers reach this point in the text, they will have learned how fibers are produced, how yarns are made from those fibers, and how fabrics can be made from yarns or fibers by weaving, knitting, or other processes. It is also possible to create products by combining two or more of these textile materials (fibers, yarns, and fabrics) into a single material. Materials created by combining several different textile products can be called *multicomponent fabrics*. Some multicomponent materials have been used for centuries. For example, quilts have long been made by placing a batt, a sheet of matted fibers, between two layers of (ordinarily) woven fabric. Other multicomponent fabrics may rely on high technology to create composite structures of fibers held within a polymer matrix and shaped within a mold.

EMBROIDERY

The technique of embroidery, which is not a method of constructing fabrics but a method of decorating them, uses two components: a fabric base and a yarn that decorates it. The effects it produces are similar to those achieved by the surface weaves discussed in chapter 15. Embroidery is often used in conjunction with appliqué.

Appliqué also uses two components: a fabric base and small decorative pieces of cloth. The cloth is cut and attached to the surface of the larger textile to create a design. The decoration of fabrics by appliqué is an old technique. Archeologists have identified appliqués from as early as the fifth century B.C. These early forms were wall hangings or carpets in which the base material was felt and the designs were formed with other, smaller pieces of multicolored felt.

Since appliqués are most often attached to the base fabric by hand stitches, they are often combined with embroidery. Embroidery is the use of yarns applied with a needle in a variety of stitches to form a decorative pattern. Embroidery is a skill that has been practiced for many centuries. Translations of writings from classical Greece include many references to fine embroideries. The ancient Greeks considered weaving and embroidery to be fitting occupations for goddesses and noblewomen. One Greek textile showing evidence of embroidery has been dated at 500 B.C. and provides some of the earliest evidence of the embroidery skills. It is believed, however, that embroidery was practiced long before this date (Wace 1948).

A wide variety of different types of embroidery and embroidery stitches has been developed in all parts of the world. Each area originated a style with a distinctive repertory of stitches and decorative motifs.

One of the most famous decorated textiles ever made was created by embroidery. Called the Bayeux tapestry, this representation of the conquest of Britain by the Normans is actually a large embroidery, not a tapestry. On its 231-foot length and 20-inch width, seventy-two embroidered pictures show the sequence of events that led to the Battle of Hastings and the conquest of England by William the Conqueror in 1066. The embroidery, made almost nine hundred years ago and now discolored with age, is displayed in a museum in Bayeux, France.

American embroidery forms originated in Europe, especially in England. From the general category of embroidery, a number of specialized forms have broken off to become separate art crafts. These include crewel embroidery, cross-stitch embroidery, and needlepoint.

In embroidery different stitches are used to outline and fill in the design. The choice of stitch is usually related to the effect the sewer wants to achieve. Different fiber and yarn combinations can provide a variety of fabric effects.

Crewel embroidery is done with crewel wool, a loosely twisted fine yarn that was probably named after the English town of Crewel. Traditional crewel embroidery uses stylized forms and a repertory of specific basic stitches.

Made of two stitches that cross in the center to form an X, the cross-stitch is one of the simplest of the embroidery forms. In Colonial American times it was the first embroidery technique taught to young girls. Combinations of the X-shaped stitches were used to make samplers or to decorate all kinds of household articles.

Needlepoint embroidery covers a canvas base with thousands of tiny stitches. Queen Elizabeth I of England was said to have preferred it to all other embroideries, and in the 1920s, Alice B. Toklas, companion to the writer Gertrude Stein, made needlepoint chair covers after designs created for her by Picasso. Needlepoint has its own repertory of specialized stitches that are selected according to the pattern they will make in the often complex needlepoint design.

Machine Embroidery

When machines create embroidery, the embroidery is not accomplished as an integral part of the weaving process but is applied to the cloth after it is completed. (See Figure 18.1.) The Schiffli embroidery process, developed in Switzerland, requires as many as a thousand needles. Designs can be applied to all weights and types of fabrics. When used on sheer fabrics, these embroideries can have the appearance of lace. Schiffli is the predominant method used for applying embroidered designs to fabric yardage.

Other machines are used to embroider individual apparel items or decorative textiles. A recently developed embroidery process can create designs from a number of colored threads with only a single needle, as it automatically changes colors and splices yarns together. (See Figure 18.2.) Not all hand embroidery stitches can be created by machines, but through computer technology design changes and stitch variations can be accomplished quickly and easily.

CARPETS

Carpets have three-dimensional structures that are achieved by stitching pile yarns into a base fabric or by special weaving processes that include base yarns and pile yarns. The first technique is called *tufting* and more than 90 percent of the carpet produced in the United States is constructed by this method.

Tufting

Tufting is the process of punching a first component, loops of yarn, through a second component, a woven or nonwoven backing material. Hand-tufting is often used in "hooking" or tufting rugs. A hook is passed through the backing material, a loop is formed on the outside of the backing, and the needle is pulled back to the wrong side, leaving the loop to form the pile on the surface of the fabric. Loops can be left uncut or can be cut to create a fluffy surface.

FIGURE 18.1

Machine-made Schiffli embroidery.

FIGURE 18.2

Six-head embroidery machine that can embroider up to 1,200 stitches per minute. Photograph courtesy of Melco Embroidery Systems.

Machine-made tufted fabrics are created in much the same way as hand-tufted fabrics except that many needles punch through the fabric at the same time. A hook holds the loop in place when the needle is withdrawn. If a cut pile is being made, this hook has a small blade that cuts the loop. (See Figure 18.3.) Tufted fabrics are easily identified by the parallel rows of stitches on the wrong side of the fabric.

For carpeting tufts of pile yarn are stitched into a woven primary backing of jute, heavy cotton, polypropylene, or other synthetic. The back of the carpet is given a coating of latex for greater stability and strength and to hold in the tufts. A secondary backing fabric may also be applied and bonded by the latex.

Compared to more traditional methods of pile carpet construction, tufting is faster, does not require such highly skilled craftspersons, and requires less expensive equipment to manufacture. Although lower in cost than most other constructions, tufted carpet is not necessarily inferior in quality. The quality of carpets is more dependent on the fibers, yarns, and backing materials and the closeness of the pile than on the construction. Types of pile seen in tufted carpets are shown in Figure 18.4.

The major limitations in tufting are in the area of design. Jacquard-type designs cannot be made, although design variations can incorporate cut and uncut pile or higher and lower levels of loops or cut pile. Recent innovations in tufting machines now make possible the use of different colored yarns to create patterns in the carpet. Designs can also be printed on the surface of the carpet.

Most tufted carpet manufacturing in the United States takes place in or near the town of Dalton in northeast Georgia. Tufting of bedspreads and other items began as a handcraft in that area in the early twentieth century. The process was mechanized and adapted for carpets in the 1950s.

Other Machine Carpet Constructions

In addition to tufting, several other major types of pile carpet construction are available to consumers. The names of the processes used for weaving carpets have become standard terminology in the carpet industry. Many of these are very sturdy and can be woven in intricate designs that help hide wear and soiling.

FIGURE 18.3

In tufting process, looper below primary backing holds loop of yarn as needle withdraws (a). For cut pile carpet (b), a knife cuts across the loop as the needle withdraws as shown in the lower sketch. Illustration courtesy of the Monsanto Company.

(a) Uncut pile

(b) Cut pile

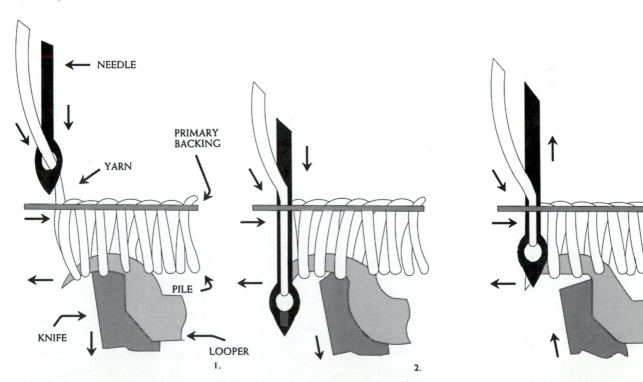

FIGURE 18.4

Various types of carpet pile. Reprinted from *How to Choose Carpets and Rugs.* Illustration courtesy of the Carpet and Rug Institute.

level loop

velvet plush

saxony

cut and loop

Velvet-Weave Carpets

Velvet-weave carpets should not be confused with velvet-surface carpets. The term *velvet weave* refers to the construction of the carpet, the pile of which may be either cut or uncut. Simple in construction, the weave is similar to the construction of lighter weight pile fabrics made by the wire method. (See Figure 18.5.) The pile is formed by wires inserted between the pile warp and ground yarns. The loops that are formed are held in place by the interlocking of filling yarns with the pile. The ground warps are also interlocked with the filling. Velvet-weave carpets are usually made in solid colors, but tweed effects can be created with multicolored tweed yarns. The cost of these carpets is moderate to low.

FIGURE 18.5

Velvet-weave carpet construction. Illustration courtesy of Bigelow-Sanford, Inc.

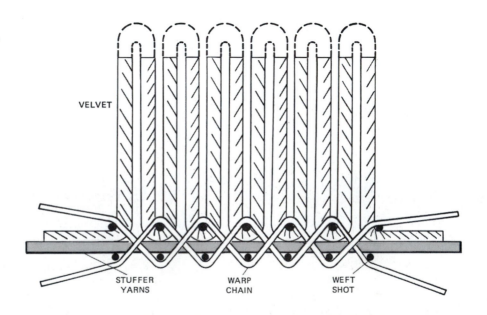

VELVET

STUFFER YARNS

WARP CHAIN

WEFT SHOT

Wilton Carpets

Wilton carpets are made on a special Wilton loom. This loom is essentially a velvet loom with a jacquard attachment that can work with up to six different colors. Patterns in Wilton carpets are woven, not printed. When yarns are not utilized in the surface design, they are carried along in the back of the carpet. (See Figure 18.6.) This makes for a dense, strong construction. Wilton carpets of good quality are among the longest-wearing machine-made domestic rugs. Piles may be cut or uncut; loops may be high or low.

Both velvet-weave and Wilton carpets are extremely durable and are often found in offices and public buildings ("contract installations" as opposed to home, or "domestic," use).

Axminster Carpets

Axminster carpets have the greatest versatility in machine-produced carpets in utilizing color. The loom draws pile yarns from small spools wound with yarns of various colors as they are needed for the design. These carpets have a one-level, cut pile, although textured effects may be attained by varying the twist or type of yarn used. (See Figure 18.7.) Carpets made on an Axminster loom are readily identifiable because the construction produces a heavy ridge across the back of the carpet, and the carpet can be rolled only in the lengthwise direction. The quality of carpets made on the Axminster loom is medium, but they are the only machine-made carpets that can have woven-in designs similar to those in oriental carpets. Recent advances in gripper weaving technology have increased the speed of Axminster looms, making this method more competitive with tufting.

Chenille Carpets

Chenille carpets are the most expensive and the most luxurious of all machine-made carpets and are rarely found. They are constructed on two looms. On one loom a fabric called a chenille blanket is woven. This blanket is cut into long strips called *caterpillars*, which have a fuzzy surface. A second loom weaves the strips into the carpet. These strips are used in the filling direction, and are actually sewn into place. Chenille carpet

WILTON

BACKING YARNS
(WARP)

CROSSWISE BINDING
(WEFT)

FIGURE 18.6

Wilton carpet construction.
Illustration courtesy of Bigelow-Sanford, Inc.

FIGURE 18.7

Axminster carpet construction. Illustration courtesy of Bigelow-Sanford, Inc.

pile is cut, carpets are made in solid colors, and the pile is dense, close, and velvety in texture.

Carpets can also be made by knitting, needle punching, as discussed in chapters 16 and 17, and flocking, as described later in this chapter. Designs can be added to carpets by printing as well as by weaving.

Consumer Brief 18.1 discusses the construction and use of residential wall-to-wall carpet.

Hand-Made Carpets

In addition to mass-produced, machine-made carpets, one-of-a-kind, handwoven carpets are also made. The reference list for this chapter includes some references for further reading about hand-woven and specialty carpets.

Many hand-woven carpets are made in the Near or Far East, using traditional designs, and are known as *oriental carpets*. Both antique and contemporary versions of these traditional design carpets can be purchased. Oriental designs can be printed or woven into machine-made carpets, but true orientals are made by hand-knotting a pile of wool or silk yarns to a woven base of cotton or wool. The quality of these carpets depends on the density rather than the length of the pile. There is a lively trade in new and antique oriental carpets, and prices are high. Purchasers should deal only with reputable merchants who can be depended on not to sell counterfeit merchandise.

Rya rugs, another hand-made area rug type, are imported from the Scandinavian countries. These rugs have a long "shag" pile and are generally woven in contemporary designs.

Some traditional early-American-style rugs are made not by weaving but from strips of cloth braided or sewn together. Still others are made by hooking, a hand process similar to tufting in which yarn or fabric strips are punched or pulled through a woven backing with a special hook.

CONSUMER BRIEF 18.1 Residential Wall-to-Wall Carpet

Textile floor coverings are generally referred to as carpets or rugs, terms that are often used interchangeably. The term *wall-to-wall carpet* is used to distinguish carpeting that covers the entire floor of a room from an *area carpet*, a rug that covers only part of the floor. Although the following discussion focuses on wall-to-wall carpet, the principles would apply to area rugs of the same construction as well. Wall-to-wall carpet is one of the most costly textile products purchased by consumers. For such a major investment, informed purchase is essential.

The first step in making an informed choice is to analyze the area to be carpeted. What kinds of activities will take place in the area? What will the traffic patterns be? Who will use the area—adults? children? pets? Armed with a thorough understanding of the demands that will be made on the carpet, the consumer can move on to examine available alternatives.

Carpet is usually made from nylon, olefin, polyester, acrylic, or wool fibers. (Individual chapters on fibers give detailed description of their properties.) The qualities of these fibers contribute to their use in carpets.

Nylon accounts for about 80 percent of carpet pile fibers. It resists abrasion, wear, and staining; dyes to a wide variety of colors; and is easy to clean. Olefin (polypropylene) resists abrasion and is readily cleaned. Generally, the color is added before the fiber is formed, making it colorfast. Resistant to stains, moisture, and mildew, olefin carpeting is often used outdoors as well as indoors, especially in areas such as playrooms and kitchens. Polyester can have an attractive texture, clear colors, and high luster. It is resilient, resists water-soluble stains, and is easily cleaned. Acrylic fibers resist moisture, mildew, and water-soluble stains. They can look and feel much like wool. The vast majority of carpets are made from manufactured fibers such as these; only about 3 percent are wool, which is generally more expensive. Wool is resilient and durable, can be dyed a wide range of colors, and has a luxurious appearance.

Many fiber manufacturers produce trademarked fibers specially for carpet use. Retailers can readily supply information about whether fibers have been engineered or carpets finished to incorporate antistatic or antisoiling qualities.

This chapter describes in detail the manufacture and construction of the various types of carpet. The type of pile will affect the appearance and performance of the carpet. Pile can be cut or uncut (also called *loop pile*) or a combination of *cut and loop pile*, which produces a sculptured surface effect. *Single level loop pile* has a smooth surface with all loops the same size. In *multilevel loop pile*, the loops are two or three different heights, often producing an interesting patterned effect on the surface. Cut pile carpets include *velvet* (not to be confused with velvet construction), or *plush*, surfaces. Their yarns have little twist and a level surface. *Saxony pile* carpets, made with yarns of two or more plys heat-set to lock in twist, produce a texture in which individual yarns are more distinct than velvet pile. *Frieze pile* yarns are tightly twisted to produce a nubby effect. Figure 18.4 illustrates some common varieties of carpet pile.

The most important factor in durability is pile density: the closer and more dense the pile yarns, the better a carpet will wear. To evaluate pile density, fold the carpet back upon itself and look through the pile at the backing. The more visible the carpet backing, the lower the density of the pile. Pile with yarns of the same length distributes wear evenly across the surface of the pile. Footprints do not cause flattening or shading of pile made with tightly twisted yarns, like those in frieze and some uncut pile carpet, which tend to be more durable and suitable for high-traffic areas.

Generally, wall-to-wall carpet is installed over a carpet pad or cushion. The carpet manufacturer will have informed the retailer of the type of padding appropriate for a particular carpet. Incorrect installation or use of improper padding may void carpet warranties; therefore, purchase from and installation by a reputable dealer is essential.

Although construction, fiber content, and installation determine the wear life of a carpet, its selection is based to a significant extent on the consumer's preferences for certain colors, textures, or printed or woven designs. A natural characteristic of cut pile fabrics is the "shaded" effect that results from light reflecting off different areas of pile, which do not all fall in the same direction. Footprints are more apparent in cut pile carpets.

Color and design are related not only to appearance but also to performance. Soil is generally tracked onto carpets from uncarpeted areas or from the out-of-doors. Consumers living in geographic locations where the soil is dark will find darker-colored carpets more practical, but those

continued

with light-colored soil will notice that dark carpets will show soil, dust, and lint. For these consumers lighter colors may be more practical. Tweeds, multi-colored patterns, and nubby textures tend to hide soil. Many carpets sold today have been treated with a stain-blocking finish.

Other than soiling, the most serious consumer concern with cut pile carpeting is wear. In heavy traffic areas carpet will begin, after some time, to look worn down and matted. This is because the tips of the pile yarns untwist and flatten, becoming en-tangled with their neighbors. When this happens, the yarns have lost their tuft definition, and the carpet has lost its new appearance. Carpets with higher twist pile yarns, and higher pile densities, will retain a

better appearance longer because the yarns will not untwist as easily.

Proper care can extend the wear life of carpet-ing. Soil accumulating at the base of carpet pile abrades and cuts the fibers, so frequent vacuuming to remove soil particles is important. Stains should be removed immediately. Carpets also require periodic cleaning that goes beyond vacuuming. The Carpet and Rug Institute recommends that deep cleaning be done once every 12 to 18 months. If you do it yourself, check with your retailer about procedures. Do not rub carpeting vigorously, either to remove stains or for general cleaning, as this will accelerate the loss of tuft definition. Most communities have reputable professional carpet cleaning services.

QUILTED FABRICS

Quilted fabrics have been made for centuries. Quilted fabrics use at least three components, as a general rule. A filling material (usually cotton batting, wool, or down) is sandwiched between two layers of decorative outer fabric. These layers are sewn together with strong thread in selected areas to keep the filling material from shifting about. The location of the stitches forms a padded design that might take geometric, floral, or other shapes. (See Figure 18.8.)

Many quilted fabrics are produced commercially for apparel or household use. Polyester fiberfill has, to a large extent, replaced the natural fillers because of its easy-care aspects.

The performance of quilted fabrics is related to the closeness of the quilting stitches, the size of the stitches, the type of thread used for stitching, and the durability of the outer fabric. If stitches are spaced too far apart, the filling will shift about and become uneven. If quilting stitches are too large, stretching of the cloth will tend to break the thread. The outer fabric layer should have high fabric count and a balanced weave. Well-balanced fabrics will have better abrasion resistance and durability. A close weave is also important if the filling is not to work its way out through the covering fabric. Down-filled comforters or quilts require the use of an inner layer of downproof ticking, a dense, closely woven fabric that prevents the escape of small bits of down.

New Techniques of Quilting

Changes have taken place in the methods by which some quilted fabrics are produced. Instead of sewing quilted fabrics with thread, bonding may be done with heat or adhesives. Thermal bonding requires that all components be thermoplastic. The heat application causes the components to fuse together in the heat-stitched areas.

FIGURE 18.8

Nineteenth-century appliquéd and pieced quilt. Photograph from the collection of the Huntington Historical Society, Huntington, N.Y.

One of these techniques uses high-frequency, ultrasonic vibrations to generate the heat in the stitching device. (See Figure 18.9.) This *sonic sewing* can be used to construct apparel and household textiles made from synthetic fibers.

Another technique used to produce raised surface patterns with layered fabrics places a layer of fabric that is not thermoplastic over fabric, foam, or fiberfill that is thermoplastic. A design is printed on the fabric with a special chemical, which holds the layers together in the printed area. The fabric is subjected to heat, which causes the backing fabric to shrink, thereby producing a raised pattern on the face fabric.

LAMINATED OR BONDED FABRICS

The terms *laminated* and *bonded* have been defined by the ASTM (1998) as follows:

> *bonded fabric*—a layered fabric structure wherein a face or shell fabric is joined
> to a backing fabric, such as tricot, with an adhesive that does not signifi-
> cantly add to the thickness of the combined fabrics (p. 11).

FIGURE 18.9

Close-up photograph of sonically quilted fabric in which heat has been used to fuse thermoplastic elements of the quilt.

laminated fabric—a layered fabric structure wherein a face or outer fabric is joined to a continuous sheet material, such as polyurethane foam, in such a way that the identity of the continuous sheet material is retained, either by the flame method or by an adhesive, and this in turn normally, but not always, is joined on the back with a backing fabric such as tricot (p. 28).

Several different methods can be used to join fabric to fabric, fabric to foam, or fabric to foam to fabric.

Fabric-to-Fabric Bonding

When two layers of fabric are joined, the purpose is to provide greater stability and body to the face fabric or to create a self-lined fabric. The underlayer in bonded fabrics is often knitted tricot or jersey, used because they have good flexibility, are relatively inexpensive, and slide readily, making them easy to don over other garments. For the most part, fabrics used in bonding are less expensive and lower-quality fabrics that can be upgraded by this process.

Two methods can be used for attaching fabric to fabric. The *wet-adhesive method* places an adhesive material on the back of the face fabric, and together the fabrics are passed between heated rollers that activate and set the adhesive. (See Figure 18.10.)

The second method is known as the *flame-foam method*. A thin layer of polyurethane foam is melted slightly by passing it over a flame. The two layers of fabric are sandwiched around the foam, which then dries, forming the bond between the two layers of fabric. Ideally, the layer of foam should be so thin that it virtually disappears. (The foam in the finished fabric is about 0.010 inch thick.) The foam does, however, add body to the fabric and produces a somewhat stiffer fabric than does the wet-adhesive method. It is preferable that the flame-foam method not be used with open-weave fabrics because of the possibility that some of the foam may appear on the surface of the fabric.

FIGURE 18.10

Flame-foam and adhesive bonding. Illustration courtesy of Hoechst-Celanese Corporation.

Fabric-to-Foam Lamination

Fabrics are laminated to polyurethane foam when it is desirable to provide some degree of insulation. Winter coats and sportswear, for example, are made from these fabrics. The flame-foam process can be used to manufacture such fabrics. A thick layer of foam is utilized. Only one side of the foam, that to which the fabric attaches, must be heated. Still another foam process flows the sticky foam onto the fabric, cures the fabric, and causes the foam to solidify and adhere to the fabric at the same time.

When laminates first entered the retail market, customers found wide variation in the permanence of the bonding. Some fabrics separated during laundering, others separated during dry cleaning, and still others separated during use. Often the backing and face fabrics shrunk unevenly, causing wrinkling and puckering. Today, many of these problems have been overcome. Although laminated fabrics of varying quality are still sold, many of these fabrics are labeled with guarantees of serviceability. The label *Certifab* guarantees bonding and dimensional stability in dry cleaning or laundering for one year. *Celabond* offers the same guarantee but is applied to fabrics laminated with certain acetates.

Recent Developments in Lamination

The older technique of lamination has been applied to some newer materials. With the success of Gore-Tex®, special attention has been given to the creation of fabrics made by layering conventional fabrics with thin, microporous films that transmit moisture. (See discussion of water repellency in chapter 23.) Such fabrics require extreme precision in application of adhesive materials if the finished product is to transmit vapor and also drape well. In addition to its use in rainwear, vapor-transmitting film laminates are used in clean-room clothing, (i.e.: free of contaminants) medical barrier products, and molded automotive parts.

Molded automobile seats traditionally required a labor-intensive sewn upholstery process. In the laminated process molded seats are covered with a film component to which a urethane foam is attached, and then the upholstery fabric is laminated to the urethane foam.

FLOCKED FABRICS

A surface effect that is similar to a nap or a pile may be created by flocking, a process in which short fibers are "glued" onto the surface of fabrics by an adhesive material. If the adhesive coats the entire surface of the fabric, the flocking will cover the entire surface of the fabric, but if the adhesive is printed onto the fabric in a pattern of some sort, the flock will adhere only in the printed areas. All-over flocked fabrics may have a suedelike appearance.

Short lengths of fiber flocking can be made from any generic fiber type. Rayon is often used for flocking. Nylon may be selected for situations that require good abrasion resistance.

FIGURE 18.11

Application of flock to fabrics.

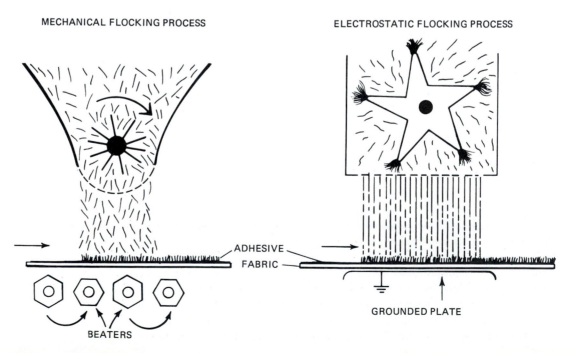

MECHANICAL FLOCKING PROCESS

ELECTROSTATIC FLOCKING PROCESS

ADHESIVE
FABRIC

BEATERS

GROUNDED PLATE

Fibers for flocking are made from bundles of tow fiber (continuous filament fibers without twist). The tow is fed through a finish removal bath and then into a bank of cutters that cut flock of the desired length. The fibers may be dyed before they are attached to the fabric, or the completed fabric may be dyed.

The flock is applied to the fabric in one of two methods. The mechanical flocking process sifts loose flock onto the surface of the fabric to be coated. A series of beaters agitate the fabric, causing most of the fibers to be set in an upright position, with one end of each fiber "locked" into the adhesive. (See Figure 18.11.)

The second method causes the fibers to be attached in an upright position by passing them through an electrostatic field. The fibers pick up the electric charge and align themselves vertically. One end penetrates into the adhesive, and the flock is formed. Electrostatic flocking ensures more complete vertical positioning, and the resultant fabrics are of better quality. It is a more costly process. When buying fabrics, a consumer cannot tell which process was used.

The durability of flocked fabrics depends largely on the adhesives that hold the flock firmly during either laundering or dry cleaning. In some cases, flock may be removed by dry-cleaning solvents. Permanent care labels should tell the consumer how to handle flocked fabrics. A second factor in the durability of flocked fabrics has to do with the fiber from which the flock has been made.

FIBER AND TEXTILE WALL COVERINGS

Textile products used in interior design include laminated materials that are affixed to walls. They are generally made by attaching fibers or fabrics to cloth, foam, or paper backings. The backing is attached to the wall with adhesives. Fibers often used include linen, silk, cotton, wool, jute, manufactured fibers, or blends. Other popular materials include simulated suede produced by flocking and flocked printed designs.

When selecting textile wall coverings, consumers should avoid those made in wide sections, as the fabrics may sag. Fibers or fabrics that do not shrink are important if climates are humid and because moisture from the water-based adhesives can pass through to the surface. Woven fabrics should have a close weave and be of at least medium weight so that stains from the adhesive will not pass through the fabric.

Many of these wall coverings are treated so that they are washable. Selection of fiber or fabric wall coverings should take into account the properties and characteristics of fibers, yarns, and fabric structure as it relates to the anticipated use of the areas where they are placed. For example, if fabrics, especially simulated suede or flocked materials, are located in high-traffic areas where they are subject to abrasion, the surface fibers may wear off. Wall coverings made from fibers that are damaged by sunlight or fabrics colored with dyes that are not colorfast to sunlight should not be used in areas that have extended exposure to direct sunlight.

HYBRID FABRICS USING POLYMER FILMS

Fabrics coated with polymer films are used for a variety of products ranging from apparel to tablecloths. ASTM defines a *coated fabric* as "a flexible material composed of a textile fabric and an adherent polymeric material applied to one or both surfaces" (ASTM 1998, 14). Coatings may be solid films or *poromerics*, products with microscopic, open-celled structures used to produce leatherlike materials. These multicomponent coated fabrics should be distinguished from fabrics that may have a special finish applied. (See chapter 23 for a discussion of functional finishes.)

Coated Fabrics

Fabrics may be coated with thin polymer films to provide protection or to simulate leather or other materials. Polymers most often used are polyvinyl chloride (PVC) and polyurethane.

PVC-coated fabrics, often just called vinyls, are used to produce leatherlike and protective materials. Vinyl-coated fabrics may have an imitation leatherlike grain embossed on the surface. These are the least satisfactory leather imitations both in terms of aesthetics and performance. Fabrics are cold and hard to the touch and do not allow the transmission of moisture vapor. Expanded vinyls are manufactured so as to have internal air bubbles that improve flexibility and cause the material to feel warmer and softer. Urethane-coated fabrics are even more leatherlike in their qualities.

Lamination of extremely thin films to fabrics of Lycra® spandex/nylon has been used in the manufacture of lightweight, stretchable fabrics. The Lycra®/nylon layer is bonded to a urethane film with a special urethane adhesive system. Marketed under the trademark of Darlexx®, these fabrics are capable of passing moisture vapor for comfort. Darlexx® fabrics are said to be particularly suitable for active sportswear, in particular for racing swimwear and windsurfing suits.

Garments for weather and water protection or protection from harmful substances are often made from coated fabrics. Vinyl films may be bonded to fabrics for rainwear or more resistant polymer materials can be used. Elastomeric polymers can provide more stretch, and therefore comfort, than vinyl coatings. Chloroprene synthetic rubber is a good coating for garment fabrics for industrial workers who may be exposed to chemical spills or splashes.

Apparel items made from film-coated fabrics vary in their care requirements. Consumers should follow care label instructions carefully as some products must be laundered; others can withstand dry cleaning.

Poromerics

Poromeric structures more closely match the moisture vapor permeability and other qualities of real leather. Many of their applications fall outside of areas that would be considered as textile products. In simplified terms, the process of producing poromerics consists of forming a microporous web of urethane which is extruded onto a suitable support, usually a woven, knitted, or nonwoven fabric structure. A suedelike finish may be achieved by brushing and napping the polyurethane surface.

Certain of the techniques for creating suedelike fabrics, however, rely on recently developed, highly sophisticated fiber-forming technologies. Ultrasuede®, the trademark name of a suede-type fabric, is manufactured in Japan and distributed in the United States by the Skinner Division of Springs Mills. It is a multicomponent nonwoven fabric composed of polyester microfibers. (See chapter 5 for a discussion of microfibers.) The nonwoven web is mechanically bonded by needle punching or hydroentangling. The fabric is then impregnated with polyurethane and the surface brushed to create the suedelike texture.

The soft hand and smooth suede appearance of the fabric are attributable to the microfibers in the structure. Promotional materials from Skinner indicate that Ultrasuede® will not stretch out of shape, pill, fray, crock (lose color through rubbing of the surface), or wrinkle. It is hand or machine washable, dry-cleanable, colorfast, and will not water spot or stiffen.

Ultrasuede® is used for apparel of all kinds, for furniture, wall coverings, and for luggage. Special care must be used by home sewers using this fabric. In the fabric all face fibers run in the same direction, so all garment pieces must be cut in the same direction. Needle and pin holes will remain, so care must be taken to avoid ripping and pinning in areas where holes would be evident.

FIBER-REINFORCED COMPOSITES

Fiber-reinforced composites (FRC) are among the newest technological developments in the textile field. FRCs generally consist of one or more textile components impregnated with or imbedded in a resin matrix. (See Figure 18.12.) The textile components may be fibers, yarns, nonwoven mats, or woven fabric structures. The resulting products have high strength and light weight and can be molded into a variety of shapes. In most FRCs the fibrous materials make up 65 percent or less of the total volume.

Briefly summarized, the process for forming FRCs includes these steps. Fibers, yarns, or fabrics are impregnated with resin. Any of a number of high-technology fibers can be used, but at present these are most likely to be glass, carbon, or aramid fibers. Cellulosic fibers are also being used in composites. Polymers commonly found in the matrix phase of composites are polyester, polypropylene, polyethylene, and epoxy. Resin application may be done by a wet lay-up system, or materials may be delivered as already resin-impregnated sheets called *pre-pregs*.

The fiber resin layer is placed in a mold of the selected shape. Layers can be arranged as required for purposes of the final product. For example, reinforcing fibers may be laid one over the other with fibers running in the same or different directions to provide strength in a particular area. The layer or layers are pressed into the mold. After or during this shaping, heat is applied which cures the resin and sets the shape. Additional curing processes may be needed, depending on the resin that was used.

A newer process that eliminates the pre-pregs is reaction injection molding (RIM). The fiber reinforcement is placed in the mold and the monomers that will

FIGURE 18.12

Structure of a fiber-reinforced composite in which fibers are embedded in a matrix. Illustration reproduced from *Textiles Magazine*, a publication of the Textile Institute, U.K. Easton, P. M., Fibre-reinforced composites vol. 15 (no. 2), 1986. Manchester, U.K.

make up the polymer resin are injected. They react to form the polymer and then fill the mold around the fibers.

If hollow or spherical components are required, an alternate construction method called *filament winding* may be used. In this process a continuous yarn or roving is fed through a resin bath, then wound on a form of the correct shape. When the desired thickness is reached, the FRC is cured.

Like the reinforcing cords in tires, one of the most important factors in FRC production is the adhesion between the reinforcing material and the matrix. The reinforcing fibers are added to the composite to increase the tensile, compressional, or impact strength of the matrix material. To do this, the load must be transmitted from the matrix phase to the fiber phase. If the fiber and resin phases separate, the load sharing is not maximized. Glass fibers, for example, are treated with coupling agents to increase their adhesion to polyethylene and polyester resins.

Uses for FRCs were discussed in chapter 11 under high-performance fibers. They can be seen not only in aerospace structures but also in sporting equipment and molded automobile parts. It is predicted that in the next century 60 percent of the structural materials used in aircraft will be FRCs (Hongu and Phillips 1997, 8).

EFFECTS OF MULTICOMPONENT FABRIC STRUCTURE ON PRODUCT PERFORMANCE

Durability Factors

In multicomponent fabrics, each part of the structure plays a role in the durability of the final product. As has been seen in Consumer Brief 18.1 on carpets, fiber and yarn structure, as well as the type of carpet construction all contribute to the durability of a carpet. In some products, however, one part of the fabric may be subjected to the greatest amount of wear. For example, in a multilayered quilt, the external fabric will be subject to abrasion to a far greater extent than the fibers within the quilt. Consumers must, therefore, look at durability of fibers, yarns, and fabrics that are likely to be subjected to the greatest stress.

Appearance

The visible part of a multicomponent fabric also requires evaluation in relation to how well its fiber, yarn, and fabric components can be expected to maintain an attractive appearance. Appearance is an important feature for embroidered, quilted, and carpeting fabrics, less so for those that are primarily functional or have industrial uses.

Comfort Factors

Multicomponent fabrics are often used in clothing or household products to maintain warmth. Fabric thickness is usually considered to be the most important single variable in determining thermal comfort. However, there is a limit to how thick the fabric can be without adding too much weight. Multicomponent fabrics such as quilts are thick, but their inner layers of fibers or down have a high volume of air and therefore little weight. This is why down comforters and jackets are so warm. The down feathers between the outer layers allow for a larger volume of dead air to serve as resistance to heat transfer. The glass fiber insulation in buildings is in a loose mat form for the same reason—to provide a significant volume of dead air space.

The ability of fabrics to breathe is a significant comfort factor. Coated, and some bonded and laminated fabrics, have decreased breathability, and this characteristic must be balanced against safety in selecting materials for protective clothing. Poromeric laminates can provide both comfort and weather protection.

The feel of many of these products may also be of interest to consumers. Here the fibers and exterior fabrics used will play an important role.

SUMMARY

Multicomponent fabrics are created because no single component—fiber, yarn, or fabric—can be as effective as a fabric that combines several components. Case Study 26.2 (Chapter 26) explores considerations in the choice of outdoor clothing to include not only multicomponent fabrics, but also the practice of putting together layers of clothing. The discussion, therefore, summarizes not only considerations in relation to multicomponent fabrics, but also the selection of fibers, yarns, and fabrics to accomplish a specific objective. With its focus on a variety of fabric structures, it serves to close the sections of this text that deal with fiber, yarn, and fabric structures.

References

ASTM. 1998. *Annual book of ASTM standards.* West Conshohocken, Pa.: American Society for Testing and Materials.

Hongu, T., and G. O. Phillips. 1997. *New fibers.* Cambridge, U.K.: Woodhead.

Wace, A. T. B. 1948. Weaving or embroidery? Homeric references to textiles. *American Journal of Archeology* 52 (1): 51.

Review Questions

1. What are the limitations of machine embroidery as compared with embroidery done by hand?
2. What types of designs are possible on carpets that are made by tufting?
3. What should a consumer look for when examining a carpet sample to determine its probable quality and durability?
4. What should a consumer look for when examining a quilt to determine its probable quality and durability?
5. What is the difference between a laminated, a bonded fabric, and a coated fabric? Give an example of one kind of product in which each process would be used.
6. How have new fiber-forming technologies been used to create suedelike fabrics?
7. Describe three processes used to produce fiber-reinforced composites. What properties are important in selecting the textile reinforcement in composites?

Recommended Readings

Devine, J. 1994. Understanding ultrasonics. *Bobbin* 35 (March): 74.

Easton, P. M. 1986. Fibre-reinforced composites. *Textiles* 15 (2): 35.

Fulmer, T. D. 1994. Coated fabric use increasing. *America's Textiles International* 23 (June): 86.

Kirby, J. 1993. Fibre and textile wallcoverings. *Textiles* 22 (1): 22.

Lomax, G. R. 1992. Coating of fabrics. *Textiles* 21 (2): 18.

Mansfield, R. 1990. Specialty composites. *America's Textiles International* 19 (June): 88.

Mohamed, M. 1990. Weaving of fabrics for composite applications. *America's Textiles International* 19 (February): 55.

Novina, T. 1993. Quilting market a rising star. *America's Textiles International* 22 (December): 82.

Southern, J., et al. 1991. Fundamental physics of carpet performance. *Journal of Applied Polymer Science* 47 (1991): 355.

Svensson, N. 1998. Textile structures for load-carrying composites. *Textiles Magazine* (2): 7

Walters, B. J., and J. O. Wheeler. 1984. Localization economics in the American carpet industry. *Geographical Review* 74 (2): 183.

Ward, D. 1998. Carpet machinery: performance advances through latest technology. *Textile Month* (June): 27.

Woodruff, F. A. 1998. Laminating: Latest adhesive and machinery developments. *Textile Month* (November): 62.

Wyner, D. 1990. Succeeding with sensitive laminates. *America's Textiles International* 19 (May): 74.

19

Preparation of Fabrics for Dyeing and Finishing

Woven, knitted, and other textile fabrics almost always undergo some type of finishing after they are constructed. These finishes may be classified on several bases. Certain finishes, that are routinely given to fabrics before dyeing or final processing, are sometimes referred to as steps in fabric preparation rather than finishes. These are performed on greige (or unfinished) fabrics.

Special finishes may be given to fabrics after preparation to modify their appearance or their behavior, or both. Some finishes involve the mechanical manipulation of the fabric, while others are chemical or thermal treatments that produce some change in fabric properties.

The discussion in this chapter concentrates on routine finishes that are applied to prepare fabrics for further processing. Finishes that affect fabric hand and/or appearance are covered in chapter 22 while those that improve or alter performance or function are described in chapter 23.

APPLICATION OF FINISHES

Preparation steps, as well as many dyeing and finishing processes, involve wet treatment of fabrics. Application of treatment chemicals or finishes from a solution is generally accomplished through the steps of padding, drying, and/or curing. Figure 19.1 depicts this traditional process.

Padding

In the padding stage, the fabric is wet by the finishing solution. Then, as the fabric passes between two rolls, the excess liquid from the padding solution is squeezed out. The fabric is then dried by one of several processes. Fabrics treated with finishes that react chemically with the fibers undergo curing at a higher temperature as a final step. This is often the case with the finishes discussed in chapter 23.

Considerable amounts of energy are required to dry the fabric after padding. Because energy use contributes significantly to the cost of making textiles, manufacturers have devoted a good deal of effort to the development of processes that are less energy intensive. A basic goal in developing these finishes is to decrease drying time. This is done by removing substantial quantities of liquid from the fabric before drying, using low-wet-pickup techniques to wet the fabric less during finishing, or combining several finishes into one so that instead of drying fabrics several times, they need be dried only once. Similar principles and techniques are used in some types of dyeing to save energy.

Some examples of low-wet-pickup processes are (Fulmer 1984):

1. *Vacuum extraction.* A vacuum slot is placed after the pad bath to extract some of the water before drying.
2. *Transfer padding.* A loop belt that picks up the finish solution is then squeezed against the fabric.
3. *Kiss roll.* A roller, instead of a loop belt, picks up the finish solution and transfers it to the fabric.
4. *Spray.* Finishing solution is sprayed onto the surface of the fabric.
5. *Foam finishing.* The finish solution is applied as a foam, rather than as a liquid.

Drying

Every type of fabric is dried at least once and often more times during processing. Drying is costly both in terms of time and energy. As the application of heat to dry the cloth is the most expensive part of this operation, mechanical devices such as

FIGURE 19.1

Pad-dry-cure textile finishings. Diagram from M. Grayson, ed (New York: Wiley), 468. *Encyclopedia of Textiles, Fibers,* and *Nonwoven Fabrics.* Reproduced courtesy of John Wiley and Sons, Inc.

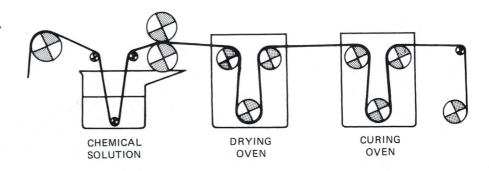

CHEMICAL SOLUTION   DRYING OVEN   CURING OVEN

mangles, which squeeze off water; suction dryers, which pull off water by vacuum extraction; or centrifuges, which spin off water, may be used to remove as much water as possible before thermal drying.

Thermal drying requires the application of heat. Passing the cloth over heated cylinders, called "dry cans," is one such drying technique. This would be comparable, in principle, to ironing a wet garment to dry it. This drying technique is not suitable for pile fabrics, as it would crush the pile.

Another method uses hot air in a tentering machine. Tentering both dries and stretches the fabric smooth and free from wrinkles. Fabrics are stretched between two parallel chains of correct width. (See Figure 19.2.) The fabric is held in place on the tenter frame by pins and clips. Examination of the selvage of fabrics dried in tentering frames will usually reveal either small pinholes or marks from the clips.

The tenter frame carries the fabric into a drying apparatus, where the fabric is dried under tension and made wrinkle free. Fabrics that have not been set on the tenter frame straight will be off-grain. That is, the warp and filling yarns will not cross at right angles. Some fabrics that are off-grain can be straightened by pulling the yarns into the correct or straight position. However, fabrics that have had heat-setting or resin treatments cannot be straightened and will always be off-grain. The serviceability and aesthetic qualities of fabrics are, therefore, adversely affected by poor tentering.

Drying fabrics with hot air is more expensive than drying with heated rollers. For this reason, some fabrics may be tentered after being passed over heated rollers

FIGURE 19.2

Fabric entering tenter frame. Photograph courtesy of West Point–Pepperell.

for preliminary partial drying. Infrared "pre-dryers" can also be used. In any case, after the last drying, the fabric should have a controlled width and length.

Radio frequency waves and microwaves have been used to dry fabrics. This method is similar to microwave ovens in that only the material being processed and not the equipment itself is heated. Advantages over conventional drying systems are faster drying, greater economy of energy consumption, flexibility of design, selective drying of damp areas, and the ability to efficiently dry bulky items such as yarn packages.

PREPARATION OF FABRICS

The preparation steps for fabrics are highly dependent on the fiber content. Natural fibers have impurities such as grease and vegetable matter in wool, gum in silk, or vegetable matter and waxes in cotton. Optimum conditions for spinning fibers into yarns, however, require some lubrication of fibers. Also, in synthetic fibers some means must be found to decrease the static electricity that builds up during spinning. For these reasons, natural lubricating substances in cotton are not removed before spinning, and other fibers generally have had substances added that aid in spinning. During weaving, temporary sizes, such as starch or polyvinyl alcohol (PVA), or other special additives such as identifying dyes may have been used. If fabrics become soiled during weaving, these substances and soils must be removed before further treatment is given to the fabrics. The special preparation treatments given to different fiber types are discussed later.

COTTON AND COTTON BLENDS

Singeing

To produce a smooth surface finish on fabrics made from staple fibers, the fabrics are passed over a heated copper plate or above a gas flame. (See Figure 19.3.) The fiber ends burn off. The fabric is moved rapidly, and only the fiber ends are destroyed. Immediately after passing the flame, the fabric enters a water bath that puts out any remaining sparks.

The burning characteristics of fibers must be taken into account when this process is applied, as heat-sensitive fibers melt, forming tiny balls on the surface of the fabric. These balls interfere with dye absorption, so that, as a general rule, heat-sensitive fibers would be singed after dyeing or printing. The tendency of some manufactured fibers to pill may be decreased by singeing.

Filament yarns do not require singeing, as there are no short fiber ends to project onto the surface of the fabric. Fabrics that are to be napped are not singed.

Desizing

So that subsequent dyeing and finishing materials can be absorbed as evenly as possible, all sizing material must be removed from fabric completely and uniformly. These materials are removed either by a hot water wash for PVA or by enzymes for starch sized fabrics. The enzymes break up the starch polymers into smaller molecules that can be washed away. In order to allow time for the enzymes to work, the fabric is steeped or held in a moist condition before washing away the enzyme residue.

FIGURE 19.3

Fabric passes over gas flame that singes or burns off excess surface fiber. Photograph courtesy of West Point–Pepperell.

Scouring

Scouring removes waxes and destroys vegetable matter residues in cotton and cotton blend fabrics. Sodium hydroxide (caustic soda) is applied to the fabric, and in a chemical reaction with the waxes, and fats on the cotton fibers, forms a soap. This "soap" then serves to emulsify the remaining waxes and wash away any dirt or other impurities.

Scouring was traditionally done in a *kier vat*, a large iron vessel in which the fabric was boiled in the alkaline solution. Economic considerations have largely caused this batch method to be replaced by continuous processes. The fabric can be passed over a series of rollers in a pad bath, so that it is repeatedly exposed to the scouring solution. (See Figure 19.4.) Knitted goods are processed in a beck/jet machine in which the process is integrated with dyeing of the fabric. (See Figure 20.5, page 420, and Figure 20.7, page 421.)

Another system uses a saturator to apply the scouring solution and then passes the fabric through pressure rollers into a large J-shaped steam chamber. The fabric is allowed to collect in the bottom of the *J-Box*, is held there to allow the scouring solution to take effect, and is then washed. (See Figure 19.5.) This is a versatile process in which the fabric can be held at its full width or can be treated in the form of a loose rope.

Bleaching

Cotton fabrics are naturally off-white to tan in color, depending on the amount of pigmentation in the fiber. Problems can arise in dyeing if any small amount of impurity that is highly colored remains. Even manufactured fiber fabrics, especially those that have been heat-set, may become yellowed as a result of processing. Therefore, fabrics may require bleaching or whitening to prepare them for dyeing or printing or to produce a clear white fabric.

FIGURE 19.4

Fabric is scoured on a continuous basis as it passes through cleansing solution. Photograph courtesy of West Point–Pepperell.

FIGURE 19.5

Schematic of continuous processing in a J-box.

Bleaches are chemical substances that oxidize colored compounds, removing the color. Most bleaches used by industry are either chlorine bleaches or peroxygen bleaches. The peroxygen bleaches, and particularly hydrogen peroxide bleaches, are used most frequently in commercial bleaching of greige goods, although for some fabrics other types of bleaches must be used.

Mill processes include saturating the fabric with the bleaching agent, steaming it to effect the bleaching reaction, and washing the fabric thoroughly, usually with a dilute mineral acid to neutralize any residual alkali. This last step is called *souring* and in earlier times was done with buttermilk. (Home bleaching is discussed in chapter 24.)

Combination Processes

The desizing, scouring, and bleaching processes can be combined into two steps, or even one step. The savings in energy, space, and water use are significant for combined continuous processing. The two-stage method consists of two sequences of padding, steaming (usually in a J-box), and washing. Chemicals for all three operations can also be combined in a saturator or pad bath to accomplish desizing, scouring, and bleaching in one step.

It is important to carefully control the solution formulation when combining steps. Exposing too alkaline a fabric to a strong oxidizing bleach can damage the cotton fibers. With judicious choices however, efficient combinations can be applied. Peroxide, with some caustic soda added, can remove starch, enabling desizing and scouring to be carried out simultaneously. For PVA- sized fabrics, the hot conditions of the scouring process can remove the size. New methods for scouring with enzymes hold the promise of combining this step with desizing fabrics sized with starch (Li and Hardin 1997).

Mercerization

Singeing, desizing, scouring, and bleaching are routine finishing processes, whereas *mercerization* is an optional step in the finishing of cotton and cotton-blend fabrics. In 1851 John Mercer discovered that the treatment of cotton with a strong solution of sodium hydroxide altered the strength, absorbency, and appearance of the fabric. Because fabric treated in this way shrunk as much as 25 percent of its length, the finish was not applied commercially until an English chemist, H. A. Lowe, discovered that applying the finish under tension not only minimized shrinkage but also increased luster.

In mercerization, as this finish is called, the cotton fabric is immersed under tension in a strong solution of sodium hydroxide for a short, controlled period of time (usually 4 minutes or less), the alkali is washed off, and any excess alkali is neutralized. The sodium ions in the solution displace the hydrogens on the cellulose–OH groups, pushing the polymer chains farther apart and swelling the fiber.

Mercerized cotton fabrics have greatly increased luster. During mercerization the fiber swells, the natural convolutions of cotton are largely lost, and the fiber retains a fuller, rounded diameter. This smooth surface reflects more light than does the untreated, flatter fiber.

The strength of the fiber is increased as much as 20 percent. The cotton becomes more absorbent and has a greater affinity for moisture and for dyes. Vat-dyed cotton fabrics that have been mercerized have excellent colorfastness, and less dye is required to produce colors. Some decorative effects can be achieved by combining mercerized yarns and unmercerized yarns in one fabric because mercerized fibers dye to darker shades than untreated fibers.

Mercerized fabrics are also more reactive. As a result, they are more easily damaged by acids and oxidizing agents, but mercerized fabrics are more receptive to resin finishes.

Mercerization can be applied to either yarns or fabrics. Most good-quality cotton sewing threads are mercerized to improve their strength. *Slack mercerization,* or mercerization of fabrics that are not held under tension, can be used to produce stretch fabrics. During slack mercerization yarns shrink and develop a higher degree of elasticity. The finished fabric can be stretched, and when the tension is removed, the goods will return to their original length. Yarns that have been slack mercerized do not have the high luster of yarns mercerized under tension. This process is not widely used.

Mercerization is both inexpensive and permanent, and for these reasons it is widely used on cotton goods. Linen can also be mercerized, and since it has a natural luster and good strength, the major advantage of mercerizing linen is to improve the dyeability and receptivity of linen to other finishes.

SILK

In preparation for dyeing and finishing silk fabrics are scoured and usually bleached. In addition to removing the soil or additives used while weaving silk, scouring removes any sericin (gum) that remains on the silk. Often a quantity of the natural gum has been allowed to remain on the silk fiber to give it additional body and to make it easier to handle in spinning and weaving. Although for raw silk fabrics the gum is retained purposely to provide body or produce a different texture, most silk fabrics are degummed as a part of the finishing process. The resultant fabric has a much softer hand and a whiter appearance. Silk is usually bleached with dilute solutions of hydrogen peroxide.

WOOL

As with cotton, wool fabrics routinely go through a number of finishing steps. These include carbonizing, scouring, fulling, and bleaching.

Carbonizing

Wool fabrics that have some vegetable matter clinging to the woven or knitted yarns must be *carbonized*. Carbonizing is accomplished by the immersion of wool in sulfuric acid or hydrochloric acid. Because strong acids readily attack the cellulose of the vegetable matter and do not immediately harm protein fibers like wool, the burrs, sticks, leaves, and the like that remain in the wool are destroyed. The treatment is carried out under carefully controlled conditions so that the wool is not damaged, and the fabric is given a careful scouring afterward to remove or neutralize all the acid that remains.

Crabbing

Crabbing is a preparation step that sets wool fabric in a flat form to inhibit creasing in subsequent processing steps. It involves wetting the fabric in hot water, drying it, and then exposing the hot fabric to cold water. The "thermal shock" of the cold water sets the flat fabric (Schneider et al. 1998). Crabbed fabrics can then be treated later in rope form. Originally a batch process with the fabric wound on rollers, crabbing can now be done continuously.

Scouring

The scouring of wool is done in solutions of less concentration and at lower temperatures than the scouring of other fibers because the alkalinity of most scouring solutions damages wool. Mild detergents and sodium carbonate are frequently used. This step can be combined with the subsequent milling process.

Fulling

Wool fabrics are *fulled*, or *milled*, to give them a more compact structure. In a type of preshrinking, fabrics are subjected to moisture, heat, soap, and pressure. In the milling machine, the wet fabric is pounded with hammers or is alternately stretched and compressed for mechanical action.

Fulling causes the yarns to shrink and to lie closer together and gives the fabric a denser structure. Wool cloth may be given more or less fulling, depending on the desired characteristics of the resultant fabrics. Melton cloth, for example, is one of the most heavily fulled wool fabrics and has a dense, feltlike texture.

Bleaching

Although wool fabrics may be finished in the natural color or dyed without bleaching, often bleaching is necessary. Traditionally, wools were bleached by a process called stoving, which exposed the fabric to sulfur dioxide. Current processes use hydrogen peroxide and mild temperatures to avoid damage to the fibers under alkaline conditions.

FLAX AND OTHER BAST FIBERS

Cellulosic bast fibers must generally be prepared in the same manner as cotton. However, since these fibers contain more impurities and also exist as bundles, the processes must be modified. The scouring and bleaching operations are milder than for cotton because strong alkaline solutions can separate the fiber bundles, leaving extremely short fibers. For this reason, it may not be desirable to bleach the fabrics to a very white color.

MANUFACTURED FIBERS

The stringent preparation processes necessary for natural fibers are not required for manufactured fibers because they do not contain the impurities and coloring matter. They may, however, have picked up dirt and other soils, the yarns will have had lubricants applied, and any applied sizing must be removed. A mild scouring process is usually sufficient to clean the fabrics and remove PVA sizes. Enzyme solutions may be necessary if starch was used to size the warp yarns.

INSPECTION AND REPAIR

Before a fabric is ready to leave the factory, a visual or electronic inspection of the goods is made. This may be done after preparation, if the fabric will be transported to another company or destination for dyeing and finishing. In vertically integrated operations, the final inspection if often done after the fabric is dyed and finished.

If the inspection is done visually by a worker, the fabric is run over a roller. The process is called *perching*, and the machine used is known as a perch. Originally perch

FIGURE 19.6

Hand inspection and repair of woolen fabric.

apparatus resembled the uprights on a foorball goal. A light is often placed behind the fabric for better visual inspection. (See Figure 19.6.)

The more sophisticated electronic scanning of today is done by a laser that generates selvage markings of defective areas and a computer map showing where all the defects in a roll are located. This map can be used by apparel manufacturers with the aid of computer-controlled cutting systems that automatically cut around defects in the cloth. The data generated by electronic inspection can help to pinpoint sources of defects so that these can be corrected. (See Figure 19.7.)

For woolens and worsteds, both *specking* and *burling* may have to be done. *Specking*, usually done with tweezers or a burling iron, is the removal from woolens and worsteds of burrs, specks, or other small objects that might detract from the final appearance of the fabric.

Burling is the removal of loose threads and knots from woolens and worsteds by means of a burling iron, a type of tweezer. Many knots must be pulled or worked to the back of the fabric because pulling them out might leave a small hole in the fabric. These inspection and repair steps are often done before milling because the yarns are not tightly compacted and defects are easier to see.

FIGURE 19.7

Computer monitor reports results of inspection of sheets made on an authomated machine that cuts, sews, and folds the finished product. Photograph courtesy of CMI Industries, Inc.

SUMMARY

Fabrics as they come from the loom or knitting machine must undergo preparation processing before being dyed and finished. These processes are fairly standard, but are also specific to the fibers of the which the fabric is composed. They involve removing impurities and any soils from the fabric and bleaching it to a white color. Sometimes cotton, linen, wool, or silk fabrics are not bleached because the natural coloring of the fibers is desired in the final textile product.

References

Fulmer, T. D. 1984. Low-wet-pickup techniques in finishing. *America's Textiles* (May): 62.

Li, I., and I. R. Hardin. 1997. Enzymatic scouring of cotton: Effects on structure and properties. *Textile Chemist and Colorist* 29 (8): 71.

Schneider, A. M., N. A. Michie, and D. H. Tester. 1998. An investigation of fabric conditions during continuous crabbing. *Journal of the Textile Institute* 89 Part I (4): 669.

Review Questions

1. Describe the ways that finishes can be classified.
2. What is meant by low-wet-pickup finishes? Why is the textile finishing industry placing emphasis on these finishes?
3. Explain the differences in batch and continuous fabric preparation processes.
4. List and give the purpose of each of the preparation steps for:

   cotton   silk

   wool   linen

   manufactured fibers

Recommended Readings

Abrahams, D. H. 1994. Improving on mercerizing processing. *American Dyestuff Reporter* 83 (September): 78.

Cook, F. L. 1994. Less is more in applying chemicals to textiles. *Textile World* 144 (January): 59–65.

Hodgson, A. 1982. Desizing and bleaching. *Textiles* 11 (Spring): 10.

Peters, R. H. 1967. *Textile chemistry. Vol. II: Impurities in fibres, purification of fibres.* Amsterdam: Elsevier.

ADDING COLOR TO TEXTILES

Most objects made by human beings are decorated in some way. Textiles are no exception. The decoration of textiles may be achieved through varying the construction of the fabric, by adding color through dyeing, or by applying color in patterns by printing.

Even the earliest fabrics excavated by archeologists show evidence of ornamentation, through the use of natural fibers of contrasting colors or by embroidery or dyes. The first addition of color to fabrics may have been done by painting designs on the cloth.

DYES AND PIGMENTS

Dyes are colorants that are applied to, or formed in, a textile substrate in a molecularly dispersed form (AATCC 1997, 375). They derive their color from the conjugated double bonds in their molecular structure. (See chapter 2, page 34.) The definition stresses that for use in textiles, dyes must be soluble or capable of being made soluble in the medium in which they are applied, or they must themselves be molecularly dispersible into the fibers. It is this property that distinguishes them from pigments.

Natural Dyestuffs

The paints used on pottery or stone were not always serviceable on fabrics, but certain substances did have a particular affinity for cloth. These dyestuffs came from a wide variety of animal, vegetable, and mineral matter. The difficulty with most of the natural dyestuffs was that they lacked colorfastness, or permanence. As a result, those dyes that proved to have excellent colorfastness became important items of international trade.

Few of these early dyes could be relied on to produce strong colors on all fibers. The coloring of fibers results from the chemical or other reaction of the functional groups within the fibers and those within the dyestuff. The varying chemical composition or structure of the natural fibers caused each to react differently with the chemicals in each of the dyestuffs then available. The treatment of the fabrics with appropriate natural acids or oxides did, however, improve their colorfastness. These substances, called *mordants*, react both with the dyestuff and the fiber to form a *colored lake*, an insoluble compound, thereby "fixing" the color within and on the fiber. The effect of mordants probably was discovered accidentally when it was realized that washing undyed fabrics in the water of some streams (those high in certain metallic compounds) resulted in their taking and holding colors better.

Some mordants were more effective on animal fibers such as silk and wool; others were preferable for cotton and linen. Workers in the dyer's trades developed skill in using mordants to make fabrics of fairly good colorfastness, although it was not possible to obtain consistently excellent colorfastness until after the invention of synthetic dyes in the nineteenth century.

Vegetable dyes could be made from flowers, leaves, berries, barks, roots, grasses, weeds, vines, and lichens. Woad, a blue dye made from the bark of the woad plant, was produced in Europe from Roman times to the end of the Middle Ages when it was supplanted by indigo, a more effective blue dye imported from India. Madder, a source of reds, also had the peculiar quality of producing several different colors or color intensities when it was employed in combination with different mordants. The chemical reaction of the metallic salts in the various mordants with the chemical compound in madder resulted in colors that ranged from yellow to rose to red. Fustic for yellow, logwood and cutch for browns, and safflower for red were other widely known dyes. By combining the primary colors of red, blue, and yellow, it was possible to create additional colors in the green, purple, and orange ranges. A good, fast, dark black was exceedingly difficult to achieve.

Some iron oxides were employed, but in general mineral colors were less often used than were plant or animal substances. Animal sources provided some of the most effective dyestuffs. Kermes, a brilliant scarlet dyestuff, was obtained in ancient times from the bodies of small insects that lived in oak trees. This dye was replaced by cochineal from small insects that are native to South America and that had been used by the Indians as a dyestuff for many centuries. This cochineal bug, which became a major item of trade between the New and Old Worlds, produced a vivid red of excellent fastness.

The color purple has been associated with royalty for centuries. The origins of this association are based on the production of Tyrian purple, a color made from the juice secreted by a small shellfish. The technique for making the dye was known as early as 1000 B.C. and required a lengthy and complex series of steps. First, the dye was "milked" from the shellfish. This white liquid, as it oxidized, turned from milky white to green, to red, to deep purple. Careful control of the color range could be used to produce a wide range of red-purple colors, the most desirable being a deep, rich red-purple. The process was time consuming, difficult, and the supply of the dye limited. Fabrics dyed with Tyrian purple were extremely costly and therefore available only to the rich and, in particular, to the nobility. Royalty eventually gained a monopoly on the color, and so it has come to be known as "royal purple" (Gerhard 1964).

Synthetic Dyes

William Perkin, an English chemist, discovered that a coal tar derivative, *aniline*, colored white silk. After further experimentation, Perkin was able to make a dyestuff that had potential commercial application. It was a reddish-purple in color, called mauve.

Perkin's discovery in 1856 stimulated additional research with other coal tar derivatives and related compounds, and the synthesis of a wide range of manufactured dyestuffs resulted. Gradually, an enormous range of synthetic dyes made from many chemical substances was developed. These have almost completely replaced natural dyes for commercial production.

The selection of dyes for coloring fabrics is a decision requiring the attention not only of the highly trained dye technician but also of designers, stylists, and business managers who are knowledgeable about current fashion trends. Although some types of dyed fabrics can be bleached and redyed another color, or designs printed over plain-colored fabrics, dyeing a fabric to an unpopular color may spell financial disaster for a manufacturer of piece goods.

In addition, the choice of hue is only the first of many decisions about adding color to fabrics. It must be decided at what point the color will be added and the type of dye that will be used.

Each fiber reacts differently to dyes; therefore, the use of an appropriate dye is crucial to colorfastness. Since loss of color in use is a major source of consumer dissatisfaction, reputable manufacturers must choose dyes carefully.

Color is one of the areas in which the chemistry of textiles is particularly important. The combination of fibers with dyes may involve not only physical but also chemical reactions.

Pigments

Pigments are colorants "in a particulate form which is insoluble in a textile substrate, but which can be dispersed within the substrate to modify its color" (AATCC 1997, 377). They are not molecularly dispersed as are dyes, but are small particles, similar to the pigments in paints.

THE DYEING PROCESS

The science of dyeing is highly complex, and the mechanisms of dyeing are not completely understood. This discussion is necessarily superficial and does not provide an in-depth exploration of the subject. For additional background, readers may consult the sources listed at the end of the chapter.

The medium most often used to dissolve or disperse dyes for application to textiles is water. The dye solution, called the *dye liquor*, is agitated or circulated to increase the migration of the dye to the fiber surface. The attraction or *affinity* of the dye for a particular fiber is influenced by several factors. Different dye types are attracted chemically or physically to specific fibers. Fibers often undergo swelling in aqueous dyeing processes, increasing dye absorption. For hydrophobic fibers that do not swell in water, organic solvents can be used as swelling agents or "carriers" for the dye. Mordants can be added to increase the acceptance of dyes. Dyebath additives such as these are classed as *dye auxiliaries*.

Surface features such as the scales on wool or waxes or finishes on fibers can inhibit attraction of the dye to the fiber. Careful preparation of fabrics for dyeing minimizes this effect by removing waxes and sizes. Further, application of aesthetic and functional finishes usually follows the dyeing process, so that the finishes do not compete for dye sites on the fiber.

Once dyes are attracted to the fiber, they should diffuse through it rather than remaining adsorbed on the surface. Dyes are absorbed into the fiber predominantly in the amorphous areas, and making these areas larger or more accessible enhances the dyeing process. Mercerization of cotton, which moves the polymer chains farther apart, allows more dye in. Higher temperatures, around the glass transition phase of thermoplastic fibers, cause some of the crystalline areas to move and separate more, increasing dye accessibility. Nylon fibers have a low glass transition temperature and can often pick up dyes from other fibers.

Exhaustion is the amount of transfer of dye from the bath to the fiber, either by adsorption or absorption. It is possible for all the dye to be removed from the bath and for the dyebath to be clear at the end of the process. Some dye classes exhaust better than others. It is not always prudent, or even necessary, to dye to complete exhaustion of the bath.

A concern in dyeing is how evenly distributed the dye is in the fiber, a characteristic known as *levelness*. Low leveling will result in a streaked appearance of the fabric. Dyes may be only adsorbed on the fiber surface, or dyes that have been absorbed by fibers may migrate back to the surface when the textile is dried, resulting in uneven dyeing. Leveling agents and retarders are dyebath auxiliaries than can promote even dye absorption.

Once the dye has entered the amorphous regions of fiber, it must be retained within the fiber not only during the dyeing but also when fabrics are laundered or dry cleaned during use. Several factors make for dye retention. The nature of the chemical bonds and physical attraction between fiber and dye is a crucial element. Dyes may be physically bound to fibers by forces such as hydrogen bonding or ionic forces. Ionic forces are the attraction between positively and negatively charged ions, one on the dye, the other on the fiber. The chemical structure of dye and fiber may allow the formation of covalent chemical bonds between fiber and dye. Dyes that are absorbed into swollen fibers can be physically trapped when the fibers are cooled and dried. Dyes that are soluble in water, which may also swell some fibers, can be removed when the textile is wetted.

Pigment colors are not soluble, cannot penetrate fiber surfaces, and therefore must be attached to the surface of the fabric by a binder. A polymeric resin serves as the binder. When the resin is cured, or permanently fixed to the fabric, the dye is also fixed on the fabric surface. The retention of pigment colors is dependent on the durability of the binder, not the pigment. As discussed later, pigments can also be used to color manufactured fibers before spinning.

COLORFASTNESS

A fabric that retains its color during care and use is said to be *colorfast*. Fastness, that is affected by the factors discussed above, is an important concern of consumers. Small aggregates of dye molecules distributed evenly throughout the fiber make for a more satisfactory result than do surface applications of color.

Fabrics may be more or less colorfast to a variety of different substances or conditions. The importance of colorfastness depends on the use of the fabric. Colorfastness to laundering is, of course, important in those garments and household textiles that must undergo frequent laundering. Some colors are not fast to laundering but are fast to dry cleaning, or vice versa.

Perspiration may cause some color change and/or color transfer, and some colors are may be lost or diminished by heat. Colorfastness to sunlight may be important in evaluating the usefulness of fabrics for curtains, draperies, carpets, and outdoor clothing. Light fastness is usually a function of the dye structure rather than its retention within the fibers. The molecular structure that provides the color can be interrupted by light, particularly ultraviolet light. Additives or finishes are available to stabilize dyes from this type of action.

Some dyes tend to *crock*, or rub off on fabrics or other materials with which they come in contact. Others will *bleed* into water during laundering and may be picked up by lighter-colored fabrics. Chlorine bleaches will remove color from most dyed fabrics, but some dyes are more sensitive than others to the action of chlorine bleaches.

Even dyes that belong to the same class can have differing degrees of colorfastness to the same condition, so that the consumer has no real guarantee of color permanence unless a label specifies that a particular fabric is colorfast. Dye performance labeling is not required by any form of legislation or regulation. Some manufacturers do, however, include colorfastness information on labels. Such labels will generally describe the conditions under which the fabric is colorfast, such as "colorfast to laundering, but not to chlorine bleaching" or "colorfast to sunlight." A few terms may be found on labels that carry an assurance of colorfastness, such as trademarks that have been applied to solution-dyed synthetic fibers. The colorfastness of one class of dyes, the vat dyes, is so consistently good for laundering that the term "vat dyed" on labels has come to be accepted as an assurance of good colorfastness.

DYEING AT DIFFERENT PROCESSING STAGES

Color may be added to fabric at any one of four steps in its processing. Color can be added to manufactured fibers before the fiber is extruded, or dyes can be applied to fibers, to yarns, or to constructed fabrics or finished products.

Mass Coloration

Mass coloration is the addition of color to manufactured fibers before they are extruded. These fibers have been variously known as *spun-dyed, solution-dyed* or *dope-dyed* fibers. Pigment is dispersed throughout the liquid fiber solution. When the fiber is extruded, it carries the coloring material as an integral part of the fiber.

This "locked-in" color is extremely fast to laundering (that is, it will not diminish); however, such colors can be sensitive to light and bleaching or may fade. The range of colors in which solution dyeing is done is rather limited for economic reasons. The fiber manufacturer must produce substantial quantities of fiber to justify the expense of adding an extra step during the manufacturing process. Furthermore, fiber production takes place well in advance of the time when fabrics reach the market. Fashion color trends may change fairly rapidly, so that, by the time a mass colored fabric reaches the market, the color may be out of fashion and not salable. For this reason, spun-dyed fabrics are generally produced in basic colors.

Mass coloration is used on acetate to prevent gas fading. Gas fumes in the air may turn some blue or green dyes used for acetate to pink or brown.

Dyeing Fibers

When color is added at the fiber stage, this process is known as *fiber dyeing* or *stock dyeing*. It is a batch process in which loose (usually staple) fibers are immersed in a dyebath, dyeing takes place, and the fibers are dried. Exhaustion is quicker in fiber dyeing because the dye liquor has better access to fiber surfaces. Levelness may be a problem but its effect can be minimized by blending fibers later during yarn processing.

Stock-dyed fibers are most often used in tweed or heather effect materials in which delicate shadings of color are produced by combining fibers of varying colors. (See Figure 20.1.) The yarns in Harris Tweed fabrics are a distinctive example of fiber dyeing. Fiber-dyed fabrics can be identified by untwisting the yarns to see whether the yarn is made up of a variety of different colored fibers. In solid-colored yarns untwisted stock-dyed fibers will be uniform in color, with no darker or lighter areas.

FIGURE 20.1

Tweed effect created by using filling yarns made from stock dyed fibers.

Fibers for worsted wool fabrics are sometimes made into a sliver before they are dyed. This variation of fiber dyeing is known as *top dyeing*. By dyeing the fibers after they have been combed, the manufacturer avoids the wasteful step of coloring the short fibers that would be removed in the combing process. The dyed tops can be drawn or gilled to produce heather effects in the yarns.

Yarn Dyeing

If color has not been added either to the polymer or the fiber, it can be applied to the yarns before they are made into fabrics. Yarns may be dyed in skeins, in packages, or on beams. Special dyeing equipment is required for each of these batch processes.

In skein dyeing, large skeins of yarn are loosely wound on sticks and placed in a vat for dyeing. In package dyeing, the yarn is wound onto a number of perforated tubes or springs. The dye is circulated through the tubes to ensure that the yarns have maximum contact with the dye. (See Figure 20.2.) Beam dyeing is a variation of package dyeing, which uses a larger cylinder onto which a set of warp yarns is wound.

Many types of fabrics utilize yarn of differing colors to achieve a particular design. Stripes in which contrasting sections of color alternate in the length or crosswise direction, chambrays in which one color is used in one direction and another color is used in the other direction, complex dobby or jacquard weaves, and plaids may all require yarns to which color has already been added. (See Figure 20.3.)

Yarn-dyed fabrics may be identified by unraveling several warp and several filling yarns from the pattern area to see whether they differ in color. Not only will each yarn be a different color, but the yarns will have no darker or lighter areas where they have crossed other yarns.

Usually yarns are dyed to one solid color, but in a variant of the technique called *space dyeing*, yarns may be dyed in such a way that color-and-white or multicolored effects are formed along the length of the yarn.

FIGURE 20.2

Package dyeing of yarns.

FIGURE 20.3

Examples of fabrics in which designs are created by using yarns dyed to different colors.

a

b

c

Piece Dyeing

Fabrics that are to be a solid color are usually piece dyed. In piece dyeing, the finished fabric is passed through a dyebath where the fibers in the fabric absorb the dye. A number of different methods are used for piece dyeing, each of which differs slightly in the way in which the fabric is handled.

Fabrics may be dyed in either continuous or batch processes. In continuous dyeing, the cloth continually passes through the dyebath. This is the cheaper process and, where possible, is used for dyeing large yardages. Batch dyeing is used for shorter fabric lengths. Some fabrics are dyed in open, flat widths. Knitted fabrics and those woven materials that are not subject to creasing are handled in "rope" form, that is, bunched together and handled as a narrower strand. They are usually attached at the ends to form a continuous loop. Some dyeing methods are especially suitable for certain types of fabrics and unsuitable for others. Many different kinds of machines can be used for piece dyeing. The processes used are summarized in Table 20.1.

Batch Processes

Beck and *jet* dyeing are batch processes for fabric in rope form. Beck dyeing, also called *box* or *winch* dyeing, is frequently used for dyeing wool fabrics and knits, as it

TABLE 20.1
Dyeing Processes

Batch		Continuous
Rope Form	**Flat Width**	
Beck	Jig	Pad-dry/Steam
Jet	Beam	Vacuum impregnation

places relatively little tension on the fabric during dyeing. The loop of fabric is pulled in and out of the dyebath by a winch, and large sections are allowed to accumulate in the bottom of the beck to increase the residence time in the bath. (See Figure 20.4.) Up to twelve ropes of fabric can be dyed side by side at the same time. Devices in the machine keep the ropes separate.

Jet dyeing is a newer method that uses propulsion of the dye liquor through the fabric to improve dye penetration. Dyeing takes place in a closed system that carries a fast-moving stream of pressurized dye liquor. A fluid jet of dye penetrates and dyes the fabric. After it passes through this jet, the fabric is floated through an enclosed tube in which the fluid moves faster than the fabric. This prevents the fabric from touching the walls, keeping it constantly immersed in the dyebath. Turbulence is created by locating elbows in the tube. The turbulence aids in diffusing dyes and dyebath auxiliaries. (See Figure 20.5.) Since no pressure is put on the fabric, even delicate fabrics can be dyed by this process. Jet dyeing has the advantage of being economical in operation and at the same time allowing a high degree of quality control.

Batch processes that dye fabric in flat widths are *jig* and *beam* dyeing. Jig dyeing is a process that places greater tension on the fabric than the beck and jet machines. Fabrics are stretched across two rollers that are placed above a stationary dyebath. The fabric is passed through the dyebath and wound on one roller. The motion is then reversed until the desired exhaustion or depth of shade is achieved. (See Figure 20.6.) The tension created by placing the fabric on the rollers means that this process must be reserved for fabrics with a fairly close weave that will not lose their shape under tension.

Beam dyeing, which is used for lightweight, fairly open-weave fabrics, utilizes the same principle as beam dyeing of yarns. The fabric is wrapped around a perforated beam and immersed in the dyebath. (See Figure 20.7.) Tightly woven fabrics would not allow sufficient dye penetration; hence, this method must be applied to loosely woven cloth. It has the added advantage of not putting tension or pressure on the goods as they are processed.

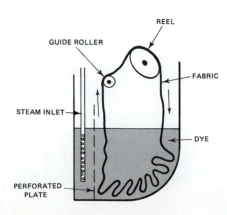

REEL
GUIDE ROLLER
FABRIC
STEAM INLET
DYE
PERFORATED PLATE

FIGURE 20.4

Side view diagram of a typical dye beck showing movement of fabric through the dyebath.

FIGURE 20.5

Hiska jet-dyeing machine. Reprinted by permission of National Knitwear and Sportswear Association.

1. Fabric guide roll
2. Loading and unloading port
3. Header tank
4. "U" tube
5. Suction control
6. Suction control
7. Suction control
8. Delivery control
9. Main Pump
10. Filter
11. Heat exchanger
12. Service tank

Continuous Processes

Continuous dyeing, used in producing large quantities of piece-dyed goods that can withstand tension and pressure, generally follows some variation of the pad-dry-cure sequence. (See Figure 19.1, page 400.) The last steps can be a steam setting process rather than drying and curing. Fabrics pass through a dyebath, then through pads or rollers that squeeze out the excess dye, and finally into a steam or heated chamber in which the dye is set. An example is the Thermosol® process, developed by DuPont for application of disperse dyes to synthetics. Predrying with infrared heaters can be done before the fabric enters the heating chamber.

The process, while efficient, is not without its disadvantages. Leveling can be a problem because the dye absorption may not be uniform and dye migration to the surface may occur during drying. In addition, as dye is picked up, the bath becomes depleted and fresh dye liquor must be added.

Variations of this continuous process are *vacuum impregnation* and *foam application*. The vacuum method was introduced to improve the dyeing of heavyweight fabrics. Trapped air, caught in denser fabrics such as corduroy and heavyweight ducks

FIGURE 20.6

Diagram of jig dyeing method. Rollers reverse and fabric is passed through the dyebath multiple times.

FIGURE 20.7

Beam dyeing of fabric. Photograph courtesy of Allied Chemical Corporation–Fibers Division.

makes dyeing them difficult. In this system, a perforated stainless steel cylinder imposes a vacuum as the dye liquor is applied to the other side of the fabric. The result is more thorough dye penetration. The vacuum system has been particularly useful in dyeing pile fabrics as it allows equal dye penetration of both the pile and the ground fabric.

In foam dyeing the dye solution is spread over the fabric as a foam, that then collapses carrying the dye into the fiber. Level application has been difficult to achieve and this method is little used.

Other Piece Dyeing Techniques

Some specialized piece dyeing techniques exist for achieving solid or mixed colors in fabric blends. *Cross-dyeing* produces a multicolored fabric in one operation. It is done by mixing several dyes, each of which is specific to one fiber, in one dyebath. Each fiber picks up only its specific dye. Plaids or stripes can be created in a fabric by alternating yarns of different fibers, so that, for instance, nylon yarns are dyed red and polyester yarns are dyed blue to make a blue and red stripe.

Union dyeing produces solid colored blended fabrics by piece dyeing. Dyes of the same color for each fiber in the blend are carefully selected and mixed. The fabric is then placed in the dyebath, and ideally a uniform color is produced. Solid coloring of blends with pigments applied to the fabric surface is increasingly done because it produces a more consistently even color.

A subtle method of creating pattern with color is seen in *tone-on-tone or differential* dyeing. Here, two different types of the same generic fiber might be used. Both types respond to the same type of dye, but one may be less reactive so that, for example, a lighter and darker shade of the same color results. Shaded carpets are often dyed this way, where two or three nylon fibers with differing degrees of affinity for the same dye are blended in the carpet yarns.

Garment Dyeing

Except for dyeing socks and narrow fabrics, *garment dyeing*, or the process of dyeing completed garments, remained a rather unimportant novelty until the second half of the 1980s. Industry sources credit two factors with a sharp increase in the amount of garment-dyed apparel. First, fashion demanded small lots of garments from fabrics with stonewashed, ice-washed, tie-dyed, overdyed, and distressed effects. These effects were more readily achieved through garment dyeing than traditional dyeing methods. The second factor was the ability of manufacturers to achieve Quick Response or Just-In-Time production (discussed in chapter 1) through garment dyeing.

The lead time required for delivery of orders in the traditional dyeing system is about eight weeks. For garment-dyed products lead time is about two weeks. Although the process of garment dyeing is more costly than traditional piece dyeing (estimated at $1 to $3 per item), savings are achieved in the long run because manufacturers and retailers need not maintain large inventories. If undyed merchandise is left from one season, it can be dyed for sale the following season. However, if it has already been dyed and a different color is wanted, it must be overdyed, given a second dyeing to a different color. Manufacturers can be more responsive to fashion trends by producing small dye lots.

Garment dyeing is primarily applied to cotton fabrics; however, high-pressure equipment can be used to process polyester and cotton blends. To achieve consistently good results with garment dyeing, manufacturers must exercise care in a number of areas.

1. *Fabric.* All fabric used in one garment must come from the same bolt of fabric. If, for example, one trouser leg of a pair of jeans is cut from one bolt of fabric, and the other from another bolt, each leg may dye to a different shade. The result would be jeans in which the legs do not match.
2. *Shrinkage.* Fabric must also be tested for shrinkage before cutting of garments, and garments must be cut large enough to allow for shrinkage so that sizes will be accurate.
3. *Thread.* Thread must be chosen carefully and tested to be sure it will accept the dye in the same way as the fabric. One hundred percent cotton thread is preferred, but even with all-cotton thread there may be problems. For example, mercerized thread will dye to a darker shade than unmercerized garment fabric. This will make the stitching stand out from the background fabric.
4. *Labels, buttons, zippers.* All of these supplies must be compatible with the garment fabric in terms of reaction to the dye and shrinkage.

The machines used for garment dyeing are called *paddle machines*. To avoid entanglement during dyeing, garments are generally placed inside bags. Paddles in the machine rotate, changing directions periodically, to make sure that all pieces being dyed are equally exposed to the dye liquor. Garments are generally washed before dyeing, to remove any finishing materials that would interfere with dyeing, and after dyeing to remove excess dye.

Special Washing Techniques

The fashions that provided the impetus for the growth in garment dyeing often had a distressed look in which garments had uneven colors. To achieve this effect, denim or other fabric was treated to destroy color randomly on the garment. Although the most widely used term for this process was *stone washing*, other names to describe the random removal of color included ice washing, white washing, acid washing, frosting, super washing, and snow washing.

Both indigo and sulfur-dyed denims lose color when exposed to oxidative bleaches. Stone washing is most commonly done by soaking a rather porous pumice stone in sodium hypochlorite or potassium permanganate, adding these stones to a load of garments in a type of washing machine without any water, and running the machine for a specified time. The contact of the cloth with the bleach removes color at random on the garment. This treatment is followed by another wash (in a different machine, as a rule) to remove any excess bleach.

Cellulase enzymes (see chapter 19, page 402) are also used to produce a stone-washed appearance on fabrics. If enzymes are used in combination with stone washing, the capacity of processing machines can be increased, thereby speeding up production.

DYE CLASSES

Dyes are divided into a number of classifications. Within each of these classifications there exist a range of colors, and each of these colors may vary somewhat in its fastness to different conditions. The names given to the dye classes generally relate to the method of application and, to a lesser extent, the chemical composition of the dye class. All currently used dyes are listed by class in the *Colour Index*, a set of volumes published jointly by the Society of Dyers and Colourists in the United Kingdom and the American Association of Textile Chemists and Colorists (AATCC) in the United States.

In the following discussion of dye classes, the classes are grouped according to the fiber types for which they are most widely (though not exclusively) used.

Dyes Most Often Used on Cellulosic Fibers

Azoic Dyes

Azoic dyes (also called naphthol dyes) are used primarily on cotton fibers, but they can also be applied to acetates, olefins, polyesters, and nylons. The reaction that produces dyeing takes place when two components, a diazonium salt and a naphthol compound, join together to form a highly colored, insoluble compound on the fabric. These dyes are also known as *ice dyes* because the reaction takes place at lowered temperatures. They have good colorfastness to laundering, bleaching, alkalis, and light. They do tend to crock somewhat, however. Colors are mainly in the red range.

Direct Dyes

Direct dyes, historically referred to as substantive dyes, are water soluble dyes used primarily for cotton and rayon, although some polyamide and protein fibers are also dyed with these compounds. These dyes have the advantage of being applied directly in a hot aqueous dye solution in the presence of common salts required to stabilize the rate of dyeing, making the process relatively inexpensive. They also possess the disadvantage of poor fastness to laundering because they are primarily physically bound to the fibers and are soluble in laundering solutions. Aftertreatment with cationic (positively charged) compounds can improve wet fastness.

Vat Dyes

Vat dyes are insoluble in water. By chemical reduction they are converted to a soluble form. The dye is applied to the fibers, and then the dye, now within the fiber, is reoxidized to the insoluble form. This creates a color that is fast to both light and washing. These dyes are expensive, however, and are not manufactured in the United States because of environmental concerns.

Because vat dyes must be applied in an alkaline solution, they are not suitable for use with protein fibers. Primarily used with cottons and rayons, vat dyes can also act as disperse dyes on polyester. These dyes provide a wide range of colors except for reds and oranges. Denim is a popular fabric in which the warp yarns are traditionally dyed with the vat dye indigo. The yarns are dyed prior to scouring, so a wetting agent is applied to provide better penetration of the dye (Etters 1999).

Sulfur Dyes

Sulfur dyes produce mostly inexpensive dark colors, such as black, brown, or navy and are applied in an alkaline solution to cottons and rayons. Fabrics dyed with sulfur dyes must be carefully processed or a buildup of excess chemicals on the fibers will eventually weaken the fibers. Like vat dyes, sulfur dyes are applied to textile materials in a soluble form and then oxidized to an insoluble form within the fiber. Colorfastness of sulfur dyes is good to washing and fair to light. Black and yellow sulfur dyes may accelerate light degradation of cellulosic fibers.

Reactive Dyes

In this class of dyes, the dyestuff reacts chemically with the fiber to form covalent bonds. Reactive dyes are applied most commonly to the cellulosic fibers, cotton, rayon, and linen. They are easy to apply and can produce a wide range of bright colors. Reactive dyes have good wash fastness because the chemical bonds between dye and fiber are strong.

Wool can also be colored with reactive dyes, although wools that have been chlorinated, bleached, or shrink-proofed tend to have poor wetfastness. Reactive dyes are, however, a good choice for washable wools and silks because of their colorfastness to laundering.

Dyes Used Primarily for Protein Fibers

Acid Dyes

Acid dyes have one to four negatively charged functional groups. Applied in acid solution, they react chemically with the basic groups in the fiber structure to form ionic bonds. Because wool has both acid and basic groups in its structure, acid dyes can be used successfully on wools. These dyes are also utilized for dyeing nylon and, to a lesser extent, for acrylics, some modified polyesters, polypropylene, and spandex. They have little affinity for cellulosic fibers. Colorfastness of acid dyes varies a good deal, depending on the color and the fiber to which the dye has been applied.

Metal complex dyes, or *premetallized dyes*, are usually classified with acid dyes. These are dyes that have been reacted with a metal mordant, such as chromium or cobalt, before application to the fiber. The resulting dyes are very stable, with excellent light and wash fastness, but the resulting colors are not as bright as those of unmetallized acid dyes. Major applications are for protein fibers and nylons.

Chrome, or Mordant, Dyes

Used on the same general group of fibers as acid dyes, chrome dyes (also called mordant dyes) are applied with a metallic salt that reacts with the dye molecule to form a relatively insoluble dyestuff with improved wet- and lightfastness. As the name of the dye indicates, chromium salts are most often used for the process. Especially effective for dyeing wool and silk, these dyes have excellent colorfastness, but residual metals may be harmful, especially to silk fabrics. Chrome dyes usually produce duller colors.

Dyes Used Primarily for Manufactured Fibers

Basic Dyes

Basic dyes contain positively charged amino groups that are attracted to negative groups in fibers; for this reason, they are also known as cationic dyes. Wool and silk have negative acid groups and acrylic fibers usually have sulfonic acid groups added to the polymer for dyeing with basic dyes. Modified nylon and polyester fibers can also be dyed with basic dyes.

The colors that these dyes produce are exceptionally bright. Silk is often dyed with basic dyes because of their bright colors, but the fastness to laundering is poor. Recent developments of basic dyes for synthetics produce excellent colorfastness.

Disperse Dyes

Developed for coloring acetates, disperse dyes are now used to color many other manufactured fibers. The dye is sparingly soluble in water. Particles of dye disperse in the water without dissolving but, rather, dissolve in the fibers.

Disperse dyes can be applied to a wide variety of fibers, including acetate, acrylic, aramid, modacrylic, nylon, olefin, polyester, and triacetate, and are really the only practical means of coloring acetate and polyester fibers.

Colors produced with disperse dyes cover a wide range and generally have good fastness. Blues, however, tend to be discolored by nitrous oxide gases in the atmosphere and may gradually fade to a pinkish color. Greens may fade to brown. This fume fading is apparent primarily in disperse-dyed acetate. The main source of fumes in homes is gas-fired stoves and heaters. (See chapter 6).

Fugitive Tints

Colors that are not permanent are sometimes called *fugitive tints*. In most dyeing processes, the manufacturer wishes to produce a color that is permanent and one that will not disappear in use or in processing. Fugitive dyes, on the other hand, are used to identify fibers or yarns during the manufacture of fabrics. By coloring fibers or yarns of a particular generic type to a specific tint, the manufacturer has a readily identifiable color code. When the processing of the materials is complete, the manufacturer can remove the color by a simple wash, often in cold water.

Heat-Sensitive Dyes

Fabrics have been dyed and printed with *heat-sensitive inks* that contain thermotropic liquid crystals, like the displays on watches and clocks. Thermotropic liquid crystals are formed or changed by changes in temperature. Heat-sensitive dyes, used in the "mood change" fabrics, reflect different wavelengths of light at different temperatures. The inks are sensitive to either body or atmospheric heat. They can be applied by screen printing or by heat transfer printing. (See chapter 21 for a description of these processes.) Care labels generally recommend that garments colored with these inks should be washed in cold water without bleach, and that the fabrics not be ironed. Some trade terms applied to these products include hypercolor and chameleon colors.

SUMMARY

Dyes and pigments can be used to color textiles. Dyes are absorbed by the fibers in a yarn or fabric, whereas pigments are adhered to the fabric surface with an adhesive substance. The attraction of dyes for fibers depends on the chemical structure of fiber and dye, on the fiber morphology, and the dyeing conditions.

Dyeing may be done at the fiber, yarn, fabric, or garment stage in production of a textile product. A number of dyeing processes and machines have been developed for the different dyeing stages. Dyes are grouped into classes according to their chemical structure and mode of action. Different classes are more effective on some fiber types than on others.

Colorfastness is the retention of dyes as the textiles are exposed to laundering, light, and other conditions. This property is of considerable interest to consumers, but may not be specifically labeled or readily apparent. The care labels on products can provide information on proper laundering or dry cleaning conditions to guard again fading and running of dyes. Textiles that would normally be used out of doors are usually colored with dyes that are fast to light.

References

AATCC. 1997. *Technical Manual,* Research Triangle Park, NC: AATCC.
Etters, J. N. 1999. Chemical conservation in denim manufacturing. *Textile Chemist and Colorist* 31 (2): 32.
Gerhard, P. 1964. Emperor's dyes of the Mixtecs. *Natural History* 73 (January): 26.

Review Questions

1. What is the difference between dyes and pigments?
2. Before the discovery of synthetic dyes, what kinds of substances were used to dye fabrics? When were the first synthetic dyes made, and what were they made of?
3. Define the term *colorfastness.* What are some of the conditions that may affect the colorfastness of dyed textiles?

4. What are some of the factors that make for good dye retention in a textile fabric?
5. Identify the stages of fiber and fabric manufacture at which color can be added to a textile.
6. Compare batch and continuous dyeing processes.
7. What is the basis of the names given to the various dye classes? Explain why all dye classes are not equally useful for fabrics made from all textile fibers.
8. What are the advantages and disadvantages of garment dyeing?

Recommended Readings

Aspland, J. R. 1991–1993. Series of articles on dyeing. *Textile Chemist and Colorist*. Appearing monthly from October 1991 (vol. 23) to November 1993 (vol. 25). See individual issues for a wide range of specific topics.

Bide, M. 1992. Wool dyeing: What's new? *Textile Chemist and Colorist* 24 (April): 17–22.

Fox, M., and J. Pierce. 1990. Indigo: Past and present. *Textile Chemist and Colorist* 22 (April): 13.

Fulmer, T. D. 1993. Dyeing textiles for automotive interiors. *America's Textiles International* 22 (December): 88.

Hunt, P. K., and J. N. Etters. 1994. The dyeing process in wearable art. *American Dyestuff Reporter* 83 (September): 112.

Lopez, J., and J. Farrell-Beck. 1992. What colored the transition from madder to alizarine? *Clothing and Textiles Research Journal* 10 (Spring): 36–43.

100 years of synthetic indigo. 1997. *Textiles Magazine* (2): 7.

Perkins, W. S. 1991. A review of textile dyeing processes. *Textile Chemist and Colorist* 23 (August): 23.

Rivlin, J. 1992. *The dyeing of textile fibers: Theory and practice.* Philadelphia: Philadelphia College of Textiles and Science.

Water-soluble dyes. 1992. *Clothes Care Gazette,* 65 (December).

CHAPTER 21

TEXTILE PRINTING AND DESIGN

Important decisions in the creation of a textile product must be made when its design and/or its color are chosen. Although many thousands of yards of fabric are processed in solid colors, thousands more yards have designs applied through printing.

The application of a pattern to fabric by the use of dyes, pigments, or other colored substances may be effected by a variety of hand or machine processes. Freehand painting of designs on fabrics is probably the oldest technique for applying ornament, but hand painting is a time-consuming procedure. Furthermore, it does not always result in a uniform repeat of a motif that is to be used more than once. If a design is transferred to a flat surface that can be coated with a dye and then stamped onto the fabric, the same design can be repeated many times over simply by pressing the decorated surface against the fabric. This process is known as *printing*. Over many centuries a variety of techniques for printing designs have evolved. Printing can be applied to warp yarns, to fabrics, or to apparel pieces—for example, slogans or pictures on T-shirts.

In general, printing is a cheaper way of creating designs on fabric than weaving or knitting with different colored yarns. Printing can be done with dyes or pigments. For pigments it is necessary to use an adhesive to bind the colored substance to the fabric.

Different methods for applying designs can be combined with a number of printing tools or machines to provide the printer with a variety of processes. The methods and machinery are discussed separately below.

429

DIRECT PRINTING

The principle of direct printing is creation of a colored design by applying a dye or pigment directly onto a textile substrate (yarn or fabric).

Block Printing

Block printing appears to be the oldest direct printing technique. Printed fabrics from the Caucasus in Russia appear to date from 1000 B.C. Blocks that were used in printing textiles have been recovered from Egyptian graves of the fourth century A.D. (Haller 1939). This is the simplest of the printing techniques and requires only a limited technology. A block of material (usually wood) has a design drawn on one flat side. The design is carved by cutting away the spaces between the areas that form the pattern, thus placing the design in a raised position. Color is applied to the surface of the block, and the block is pressed onto the cloth. Anyone who has ever made a potato or linoleum print should recognize the technique. Sometimes during printing, the block was tapped with a mallet to ensure complete contact of the block with the fabric.

To make the best possible print, the dye had to be in a viscous or pastelike form; otherwise, the incised areas would have been filled in by the dye mixture, and the block would not have carried sufficient dye to make a clear image.

Mordant Printing

Inventive printers found another means of combining printing and dyeing to add color patterns directly to fabrics. Since colorfastness without mordanting was very poor, the mordant rather than the dye could be printed onto the surface of the fabric and then the entire cloth passed into the dyebath. The mordanted areas absorbed the dye permanently; the rest of the cloth picked up dye only on the surface. When the fabric was rinsed after the dyebath, the dye washed out of the unprinted areas and left a colorful design on the section that had been impregnated with the mordant.

By using different mordant materials, different colors could be produced from the same dyestuff. When the dyer printed the surface with several different mordants, immersed the fabric in the dyebath, and rinsed away the excess dye, a fabric printed with two or three different colors resulted.

Blotch Printing

In blotch prints, both a colored background and design motifs are printed onto the fabric. Background colors of blotch-printed fabrics usually have a lighter color on the wrong side than on the right side of the fabric. Sometimes, too, minute, uncolored areas appear between the sections of background color and the design. Blotch prints can be made on either a rotary screen printing machine or on a roller printing machine. Blotch-printed fabrics made by screen printing may have better color penetration in background color areas than those made by roller printing. (See Figure 21.1.)

Overprinting

Overprinting is application of a design on a fabric that has already been piece dyed. An overprinted fabric can be distinguished from a blotch print because the overprint will have the same depth of shade on both the face and back. To be successful the color of the printed design should be darker than the background. A lighter–colored dye will not show up with a darker background. Use of pigments, however, in this method al-

FIGURE 21.1

Blotch print. In blotch prints background color is lighter on the underside of the fabric, whereas in an over-printed fabric the background has the same depth of color on both face and back sides. (a) Back; (b) face.

lows more flexibility in color selection. The pigments are not absorbed by the fibers but remain on the surface, and their color is not affected by the background.

Warp Printing

Warp yarns can be printed before they are woven into the fabric. The resulting fabrics have a delicate, shimmery quality that is achieved by the indistinct patterns created in warp printing. (See Figure 21.2a.) The indistinct edge of the design is due to the slight variations in the position of the warp yarns as the filling yarns are inserted and beaten into the fabric structure.

a

FIGURE 21.2

(a) Warp-printed silk fabric; (b) roller-printed cotton fabric made to simulate indistinct pattern of a warp-printed fabric.

b

Warp printing is applied to higher-priced fabrics. This blurred effect can be simulated in a cheaper process by directly printing a design with indistinct edges. (See Figure 21.2b.)

RESIST PRINTING

In *resist printing* a substance coats the fabric in preselected areas, thus preventing the fabric from absorbing dye in those areas. Resist materials have included starch, clay, and wax. The technique has been used to produce designs in textiles in many different cultures, including those of Persia, India, South America, Egypt, and the Far East. Although the pattern of the resist material can be said to be "printed" onto the fabric, the application of color takes place by dyeing, just as in mordant printing.

Batik

Batik cloth is made by a wax-resist process. The name *batik* originates in the Indonesian Archipelago, where resist printing has become an important art form. Wax is applied to the areas that the printer does not want to dye. In Indonesia a small, spouted cup with a handle called a *tjanting* is used to apply the wax. (See Figure 21.3.) Melted wax is poured from the tjanting onto the cloth. When it hardens, the wax coats the fabric so that the dye cannot reach the fibers.

If several colors are to be used, the process becomes somewhat more complex. For example, if a fabric is to be colored white, red, and blue, the artisan begins with a creamy-

FIGURE 21.3

Indonesian woman uses *tjanting* for applying wax to a batik fabric. Photograph courtesy of Exxon Corporation.

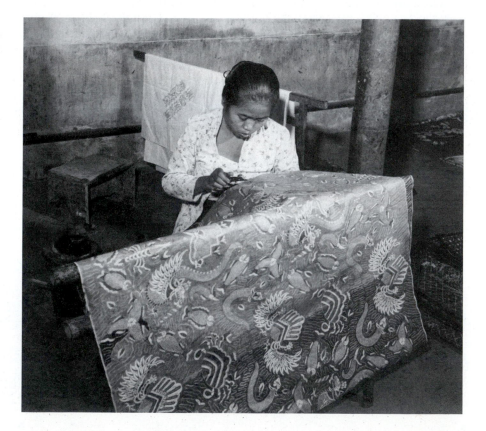

white cotton cloth. Those areas that are to remain white and those that are to be red are coated with wax. The fabric is now subjected to a blue dyebath, and the exposed areas take on the blue tint. The wax is boiled off and reapplied to cover the blue and white areas. When the fabric is placed in the red dyebath, the color penetrates only the uncovered areas of the design. After dyeing is complete, the fabric is treated with a fixative (a mordant) to make the colors fast, and a final rinse in hot water removes all traces of wax.

For faster production a technique was devised whereby the wax could be printed onto the surface of the fabric with a device called a *tjap*. The design is carved on a tjap block, the block is dipped in wax, and pressed onto the fabric to imprint the molten wax. Although to the untrained eye tjap-printed fabrics look much the same as those made with the tjanting, connoisseurs consider them inferior in quality.

Tie Dyeing

Resist designs can be produced by the tie dyeing, or tie-and-dye, method in which parts of the fabric are tightly wound with yarns, or the fabric may be tied into knots in selected areas. When the fabric is placed in a dyebath, the covered or knotted areas are protected from the dye. Careful attention to the shape of the wrapping and the placement of the tied areas can produce intricate and attractive patterns. (See Figure 21.4.) In Indian textiles the tie dyeing method is known as *bandanna*. Often used for T-shirts, dresses, skirts, and other garments, tie-dyeing has become a popular craft technique today.

FIGURE 21.4

A tie-dyed fabric. Photograph reprinted by permission from the Metropolitan Museum of Art. Gift of Fay Halpern.

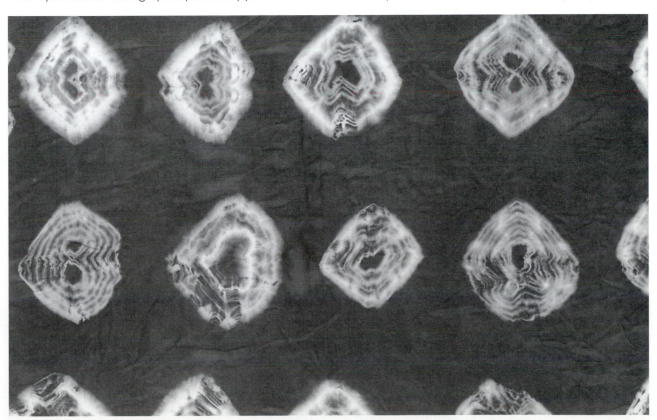

FIGURE 21.5

(a) Ikat fabric; (b) printed fabric made to imitate a woven ikat fabric.

a   b

Ikat

A complex and unusual variation of resist printing has been practiced in many places. The process, called *ikat*, from the Malaysian word menigikat meaning tie or knot, required the weaver to prepare the warp yarns on the loom. Selected sections of the yarns were then covered with a resist material—wax, clay, or other yarns as in tie dyeing. The warps were dyed, and the covered area did not absorb the dye. If a more complicated pattern were required, the warp yarns might be treated several times, as in the batik procedure. When dyeing was completed, the resist material was removed, and the filling was woven into place. This produced a fabric design of blurred, indistinct patterns. Ikat fabrics often have a beautiful shimmering, soft quality. (See Figure 21.5a.) Warp printing grew out of the ancient ikat process, and like warp printing ikat can be imitated by printing a design with indistinct edges. (See Figure 21.5b.)

Block printed, batik, and tie-dyed fabrics are often created by persons using these techniques as hobbies or art forms. Such fabrics are sometimes produced commercially in small quantities, usually at extremely high prices.

DISCHARGE PRINTING

Piece-dyed fabrics may be printed with a substance known as a *discharge paste* that removes color from specific areas of the fabric. Discharge printing is used only for small, light-colored or white designs on dark background. If fabrics are not processed carefully to remove all the discharge paste, these chemicals may eventually weaken the fabric in the areas from which color has been discharged. Discharge prints are recognizable because the color of the background design of the fabric is the same on both the front and back sides. (See Figure 21.6.)

FIGURE 21.6

Discharge print. This fabric has been dyed, then the light area has had the color removed to create the design. (a) Face; (b) back.

HEAT TRANSFER PRINTING

Heat transfer printing, or sublimation printing,[1] is a system in which dyes are printed onto a paper base and then transferred from the paper to a fabric. The transfer of colors takes place as the color vaporizes or "sublimes." Transfer printing is achieved by

---

1. Sublistatic printing, a term often used in conjunction with heat transfer printing, is the trademark of the Sublistatic Corporation, a major producer of heat transfer printing paper.

FIGURE 21.7

Transfer-printed designs on T-shirts.

rolling or pressing the paper and the fabric together under pressure and at high temperatures (424°F or 200°C). Sublimation printing achieves a sharpness and clarity that other types of printing cannot match. One disadvantage of heat transfer printing, however, is off-grain printing. Some dyes used on nylons and acrylics have displayed variations in shade depth and, in some cases, problems with fastness to laundering. Heat transfer printing also consumes a large quantity or print paper that cannot be reused and may present a disposal problem.

Transfer printing can also be used to apply designs to garments such as T-shirts and jackets. Often the design is comprised of pigment colors on a paper sheet. When this is placed on the textile item and a hot press is applied the pigments adhere to the fabric in the design pattern. The design area is usually somewhat stiffer than the rest of the fabric. (See Figure 21.7.)

Initially, heat transfer dyes were disperse dyes mostly effective on nylons and polyesters. Disperse dyes can also be used on acrylics, triacetates, and polyester and cotton blends where the proportion of polyester is relatively high. In the early 1990s development of several alternative processes have extended heat transfer printing to silk, cotton and other cellulosic fabrics, and wool.

OTHER PRINTING TECHNIQUES

Photographic Printing

Photographic printing is done in a manner similar to the photochemical preparation of screens for screen printing. A photosensitive dye is coated on the fabric, a negative is placed over the fabric, light is applied, and a photographic type of printing takes place. (See Figure 21.8.)

FIGURE 21.8

Cotton fabric with a photographic print of citrus fruits.

FIGURE 21.9

Flocked design printed on a sheer nylon fabric.

Electrostatic Printing

Electrostatic printing is an experimental process in which a plate with an electrostatic charge is placed behind the fabric. A stencil in the form of the pattern is placed over the fabric. Special powdered inks that can be attracted by the electrostatic charge are passed over the surface fabric, and the inks are attracted into and color the fabric in the open areas of the stencil.

Flock Printing

By imprinting an adhesive material on the surface of a fabric in the desired pattern, and then sprinkling short fibers over the adhesive, a *flocked print* may be created. Flocking as a type of finish is discussed at length in chapter 22. (See Figure 21.9.)

PRINTING MACHINERY

Some of the hand printing techniques have evolved into, or been modified for, mechanized printing of large yardages of fabric. Other processes have been developed specifically for high demand and specialty markets. Following is an overview of common production equipment and new technologies in textile printing.

Screen Printing

Silkscreen, or screen, printing is a method of applying a colored design created either by hand or by an automated process. In hand screen printing, the fabric to be printed is spread out on a long table. A screen is prepared for each color of the design. At the time this procedure was developed, fine screens of silk were used—hence the name silkscreen printing. Today, screens of synthetic fibers or metal mesh are used for industrial processes.

To produce printing screens a lacquer coating is applied to close off all areas of the screen except the area through which one of the colors of the design is to be printed. For example, if a red rose with green leaves is to be printed, one screen is made that closes off all but the red rose area, and another is made that closes off all but the green leaves. A screen is prepared for each color of a design by coating it with a photosensitive material, covering it with a negative, and exposing it to light. The light degrades the coating in the exposed area, which can then be washed out.

The printer takes the screen for one color, which is mounted on a frame, and places it in the correct position above and against the fabric. A viscous dye paste, rather than an aqueous dye solution, is used to prevent running of the applied design. The dye paste is coated on the top of the screen; the fabric is underneath. A squeegee is run across the screen and presses the dye through the open area of the screen, onto the fabric. To color the next section of the fabric, the screen is moved farther along the fabric. After one color has been applied, a second color is added as are additional colors if they are required.

Hand screen printing was a slow process. Automation has been achieved in the manufacture of flatbed screen prints by making the frames stationary and moving the fabric along on a belt from screen to screen. The squeegee action, too, is done automatically. (See Figure 21.10.) Flatbed screen printing machines have limited production speeds when compared with rotary screen printing and roller printing, but they do allow very large design repeats.

FIGURE 21.10

Silk screen printing of carpets. Photograph courtesy of *Modern Textiles* magazine. Reno, J. C. and F. C. Klindt, Continous printing and continuous dyeing, January 1972, p. 3.

Flat-bed Zimmer carpet printing machine lays down each color separately form printing paste applied by means of two magnetic roller squeegees. Pressure is controlled by the selection of heavy or light squeegees and by varying the current going to the electromagnet. Endless belts fitted with needles assure a positive drive for good register.

The BDA Screen printer uses a series of screens, one for each color; the basic unit is sketched above.

Rotary Screen Printing

In addition to flatbed screen printing, a rotary screen printing technique has been developed that makes possible an output of quantities of 25 to 100 meters per minute. Instead of using a flat screen, screens are shaped into cylinders or rollers. As in the hand process, a screen is prepared for each color. The dye feeds through the unscreened area, pushed out from inside the roller by a squeegee. Fabrics move continuously under the rollers, and up to twelve colors may be printed on one fabric. (See Figure 21.11.) The maximum length of the design repeat is limited to the circumference of the roller. The production of screens for rotary screen printing is less costly than the engraving of the heavy copper rollers used for roller printing, and rotary screen printing techniques have become standard in the industry.

FIGURE 21.11

Rotary screen printing machine. Each cylinder on the machine adds a different color and a different part of the total pattern. Photograph courtesy of the American Textile Manufacturers Institute.

Roller Printing

Like rotary screen printing, roller printing uses a series of rollers, each imprinting a different color on the fabric. Up to sixteen different colors can be used on one fabric. As with rotary screens, the length of the repeat is determined by the circumference of the roller.

The rollers are made of copper, plated with chromium for durability. The design of each color is transferred accurately to the roller by one of several processes. In photoengraving, a photographic image of the design is etched onto the roller, or a pantograph may be used to transfer the design from a flat surface to the roller. This device allows markings to be made on the roller simultaneously with the tracing of the design from a master design.

Once the rollers have been prepared, they are installed in exact position on the printing machine. The fabric to be printed moves over a rotating drum. Behind it is placed a layer of fabric that absorbs excess dye and keeps it from being deposited on the drum. The design roller also rotates, moving against a rotary brush that rotates in a tray of print paste. This brush furnishes color to the roller. A *doctor blade* scrapes off excess dye from the roller, and the roller then rotates against the cloth and the design is imprinted. The fabric moves on to the second roller where a second color is imprinted, and so on, in a continuous printing operation. (See Figure 21.12.)

Rollers must be aligned perfectly to keep the print in registration. If rollers are not positioned correctly, the resulting print will have one or more colors that do not fall in quite the correct position, causing the print to be distorted. The printed cloth is dried immediately and then passes to a chamber in which steam or heat sets the dye.

FIGURE 21.12

Diagrammatic view of a roller printing system. Courtesy of Allied Chemical Corporation, Fibers Division.

Roller printing is superior to other types of printing for fine or precise designs. However, roller printing requires skilled labor and much heavy manual work in the changing of the color troughs and rollers. The initial investment of time and money in the preparation of rollers for roller printing and in setting up the machine is such that production of small quantities of printed cloth is not economical. Roller printing is used more advantageously for lengthy runs of the same pattern.

Use of roller printing is declining in the United States as rotary screen printing increases. Roller printing can be used for carpets by mounting hard and soft rubber materials on a wood roller. These materials take up the dye from a dye trough and apply them to the carpet without flattening the pile.

Duplex Roller Printing

Duplex printing is done with rollers on a special machine that imprints designs on both sides of the fabric at the same time. Most often, the same design is printed on opposite sides, although different designs can be printed on each side. The resulting fabric looks like fabric with a woven design. (See Figure 21.13.) This process is seldom used now, as it is almost as expensive to create duplex prints as it is to weave designs.

Heat Transfer Roller Printing

Like traditional roller printing, heat transfer printing is done by passing the fabric around a central drum or cylinder where it contacts a roller for transferring the design. The roller is followed by a heating zone to effect the sublimation of the dye. (See Figure 21.14.) Since all colors are applied to the fabric at the same time, however, the operation is simpler with lower processing costs and fewer personnel required.

Production can change rapidly from one design to another simply by changing the design paper, whereas in roller or screen printing, each separate roller or screen

FIGURE 21.13

Duplex print. Note that the same design has been printed on both sides of the fabric, thereby giving the appearance of a woven design. (a) face (b) back.

a   b

FIGURE 21.14

Heat transfer printing. This schematic diagram shows transfer-printing process. Unprinted fabric roll is at top to the right of the heat outlet. Greige fabric moves down to the drum where it is almost immediately joined by transfer paper from the right. The two pass through a bank of infrared heaters. Used transfer paper exits left and to the bottom, while printed fabric goes to the roll at top left of the heat outlet. Schematic coutresy of *Textile World* magazine. Copyright © 1972 by McGraw-Hill, Inc.

must be removed from the machine and the machine set up for a new design with different rollers or screens. Short runs are feasible, fast deliveries are possible, given shorter time for processing, and companies need not keep costly inventories of fabric in stock. On the other hand, heat transfer printing is slower than is either roller or screen printing. Ten to 15 meters of printed fabric are produced per minute in transfer printing operations.

Heat transfer printing has proved especially successful in printing knitted fabrics. Knitted goods are less dimensionally stable than are woven fabrics. Manufacturers using conventional screen and roller printing techniques on knit fabrics experienced difficulties in making multicolor prints in which the segments of the print must fit together accurately. In transfer printing, all parts of the design are applied at once, eliminating the problem of fabrics stretching as they move from one roller to another.

Losses of fabric through faulty printing are substantially lower during heat transfer printing than are losses in conventional roller printing. Energy requirements are also lower. Garments and garment pieces can be printed, and precise placement of decorative motifs on a completed garment is possible.

Jet Printing

Some of the latest technological advances have been in the area of *ink jet printing*. Ink jets are similar to the computer-controlled paper printers used for office applications. They eject small droplets of dye liquid onto a textile fabric in a predetermined pattern. The Milliken Company's Millitron® system for printing carpets was one of the prototypes of these machines. (See Figure 21.15.) Consumer Brief 21.1 provides some detail on the technology and current use of ink jet printers for textiles.

FIGURE 21.15

Carpet printed by the Millitron®, printing machine is inspected. Photograph courtesy of the Milliken Company.

CONSUMER BRIEF 21.1   Ink Jet Printing

Ink jet printing has been a staple for office printing for a number of years. It has now made its way into the textile world and is generating much interest in our quick response and just-in-time industry. Current ink jet machines are of two types: continuous ink jet (CIJ) and drop-on-demand (DOD).

CIJ machines eject a continuous stream of dye that is broken into drops for placement on the fabric. The first successful application of this technology was the *Millitron®* unit, developed by the Milliken Company for printing carpets. The placement of the drops is controlled by air valves that deflect the drops to specific places on the carpet (Tincher et al. 1998). This was a breakthrough in carpet printing technology because it allowed good pattern clarity on carpets without distorting the pile with rollers or screens. Its other advantage was the production of relatively short runs economically.

Following developments in office printers, machines with more advanced techniques for selecting and placing ink drops are now being used. DOD machines require some kind of stimulus to eject a drop of color. In bubble jets, for example, the stimulus is a thermal impulse that creates a bubble in the ink, which then ejects a drop. The impulse for producing a drop of a specific color or combination of colors is supplied by a computer. The placement of the drops is controlled by an electrostatic plate in the print head that directs the jets of dye. Bubble jet printers produce designs with high clarity, or resolution, and the designs can be easily changed through computer control. As noted in chapter 1, ink jet printing can be used in mass customization of garments. The garment will not only be individually sized, but printed designs can be selected by the customer.

Ink jet printing is used extensively for making fabric "proofs," or sample fabric designs, before investing in engraving screens or rollers for large production runs of fabric (Stefanini 1996). The pattern can be checked or altered and shown to customers quickly and cheaply.

Future developments will likely focus on ink jet printing of wider widths of fabric at higher speeds and modification of dye and pigment formulations. The inks used in this type of printing must be less viscous than ordinary print pastes. High viscosity liquids will not easily form the ink drops necessary for jet printing. The dyes must be of high purity because impurities can clog the jets.

As many of us know from use of ink jet paper printers, the print heads are extremely sensitive, requiring

continued

CONSUMER BRIEF 21.1 *continued*

frequent cleaning and replacement. More rugged print heads are required for printing large runs of fabric. Further, machines with more than the four basic colors of black, cyan, magenta, and yellow will probably be needed to provide designers with the color variations with which they are used to working.

As these challenges are being undertaken by printing machine manufacturers, the advantages of ink jet printing for textile products can be emphasized. The ability to produce customized apparel or furnishings, to print short-run fabric lots, to facilitate merchandising planning through production of samples, and to take advantage of the growing investment in e-commerce all augur for expansion of this technology.

Summary

Printing of textiles with dyes and pigments is an age-old process that continues to develop today. The color for printed designs can be applied by direct, resist, discharge, transfer, or other methods. Yarns can also be printed before fabrics are woven. For most applications, printing substances are in a paste, or viscous, form so that they will not run when they contact the fabric. Some methods, however, are really combinations of printing and dyeing, that involve blocking or bleaching fabric areas before or after piece dyeing.

A number of different machines are available for applying printed designs. Screen printing is done with flat or rotary screens that only allow the dye paste to penetrate in selected areas. Roller printing machines, like ink stamps, have the design etched or carved on the roller surface. Designs can also be transferred from paper prints onto fabric. The new technologies of ink jet printing are borrowed from the computer paper printing arena.

References

Haller, R. 1939. The technique of early cloth printing. *CIBA Review* 26 (October): 933.

Stefanini, J. P. 1996. Jet printing for the textile industry. *Textile Chemist and Colorist* 28 (9): 19.

Tincher, W. C., Q. Hu, and X. Li. 1998. Ink jet systems for printing fabric. *Textile Chemist and Colorist* 30 (5): 24

Review Questions

1. Describe the way that batik, tie dyeing, and ikat printing are done, and explain why these are called "resist" printing techniques.
2. Describe screen printing, rotary screen printing, roller printing, heat transfer printing, and ink jet printing. Listed below are descriptions of several different

types of fabric. Which of these printing processes would be the most logical choice for making each of these fabrics? Explain your choice.

a. A multicolored fabric with fine designs that sells large quantities of fabric year after year

b. A fabric with an exceptionally large repeat that will be used in high-priced fabric for interiors

c. A fabric whose relatively small repeat motif is a fad that will probably not be popular after this year

d. A knitted polyester-cotton blend fabric for a retailer who wants to participate in Quick Response merchandising

3. What are the unique aspects of the following types of printing?

duplex printing   overprinting

blotch printing   warp printing

discharge printing

Recommended Readings

Carr, W. W. 1991. Printing textile fabrics with xerography. *Textile Chemist and Colorist* 23 (May): 33.

Doujak, R. 1994. Automation in the textile printing industry. *American Dyestuff Reporter* 83 (September): 76.

Fabrics that change color with temperature. *Apparel International* 19 (June): 15.

Fulmer, T. 1989. Printing. Where is it now? Where will it go? *America's Textiles International* 18 (December): 64.

Graham, L. 1989. Ink jet systems for dyeing and printing of textiles. *Textile Chemist and Colorist* 21 (June): 27.

Liquid crystals, red, hot, and blue. 1991. *The Economist* 319 (May 18): 92.

Shore, J. 1990. Textile coloration: Part 2: Application by printing. *Textiles* 19 (1): 19.

Zimmer, R. 1994. Automating the textile printing industry. *Canadian Textile Journal* 111 (June): 12.

FINISHES THAT AFFECT APPEARANCE

After fabric preparation and coloring, finishes can be applied to modify the appearance, hand, and/or texture of the textile. These finishes may change the surface appearance or texture, add a design feature, or alter the body and hand of the fabric. They are well described by *A Dictionary of Textile Terms* (1967): "the application of a pleasing or appealing effect to the fabric, comparable with the application of cosmetics to improve the facial effects of those who use them" (p. 41).

These finishes, and the functional finishes described in chapter 23, may be classified as permanent, durable, and temporary. Permanent finishes will last for the lifetime of the product, durable finishes can be expected to function reasonably well for most of the lifetime of the fabric, and temporary finishes are removed after one or more launderings or dry cleanings.

Temporary, but renewable finishes, such as some fabric softeners, can be added to fabrics when the original finish has been diminished or destroyed through use or care. Durable finishes usually involve a *resin* treatment, which involves applying a polymer to modify the fabric or to set another finish. Some finishes are made permanent by utilizing the thermoplastic characteristics of synthetic fabrics. When heat-sensitive fibers are subjected to finishes involving heat treatment, creases or designs may be permanently set in the fabric.

SURFACE FINISHES

Many finishes are used because of the effect they have on the appearance of the fabric. Sometimes these finishes also produce a related change in texture or hand.

Calendering

Calendering is a broad, general term that refers to a mechanically produced finish achieved by passing fabrics between a series of two or more rollers. The object of calendering is to smooth the fabric and/or create interesting surface effects.

Simple Calendering

The simplest form of calendering is comparable to ironing a fabric. The calender rolls are heated, and the dampened cloth is passed between the cylinders to smooth and flatten the fabric, producing a wrinkle-free, slightly glossy surface.

Glazing

A special calender called a *friction calender* produces fabrics that have a highly glazed or polished surface, such as chintz or polished cotton. Before the fabric is passed through the calender, the cloth is saturated with either starch or resin. The fabric is dried slightly and then fed into the machine in which a rapidly moving, heated roller polishes the surface of the more slowly moving fabric. If starch is used to produce the glaze, the finish is temporary. If resins are used, the glaze is durable.

Ciréing

Ciré fabrics are characterized by a high surface polish. A fashion term, "the wet look," has sometimes been used to describe ciré fabrics. Made by much the same process as friction calendering, ciré effects on natural fibers or rayon are produced with waxes and thermoplastic resins. Heat-sensitive synthetics are given a permanent wet look when the thermoplastic fibers fuse slightly under the heat of the rollers.

When hydrophobic fibers are given a ciré finish, some degree of water repellency results. This occurs as a result of the slight glazing or fusing that the fabrics undergo.

Embossing

Embossed effects are produced by pressing a pattern onto fabrics. Like other calendered finishes, the designs may be permanent when applied to thermoplastic fibers, durable when applied to fabrics that have been resin treated, and temporary on other fabrics.

Some embossed designs are relatively flat, as in a velvet with flattened embossed areas. The pattern is created by running an embossed roller with a raised pattern across the fabric. The opposite roller is made of paper and has a smooth surface. Because the paper roll can "give" with the pressure, the embossed roller "prints" the colorless design by flattening some sections of the cloth.

Three-dimensional embossed designs are also made with embossed rollers. In this method the embossed roller first presses the design onto the surface of the paper roller; then, when the fabric is passed between the rollers, both the engraved roller and the shaped paper roll work together to mold the shape of the pattern into the cloth. (See Figure 22.1.)

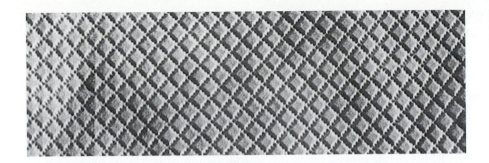

FIGURE 22.1

Embossed cotton fabric.

Embossed designs provide surface texture at a lower cost than do woven designs. If embossing is applied to nonthermoplastic fibers without special resin finishes, it will be lost sooner or later. Embossed fabrics should not be ironed or pressed, as the design may be diminished by the pressure.

Schreinering

The Schreiner calender produces fabrics with a soft luster and a soft hand. One of the calender rolls is embossed with about 250 fine diagonal lines per inch. This roller passes over the fabric, flattening the yarns and producing a more opaque fabric with soft luster and hand. Unless the fabric is thermoplastic, the finish is temporary. Thermoplastic fibers are set permanently into position by the Schreiner calender's heat. If fabrics are given a resin treatment before Schreinering, the finish will be fairly durable.

The Schreiner finish is designed to give fabrics a soft luster. Damask table linens and cotton sateens are among the fabrics given this finish routinely. Thermoplastic tricots are treated with the finish to enhance surface luster.

Moiré

The fashion side of *moiré* fabrics has a watered or clouded surface appearance that is sometimes called a "wood grain" pattern. (See Figure 22.2.) The original technique for producing moiré fabrics is an old one and was used to produce many luxurious silks of the eighteenth and nineteenth centuries.

FIGURE 22.2

Faille fabric with a moiré finish.

The moiré pattern is temporary, durable, or permanent depending on the fiber and/or chemicals used. In watermarked moiré fabrics, such as those produced a hundred years ago, the pattern would be destroyed by laundering. Resin treatment makes the pattern reasonably durable to cleaning and laundering, and the use of heat setting of thermoplastic fibers creates a permanent finish.

To achieve an effective moiré pattern, ribbed fabrics such as taffeta, faille, or bengaline are usually selected. One of two methods is employed. In the first and more traditional method, two lengths of a fabric from the same bolt are placed face to face, with one layer slightly off-grain in relation to the other. Enormous pressure is put on the fabrics by the smooth moiré rollers, and the ribs of one fabric press down on those of the other, so that the ribs of each fabric flatten those of the other fabric, causing light to be reflected differently across the surface of the fabric. The moiré produced in this manner has a random pattern with no discernible repeats.

The second method uses a roller with a moiré pattern etched into its surface. In this procedure the roller flattens or distorts one area more than another, creating the same effect as in the first method. Here, however, the patterns are repeated at regular intervals.

Beetling

Linens and cottons that are intended to look like linens are beetled, a process in which the fabric is pounded (in a machine equipped with hammers that strike over the surface of the fabric), flattening the yarns and making them smoother and more lustrous. (See Figure 22.3.) Unless a resin treatment has been given to the fabric before beetling, the finish is temporary.

Napping and Sueding

Napped and *sueded* fabrics are fabrics in which fiber ends are brushed up onto the surface of the fabric. Napping and sueding are applied to woven or knitted goods, and although the term *pile* is often used to refer to the fiber ends that appear on the surface of the cloth, these fabrics should not be confused with pile fabrics in which a separate set of yarns is used to create the pile through weaving.

Sueding develops a low pile on the surface of the fabric, and the surface of the fabric can be finished to look and feel like suede leather. An abrasive material, a type of sandpaper, is used to achieve the finish. The fabric is rotated against the abrasive material, and the hand and appearance of the fabric are determined by the type of fiber used, the size of the yarn, and the intensity of the contact between the fabric and the abrasive material. This process is sometimes referred to as *sanding*, and is one of the ways that so-called sandwashed silk is produced.

In periods when suedelike fabrics have been fashionable, woven and knitted fabrics finished on sueders have been widely available. Attempts to simulate suede leather have ranged from the development of nonwoven fabrics such as Ultrasuede®, which approximates the hand and appearance of suede leather closely, to those in which finishing with a sueder provides the appearance of suede surface while maintaining the hand and drapability of woven or knitted cloth.

Napped fabrics, like suede fabrics, have a pile or nap on the surface of the fabric. Napping generally develops a deeper nap and is produced by machinery different from sueding. The nap is created by rubbing the surface of the fabric with a rough device. Napped fabrics are generally made from yarns with a fairly loose twist, so that the surface fibers will brush up easily. Long ago this was done with teasels (plant heads with many fine, hooklike, sharp projections). Today, napping is more likely to

FIGURE 22.3

Lustrous linen damask fabric reflects light as a result of beetling.

be done with machines equipped with small, fine wires that approximate the teasel spine. These small, hooklike projections catch fibers and pull them up to the surface of the fabric, creating a fuzzy, soft layer of fibers on the surface that are also caught into the yarn. Some fine napped wools are still made by using natural teasels. The terms *gigging* and *raising* may also be used to describe the napping process.

Excessive napping may tend to weaken fabrics by pulling up too many fibers, thereby weakening the basic structure of the fabric. The special knit fabric Polartec®, that is made from recycled polyester is highly napped, but the strong polyester fibers are able to withstand the treatment.

Napped fabrics are used for clothing and household textiles in which warmth is desired. The loose fiber ends trap air that serves as insulation. Blankets, sleepwear, coating fabrics, sweaters, warm activewear, and the like are often made from napped fabrics. Fabrics intended for apparel are generally napped on one side, whereas those for blankets are napped on both sides. (See Figure 22.4.)

Brushing

Fabrics made from staple fibers may be brushed to remove loose fiber from the surface of the fabric. This is done to improve the appearance of the fabric.

Some fabrics with names such as *brushed denim* or *brushed tricot* are created by napping or sueding or brushing fibers up onto the surface of the fabric to create a soft

Figure 22.4

(a) Cotton fabric before napping; (b) cotton fabric after it has been napped on one side.

a   b

surface texture. The surface fibers are less dense than in napped or sueded fabrics. Microfiber fabrics can be brushed to create a "peach skin" effect.

Many napped and pile fabrics are brushed in such a way that the nap or pile runs in one direction. When this has been done, one's fingers can be run across the surface of the fabric to feel that the fabric is smooth in one direction and rougher in the other. Items cut from such fabrics must be handled so that the direction of all pieces is the same. If this is not done, a fabric in which the grain runs down may reflect light differently from one in which the grain runs up. This difference in light reflection may cause pieces placed side by side to appear to be different in color.

Shearing

Shearing removes unwanted fibers projecting onto the surface of fabrics. Worsted wool fabrics are often sheared to give a clean, clear surface. Napped or pile fabrics may be sheared to make the nap or the pile the same thickness in all parts of the fabric.

The shearing is done in a machine in which sharp, rotating blades cut off fibers or cut the pile or nap to the desired length. The machine has been compared by Potter and Corbman (1967) to a lawn mower. If some sections of the pile or nap are flattened, and other areas sheared, the uncut sections can be brushed up to achieve a sculpted effect.

Enzyme Treatment

Cellulase enzymes are used in finishing cotton, rayon, and lyocell to produce smoother surfaces, softer hand, and a decrease in pilling. The enzymes degrade cellulosic fibers on the surface of the fabric, and mechanical action removes the weakened fibers from the surface. As a result, the fabric becomes softer and smoother. The Danish firm Novo Nordisk calls its enzyme finishing process *BioPolishing*.

If enzyme finishing is applied after fabrics or garments have been dyed with vat, sulfur, or pigment dyes, the effect is similar to that of stone washing (see page 423). The treatment does result in some loss of strength and reduction in weight, so it must be carefully controlled. It is most frequently applied to denim, but can be used on any number of cellulosic fabrics.

DESIGN FINISHES

A number of primarily chemical finishing processes have been developed to create designs on fabrics. Applying these finishes is similar to printing. (See chapter 21.)

Burn-out Designs

Chemicals that dissolve some fibers can produce alterations in fabric appearance. One can create open areas in fabrics by imprinting a cellulosic fabric with a sulfuric acid paste that dissolves the printed area. Such fabrics are likely to fray around the edges of the dissolved area and are not especially durable.

In blended fabrics, this technique can be used to create interesting effects. Two different fibers are used. When the dissolving material is imprinted on the fabric, one of the fibers is dissolved, leaving the other unharmed. Areas with no chemical imprinted on them remain intact and create the design. By contrasting the texture, luster, or color of the "burned out" fiber with that of the second fiber, attractive decorative effects can be achieved. (See Figure 22.5.)

Acid Designs

Treating cotton fabric with acid causes it to become more transparent as some of the surface fibers are dissolved away, creating fabrics with a "frosted" design. Fabric areas are coated with acid-resistant materials. When the finish is applied, these areas remain opaque, while the acid-treated areas become transparent.

FIGURE 22.5

Burn-out design. Chemicals printed onto this fabric have dissolved away the dark-appearing sections. For photographic purposes the fabric has been placed against a dark background; when the fabric is in use those areas would be more sheer and translucent than the leaf-shaped design.

FIGURE 22.6

Cotton plissé puckered design created by printing the fabric with sodium hydroxide on the background to shrink the fabric, leaving puffed, untreated areas between.

Plissé Designs

A puckered effect called *plissé* is achieved in fabrics by imprinting them with chemicals that cause the fabric to shrink. When these chemicals are printed in a design, some areas of the fabric shrink while others do not. This causes untreated areas to pucker or puff up between the treated areas. (See Figure 22.6.) Cottons and rayons react in this way when treated with sodium hydroxide, an alkali, as do nylons printed with phenol, an acid. Although plissé is a fairly durable finish, such fabrics should not be ironed because the pressing of the plissé flattens the surface. Thermoplastic fibers can also be embossed to simulate plissé.

FINISHES THAT AFFECT HAND OR TEXTURE

Since fabric hand is an important consideration in consumer selection of textile products, the effect of softeners and other aesthetic finishes on hand has been the subject of much study. The American Association of Textile Chemists and Colorists (AATCC) defines fabric hand as "the tactile sensations or impressions that arise when fabrics are touched, squeezed, rubbed, or otherwise handled" (AATCC 1997, 376). Fabric hand is a complex phenomenon involving a number of different fabric characteristics.

One factor in hand is the smoothness of the material. Filament yarns and fine combed spun yarns feel smoother than textured or crepe yarns. In addition, a fabric that compresses easily and recovers from compression or squeezing feels soft. This feeling is enhanced by resilient fibers and yarns with high loft that are not compact. Consider the difference in feel between a bulky wool sweater knit and a wool gabardine. Finishes that add body or bulk can provide a more pleasing hand to fabrics.

The shearing and bending behavior of fabrics affects hand as well as drape. Fabrics with low resistance to shearing and bending will feel soft. Fabric softeners decrease the friction between fibers and yarns so the fabric shears and bends more easily.

Adding Body

To add body to fabrics, some type of sizing is often applied. This may be in the form of starch, gelatin, or resin or a combination of these with softening substances such as oils or waxes.

Starches and gelatins are temporary sizings and are removed during laundering or dry cleaning. Inexpensive cotton or rayon fabrics are often heavily starched and after laundering may become limp. It is possible to determine how heavily sized a fabric sized with starch or gelatin is by rubbing a section of the fabric hard. If you remove small flakes of starch, the fabric has obviously been sized. By holding the same fabric up to the light, one can often see more light through the area in the section from which the sizing has been removed than in other areas.

Gelatins are used as sizing on rayons because they are clear in color and do not dim the luster of the fabric. The application of the sizing, plus a hard press, may create a deceptively full hand and surface luster that is later lost after laundering.

Various resins can also be used to add body to fabrics. Acrylic emulsion finishes known as *hand builders* can give fabrics a more substantial hand. These compounds are similar, not to acrylic fibers, but to the binders used for pigment printing.

Permanent Stiffening of Cottons

A special acid treatment known as *parchmentizing* is used to give some cottons a permanently stiff character. The application of a carefully controlled acid solution causes the surface of the yarn to become softened and gelatinlike. An afterwash in cold water causes the gelatinous outer surface to harden, forming a permanently stiffened exterior. Permanently finished organdy, for example, is made by this process.

Softening

Some fabrics may feel harsh after production or heat setting of manufactured fabrics, durable press finishes, and some treatments given to acrylic fabrics may produce an unpleasant hand. Applying fabric softeners during finishing can overcome these negative qualities. The chemical compounds used penetrate intersections between yarns and fibers to allow a certain amount of slippage, thereby creating a more supple, smoother, and more pleasant-feeling fabric.

Silicone polymers and ionic ammonium compounds have been used for many years to soften fabrics. They can be applied in a pad bath at the same time as durable press, flame retardant, or other functional finishes. Some of these products are available for use in home laundering, and are discussed in chapter 24.

SUMMARY

Fabrics, of whatever construction, can be made more appealing by the application of finishes that modify their appearance, texture, and hand. Finishes that change the surface design or texture of fabrics are visually apparent, but may also affect other properties such as durability. The hand or feel of fabrics may be changed by applying a finish to add bulk or increase softness. These qualities can be subjectively evaluated by designers, buyers, and consumers but are usually not included in product labels.

References

AATCC, 1997. *Technical Manual,* Research Triangle Park, NC: AATCC.

A dictionary of textile terms. 1967. Danville, Va.: Dan River Mills.

Potter, M. D., and B. P. Corbman. 1967. *Textiles, fiber to fabric.* New York: McGraw-Hill.

Review Questions

1. What properties must a fabric have to make it appropriate for each of the following finishes:

embossing	enzyme treatment
moiré	plissé
napping	parchmentizing
sueding	

2. How can body be added to fabrics?
3. Why are softeners applied to fabrics?

Recommended Readings

Cowhig, W. T. 1974. What is moiré? *Textiles* 4 (June): 46

Finishing fabrics in the nineties. 1994. *Canadian Textile Journal* 111 (November): 28.

Goldstein, H. E. 1993. Mechanical and chemical finishing of microfabrics. *Textile Chemist and Colorist* 25 (2): 16.

Tyndall, R. M. 1992. Improving the softness and surface appearance of cotton fabrics and garments by treatment with cellulase enzymes. *Textile Chemist and Colorist* 24 (6): 23.

FINISHES THAT AFFECT PERFORMANCE

This chapter concentrates on finishes that are more functional than aesthetic and that are produced chiefly through the use of chemical applications, although some may be achieved by mechanical means as well. Finishes for shrinkage control, for example, include both mechanical techniques or chemical finishes or a combination of both.

SHRINKAGE CONTROL

A reduction in the length or width of a fiber, yarn, or fabric is known as *shrinkage*. If fabrics shrink after they have been made into garments or household items, they may decrease in size to such an extent that the item is no longer serviceable. For example, a garment with a 25-inch waist size will decrease by 1 1\4 inches if it shrinks 5 percent. *Growth* occurs when a fabric increases in dimension.

Some fibers such as wool, cotton, and rayon swell more in water than do others. Fabrics made from these fibers are less dimensionally stable than fabrics made from fibers with lower moisture absorbance.

Wetting a fabric causes the tension that has been applied during its manufacture to be relaxed, so that fabrics generally shrink after the first and subsequent launderings. As discussed in chapter 2, this type of shrinkage is known as relaxation shrinkage. It occurs because the moisture within the fibers allows them to return to the dimensions they occupied before they were stretched during processing. The amount of relaxation shrinkage depends on the amount of stretching the fibers underwent during manufacturing. Wool and rayon, which are more extensible, will stretch more and therefore have greater potential for relaxation. Successive heating and drying cycles may produce progressive shrinkage, where the fabric continues to shrink.

Woven fabrics generally shrink more in the warp than in the filling direction because the warp yarns are under greater tension during weaving. When the fabric is later subjected to moisture, or heat in the case of thermoplastic fibers, the stresses within the fibers are relieved, and the fabric relaxes. Fibers that are moisture-absorbent absorb a significant amount of water and swell. Accordingly, the yarn diameter increases, and the yarns in each direction must move closer together to accommodate the yarns in the opposite direction. This is a less strained position for the yarns and results in a permanent increase in crimp, especially in warp yarns. This relaxation is illustrated in Figure 23.1.

FIGURE 23.1

Effect of yarn swelling on fabric shrinkage. Cloth length represents the space between adjacent filling yarns, that decreases as fabric shrinks in the warp direction. (a) Stretched fabric. (b) Original dry state of fabric. (c) Filling yarn swelling increases amplitude of warp yarn path; hatched area represents strain in warp yarn. (d) Filling yarns move closer together to minimize strain. Diagrams reproduced from H. Mark et al., *Chemical Aftertreatment of textiles*, H. F. Mark, N. S. Wooding, and S. M. Atlas New York: Wiley, 1971, p 163. Reprinted by permission of John Wiley & Sons, Inc.

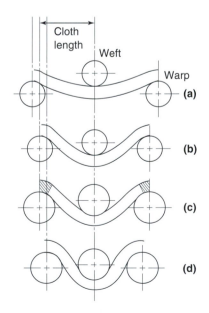

Knit goods tend to stretch more during manufacture than woven goods, and therefore knit goods are likely to shrink and change shape even more than woven goods.

Procedures and solvents used in commercial dry cleaning, as a rule, do not permit fabrics to relax, as washing does, so that items that are dry cleaned may not shrink as readily. Shrinkage in dry cleaning generally results from the high moisture content in the solvent or from steaming the fabric during pressing.

Compressive Shrinkage Control

For fabrics subject to relaxation shrinkage, such as cotton, linen, and rayons, it would seem logical to "wash" or wet the fabrics to allow them to return to their true dimensions. This is not, however, practical for the manufacturer, not only because the process would be time and energy consuming but also because the required equipment would take up a great deal of space. Instead, a method has been devised in which the fabric is mechanically reduced to its correct dimensions.

A sample of fabric is measured, the measurements are recorded, and the fabric is laundered in such a way as to produce maximum shrinkage. The shrunken fabric is measured, and the percentages of warp and filling shrinkage are calculated. This tells the processor how much to compress the fabric.

In compressive shrinkage control processes, the fabric is dampened and is placed on a machine equipped with a continuous thick woolen or felt blanket. The blanket travels around a small roller carrying the fabric with it as it stretches around the curve of the roller. As the carrier moves from the curve to a straight area, it squeezes or compresses into a smaller, flat area. When the carrier compresses, the fabric it carries is also compressed and is then heated to set in this compressed structure. (See Figure 23.2.) The blanket is continuously pulled around two rollers to process the fabric as it is fed in. The various patented processes of the compressive shrinkage type guarantee residual (or remaining) shrinkage of less than 1 percent unless the fabric is tumble dried.

FIGURE 23.2

Schematic of machine for compressive shrinkage.

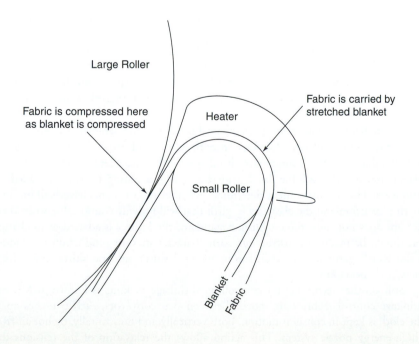

Large Roller

Fabric is compressed here as blanket is compressed

Heater

Fabric is carried by stretched blanket

Small Roller

Blanket

Fabric

The Sanforized Company has developed a number of different compressive shrinkage control processes for different types of fabrics. All provide for shrinkage of less than 1 percent. The trademark Sanforized® is used on woven cotton and cotton blends. Sanfor-set® is used on easy-care 100 percent cotton and cotton blends. In this latter process, cotton fabric is treated with liquid ammonia, which causes the fiber to swell and relax. Then the fabric is subjected to mechanical, compressive shrinkage control treatment. When the treatment is complete, the ammonia is removed from the cotton and recycled. The resulting fabric is both shrinkage and wrinkle resistant. It can be laundered in the same way as any cotton fabric by being washed and tumble dried, although prompt removal from the dryer is recommended.

Shrinkage Control for Knits

During knitting and finishing, knit fabrics are subject to tension and stretching, especially in the lengthwise direction. The construction of most knits allows for greater stretch. They often shrink far more than comparable woven goods. Shrinkage may be particularly pronounced in the lengthwise direction, often accompanied by growth in the crosswise direction.

Techniques used to control shrinkage in knitted fabrics include subjecting fabrics to treatment with resin-containing solutions, wetting then drying fabrics to relax tensions applied during processing, and compressive shrinkage processes similar to those described for woven fabrics.

Excellent results can be obtained by wetting fabrics to at least 40 percent humidity and then drying them in a rotary tumbler, but while dimensional stability of fabrics is excellent, the process is costly because lots must be small and fabrics tend to become knotted or tangled during tumbling. Knots must then be untangled manually. A variation of this process called the VH-Tric-O-Dry system utilizes the same principle. Fabrics are wet to at least 40 percent humidity. They are then passed through a closed-channel system in which fabrics bump against the walls of the channel, rather than tumbling; finally, they are relaxed and dried in a larger chamber so that knots do not form. The manufacturer of the equipment indicates that larger lots can also be processed (Skieller 1989).

Compressive shrinkage processes for knits use different methods to return fabrics to their relaxed position. Among these is a process that feeds fabric through a machine in which a series of rollers operating at different speeds causes the fabric to become compressed. In another process, knitted fabrics are stretched in the crosswise direction.

Sanfor-Knit®, another shrinkage control process of the Sanforized Company, addresses the problem of knit shrinkage in both length and width. In this process, test garments that have had compressive shrinkage control treatment are made up in the desired size, washed, tumble dried, and checked by a testing instrument called the Knitpicker. The test instrument determines whether the garments have held both the length dimension and the elasticity in girth that will provide comfortable wear. If the garment does not meet the established standard, the knitter is advised as to changes that should be made in construction, yarn characteristics, or production techniques. Sanfor-Knit® garments are available in men's T-shirts, athletic shirts, polo shirts, briefs, and sports knits.

Still another technique for controlling shrinkage in knits is known as Micrex® shrinkage control. Fabrics are moved between two conveyors, each 6 inches apart. The cloth is kept in constant motion, both vertically and horizontally, by hot air from a high-energy nozzle system. This action allows the relaxation of the tensions that were imposed in previous operations, thereby allowing the fabric to relax to its original dimensions.

Synthetic knits are stabilized by heat setting. If heat setting has not been done, the fabrics will shrink. Low-priced double knits, for example, may shrink as a result of inadequate heat setting.

Shrinkage Control for Rayon Fabrics

Viscose rayon fabrics may shrink progressively, although high-wet-modulus rayon fabrics exhibit less shrinkage. Shrinkage control for rayons is most effective when compressive shrinkage control treatments are followed by a resin finish to stabilize the fabric.

Careful control is needed when chemical resins are applied, as excessive concentrations can lower the quality and durability of the fabric. However, if applied correctly, chemical resins penetrate the fibers to prevent further shrinkage.

Shrinkage Control for Wool

Wool and animal hair fibers are among those few fibers that show progressive shrinkage. This continuous shrinkage is due to the scale structure of the wool fiber, which also causes felting. (See chapter 4, page 106.)

In addition to felting shrinkage, wool fabrics display the same type of residual shrinkage from relaxation that other fibers show. Unlike cotton fabrics, however, wool may continue to shrink if the relaxation of the fibers is not complete after one or two washings. Shrinkage treatments for wool are of two types: those that alleviate the problems of relaxation shrinkage and those that eliminate or ameliorate felting shrinkage.

Relaxation Shrinkage

Wool fabrics can be set by a number of processes that use moisture to relax the fabric. Because these processes do not protect against felting shrinkage, fabrics that have these finishes should be dry cleaned or handled carefully during laundering.

1. *Damp relaxing or steam relaxing.* High-quality worsted fabrics are subjected to a step that permits them to relax before they are cut into garments. The fabric is dampened or steamed and then permitted to dry in a relaxed state. The tensions applied to the fabric during processing are thereby removed. The process is also referred to as *London shrinking*, or *sponging*, although the former term is not often used by American textile manufacturers.
2. *Decating of decatizing.* In this process wool fabric is wound on a perforated cylinder, with a blanket of another fabric between the layers. Jets of steam are released through the holes in the cylinders, causing the fabric to be dampened and relaxed. Cold air is then blown through to set the fabric. Not only does this process set the wool fabric, but it also increases its luster.
3. *Potting or boiling.* For napped, sueded, and fine wools, the fabric may be wound on a roller, wrapped in cotton, and immersed in high-temperature, but not boiling, water.

Washable Wools

Attempts to produce washable wool fabrics that will not show felting shrinkage have led to the development of processes that alter the scale structure of the fiber. Superwash® is the Wool Bureau's trademark for fabrics that meet their standards for dimensional stability and colorfastness.

Degradative Processes. Because the scale structure of wool is responsible for felting shrinkage, techniques have been developed to alter the scale structure in some way. Used alone, these processes may not meet "machine washable" standards, but they are adequate for products designated as "hand washable."

The most common degradative processes use chlorine gas or liquid chlorine compounds to apparently partially dissolve the edges of the wool fiber scales, thereby decreasing their tendency to catch on each other. This chemical is, however, destructive, and unless the process is carefully controlled, it can weaken or seriously damage the cortex of the fiber. The texture of the fabric tends to become rough and harsh.

Fibers that have been subjected to chlorination are often blended with other wool or manufactured fibers. When blended with other wool fibers, chlorinated fibers may lead to uneven dyeing because they tend to accept dyes more readily than do untreated fibers.

Alternative processes utilize other oxidative or reductive agents, or, increasingly, enzymes.

Polymer-based Processes. A second method for the creation of washable wools is the application of a thin polymeric layer to the surface of the fabric. The polymer coats the scales, inhibiting the interlocking action. Different processes utilize varying resins. Hercosett® is a branded process for polymer treatment of wool for shrinkage control. It is usually done on wool sliver and preceded by chlorination.

Fibers can also be "spot welded" with synthetic resins to prevent their migration within the fabric structure. This process is most effective for garments, especially sweaters.

Problems encountered in the use of resins or polymers include a tendency for the fabrics to become stiff or harsh to the touch when enough resin or polymer is used to make the fabrics completely shrinkproof. Also, some resin or polymer is lost after a number of launderings.

Shrinkage Control Through Heat Setting

Fabrics made from thermoplastic fibers may be stabilized through heat setting. Synthetics can be permanently set into shape by subjecting them to heat near their glass transition temperature. The heat allows the molecules to relax so the fiber will not exhibit further shrinkage. This process is used to establish permanent dimensions for these fabrics. Synthetic knits, for example, are relatively free from shrinkage problems during laundering if they are properly heat-set. They may, however, undergo thermal shrinkage when subjected to high heat.

FINISHES THAT MINIMIZE FABRIC CARE

Wrinkle Resistance and Recovery

Resistance to the formation of persistent wrinkles can be imparted to fabrics by different means. First, the fiber itself may recover naturally from wrinkling because of its resiliency. This is true of many synthetics and of wool. Second, because of their construction, certain fabric types recover from or disguise wrinkling. Terry cloth, knits, seersucker, plissé, and some "busy" prints with small close designs covering the fabric are examples of such fabrics. Or special finishes may be applied to fabrics to improve their wrinkle resistance.

Since cellulosic fibers are most prone to wrinkling, most wrinkle-resistant finishes were applied to fabrics made from these fibers or their blends. Wrinkle-resistant finishes date back to 1929 when Tootal Broadhurst Lee, Ltd. patented a finish that could be used on cottons and rayons. The Tootal process utilized urea-formaldehyde resin. The theory behind this process—accepted at the time the process was developed but later modified was that the urea-formaldehyde compound penetrated into the fiber and formed a polymeric resin inside the fiber. It was called a thermosetting resin because it formed a crosslinked network that was "set" by curing it with heat. Once inside, the resin was thought to "stuff" the fiber so that it was less flexible and therefore resisted wrinkling. Later work led to the durable press finishes described below, which confer wrinkle resistance by cross linking the cellulose molecules.

In the 1950s the terms *wrinkle resistant* and *crease resistant* gave way to *wash-and-wear*. This emphasized that the finish would eliminate the need for ironing after items were laundered. Many of these wash-and-wear finishes although did require some touch-up pressing before use.

Durable Press Finishes

Durable press finishes, also called *permanent press finishes*, were the successors to the wrinkle resistant treatment developed earlier. They are applied to cotton or cotton blend fabrics to enhance their wrinkle recovery and smooth drying properties. These compounds have at least two functional groups that react with adjacent cellulose molecules. They are thus reactant finishes, because they react with the cellulose rather than forming a network with themselves. Strong covalent bonds replace the weaker hydrogen bonds, crosslinking the cellulose chains and providing greater stability in the position of the molecules. Upon deformation, the molecules are pulled back into alignment, preventing the formation of wrinkles. Fabrics exhibiting this property are called *wrinkle free* as well as durable press.

The most commonly used durable press treatment is dimethyloldihydroxyethyleneurea (DMDHEU). It has two $-OH$ (hydroxyl) groups and two $-NH_2OH$ (methylol) groups that can react with cellulose. The covalent bonds that provide the crosslinks are ether bonds. When blends consisting of cellulose fibers and synthetic fibers are treated, the resin reacts only with the cellulosic fibers in the blend.

Durable Press Processes

The manufacturer applies the durable press treatment, dries the fabric, and then follows with a "cure" period at higher temperature. It is during the curing step that the chemical reaction takes place. The cure may be applied either before the goods are constructed into garments or other items or after construction. (See Figure 23.3.)

Fabrics given a *precure* (also called *flat-cure*) treatment are finished before delivery to the manufacturer. The finish is padded onto the fabric, which is then dried and cured, setting the fabric in a flat position. Durable press yard goods used by home sewers are made by the precure process.

When precured goods of blended fibers are used in manufactured items, the items are pressed with a hot-head press. The heat and pressure of the press shape the item, chiefly by heat-setting the thermoplastic fibers in the blend. Precured fabrics have been made into plain dresses or blouses, curtains, table and bed linens, and draperies, all of which require relatively little shaping.

Manufacturers found that precured fabrics were difficult to handle in manufacture. Furthermore, these fabrics were not easily pressed into permanent shape because

FIGURE 23.3

Comparison of the sequence of
processing durable press
treatments.

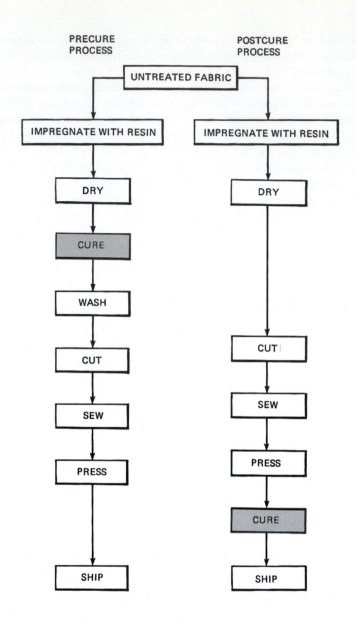

they had been set as "flat." An alternative method of producing durable press items
was, therefore, required.

In an alternative *postcure* process, the fabric is impregnated with the finish and
dried. In this state, the treated but not cured fabric is shipped to the manufacturer.
Garments or other items are manufactured from the cloth, and then the finished
items are cured in a special curing oven. Creases, pleats, hems, and the like are "permanently" set in this way. Care must be taken to be sure that the fabrics are free from
wrinkles or puckers, or these, too, will be permanently set.

Problems of Durable Press

Manufacturing. The production of durable press items raises the cost of manufacture. The additional steps required and the cost of special equipment for finishing

both contribute to the increase in price, which is passed along to the consumer. Most consumers, however, appear to be willing to pay more for a product that requires less care.

In constructing items, the garment manufacturer must make changes in sewing techniques. Stitching of long seams may cause puckering unless special thread is used and unless changes in sewing machine tension, type of needle, and length of stitching are made. It is also important for the garment manufacturer to select findings such as interfacings, linings, hem tape, and the like that will be compatible with durable press. They must not wrinkle or shrink differently from the fashion fabric.

Use and Care. Durable press fabrics, like their forerunners the crease-resistant and wash-and-wear fabrics, exhibit some loss in strength and particularly a decrease in abrasion resistance. One hundred percent cotton fabrics have been known to undergo loss in strength as high as 50 percent when given durable press finishes. In blends, areas such as collars and cuffs of men's shirts or the knees of children's pants often show the results of abrasion by fraying or frosting. *Frosting* is a change in color that results from the breakage and loss of fibers because of abrasion. The soft, fuzzy ends of the fibers give abraded areas a lighter or darker shade of color, depending on the color of the synthetic fibers that have not been worn away. (See Figure 23.4.)

Blending cellulosic fibers with synthetics, especially with polyesters that have increased abrasion resistance, can overcome the abrasion problem to a great extent. Even with blends, however, the problem of different rates of abrasion for each fiber remains.

A variety of different blends of thermoplastic and cellulosic fibers are used for durable press. The most common of these are polyester (from 40 to 75 percent) and cotton (from 25 to 60 percent), polyester (from 50 to 65 percent) and high-wet-modulus rayon (from 35 to 50 percent), and varying other combinations such as rayon or cotton with nylon. Spandex is sometimes incorporated for its stretch properties.

A number of problems with durable press finishes were noted in the 1970s. One was increased attraction of oils and reduced water penetration. As a result, oilborne

FIGURE 23.4

Close-up view of durable press fabric in which frosting has taken place. Darker cotton fibers have worn away, leaving a line of lighter polyester fiber.

soils were absorbed by durable press fabrics, and since the fabrics resisted wetting, laundering (even with detergents that would normally remove oil-based soils) did not clean them effectively. Special soil-releasing finishes (discussed later in this chapter) were developed to overcome these difficulties.

Another problem was that the quantities of finish needed to produce satisfactory durable press made some of these fabrics rather stiff. They did not drape as well and were less comfortable to wear in warm weather than untreated fabrics. Also, if fabrics were not given an adequate after rinse, they had a "fishy" odor. This odor was generally lost after one or more launderings. Many of these problems have been overcome with the development of better finishes, such as DMDHEU, and by using lower levels of finish.

Safety. Formaldehyde is an important component of easy-care and durable press finishes. Under hot, humid conditions, the reaction forming the finish can reverse, releasing formaldehyde. Debate has focused on what constitutes a safe level of formaldehyde in the environment, and revised Occupational Safety and Health Act (OSHA) standards may mandate still lower levels in the workplace. Manufacturers have thus decreased the amount of formaldehyde-containing finishes being applied to fabrics and are developing newer finishes without formaldehyde.

One approach has been to alter the methylol groups in DMDHEU that are the source of formaldehyde. Finishes based on this approach show minimal formaldehyde release but are not as cheap or effective as the traditional commercial finish. Current research is focused on polycarboxylic acids, compounds with multiple acid groups that can react with cellulose molecules forming ester bonds. Fabrics finished with polycarboxylic acids have good durable press features with better strength retention and abrasion resistance, but are either expensive or such finishes cause yellowing of the fabric.

Consumer Brief 23.1 summarizes performance and care aspects that consumers should be aware of when selecting products made from 100 percent cotton durable press fabrics.

SOIL AND WATER REPELLENCY

Soiling results when a textile comes into contact with soiled surfaces or with air- or waterborne soils. Soil is retained either by mechanical entrapment of soil particles within the yarn or fabric structure or by electrostatic forces that bond the soil to the fabric.

One way to approach the problem of soiling is to prevent its deposition on the fabric. Another is to seek ways to facilitate its removal. Special finishes have been developed that have taken both of these approaches.

Stain Repellency

Scotchgard® and other finishes that repel water and oil may be classified as stain-resistant finishes. These finishes decrease the surface energy of the fabric so that water or oil beads up rather than penetrating the fiber. Figure 23.5 illustrates this principle with two different stain-repellent finishes: fluorochemical and silicone. The fluorochemical finish, like DuPont's Teflon® finish on cookware, prevents both oil and water from penetrating the fabric surface. The silicone finish, which also coats the fabric, repels water but not oil.

CONSUMER BRIEF 23.1   Durable Press Fabrics of 100 Percent Cotton

Cotton fabrics, as we all know, become wrinkled during use and after laundering. The cause of this wrinkling is described in chapter 4. Durable press finishes were developed to provide cotton fabrics that did not require ironing after washing. These finishes react chemically with the cellulose chains in cotton fibers to prevent deformation of the fibers, which results in wrinkling of the fabric.

Consumers like the comfort of all-cotton fabrics for apparel as well as for home furnishing items such as sheets. Application of durable press finishes to cotton fabrics increases their consumer acceptance in many end uses. Products made from the finished fabric may be designated as *wrinkle resistant, wrinkle free, or easy care.*

Current commercial finishes can be applied to both cotton and cotton blend fabrics. Blending synthetic fibers, such as polyester, with cotton enhances the fabric's smooth-drying properties, and such blends require less of the durable press finishing material. All-cotton fabrics finished with durable press resins exhibit significantly higher wrinkle resistance after washing and drying than unfinished fabrics. These wrinkle-resistant cotton garments are enjoying a market surge, especially in men's casual clothing. The cost is slightly higher for durable press products, but consumers seem willing to pay for the convenience of easy care. Labels on such products should tell consumers that the products are wrinkle resistant or wrinkle free.

Both precure and postcure processes are used for durable press cotton products. The precure process is best for fabric that will be made into items without creases or pleats. These include sheets, shirts, and knits. Postcuring is used for products that have permanent creases or pleats, such as men's pants. For both processes accurate control of the curing step is the key to ensuring high-quality manufactured products.

Even though the wrinkle-resistant properties of cotton are enhanced by durable press finishes, the fabrics may still need touch-up ironing, especially at seams and other stitched areas, to achieve the appearance desired by some consumers. The finishes will therefore be more effective on cotton garments or home furnishings with less stitching and fewer details.

Durable press finishes also allow the setting of durable creases and pleats in garments of 100 percent cotton. The postcuring process, for example,

can set creases in pantlegs of men's trousers. However, once creases and pleats are permanently set, making alterations to garments is difficult. It is easier to shorten skirts or trousers than it is to lengthen them, even though it may be difficult to get as crisp a press as the fabric had when it came from the manufacturer. The crease mark of the original hem will always show in a lengthened garment. For these reasons, durable press garments should be bought to fit and should not be given extensive alterations.

Durable press finishes not only produce wrinkle resistance, but they also inhibit shrinkage, a property that has led to increased use of these finishes in knit goods. Cotton knits do not wrinkle as much as woven cotton fabrics, but they usually shrink more, and the durable press finishes stabilize the fabric dimensions. Several companies are beginning to market 100 percent cotton knit shirts with shrinkage control.

Special care in home laundering is required to produce optimum durable press performance. Washing should be done at warm rather than hot temperatures. Best results are seen when a warm wash cycle is followed by a cool rinse. Durable press finishes are designed for use in automatic laundering equipment, especially tumble dryers. If items must be line dried, they should be washed in a durable press cycle or removed from the washer before the spin cycle, in which fabrics may become creased.

Dry fabrics should be removed from the dryer immediately after the cycle ends to keep creases from forming while the item lies wrinkled at the bottom of the dryer. Durable press cycles, a feature of most modern dryers, have an initial warm-drying phase, followed by a cool-air phase that prevents this problem. If items do become wrinkled, they can be placed in a warm dryer for a few minutes with a damp item and then immediately removed.

Although durable press resins increase the smooth-drying property of cotton fabrics, they also decrease their strength and abrasion resistance. Some of the earlier wash-and-wear finishes caused losses in fiber strength and toughness. Consumers should recognize that although this problem is no longer so severe, the wear life of cotton durable press fabrics is shorter than that of unfinished fabrics. The problem is greater with shirt-weight fabrics because they are weaker to begin with than the heavier-weight fabrics used for pants and trousers.

Cotton fabrics with a durable press finish may have decreased absorbency. The decrease, however, is

continued

CONSUMER BRIEF 23.1   *continued*

not large and should not noticeably affect the comfort of the fabrics. Finished cotton fabrics also have an increased attraction for grease and oil. To improve performance in this area, most manufacturers couple the wrinkle-resistant finish with a soil-release finish.

Another problem with durable press cotton fabrics has been the release of formaldehyde from the finish under hot, humid conditions. Garments, curtains, or sheets that have been stored in plastic wrappers for some time may release detectable formaldehyde when the plastic is opened. The improved finishing methods currently used have significantly decreased the formaldehyde release, but to minimize exposure consumers should prewash any durable press items before use. Research has shown that laundering easily removes released formaldehyde. Researchers are experimenting with finishes without formaldehyde, but such finishes are not yet commercially available.

Stain-resistant finishes are applied to fabrics used in products such as upholstery and tablecloths to prevent soiling by staining. Since the soils do not penetrate they are readily lifted away when the fabric is laundered or cleaned. They may be applied to an upholstery fabric at the time of manufacture in a liquid form or sprayed onto the fabric after the fabric has been applied to a piece of furniture. Aerosol spray containers of some of these finishes can be purchased for home application. The finish tends to diminish with laundering but can be renewed by using the sprays again.

FIGURE 23.5

(a) The drop of liquid on the left is oil, that on the right, water. Note how the fluorochemical strain-resistant finish enables this nylon upholstery fabric to resist both oil- and water-based strains and soil. (b) The silicone finish applied to this nylon upholstery fabric enables it to resist only water-based stains. Oil-based stains are absorbed by the silicone-treated fabric. (Note, however, that application of silicone finishes over fluorochemical finishes will cancel out oil repellency.) Photographs courtesy of 3M Company.

b

Soil-Release Finishes

Soil-release finishes were developed largely as a result of the tendency of durable press and polyester fabrics to absorb and hold oilborne stains. The soil-releasing finish should not be confused with stain-repellent finishes, although Scotchgard® is both stain resistant and soil releasing.

Soil-release finishes alter the characteristics that cause soil to bond to the fibers. Agents such as polyethylene glycol derivatives may be added to the polymer solution before extrusion to make the nonabsorbent fibers more hydrophilic ("water loving" or having a strong affinity to water). Other finishes may form hydrophilic grafts on the fiber resulting in improvements in soil release and soil redeposition. Most soil-releasing finishes are applied during the finishing of the fabric and are compatible with durable press finishes.

Some fluorochemical finishes are dual-acting. They are block copolymers of fluorocarbons and polar segments such as esters. In air the fluorocarbon sections come to the surface to repel oily substances. When the finished fabric is immersed in water, however, the polar hydrophilic sections predominate on the surface, attracting water to help release soils.

At the same time that soil-releasing finishes increase the receptivity of fibers to water, a second benefit is gained. Static electricity buildup is decreased as absorbency is increased. Increased absorbency also increases the comfort of the garment in warm weather. Fuzzing and pilling seem to be decreased by soil releasing finishes as well, because the finish also lubricates the fabric.

Effective soil-releasing finishes should result in fabrics from which common soil is removed during home laundering with normal detergents. Oily stains, often hard to remove from durable press fabrics, should be removable in home laundering. The disadvantage of most of these finishes is that they are gradually diminished through laundering.

Stain-Resistant Finishes

Stain-resistant finishes for nylon carpets were developed to increase the resistance of these carpets to food and other common stains. The finishes are generally sulfonated aromatic condensation (SAC) compounds that function essentially as colorless dyes. The stain blockers, which have negative charges, are attracted to the positive sites in the nylon fibers, tie up the dye sites, and set up a barrier layer to staining materials. Many food stains, for example, which are negatively charged like the stain resist molecules, are not absorbed as easily.

Today, stain-resistant finishes are used on most nylon carpets for residential use. One trademark is DuPont's Stainmaster®.

Water Repellency

Waterproof Fabrics

A fabric that is waterproof allows no water to penetrate from the surface to the underside. Coatings made from rubber or synthetic plastic materials can create fabrics that are completely waterproof; however, these fabrics tend to be warm and uncomfortable because they create a barrier that traps air and perspiration close to the body. (See chapter 17.)

The dilemma of providing protection and comfort was resolved by the development of fabrics that are described as *waterproof and breathable* (*WP/B*). The general principle behind these fabrics is that they keep out water from rain and snow but allow the passage of moisture vapor from perspiration. They are promoted for use in outdoor clothing and for active sports. One of the first of these products was Gore-Tex®, made by placing a membrane of fluoropolymer underneath a layer of outer fabric. The membrane is porous. The pores are smaller than a drop of water that contains many water molecules, but they are larger than a molecule of water vapor. This structure keeps out rain but allows moisture from perspiration to escape. (See Figure 23.6.)

The success of Gore-Tex® has led to the production of other products using similar principles. Many of these use polyurethane coatings with microscopic pores. Sympatex®, a polyester membrane for lamination, is nonporous but breathable. A charged outer surface attracts polar water molecules which are drawn through the membrane. Also helping to "push" moisture vapor through is the high vapor pressure on the body side (Sympatex 1988).

Performance of waterproof garments is closely related to their construction. Seamlines must be sealed, so that water does not pass through the fabric by way of the holes left by the sewing needle. Tears, rips, or worn spots are also areas in which leaks can occur. The manufacturer recommends that Gore-Tex® garments not be laundered in liquid detergents, as these tend to leave surfactants on the surface that may allow the wetting of the fabric. Instead cold-water temperatures and powdered detergent should be used.

Water-Repellent Fabrics

The term *water repellent* should not be confused with the term *waterproof*. Water-repellent fabrics resist penetration by water but are not completely waterproof. Such fabrics represent a practical alternative to fabrics that keep out water and air, since

FIGURE 23.6

Manufacturer's diagram shows how Gore-Tex® membrane repels water but allows moisture vapor to pass through pores that are too small to permit the passage of water. Courtesy of W. L. Gore and Associates.

they resist wetting and also allow the passage of air. The passage of air is imperative if one is to have a garment that is comfortable to wear.

Water repellency is conferred through a combination of appropriate selection of fiber content and fabric construction and the application of finishes that are classified as either renewable or durable. Fibers that are nonabsorbent and fabrics with high fabric counts or other compact structures help to repel water. For higher levels of protection, finishes are required.

Renewable Finishes. Renewable water-repellent finishes are removed during laundering and dry cleaning. These are relatively inexpensive and easily applied, so that they can be renewed after each laundering or dry cleaning.

Either wax emulsions or metallic soaps are used to secure renewable water repellency. Both these materials are naturally water repellent, and when they are applied in such a way that they coat the yarns of the fabric, they permit the passage of air between the yarns but prevent the passage of water. Of course, in conditions in which the fabric is subjected to long periods of exposure and sufficient force, water will eventually penetrate any water-repellent fabric.

Durable Finishes. Some of these finishes provide water repellency only while others repel both water and oil. Water-repellent finishes begin with fatty or oily substances that possess natural water repellency; these substances are then treated with other chemicals to form compounds that can be absorbed by the fiber and are also insoluble in dry cleaning or soap solutions. Pyridinium compounds, methylol stearamides, and ammonium compounds are used. Silicone compounds are also effective in producing durable water-repellent fabrics.

These finishes are serviceable for products in which only water repellency is required. However, by using the fluorochemical compounds described above, it is possible to produce finishes that repel both water and oil. Scotchgard® is the trade name of one such finish. (See Figure 23.5.)

Some of the durable finishes are durable only to laundering or only to dry cleaning. It is especially important, therefore, for the consumer to follow care instructions attached to these products.

FLAME RESISTANCE

The terminology employed in a discussion of flame resistance can be confusing. The following definitions and descriptions are currently accepted, although usage may vary, particularly from country to country.

1. *Flame resistance* is defined by American Society for Testing and Materials (ASTM) (1998, 23) as "the property of a material whereby flaming combustion is prevented, terminated, or inhibited following application of a flaming or non-flaming source of ignition, with or without the subsequent removal of the ignition source." The material that is flame resistant may be a polymer, fiber, or fabric.

2. Use of the terms *flame retardant* and *self-extinguishing* is discouraged (ASTM 1998, 23, 40). *Flame-retardant treated* and *flame-retardant treatment* are, however, acceptable terms and *flame retardant* is used in other countries. ASTM does not approve the use of the term *self-extinguishing* to describe a textile product because it is meaningful only when applied to specific circumstances.

3. A *thermally stable* material (fiber or polymer) is one that has a high decomposition temperature and is thus inherently flame resistant because of chemical structure (rather than through the presence of added flame-retardant treatments) (Clark and Tesoro 1974).

Flammable Fabrics Act

Flammability of textiles is an important contributor to serious injuries and loss of life and property in fires. This was recognized with the passage of the Flammable Fabrics Act in 1953. The legislation banned the use and sale of *highly* flammable materials for clothing. The law was amended in 1967 to extend coverage (excluding some types of accessories) to carpets, draperies, bedding, and upholstery.

The Flammable Fabrics Act is a federal law. Local and state laws and other regulations may impose restrictions on the use of flammable textile materials in public buildings, but there is no *national* regulation of such items as draperies or curtains for home or public places, other than that they may not be "highly flammable."

Since 1967 the regulations have been modified still further. Originally only those materials that are *highly* flammable were prohibited, but now the manufacture of *all* flammable carpets, mattresses, and children's sleepwear (sizes 0 to 14) is banned.

In 1972 responsibility for administering and enforcing the law was given to the federal Consumer Product Safety Commission (CPSC). Products found to be in violation of the law may be confiscated and destroyed. Persons found guilty of any of the following are subject to fines and/or imprisonment: manufacturing for sale, offering for sale, or selling items that do not comply with the law. The secretaries of the Commerce and Health and Human Services departments are required to sponsor research concerning fire-related hazards. When, on the basis of these investigations, the secretary of commerce determines that a new standard is needed, the National Institute of Standards and Technology (NIST) is given the responsibility of conducting research analyses and developing test methods.

Standards that products must meet are established in a two-step procedure. Notice is given by the commission that there may be a need for a new standard, and a proposed standard is set forth. Individuals are invited to offer their opinions about the proposals. Finally, the standard and test method(s) are announced together with effective dates.

Flammability Standards

Current flammability standards for textile products sold in the United States are prescribed in Title 16 of the Code of Federal Regulations (CFR). Different sections, or parts, of the code address different products. At the present time there are standards for clothing textiles (Part 1610), vinyl plastic film (Part 1611), children's sleepwear, sizes 0 to 6X (Part 1615) and sizes 7 to 14 (Part 1616), carpets and rugs (Parts 1630 and 1631), and mattresses and mattress pads (Part 1632). These standards specify criteria that materials have to meet in order to pass the flammability test.

Clothing Textiles

The standard for clothing requires that "a piece of fabric placed in holder at a 45 degree angle and exposed to a flame for 1.0 second must not spread flame up the length of the sample in less than 3.5 seconds for smooth fabrics or 4.0 seconds for napped fabrics." (CPSC 1974, 1). Five specimens measuring 2 inches by 6 inches are required for each test. The time of flame spread is taken as an average of five specimens.

In 1983 the CPSC issued a rule that allows persons and firms performing testing of fabrics to use apparatus and procedures other than the ones specified in the standard, "provided that the apparatus or procedure is as stringent or more stringent than the apparatus and procedure prescribed by the Standard."

Carpets

Carpet standards require that manufacturers test samples of carpet before marketing. Eight samples are tested by the "methenamine pill" test. This pill, which simulates a source of flame such as a match, is placed in the center of a bone-dry sample of carpet and ignited. If the resulting flame does not extinguish itself before it spreads 3 inches in more than one of the samples, the carpet will not pass the test and must not be sold in the United States.

The pill test determines only surface ignition. It does not assess the contribution of carpets to the spreading of fires, the behavior of carpets in an environment created by a general fire, or the toxicity of the fumes produced.

There are several exceptions to carpets covered under flammable fabrics legislation. One-of-a-kind carpets need not meet the standards. Handcraft items, oriental carpets, and the like are not covered by this law. Carpets that are 6 feet by 6 feet or smaller than 24 square feet that do not pass the pill test may be sold, provided that they are clearly labeled as being flammable.

Children's Sleepwear

Since 1972 children's sleepwear in sizes 0 to 6X has been regulated under the Flammable Fabrics Act. For the first year that the law was in effect, sleepwear that did not meet the standards established had to be labeled as flammable. After July 1973 flammable children's sleepwear was banned. Coverage under the law was extended in May 1975 to sleepwear sizes 7 to 14.

Standards for children's sleepwear sizes 0 to 6X and for sizes 7 to 14 are virtually the same. The general requirements of the standard are described as follows: "Five conditioned specimens, 8.9 × 25.4 cm. (3.5 × 10 in.) are suspended one at a time vertically in holders in a prescribed cabinet and subjected to a standard flame along their bottom edge for a specified time under controlled conditions. The char length is measured." Test criteria that must be met are:

1. Average char length of five specimens shall not exceed 17.8 cm (7 in.).
2. No individual specimen shall have a char length of 25.4 cm (10 in.). (Code of Federal Regulations 1989, 517)

These standards must be met not only by new fabrics but also by those that have been laundered fifty times. All sleepwear must be labeled permanently with instructions as to the care required to maintain the flame resistant properties. Both manufactured sleepwear items and fabrics intended for use in sleepwear must meet the standard. This includes fabrics and wearing apparel such as pajamas, nightgowns, robes, sleepers, and underwear that is sold in children's sleepwear departments.

In 1996 the CPSC exempted tight fitting children's sleepwear and infants' sleepwear under size nine months from the mandatory standard. The rationale for this change is that infants six months or younger do not have sufficient mobility to come close to sources of ignition. The commission took the same action on exempting tight-fitting children's sleepwear because "tight-fitting garments can reduce the amount of trapped air needed for combustion, reduce the possibility of contact with a flame, and shorten the reaction time of the wearer" (CPSC 1994).

Mattresses and Mattress Pads

After December 1973 it became illegal for manufacturers to make mattresses and mattress pads that are combustible. The flammability of mattresses is tested using lighted cigarettes, which were selected as a source of ignition because statistics showed that the greatest number of mattress fires were caused by smoking in bed.

This testing procedure requires that nine cigarettes be placed at various points on the mattress and another nine cigarettes between two sheets on the mattress. To pass the standard the char length on the mattress surface may not be more than 2 inches in any direction from any cigarette. The legislation applies to mattress ticking filled with "any resilient material intended or promoted for sleeping upon" and includes mattress pads. Pillows, box springs, and upholstered furniture are excluded.

Upholstered Furniture

In November 1978 the CPSC considered a draft of a mandatory standard for flammability of upholstered furniture. In response to this move by the CPSC, the Upholstered Furniture Action Council (UFAC), a trade organization for the furniture industry, proposed that a voluntary plan devised by the industry be utilized. The industry plan, as it evolved, included a fabric rating system, criteria for construction of furnishings, a labeling plan, and compliance procedures.

The CPSC gave the industry an opportunity to try the voluntary plan. The rating system grouped all upholstery fabrics into one of two classes, based on fiber content. Fabrics containing at least 50 percent thermoplastic fibers, which are less likely to ignite, are placed in Class I; all other fabrics are placed in Class II. Class II fabrics can be upgraded to Class I if they can pass a cigarette ignition test. Cigarettes are responsible for many of the fires that start in upholstered furniture.

Furthermore, various components of furniture such as welting, filling and padding, decking materials, and substances placed as a barrier between Class II fabrics and the cushion filling must be able to withstand cigarette ignition tests. Only furniture meeting the Class I standards could carry the UFAC approval label.

Compliance was monitored through the UFAC by periodic inspections. The commission considered that the voluntary standard provided adequate protection and did not impose a mandatory standard for furniture. Following a petition by the National Association of State Fire Marshals, however, the CPSC is now preparing such a mandatory standard.

The Boston Fire Department and the state of California have established stringent mandatory standards for flammability of upholstery fabrics and other interior textiles. The Boston city code requires a 45 degree angle test, but with a larger ignition flame and a longer ignition time. In addition, the burning time after removal of the ignition source is measured. California has standards for upholstered furniture that include testing of furniture components as well as mock-ups of the furniture model.

Flame-Resistant Textiles

Textile products can be made flame resistant by using fibers that are inherently flame resistant or by application of a flame-resistant finish. Modacrylic fibers offer adequate flame resistance at a moderate cost and have some use in carpets, curtains, and children's sleepwear. Many other synthetic fibers shrink from ignition flames, providing some protection. Untreated polyester and nylon, for example, will pass the test for children's sleepwear based on this characteristic.

The more thermally stable materials such as asbestos, glass fiber, the aramids, PBI, and PBO could be called fireproof substances that will not burn. Glass fiber has many industrial uses and may be used to a limited extent in household textile products such as window shades or lamp shades. Thermally stable synthetic fibers have not been developed for general use but rather are intended for specialized protective clothing for industrial and military uses. Not only are they expensive, but they also lack the aesthetic features that would make them useful in consumer products.

For fibers that are not flame resistant, a flame-retardant treatment can be applied. Durable finishes for cotton and cotton blend fabrics contain phosphorus which reacts chemically with the fibers and inhibits the production of compounds that fuel the flame. Commercial flame-retardant finishes are Pyrovatex®, Proban®, and PyronO®, the latter produced by Ciba Chemicals.

Finishes for synthetic fibers have bromine that quenches the flame by reducing the generation of flammable gases. Tris-2, 3-dibromopropyl phosphate (TRIS) was used for several years to impart flame resistance to nylon and polyester, but was suspected of causing cancer in laboratory animals. Since its removal from the market, and modifications in the test procedure for children's sleepwear, nylon and polyester are not usually finished with a flame-retardant treatment.

A particular problem in textile flammability is the burning of cotton/polyester blends. Since polyester is less flammable than cotton, one would expect blended fabrics to be less hazardous than all cotton fabrics. This is unfortunately not the case, because the char left as the cotton burns serves to hold the melting and dripping polyester in the flame. This is referred to as a "scaffolding" effect that prevents the polyester from dripping away, as it would do in a 100 percent polyester fabric. The polyester remains in the flame and contributes to the burning.

Wool is inherently moderately resistant to burning and provides some protection in apparel and interior furnishings. For more stringent uses such as airplane seats, however, wool is given a flame-retardant treatment. A common finish for wool is Zirpro®.

Flame resistance conferred through finishing, as opposed to that achieved by use of thermally stable and inherently flame resistant materials, may be lost or diminished through normal use and care of products. Ammonium phosphate, which is a nondurable flame-retardant treatment, is lost in laundering and must be reapplied. Chlorine bleach, soaps, low-phosphate detergents, and some fabric softeners can harm durable flame-resistant finishes. Laundering in hard water will also decrease the effectiveness of the finish.

Flammability Testing

Testing for flammability is required under the Flammable Fabrics Act. The requirements of that legislation and the performance standards that materials are required to meet are set forth in the CFR. These tests described above usually have a single pass/fail criterion. A wide variety of additional tests for flammability can be conducted to provide information on burning behavior and effectiveness of finishes. (See Figure 23.7.)

Many of these methods require test samples of considerable size or even whole garments. DuPont, Eastman Kodak, and the University of Minnesota have developed thermal testing manikins with heat sensors located in various parts of the figure. Tests performed using these figures can determine not only the combustibility of the fabric being tested but also the location of hot spots and can furnish data about the transfer of heat. They can also assess effects of fabric layers such as a cotton dress worn over a nylon slip.

FIGURE 23.7

Flammability tester used to test vertically oriented textile products, in this case a plush child's toy. The specimen is mounted on the rectangular frame at the center of the upright section of the tester. Ignition is from the small nozzle just below the foot of the toy. Photograph courtesy of James H. Heal & Company, Ltd.

There are tests for carpets other than the pill test required by the federal standard. The Flooring Radiant Panel Test is said to simulate conditions of interior fires more effectively than other carpet tests. As a result, it is likely to be used by governmental and other regulatory agencies that require the more extensive product evaluation that carpeting installed in hospitals and facilities participating in Medicare and Medicaid programs must meet.

An area of considerable interest in flammability testing of interiors is computer simulation or virtual tests to determine the hazards of real-life situations. For example, data on the furnishings in a prototype room can be used to predict the results of a fire (Gorman 1994). More realistic measures of fire hazards can be obtained and used in such predictive models. These measures, including total heat release, rate of heat release, and toxic gases evolved, are the real dangers from fires involving textiles.

Consumer Reaction

Consumer and research interest in fabric flammability reached its peak in the ten-year period beginning in the late 1960s. When the flame-resistant finish TRIS was banned in 1977, much of the public quickly became suspicious of fire-retardant treatments in general. As a result, interest in the development of finishes waned. At the present time there is renewed activity in the area of flammability and it is predicted that world markets for flame-retardant finished fabrics will grow (Holme 1999).

ANTISTATIC FINISHES

Synthetic fibers, being poor conductors of electricity, tend to build up static electric charges. Electricity causes garments to cling or to build up charges that are dissipated through unpleasant, though mild, electric shocks when the wearer touches a conductor such as a metal doorknob or another person's hand.

Finishes have been developed that attempt to decrease static buildup. However, these finishes tend to have limited effectiveness, largely because they are gradually lost during laundering. Antistatic finishes work on either of two principles: either they coat the surface of the fiber with a more conductive substance, or they attract to the fiber small amounts of moisture that increase its conductivity.

More successful decrease in static buildup of synthetics is achieved through the modification of the polymer before extrusion. This method permanently incorporates compounds in the fiber structure that increase moisture absorbency, which, in turn, increases conductivity.

Another approach is to use special, high-performance antistatic fibers. Metal, metallized, and bicomponent fibers containing metal or carbon are among those used. A small proportion of these fibers is blended with conventional synthetic fibers. Being more conductive, they serve to dissipate the static charges.

Antistatic sprays can be purchased for home use. Fabric softeners applied in the final rinse during laundering will also provide some reduction in static buildup.

SPECIAL PURPOSE FINISHES

Finishes have been developed to overcome problems of individual fibers or to meet a particular need. Such finishes are applied on a fairly limited basis to particular fibers, yarns, or fabrics, many intended for rather specialized uses.

Finishes that Increase Absorbency

Ammonium compounds may be applied to cellulosic fibers used for diapers, towels, or other items in which absorbency is important. These compounds increase the absorbency of the fabrics somewhat and many also soften the fabrics.

Some success has been achieved in increasing the absorbency of synthetic fibers. Antistatic and soil-releasing finishes make synthetic fibers more hydrophilic. Surface degradation of polyester using sodium hydroxide can also increase absorbency, although this process is not used on a large scale.

Antislip Finishes

Smooth filament yarns may have a tendency to slide against one another, creating flawed areas in a fabric or problems of seam slippage. This is known as yarn *slippage*. Resins coated on the surface of these fabrics will keep the yarns in place, because the resin holds yarns together at the points where the yarns interlace. Resin antislip finishes are durable.

Other antislip finishes can be created by coating silica compounds on fabrics. However, these finishes are only temporary.

Antimicrobial Finishes

Antimicrobial finishes help to protect fabrics against mold, mildew, and bacteria. In addition to the finishes described here, several manufactured fibers are produced with antimicrobial agents incorporated into the fiber structure. These modified acetates, acrylics, and olefins can provide durable protection against growth of microbes.

Antimildew and Antirot Finishes

Mildew, a fungus or mold, is a whitish growth that affects certain textile fibers when they are stored in a damp condition in a warm place. This growth damages the fiber and causes serious staining. Cellulosic fibers are most susceptible to mildew. Protein fibers are less likely to be attacked.

The best protection against mildew is to make certain that the fabrics are dry and clean when stored and that they do not become damp during storage. Mildew is an especially serious problem in warm, humid climates. Mildew weakens fabrics, and home treatments to remove mildew stains may further degrade the fabrics.

Rotting is an acute problem with bast fibers, such as jute and hemp, used for bags, ropes, and other materials that are exposed for long periods to water, damp soil, or wet floors. Rot- and mildew-resistant fabrics can be made by treating the fabrics with antiseptic substances. Since copper has bactericidal power, copper solutions may be used to confer rot resistance to fabrics. A variety of other chemical substances (among them phenol, formaldehyde, and pentachlorophenol) that are not harmful to the fabric and inhibit the growth of microorganisms are also used.

Experimentation with melamine resin finishes for crease resistance revealed that these finishes retarded mildew and rotting. Home processes can be used to guard against mildew. An after-rinse with boric acid will retard the formation of mildew.

Antibacterial Finishes

Chemical substances that inhibit the growth of bacteria are also used to finish goods that will be used in health care products, apparel, home furnishings, or fabrics used in the hotel and restaurant industry. These finishes, also called biocides, can be metal compounds that are toxic to bacteria or organic substances such as phenols and anilides.

Although these finishes are classified as either renewable or durable, even so-called durable finishes are removed gradually during laundering. Renewable finishes can be replaced during laundering. A recent development in renewable finishes is an inactivated biocide that is chemically bonded to the fiber. The finish is activated during laundering with chlorine bleach. The chlorine serves as the antibacterial agent, and the activated agent can be regenerated when the fabric is bleached again (Sun and Xu 1999).

Certain specific organic ammonium compounds are known to combat diaper rash. Many diaper services routinely apply this finish to the diapers that they launder. Antimicrobial finishes are also applied to nonwoven fabrics used in surgical and medical products such as instrument packs, surgical packs, and surgical draping fabrics.

Mothproofing Finishes

Wool and other animal hair fibers are attacked by the larvae of the clothes moth. Silk is not attacked by moths as it lacks cystine, a sulfur-containing amino acid moths seem to require.

Finishes that prevent moth damage can act as insecticides to poison the moth larvae, or can alter the fiber in some way that makes the wool unpalatable to moth larvae, thereby starving the grubs. These insecticide finishes may be applied during manufacture or during dry cleaning. Some of these finishes are durable, whereas others must be renewed with each cleaning. The second type of finish replaces the disulfide crosslinks in wool with longer linkages that the moths cannot digest. These finishes are permanent.

Temperature-Regulating Finishes

Temperature-regulating fabrics are sensitive to the surrounding temperature or to body heat. Finishes that provide this adaptation include substances called phase change materials (PCMs) (Lennox-Kerr 1998). These substances change from solid to liquid or liquid to solid depending on the temperature. The example we are probably most familiar with is ice changing to water when the temperature rises and then changing back to ice again when cooled. Ice absorbs heat to melt and water gives off heat when it becomes solid. PCMs work the same way but are selected to undergo this phase change around normal skin temperature.

One such finish is polyethylene glycol (PEG), which is applied to fabrics along with a methylol agent such as DMDHEU. The result is a network polymer that is insolubilized on the surface of the fibers. The polymer absorbs and holds heat energy at high temperature, and then releases the stored energy under cooler conditions. The finish is durable to wear and laundering, because it is crosslinked on the fabric.

Not only do these finishes help to warm or cool the body, but they also increase the moisture absorbency of fabrics, thereby further enhancing comfort. Other improved properties are resistance to static, wrinkling, abrasion, pilling, and soil. The PEG finish has been used on T-shirts, underwear, socks, activewear, and biomedical products.

In another form, PCMs have been applied to fabrics as microcapsules in coatings, used in nonwoven bonding materials, or included in spinning solutions of manufactured fibers. Outlast Technologies, Inc. produces the microcapsules. Acordis Fibers has produced a version of their Courtelle® acrylic fibers with the PCM embedded in them. The fabrics made with these fibers are targeted for outdoor apparel, particularly for cold climates. PCM-containing textile fabrics are expensive because the encapsulation process is technology intensive.

Heat-Reflectant Finishes

An increased level of insulation can be provided in garments and draperies by the addition of heat-reflectant finishes. Most of these products are treated with a spray coating of metal and resinous substances. The heat-reflectant material is sprayed onto the surface of a closely woven fabric. The finish is designed to keep heat either on one side or the other side of the fabric. The finish is effective only with radiated heat.

Lining fabrics are usually constructed so that the finish is applied to the inside of the fabric. The finish reflects the body heat back toward the wearer, thus providing added warmth. In protective clothing to be worn under hot conditions, the finish is worn to the outside to deflect heat away from the body. Draperies may also be treated to provide greater insulation for homes. Treated draperies placed inside windows may serve to keep heat inside the home or to reflect heat outward, preventing it from warming the house.

Some of the processes designed to produce heat reflectance use aluminum in the finish, because it provides excellent reflectancy. A variant of this principle is utilized in fabrics coated or laminated with a thin layer of aluminum, foams, resins, or synthetic rubber.

Light-Reflectant Finishes

Light-reflectant finishes are created by the application of microscopic reflective beads to the surface of a fabric. The increased number of persons who jog or ride bicycles after dark is probably responsible for the application of this finish to a variety of garments for sports and to other items such as backpacks. A reflective finish called Scotchlite® is produced by the 3M Company. The manufacturer notes that the finish does not alter the color or appearance of the garment by day, but after dark the fabric "lights up" when directly in the path of the lights of an oncoming vehicle. (See Figure 23.8.)

Light-Resistant Finishes

Many textile fabrics are deteriorated by exposure to sunlight, so attempts have been made to protect fabrics from light damage. Of all the types of rays in the sun's spectrum, ultraviolet rays are the most destructive of fibers. Although antilight finishes have yet to be perfected, those that are being tried either coat the fabric or impregnate the fibers with materials that absorb ultraviolet rays but are not themselves damaged by or removed by exposure to these rays. Such finishes are particularly important in olefin fabrics, which are degraded by sunlight unless ultraviolet stabilizers are added. Such additives to olefin fibers are permanent and are not lost during usage.

Synthetics that have been delustered with titanium dioxide are especially subject to damage from sunlight. This chemical apparently accelerates damage to the fiber and fading of dyes. The addition of certain chemical salts to the melt solution before spinning can ameliorate this problem.

The relationship between exposure to the ultraviolet light of the sun and skin cancer is well known. Many people assume that fabrics prevent exposure to any part of the body that is covered; however, research shows that fabrics do allow passage of ultraviolet light. Knitted fabrics, which usually have a more open structure, generally allow more ultraviolet light through than woven fabrics; lightweight summer fabrics allow more ultraviolet light to reach the skin than heavier fabrics with more opaque yarns.

Ultraviolet protection is now being built into fibers and fabrics. Most of the techniques are proprietary processes, so details of how the protection is provided are limited. Kuraray, a Japanese firm, produces Esmo®, a polyester staple fiber to which powdered ceramics have been added to absorb and reflect ultraviolet rays. A similar fiber called Aloft® is produced by the Japanese firm Toray, and other Japanese firms produce fabrics that are given special protective finishes (Development of new fibers. . . 1992).

Australian researchers have developed a chemical finish called Rayosun® that is said to be washfast, colorfast, and lightfast. The finishing material contains a "two-part molecule," one part of which absorbs ultraviolet rays while the other part reacts with the fabric, thereby making the finish durable (Sun-proof clothing 1993, 72).

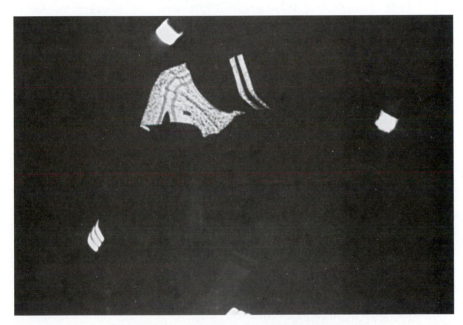

FIGURE 23.8

Runner wears garments with Scotchlite® light-reflective finish. At night, light is reflected from headlight beams to alert motorists to the presence of the wearer. Courtesy of 3M Company.

Other Specialty Finishes

Several additional finishes produce special effects. In one, a powdered material is applied to fabrics to decrease the loss of body heat. In another, the finishing material contains microencapsulated fragrances that gradually release perfumed oils as the fabric is abraded during wear. The scented finishes have been used in fabrics for mens' suits. New, too, are finishes for odor control. These compounds entrap the volatile molecules that cause unpleasant odors.

SUMMARY

Whereas the finishes discussed in chapter 22 were compared with "cosmetics," used to enhance the physical properties of fabrics, the finishes discussed in this chapter are designed to modify the actual behavioral properties of textiles. Although finishes may change the appearance, texture, and hand of a fabric, they do so for more than cosmetic reasons. Finishes that modify, or in some way improve, inherent fiber properties may result in an increase in price and/or a change in care requirements, but consumers have generally been receptive to the improvements and are willing to pay for them. But the costs of some finishes cannot be measured only by a price increase on the product. Durable press finishes do result in shorter wear life and may result in more frequent replacement of garments, and there are other trade-offs involved. For example, proper laundering of some flame resistant products requires the use of phosphate-containing detergents. Phosphates have been cited as a cause of water pollution. The choice is between one kind of hazard and another. There are no easy answers and no simple solutions.

References

ASTM. 1998. *Annual book of ASTM standards*, 7.01. West Conshohocken, Pa.: American Society for Testing and Materials.

Clark, J. E., and G. Tesoro. 1974. Textile flammability. Paper presented to the American Chemical Society's State of the Art Symposium on Man-made Fibers, held in Washington, D.C. (June).

Code of Federal Regulations. 1989. 16 CFR, chapter 11 (January 1).

CPSC. 1974. *Fact sheet.* Washington, D.C.: Consumer Product Safety Commission (June).

CPSC. 1989. U.S. Consumer Product Safety Commission memorandum, July 13.

CPSC. 1994. CPSC votes to continue rulemaking on children's sleepwear. *News from CPSC*, August 3.

Development of new fibers with sophisticated functions as high added-value products. 1992. *Knitting International* 99 (June): 42.

Gorman, M. 1994. Update: E-5; the fire standards committee reaches into the 1990s. *Standardization News* 22 (11): 30.

Holme, I. 1999. Fireproof future. *Textile Horizons* (May): 23.

Lennox-Kerr, P. 1998. Comfort in clothing through thermal control. *Textile Month* (November): 28.

Skieller, E. 1989. Eliminating shrinkage problems in knitted cotton fabrics. *American Dyestuff Reporter* 90 (September): 30.

Sun, G., and X. Xu. 1999. Durable and regenerable antibacterial finishing of fabrics: Chemical structures. *Textile Chemist and Colorist* 31 (5): 31.

Sun-proof clothing. 1993. *Textiles* 22 (3): 6.

Sympatex: Breathable fabrics without pores. 1988. *America's Textiles International* 17 (November): 72.

Review Questions

1. Explain the difference between relaxation shrinkage, progressive shrinkage, and consolidation shrinkage.
2. Identify and describe the ways that fabrics can be preshrunk without being made wet. Why is it not desirable to wet or launder fabrics to prevent shrinkage?

3. How is the largest quantity of fabric given durable press finishes? Explain the chemical changes that take place within the fibers, and identify other properties that may be affected.

4. What is the difference between stain-repellent and soil-releasing finishes? Explain how each is achieved.

5. What is the difference between a fabric that is waterproof and one that is water repellent? What is the difference between a fabric that is waterproof and one that is waterproof and breathable? How is breathability achieved?

6. Which generic fibers are flame resistant? How can other fibers or fabrics that are not flame resistant be made safer?

7. What kinds of products are subject to strict regulation under the Flammable Fabrics Act and must meet specified standards? What kinds of products are encouraged to meet voluntary standards?

8. Identify five or more finishes that have been developed to improve specific properties of fibers that consumers find troublesome. Explain which properties the finish changes and how.

9. Identify two finishes that might be described as providing additional safety or protection to consumers who wear apparel made from these products. How do these finishes function?

Recommended Readings

Andrews, B. A. K. 1992. Safe, comfortable, durable press cottons: A natural progression for a natural fiber. *Textile Chemist and Colorist* 24 (November): 17.

Brown, R. O. 1994. Enhancing the performance of wrinkle resistant cotton garments. *American Dyestuff Reporter* 83 (September): 106.

Czech, A. M., J. Pavlenyi, and A. J. Sabia. 1997. Modified silicone softeners for fluorocarbon soil release treatments. *Textile Chemist and Colorist* 29 (9): 26.

Dockery, A. 1993. New process lets polyester breathe. *America's Textiles International* 22 (October): K/A 12.

Ferguson, C. 1982. Hydrophilic finishes for polyester: Durability and processing advantages. *American Dyestuff Reporter* 71 (June): 43.

Flame retardant fibers for interior use. 1990. *JTN* no. 426 (May): 43.

Gurian, M. 1997. The finishing needs of the evolving commercial interior fabrics industry. *Textile Chemist and Colorist* 29 (10): 21.

Hamlyn, P. F. 1990. Talking rot . . . and mildew. *Textiles* 19 (2): 46.

Huang, X. X., Y. K. Kamath, and H.-D. Weigmann. 1993. Photodegradation and the loss of stain resistance of stain blocker treated nylon. *Textile Chemist and Colorist* 25 (November): 293.

LeBlanc, R. B. 1997. The durability of flame retardant-treated fabrics. *Textile Chemist and Colorist* 29 (2): 19.

North, B. F. 1991. Reactants for durable press textiles: The formaldehyde dilemma. *Textile Chemist and Colorist* 23 (October): 21–22.

Sabia, A. J. 1994. Use of silicones to enhance the aesthetic and functional properties of microfibers. *Textile Chemist and Colorist* 144 (August): 13–16.

Townsend, M. W. 1983. Moths and wool. *Textiles* 12 (Spring): 9.

Vigo, T. L., and J. S. Bruno. 1993. Fibers with multifunctional properties: A holistic approach. In *High technology fibers, Part C*, ed. M. Lewin and J. Preston, 317. New York: Marcel Dekker.

Zhou, Y., and P. C. Crews. 1998. Effect of OBAs and repeated launderings on UVR transmission through fabrics. *Textile Chemist and Colorist* 30 (11): 19.

CHAPTER 24

THE CARE OF TEXTILE PRODUCTS

Attention to the correct procedures for cleaning and maintaining textile products will extend the useful life of the product. Improper cleaning and storage can result in either severe damage to the fabric or an increased rate of wear over a period of time.

The accumulation of soil on fabrics is one of the factors that causes them to deteriorate. Spilled food, for example, can make a fabric that is normally unappetizing to insects into an attractive meal for moths and carpet beetles. The "ground-in dirt" that television commercials decry can increase the abrasion of yarns as gritty soils rub against fibers, causing them to break. Soil removal is, therefore, one of the most important aspects of caring for fabrics if they are to be maintained in good condition.

Soil deposited on fabrics is made up of different materials. Some types of soil are soluble; other types are insoluble. Soluble dirt is made up of organic acids, mineral acids, alkaline substances, blood, starches, and sugars. All these substances dissolve in cool or warm water, and although they may sometimes require special stain-removal techniques, these soluble substances present no extraordinary problems in cleaning.

Water alone will remove soluble soil, but insoluble soils may be held onto the fabric by physical attraction or in films, greases, or oils. Such soil requires the use of some kind of cleaning aid.

HISTORICAL DEVELOPMENT

Soaplike materials dating from 2500 B.C. have been found in clay cylinders from the city of Babylon in the Near East, but whether this substance was used as a cleaning agent or as a dressing for the hair is not known. Other references from antiquity likewise provide no clear description of the uses of soap, although the Roman writer Pliny describes the process by which it was made. By the Middle Ages the craft of soapmaking was well enough developed that guilds or associations of soapmakers had been formed.

For many centuries the making of soap from natural materials was a major household task. Animal fats and lye, made by soaking wood ashes in water, were boiled together to make a strong soap. Commercial soapmaking coexisted with the home process. Over time the commercial processes gradually improved and eventually replaced the homemade product as chemists found better ways of isolating and manufacturing the components used in the soapmaking process.

Soap is a good cleaning agent, but it does not perform well in hard water. Hard water is generally found in areas of limestone rock and contains higher concentrations of minerals such as calcium and magnesium. The minerals in the water combine with soap to form an insoluble gray curd, or scum. Once the soap has combined with these minerals, less soap is available for cleaning, and larger quantities of soap must be used. Also, the hard-water scum may be deposited on clothing, leaving it gray or dull looking.

An alternative cleaning agent to soap was developed during World War I in Germany when fats and oils normally used for making soap were in short supply. This substance, a synthetic detergent, had another advantage: it did not form a scum with minerals such as calcium and magnesium that make water "hard."

The term *detergent* can create some confusion. Cleaning agents are commonly known as detergents. Both soaps and synthetic detergents are, technically speaking, detergents, even though the term *detergent* is often used by the general public to refer only to synthetic detergents. For purposes of this discussion, *detergent* will be used to refer to synthetic detergents and to both soaps and detergents where those terms are interchangeable.

Although synthetic detergents were produced in the United States as early as the 1930s, it was only following World War II that their use increased dramatically. Today, synthetic detergents dominate the home laundry market, and only a few brands of laundry soap remain.

SOIL REMOVAL

Soil can be removed from fabrics by laundering or dry cleaning. These processes can be carried out in the home or by professional cleaners. The principles used are the same in both instances, but the equipment and laundry or dry-cleaning products will vary.

Laundering

The process of laundering soiled fabrics consists of wetting the fabric and its soil, removing the soil from the fabric, and holding the soil in suspension so that it does not redeposit on the fabric during washing. Detergents increase the cleaning ability of water. The addition of detergent to water decreases the surface tension of water, that is, the molecular forces in the outer layer of the water. The lower surface tension increases the wetting power of water allowing it to penetrate textiles more completely. Essentially detergents make water "wetter."

A simple experiment will demonstrate this principle. Take a small piece of nylon fabric and float it on the surface of a small bowl of water. The surface tension of the water enables the nylon to float for a time, until it becomes wet throughout. Drop a few drops of liquid detergent into the water. The fabric will become wet immediately and sink.

In laundering the wet fabric is agitated by the motion of the washing machine or by hand scrubbing. The soil is broken into smaller particles, surrounded (emulsified) by the detergent, and then lifted off the fabric by the action of the detergent molecules. The detergent surrounding the soil particles prevents them from being redeposited on the fabric as the washing progresses. When fabrics are rinsed, the soil and detergent are rinsed away.

Soaps

Soap is made from fatty acids and alkali that react together to form the soap. Some degree of alkalinity is necessary for cleaning, and as the soap dissolves, the washing water becomes somewhat alkaline in reaction. Much soil is acid in chemical reaction and will tend to neutralize some of the alkalinity of the soap and decrease its effectiveness. Therefore, more heavily soiled items require more soap.

To ensure that adequate alkalinity is present for thorough washing, extra alkali is added to increase the effectiveness of the soap. Soaps with added alkali are known as *built* or *heavy-duty* soaps and are designed for general laundering. Less alkaline soaps are also available for laundering more delicate fabrics. Because protein fibers are damaged by excessive alkali, mild detergents should be used for washing wool, silk, and other delicate fabrics.

Nonsoap Detergents

Synthetic detergent products are made from petroleum and natural fats and oils. Unlike soaps, synthetic detergents do not form hard-water scum but dissolve readily not only in hard water, but also in soft water that contain few minerals. The specific formulation of each synthetic detergent varies, of course, from one product to another. Laundry detergents are produced in both liquid and powder form. The use of heavy-duty liquid detergents has grown in recent years. One reason for the increased use of these products is that they can be formulated more readily without phosphates than can powdered detergents.

1. *Surfactants.* Surfactants, the active ingredient in synthetic detergents, are organic chemicals that alter the properties of water and soil so that dirt can be removed. The surfactant molecule has a hydrophobic ("water-hating" or repelled by water) body that is attracted to oily substances, and a hydrophilic head that attracts water and other polar and charged compounds. The action of the surfactant breaks up water droplets that surround soil particles by lowering the surface tension and allowing water to penetrate. Groups of surfactant molecules (called *micelles*) surround the soil, with the hydrophobic body of the molecule attached to the soil and the hydrophilic head of the molecule oriented toward the water in which the particles become suspended. (See Figure 24.1.)

FIGURE 24.1

Diagram showing the action of a surfactant removing and suspending greasy soil.

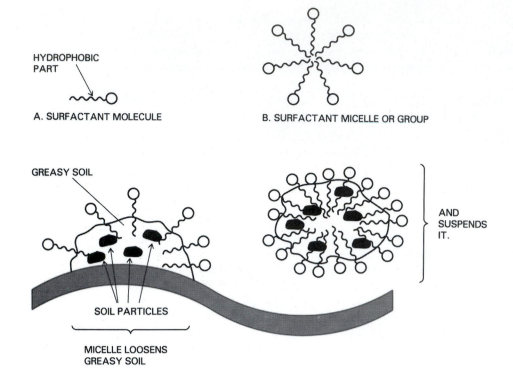

The most commonly used surfactants are linear alkyl benzene sulfonate (LAS), alcohol sulfates (AS), nonionic surfactants, and soap. Both LAS and AS surfactants and soap are anionic, that is, they generate negative charges in water. Similar electric charges repel each other. Most fabrics also carry negative charges, so that the negative charge of the surfactant molecules surrounding the soil particles is effective in preventing the redeposition of soil on the fabrics being washed. Nonionic surfactants do not carry electric charges as they dissolve. They are more effective in removing oily soil than are anionic surfactants. Concern about the slow decomposition of some detergents in sewage treatment and in surface water has led to the use of biodegradable surfactants, which are readily decomposed after use.

2. *Builders*. Builders are substances that soften water and maintain alkalinity. Until recently, the majority of builders used in detergent formulations were phosphates, which are especially effective in counteracting water hardness. They also disperse and suspend dirt and maintain alkalinity, which is necessary to neutralize many soils that tend to be acid in chemical reaction.

Fears that phosphates contribute to water pollution have led some states and communities to restrict the use of phosphate-containing detergents. As a result, detergent manufacturers have developed a variety of nonphosphate or low-phosphate detergents that contain other builders. These nonphosphate builders include sodium silicate, sodium carbonate, sodium sulfate, and sodium citrate.

Some detergents do not contain builders, relying instead primarily on surfactants to keep soil suspended and to combat water hardness. Nonionic surfactants are especially good for the latter purpose because they do not react with minerals that cause water hardness.

3. *Suds control agents.* Some detergents are made to maintain low suds levels, whereas others produce more suds. All suds levels clean equally well, but low-suds formulations are often necessary for optimum cleaning in front-loading washers, in which the laundry is carried up and around as the basket rotates. When the wet laundry reaches the top of the basket as it rotates in a circle, the laundry drops to the bottom, thereby providing the agitation necessary for releasing soil. High-suds detergents break the fall of the fabrics, thereby decreasing the washing action in front loading machines. They are, however, appropriate for machines with oscillatory agitation that are widely used today. Soap is an additive that can control sudsing and foaming.

4. *Processing aids.* Materials added to maintain good powder properties in powdered detergents include sodium silicate (also cited previously as a builder) and sodium sulfate. Liquid detergents may contain alcohol as a solvent to help maintain the detergent in liquid form under colder conditions.

5. *Agents to protect washing machine parts.* Silicates in detergents help to prevent corrosion of the parts of the washer that are exposed to water and detergents.

6. *Antiredeposition agents.* Although anionic surfactants help to prevent the redeposition of soil, other agents are also added to the detergent to prevent redeposition. The most common chemical used for this purpose is sodium carboxymethyl cellulose.

7. *Fragrances.* Many detergents contain fragrances. These products give the laundered items a more pleasant odor.

8. *Other additives.* Enzymes, oxygen bleaches, fluorescent whiteners, bluing, and/or fabric softeners may be added to some detergents to create what the industry calls *multifunctional products.* Each of these additives can also be purchased by the consumer and used separately from the detergent.

Laundry Disks

Spurred by environmental concerns over the use of detergents with phosphates and other additives, alternative products that are claimed by their manufacturers to clean by a different mode of action have been introduced, primarily in Europe and the Far East. These products, known variously as laundry disks, balls, or spheres, emit a negative charge or electromagnetic radiation that separates aggregated water molecules into individual molecules or even separate hydrogen hydroxyl ions (Lumley and Gatewood 1998). This action enables water to penetrate the textile structure more easily and aids cleaning. Assessments of these products have concluded that they are not more effective than water alone.

Water Softeners or Conditioners

Synthetic detergents do not produce hard-water scum as soaps do, but it is necessary to use larger quantities of detergent in hard water than in soft water. (Soft water is free from these dissolved minerals.) Many families, therefore, find it helpful to decrease the hardness of water by some form of water conditioning. Hard water can be softened either by commercial softening systems installed in the home to soften all water used in the household or by the addition of powdered water softeners to the laundry. Powdered softeners are of two types: precipitating and nonprecipitating.

Precipitating water softeners combine with the minerals that cause water to become hard to form a compound that precipitates, or settles out of solution, into visible granules. More common are the nonprecipitating water softeners that keep hard-water minerals tied up in chemical combination and in solution so that neither soap scum nor a precipitate is formed. Nonprecipitating softeners can dissolve soap scum formed before the softener was added to the water and can strip scum left in clothes from previous washings in hard water.

Minerals, such as iron or manganese, in water may stain fabrics. The addition of bleach to such water may cause the formation of colored salts that, when deposited on fabrics, cause discoloration. Nonprecipitating water softeners will prevent such staining by tying up the minerals. Calgon® is a nonprecipitating water softener.

Bleaches

Bleaches are often used along with soaps and synthetic detergents in laundering. It is important to remember that bleaches do not *clean* clothing. Detergents do the cleaning; bleaches are used to whiten fabrics and remove stains.

Bleaches oxidize the coloring matter in fabric, and some stains are removed by the oxidation of the coloring matter in them. Two basic types of bleaches are used in the home: chlorine bleaches and perborate bleaches.

Chlorine bleaches are the stronger of the two types. They contain active chlorine to oxidize colored matter. But after the chlorine has oxidized all stains, color, and so on, it begins to oxidize susceptible fibers. For this reason, chlorine bleaches need to be used in correct concentrations, must be dissolved thoroughly before application, and must be rinsed out thoroughly, or they may damage the fibers. Some dyes are damaged by chlorine bleach; therefore, it is rarely recommended that colored fabrics be bleached with chlorine bleach.

The following are the most frequent mistakes made in handling chlorine bleach.

1. *Using too much bleach.* Follow directions on the package. Do not assume that if a little bleach is good, twice as much is better.
2. *Pouring bleach directly onto clothing.* Bleach should be added to a full tub of water and agitated thoroughly before any laundry is added. Adding concentrated bleach to a washer full of clothing will result in concentrated bleach being poured over some garments, which may damage them. Many washing machines today have bleach dispensers to measure the bleach and add it at the appropriate time.
3. *Bleaching items that should not be bleached.* Read care labels carefully. Some resins or fibers such as spandex will yellow on contact with chlorine bleach. Chlorine bleach damages fibers such as silk, wool, or spandex.
4. *Soaking heavily stained items in concentrated bleach solutions.* Exposure to concentrated bleach solutions may damage certain fibers and should be avoided. Items should not be soaked in even low concentrations of chlorine bleach for longer than 15 minutes.

Chlorine bleaches are sold in both dry and liquid forms under a variety of trade names. Clorox® and Purex® are trademarks of chlorine bleaches. It is important to rinse bleached fabrics carefully, or deterioration of the fibers can continue for as long as any bleach remains in the material.

Oxygen bleaches do not use chlorine for oxidation but use other chemicals such as sodium perborate, hydrogen peroxide, and potassium monopersulfate. They also do not whiten as efficiently in a short period of time. These bleaches will work best if used in hot water; new formulations however have been developed to function at the lower, "energy saving" washing temperatures of today. Like chlorine bleaches, oxygen bleaches should be diluted before addition to the wash, as some colors may be sensitive to the bleaching action of these products. Trade names of oxygen bleaches are Clorox-2® and Purex All Fabric Bleach®. Hydrogen peroxide is sold in drugstores as an antiseptic.

Pretreatment Products

Certain types of stains are especially hard to remove. Among these are protein-based stains such as body soils, blood, eggs, baby formula, grass stains, and chocolate. Special enzyme presoak products contain selected types of enzymes that may break down these soils to simpler forms that are then more readily and completely removed by the laundry soap or detergent. Fabrics are soaked from 30 minutes to overnight, depending on the instructions and the age and amount of the stain. Enzymes are commonly incorporated into the formulations of multifunctional detergents.

Aerosol prewash soil and stain removers that contain perchlorethylene or other petroleum-based solvents are sold for use on synthetics and durable press fabrics. They help to remove greasy stains such as those made by lipstick, bacon fat, coffee with cream, and ballpoint pen. Instructions on the label generally recommend that they be applied to fabrics five minutes or longer before washing.

Fluorescent Whiteners, or Optical Brighteners

Most detergent formulations contain fluorescent whiteners. It is also possible to purchase fluorescent whiteners—referred to as optical brighteners—for use in the home. Fluorescent whiteners absorb light in the visible wavelength range and reemit it in the ultraviolet range. As a result, fabrics treated with brighteners look bluer. These agents do not attach themselves to different fibers to the same degree, so their effectiveness may vary from fiber to fiber. Also, chlorine bleach may destroy the active ingredients in fluorescent whiteners, so that the two products should never be added to the laundry at the same time.

Before optical brighteners for household use were developed, white laundry could only be treated with *blueing*. Blueing is a laundry product available in liquid or powder form that is added to the rinse cycle. It contains small quantities of blue dye that masks yellow color by reflecting blue-white light. When using blueing, one must follow directions carefully. Too great a concentration of the dye may give white laundry a bluish tint, instead of just canceling out the yellow color.

Disinfectants

One of the purposes of laundering clothing and household items is to destroy bacteria. Ordinary laundering procedures using detergent and hot water will destroy many bacteria. Recent trends toward using cooler washing temperatures may have the effect of allowing more bacteria to survive, however, so that when there is illness or infection in a home, special care may be required to sanitize items being washed.

To be suitable for sanitizing laundry, a disinfectant should kill bacteria without injuring or discoloring fabrics. Furthermore, disinfectants should not leave a residue that is harmful to the user and they must be compatible with detergents. Four types of products meet these criteria:

1. *Liquid chlorine bleaches.* Labels should state that the bleach contains 5.25 percent of sodium hypochlorite.

2. *Quarternary disinfectants.* These are colorless and odorless compounds that are effective in hot, warm, or cold water. Such substances are available in drugstores, mass merchandisers, grocery stores, and from janitorial, hospital, or dairy supply houses.

3. *Pine oil disinfectants.* These products are effective in hot or warm water. They have a characteristic odor that does not remain after laundering. The label should state that the product contains at least 70 percent steam-distilled pine oil. Pine oil disinfectants are sold in supermarkets or grocery stores.

4. *Phenolic disinfectants.* Effective in warm or hot water, these products should be used according to directions on the package. Lysol® is the brand name of one of the better-known phenolic disinfectants.

Fabric Softeners

Fabric softeners deposit a waxy, lubricative substance on fibers that causes fabrics to feel softer. Fabric softeners used by consumers as laundry aids are based on quarternary ammonium compounds. Although different chemical compounds are used, all have a long fatty chain that imparts the soft feel to the fabric. The softening effect is especially desirable for fabric with a napped or pile surface that may become harsher after laundering, particularly if the fabrics are line dried rather than tumble dried. Towels, washable blankets, diapers, corduroy or other pile fabrics, and sweaters are often washed with fabric softeners.

In addition to making fabrics feel softer, fabric softeners cut down static electricity, make ironing easier, and improve the performance of durable press finishes, often making touch-up ironing unnecessary. At the same time, the continual use of fabric softeners causes a buildup of the softener on the fibers, thereby decreasing absorbency. On items where absorbency is an important function, such as towels or diapers, it is recommended that fabric softeners not be used in every wash but in alternate washings or periodically.

Fabric softeners are designed for addition to the wash, the rinse, or the drying cycle. Wash-added liquid fabric softeners should be added to the wash water *before* the detergent and the clothes are placed in the water to prevent fabric staining. These products can generally be used in the final rinse cycle as well.

Rinse-added fabric softeners cannot be used in the wash cycle, nor should they be used along with other laundry additives such as blueing or water softeners. These products and detergents may interfere or react adversely with the softener. They should be diluted, unless machine dispenser instructions state that this is not necessary, and they should not be poured directly onto fabrics as they may cause staining.

Dryer-added fabric softeners are added to a load of clothes in the dryer and are usually supplied in sheet form. Sheet-type softeners are impregnated into a nonwoven fabric or polyurethane foam sheet. The heat of the dryer and the tumbling action of the clothes cause the softener to be transferred to the clothes and spread evenly on the fabric surfaces.

Packages of fabric softeners provide specific instructions that should be followed carefully to achieve best results.

Starches

Starches are sizings that are added during home laundering. They help to restore body or stiffness to limp fabrics. Starches help to keep fabrics cleaner, because dirt tends to slide off the smooth finish produced by starching. Also, soil may become attached to the starching material rather than to the fiber, making the soil easier to remove.

Since vegetable starches were used originally for this purpose, the term *starch* was given to these products. Today, however, "starches" may be either vegetable or resinous compounds. Liquid or dry sizings are added in the rinse cycle of laundering. Aerosol sprays are added at the time of ironing. Vegetable starches must be renewed after each washing. Resins penetrate the fiber more thoroughly and will last through several washings.

Laundry Equipment

Washing Machines. Except for hand-laundered items, most laundry in the home is done in washing machines. Washing machines may be of three types: automatic, semiautomatic, and wringer style. Many households use automatic dryers. Each of these appliances differs in its construction, features, and operation. It is beyond the scope of this book to discuss the variety of types of laundry equipment in relation to the care of fabrics.

Although some fully automatic washers have programmed cycles that require only the selection of a suitable term, such as *permanent press*, it is more likely that the user will have to select water temperature, time duration for washing, and type of agitation. Most washers offer a low, moderate, or high water temperature; washing time durations of from 2 to 14 minutes; and either gentle or normal agitation. Washing machine instruction manuals give specific directions for selecting settings for varying types and loads of laundry. Of course, the user must select the detergent and other laundry additives such as bleach, water softener, fabric softener, and so on that are to be used in the wash. Table 24.1 offers typical time, speed of agitation, and water temperature for various fiber groups.

The expansion of the use of durable press finishes has led to the manufacture of washers and dryers that have permanent press cycles. These cycles are designed to produce optimum performance from durable press finishes by using varying water temperatures in washing and rinsing, by offering decreased agitator speeds in extracting water, and by ending the drying cycle with a cool temperature to avoid heat-setting wrinkles into dried clothing. During the extraction of the water in the spin cycle, clothes are compressed against the basket walls. If the fabric is warm, the cooling that takes place will cause the fabrics to wrinkle, whereas the cool water cycles of the special durable press cycle provide better wrinkle resistance. If the clothes are to be dried in an automatic dryer, these wrinkles will be tumbled out of the fabric. If clothes are to be line dried, however, durable press items should be removed from the washer before the final spin cycle.

TABLE 24.1
Washing Machine Settings for Various Fibers

Fiber	Cycle Time	Water Temperature	Agitation and Spin Speed
Wool	1–3 min	110°–120°F	Slow
Cotton and linen	10–12 min	120°–140°F	Normal
Manufactured and durable press	5–7 min	110°–120°F	Slow

Energy savings is an issue with many consumers. Since heating of water is energy intensive, detergents have been developed that are effective at lower temperatures. In addition newer front loading washing machines are available that use less water. These machines have a reversing tumbling action that provides agitation and pulls the water through the textile items for optimum cleaning. As mentioned earlier, low-sudsing detergents should be used with these washing machines.

Laundry Procedures

Although the washer and dryer do the physical work of laundering, the selection of appropriate laundry procedures is essential for efficient cleaning. Sorting, selecting washing time and water temperature, pretreating spots and stains, and carefully selecting laundry products for use all require that decisions be made by the person doing the washing.

Laundry should be sorted carefully according to color, fiber type, degree of soil, and delicacy of construction. Items requiring the same laundry products, water temperature, length of washing, and speed of agitation should be grouped together.

White items should be washed together. White permanent press and nylon fabrics are most prone to discoloration if washed with items of color and should be washed only with other whites. Colorfast items may be laundered together, even if the colors are not the same, but it is advisable to separate light and dark colors at least until it has been ascertained that the dark colors will not bleed. Items that are not colorfast should be washed separately; in some cases they may have to be washed by hand. The care labels on products often provide information that is helpful in sorting items.

Fabrics that produce lint, such as bath towels, chenille fabrics, terry cloth items, and the like, should be washed separately from those that attract lint; that is, corduroy, synthetic fabrics, and durable press. It is especially important to separate light-colored lint-producing fabrics from dark-colored lint attractors, such as dark nylon underclothing or socks.

Loads should, as much as possible, be balanced with some small and some larger items. This will provide better washing action. However, lightweight manufactured fiber items should be dried separately from heavy cellulosic fabrics, such as towels, because the manufactured fiber items will dry first and then become overheated during the time required for the heavier, cotton fabrics to dry.

Heavy items such as blankets or bedspreads may have to be washed alone because of their size. When a heavy load is put into a washer, it should be arranged carefully so that the washer balance is maintained during spin cycles. Most washing machines automatically shut off if the load becomes too unbalanced.

Heavily soiled items should not be washed with lightly soiled items, but alone. The lightly soiled items may pick up soil or discoloration from the wash water, and the heavily soiled fabrics may need a more rigorous wash cycle.

Before laundering, clothing should be checked carefully. Pockets should be emptied since coins or other items left in pockets can damage washers or dryers, and tissues left in pockets will produce lint that will be picked up by garments. Lint and dirt should be brushed out of pant cuffs. Zippers and hooks should be closed so that they do not catch onto other items and tear them. Pins, heavy ornaments, and buckles may also cause damage to fabrics and should be removed. Tears should be mended before laundering, as the agitation of washing and drying may cause them to be enlarged.

Some items may require pretreatment for optimum cleaning. Soil lines that are formed around collars and cuffs may be difficult to remove from synthetic and durable press fabrics. The area may be pretreated by dampening the area and then rubbing liquid detergent or a paste made of powdered detergent and water over the soiled area.

Stain Removal

Stains, which are specific substances spilled on a fabric as opposed to general soiling through use, should be treated as soon as possible. The longer a stain remains on an item, the harder it will be to remove.

In treating fabrics to remove stains, the first consideration must be the composition of the material that has been stained. Knowledge of fiber content may help to determine appropriate solvents. For example, attempting to remove a nail polish stain on an acetate fabric with nail polish remover that contains acetone would destroy the fabric. Once fiber content has been taken into consideration, then fabric structure must be evaluated. Rubbing hard on a stain on a pile fabric will flatten the pile. Rubbing may abrade the surface of a satin weave fabric.

Stain removal is easiest immediately after the fabrics have been subjected to staining. It is important to know the kind of material that caused the stain and the fiber of which the fabric is made. The selection of the method to use in removing the stain will be determined by the type of stain, and the type of stain remover to be used may be limited by the type of fabric.

Before any stain remover is used, the fabric should be tested to determine whether it is colorfast to the stain remover or whether it may have a finish that the stain remover will harm. Fabrics can be tested by sponging a small amount of stain remover onto a seam, hem, or other hidden part of the item. If a suitable stain remover cannot be found, the item should be taken to a professional dry cleaner for treatment.

Table 24.2 lists a wide variety of materials that may produce stains on fabrics and suggests appropriate treatments for fabrics that (1) are washable and (2) have fiber content and fabric structures that are compatible with the recommended treatment. Some stains cannot be removed. Extensive staining by hard-to-remove substances or stains on delicate and/or nonwashable fabrics are probably best removed by a professional dry cleaner who has a variety of spot- and stain-removing chemicals and an expert knowledge of stain removal. It is always helpful to the cleaner, however, if the customer points out the stain and identifies the staining substance.

Drying

Automatic dryers generally provide both time and temperature settings. Temperatures for drying may range from no heat to moderate and high temperatures. The drying time is determined by the size of the load and the weight of the fabrics being dried. Some dryers have an automatic moisture sensor that turns off the dryer when the wash is dry, whereas others will continue to tumble for the length of time set on the dial, even after the laundry is dry.

Fabrics that have been laundered may be either line dried or dried in an automatic dryer. Some fabrics should not be dried in dryers, because the heat and action of the dryer may cause some shrinkage in heat-sensitive fabrics. Elastics made with natural rubber may lose their elasticity over a period of time if dried in an extremely hot dryer. Care labels should be consulted to ascertain whether fabrics should be placed in a dryer.

Heat-sensitive fabrics, such as those made with olefin or acetate fibers, should be dried at low-heat or no-heat settings. Durable press and synthetic fabrics should be removed from the dryer immediately after completion of the drying cycle to prevent

TABLE 24.2
Stain Removal Chart

Stain	Treatment
Adhesive tape, chewing gum, rubber cement	Apply ice or cold water to harden surface; scrape with a dull knife. Saturate with cleaning fluid. Rinse; then launder.
Baby formula	Soak in a product containing enzymes for at least 30 minutes (several hours for aged stains). Launder.
Beverages (coffee, tea, soft drinks, wine, alcoholic beverages)	Sponge or soak stain in cool water. Then pretreat with prewash stain remover, liquid laundry detergent, liquid detergent booster, or paste of granular laundry product and water. Launder using chlorine bleach, if safe for fabric, or an oxygen bleach. Older stains may respond to soaking in a product containing enzymes, then laundering.
Blood	If stain is fresh, soak in cold water. For dried stains, soak in warm water with a product containing enzymes. Launder. If stain remains, rewash using a bleach safe for fabric.
Brown or yellow discoloration from iron, rust, manganese	Use a rust remover recommended for fabrics; launder. Do not use a chlorine bleach to remove rust stains because it may intensify discoloration. For a rusty water problem, use a nonprecipitating water softener in both wash and rinse water. For severe problems, install an iron filter in the system.
Candle wax	Scrape off surface wax with a dull knife. Place stain between clean paper towels and press with a warm iron. Replace paper towels frequently to absorb more wax and to avoid transferring stains. Place stain face down on clean paper towels. Sponge remaining stain with cleaning fluid; blot with paper towels. Let dry. Launder. If any color remains, rewash using a chlorine bleach, if safe for fabric, or an oxygen bleach.
Chocolate	Prewash with a product containing enzymes in warm water or treat with a prewash stain remover. Launder. If stain remains, rewash using a bleach safe for fabric.
Collar, cuff soil	Pretreat with prewash stain remover, liquid laundry detergent, or paste of granular detergent and water. Launder.
Cosmetics	Pretreat with prewash stain remover, liquid laundry detergent, paste of granular detergent, or laundry additive and water or rub with bar soap. Launder.
Crayon	For a few spots, treat same as candle wax. For a whole load of clothes, wash with hot water using a laundry soap and 1 cup baking soda. If color remains, launder using chlorine bleach, if safe for fabric. Otherwise, soak in a product containing enzymes or an oxygen bleach using hottest water safe for fabric, then launder.
Dairy products (milk, cream, ice cream, yogurt, sour cream, cream soups)	Treat as for baby formula. Soak in a product containing enzymes. Launder.
Deodorants, antiperspirants	Pretreat with liquid laundry detergent. Launder. For heavy stains, pretreat with prewash stain remover. Allow to stand 5 to 10 minutes. Launder using an oxygen bleach.
Dye transfer	You can attempt restoration of white fabrics that have picked up color from other fabrics by using a packaged color remover, following label directions. Launder. If dye remains, launder again using a chlorine bleach, if safe for fabric. For colored fabrics and whites that cannot be chlorine bleached, soak in oxygen bleach. Launder. This type of stain can be prevented if proper sorting and laundering procedures are followed.
Egg	Treat as for baby formula. Soak in a product containing enzymes. Launder.
Fabric softener	Dampen the stain and rub with bar soap. Rinse out, then launder.
Fruit, juices	Wash with bleach safe for fabric.
Grass	Soak in a product containing enzymes. If stain persists, launder using chlorine bleach, if safe for fabric, or oxygen bleach.
Grease, oil (car grease, butter, animal fats, salad dressings, cooking oils, motor oils)	Pretreat with prewash stain remover, liquid laundry detergent, or liquid detergent booster. For heavy stains, place stain face down on clean paper towels. Apply cleaning fluid to back of stain. Replace paper towels under stain frequently. Let dry, rinse. Launder using hottest water safe for fabric.

(continued)

TABLE 24.2
(continued)

Stain	Treatment
Ink	Some inks in each of the following categories—ballpoint, felt tip, and liquid— may be impossible to remove. Laundering may set some types of ink. Try a pre-treatment method using a prewash stain remover, denatured alcohol, or cleaning fluid.
	Use one of the following methods with denatured alcohol or cleaning fluid. First, sponge the area around the stain with the stain remover before applying it directly on the stain. Place stain face down on clean paper towels. Apply denatured alcohol or cleaning fluid to back of stain. Replace paper towels under the stain frequently. Rinse thoroughly. Launder.
	Another method is to place the stain over the mouth of a jar or glass and hold the fabric in a taut position. Drip the stain remover through the spot so that the ink will drop into the container as it is being removed. Rinse thoroughly. Launder.
Mildew	Badly mildewed fabrics may be damaged beyond repair. Launder stained items using chlorine bleach, if safe for fabric. Or soak in oxygen bleach and hot water; then launder.
Mud	When dry, brush off as much as possible. Pretreat with a paste of granular detergent and water, liquid laundry detergent, or a liquid detergent booster. Launder. For heavy stains, pretreat or presoak with a laundry detergent or a product containing enzymes. Launder.
Mustard	Pretreat with prewash stain remover. Launder using chlorine bleach, if safe for fabric.
Nail polish	May be impossible to remove. Try nail polish remover but do not use on acetate or triacetate fabrics. Place stain face down on clean paper towels. Apply nail polish remover to back of stain. Replace paper towels under stain frequently. Repeat until stain disappears, if it does. Rinse and launder.
Paint	**Water-based:** Rinse fabric in warm water while stains are still wet; then launder. Once paint is dry, it cannot be removed.
	Oil-based and varnish: Use the same solvent the label on the can advises for a thinner. If label is not available, use turpentine. Rinse. Pretreat with prewash stain remover, bar soap, or laundry detergent. Rinse and launder.
Perfume	Pretreat with prewash stain remover or liquid laundry detergent. Launder.
Perspiration	Use a prewash stain remover or rub with bar soap. If perspiration has changed the color of the fabric, apply ammonia to fresh stains, white vinegar to old stains and rinse. Launder using hottest water safe for fabric. Stubborn stains may respond to washing in a product containing enzymes or oxygen bleach in hottest water safe for fabric.
Pine resin	Sponge cleaning fluid into the stain; let dry. Mix liquid laundry detergent and ammonia; soak stain in the solution. Launder using liquid laundry detergent.
Scorch	Treat as for mildew. Launder using chlorine bleach, if safe for fabric. Or soak in oxygen bleach and hot water, then launder.
Shoe polish	**Liquid:** Pretreat with a paste of granular detergent and water; launder.
	Paste: Scrape residue from fabric with a dull knife. Pretreat with a prewash stain remover or cleaning fluid. Rinse. Rub detergent into dampened area. Launder using a chlorine bleach, if safe for fabric, or an oxygen bleach.
Tar	Scrape residue from fabric. Place stain face down on paper towels. Sponge with cleaning fluid. Replace paper towels frequently to absorb more tar and to avoid transferring stains. Launder in hottest water safe for fabric.
Tobacco	Dampen stain and rub with bar soap. Rinse. Soak in a product containing enzymes; then launder. If stain remains, launder again using chlorine bleach, if safe for fabric.
Typewriter correction fluid	Let stain dry thoroughly. Gently brush excess off with a clothes brush. Send to professional dry cleaner and mention the type of stain.
Urine, vomit, mucous, feces, or stool	Soak in a product containing enzymes. Launder using chlorine bleach, if safe for fabric, or use oxygen bleach.

Source: Reprinted courtesy of the Soap and Detergent Association.

the setting of wrinkles. These fabrics should not be line dried, because the wrinkles are not removed as they are in tumble drying.

Dryers in coin-operated laundromats often operate at much higher temperatures than home units. Synthetics that dry quickly and are thermoplastic sometimes melt when they come in contact with the sides of the hot dryer drum when these machines are used.

As in washing, fabrics of similar colors should be dried together. It is possible for colors to run from one fabric to another if damp, noncolorfast fabrics are placed on top of other fabrics during drying.

Pressing

Although many synthetic and durable press fabrics do not require pressing, other items will need touch-up pressing before use. Linens and cottons require the highest temperature settings, synthetics the lowest. Even though irons have temperature settings for different fabric types, the iron temperature should be tested in an inconspicuous part of the item, as thermostats of irons vary in accuracy.

Fabrics of absorbent fibers are best pressed when they are slightly damp or with steam, as wrinkles are removed more easily. Dark-colored fabrics of all fibers, silks, acetates, and rayons should be ironed from the wrong side to prevent shine. When these fabrics require pressing on the right side, press over a press cloth, not directly on the fabric.

Wool fabrics should be pressed with steam or a dampened press cloth. Silk should be pressed with a dry press cloth. Fabrics with textured surface should be tested carefully to see if ironing will flatten the surface. Sometimes these fabrics can be pressed lightly on the wrong side over a folded terry cloth towel or other soft surface. Corduroy can be pressed in this way, although it is better to use a special pressing board called a needle board. Velvets, velveteens, and plushes also require the use of a needle board. These fabrics may respond better to steaming (holding a steam iron or a "wrinkle remover" steamer several inches away), then hanging to dry to allow the wrinkles to hang out. The same effect may be achieved by hanging items in a bathroom that is warm and moist from a hot shower.

Commercial Laundering

Commercial laundering procedures are used by local dry cleaning establishments to clean washable items such as men's shirts or household linens. Commercial laundering procedures are similar to those used in the home, except that the conditions under which laundry is done commercially are more controlled and wash loads are considerably larger than in the home laundry. These large wash loads are made up of items from a number of different customers, so that identification numbers or tags must be affixed to each item for identification purposes.

The first step in the commercial laundering process is to sort the fabrics. Items are separated accordingly to color, fiber content, and degree of soil. As many as twelve different classifications can be used.

Different laundries utilize different detergent formulations and procedures, but, in general, bleachable items are subjected to several sudsings with soap or detergent and added alkali at temperatures of 125 to 160°F, a chlorine bleaching at 160°F for three to five minutes, three or four rinses at different temperatures, each one lower than the last, an acid sour, and blueing. In the rinse, starch is added for those items for which customers have requested it.

The purpose of the acid sour is to neutralize the alkalinity of the water, to remove iron stains, to kill bacteria, and to destroy excess or unused bleach. Some typical sours are acetic acid, sodium bisulfite, sodium acid fluoride, and oxalic acid.

Light-colored fabrics are washed at lower temperatures than are white fabrics, generally, 100 to 120°F, and no chlorine bleach is used. Dark-colored fabrics are laundered at still lower temperatures, 90 to 100°F, as they are more likely to lose color or bleed at higher temperatures. They, too, are not bleached.

After the final rinse, fabrics are spun in an extractor to remove excess water. The extraction may be done by the same machine that washes the items, or it may be done by a separate piece of equipment. This step is comparable to the spin-dry cycle on home washers. After extraction the fabrics are dried in a dryer and, if the customer wishes, pressed. Different types of pressing equipment are used for various items. Flat pieces are ironed on a machine called a *flatwork* ironer. A smooth, heated iron plate provides the heat and pressure, while the fabrics travel across a rotating, padded roll. Special equipment is made for ironing shirts, small pieces, and oversized items such as curtains.

Customers may send washable silk and wool garments to commercial laundries. These are handled in special machines and without the use of chlorine bleach. Neutral soaps and detergents are used without additional alkali, and the washing machine uses a gentle agitation. Three to five rinses are needed to remove all the soap and detergent, so that discoloration of the fabric does not take place. An acid sour is used. Extraction is done gently.

Dry Cleaning

The term *dry cleaning* derives from the use of special cleaning solvents that dry quickly. Washing of cloth has been the chief method of cleaning washable fabrics since before the beginning of recorded history. Dry cleaning is a relatively recent development, supposedly discovered in 1825 by a Frenchman, Jean Bapiste Jolly, who observed that a tablecloth over which the contents of a paraffin lamp were spilled lost its staining in the area of the spill. He recognized that he might be able to clean clothing using this solvent and established the first dry cleaning business. Benzene replaced paraffin as the solvent fairly early, but the technique was still a far cry from present-day dry cleaning processes. Originally, the entire garment was taken apart, and each piece was cleaned separately by dipping it into pans of benzene. The pieces were brushed on a scouring board, dipped again, dried in a warm oven, and ultimately reassembled.

Benzene was replaced by other solvents considered to be less hazardous. Perchloroethylene (known as perc) became the industry standard, but recently concern over the environmental effects of chlorocarbons has prompted a search for other alternatives. Candidate solvents being explored are petroleum spirits, that were used by dry cleaners before perc, and liquid carbon dioxide.

For both economic and environmental reasons, used dry cleaning solvents are not discarded; instead, they are recycled and reused. Solvents are purified, and accumulated soil is removed either by filtration or distillation. The continual use of dirty solvent will interfere with cleaning.

After cleaning, the garments are checked for spots or stains that have not been removed in the dry cleaning. Spotters are trained to handle different fabrics and stains as effectively as possible.

If dry cleaning and spotting have not been adequate to remove all soil, the garments may have to be wet cleaned. Wet cleaning is not laundering, but rather involves treating fabrics with small amounts of water to remove soil.

Final touches are given to the clean garment in the finishing department. Buttons or trimmings that have been removed are replaced, garments are steamed or, if necessary, pressed, and minor repairs are made.

STORAGE OF TEXTILE PRODUCTS

Between uses, textile items may be put away for either short or long periods of time. Some attention to the way in which clothing is stored may help to prolong the life of textile products.

Textile products will wear longer if given a chance to "rest" between uses. Rotating items in use, either clothing or household textiles, will provide this rest period. Storage practices may encourage this rotation. For example, towels or bed linens that have been laundered may be placed at the bottom of the stack of items, and the next item to be used taken from the top of the stack.

When table linens, bed linens, or other items are pressed, care should be taken to fold these items at different places. Continuous folding of fabrics, especially where sharp creases are pressed into the material, in the same place will cause the yarns to break or wear first in those spots. This is particularly the case for items made of linen and cotton that have low recovery from creasing and low resistance to edge abrasion.

Fabrics that are to be put away for long-term storage should always be put away clean. Moths or other insects and fungi will more readily attack soiled fabrics. Furthermore, some spots or stains that are only slightly evident may be oxidized. Oxidized stains darken and are exceedingly difficult to remove. Fabrics should not be put away with pins left in them, as the pins may rust and cause stains to appear around the pinned area.

Fabrics that are subject to attack by insects and mildew should be stored carefully. The resistance of specific fibers to microorganisms was discussed in the chapters dealing with each fiber. Wool and animal hair fabrics can be mothproofed before storage or stored in tightly closed containers with moth repellents. (See Figure 24.2.)

Fabrics that are susceptible to mildew should be stored clean and dry, in a dry place. The fairly widespread use of central or room air conditioning has decreased humidity in many buildings. Closed closets can hold humidity, so that leaving doors slightly ajar or using ventilated doors will help to prevent humidity buildup in closed areas.

If fabrics that are normally starched are to be stored for a long period of time, it is best to store them without starching, as silverfish find the starch especially appetizing. If starch is required later, garments can be spray starched before use. If starched garments are stored, they should be put away in a closed container that insects cannot penetrate.

Historic Costumes and Textiles

Historic costumes and/or textiles may be collected by museums, historical societies, and individuals. Once acquired, these materials are generally stored and may be displayed periodically. The general storage principles outlined earlier apply to historic materials, but given their age and fragility, additional cautions should be observed.

As in selection of any care procedure, the fiber from which the item is made must be considered. Historic fabrics are generally made from natural materials: cotton, linen, silk, or wool. The most important considerations in storing these materials is that they be stored away from light and in acid-free containers.

FIGURE 24.2

Areas that show up as light spots on this photograph are holes created by moth larvae.

Ordinary paper contains acid residues that may cause deterioration of fabrics. Special acid-free boxes and tissue paper are manufactured. The names of several firms that sell these supplies are listed at the end of this chapter in the section Sources of Storage Materials for Historic Textiles. Items should not be stored in plastic bags because these bags will deteriorate and release substances that may harm the fabrics, a phenomenon referred to as *off-gassing*. Ideally, temperature and humidity should be maintained at 70°F, 60 percent relative humidity.

As with other materials, it is best if historic fabrics are clean when stored; however, ordinary laundering and dry-cleaning processes may be too harsh for these materials. Some items made from cotton or linen can be laundered by hand if special precautions are taken. The Recommended Readings section at the end of this chapter includes several references in which specific instructions for laundering of historic textiles are given.

Wool and silk garments cannot be laundered. Nor should they be dry-cleaned except by an expert in historic conservation who has been trained to handle these materials. To remove loose dust and soil, silk and wool garments can be vacuumed using a small hand vacuum cleaner. Such items should be placed on a flat table for support. Synthetic netting should be placed between the item to be cleaned and the vacuum cleaner. Trimmings should be handled carefully to avoid damaging them. See Consumer Brief 24.1.

The names and addresses of organizations devoted to the study of historic textiles and costumes are listed at the end of this chapter, and a list of publications dealing with the care, preservation, and restoration of historic material is included in the bibliography in Appendix A.

CONSUMER BRIEF 24.1   Preserving Antique and Heirloom Textiles

Consumers may want to preserve such diverse items as a recently worn wedding dress, vintage clothing, or antique quilts and samplers. When handling textiles that you want to preserve, be sure you are working in a clean area, that your hands are clean, and that you are not wearing jewelry that will catch on delicate fabrics. Support fragile items so that no one place in the fabric must sustain the full weight of the fabric. It is generally a good idea to wear cotton gloves when working with historic textiles because the oil from your fingers can be transferred to the fabric.

Do not allow newsprint, gummed tape, wood, or iron to remain in contact with objects during storage or display. If objects are to be displayed, use only acid-free backing materials, use no glue or adhesives, minimize exposure to light, rotate pieces, and display behind glass that filters out ultraviolet light.

The following are some common problems encountered in long-term preservation of both old and new textiles and the recommended means of preventing or solving those problems.

Problem	Solution
Loss of strength	Store away from the light, preferably in acid-free materials or wrapped in clean, undyed cotton fabrics. Weighted silks dating from the late nineteenth century up to the 1920s are likely to break apart. Nothing can be done to prevent this, nor can damaged fabrics be repaired.
Color changes	White silk and wool will usually yellow over time; this cannot be prevented. Acetate may be subject to fume fading. Store so that items are not exposed to atmospheric gases.
Development of stains	Put items away clean so that spills that may not show at the time of last usage during storage do not oxidize and appear later. To avoid rust spots, be sure no pins are left in items, and wrap metal zippers, hooks, snaps, and buttons so that they will not touch the fabric.
Damage from moths or carpet beetles	Put away clean. Store in closed container with moth repellent, or if odor from moth repellent is a problem, store for a week in an airtight container with moth insecticide, remove, put away, and monitor material for signs of insect activity.
Damage from mildew	Store only in dry, well-ventilated area. Do not wrap in plastic.
Development of cracks or breaks at folds	If possible, roll large items around a cardboard tube or dowel covered with acid-free paper. Multicomponent or pile fabrics should not be rolled, however, because the inner layer will wrinkle. Cover items with clean, undyed cotton fabric. If items must be folded, pad folds with acid-free tissue, and change the position of the folds periodically.
Yellowing of starched cottons and linens	Put items away unstarched. Starch also makes cotton and linen materials appetizing to silverfish.
Mysterious holes in vintage garments of the 1940s and 1950s	Nitrocellulose plastics used in buttons can decompose and, if garments are stored where there is no air circulation, release nitric acid fumes that damage or discolor the fabric. If items are believed to have buttons of this type, remove before the item is stored.

PERMANENT CARE LABELING

In 1972 the FTC published a Permanent-Care Labeling Ruling which specifies that wearing apparel and fabrics sold by the yard must carry a permanently affixed label giving instructions for the care of the item. The provisions of the ruling are detailed in the following section.

Labeling Requirements

All textile wearing apparel and piece goods sold for making apparel are subject to the legislation except shoes, gloves, hats, and items not "used to cover and protect the body," such as belts, neckties, handkerchiefs, and suspenders. Nonwoven, one-time use garments are also excluded, as are manufacturers' fabric remnants up to 10 yards in length when the fiber content is not known and cannot easily be determined, and trim up to 5 inches wide. These provisions apply whether the items were manufactured in the United States or abroad.

Manufacturers are required to provide full care instructions about regular care or to provide warnings if a garment cannot be cleaned without harm. Care labels are attached to finished garments before they are sold. These labels must remain legible throughout the useful life of the garment. Piece goods information is to be provided on the end of each roll or bolt. Consumers, therefore, need to make note of care procedures themselves when purchasing piece goods, as copies of instructions are not provided.

Labels must be placed so that they can be seen or easily found by consumers at the point of sale. If packaging obscures the label, additional information should appear on the outside of the package or on a hang tag fastened to the product.

Some types of products, however, need not include any care instructions. These are products sold to institutional buyers for commercial use, such as employee uniforms that are purchased by and cared for by a hospital, garments custom made from fabric provided by the customer, and completely washable items sold at retail for $3.00 or less.

Some other products need not have permanently affixed labels but have to be provided with temporary labels. Totally reversible clothing without pockets and those products granted exemptions because a label would harm their appearance or usefulness are cited in the rule, although special permission for items in the latter category must be obtained through petition. Products that may be washed, bleached, dried, ironed, or dry-cleaned by the harshest procedures available are also exempt, provided that the instruction "Wash or Dry Clean, Any Normal Method" appears on a temporary label that is conspicuous at the point of sale.

The directions to manufacturers as to the contents of the care label make the following stipulations. The label must have either a washing or dry cleaning instruction. If a product can be both washed and dry-cleaned, it need carry only one of these instructions. If it can be neither washed nor dry-cleaned, the label must say "Do Not Wash—Do Not Dry Clean." The rule included a glossary of terms to be used when applicable.

If a garment is labeled as washable, the label must say whether the product should be washed by hand or machine, and if regular use of hot water will harm the product, a water temperature must be stated. For example, a label that says "Machine Wash, Cold" means that the consumer can machine wash the garment but only in cold water. A label that says "Machine Wash" means that any temperature ranging from cold to hot could be used. The word "wash" cannot be used alone but must stipulate whether the item should be machine or hand washed.

If all commercially available bleaches can be used on a regular basis, the label need not mention bleach. If chlorine bleach would harm the garment, but nonchlorine bleach would not, the label should say "Only Nonchlorine Bleach When Needed." If all commercially available bleaches would harm the product, the label should say "No Bleach" or "Do Not Bleach."

The appropriate drying method must be stipulated, and if regular use of high temperature would be harmful, the appropriate temperature setting must be given. "Machine Wash, Tumble Dry" would indicate that there are no restrictions of washing or drying temperatures.

Ironing information is to be given if ironing will be needed on a regular basis. As in washing and drying instructions, ironing temperature should be stipulated unless a hot iron can be used without harm.

The rule also requires that consumers be warned against processes that they might be expected to use that would harm the product. For example, if ironing would be harmful to a garment that consumers might touch up occasionally, the label should read "Do Not Iron." If an item is not colorfast, it must be labeled "Wash Separately" or "Wash with Like Colors." It is not necessary to warn users about alternate procedures that may be harmful to the item. For example, if instructions say "Dry Flat," it is not required that labels also say "Do Not Tumble Dry."

For items labeled as dry cleanable, other provisions apply. If all commercially available types of solvents can be used, the label need not mention any type of solvent. If one or more solvents would harm the product, a solvent that is safe to use must be mentioned. If any part of the dry cleaning process will harm the garment, the label must warn "Do Not . . ." or "No . . ." or provide other wording that would clarify appropriate procedures. For example, "Professionally Dry Clean, No Steam" would indicate that no steam should be used in pressing or finishing the garment. If the words "Dry Clean" are used without the word "Professionally" in front of it, the item should be dry cleanable by any machine process with no restrictions on solvents, moisture content, heat, and steam. "Professionally Dry Clean" is used when the normal dry cleaning process must be modified in some way. This term is not used alone but must be followed by a description of the modifications that are needed. For example "Professionally Dry Clean, Short Cycle, No Steam" would mean that any commercially available solvent could be used, the cleaning time should be reduced, and steam should not be used during pressing or finishing (FTC 1984).

The problems that can result from an improper care label are illustrated in Figure 24.3 and Consumer Brief 24.2.

International Care Symbols

As international trade in textiles has increased, the need for globally consistent care labels has been recognized. The International Organization for Standardization, working with national organizations in various countries, developed a set of textile care symbols that could be used by consumers worldwide.

There are five basic symbols: a washtub, a triangle to represent bleaching, a square for drying methods, an iron, and a circle for dry cleaning recommendations. Temperatures and other conditions are printed below the symbols. An X through a symbol designates a prohibition against that method. (See Figure 24.4.)

a

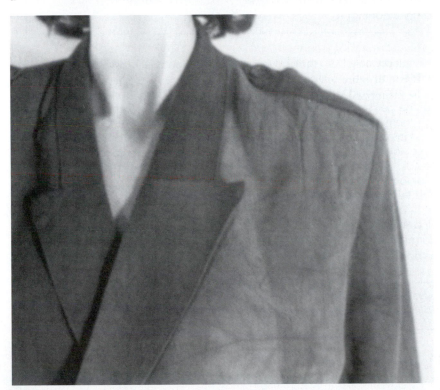

b

FIGURE 24.3

Garments with faulty care labels: (a) Garment with "Dry clean only" label has white surface dots that were not resistant to dry-cleaning solvent. The solvent caused them to dissolve and transfer to other portions of the garment. (b) Dry cleaning is recommended on care label; however, after the garment was dry-cleaned, one sleeve and one side of the front showed severe color loss. The manufacturer apparently used two different bolts of fabric in the one garment, and one bolt was colored with dye that was not fast to dry cleaning. It is the manufacturer's responsibility to ascertain that garments can be handled according to care labels. Photographs courtesy of the International Fabricare Institute.

| CONSUMER BRIEF 24.2 | The Dress That Can't Be Cared For |

This is the story of a white dress with blue sequins that had two distinct care labels. The story was originally reported in *Clothes Care Gazette*, November 1991.

These two care labels were attached to the same sequined dress.

> DRY CLEAN ONLY
> REMOVE SEQ TRIM

USE A PROFESSIONAL DRY CLEANER ONLY
INSTRUCT CLEANER TO USE SHORT CYCLES—5 MINUTES
INSTRUCT CLEANER TO USE PURE PERCHLORETHYLENE ONLY
INSTRUCT CLEANER TO USE MAXIMUM 120F IN DRYCLEANING PROCESS
INSTRUCT CLEANER NOT TO PRESS OR STEAM GARMENT
Do NOT allow perfume, deodorant, hair spray, or alcoholic beverages to come into contact with sequins.
  If garment should become dampened with perspiration or water:
  1. Do NOT place garment in airtight container or plastic bag.
  2. Dry garment in air. Do NOT use heat.
  3. Be certain garment is dry before dry cleaning.

The smaller care label recommends dry clean only, **remove sequin trim**. This is impossible. The many sequins on the article are actually sewn to it. It would be impossible for anyone to remove the sequins, clean the garment, and then reattach them. Obviously, this label was not intended for a garment of this type. Furthermore, the larger care label has other problems in that it recommends the dry cleaner use perchloroethylene only. Unfortunately, perchloroethylene dissolved the dye on the sequins almost immediately and this caused many of the blue sequins to turn white after cleaning. In addition to this, the instructions suggest the garment should be dried in the air, which is against all regulations that govern the professional dry cleaner using perchloroethylene.

In this case, the dry cleaner cleaned it in a short, two-minute cycle, which is in line with the care label, only to experience drastic loss of color on some of the blue sequins. Additional colorfastness tests indicated the sequin trim would be colorfast to a washing procedure, but the extensive finishing details on the article would not withstand a washing process. This garment is fabricated in such a way that it cannot be successfully dry cleaned or washed—certainly not according to the care instructions given on either label.

Source: Reprinted by permission of International Fabricare Institute. "The Dress That Can't Be Cared For," November 1991. Copyright © 1991 by IFI, all rights reserved.

FURTHER SOURCES OF INFORMATION

Many organizations publish booklets or pamphlets that offer information to the consumer about the care of textile products. Soap and detergent manufacturers and consumer magazines frequently publish materials that instruct the consumer in the appropriate care techniques for textiles of all kinds.

FIGURE 24.4

Symbols to be used on care labels. Courtesy of Soap and Detergent Association.

a

b

Consumers who wish to obtain further information about textile cleaning, storage, and maintenance can often find current information on these subjects from the Department of Agriculture and from state or local Cooperative Extension Offices. Lists of publications of the U.S. Department of Agriculture can be obtained from the U.S. Government Printing Office, Washington, DC 20402. Most of these materials are published as "Home and Garden Bulletins." Lists of state extension publications are generally available from the land-grant college in each state.

Manufacturers of detergents and other laundry products also write and distribute a variety of informational materials for consumers and professionals. The Soap and Detergent Association holds symposia for its members and others at which new developments are examined. The proceedings of these meetings are published and can be obtained by those who are unable to attend meetings. The International Fabricare Institute, an organization that does research and supplies current information to dry-cleaning establishments, publishes newsletters and fact sheets about dry-cleaning practices and problems. These materials can be obtained by purchasing a membership in the institute for a reasonable fee.

References

FTC. 1984. *Writing a care label* (pamphlet). Washington, D.C.: Bureau of Consumer Protection, Federal Trade Commission.

Lumley, A. C., and B. M. Gatewood. 1998. Effectiveness of selected laundry disks in removing soil and stains from cotton and polyester. *Textile Chemist and Colorist* 30 (12): 31.

Review Questions

1. Describe the purpose of each of the following substances during laundering of soiled textiles, and explain how each substance accomplishes its purpose.

detergents	bleaches
fluorescent whiteners	builders
water softeners	enzymes
fabric softeners	

2. Explain why it is desirable to have a cool rinse as the final cycle in laundering durable press garments.
3. Make a list of dos and don'ts that you would give to consumers if you were assigned to advise them about laundering procedures.
4. Make a list of dos and don'ts that you would give to consumers if you were assigned to advise them about having clothing dry-cleaned.
5. Develop five generalizations about stain removal procedures that you can derive from Table 24.2.
6. Based on what you have learned about the properties of textile fibers and fabric constructions, develop care labels with symbols that meet permanent-care labeling requirements for each of the following imaginary textile products. Explain why you chose these care procedures.
   a. Plain weave 100 percent cotton shirt dyed dark navy blue, with no functional finishes
   b. White 100 percent silk chiffon blouse with white silk embroidered decoration
   c. Jersey knit sweater of 100 percent acrylic fiber

Recommended Readings

Bevan, G. 1979. Mechanism of soiling of textiles. *Textiles* 8 (October): 69.

Drycleaning. 1994. *Textiles Magazine* 23 (2): 11.

Harvey, E. 1993. Handling antique items. *International Fabricare Institute Bulletin* (July).

Keesee, S. H. 1998. EPA's garment and textile care program: An eye to the future. *Textile Chemist and Colorist* 30 (11): 9.

Lusk, C. B. 1975. The invisible danger of visible light. *Museum News* (April): 22.

Making your clothing last—a practical guide. 1994. *Clothes Care Gazette* no. 86 (September): 1.

McCall, R. E., F. M. A. Patel, G. Mock, and P. L. Grady. 1998. Solvent and ultrasonic alternatives to perchloroethylene drycleaning of textiles. *Textile Chemist and Colorist* 30 (11): 11.

Pullen, J. A. 1997. Decoding the ASTM care symbol system. *Textile Chemist and Colorist* 29 (12): 28.

Soap and Detergent Association. *A handbook of industry terms.* 1987. New York: Soap and Detergent Association.

Wedding gowns: Preserving your memories. 1999. *Clothes Care Gazette* 142 (June): 1.

Sources of Storage Supplies for Historic Textiles

Conservation Materials Ltd., 1395 Greg Street, Suite #110, Sparks, NV 89431

Conservation Resources International, 8000-H Forbes Place, Springfield, VA 22151

Talas, 213 West 35th Street, New York, NY 10001

University Products, P.O. Box 101, Holyoke, MA 01041

Organizations that Study Historic Costumes and Textiles

Costume Society of America, 55 Edgewater Drive, P.O. Box 75, Earleville, MD 21919

The Textile Conservation Group, c/o Department of Anthropology, American Museum of Natural History, Central Park West at 79th Street, New York, NY 10024-5192

Textile Society of America, c/o 4401 San Andreas Ave., Los Angeles, CA 90065

TEXTILES AND THE ENVIRONMENT, HEALTH, AND SAFETY

Growing awareness of the relationship between individual, business, and industry practices and a healthy and safe environment for consumers and workers has led to concerns about the ecological impact of textile use, production, and processing. As a result, some consumers purchase products they believe are environmentally friendly, have changed their practices in caring for textile products, or engage in recycling. Other environmental, health, and safety problems may be less obvious to the general consumer but have important economic implications for the textile industry.

LEGISLATION AND REGULATION

The generation of air, water, and soil pollution and health hazards for textile workers and consumers has led governmental bodies to enact laws and regulations that are intended to protect individuals and the environment. A number of those laws have a significant impact on textile product manufacturing and use. Of particular importance to the textile industry in the United States are the Occupational Safety and Health Act (OSHA), which regulates the safety of the workplace, the Toxic Substances Control Act (TSCA), which regulates the management of toxic substances within the workplace, and licensing requirements and pollution limits imposed by the Environmental Protection Agency (EPA) under the Clean Water Act and the Clean Air Act.

The Clean Water Act regulates the discharge of pollutants into waterways and authorizes EPA to set water quality standards. Discharge of materials into waterways is also controlled under the Safe Drinking Water Act. The Clean Air Act was passed to control air emissions through National Ambient Air Quality Standards. The 1990 amendments to this act addressed specific problems such as acid rain and ozone depletion. The Resource Conservation and Recovery Act regulates the production, transportation, storage, and disposal of hazardous wastes.

The Pollution Prevention Act of 1990 signaled a trend toward source prevention rather than regulation diminishing the downstream problems of remediation and disposal. It requires that businesses submit source reduction and recycling reports each year. The various federal laws relevant to the environment are listed in Table 25.1.

Many states have also enacted environmental legislation that affects textile industries. While these laws have improved the safety of textile production and have helped to protect the environment, they have also had an impact on industry productivity, profitability, and competitiveness with imported products from countries

TABLE 25.1
Environmental and Safety Legislation

Title	Date	Purpose
Occupational Safety and Health Act	1970	Ensure workplace safety
Federal Water Pollution Control Act	1972	Regulate discharge of pollutants into waterways
Clean Air Act	1970	Establish air quality standards
Resource Conservation and Recovery Act	1976	Control hazardous waste from generation to disposal
Toxic Substances Control Act	1976	Control hazardous substances before they are produced and sold
Clean Water Act	1977	Control discharge of toxic pollutants into waterways[a]
Pollution Prevention Act	1990	Reduce generation of pollution at source

[a]Amendment to Federal Water Pollution Control Act

that do not have comparable environmental legislation. It should also be noted that although the textile industry contributes to environmental pollution, it is not on the list of major polluters targeted by the federal government.

ENVIRONMENTALLY IMPROVED TEXTILE PRODUCTS

Consumers with a strong commitment to protecting the environment are ecologically conscious shoppers. They look for products manufactured in ways that do not harm the environment and products that will save natural resources during or after use. The textile industry has responded by publicizing those products that are environmentally friendly and designating them as *environmentally improved textile products* (EITP). Examples include the new regenerated cellulosic fiber lyocell, organically grown cotton, naturally colored cotton, naturally dyed fabrics, and recycled textiles.

Organic cotton, which is grown without the use of pesticides, is increasing as a proportion of cotton production in the United States. Consumers pay a higher price for organic cotton, but cost should be reduced if demand increases. Organic wool is also seeing some usage. The wool is subjected to processes that are less harsh and the waste from scouring and milling is decreased.

Concerns about use of synthetic dyes have led to consumer interest in purchasing products dyed with natural dyes. Natural dyes from plants, insects, and minerals are being used in modern mills to color fabrics. The consistency of the dye lots is lower than with synthetic dye processes, and the fabrics are not as colorfast; however, the response of environmentally conscious consumers to the products has been extremely good. Undyed fabrics are also considered to be environmentally improved products.

It is not just the manufacture of textile products that affects the environment. Studies have shown that most of the environmental impact from textile products occurs during their use (Ecolabelling 1994). Energy and water are consumed in caring for textile products and pollution may be produced by laundering and dry cleaning.

Some apparel manufacturers and retailers help to support the environmental efforts of manufacturers by purchasing fabrics from companies that emphasize waste reduction. According to David Mention, manager of process improvement at L. L. Bean, "When we rate our suppliers, environmental soundness is right there with quality goods, timely delivery, innovations, and the soundness of their business. . . ." (Maycumber 1994, 2).

Marketing EITP

Marketing to environmentally conscious consumers may result in *ecolabeling* of products. One such scheme is the labeling by member countries of the European Union (EU) of textile products according to the environmental impact of their manufacture as well as their use and ultimate disposition. Biodegradability and recycling of components in a textile product are areas of significant research and development, and as advances are made, the economic viability of these processes increases. The company Patagonia®, Inc. uses key symbols to label their products as recycled or made with organically grown cotton. (See Figure 25.1.)

The Federal Trade Commission, working with EPA, has developed some guidelines for marketers to avoid claims that are erroneous or can be misleading to consumers (FTC 1999). Labeling should include specific information rather than general claims such as "Environmentally safe." If organically produced fibers or natural dyes

FIGURE 25.1

Examples of promotion of environmentally improved textile products by Patagonia®, retailer of active sportswear. (a) Key that is printed in their catalog. (b) and (c) Examples of how the key is used within the catalog. Photographs courtesy of Patagonia®, Inc.

indicates products made from post-consumer recycled soda bottles.

ORGANIC COTTON indicates products made from organic cotton.

a

PRINT BIG ZIP

The Minnehaha print takes its name from Longfellow's poem and its design from Navajo "eye dazzler" rugs. Deep Under proves that fleece can go tropical. Both prints adapt nicely to the jumbo comfort of this Lightweight Synchilla® pullover. Reflective collar for safety; handwarmer pockets hide cordlock for the adjustable hem. Oversized fit. Made in USA. **[ID]**

b

To Order
1-800-

ORGANIC COTTON **SUMMER SHADE**

A classic baseball cap style with appealing features: a shady, shapeable bill, a web buckle for fit and a soft, comfortable inner sweatband. Made in organic cotton with a choice of twill, canvas or dobby cord. Machine wash. Made in USA.

c

were used, this could be emphasized. The terms *recyclable* and *biodegradable* should be used cautiously in consumer labeling. A technically biodegradable material may nevertheless remain intact in a landfill for many years.

ENVIRONMENTAL MANAGEMENT

The commitment of major retailers such as L. L. Bean emphasizes that environmental awareness has become an important factor in manufacturing. Not only manufactured fibers but also natural fibers create pollutants, as in the scouring of wool and in many of the dyeing and finishing operations. The concern with industrial pollution of air, soil, and water has focused attention on by-products of textile manufacture. Textile companies must comply with federal, state, and regional standards for air, water, and hazardous solid waste, and, if they are to be leaders, must be proactive in developing and adopting environmentally responsible operations. There are challenges in reducing pollution in textile wet processing and in decreasing energy consumption in the industry. Again the preferred method for dealing with environmental problems downstream is source reduction at earlier stages of manufacturing.

The legal requirements for meeting clean water standards imposed by local, state, or national governments have led the textile industry to look for means of waste disposal that do not pollute streams. Recycling of water or other processing materials (such as sizing), treating the water in special wastewater treatment facilities to render it safe or remove pollutants, and using biodegradable substances are techniques used by manufacturers to maintain clean water. Difficulties encountered in meeting clean water requirements have led some textile companies to discontinue the manufacture of some products, such as rayon. (See chapter 6.)

ISO 14000

Meeting pollution standards and production of EITP require industrial firms to analyze and control all the steps in their manufacturing processes. The International Organization for Standardization (ISO) has developed a system, *ISO 14000*, that provides guidance in this area, not just for textiles but for all types of manufacturing. Analogous to the ISO 9000 standards for quality control (see chapter 1), these environmental standards, if adhered to, can allow producers who are compliant to become certified by the ISO for adherence to ISO 14000 standards.

To be certified (Shaver 1999) companies must:

1. articulate an environmental policy.
2. develop a plan that includes objectives and targets for reducing environmental hazards.
3. implement the plan and provide documentation that objectives are met.
4. monitor operations and institute corrective actions when appropriate.
5. review operations and modify the plan when needed.

The plan and implementation are reviewed and monitored by a third party before certification is granted.

The American Textile Manufacturers Institute (ATMI) launched its Encouraging Environmental Excellence (E3) campaign in 1992 to promote environmental awareness and good practice in the industry. Member companies pledge to adhere to a ten-point plan of action that includes performing environmental audits, developing spill prevention and control plans, conducting employee training in environmental practices, distributing recycling bins, and providing environmental expertise to cities and towns. Companies are working together to minimize waste in manufacturing processes and with suppliers to reduce the waste coming into plants.

THE PRODUCT LIFE CYCLE

Much of the environmental impact of a textile (or any other) product is determined at the design stage by the materials and processes selected (Heeley and Press 1997). Whether the area of concern is manufacturing processes that contribute to pollution or problems in waste disposal, the journey and fate of textile products are affected by initial decisions made by those involved in the design and development of products. Judgments should be based on accurate information and sound knowledge of the principles and costs of textile materials and processing. Environmental impact should be weighed against cost and other environmental effects. (See Figure 25.2.)

Material Selection

Selecting the fabric for a textile product requires understanding of the interrelations among fiber, yarn, and fabric processing. The ultimate price and the target market for

FIGURE 25.2

The product life cycle concept.
Courtesy Textiles Magazine.
Heely, J. and M. Press. 1997.
Design and the Environment,
Textiles Magazine (1): 22.

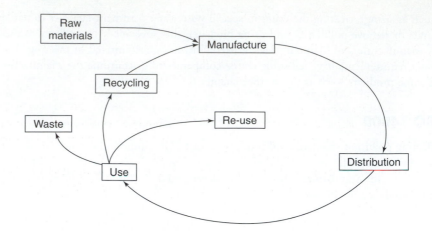

the product must be taken into account. As noted earlier, producers and retailers can market to the growing numbers of environmentally conscious consumers.

Many consumers who are concerned about the environment believe that a return to the use of larger quantities of natural fibers will have a positive effect on the environment. The issue, however, is more complex than it appears. There are not enough natural fibers to supply the demands of consumers from all over the world. Furthermore, natural fibers also require energy for their production and processing, so that these fibers are not "energy free." Many fertilizers are made from petrochemicals, and tractors and other farm machinery are run on petroleum fuels.

Organically grown or colored cotton may seem an obvious choice in designing an environmentally improved cotton fabric. Organic cottons are, however, more expensive because crops are more susceptible to insect damage than are those treated with pesticides. The yield per acre is less and harvesting is less standard. Naturally colored cotton offers an appealing alternative to expensive dyeing processes with synthetic dyes. Some colored cottons are, however, weaker and more difficult to spin into yarns.

Manufactured fibers are often cheaper than natural fibers, but synthetic materials are not as easily biodegraded. On the other hand, manufactured fibers are produced in filaments that can be easily formed into yarns, eliminating the costly steps in spinning staple yarns.

Decisions on dyeing and finishing processes must be made. Bleaching, which requires water, heat, and waste treatment, can be eliminated for a natural look for cotton, wool, or linen fabrics. Inclusion of a durable press or soil-resistant finish can decrease some of the costs involved in caring for the textile product during use.

Processing

The greatest environmental problems in textile processing occur at the dyeing and finishing stages because these steps require using chemicals and large quantities of water. Dyes that are not exhausted onto fibers can be discharged into waterways and residuals from preparation and finishing can also be found in industrial effluents. In addition, heat causes the vaporization of organic compounds used in such finishes as durable press or coating of fabrics. They are carried off as airborne gases, and must be controlled to reduce air pollution. Companies signing on to the ISO 14000 standards attempt to prevent pollution and also save money by process modifications.

The component materials selected for a textile product, and specifications for the final product, determine to a great extent the dyeing and finishing processes downstream. There may also be trade-offs in performance level and pollution reduction. In striving for good environmental management, processors continue to modify their operations to effect point source reduction of pollutants.

An example that illustrates these challenges is dyeing of cellulosic fabrics with reactive dyes. Reactive dyes are a good choice for cellulosic fabrics because of their excellent colorfastness and wide range of colors. Achieving good exhaustion of reactive dyes, however, requires large amounts of a salt, usually sodium sulfate, which ends up in the plant waste stream (Schlaeppi 1998). A new reactive dye for cellulose has been developed that dyes fabric well with significantly less salt added to the dyebath. This presents an opportunity to reduce the amount of sulfate discharged. (See chapter 20, pages 418–419.)

Cotton/polyester blends are popular fabrics for both apparel and household linens. Dyeing them requires essentially two processes with different dyes for each fiber. Cotton is traditionally dyed in a batch process and polyester in a continuous operation using disperse dyes. A number of variations of this model have been used to decrease the steps and separate washings of the fabric. They include washing off the unattached dye on a beam rather than in a beck and bleaching after dyeing rather than before. Any step eliminated saves money and benefits the environment. Bleaching after dyeing, however, could not be done on fabrics that require extremely bright colors.

Dyebath reuse, in which the dye liquor is replenished with dye and the same bath used for another run of fabric, has been highly successful in dyeing carpets. Since carpets are large pieces of fabric, with a high weight of fibers, dyeing processes require significant volumes of water. Recycling dyebaths can reduce the dyehouse effluent. To maintain good quality in the dyeing, the bath should be filtered between runs to remove loose fibers and spin finishes from the fibers.

As with much of the chemical industry, computer process control of operations not only saves labor costs, but also ensures precise measurement of ingredients to prevent waste of costly chemicals. Recovery and reuse of chemicals is a good approach as well. Of course selection of dye, fabric, and auxiliaries to promote high exhaustion leaves less dye to be recovered. (See chapter 20, page 414.)

Energy use is another area of concern. Conservation efforts in the textile industry were spurred by disruption of oil supplies in the 1970s. Not only are petroleum and petroleum by-products the single most important raw material used in the manufacture of synthetic fibers, but fuel for energy is also a major cost in the production of fibers, yarns, fabrics, and finishing materials. Dyeing and finishing are aspects of the manufacture of textiles that are especially energy intensive. Low-wet-pickup finishing processes, microwave and infrared drying, and use of dyes that are effective at lower temperatures are all energy-saving innovations that have been adopted. The development of combined desizing, scouring, and bleaching processes for cotton-containing fabrics has also contributed to more efficient processing of textiles.

Laundering and Dry Cleaning

Consumers, as they care for textile products, should be aware of the energy demands and potential pollution problems inherent in laundering and dry cleaning. Washable fabrics are preferable because of the cost of dry cleaning and the hazards of the solvents used. Washing, drying, and ironing, however, all require the expenditure of energy. One study reported that fiber production accounted for less than 15 percent of the total energy required for production and manufacture of a garment, whereas care of the garment after purchase accounted for 55 to 80 percent (Van Winkle et al. 1978). The selection of fabrics that require shorter drying time or can be line dried, as well as those that can be washed in cooler water or do not require ironing, has the end result of costing the consumer less money because less energy will be used in their care.

Home laundry equipment manufacturers are seeking to design more energy-efficient products. High-efficiency front-loading machines are being promoted. (See chapter 24.) These machines consume less water and energy than top-loading machines with oscillating agitators currently used in most washers.

Concern over the use of phosphates in laundry detergents to enhance detergent performance led to their replacement by other compounds. (See chapter 24 for a discussion of the role of builders in laundry detergents.) Although phosphates posed no problem to human health, they promoted growth of algae and depletion of oxygen (eutrophication), thereby changing the ecosystems in rivers, lakes, and bays.

Detergent manufacturers are also producing a wide range of detergents that are more biodegradable; that is, substances that decompose more rapidly during sewage treatment. Like manufacturers of other products, they are packaging detergents and other laundry aids in recycled cardboard boxes and refillable bottles.

Dry cleaning can also be a source of pollution. There is environmental concern over the chlorinated hydrocarbons used in dry cleaning. Dry cleaners routinely recycle cleaning fluid so that its disposal will not be a problem. Dry cleaners deliver clean clothing to customers on hangers inside plastic bags. Some cleaners encourage customers to return hangers and collect the plastic bags for recycling. Dry cleaners may provide regular customers with reusable cloth bags for delivery and return of laundry.

An increased consumer emphasis on durability may also contribute to a reduction of energy needs. If textile items are used longer, they will have to be replaced less often, thereby reducing the amount of raw materials needed. Longer use before disposal will also decrease the problem of disposal of used textiles. Conversely, though, the most durable fabrics are generally made with synthetic fibers that do eventually pose a waste disposal challenge. Fashion, however, is such an important aspect in the apparel industry that many items are discarded before they are outworn. Consumers may find it useful to identify certain of their purchases as "fashion" items in which durability may not be so important as it is in "classic" or other items that do not go out of style quickly.

Waste Disposal

When textile products are no longer considered serviceable, they are discarded or disposed of in some way. The manner of disposal of these products should also be a factor in design and product development. Fortunately this area is one that has received much attention by industry, researchers, and consumers, and also offers considerable flexibility in determining approaches. Landfilling, incineration, reuse, and recycling are all options available.

Solid waste materials that require disposal are many and varied. Some waste products from fiber synthesis and spinning, finishing, and dyeing may be contaminated with toxic chemicals. Not only yarn and fabric scraps but also storage, packing, and shipping materials add to the solid waste stream.

The volume of discarded textiles has increased greatly. Disposable nonwovens used in medical institutions and disposable diapers and wipes have increased significantly during the past decades. Interior furnishing fabrics, usually large pieces such as carpeting, have presented particular disposal problems. Figure 25.3 gives a quick overview of the sources of solid textile waste from manufacturers and consumers.

FIGURE 25.3

Typical flow of textile fibers in process and the resulting generation of textile waste at each step of production and consumption.

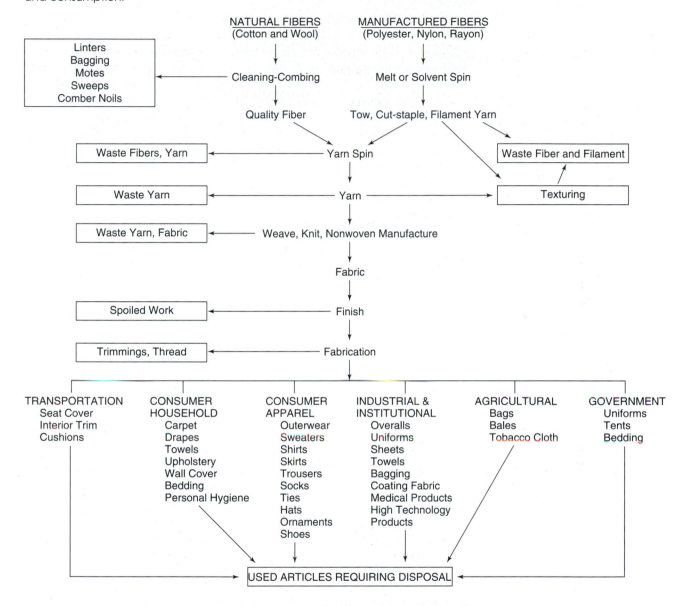

Landfilling

Much of the textile waste produced by manufacturers and consumers has been buried in landfills to biodegrade. In landfills natural fibers are biodegradable and will eventually break down, but synthetics are more resistant and are not so easily disposed of. Olefin fibers are degraded by sunlight, but will not have great exposure to the sun when buried in a landfill. Fibers and films for some newer products are being constructed of easily biodegraded materials such as starch and polylactic acid (PLA).

Disposable diapers provide an interesting overview of many of the difficulties that arise from the use of disposable items. Sales of disposable diapers grew rapidly during the 1970s and 1980s. Present estimates of the quantity of diapers to be disposed of range from 3.6 billion to more than 5 billion pounds of diapers a year. Environmentalists claim that these products are clogging landfills and that associated viruses and bacteria are leaching into groundwater. About two dozen states have either enacted or proposed legislation to discourage or tax use of disposables. The industry responds that diapers make up less than 2 percent of total solid waste in municipal landfills and that there is no evidence of any cases of disease caused by diaper disposal. Industry spokespersons also note that care of cloth diapers, the alternative preferred by some environmentally minded consumers, consumes up to six times as much water as is used in the manufacture of disposables and that laundering cloth diapers creates nearly ten times as much water pollution as manufacturing disposables (Joseph 1990). Work continues on producing disposable diapers that are more easily biodegraded.

An alternative to burial has been composting, which is above-land biodegradation. Materials in a compost have greater exposure to light and water, and the compost is stirred periodically to provide more air for microorganisms. Among the drawbacks are the labor required for stirring the compost and odors evolved as the materials decay. Mature composts can, however, be subsequently used to enhance the organic matter in soils.

Disposal of solid wastes from textile firms and from chemical companies associated with the textile industry is another difficulty. Burial may lead to the contamination of groundwater, fires, or the generation of noxious gases from the indiscriminate mixing of chemical substances.

Incineration

Incineration is a commonly used method for disposing of garbage, but it too has its problems, such as evolution of heat and hazardous gases. Incineration can, however, contribute to ameliorating other problems by harnessing the heat produced as an energy source for industry. This is indeed being done, especially with carpet waste.

Reuse

Textile items that are discarded can be fed back into the product life cycle by reusing them without destroying the original form. Consumers often donate apparel and other textiles to nonprofit organizations or sell them to secondhand stores (Chang et al., 1999). Secondhand stores have increased in popularity recently as a source for fashion apparel and accessories that may still be serviceable but can be obtained at low cost. Another reuse approach is conversion of discarded textile items into other useful products. Some apparel designers have shown that innovative clothing can be made from used jeans, neckties, socks, sports pennants, or woven fabrics with strips of used fabric as filling. (See Figure 25.4.)

Recycling

Perhaps the greatest area of success in dealing with textile waste has been in the area of recycling. A number of states actively encourage recycling through tax credits to businesses that recycle or by assigning recycled products preference when being purchased by state-funded agencies.

Preconsumer Waste

Both small and larger textile scraps are produced during the spinning of yarns, fabrication of cloth, and manufacture of garments. These items that have not yet been

FIGURE 25.4

Another form of recycling: evening dress made from neckties. Design called "Re-tied" by Shu-Hwa Lin. Photograph by Shu-Hwa Lin.

used by consumers are known as *preconsumer waste*. Textile firms may use their waste materials or purchase them from other manufacturers and reprocess them. The Wool Products Labeling Act and its requirement that recycled wool be labeled as such shows clearly that, in some parts of the industry, the waste materials from manufacture have traditionally been reclaimed.

Reprocessing generally produces lower value items, because it employs shredding that may damage the fibers. Products include stuffing, pads, bags, disposables, and reinforcement for composites. While reclamation of fiber waste from yarn production has been fairly widespread, reclamation of colored fibers and waste from previously woven or knitted goods made from a variety of different natural and manufactured fibers has been limited. Furthermore, customers who used to look with disfavor on products made from "reused" products are likely to be positively disposed toward "recycled" products.

Postconsumer Waste

In the textile recycling industry, items discarded after use are referred to as *postconsumer waste*. The recycling industry processes 2.5 billion pounds of postconsumer waste each year (about 10 pounds for every person in the United States).

Textile waste from manufacturers of garments or other textile products is relatively easy to process, since the manufacturer can identify the textile fiber. During reclamation, fibers must be sorted into different generic categories, and the identification of unknown manufactured fibers or blends is difficult. Chemical analysis for identification purposes may be necessary. Recycling textiles used and discarded by consumers is extremely difficult. Not only is fiber content unidentified, but the quality of fibers may also be uneven as a result of wear.

Natural fibers and rayon present relatively few problems of identification and recycling. Wool is recycled and is made into "new" fabrics. Cotton, linen, and rayon can be utilized in the production of paddings and fine rag paper battings.

The separation of blends into their component parts is more difficult. Often this is achieved by identifying the components of the blend and then dissolving out one of the fibers, leaving the other intact. Manufactured fibers can be reused in making flock, as industrial fillers in the manufacture of plastic, or in the regeneration of synthetic fibers. Some thermoplastic fibers can be recycled by melting and forming them into nonfibrous materials such as polymer films or tubes. However, some thermoplastics, like acrylics, decompose during melting.

Special finishes that are applied to fabrics may create additional problems for recycling. Many of these finishes are virtually impossible to recycle, and they contaminate the fibers, making their recycling impossible too.

As the raw materials from which many textiles are made become more scarce, recycling textile products becomes increasingly important. It is imperative that priority be given to intensive research into ways to turn discarded textile products into usable raw materials. Figure 25.2 summarizes the flow of products in textile waste utilization.

Success Stories

Carpets. Recycling of carpets has received considerable industry attention over the past few years for several reasons. First, the large volume of carpet waste (about 4 billion pounds in the United States alone) represents a significant potential environmental impact as successful recycling measures are developed. Second, most carpets have a fairly standard (and known) composition: nylon, polyester, or polypropylene pile; polypropylene backing; and latex synthetic rubber adhesive. This makes identification of components easier and application of separation techniques more feasible.

Early recycling processes shredded the carpet fibers and ground them into a polymer mixture. Compatibilizers are added to facilitate mixing of the polymers. These substances can bond to two different polymeric materials, holding them together. The mixture is melted and reformed into automobile parts or plastic structures. The shredded fibers can also be compressed and burned as fuel.

Later technologies have aimed at taking the pile fibers, over 50 percent of the carpet weight, back to the original monomeric materials. Nylon 6 is converted to caprolactam by treatment with steam and phosphoric acid. The caprolactam is in a pure enough form to be used as the starting material for polymerization of new nylon. This is called "closing the loop" in recycling by regenerating the original material. DSM, a Dutch chemical company, has joined with AlliedSignal to construct a carpet recycling plant in Georgia based on an enhanced nylon recovery process. The new process does not require phosphoric acid, disposal of which could be a problem. It relies instead on selective pyrolysis, or burning, to liberate the caprolactam.

DuPont has a commercial plant in Tennessee to convert nylon carpet waste into hexamethylene diamine, one of the building blocks for nylon 66. The fibers are chemically treated with ammonia at high pressure and temperature. This is again a closed-loop system.

Recycled Polyester from Plastics. Probably the most successful of the recycling efforts for textiles has been the production of polyester fibers from plastic soft drink bottles. These bottles are blow-molded polyethylene terephthalate, the same polymer as the fibers. They are collected and sorted (primarily according to color), then melted and extruded as fibers. Fortrel® EcoSpun™ is a recycled polyester fiber produced by Wellman, used in a variety of products. (See Figure 25.5.) Trevira II®, made by

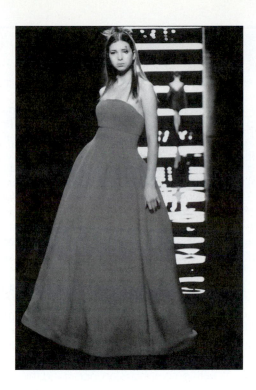

FIGURE 25.5

Evening dress made from
polyester fiber recycled from
soda bottles. Designer Amsale
Abera, model Ivanka Trump,
photograph by Eric Weiss.
Photograph courtesy of
Wellman.

Hoechst Celanese from a blend of 50 percent recycled polyester and 50 percent non-recycled polymer, has been made into T-shirts, baseball caps, tote bags, and cold weather performance fabrics.

Consumer Brief 25.1 describes some of the uses of recycled polyester.

HEALTH HAZARDS

Some of the safety and health hazards connected with manufacturing and use of textile products were alluded to in earlier chapters. Asbestos and cotton dust, chemical finishes and dyes, and flammability are examples. The following discussion concentrates on health problems for which there is some regulation or government oversight.

Hazards for Textile Workers

Lung Disease

The deleterious effect of inhaling minute, invisible particles of grit or hard inorganic matter has been recognized for many years. The constant exposure of the lungs to these irritants is harmful and may eventually produce lung disease in many of those exposed to it.

This type of exposure has long been recognized as a hazard in the production of asbestos. Recently, two similar problem areas in textile processing have been given increased attention. Glass fibers are hard and fairly durable. Questions have been raised about whether the inhalation of fibers of glass may cause lung disease. To date, research into this question is continuing, and researchers are searching for evidence of a relationship between inhaling glass fiber and lung disease.

CONSUMER BRIEF 25.1   Recycled Polyester

The environmental movement has spurred development of recycling processes for both industrial and consumer waste. This recycling can take one of two forms: waste can be reintroduced into the same production process to produce the same good, or a solid waste can be made into a completely different product. A significant advance in the second area has been the reprocessing of polyester products into polyester fibers. Companies in the United States are using 2-liter soft drink bottles, as well as film and fiber waste from manufacturers, to make new polyester fibers.

Soft drink bottles are composed of the same polymer as polyester fibers: polyethylene terephthalate (PET). Several fiber producers have developed processes for collecting the used bottles, melting them, and extruding the PET as fibers. Soft drink bottles are collected from consumers and recyclers and crushed and compacted for shipping to recycling plants. Initial processing involves separation of the polyester bottles from other foreign materials such as aluminum caps, paper labels, and the rigid base cups used in some bottles. Clear and green bottles are separated, to give clean streams of each.

The clear bottles are processed into polyester fibers for use in sleeping bags, carpeting, pillows, quilted jackets, and other products. Polyester waste from film and fiber producers is often added to the waste stream for fiber production. Producers may also add virgin polyester polymer to the melt before extrusion. At least one producer is molding packaging materials from a melt of recycled and virgin PET.

The green bottles can be reprocessed into green polyester fiber that is made into needle-punched nonwoven geotextiles for erosion control and other engineering applications. The black base cups that are used in 2-liter bottles for stabilization are composed of polyethylene and must be separated from the PET before reprocessing. Although the base cups can also be reprocessed into packaging materials, separating them from the bottles increases the cost of reprocessing. Increasingly, soft drink bottles are made without the base cup, with a ridged bottom providing the necessary stability for the filled bottles.

Work on refining recycling processing continues, with an emphasis on increasing the quality of the recycled fibers. The recycled fibers of today are appearing in apparel and other higher-end products. Wellman, the pioneer in recyled polyester fibers, produces their fiber Fortrel® Ecospun® for many different end uses. Each year the company sponsors a scholarship program that pairs design students with leading American designers to develop a Master Apprentice Collection of apparel made with Ecospun®.

For many years it has been known that cotton industry workers may, after a period of exposure to cotton dust, develop byssinosis, or "brown lung" as it is called by the workers. Researchers had thought that the sand and other gritty particles present in bales of cotton might be responsible for the development of byssinosis. The most recent research, however, tends toward the conclusion that the cause of byssinosis is probably toxins from bacteria or fungi that are present in the leaf dust that is part of the raw cotton. The precise cause, however, is still not clear.

OSHA has established maximum allowable levels of cotton dust that may be present in the air of factories where cotton is being processed. In the United States the problem has been brought under control by the development of equipment and manufacturing operations that have substantially decreased worker exposure to cotton dust. Closed systems for processing raw cotton, improved air ventilation, and personal safety devices, rather like gas masks, are among the technologies that have been put into place.

Chemicals

Some of the chemical substances with which textile workers come into contact are highly toxic. For the most part, companies have been able to identify these substances and to protect workers from contact with them.

From time to time, research findings attribute harm to materials that were not previously identified as presenting any serious health problems. Vinyl chloride is such a chemical. An important ingredient in the production of polyvinyl chloride (PVC) plastics, vinyl chloride is used in the production of plastic backings and coatings for fabrics. Evidence indicates that continued exposure to vinyl chloride monomers will produce cancer of the liver in some of the persons exposed. PVC plants are carefully monitored to detect escape of the monomer during polymerization processes.

Some dyes have been proven to be harmful to workers. When evidence is found linking dyes to health hazards, their use may be discontinued. For example, some dyes with excellent colorfastness characteristics have been removed from use because of health hazards.

Formaldehyde is another chemical widely used in the textile industry. Research has indicated that high levels of formaldehyde are associated with nasal cancer in rats. Whether it is a carcinogen in humans has not been proven. Long-term studies of workers exposed to formaldehyde have been inconclusive. The American Cancer Institute is conducting additional studies that may yield more reliable data.

About 1.5 million workers are estimated to be exposed to formaldehyde in the workplace; about 970,000 of these work in the textile and apparel industries. Present allowable levels of formaldehyde in the workplace are 1 part per million (ppm). It is possible that further reductions may be mandated. Although a final resolution has yet to be made about the formaldehyde issue, formaldehyde levels in textile mills and apparel factories have been reduced considerably. Several finishing techniques that reduce the quantity of formaldehyde used or the amounts released into the atmosphere have been developed (see "Problems of Durable Press" in chapter 23).

As of May 1986, OSHA employee health protection rules required that information about hazardous chemical substances be communicated to employees by the employer. In summary, the requirements are:

1. Hazard information must be conveyed to employees through appropriate labels on the products that they use.
2. Material Safety Data Sheets provided to employees must identify hazard information.
3. Affected industries must have a written hazards information communications program.
4. Industries must establish and conduct employee chemical hazard training programs.

The specific means by which these requirements are met are not mandated, but both the producers of chemicals deemed hazardous and the industries using the chemicals must comply. The textile industry sectors that manufacture or process a wide variety of textile products are therefore affected.

Noise

Noise levels in textile manufacturing plants can be extremely high. Governmental standards regulate noise levels in the workplace. These standards were imposed because of the relationship between high noise levels and hearing loss. The standards limit noise based on the employees' length of exposure and also require periodic hearing tests for machine operators.

Textile manufacturers meet these standards in a number of ways. The problem is most acute in factories using older equipment, which operates at much higher sound levels than does newer equipment, which is engineered to satisfy noise-level regulations. Shuttleless looms, now rapidly replacing shuttle looms, are an example of a newer type of textile machinery that has made a significant contribution to reducing sound levels. Those working in areas with high sound levels are required to wear ear protectors.

Hazards to Consumers

Hazards to consumers from textiles might be divided into dangers posed by flammable fabrics, fibers or finishing materials that may pose health risks, and individual sensitivity or allergy to certain types of textile products.

Flammability

Some textile products can ignite and burn, and individuals may suffer injury if garments, mattresses, bedding, or upholstery catch fire. Regulation of highly flammable fabrics was enacted as early as 1953. Additional products have been subject to regulation in the intervening years. See chapter 21 for a full discussion of flammability.

Hazardous Substances

When textile products are shown to be dangerous to health, they are withdrawn from consumer products, as was the case with asbestos. Probably the best-known instance of public concern with textile chemicals is the TRIS case. As explained in chapter 23, TRIS was a chemical finish used to make some polyester, acetate, and triacetate children's sleepwear fabrics flame resistant. When TRIS was found to be an animal carcinogen, TRIS-treated garments were withdrawn from the market, and its use was prohibited. Much of the public failed to realize that not all sleepwear fabrics were being treated with this particular chemical, and many consumers rejected sleepwear of cotton and other fibers treated with safe substances.

The issue of safety has also been raised in regard to formaldehyde-finished products. The Consumer Product Safety Commission has concluded that consumers are not at risk because garments do not give off enough formaldehyde to affect wearers. Evolution of formaldehyde from building materials such as plyboard and particleboard still remains a problem.

The chemical 4-PCH (4-phenylcyclohexene) is used in carpet finishing and associated with "new carpet" odor. Reports of ill effects and death of laboratory mice exposed to carpeting subjected to heating resulted in speculation that 4-PCH might have been the cause. Further laboratory tests on mice indicated no adverse effects even at levels more than a thousand times higher than those that can be expected in new carpet installation (Tests show no ill effects. . . 1993).

Dermatitis

Dermatological problems associated with textile use are sometimes reported by consumers. In some instances, skin irritation may result from continued contact with coarse wool fabrics or fabrics containing glass fiber. Some dyes, especially those used on nylon and polyester, and some chemical finishes have also been associated with consumer complaints. Individual consumers may be allergic to specific fibers, dyes, or finishing materials that do not cause problems for the general population.

Consumers may also report irritation or allergic reactions to laundry products. Laundry products most likely to be identified as the source of perceived dermatological problems are soaps and detergents, fabric softeners, and bleaches (Dallas et al. 1992).

SUMMARY

Both industry and the public have obligations for the protection of the environment. Whereas at first glance industry would seem to be more responsible for pollution, a deeper examination of the issues leads inexorably to the conclusion that this is a shared responsibility. In the long run, the public must be willing to pay for the improvements in pollution control that industries make. Manufacturing of EITP is expensive. Although recent advances are lowering costs, cleaner factories and mills will be paid for by increasing prices of the items that are marketed. More successes such as carpet recycling and conversion of plastic bottles into polyester fibers should help both consumers and producers of textile products. As more producers become certified by ISO 14000, better industry practices will be put into effect.

At the same time, consumers must recognize that imported fabrics and apparel are often produced in countries that have little or no regulation of the workplace environment. Such goods compete with domestically produced fabrics into which the costs of more environmentally sound processing must be calculated. No one relishes increases in the cost of textiles, but the trade-off for lower prices would be to continue the deterioration of the environment that future generations will inherit.

References

Chang, Y., H.-L. Chen, and S. Francis. 1999 Market applications for recycled post-consumer fibers. *Family and Consumer Sciences Research Journal* 27 (3): 320.

Dallas, M. J., et al. 1992. Dermatological and other health problems attributed by consumers to contact with laundry products. *Home Economics Research Journal* 21 (September): 34.

Ecolabelling. 1994. *Textile Horizons*, June, 17.

Federal Trade Commission. 1999. Sorting out 'green' advertising claims. www.ftc.gov. /bcp/conline/pubs/general/sortgrn

Heeley, J., and M. Press. 1997. Design and the environment. *Textiles Magazine* (4): 13.

Joseph, L. 1990. The bottom line on disposables. *New York Times Sunday Magazine*, September 23, 26.

Maycumber, S. G. 1994. Environmental issues rank up with QR when choosing vendors: L. L. Bean exec. *Daily News Record* 26 (April): 2.

Schlaeppi, F. 1998. *Textile Chemist and Colorist* 30(4): 19.

Shaver, J. A. 1999. Applying ISO-14001 to environmental regulation. *Textile Chemist and Colorist* 31 (5): 27.

Tests show no ill effects from use of 4-PCH on carpets. 1993. *Textile Chemist and Colorist* 25 (March): 6.

Van Winkle, et al. 1978. Cotton versus polyester. *American Scientist* 66 (September-October): 280.

Review Questions

1. Identify five specific actions consumers can take in relation to textile products that would have a beneficial effect on the environment. Explain the impact of each action you have identified.

2. Discuss the environmental impact that design and development decisions can have at each stage of the textile product life cycle. For each stage:
   a. Identify the impact.
   b. Describe the considerations in selecting materials and processes using a specific example for each.
3. What organization is charged with the responsibility of monitoring the workplace to ascertain whether conditions for workers are safe? What are some of the potential threats to the health and safety of textile employees?
4. Imagine that your employer required you to defend the idea that a shirt made from 100 percent cotton fabric would be more environmentally safe than one made of 100 percent polyester. Develop a list of reasons to support this position. Now imagine that you were required to argue against this position. Develop a list of arguments supporting polyester.

Recommended Readings

Bockner, B. 1994. Pollution prevention: Key to survival for the dyestuff industry. *American Dyestuff Reporter* 83 (August): 29.

Closing the loop. 1999. *Textile Month* (June): 61.

Glover, B., and L. Hill. 1993. Waste minimization in the dyehouse. *Textile Chemist and Colorist* 25 (June): 15.

Gross, P., and D. C. Braun. 1984. *Toxic and biomedical effects of fibers*. Park Ridge, N.J.: Noyes.

Grove, N. 1994. Recycling. *National Geographic* 185 (July): 93.

Gund, N. 1995. Environmental considerations for textile printing products. *Journal of the Society of Dyers and Colorists* 111 (1/2): 7.

Kim, H. S., and M. L. Damhorst. 1998. Environmental concern and apparel consumption. *Clothing and Textiles Research Journal* 16 (3): 126.

Kumar, S. 1997. Carpet recycling technologies. *AATCC book of papers*, 220. Research Triangle Park, N.C.: AATCC.

Moore, M. A., A. Money, and B. Orzada. 1999. An examination of environmental awareness in the textile industry. *Textile Chemist and Colorist* 31 (4): 27.

The go-betweens. 1994. *The Economist* 333 (October 1): 109.

TEXTILE PRODUCT PERFORMANCE

Throughout this text readers have looked at the contributions of fiber, yarn, fabric, and finishes to the performance of textiles in the areas of durability, appearance, and comfort. These evaluations of the likely performance of a product have been based not only on understanding the general properties of the various components of textiles, but also on subjective responses to the final products. However, in some situations the judgment of a textile product cannot be based on general knowledge and personal preferences alone, but requires some more objective means of evaluation. Standard specifications and objective tests are used for this purpose.

A *standard specification*, as noted in chapter 1, is a defined level of performance that a product must achieve to be considered acceptable for use. Except in the case of some flammability standard specifications, manufacturers are not required by law to conform to textile product standards. Some retailers, however, insist that wholesale manufacturers from whom they buy must produce goods that meet specifications. The Department of Defense establishes minimum specifications for textiles used by the military and some federal agencies. Funding regulations for federally financed construction projects require that carpets, draperies, and the like conform to stated specifications. Standard specifications also provide a basis for different researchers to compare the results of textile studies and new products. Although the general public does benefit from the use of standards by segments of the textile industry, most consumers are unaware of their existence. The organizations that establish standards were identified and described in chapter 1, pages 21–22.

Textile testing is used to determine whether products meet established standards. These testing methods have been proven to be both valid and reliable. Not only do industry and government require testing of materials in ways that are accepted as reliable and standardized, but researchers also require a body of accepted tests for use in comparing data accumulated by different researchers working in different laboratories. Test methods are published by AATCC and ASTM so that they can be obtained by those interested in performing such tests.

In the pages that follow some of the most widely used tests are described briefly and photographs of some of the equipment used to make these tests are provided. Those who pursue advanced studies in textiles will become familiar with many of these tests and devices. Those who work in any area of the textile field in which quality control plays a role will benefit from some elementary understanding of such tests.

TESTING

To ensure accuracy and reliability, textile testing must be carried out under carefully controlled conditions. Atmospheric conditions (particularly the amount of moisture present that might be picked up by fibers) affect the performance of textiles. For this reason, testing is done with temperature and humidity being maintained at standard levels: 70°F (21°C) and 65 percent relative humidity. Testing equipment must conform to specifications established in the test methods and fabric specimens must be of uniform size. Test measurements are repeated a number of times because of variability in results from one specimen to another. Results are averaged. Those overall measurements more accurately characterize the materials being tested than does the measurement of a single sample that might possess some atypical quality.

Laboratory testing has limitations in that these tests do not simulate exactly the conditions under which textiles will be used. Consumers will differ from each other in the stresses to which they subject textiles. A farmer will place different demands on a pair of jeans than will an urban high school student. The research literature that deals with the evaluation of textile products contains numerous studies of actual wear tests or of correlations between consumer evaluations of products and standard testing procedures. Studies such as these add another dimension to the testing of textiles. Technical and research publications in the field regularly report new developments in testing as well as the results of tests performed in studies of various aspects of textile performance. In addition standard test methods undergo periodic reexamination by professionals to ensure their continued validity and to include new instrumentation that is developed.

Basic Physical Properties

The basic physical properties of fabrics are usually measured before performance testing, so that results can be correlated. Physical characteristics routinely determined are weight, thickness, and fabric count. Weight is expressed as ounces per square yard, ounces per linear yard, or grams per square meter. Fabric thickness can be measured by using any of a number of thickness gauges or compressometers. Fabric count, the number of yarns per inch or centimeter in a woven fabric, is made with a linen tester. (See chapter 14, Figure 14.15.)

TESTING FACTORS RELATED TO DURABILITY

Mechanical Properties

Fabric strength evaluations are made in terms of breaking strength, tearing strength, or bursting strength. A variety of machines is used to measure strength, and fabric samples are prepared for testing according to ASTM test method procedures.

Breaking strength, the force required to break a woven fabric when it is pulled under tension, is measured on a tensile testing machine. (See Figure 26.1.) The strength is reported in pounds or newtons of force required to break the fabric. Half the specimens are prepared with warp yarns running in the direction of stress, and the other half have the stress in the filling direction.

At the same time that breaking strength is being tested on a tensile testing machine, the degree of elongation that the fabric undergoes before breaking may be determined and reported as a percentage of the original length. Fabrics may also be tested for recovery from elongation. They are stretched to certain percent of their original length and then permitted to recover for a specified time.

FIGURE 26.1

Instron Tensile Tester with fabric specimen mounted in clamps. Photograph by Prather Warren, Louisiana State University Public Relations.

Tearing strength of a fabric, expressed in pounds or grams, is the pressure required to continue a tear or rip already begun in a woven fabric. Strength can be measured on a tensile tester by cutting a slit in a fabric specimen and mounting the two parts, or "tongues" in the clamps of the machine. Other instruments provide alternate methods for holding the two split ends of the sample before tearing.

For breaking and tearing strength tests, warp and filling results are reported separately. If yarns in one direction have a loss in tearing or breaking strength, performance will be affected. High levels of strength in one direction do not counterbalance low strength in the other.

Bursting strength is the force required to rupture a fabric. In this case, the force is applied in many directions at once by either pushing a ball through the tautly held fabric or by air pressure. Bursting strength tests are commonly used to evaluate the strength of knitted and nonwoven fabrics, where the elongation or resistance to stretch in all directions is important.

Abrasion Resistance and Pilling

Abrasion resistance can be determined on several different types of abrasion-testing machines. The results of tests run on different machines cannot be compared, as each machine tests with a different motion and each holds the fabrics in different positions. Some instruments determine only flat abrasion, while others can measure resistance to edge and flex abrasion. The CSI surface abrader pictured in Figure 26.2 is one of the latter type.

FIGURE 26.2

CSI Surface Abrader for testing surface abrasion. Other instruments will test for flex abrasion and edge abrasion. Photograph courtesy of Custom Scientific Instruments, Inc.

Abrasion results depend not only on the type of machine action but also on the following factors (Price and Cohen 1994):

1. Type of abradant
2. Pressure between fabric and abradant
3. Frequency and time duration of the abrading sequence
4. Tension of the fabric while being abraded

Results can reported as the number of rubbing cycles to produce a hole or as the loss in strength, weight, or thickness after a specified number of cycles.

Pilling is a result of abrasion but can also affect the appearance of a fabric. It is often important to determine a fabric's tendency to pill when evaluating its serviceability. The Random Tumble Pilling Tester can be used for this purpose. (See Figure 26.3.) Specimens are tumbled in cork-lined cylinders and then the number of pills in a specified fabric area can be counted. Alternatively, pilled fabric specimens can be subjectively rated against photographs representing different pilling levels.

FIGURE 26.3

Random Tumble Pilling Tester for determining the pilling and fuzzing characteristics of all types of fabrics. Photograph courtesy of Atlas Electric Devices Co.

Abrasion is one of those factors most likely to be affected by each individual's unique use of textiles. For example, the linings of overcoats are subject to abrasion from garments worn beneath them. A person who favors soft, smooth-textured clothing would subject the lining of a coat to considerably less abrasion than one would who prefers coarse-textured, rough-surfaced textiles.

Tests Evaluating Finishes

It is sometimes desirable to determine whether special finishes have been applied to textiles. The presence of some finishes, for example, would interfere with textile recycling. The identification of such finishes is difficult. Except for mechanical finishes that can easily be identified by eye (such as embossing and napping), the determination of chemical finishes may require extensive laboratory procedures. AATCC Test Method 94 outlines a variety of tests for the identification of textile finishes.

Researchers may use testing methods to make comparisons between control samples of unfinished fabrics and fabrics with finishes. Tear and breaking strength tests and abrasion tests, for example, may be used to ascertain whether finishes used to improve wrinkle recovery will affect the durability of fabrics.

A number of tests have been devised to determine the effectiveness of finishes. These tests cover such areas as durability of applied designs and finishes to dry cleaning, oil repellency, soil release, durable press, water resistance and repellency, and weather resistance. Specific instructions for testing in these and other areas are included in the AATCC's *Technical Manual* and in the *ASTM Book of Standards*.

TESTING FACTORS RELATED TO APPEARANCE AND HAND

Fabric appearance is affected by several factors and testing usually involves measuring the components separately.

Dimensional Stability

Shrinkage or growth of fabric during wear and care can render an apparel or household textile item both unappealing and unusable. Consequently a required level of dimensional stability is often specified when selecting fabrics for textile products. It is traditionally determined by placing marks on the fabric, subjecting it to laundering, dry cleaning, or other conditions, and then remeasuring the marked area. The shrinkage or growth is reported as a percentage of the original dimensions. Changes in the lengthwise and crosswise directions are reported separately. The effectiveness of a shrink-resistant finish can be determined by comparing the shrinkage of finished and unfinished fabrics.

Not only may fabrics shrink, but they may also twist or skew during laundering. Knits and twill weaves are especially susceptible because there are twist stresses built up during the processing of these fabrics. A test method was developed by AATCC for determining skewness change in fabrics. The diagonal lines of a marked square are measured, and the percent change in their length calculated. (See Figure 26.4.)

Wrinkle Recovery

Wrinkle recovery of fabrics is measured by creasing small fabric samples for a specified time, allowing them to recover, and calculating the angle that the two creased ends form.

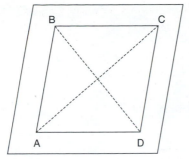

FIGURE 26.4

Diagram shows how markings are made on fabrics being tested for skewness or twisting. Skewness is calculated by subtracting the length of BD from the length of AC and dividing by the sum of the two lengths. It can be seen that if there is no skewness after laundering, BD will equal AC and the skewness change will be zero. AATCC Test Method 179–1994. Reproduced courtesy of the American Association of Textile Chemists and Colorists.

Fabrics with good recovery will result in measured angles that are high, around 150 degrees. Untreated cotton fabrics usually have recovery angles less than 100 degrees.

Retention of a smooth fabric appearance after laundering can be determined by comparison with standard plastic replicas representing different levels of wrinkling. Fabrics are laundered and visually compared to the replicas. Ratings for smoothness appearance (SA) range from 1 (poor) to 5 (very good). Standard test methods also exist for determining the appearance of creases in durable press items after laundering and the appearance of finished garments and other textile products.

Drape and Hand

Drape and hand of fabrics are affected by shearing and bending behavior, resistance to stretching and compression, and surface properties. Several different instruments have been constructed over the years to measure drape directly and to measure the separate properties that affect drape and hand. The most successful of these are the Drapemeter, the Kawabata Evaluation System for fabrics (KES), and the Fabric Assurance by Simple Testing (FAST) system.

The Drapemeter contains a pedestal over which a circular fabric sample is draped. A light casts a shadow of the draped fabric sample that is captured and compared to an undraped sample.

The KES, developed by Dr. Sueo Kawabata, takes into account the fabric mechanical properties that affect hand and relates objective measurement of these properties to subjective evaluation (Kawabata 1980). The subjective component of the system was supplied by a team of textile experts in Japan who evaluated a large number of apparel fabrics. The objective component was determined by a series of instruments designed by Kawabata. These instruments measure fabric responses to small deformations such as those that occur in ordinary wear or other use of textiles; that is, the forces applied are much less than those used in breaking or tearing strength tests.

The four instruments in the KES are:

1. *Tensile and shear tester.* Measures response to slight stretching and recovery from stretching, as well as resistance to shearing and recovery from shearing.
2. *Pure bending tester.* Measures resistance to bending and recovery from bending. (See Figure 26.5.)

FIGURE 26.5

Kawabata Pure Bending Tester. Fabric is being bent between holding clamps.

3. *Surface tester.* Measures surface roughness and resistance to friction.
4. *Compression tester.* Measures resistance to compression and recovery from compression.

The objective measurements can be used to predict specific hand properties which are used in Japan and other parts of the world in specifying fabric properties in apparel production.

The FAST system is a set of instruments, somewhat simpler in operation, that evaluate appearance, hand, and performance properties of textiles. Compression, bending resistance, and elongation are measured, as well as dimensional stability to wetting and pressing. Results can be used to predict processing of fabrics, particularly wool fabrics, into apparel.

Colorfastness

The colorfastness of fabrics to a variety of substances and conditions can be measured by the use of specific testing methods and machinery. The details of these test methods are described in the *Technical Manual* published by AATCC.

Color change is ascertained by keeping a *control*, an untreated sample of the fabric being tested. Tested samples are then checked against the original. A scale called the *Gray Scale*, established by AATCC, makes it possible to determine more precisely the degree of color change that has taken place. Samples of both treated and control samples are compared under standard lighting conditions, and the standard scales and numerical ratings are applied. (See Figure 26.6.) Although visual evaluation can yield reasonably consistent results, computerized color evaluation instruments are more accurate, and visual evaluations are being superseded by electronic measurement.

Fading from exposure to sunlight is measured in a machine that simulates, at an accelerated rate, the fading action of the sun. Samples can be exposed for varying pe-

FIGURE 26.6

MacBeth Color Matching Booth for evaluation of color change. Photograph by Prather Warren, Louisiana State University Public Relations.

riods of time and tested samples compared to control samples. Among the machines most often used for such tests are the Fade-Ometer and the Weather-Ometer.

Colorfastness to laundering and dry cleaning are done in machines such as the Launder-Ometer. Fabric samples and detergent solution are placed in small sealed cylinders and rotated in a temperature-controlled water bath for a specified time. Similar procedures are used to ascertain fastness to dry cleaning, but instead of water and detergent, dry-cleaning solvents are used. One cycle in a laundering machine is said to be the equivalent of five home or commercial launderings (AATCC 1997, 87).

After the test, specimens are examined for color loss. If samples of a special cloth containing yarns made of a number of different fibers are added to the cylinders along with test specimens, it is possible to determine whether other fabrics are likely to pick up color from the tested fabric during laundering or dry cleaning.

Both wet and dry crocking can be tested on a device called a Crockmeter that rubs the test sample across a white fabric sample. Color transfer from the test sample to the white sample indicates that the test sample is subject to crocking. (See Figure 26.7.)

A device called the AATCC Perspiration Tester evaluates not only colorfastness to perspiration but also to chlorinated water (as in swimming pools), seawater, water spotting, and the like. The fabric sample is soaked in one of these liquids and then subjected to heat and pressure. (See Figure 26.8.) Up to twenty specimens can be tested simultaneously.

TESTING FACTORS RELATED TO COMFORT

As with many other fabric properties, comfort is affected by different fabric components and is difficult to measure in a composite sense. What is comfortable for one person may be related to the feel of a textile fabric, to the thermal properties of a fabric, or to the way a garment fits. (See Figure 26.9.)

FIGURE 26.7

AATCC Crockmeter that
provides standard motion and
pressure for determining
colorfastness to crocking.
Photograph courtesy of Atlas
Electric Devices Co.

FIGURE 26.8

AATCC Perspiration Tester for
testing colorfastness to
perspiration, and to chlorinated
pool, sea, and distilled water.
Photograph courtesy of Atlas
Electric Devices Co.

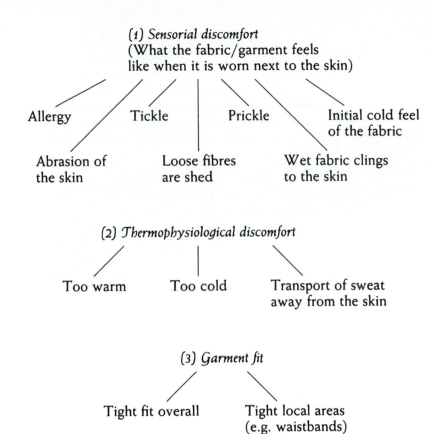

FIGURE 26.9

Factors that are related to physiological discomfort. Reproduced from *Textiles Magazine*, a publication of the Textile Institute, U.K. Smith, J.E. 1993. The comfort of clothing. *Textiles* 22 (1): 18.

Sensorial Comfort

Sensorial comfort is related to surface and softness properties of fabrics. Surface fabric properties can be measured on the Kawabata Surface Tester. Allergies and adverse reactions to abrasion and roughness are really in the realm of medical testing.

Tests for the bending stiffness of fabrics affect not only hand but comfort and softness. The Kawabata Pure Bending Tester can give a measure of fabric stiffness. These is also an ASTM method to determine bending resistance. A strip of fabric is moved off the edge of a platform until it touches the angled side of the platform. The longer the length of fabric it takes to touch the side, the stiffer is the fabric.

Thermal Comfort

Thermophysiological comfort depends largely on heat transfer and moisture vapor transport, as well as the permeability of the fabric. While these properties can be measured physically, such measurements should be related to subjective evaluations of comfort, which can often be specific to individuals. Textile technologists have defined a unit for measurement of thermophysiological comfort. This unit, the *clo*, represents the insulation or resistance necessary to keep a resting human being (producing heat at a standard rate) comfortable at 70°F (21°C) and air movement of 0.1 meter/second. The clo value is analogous to the R-value used in evaluating home insulation and window coverings.

Heat Transfer

The guarded hot plate and the heated manikin are used test the effectiveness of fabrics in maintaining thermal comfort. In the hot plate, the fabric sample is placed between a bottom heated plate and a top "guard plate." The amount of heat that the fabric allows through is measured. The heated manikin, on the other hand, works much the same as the manikin for testing flammability. (See chapter 23.) Thermocouples on the manikin measure the temperature at various points on the body.

Water Repellency and Moisture Vapor Transport

Water repellency and the ability of a fabric to transmit moisture vapor or liquid water affects its comfort, especially in hot humid conditions. In one method for testing water repellency, water is sprayed on a fabric sample that is placed over a blotter. The quantity of water absorbed by the blotter is a measure of the water resistance of the fabric. Other methods subject specimens to water pressure until they leak, tumble specimens in water for a fixed period of time and measure the water absorbed, or spray water on a specimen and compare the pattern of wetting to a photographic rating chart.

Moisture vapor transmission is evaluated by any of several devices that place textiles as a barrier between a drier and a more moist environment. The quantity of moisture that moves from the moist to the dry environment is measured. Wicking of liquid moisture can be determined by submerging the end of a fabric strip in a dye solution and measuring the height the colored liquid migrates up the strip.

Air Permeability

The basic principle of testing for air permeability is to force compressed air through a fabric specimen and to measure the rate of air flow through the specimen. The air pressure used in testing is much higher than one would normally encounter in apparel use, so these test do not really simulate every day conditions. Even so, they can be used for comparative purposes (Collier and Epps 1999, 299).

SUMMARY

A number of different tests may be given to textiles in order to evaluate them for specific uses, and in addition several tests may be required to determine whether a fabric can perform well in a particular use. The concluding section of this chapter serves as a summary of the ways in which information gained from such testing can be used to evaluate fabrics for a specific end use.

The summary for this chapter, and indeed for the entire text, is the case studies that put together the components of a textile fabric. As is true for all other choices among textiles, predicting textile performance requires that manufacturers, consumers, or craftspersons recognize that fiber content, yarn structure, fabric construction, and finish all contribute to the properties of the final fabric.

Sometimes there are trade-offs among the various components, and cost and environmental impact must be factors in selecting materials and processes. Fabric components may also complement each other, making the product more than the sum of its parts.

In all cases, it is important to focus on the intended end use of the textile. In product development this end use is specified, and manufacturers select fabrics that meet the requirements. Where it is important to predict the performance of fabrics, the effects of all the structural characteristics should be taken into account. Prediction involves testing, and quality assurance requires that fabrics meet the specification of levels of performance required by buyers.

The concluding product case studies, that "put it all together," combine the requirements for a specific product with discussion of how the properties and characteristics of particular fibers, yarns, fabric structures, coloring processes, and finishes can meet these needs.

Putting it all together for . . .

Sailcloth

Fabrics for sailcloth have a number of different requirements in terms of strength, elongation, weight, flexibility, porosity, absorbency, and environmental resistance. Designing or selecting sailcloth fabric must balance the requirements for each of these properties while maintaining a reasonable cost.

Tensile Properties

The tensile properties important in sailcloth are high strength and low elongation. Sails must withstand the forces of the wind without stretching out of shape. This requires first of all a strong fabric with strong yarns. Sailcloths of polyester or nylon filament yarns have the requisite strength.

A further necessity for sailcloth is resistance to stretch or elongation. Fibers with higher modulus will have initial resistance to stretch, and for this reason, polyester is a better choice than nylon. The new gel-spun polyethylene fibers have high strength and modulus and were originally considered appropriate for sailcloth. The creep exhibited by textiles of these fibers, however, made them unacceptable in terms of elongation and recovery. Kevlar® aramid fibers have very desirable properties but because of their cost are mainly used only in racing sails in competition.

Because of the way they are used, sails are subjected to forces in all directions. Woven fabrics normally would have less stretch than knits, but even wovens with high strength and low elongation in the warp and filling directions still stretch in the bias direction. If this happens, the sail loses its aerodynamic efficiency. For this reason, many woven sailcloths are stabilized by laminating a polyester film (plastic sheet) to the fabric, producing a multicomponent structure. Lamination decreases the elongation in all directions, preserving the shape of the sail. Most sailcloths used today are multicomponent laminated fabrics or have a resin coating applied to stabilize the structure.

Weight

Fabric weight is probably the second most important property for sailcloth. Lighter-weight fabrics are desirable because less wind is needed to fill them during sailing and also because they are easier to handle and to store. For many years sailcloths were made of cotton or linen. These fibers made strong, sturdy fabrics with excellent resistance to elongation. They were, however, of heavier weight than most materials used today. Polyester and nylon fibers have lower specific gravities than the cellulosic fibers, making them better candidates for sailcloths.

Absorbency

Related to the concern with sailcloth weight is the absorbency of the materials used. Fibers with high absorbency will increase in weight and be less desirable. This was another problem with cotton and linen sails, which absorbed water and became even heavier. Better fibers for sailcloths are those with lower moisture regains. Although nylon has good strength and durability, its regain, while lower than that of cotton or linen, is still higher than polyester. Furthermore, nylon can lose some of its strength when wet.

Flexibility

Flexibility is a secondary consideration in sailcloths. It is important for ease of handling and for preservation. Sailcloths undergo wrinkling and bending when they are stored after use. If they are stiff, repeated bending could permanently crease, or even crack, the sails, making them unusable. Flexible fibers and yarns, and thinner laminates, minimize such damage.

Air Permeability

Sails should have extremely low air permeability to maintain different amounts of air pressure on each side of the sail. High fabric counts, lamination, and resin coatings decrease the porosity of the sailcloth and enhance its performance.

Light Resistance

Since sails are used out-of-doors, their resistance to environmental conditions, especially sunlight, is an important factor in their performance. The fiber and film used in the sail structure must have good resistance to ultraviolet light. Fibers, such as polyprolypene, that may have other properties desired in sailcloth are degraded by sunlight.

Putting it all together for . . .

Outdoor Clothing

Vapor barriers . . . wicking . . . waterproof . . . breathable . . . down . . . microfibers . . . . The serious jogger, hiker, backpacker, and cross-country skier is faced with a bewildering array of choices when selecting clothing for strenuous outdoor activities. Consumers need to make informed choices among the various types of fibers, yarns, and fabrics available, and these choices must be made in relation to specific recreational needs. Comfort and serviceability must be placed in the context of climatic factors such as temperature, humidity, and wind; levels of physical activity; and how to maintain desirable properties over time.

Most experienced outdoor recreationists recommend manipulating layers of clothing. This provides greater flexibility and allows easy adaptation as weather, temperature, and activity levels change.

Underlayers

Fabric close to the body quickly become wet with perspiration during physical activity. The moisture absorption properties of fibers are most important here. Also, garments must be easily laundered. Cotton readily absorbs moisture but dries slowly. In hot, dry conditions cotton is a comfortable underlayer, but in cool, damp climates it feels cold and wet.

Wool can absorb a good deal of moisture without feeling wet and is a good insulator, but it does not launder easily unless given special finishes. Some persons are allergic to wool, and it is often expensive. Manufactured fibers such as polyester or polypropylene are low in absorbency and also wick moisture away from the body. This allows it to evaporate more quickly, thereby maintaining a dry, more comfortable feeling in cold and damp conditions. Manufactured fibers are easily laundered.

Underlayers also need to be flexible and to fit closely, bending and stretching as the body moves. Weft knits, especially jersey knitted fabric structures, have the requisite elasticity.

Middle Layers

The function of the middle layer is usually insulation. In cold weather air trapped by fibers helps to conserve body heat. These fibers may be on the surface of a fabric such as a sweater knitted from woolen yarns (as opposed to smoother worsted yarns) or part of a pile fabric structure. Polyester and wool serve well as insulators because they are resilient and spring back. Once flattened and matted together, fibers no longer trap air, and insulating qualities decrease.

Many garments designed to provide good insulation use down or synthetic fiberfill held between two layers of woven fabric. Outer fabric layers must have a high fabric count, so the filling will not escape, and they need good tensile and tear strength. The high strength of nylon fibers, compact yarns, and tightly woven fabrics into which nylon can be made lead to its frequent use in such fabrics.

Another consideration may be the weight of garments. Goose down and duck down fillings are warm and exceptionally light. (Goose down and duck down can, by law, incorporate up to 20 percent small feathers.) Synthetic fibers are also light. They are resilient, do not transmit heat, and can be textured to increase loft. Polyester is frequently used. Some fibers are hollow, trapping dead air not only between the fibers but also within the fibers.

Outermost Layers

The functions of the outermost layer could be divided as follows: (1) making direct contact with the physical environment, (2) serving as a windbreaker, and (3) keeping everything underneath dry.

The choice of fiber and construction of fabric are especially important for the first two functions. Tensile and tear strength are important for outer layers. Abrasion resistance is probably less important for jackets than for pants. Fabrics that have high, balanced fabric counts are usually more resistant to abrasion. Fabrics made with filament yarns snag and are more likely to be damaged by catching on thorns or bushes than those constructed of spun yarns. High-count fabrics also serve well as windbreakers because they have fewer openings between yarn intersections for wind to pass through.

Completely waterproof outer layers, made by coating fabrics to block out moisture vapor, are useful for situations in which people are relatively inactive and when the weather is cool. For active persons waterproof, breathable fabrics (see pages 469–471) are often preferable. In warmer weather and when water-repellent rather than waterproof garments are sufficient, microfiber fabrics may provide comfort for highly aerobic activities. Nylon and polyester fibers in either microfiber or regular deniers are often used in rain gear because they have good tensile strength, resiliency, low moisture absorbency, and are easy to care for.

Putting it all together for . . .

Automotive Textiles

The average car uses about 50 square yards of textile fabrics. About 25 square yards are used for interior trim, and the remainder goes into sound dampening, insulation, and hidden applications such as tires, filters, belts, hoses, and airbags (Smith 1994).

Although the ideal situation for purposes of eventual recycling would be to make all automotive textile materials from the same kind of fiber, various automobile parts use different fibers because of specific performance requirements. Major fibers used in interiors are nylon, polyester, and nylon/polyester blends. Seat belts are most often polyester; airbags are most often nylon; and carpeting is usually nylon. For tire reinforcement, steel predominates but substantial quantities of high-tenacity polyesters and nylons are also used, as well as smaller quantities of high-tenacity rayon.

Interior Fabrics

While aesthetic considerations are important in visible textile materials such as seat covers, carpets, and wall coverings, good performance is essential. Car interiors are subject to conditions that can degrade fibers, such as light exposure, high temperatures, and atmospheric gases.

Fiber Choices. Both nylon and polyester perform well as upholstery fabrics and wall coverings. Both have excellent abrasion resistance (important in withstanding the sliding of people and objects on and off seats), good strength, and good crease resistance. Nylon has better stretch and recovery, which allows fabrics to conform to the shape of seats for a smooth surface. It is somewhat less resistant to degradation from sunlight than polyester, but this problem can be overcome by using fibers with ultraviolet light stabilizers, applying ultraviolet light screening films, and dyeing with metal complex acid dyes.

Nylon is the fiber most often used for carpeting. It is preferred because of its abrasion resistance, resilience, and strength.

Colorfastness. Manufacturers can choose among solution-dyed fibers, yarn-dyed, and piece-dyed fabrics. Relatively little solution-dyed fabric is used, even though its colorfastness is superior. It is more expensive and requires a commitment to particular colors farther in advance than yarn or piece-dyed fabrics; however, industry sources predict increased use of solution-dyed fabrics in the future (Fulmer 1993).

Piece-dyed fabrics, though the least costly, have the poorest colorfastness to light. Yarn-dyed fabrics perform well and are widely used. Colorfastness is increased if fabrics have been treated with ultraviolet stabilizers. Laboratory tests have shown no difference in performance between bright and delustered fibers but indicate that as denier per filament decreases, lightfastness decreases.

Airbags

All automobiles and light trucks manufactured in the United States in 1999 and thereafter will be required to have both driver- and passenger-side airbags. Fabrics used in airbags must be capable of holding air when inflated and must be strong enough to withstand impact without rupturing. Nylon is used because of its strength, toughness, and dimensional stability during storage. Although manufacturers are experimenting with the use of polyester, nylon is likely to continue as the predominant fiber due to its greater strength, especially for driver-side airbags where performance standards are higher. Nylon airbags also can be produced at relatively low cost.

To hold the air inside the bag, fabrics are coated either with neoprene or silicone. The European automobile industry has moved to using more expensive uncoated fabrics constructed so as to be airtight, and the U.S. automobile industry may also move in that direction in the future (Smith 1994).

Other Applications

The following areas of automobiles also use textile materials.

Seat cushions, formerly made of urethane rubber foam, are now made from polyester fiber, which is lighter, more comfortable, and recyclable.

Seat belts must resist abrasion and must have high modulus and strength. They are most often made of polyester.

Automotive hoses must be strong and resistant to gasoline, oil, and other chemical substances. The most widely used fibers include polyester, rayon, and high-performance fibers such as aramids.

Insulation requires high-temperature resistance. Fibers in use include glass fiber, ceramic and silica fiber, aramid, molded temperature-resistant composites, and metalized fabrics.

References

AATCC. 1997. *AATCC Technical Manual.* Research Triangle Park, N.C.: AATCC.

Collier, B. J., and H. H. Epps. 1999. *Textile testing and analysis.* Upper Saddle River, N.J.: Prentice Hall.

Fulmer, T. D. 1993. Dyeing textiles for automotive interiors. *America's Textiles International* 23 (December): 88.

Kawabata, S. 1980. *The standardization and analysis of hand evaluation.* Osaka, Japan: The Textile Machinery Society of Japan.

Price, A., and A. C. Cohen. 1994. *Fabric science.* New York: Fairchild.

Smith, W. C. 1994. Automotives: A major textile market. *Textile World* 144 (September): 68.

Review Questions

1. What role does testing play in quality assurance and selecting fabrics?
2. What does the Kawabata Evaluation System for Fabric evaluate? How are these evaluations determined?

3. What textile tests would you recommend as the most important for the following products?

   draperies   school uniforms

   evening gowns   carpets

   cycling shorts

4. Develop a case study similar to those at the end of this chapter for one of the following products. Focus on fiber, yarn, fabric structure, coloration, and finishes. Do not be concerned about construction details of garments or household textiles.

   a. Bedsheets

   b. Sleepwear for a newborn infant

   c. Man's dress shirt

   d. Blanket for winter in cold climate

   c. Socks to be worn under hiking books for summer hikes

Recommended Readings

Abend, J. 1994. Fabric development takes the driver's seat. *Bobbin* 35 (May): 44.

Bresee, R. R., P. A. Annis, and M. M. Warnock. 1994. Comparing actual fabric wear with laboratory abrasion and laundering. *Textile Chemist and Colorist* 25 (January): 17–23.

Collier, B. J. 1991. Measurement of fabric drape and its relation to fabric mechanical properties and subjective evaluation. *Clothing and Textiles Research Journal* 10 (Fall): 46.

Epps, H. H., and M. K. Song. 1992. Thermal transmittance and air permeability of plain weave fabrics. *Clothing and Textiles Research Journal* 11 (Fall): 10.

Etters, J. N., and M. D. Hurwitz. 1985. The influence of surface texture on the colors of textile home furnishings. *America's Textiles* 14 (November): 56.

Gong, R. H., and S. K. Mukhopadhyay. 1993. Fabric objective measurement: A comparative study of fabric characteristics. *Journal of the Textile Institute* 84 (2): 192.

Hatch, K. L., et al. 1992. Skin response to fabric: A review of studies and assessment methods. *Clothing and Textiles Research Journal* 10 (Summer): 54.

Keyes, N. M. 1995. Development of a new test method: Skewness change and garment twist. *Textile Chemist and Colorist* 27 (1): 27.

Merkle, R. S. 1991. *Textile product serviceability*. New York: Macmillan.

Smith, J. E. 1993. The comfort of clothing. *Textiles* 22 (1): 18.

Vatsala, R., and V. Subramiam. 1993. The integral evaluation of fabric performance. *Journal of the Textile Institute* 84 (3): 495.

BIBLIOGRAPHY

GENERAL REFERENCES: TEXTS AND ENCYCLOPEDIAS

Belck, N. 1990. *Textiles: Decision making for the consumer.* East Lansing: Michigan State University Press.

Burnham, D. K. 1994. *Warp and weft: A textile terminology.* Toronto: University of Toronto Press.

Cohen, A. 1982. *Beyond basic textiles.* New York: Fairchild.

Collchester, C. 1991. *The new textiles.* New York: Rizzoli.

Fritz, A., and J. Cant. 1988. *Consumer textiles.* New York: Oxford University Press.

Gioello, D. 1982. *Understanding fabrics from fiber to finished cloth.* New York: Fairchild.

Grayson, M., ed. 1984. *Encyclopedia of textiles, fibers, and nonwoven fabrics.* New York: Wiley-Interscience.

Hatch, K. L. 1993. *Textile science.* Minneapolis/St. Paul, Minn.: West.

Ishida, T. 1991. *An introduction to textile technology.* Osaka, Japan: Osaka Senken.

Jerde, J. 1992. *Encyclopedia of textiles.* New York: Facts on File.

Joseph, M. L., et al. 1993. *Joseph's Introductory textile science.* New York: Holt Rinehart and Winston.

Kadolph, S. and A. L. Langford. 1998. *Textiles.* Columbus, Ohio: Merrill/Prentice Hall.

Larsen, J. L., and J. Weeks. 1975. *Fabrics for interiors.* New York: Van Nostrand Reinhold.

McIntyre, J. E., and Daniels, P. N., eds. 1995. *Textile terms and definitions*, 10th ed. Manchester, U.K.: Textile Institute.

Neilson, K. 1991. *Textiles for today's interiors.* New York: Van Nostrand Reinhold.

Price, A., and A. C. Cohen. 1999. *J. J. Pizzuto's fabric science*, 6th ed. New York: Fairchild.

Tortora, P., and R. Merkel. 1996. *Fairchild's textile dictionary.* New York: Fairchild.

Vincenti, R. 1993. *Elsevier's textile dictionary.* New York: Elsevier.

Yeager, J. I. and L. K. Taeter-Justice. 2000. *Textiles for residential and commerical interiors.* New York: Fairchild.

HISTORIC AND ETHNIC TEXTILES

Barber, E. W. 1991. *Prehistoric textiles.* Princeton, N.J.: Princeton University Press.

Broudy, E. 1993. *The book of looms—a history of the handloom from ancient times to the present.* Hanover, N.H.: University Press of New England.

D'Harcourt, R. 1987. *Textiles of ancient Peru and their techniques.* Seattle: University of Washington Press.

Gillow, J., and B. Nicholas. 1993. *Traditional Indian textiles.* New York: Thames and Hudson.

Harris, J., ed. 1993. *Textiles, 5000 years: An international history and illustrated survey.* New York: Harry N. Abrams.

Harvey, N. 1991. *Illustrated history of textiles.* New York: Random House.

Jorgensen, L. B. 1992. *North European textiles until AD 1000.* Philadelphia: Coronet Books.

King, R. R. 1985. *Textile identification, conservation, and preservation.* Park Ridge, N.J.: Noyes.

Landi, S. 1992. *The textile conservator's manual*, 2d ed. Newton, Mass.: Butterworth Heinemann.

Lebeau, C. 1994. *Fabrics.* New York: Crown.

Leene, J. E. 1992. *Textile conservation.* Ann Arbor, Mich.: Books on Demand.

Montgomery, R. 1984. *Textiles in America.* Wilmington, Del.: Winterthur.

Nylander, J. C. 1990. *Fabrics for historic buildings.* Washington, D.C.: Preservation Press.

Rathbun, W., ed. 1994. *Beyond the Tanabata Bridge: Traditional Japanese textiles.* New York: Thames and Hudson.

Sieber, R. 1972. *African textile and decorative arts.* New York: Museum of Modern Art.

Wilson, K. 1979. *A history of textiles.* Boulder, Colo.: Westview Press.

———. 1994. *Women's work: The first twenty thousand years; women, cloth, and society in early times.* New York: W. W. Norton.

Zeronian, S. H., and H. L. Needles. 1989. *Historic textile and paper materials.* Vol. II, *Conservation and characterization.* Washington, D.C.: American Chemical Society.

TEXTILES AS AN ART AND CRAFT

Albers, A. 1965. *On weaving.* Middletown, Conn.: Wesleyan University Press.

Brown, R. 1987. *Weaving, spinning, and dyeing book.* New York: Alfred A. Knopf.

Earnshaw, P. 1988. *A dictionary of lace.* New York: State Mutual Book Service.

———. 1995. *How to recognize machine laces.* Berkley, Calif.: Lacis Publications.

Meller, S., and J. Eiffers. 1991. *Textile designs: Two hundred years of European and American patterns for printed fabrics.* New York: Harry N. Abrams.

Palliser, B. 1984. *History of lace.* New York: Dover.

Regensteiner, E. 1986. *The art of weaving.* New York: Schiffer.

Ross, M. 1988. *Encyclopedia of handspinning.* Loveland, Colo.: Interweave Press.

Storey, J. 1992. *Thames and Hudson manual of dyes and fabrics.* New York: Thames and Hudson.

———. 1989. *Threads of lace: From source to sink.* Guilford, U.K.: Gorse.

Yates, M. 1995. *Textiles: A Handbook for Designers.* New York: W. W. Norton.

TEXTILE CARE

American Association for Textile Technology. 1973. *The technology of home laundering.* Textile Monograph 108. New York: American Association for Textile Technology.

Dantaygi, S. 1983. *Fundamentals of textiles and their care.* New York: Apt Books.

Mailand, H. F. 1980. *Consideration for the care of textiles and costumes: A handbook for the non-specialist.* Indianapolis: Indianapolis Museum.

U.S. Department of Agriculture. 1973. *Soaps and detergents for home laundering.* Home and Garden Bulletin no. 139. Washington, D.C.: U.S. Department of Agriculture.

TEXTILE CHEMISTRY

Billmeyer, F. W. 1984. *Textbook of polymer science.* New York: Wiley.

Carter, M. E. 1971. *Essential fiber chemistry.* New York: Marcel Dekker.

Happey, F., ed. 1979. *Applied fibre science.* New York: Academic Press.

Hearle, J. W. S. 1982. *Polymers and their properties.* Vol. 1, *Fundamentals of structure and mechanics.* Chichester, U.K.: Ellis Horwood.

Lewin, M., and E. Pearce. 1985. *Handbook of fiber chemistry, 2d edition.* New York: Marcel Dekker.

Miles, J. 1983. *Handbook of chemical specialties. Textile fiber processing, preparation, and bleaching.* New York: Wiley-Interscience.

Seymour, R. B. 1981. *Polymer chemistry: An introduction* New York: Marcel Dekker.

Stevens, M. P. 1999. *Polymer chemistry: An introduction,* 3rd ed. New York: Oxford University Press.

Trotman, E. R. 1991. *Dyeing and chemical technology of textile fibres.* Forrestburgh, NY: Lubrecht & Cramer.

TEXTILE CONSTRUCTION (TECHNICAL WORKS)

Brackenbury, T. 1992. *Knitted clothing technology.* Cambridge, Mass.: Blackwell Scientific.

Chou, T. W., and F. Kolek. 1989. *Textile structural composites.* New York: Elsevier.

Demir, A., and H. M. Behery. 1997. *Synthetic filament yarn texturing technology.* Upper Saddle River, N.J.: Prentice Hall.

Emery, I. 1966. *The primary structures of fabrics.* Washington, D.C.: Textile Museum.

Gioello, D. 1981. *Profiling fabrics: Properties, performance, and construction techniques.* New York: Fairchild.

Giroud, J-P. 1984. *Geotextiles and geomembranes: Definitions, properties, and design.* St. Paul, Minn.: Industrial Fabrics.

Goerner, D. 1986. *Woven structure and design. Part 1: Single cloth.* New York: State Mutual Book Service.

Goswami, B. C., J. C. Martindale, and F. L. Scardino. 1977. *Textile yarns, technology, structure and applications.* New York: Wiley.

Greenwood, K. 1977. *Weaving, control of fabric structure.* Watford, U.K.: Merrow.

Henshaw, D. E. 1981. *Worsted spinning.* Manchester, U.K.: Textile Institute.

Holloway, L., ed. 1994. *Handbook of polymer composites for engineers.* Cambridge, U.K.: Woodhead.

Jirsák, O., and L. C. Wadsworth. 1999. *Nonwoven textiles.* Durham, N.C.: Carolina Academic Press.

Klein, W. 1993. *New spinning systems.* Short Staple Spinning Series. Vol. 5. Manchester, U.K.: Textile Institute.

Lord, P. 1998. *Yarn production: Science, technology and economics.* Manchester, U.K.: Textile Institute.

Marks, R., and T. C. Robinson. 1976. *Principles of weaving.* Manchester, U.K.: Textile Institute.

Naik, K. 1993. *Woven fabric composites.* Lancaster, Pa.: Technomic.

Nield, R. 1975. *Open end spinning.* New York: State Mutual Book Service.

Omerod, A., and W. S. Sondheim. 1995. *Weaving: Technology and operations.* Manchester, U.K.: Textile Institute.

Peirce, F. T., and J. R. Womersley. 1978. *Cloth geometry.* Manchester, U.K.: The Textile Institute.

1978. *Production of textured yarns by methods other than the false twist method.* New York: State Mutual Books.

Schwartz, P., et al. 1982. *Fabric forming systems.* Park Ridge, N.J.: Noyes.

Slater, K. 1987. *Textile mechanics.* Shirley, U.K.: Textile Institute.

Spencer, D. J. 1989. *Knitting technology.* Oxford, U.K.: Pergamon.

Wilson, D. K. 1978. *Production of textured yarns by the false twist technique.* New York: State Mutual Books.

1990. *Woven structure and design. Part 2: Compound structures.* New York: State Mutual Book Service.

TEXTILE DYEING, PRINTING, AND FINISHING (TECHNICAL WORKS)

AATCC. *Book of papers, Technical Conference.* Published annually. Research Triangle Park, N.C.: American Association of Textile Chemists and Colorists.

AATCC. 1981. *Dyeing primer.* Research Triangle Park, N.C.: American Association of Textile Chemists and Colorists.

AATCC. 1987. *Trends in dyeing and finishing: A global view.* Research Triangle Park, N.C.: American Association of Textile Chemists and Colorists.

AATCC. 1993. *Basics of dyeing and finishing.* Research Triangle Park, N.C.: American Association of Textile Chemists and Colorists.

AATCC. 1993. *Color measurement principles and the textile industry.* Symposium papers. Research Triangle Park, N.C.: American Association of Textile Chemists and Colorists.

Datye, D. V., and A. A. Vaidya. 1984. *Chemical processing of synthetic fibres and blends.* New York: Wiley-Interscience.

De Boos, A. G. 1990. *Finishing wool fabrics to improve their end- use performance.* Manchester, U.K.: Textile Institute.

Kulkarni, S. V., et al. 1986. *Textile dyeing operations: Chemistry equipment, procedures, and environmental aspects.* Park Ridge, N.J.: Noyes.

Lewin, M., and S. B. Sello, eds. 1984. *Handbook of fiber science and technology.* Vol. I, *Fundamentals and preparation.* New York: Marcel Dekker.

———, eds. 1984. *Handbook of fiber science and technology.* Vol. II, *Functional finishes.* New York: Marcel Dekker.

Mark, H. F., N. S. Wooding, and S. M. Atlas. 1971. *Chemical aftertreatment of textiles.* New York: Wiley.

Nettles, J. E. 1983. *Handbook of chemical specialties: Textile fiber processing, preparation, and bleaching.* New York: Wiley.

Olson, E. S. 1983. *Textile wet processes.* Vol. 1, *Preparation of fibers and fabrics.* Park Ridge, N.J.: Noyes.

Rivlin, J. 1993. *The dyeing of textile fibers: Theory and practice.* Philadelphia: Philadelphia College of Textiles and Science.

Sandberg, G. 1989. *Indigo textiles.* Asheville, N.C.: Lark Books.

Slade, P. E. 1998. *Handbook of Fiber Finish Technology.* New York: Marcel Dekker.

Vigo, T. L. 1994. *Textile processing and properties: Preparation, dyeing, finishing, and performance.* New York: Elsevier.

TEXTILE FIBERS (TECHNICAL WORKS)

Brody, H., ed. 1994. *Synthetic fibre materials.* Essex, U.K.: Longman Scientific and Technical.

Cook, J. G. 1984. *Handbook of textile fibers.* Vols. 1 and 2. Watford, U.K.: Merrow, Technical Library.

Donnett, J. B., et al. (eds.) 1998. *Carbon fibers.* New York: Marcel Dekker.

Hearle, J., and D. Brunnschweiler. 1993. *Polyester.* Manchester, U.K.: Textile Institute.

Hearle, J. W., ed. 1990. *High performance fibres, composites and engineering textile structure.* Manchester, U.K.: Textile Institute.

Hearle, J. W. S., and R. Greeg. 1970. *Fiber structures.* New York: State Mutual Books.

Hongu, R., and G. Phillips. 1998. *New fibers.* Manchester, U.K.: Woodhead/Textile Institute.

Hunter, L. 1993. *Mohair: A review of properties, processing, and applications.* Manchester, U.K.: CSIRO Division of Textile Technology, International Mohair Association, and Textile Institute.

Kaplan, D., et al., eds. 1994. *Silk polymers: Material science and technology.* Washington, D.C.: American Chemical Society.

Kroschwitz, J. 1990. *Fibers and textiles, a compendium.* New York: Wiley.

Lewin, M. and J. Preston. 1985–1996. *Handbook of fiber science and technology.* Vol. III, *High technology fibers.* New York: Marcel Dekker.

Masson, J. C. 1995. *Acrylic fiber technology and applications.* New York: Marcel Dekker.

Militky, J., et al. 1991. *Modified polyester fibers.* New York: Elsevier.

Moncrieff, R. W. 1974. *Man-made fibres.* London: Newnes-Butterworth.

Morton, W. E., and J. W. S. Hearle. 1993. *Physical properties of textile fibres,* 3rd ed. Manchester, U.K.: Textile Institute.

Mukhopadhyay, S. K. 1993. *Advances in fibre science.* Manchester, U.K.: Textile Institute.

Nakajima, T., ed. 1994. *Advanced fiber spinning technology.* Cambridge, U.K.: Woodhead.

Plastics and Rubber Institute staff, eds. 1986. *Carbon fibers: Technology, uses, and prospects.* Park Ridge, N.J.: Noyes.

Postle, R., G. A. Carnaby, and S. deJong. 1988. *The mechanics of wool structures.* Chichester, U.K.: Ellis Harwood.

Seymour, R. B., and R. S. Porter, eds. 1993. *Manmade fibers: Their origin and development.* London: Elsevier.

Warner, S. B. 1995. *Fiber science.* Englewood Cliffs, N.J.: Prentice Hall.

World directory of manufactured fiber producers (published annually). Roseland, N.J.: Fiber Economics Bureau.

Yang, H. H. 1993. *Kevlar aramid fiber.* New York: Wiley-Interscience.

Ziabecki, A., and H. Kawai. 1991. *High speed fiber spinning.* New York: Wiley.

TEXTILE INDUSTRY

Berkstresser, G. A., D. R. Buchanan, and P. Grady, eds. 1995. *Automation in the textile industry: From fibers to apparel.* Manchester, U.K.: The Textile Institute.

Cohen, A. 1988. *Marketing textiles: From fiber to retail.* New York: Fairchild.

Dickerson, K. 1999. *Textiles and apparel in the global economy,* 3rd ed. Columbus, Ohio: Merrill/Prentice Hall.

Hunter, N. A. 1990. *Quick Response in apparel manufacturing.* Manchester, U.K.: Textile Institute.

Toyne, B., et al. 1983. *The U.S. textile mill products industry.* Columbia: University of South Carolina.

TEXTILE TESTING, STANDARDS, AND LEGISLATION

AATCC. *Technical manual.* Published annually. Research Triangle Park, N.C.: American Association of Textile Chemists and Colorists.

ASTM. *Annual Book of ASTM Standards.* Philadelphia: American Society for Testing and Materials.

Booth, J. E. 1968. *Principles of textile testing.* London: Newnes-Butterworth.

1994. *Chemical testing and analysis.* Manchester, U.K.: Textile Institute.

Collier, B., and H. Epps. 1999. *Textile Analysis.* Columbus, Ohio: Merrill/Prentice Hall.

Kadolph, S. 1998. *Quality assurance for textiles and apparel.* New York: Fairchild.

Mahall, K. 1993. *Quality assessment of textile damage detection by microscopy.* New York: Springer Verlag.

Merkel, R. S. 1991. *Textile product serviceability.* New York: Macmillan.

Perry, D. R., et al. 1985. *Identification of textile materials,* 7th ed. Manchester, U.K.: Textile Institute.

Rahiel, M., ed. 1996. *Modern textile characterization methods.* New York: Marcel Dekker.

Saville, B. P. 1998. *Physical testing of textiles.* Manchester, U.K., Textile Institute.

Slater, K. 1993. *Physical testing and quality control.* New York: State Mutual Book Service.

Weaver, J. W., ed. 1984. *Analytical methods for a textile laboratory,* 3rd ed. Research Triangle Park, N.C.: American Association of Textile Chemists and Colorists.

MISCELLANEOUS

Backer, S. 1976. *Textile fabric flammability.* Cambridge, Mass.: MIT Press.

Fourt, N., and N. R. Hollies. 1970. *Clothing comfort and function.* Ann Arbor, Mich.: Books on Demand.

Pratt, B. 1997. *Weaving textile reuse into waste reduction.* Washington, D.C.: Institute for Local Self-Reliance.

Slater, K. 1977. *Comfort properties of textiles.* Manchester, U.K.: Textile Institute.

PERIODICALS

American Dyestuff Reporter, Secaucus, N.J.

America's Textiles International, Billian Publishers, Atlanta, Ga.

Ars Textrina, Winnepeg, Canada.

Canadian Textile Journal, St. Anne de Bellevue, Canada.

Clothing and Textiles Research Journal, International Textile and Apparel Association, Monument, Colo.

Cotton Digest International, Cotton Digest Co., Houston, Tex.

Daily News Record, Fairchild, New York.

Fiber Organon, Roseland, N.J.

Geo-technical Fabrics Report, Industrial Fabrics Association International, Roseville, Minn.

Handwoven, Herb Companion Press, Loveland, Colo.

High Performance Textiles, Elsevier, New York.

Home Textiles Today, Cahner's Business Information, New York.

Industrial Fabrics Product Review, Industrial Fabrics Association International, Roseville, Minn.

International Fabricare Institute, Silver Springs, Md.

Journal of Coated Fabrics, Technomic Publishing Co., Lancaster, Pa.

Journal of Industrial Fabrics, RCM Enterprises, St. Paul, Minn.

Journal of the Textile Institute, Manchester, U.K..

JTN, Osaka, Japan.

Nonwovens Industry, Rodman Publishing Corp., Ramsey, N.J.

Nonwovens World, Miller Freeman, San Francisco, Calif.

Shuttle, Spindle, and Dyepot, Handweaver's Guild, Bloomfield, Conn.

Textile Chemist and Colorist, American Association of Textile Chemists and Colorists, Research Triangle Park, N.C.

Textile Hi-Lights, American Textile Manufacturers Institute, Washington, D.C.

Textile History, Leeds, U.K.

Textile Horizons, London.

Textile Month, World Textile Publications, Bradford, W. Yorkshire, U.K.

Textile Museum Bulletin, Washington, D.C.

Textile Museum Journal, Washington, D.C.

Textile Outlook International, Textiles Intelligence, Ltd., Wimslow, U.K.

Textile Progress, The Textile Institute, Manchester, U.K.

Textile Research Journal, Textile Research Institute, Princeton, N.J.

Textile Technology Digest, Institute of Textile Technology, Charlottesville, Va.

Textile World, Primedia Intertec Publishing Corp., Atlanta, Ga.

Textiles Magazine, Textile Institute, Manchester, U.K.

Threads, Taunton Press, Newtown, Conn.

GLOSSARY

Abrasion* The wearing away of any part of a material by rubbing against another surface.

Absorption* A process in which one material (the absorbent) takes in or absorbs another (the absorbate) as the absorption of moisture by fibers.

Adsorption* A process in which the surface of a solid takes on or absorbs in an extremely thin layer molecules of gases, of dissolved substances, or of liquids with which it is in contact.

Amorphous areas (in the fiber structure) Areas within fibers in which long-chain molecules are arranged in a random, or unorganized, manner.

Appliqué Attaching, usually by sewing, small pieces of cloth or other materials to the surface of a larger textile.

Bandanna Indian textiles decorated by the tie-and-dye method.

Bast fibers Fibers found in the woody stem of plants.

Batik Indonesian technique of resist printing in which areas of fabric that are to resist the dye are covered with wax.

Batt A mass of fibers slightly matted together, often formed into a sheet or roll.

Bicomponent bigeneric fiber Bicomponent fiber consisting of two generically different fibers.

Bicomponent fiber* A fiber consisting of two polymers that are chemically different, physically different, or both.

Bigeneric fiber See *Bicomponent bigeneric fiber.*

Bleaching* The procedure, other than by scouring only, of improving the whiteness of a textile material by oxidation or reduction of the coloring matter.

Blended yarn* A single yarn spun from a blend or mixture of different fiber species.

Block printing The application of printed designs by pressing dye-covered blocks onto a fabric.

Bobbin lace Lace made with a number of threads, each fastened to a spool. The pattern to be followed is anchored to a pillow, so that this lace is also called *pillow lace.*

Byssinosis A lung disease to which cotton mill workers are subject; thought to be caused by toxins in the cotton dust.

Calendering The process of passing fabric between rollers with the application of heat and pressure.

---

*Reprinted, with permission, from the *Annual Book of ASTM Standards,* Copyright © American Society for Testing and Materials, 1916 Race Street, Philadelphia, PA 19103.

Carbonized wool* A term descriptive of scoured wool processed to destroy cellulosic impurities by treating with a mineral acid or an acid salt, drying and baking, crushing, and dusting out the embrittled cellulosic matter followed by neutralization of the acidified wool.

Carding* The process of untangling and partially straightening fibers by passing them between two closely spaced surfaces that are moving at different speeds, and at least one of which is covered with sharp points, thus converting a tangled mass of fibers to a filmy web.

Casement cloth A term used to refer to a wide variety of curtain fabrics.

Ciré A shiny, lustrous surface effect achieved by applying a wax finish or by heat treatment of thermoplastic fibers.

Cohesiveness* The resistance to separation of fibers in contact with one another.

Colorfastness The ability of a textile material to retain its color during use and care.

Combing A process that follows carding that pulls fibers into more parallel alignment.

Compressive shrinkage The process of setting and setting the dimensions of a fabric to control relaxation shrinkage.

Courses* In knitted fabrics, the series of successive loops lying crosswise of a knitted fabric, that is, lying at right angles to a line passing through the open throat to the closed end of the loops.

Cover factor The ratio of fabric surface occupied by the yarns to the total fabric surface.

Covering power (optical) The ability of a fabric to hide that which is placed under it.

Crabbing Exposure of wool fabrics to hot and then cold water to set it in a flat state.

Crimp, fiber* The waviness of a fiber expressed as waves or crimps per unit length.

Crochet A technique of creating fabric by pulling one loop of yarn through another with a hook.

Crocking* Transfering of color from the surface of a colored fabric to an adjacent area of the same fabric or to another surface, principally by rubbing action.

Cross-dye effect* Variation in dye pickup between yarns or fibers resulting from their inherent dye affinities.

Crosslinking The attachment of one long-chain molecule to another by chemical linkages.

Crystallinity (in fiber structure)   Orderly, parallel arrangements of molecules within a fiber.

Curing   The application of heat to effect a chemical reaction, such as the reaction of a finish with the fibers in a fabric.

Cut   The number of needles per inch in the bed of a circular filling knit machine.

Cystine linkages   Chemical cross-linkages in the wool fiber.

Decating   Exposure of wool fabric to steam to control relaxation shrinkage.

Delustered fiber   A manufactured fiber that has had its natural luster decreased by chemical or physical means.

Denier   The weight of 9,000 meters of fiber or yarn expressed in grams.

Density, fiber*   Mass per unit volume of the solid matter of which a fiber is composed, measured under specified conditions.

Desizing   The removal of the sizing material from warp yarns after a fabric is constructed.

Detergent   Any cleaning agent.

Dimensional stability   The ability of a fiber or yarn to withstand shrinking or stretching.

Discharge printing   The creation of design by applying a discharge material that removes color from treated areas of a dyed fabric.

Doupion silk   A double strand of silk produced by two silkworms spinning a cocoon together. Also called *doupioni silk.*

Dry-jet wet spinning   The formation of manufactured textile fibers in which the polymer is dissolved in a solvent and extruded through an air gap into a chemical bath where the fibers are hardened.

Dry spinning   The formation of manufactured textile fibers in which the polymer is dissolved in a solvent that is evaporated, leaving the filament to harden by drying in air.

Dull fiber   See *delustered fiber.*

Durable finishes   Those finishes that have good durability over a reasonably long period of use.

Durable press*   Having the ability to retain substantially the initial shape, flat seams, pressed-in creases, and unwrinkled appearance during use and after laundering or dry cleaning. The use of the term "permanent press" as a substitute for "durable press" is undesirable.

Dyes   Natural or synthetic substances that add color to materials by being absorbed therein.

Elasticity*   That property of a material by virtue of which it tends to recover its original size and shape immediately after removal of the force causing deformation.

Elongation*   The ratio of the extension of a material to the length of the material before stretching.

Embroidery   The use of yarns applied to fabrics with a needle in a variety of decorative stitches.

Ends   Warp yarns.

Fasciated yarns   Yarns made from a bundle of parallel fibers wrapped with a surface wrapping of other fibers.

Felt, wool*   A textile composed wholly of any one or combination of new or recycled wool fibers physically interlocked by the inherent felting properties of wool and produced by a suitable combination of mechanical work, chemical action, moisture and heat, but without weaving, knitting, stitching, thermal bonding, or adhesives.

Fiber dyeing   See *Stock dyeing.*

Fiber morphology   The internal structural arrangement of polymer chains in a fiber.

Fiber reinforced composites   Molded materials containing embedded textile fibers to increase strength,

Fibrillation   The creation of fibers or yarns by drawing a polymer sheet in the lengthwise direction so as to cause the sheet to split into a network of fibers (that may be formed into yarns).

Filament*   Continuous fiber of indefinite length.

Filature   A factory in which silk fibers are processed.

Filet   An embroidered net, also known as *lacis.*

Filling*   Yarn running from selvage to selvage at right angles to the warp in a woven fabric.

Fineness*   A relative measure of size, diameter, linear density, or mass per unit length expressed in a variety of units.

Flexibility*   That property of a material by virtue of which it may be flexed or bowed repeatedly without undergoing rupture.

Flock*   A material obtained by reducing textile fibers to fragments, as by cutting, tearing, or grinding, to give various degrees of comminution (powdering).

Fulling   In the processing of wool or animal hair fabrics, treatment with moisture, heat, soap, and pressure that causes yarns to shrink, lie closer together, and give the fabric a more dense structure.

Garnetting   A process for recovering fibers from yarn or fabric by use of a garnett, a machine similar to a carding machine, which pulls the structure apart.

Gel-spinning   The formation of manufactured textile fibers in which the polymer is dissolved in a solvent to form a gel, which is stretched to harden the fibers.

Generic name   Names assigned by the Federal Trade Commission to the various types of manufactured fibers according to the chemical composition of the fiber-forming substance.

Gigging   Brushing up of loose fibers onto the surface of a fabric made from staple yarns; a synonym for *napping.*

Glass transition*   The reversible change in an amorphous polymer or in amorphous regions of a partially crystalline polymer from (or to) a viscous or rubbery condition to (or from) a hard and relatively brittle one.

Graft polymers*   A copolymer in which polymeric side chains have been attached to the main chain of a polymer of different structure.

Greige goods*   Textile fabrics that have received no bleaching, dyeing, or finishing treatment after being produced by any textile process.

Hackling   A step in the processing of flax fibers that is comparable to combing.

Heat setting   The treatment of thermoplastic manufactured fibers or fabrics with heat to set the fibers or fabrics into a specific shape or form.

Heat transfer printing   A system of textile printing in which dyes are applied to a paper base and are then transferred from the paper to a fabric under heat and pressure.

Heddle   A cord or wire eyelet through which warp yarns are passed on a loom.

High wet modulus   The quality in a fiber that gives it good stability when wet.

Hydrophilic   Term used to describe materials that have an affinity for water (literally, "water-loving").

Hydrophobic   Term used to describe materials that have no affinity for water (literally, "water-hating").

Ikat   A form of resist printing in which sections of warp yarns are made to resist dyes; a type of warp print. Dye is applied to the warp yarns, and filling yarns are inserted. The resultant patterns have an indistinct, shimmering pattern.

Ink jet printing   Printing method that ejects small drops of dye onto a fabric to form a printed design.

Kemp hairs   Coarse, straight hairs in a wool fleece that do not absorb dye readily.

Lacis   See *Filet*.

Latch needle   A needle used in knitting machines that has a latch that opens and closes to hold the yarn on the needle.

Linters*   The short fibrous material adhering to the cotton seed after the spinnable lint has been removed by ginning and that is subsequently recovered from the seed by a process called "delinting."

Loft   The ability of fibers to return to their original thickness after being flattened or compressed.

Luster*   That property of a textile material by virtue of which the latter exhibits differences in intensity of light reflected from within a given area of material when the angles of illumination or viewing are changed.

Macramé   A technique for creating fabric by knotting yarns together.

Malimo   See *Stitch-through*.

Man-made fibers   See *Manufactured fibers*.

Manufactured fibers   Fibers created through technology either from natural materials or from chemicals.

Matrix fiber   A bicomponent fiber in which one polymer is dispersed throughout another polymer. See *Bicomponent fiber*.

Melt spinning   The formation of manufactured textile fibers in which the polymer is melted for extrusion and hardened by cooling.

Mercerization*   The process of subjecting a vegetable fiber to the action of a fairly concentrated aqueous solution of a strong base so as to produce great swelling with resultant changes in fine structure, dimensions, morphology, and mechanical properties.

Micrometer (mm)*   One millionth of a meter, 0.001 mm.

Micron   A measurement that is 1/1000th of a millimeter or 0.000039 of an inch. See *Micrometer*.

Mildew   A fungus that grows on some fibers under conditions of heat and dampness.

Moiré   A ribbed cloth that has a wavy, watermarked pattern on the surface.

Moisture regain*   The amount of moisture in a material determined under prescribed conditions and expressed as a percentage of the weight of the moisture-free specimen.

Monofilament yarn*   A single filament; also a single filament that can function as a yarn in commercial textile operations; that is, it must be strong and flexible enough to be knitted, woven, or braided.

Monomer*   A relatively simple compound that can react to form a polymer.

Mordant   Substance used in dyeing that reacts with both the dyestuff and the fiber to form an insoluble compound, thereby fixing the color within and on the fiber.

Multifilament yarn   Yarn made from two or more, usually more, filament fibers.

Nap   The "fuzzy" raised fibers that have been brushed up on the surface of a fabric.

Needlepoint lace   Lace made by embroidering over other threads held in a pattern across a sheet of parchment.

Needle punching   Fabric formation technique in which fabric is formed by the entangling that results when a series of needles are punched through a batt of fiber.

Netting   A technique of creating fabric by looping and knotting a continuous strand of thread into an open mesh.

Novelty yarns   Yarns made to create interesting decorative effects.

Oleophilic   Term used to describe materials that have an affinity for oil (literally, "oil-loving").

Open-end spinning machine*   A textile machine for converting staple fiber into spun yarn by a continuous process in which the individual fibers or groups of fibers are caused to assemble at the open end of the forming yarn.

Optical brightener   Compound that absorbs ultraviolent light and re- emits it as visible blue light.

Orientation (of molecules within a fiber)   Arrangement of polymers in a position parallel to the length of the fiber.

OSHA   Occupational Safety and Health Act.

Padding   The process of applying a dye or finish to a fabric by passing the fabric through a solution of the dye or finish, and then through rollers to squeeze out the excess liquid.

Permanent finish   A finish that will last for the lifetime of the fabric.

Phase change material (PCM)   A substance, incorporated into a fiber or finish, that stores and releases heat by changing from the liquid to the solid phase (and back again).

Picks   Filling yarns.

Piece dyeing   Dyeing of woven or knitted fabrics as opposed to dyeing of fibers or yarns.

Pigment*   An insoluble compounding material used to impart color.

Pile (in pile fabric)*   The raised loops or tufts (cut loops) that form all or part of the surface.

Pillow lace   See *Bobbin lace.*

Pills*   Bunched or balls of tangled fibers that are held to the surface of a fabric by one or more fibers.

Pirns   Small metal pins around which yarns are wrapped. These pins are then inserted in a shuttle that carries the yarns across the fabric during weaving. Also called *quills.*

Plissé   A puckered effect achieved on cotton fabrics by shrinking some areas of the fabric with sodium hydroxide.

Ply yarns*   Yarn formed by twisting together two or more single yarns in one operation.

Polymer*   A macromolecular material formed by the chemical combination of monomers having either the same or different chemical composition.

Polymerization   The formation of polymers.

Progressive shrinkage   Shrinkage that continues after the first laundering and/or dry cleaning through successive cleanings.

Pure dye silk   Silk with less than 10 percent of weighting (or less than 15 percent if it is black in color).

Quills   See *Pirns.*

Regenerated fibers   Fibers produced from natural materials that cannot be used for textiles in their original form but that can, through chemical treatment and processing, be made into textile fibers.

Relaxation shrinkage   Shrinkage that takes place during initial laundering and/or dry cleaning as a result of the relaxation of tensions applied to yarns or fabrics during manufacture.

Residual shrinkage   Shrinkage remaining in a fabric after it has been preshrunk. Residual shrinkage is generally expressed as a percentage.

Resilience*   That property of a material by virtue of which it is able to do work against restraining forces during return from a deformed state.

Resist printing   The achieving of designs by causing sections of fabric to resist dye.

Retting   The process of decomposing the woody stem and gums surrounding bast fibers to remove the fiber.

Ring spinning   Method of spinning yarns from staple fibers in which the twist is imparted to the fibers by the concurrent movement of a spindle and a metal ring that moves around the spindle.

Roller printing   The application of printed designs to fabrics by the use of engraved rollers over which the fabrics pass.

Roving*   A loose assemblage of fibers drawn or rubbed into a single strand, with little twist. In spun yarn systems, the product of the stage, or stages, just before spinning.

Sanforization   A trademarked compressive shrinkage control process.

Schreiner finish   A finish that improves luster of fabrics that is produced by passing steel rollers engraved with fine lines over the cloth to flatten and smooth the surface.

Scouring*   A wet process of cleaning by chemical or mechanical means, or both.

Screen printing   The application of printed design to fabrics by the use of screen coated with resist materials that permit dye to penetrate through the screen only in selected areas.

Scrim   An open-weave fabric that is often used as a backing material.

Seed hair fibers   Those fibers that grow around the seeds of certain plants, such as cotton or kapok.

Sericin   The gum that holds silk filaments together in a cocoon.

Sericulture   The cultivation of the silkworm for the production of silk fiber.

Shed   The passageway between the warp yarns through which the shuttle is thrown in weaving.

Shuttle   The device that carries the yarn across the loom, through the shed, in weaving.

Shuttleless machine   Weaving machine in which the yarn is carried across the fabric by some means other than a shuttle. These machines may utilize jets of water, air, metal rapiers, metal grippers, or mechanical action.

SI*   The International System of Units (abbreviation for "le Système International d'Unités") as defined by the General Conference on Weights and Measures (CGPM); based on seven base units, two supplementary units, and derived units, which together form a coherent system.

Simple yarn   Yarn with uniform size and regular surface.

Singeing   Treatment of woven fabrics with heat or flame to remove surface fibers from fabric to produce a smooth finish.

Sizing*   A generic term for compounds which, when applied to yarn or fabric, form a more or less continuous solid film around the yarn and individual fibers.

Sliver*   A continuous strand of loosely assembled fibers that is approximately uniform in cross-sectional area and without twist.

Solution dyeing   Addition of color pigment to the liquid solution of manufactured fibers before the fiber is formed.

Specification*   A precise statement of a set of requirements to be satisfied by a material, product, system, or service, indicating, whenever appropriate, the procedure by means of which it may be determined whether the specified requirements have been met.

Specific gravity*   The ratio of the mass of a unit volume of a material at a stated temperature to the mass of the same volume of distilled water at the same temperature.

Spindle   A long, slender stick used in spinning to provide the necessary twist to fibers being formed into a yarn. Spindles may be hand devices or part of a spinning wheel.

Spring beard needle   A needle used in knitting machines that holds yarns on the needle by means of a springlike action of the flexible hook.

Spunbonding   A fabric formation technique in which extruded fiber filaments are randomly arranged and bonded together by heat or chemical means.

Spunlace   A fabric formation technique in which a fiber web is formed by air entanglement.

Standard*   A reference used as a basis for compensation or calibration; also a concept that has been established by authority, custom, or agreement to serve as a model or rule in the measurement of quantity or the establishment of a practice or a procedure.

Staple fibers   Fibers of short, noncontinuous lengths.

Stitch-through   A fabric formation technique in which fibers or yarns are held together by stitching through the materials.

Stock dyeing   Dyeing of fibers before they are made into yarns or fabrics.

Striations   Lengthwise markings on the surface of the manufactured fibers when seen through a microscope.

Sublimation printing   See *Heat transfer printing*.

Surfactant   Organic chemicals, the active ingredient in synthetic detergents, that alter the properties of water and soil so that dirt can be removed.

Tapa   Cloth made from bark.

Tapestry   Woven designs, created on a tapestry loom.

Temporary finishes   Those finishes that are removed through use and cleaning and must be renewed to be effective.

Tenacity*   The tensile stress when expressed as force per unit linear density of the unstrained specimen; for example, grams per tex or grams-force per denier.

Tensile strength   The resistance of fibers, yarns, or fabrics to a pulling force.

Tentering   Drying of wet fabrics after finishing or dyeing on a frame on which fabrics are stretched taut and flat.

Tex*   A unit for expressing linear density, equal to the mass in grams of 1 km of yarn, filament, fiber, or other textile strand.

Textured yarn   Filament yarn in which the smooth, straight form of the fibers has been altered.

TFPIA   Textile Fiber Products Identification Act.

Thermoplastic*   A material that will repeatedly soften when heated and harden when cooled.

Thread   Yarn made for the purpose of sewing together sections of garments or other items.

Tow*   (1) In bast fibers, the short fibers removed by hackling; (2) in manufactured fibers, a twistless multifilament strand suitable for conversion into staple fibers or sliver or for direct spinning into yarn.

Trademark name   A distinctive name registered with the U.S. Patent and Trademark Office by a manufacturer to identify such goods as made or sold by that firm. Registration of trademark is necessary in defending the legal right to exclusive use of the term.

Triaxial weave   A type of weaving in which three sets of yarns are utilized, with two sets of yarns moving in a diagonal direction to the third, rather than at right angles.

Tussah silk   Silk fiber from wild silkworms.

Union dyeing   The dyeing to the same color of two different fibers with different affinities for dye.

Wale*   In knitted fabrics, a column of loops in successive courses. The column is parallel with the loop axes; in woven fabrics, one of a series of raised portions or ribs lying warpwise in the fabric.

Warp*   The yarn running lengthwise in a woven fabric.

Warp knit   A hand- or machine-made knit in which the loops interlace vertically.

Warp print   A print in which the design is printed on the warp yarns before the filling yarns are interlaced. See *Ikat*.

Weft   The crosswise direction of a woven fabric; the filling.

Weft knit   A knit in which the loops interlace horizontally rather than vertically.

Wet spinning   The formation of manufactured textile fibers in which the fibers are hardened by extruding the fibers into a chemical bath.

Wicking*   Transmission of a gas or liquid along the fibers of the textile due to pressure differential or capillary action.

Woolen yarns*   Yarn spun from wool fibers which have been carded but not combed or gilled.

Worsted yarns*   Yarn spun from wool fibers which have been carded, and either gilled or combed, or both.

Yarn dyeing   The dyeing of yarns before they are woven or knitted into fabrics.

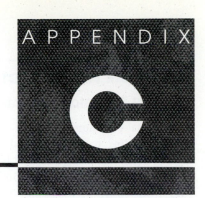

SUMMARY OF REGULATORY LEGISLATION APPLIED TO TEXTILES

APPENDIX C

The following summarizes *briefly* the major pieces of legislation and/or regulations that apply to textile products. Fuller details are provided about each of these acts or rulings in the body of the text. Only those items of legislation that have an impact on consumers are included. Those that regulate the industry, such as OSHA, are not included.

TEXTILE FIBER PRODUCTS IDENTIFICATION ACT
Passed 1960, Amended Subsequently

The TFPIA requires that each textile product carry a label listing the generic names of fibers from which it is made. These generic fiber categories are established by the Federal Trade Commission (FTC), which can add new generic categories as needed. At present there are twenty-one generic fiber categories for manufactured fibers, as well as the names for the natural fibers.

The listing of fibers is made in order of percentage by weight of fiber present in the product, with the largest amount listed first, the next largest second, and so on. Fiber quantities of less than 5 percent must be labeled as "other fiber" unless they serve a specific purpose in the product. Fibers that cannot be identified must be listed as "X percent of undetermined fiber content."

The law prohibits the use of misleading names that imply the presence of fiber not in the product. Labels must carry either the name, trademark, or registered identification number of the manufacturer. All items covered under the law must be clearly and visibly labeled as to whether they are imported or produced in the United States. (For details, see chapter 2, pages 43–47.)

WOOL PRODUCTS LABELING ACT
Passed 1939

This legislation regulates the labeling of sheep's wool and other animal hair fibers. The Wool Products Labeling Act requires that all wool products be labeled and the fibers, except for ornamentation, be identified as either new or recycled wool. The rules and regulations of the FTC established in relation to the act require that the terms *wool*, *new wool*, or *virgin wool* be applied only to wool that has never been used before. Recycled wool is either (1) wool that has never been used in any way by the ultimate consumer but has been spun into yarns or woven or knitted into cloth (these formed but unused pieces of yarns or fabrics are pulled apart and the fibers are reprocessed into fabrics) or (2) wool that has been used by consumers and is reclaimed by pulling the fabrics apart into fibers and spinning and weaving these fibers into other yarns and fabrics.

The law requires that the percentage of wool used in pile fabrics be identified as to the percentage of wool in the face and percentage of wool in the backing. The proportion of fiber used in face and backing must also be noted. Contents of padding, linings, or stuffings are designated separately from the face fabric of products, but must be listed with the same items noted. Items of wool must be clearly and visibly labeled as to whether they are imported or produced in the United States. (See chapter 4, pages 101–102.)

FUR PRODUCTS LABELING ACT
Passed 1951

This law requires that a fur product carries the true English name of the fur-bearing animal from which it comes and the name of the country of origin of the fur. (See chapter 4, page 116.)

FLAMMABLE FABRICS ACT
Original Provisions Enacted in 1953

The original provisions of the act stated that wearing apparel (excluding hats, gloves, and footwear) and fabrics that are highly flammable may not be sold. Standards were established for testing to determine whether items were highly flammable. (See chapter 23, page 472, for discussion of the standard.)

Amendments to the Act, 1967

The scope of the act was broadened in 1967 to cover a wider range of clothing and interior furnishings. The act called for the establishment of standards for flammability for items covered by the act and banned from sale carpets, mattresses, and items of children's sleepwear, sizes infant to 14, that do not meet the established standards. Some aspects of the standards have been revised periodically. (See chapter 23, page 472, for discussion of the standards.) Labels giving care instructions for children's sleepwear that is flame retardant must be placed so that they can be read at the point of purchase. These instructions must be permanently affixed to the garment. Some small carpets and one-of-a-kind carpets are exempt from the provisions of the act but must be labeled indicating that they do not meet the standard. The responsibility for administering and implementing the act was given to the Consumer Product Safety Commission. (See chapter 23 for full discussion of the legislation.)

PERMANENT CARE LABELING RULING OF THE FTC
Established 1972

This ruling requires all wearing apparel and bolts of fabric sold by the yard to carry permanently affixed labels giving instructions for care. Exempt from the ruling are household textiles, retail items costing the consumer less than $3.00, footwear, head gear, and hand coverings, and all items that would be marred by affixing a label. The kind of information that must be provided is clearly specified. (See chapter 24 for complete description of provisions.)

FTC RULING ON THE WEIGHTING OF SILK
Established 1938

No silk products containing more than 10 percent weighting except those colored black may carry a label saying that they are "silk" or "pure dye silk." Black silks can contain 15 percent of weighting. Fabrics not meeting these standards must be labeled as "weighted silk." (See chapter 4, page 120.)

INDEX